THE TRANQUILITY CHILD

Other novels by Terry Mejdrich

A MAMMOTH RESURRECTION
THE BOG LADY
THE DEVIL'S KETTLE
GHOSTS IN THE HEART

For ordering information, contact your local bookstore,
on-line book outlets,
or the author at mejdrichto@yahoo.com.

THE TRANQUILITY CHILD

A Novel

Terry Oliver Mejdrich

iUniverse, Inc.
New York Bloomington Shanghai

THE TRANQUILITY CHILD

Copyright © 2008 by Terry Oliver Mejdrich

All rights reserved. No part of this book may be used or reproduced by any means, graphic, electronic, or mechanical, including photocopying, recording, taping or by any information storage retrieval system without the written permission of the publisher except in the case of brief quotations embodied in critical articles and reviews.

iUniverse books may be ordered through booksellers or by contacting:

iUniverse
1663 Liberty Drive
Bloomington, IN 47403
www.iuniverse.com
1-800-Authors (1-800-288-4677)

Because of the dynamic nature of the Internet, any Web addresses or links contained in this book may have changed since publication and may no longer be valid.

This is a work of fiction. All of the characters, names, incidents, organizations, and dialogue in this novel are either the products of the author's imagination or are used fictitiously.

ISBN: 978-0-595-51745-9 (pbk)
ISBN: 978-0-595-62014-2 (ebk)

Printed in the United States of America

Acknowledgements

Many thanks to Donna Nelson, Darlene Mejdrich, Nancy Felknor, Therese Jacobson, and Eric Mejdrich for their help, encouragement, and suggestions.

Several Years Before

The magazine had contained a picture of a young child, maybe eight or nine, and Peter Denech could not get the image out of his mind. She was dressed in blue denim bib overalls, her dark hair hung down in two long braids, and she held a tattered doll with golden hair tightly to her breast. It was one of those appeals to help impoverished children in South America. His skepticism that any of that donated money ever made it to the children who needed it prevented him from donating in the past, but the child's face had somehow gotten to him, and it had been a spur of the moment decision to send off a check for five hundred dollars. That, he felt, would put his conscience to rest, but still the face haunted him. It didn't help that he'd torn her picture out of the magazine and taped it to the dashboard directly in front of him. Whether or not this particular child was really in need didn't matter. Millions of children worldwide lived in abject poverty. Millions were physically and sexually abused. Millions died of disease and malnutrition. The adults of the world couldn't support those children they did have and yet they continued to have more. Most claimed it was their God-given right. Yet children were fast becoming the new throwaway commodity.

For the moment, however, Peter Denech forced the vision of the young girl with long black braids from his mind. He was keeping his options open. At fifty-something years of age, job opportunities were a diminishing resource. Either you were too old to train in, or you had 'too much' experience. Essentially that meant employers would rather take a chance on a rookie at greatly reduced wages than pay someone—with years of experience and excellent references—what they deserved.

Most of his life Denech had been a 'free lance' and largely self-taught jack-of-all-trades, but more specifically an engineer going from job site to job site as a paying opportunity came along. He'd never married. Not that he had anything against women, but he tended to avoid anything that couldn't be analyzed, categorized, and eventually comprehended. Women, he found, fell inside a mutually exclusive category all their own. His few experiences with dating had left him bewildered. It was all too contrived, too false, too insincere. Too much playing, and hurtful playing at that. Engineering was steady as a rock. Either it worked or it didn't, and if it didn't there was the prospect of fixing it. Not so with relationships. A crack couldn't be welded or even duct-taped.

At the present time Denech's specialty was systems integration and networking, which mostly amounted to explaining to the empty-headed knuckleheads in middle management how to put A, B, C and X, Y, Z together in the most efficient and timely manner. In the pre-dawn hours, his current heading was along Highway 200 in central Montana en route to Butte. The headlights from the used grey sedan plowed through the darkness, and occasionally lit up the eyes of a raccoon or fox or a deer that ventured near the rural highway. The interstate would have been hours quicker, but he was a day ahead of schedule for the meeting at the Museum of Mining, and it was always nice to take 'the road less traveled', as a poet once said.

As the value of precious metals skyrocketed, there was a renewed interest in reclamation mining. He'd been asked to sit in on an informational meeting as a favor to a friend. He liked those types of meetings the best because all he had to do was sit and take notes, make recommendations, pick up his check and go home. Sometimes it would lead to other opportunities and sometimes it didn't. But what the hell, it paid the bills.

Home, yes, that was the other thing. He had none, other than a rented apartment in Spooner, Wisconsin and a timeshare in a tiny town in Arizona. He'd become the proverbial snowbird, leaving the North Country with the first November snowflakes and returning north with the robins in the spring. When he thought about it, he had few close friends, and his social circle amounted to mostly past business contacts and academics. But then, for better or worse, that was the life he chose, and if things turned sour in the end, well, yeah the end. That was another thing.

A bright flash of light in the southern sky brought him out of his reverie. The first meteor was followed rapidly by a second and then a third. One was unusual for the time of year, and he considered himself lucky to have seen three in a row. Then suddenly a burst of meteors sent blazing streaks across the sky, and he couldn't resist pulling over to get a better look.

Back toward the southeast a natural display surpassing anything he'd ever seen on any 4th of July celebration lit up the night sky. Streaks of red and green and orange and white grew in intensity. The thought occurred to him that a major satellite in low earth orbit had failed and was now raining down in myriad pieces, each burning up in the atmosphere in a fiery and spectacular death. But the sheer volume of flashes ruled out that possibility. Then a glowing red fireball became visible, leaving a vivid trail like a huge burning snake. It appeared to arch upward, but then angled downward again and raced toward him. Instinctively, he backed up a step as the ball of intense flame swept past exploding on a barren hillside a quarter of a mile distant. Even at that distance, he could see the object glowing in the darkness.

As fast as his oversized body would allow, Denech slammed his butt down behind the steering wheel. Gravel kicked up by spinning tires sprayed fifty feet behind as he rocketed toward the glowing orb. The highway took an advantageous turn and brought him within a hundred yards. He grabbed the flashlight out of the glove box and quickly checked to make sure the batteries were good. The beam of light shone briefly on the picture of the destitute child in the blue denim overalls, but there were more exciting things to attend to now. The prospect of finding an actual meteorite had him like a drug, and he bailed out of the sedan at a dead run.

There was at first a bit of disappointment. From the size of the fireball, he expected something the size of a basketball or even bigger, but the fading glow of the object indicated it was baseball sized. He knew it would only take moments for the surface heat to dissipate, since the space rock had seconds before been in the deep freeze of space. After only a few minutes wait, he threw caution to the wind and now in the increasing light of dawn, cautiously stooped to get a better view. Peter Denech knew something about meteorites and this one was not typical. Most were of the stony kind, carbonaceous chondrites, made of mostly lighter elements like carbon and silicon. A few were more densely metallic and mainly iron. Yet as he drew this one from the dirt, he immediately noted it was far too perfect to be a natural object, and the spherical shape sent his hopes to the basement.

"Artificial, after all," he said aloud. "Some part of some space junk." Still it was a nice souvenir and would make for interesting discussion with Ed Micals, a friend and astronomy professor. So, holding the tiny flashlight in the corner of his mouth, he removed some dirt with his hands. He noted markings in a language other than English, but then several countries had added to the accumulating junk pile in space.

Denech squinted curiously to get a better look. "Hello," he mumbled. "What are you?" The markings were of some pictorial language. Maybe Chinese. That seemed reasonable. But they looked more like the Mayan writing of the ancient South American natives. An eventual trip to the University in Minneapolis would solve that puzzle.

The sky had lightened to that time just between dark and daybreak that made a flashlight useless, and Denech shoved the artifact into a pocket. He turned and immediately jumped, soundly startled by the sight of a swirling cloud of brilliant rainbow colored points of light. Slowly they coalesced into a translucent form—more vaporous than solid—of the child in blue denim bib overalls and within an arm's length away. With dark hair in two long braids, she clung tightly to a ragged doll with golden hair.

"Hello," she said looking up at him. "Would you like to play a game?"

* * * *

In the full light of morning, a confused Peter Denech sat on the shoulder of the rural highway. Occasionally, a pickup swished past sending a blast of air against his back, but he hardly noticed. By his side the child with the long dark braids sat clutching his arm. In his hand he held the picture of the destitute native South American child he had taped to his dashboard. It was the spitting image of his new companion. Impossible, for sure, but there she was, a frightened soul of maybe eight or nine that had no business being alone in the wide open country of central Montana. She refused to answer when he'd asked where she'd come from, or how she'd managed to get where she was. Denech was not yet ready to believe in Little Green Men or alien children for that matter. There was some logical, earthly explanation. He just had to find it.

The child had uttered few new words since their unusual meeting, but she had reiterated several times her initial request: Do you want to play a game? Twice Denech had led her to his grey sedan, got her buckled in, only to have her immediately leave as soon as he moved around to the driver's side. Each time she went back to her present position, and he'd followed her back each time, trying to convince her that she couldn't remain alone. Yet, all attempts at reasoning seemed to fall on deaf ears, as if she were deaf, or as if he was speaking a foreign language, or, more likely, she just didn't want to answer. For the last few minutes he'd been in the midst of a one-sided conversation.

"Do you want to play a game?" she said interrupting his monologue.

"Sure. Why not? What would you like to play?'

"Not fair. You have to pick."
"Okay. How about we play twenty questions?"
"I don't know that game. How does it go?"
"We ask each other questions to get to know each other."
The child giggled. "That wouldn't be fair."
"Why not?"
"Because I already know all about you."
"Really?"
"Of course, silly."
"Okay, if you're so smart, what's my wife's name?"
"You don't have a mate."
"Oh really. Then what do I have."

The child laid her head against his arm. "You have an empty place where your children should be."

Denech didn't at first speak. It was true. Not having children of his own was one thing he'd always regret. But the usual way to have them would require first a wife, and that thought had long ago left his mind. "Yes. You're right. There is a hollow place there. How could you know that?"

"Because I know all about you."
"How is that possible? I've never met you before."
"I have been a part of you for a long time. Just hiding."
"Hiding?"
"Until you were ready. Until I was ready. Until *we* were ready."
"And now I'm ready? For what?"
"To have children, silly. And to find Mommy and Daddy."

Denech realized he was beginning to get somewhere. "So you've been separated from your mother and father? Where did you come from?"

"Is this still part of the game?"
"Yes. The game."
"I come from *here*."
"Here? You mean right *here*?"

"Yes. But I see you don't believe me."

"I want to believe you, but there's not another soul for miles in this desolate country."

The child stood and pulled gently on Denech's arm. "Get up. Follow me. I will show you where there are some pretty stones so that you will know I am from *here*."

Denech hesitated, but then decided that if humoring her was a way to keep the conversation going, then humor her he would. Eventually, she might give some information that might lead to the whereabouts of her parents. He raised his considerable bulk from the dirt, and brushed the soil from his butt. "Okay. Lead the way. Let's go find your pretty stones."

An hour later and at least two miles from the highway, the child led Peter Denech into a dry riverbed. Over eons of time it had cut down through solid layers of earth that had been a stable part of the geology for tens of thousands of years. Denech noticed a narrow vein of pure white quartz running through the dark stone. The child went directly to the intrusive layer, which was about level with her eye and pointed. "Pretty stone," she said. "Soft pretty stone."

"Pure white quartz," Denech said. "But not soft stone. Very hard."

The child shook her head. "Not hard. Very soft stone, and not white. Yellow."

Denech came within inches and squinted to get a better look. He retrieved a fist sized rock from the ground and beat the white layer several times until a piece the size of a coffee cup broke free. There, indeed, were flakes of a yellow mineral imbedded in the quartz, and a yellow nugget the size of his thumbnail protruded from the cavity. He turned to the child with a questioning look.

"Would you like to play another game?" she asked.

Denech shook his head. "Ah, no. This one suddenly has my complete attention."

A Few Years Before

Twenty five year old Marilyn Lost left her hometown in up-state New York with her two-year-old baby and recently signed divorce papers and moved in with her cousin in metropolitan New York. For a small town girl, leaving the country required nearly all the courage she could muster, but remaining where she had grown up would have been much more difficult.

There were at least two sides to every human tragedy, and Marilyn knew deep down where it hurts that the reasons for her failed marriage were not limited to her former husband. Both had stretched fidelity to the breaking point, both had failed utterly at taking each other seriously, and both had let self-interest demolish what had begun as a mutual commitment. Their final battle, more of a brawl really, had been a very public spectacle in the only grocery store in town. The confrontation had been only occasionally sprinkled with words that were *not* of the four-letter variety. Within twenty-four hours, at least a dozen different versions of their tirade had made it to the ears of every inhabitant. The embarrassment to herself and her widowed mother was the impetus that drove her to New York and a new beginning.

Still, Marilyn Lost didn't consider herself a bad person. She attended church regularly, she donated time and energy to a homeless shelter, and she hoped one day to become a nurse. Her outgoing and friendly personality landed her a job as a receptionist at a nightclub—not her lifelong dream for sure—but a beginning. Her evening work hours worked out well since she had the day to care for her child, and her cousin, Rona—not her real name but a nickname that had stuck—generously volunteered to baby-sit while she was at work.

Rona was the stereotypical New Yorker, but with a Midwestern accent. She was brash, outspoken, and fiery like her hair, and not shy about letting others know her political views, or *any* views for that matter. She reveled in one demonstration after another with protests against intrusive government her particular favorite. She believed a sinister and secret government agency existed that acted outside the law, and with total disregard for individual rights. Marilyn had warned her on one occasion to "Tone it down." Rona had merely laughed and proudly displayed a newspaper clipping depicting her and several others getting arrested in front of the White House for demonstrating without a permit. The article contained a shouted quote by her: "Since when do I need a permit to practice free speech?" Not surprisingly, she'd taped a full sized replica of the Confederate flag to the ceiling above her bed. Despite her rebel nature, or maybe because of it, Rona was generous to a fault, asked nothing of Marilyn, and even lent Marilyn her cell phone until finances improved.

On one warm sun-filled Sunday afternoon in mid April, Marilyn left her baby in Rona's capable hands and caught a cab to Central Park. The patch of green in the urban jungle was as close as she could get to her hometown roots. She brought a bag of sunflower seeds to feed whatever animals might come along. The weekly event was her personal time to unwind and reflect, and also provided the opportunity to call her mother and share the latest gossip.

Yet on that warm day in April when life was erupting into its full glory after a winter's sleep, Marilyn Lost would be unaware that she would be the *one* in the *one*-in-a-billion odds. She would be unaware that she had, through Rona's generous act, drawn the one short straw out of over seven billion possibilities. She would never know that the value of her life had been reduced to the mechanical flip of a switch.

She would never know her death would be officially listed as "suspicious but lacking evidence" and unofficially as "collateral damage".

But perhaps it was a compassionate act of Providence that in the last moments of her short life she heard her mother's voice on the phone telling her, as all mother's do, that she would always love her no matter what.

Afterwards, and as would be expected, Marilyn's mother adopted the baby as her own. But curiously contradictory to an outside observer, Rona abandoned her rebel causes and joined the establishment known as the FBI.

Chapter 1

▼

MODERN TIMES

As was his habit, Carl Walker woke just as the radio alarm went off at 6:30, and slammed the palm of his hand down on the row of control buttons on top. Each button served a different function but by hitting them all, he was sure of getting the one that cancelled the obnoxious radio station and without actually having to open his eyes. As was her habit, Mary, Carl's wife of seven years, was already returning from the bathroom shower. Wrapped only in a long light blue bathrobe, she moved directly to her closet and retrieved her uniform for the day, a white blouse and brown slacks. Carl opened one eye and watched as the bathrobe fell to the floor, and drank in the smooth curves of her slender athletic body. Oh, how he longed; no, more like ached. To caress. To do what instinct demanded.

Mary looked up, caught his glance and reading his mind, smiled and shrugged. "Caught you peeking. Your call. I'm sure we could think of something."

"Oh, so tempting."

"Try to control yourself," she said and flashed a wicked grin.

"You know I married you for your beautiful mind, not your stunning body," he said propping himself up on his elbows.

"Right. And if beautiful minds took precedence over a nice set of boobs, the human race would have died out long ago."

"Then I consider myself doubly lucky."

"Thanks for the compliment. Now get your butt out of bed. Today may just be the beginning of something …"

"Interesting?"

"Different, for sure," Mary corrected.

"Oh no. What do the little hairs on the back of your neck tell you?"

"Don't you think this is all a bit strange?"

"Like what?"

"For starters how many job offers come literally out of the blue that require a husband and wife team?"

"Not many," Carl admitted.

"More like none."

"So what's your point?"

"I have no point. It's just different. But then there's the fact that we don't really do anything."

Carl pretended hurt feelings. "Now with that I'll take issue."

"Did you actually read the job description?"

"I glanced through it."

"It said and I quote. 'Successful applicants will be part of a team of visionary thinkers and pioneers.' I mean what kind of job is that?"

"Sounds like my kind of job. I like the part where it said dress informally. We fit the parameters. Both degreed. You math. Me geology and exobiology. Married. Ranked in the upper ten percent of our graduating class."

"Not according to your grades," Mary reminded him.

"Well, I was if you only count my senior year. It took me that long to realize I actually had to study."

"More like the last half of your senior year. Which is why you now do odd jobs and work part time at the planetarium, I'm a tutor at a halfway house trying to teach first level algebra to high school dropouts, and we live in a tiny rented apartment. I hate to break it to you, but astrobiology has very limited job opportunities. At least until the aliens land."

"That would be exobiology and employers aren't falling all over themselves for people with degrees in math logic either. So what do we do? Become teachers? I couldn't stand being a teenager. I'd hate to actually have to teach them."

Mary shrugged, and began dressing. Carl rose from the bed and wandered sleepily into the bathroom, scratching his right butt cheek as he passed. His features and body fit the average mold. Not handsome but not grotesque, not flabby but not muscle-bound either. Ten minutes later, after a quick shower and shave, he returned. Mary sat in front of a long mirror combing out straight black hair that reached to the middle of her back. Her large almond shaped eyes revealed a hint of Asian ancestry. His own thick dark brown hair disheveled in typical Einstein fashion, Carl began dressing and continued the conversation. "For a couple very smart people, we aren't exactly on the road to riches."

"We both did exactly what we wanted to do. But now we need to change direction and move on. Especially if we ever intend to hear the pitter-patter of little feet."

Carl smiled. "I take it you don't mean a pet collie."

"Nope. Someone a little more connected. If we're going to have children, we have to start thinking seriously about, well, being serious, and that includes our finances."

"Agreed. So we see what this Mr. Denech has to say. If it doesn't pan out, we're not exactly over the hill. Still plenty of time for a course correction."

"There's still graduate school," Mary offered.

"And give up this life of leisure? No way."

* * * *

At ten o'clock, following the flight from Duluth to Chicago, Carl and Mary Walker parked the rented gas/electric hybrid sedan in front of a red brick building in a residential area of Downers Grove, a western suburb of the Windy City. Carl retrieved a scrap of paper from his pocket and rechecked the address: 2012 Washington Street. Mary rolled the window down to get a better look.

"Hardly looks like an office," she said. "More like someone's home, built around 1950. Not modern but practical and sturdy." She hesitated, and then continued. "Look at that birdbath in the lawn. Very unique. Shaped like a lion's head, with the pan of water on its outstretched tongue."

"My guess is it's made of copper," Carl observed.

"Now green with oxidation. Hasn't been attended to in years."

"The grass needs mowing," Carl continued.

"And the shoots in the hedge are a foot high. This can't be the right place. A 'For Sale' sign on the lawn would fit right in."

"Look at the window on the left. Cracked glass in the upper left panel. No lights on inside."

"On the other hand, there's a satellite dish on the roof. Not cable. Probably wireless internet connection."

"Or privacy protected communications."

Mary slumped back against the seat. "All this way for what? A dead end? I say we go pound on the door just to relieve our frustrations."

"Sounds like a plan. We can always say we're salesmen if this is the wrong address," Carl suggested.

"Just so we have our stories straight. What are we selling?"

"Insurance."

"That's original."

"And sure to get the door slammed in our face."

* * * *

The couple exited the vehicle and followed the cracked and weathered sidewalk the short distance to the front door. Carl pushed the white button for the doorbell, and heard it sound in the interior. Mary reached over and straightened the collar on his forest green shirt and smoothed down a patch of unruly hair just as the door opened. The slight man with black-rimmed glasses and thinning white hair seemed surprised to see them.

"Yes?" he asked. "Is there something I can do for you?"

"Is this where we do the insurance pitch or just apologize and leave?" Mary wondered aloud.

"Pardon?"

"Sorry for disturbing you," Carl continued. "We seem to be at the wrong address."

"You are not the Walker couple?"

"Why, yes."

"You have the correct address. Please excuse the—the crudeness of this residence. It does, however, meet certain important criteria."

"Very homely—I mean homey," Carl said, and received a warning look from his wife.

"I know this seems very strange to you," the door greeter continued. "You have, in fact, taken a certain amount of risk coming here. You have no idea if this is a legitimate job offer or simply a ploy to lure two unsuspecting people into a devious trap. So think very carefully now before you decide to come in and if you really feel the risk is worth it. You can very easily turn and go back to Duluth."

"We're not important enough to be led into a trap," Carl admitted, "and we can always leave after the interview."

"There will be no interview," the bespectacled man said. "At least not in the traditional sense of the term."

"I'm confused," Carl stated. "Just why did we come all this way?"

Their greeter turned his full attention onto Mary. "Why, indeed, Mrs. Walker?"

"Because," Mary began slowly thinking the situation through, "we're already hired?"

"Excellent! Now come in please. Meet Mr. Denech."

*   *   *   *

The inside of the brick house matched the exterior: Out of date, worn, and in need of repair. It smelled musty and old from the prolonged absence of human occupants. But it was clean and tidy with usable, if Spartan, facilities. The door greeter led the two to a dimly lighted room, which, judging by the multi-colored farm animals on the light green wallpaper, must have been a child's bedroom at one time. From behind a desk, a thickset man with a rounded face and bald head closed an old laptop computer and rose to greet them. While the greeter wore a dark suit and tie, this man wore what appeared to be whatever was handy when he got up in the morning. His tan shirt and slacks were crumpled and wrinkled and looked as if he'd slept in them, information that did not escape Carl or Mary. They glanced at each other, and both knew what the other was thinking.

"Allow me to introduce myself. I'm Peter Denech. My associate is Randolf Haays. Mr. Haays and I are the despised bureaucrats that make or break an organization. At this point you are wondering just what you've gotten yourself into. Please sit down, and I'll do my best to explain. Is there anything we can get for you? Coffee, tea, a beer, cola?"

"Water would be fine," Mary said. Haays disappeared for a few moments and returned with two containers of bottled water. When each had taken a sip, Carl turned his attention back to Peter Denech.

"Yes, the thought crossed my mind that this is a prank."

"But you're still here. Why?"

"Curiosity, I suppose."

"Apprehensive?"

"Not really."

"Because of your defensive skills?"

"I have never gotten into a situation I couldn't get out of if that's what you're getting at."

"Defensive skills you learned from your wife," Denech added. "Which level are you?"

"Couldn't say. I don't keep track of that."

Denech smiled, and sat back in his chair, interlocking his fingers on his broad chest. "Defensive but not offensive."

"I don't look for trouble," Carl stated.

"But here you are."

"Guess I'm just a sucker for mysteries."

"And the prospect of a full-time job that pays more than minimum wage," Mary added.

Denech removed a pen from a varied assortment in his shirt pocket protector and began rolling it between huge stubby fingers. His expression grew serious, as he leaned forward. "Right now you're on a need to know basis. I will tell you just enough to give you a broad outline of your duties, but few specifics. You must understand that this is for your own protection, and to protect the integrity of Tranquility."

"Tranquility?"

"Just the name we've given the project you may be part of. Some of the group call this particular piece plan C. No need to get into the finer points now."

Carl folded his hands in his lap and tapped his thumbs together. "Plan C implies there is also a plan A and a plan B. Somehow being part of plan C doesn't inspire a great deal of enthusiasm."

"There is also a plan F, and, yes, that implies failure, and how we might deal with that eventuality. However, these others need not concern you. None is necessarily more or less likely than the other. These things remain to be seen."

"In other words, we're being placed on a leash without knowing where we are being led," Mary surmised.

"I wouldn't call it a leash, Mrs. Walker. More like a lifeline so we can pull you back to the dock if you don't like where the boat is headed."

"Or it starts to sink?" Carl speculated.

"Indeed, yes," Denech agreed.

"But at some point there will be no lifeline," Mary guessed.

"Very perceptive and absolutely true. Still interested? You haven't asked anything about pay."

"Didn't cross my mind," Carl said, "but since you brought it up."

"There will be no paycheck," Denech said.

"So this is a prank after all. It's been nice talking to you." Carl began to rise, but his wife gently pulled him back down.

"There are other forms of compensation besides a regular paycheck," Mary offered.

Denech nodded approvingly. "Right again. You will both be issued a credit card. Open ended to cover any and all reasonable expenses you might incur."

"So if I feel like a new Jaguar, I can just go buy one? Or my own airplane? How about a paid vacation to Hawaii?"

"For the most part, yes. However, there is a credit cap, and your housing choices will be somewhat limited."

"How limited?"

"Eventually, and if all goes according to plan, your duties may be divided between a facility in Arizona and one in Montana. You will be provided a place to stay and be allotted one hundred thousand dollars forgivable credit each. Tax free. More if an emergency arises where you require more funds. The cap on the credit card is there merely so that you don't draw undo attention to yourselves. Our financial resources are in actuality quite limitless. However, extravagant purchases—like a new sports car—are, I'm afraid, unacceptable at least for now. The initial phase of your employment will be one year. After that, it could well turn out to be a lifetime project with real out-of-this-world scientific and financial possibilities."

"Mind if I ask where your gold mine is?"

"Oddly enough, you've hit very close to home. My capitol assets are primarily in precious metals and diamonds."

"Okay, your offer sounds fair. Now just who do I have to kill?" Carl said deadpan.

"I feel you are not taking this seriously, Mr. Walker."

"We're sitting in a house past due for demolition and you're offering us credit cards with hundred thousand dollar credit limits that we never have to pay back. Old house. Megabuck offer. My wife's the math whiz but even I can see something about that doesn't add up."

"And what about you, Mrs. Walker? How do you feel about this proposal?"

"So far you've told us nothing specific. Without facts about our actual duties, I can reach no solid conclusion."

"And facts you will have, but in due time. But enough about this project. Now let me tell you what I know about you."

"If you're going by our job applications, you can't know much," Carl stated.

"You were picked for this endeavor long before you received the applications. You might say we know each of you better than you know yourselves. A team of a dozen professionals has studied, categorized, scrutinized, analyzed, and documented every facet of your entire twenty-five year existence. We have accounted for every day of your lives. Illnesses, heartbreaks, education, family, friends, food preferences, pets, personality profiles, genetic history, religious affiliations or lack thereof, favorite movies, your dedication to personal fitness, quirks. Literally *everything*."

"So why didn't you just haul us away in chains? Why the applications?"

"It was just the final test. Our people are good but there was still a five percent chance you would not be suitable. The fact that you made the effort to come here, and didn't drive away when you saw the condition of this hovel has reduced that percentage to just under one percent. With nearly one hundred percent certainty, we—our organization and myself—can say that you two are all that we have hoped for."

"So what is it we will be doing?"

"You'll be part of a team—"

"Of visionaries and pioneers," Mary cut in remembering the job description. "Pretty vague."

"Let me just say for now that you have been selected from literally thousands of couples and we have great faith in your intellectual abilities."

Carl sat back in his chair. "What my wife is asking is what do we do to earn this—this free lunch?"

"Hardly free. Once into Tranquility, it will consume your every waking hour. And just to be up front about this, there are over one hundred other couples that have made the final cut, so to speak. Rest assured, regardless of the outcome, you will be fully and fairly compensated with a minimum of one-year employment, but when the project gets underway, the number of couples left will be three or four at most. And maybe only one. There will be scant time for rest, let alone social activity. But then, according to our investigations, you two don't really need social activity. You have each other, and that was the first criteria."

"The first criteria?" Carl asked.

"It put you on our list of possibles. You two met when you were both sixteen and have been together virtually every possible moment since. That you haven't grown apart, that indeed you are still remarkably civil to each other, speaks volumes about your compatibility. You have an ironclad physical and mental bond, an extreme rarity in today's hello-goodbye society. You eloped at eighteen at which time you were already half way through college pursuing academic courses considerably more challenging than basket weaving. Though you certainly don't lack for intelligence, neither of you have gone much beyond your four-year degrees, though I also know you, Carl, have continued your interest in exobiology on your own. This was also an important criteria."

Carl shifted position in his chair. "Maybe our post-graduate work is merely on our to-do list. As far as your project goes, if it's scientists you need, there are certainly many brilliant people out there who know far more than either of us."

"Of course your poor grades in your first three years of college were a concern. But then we learned that you never cracked a book and still passed—albeit sometimes barely—the most difficult courses. Physics, biology, geology, calculus and the like. A great deal of your time, in fact, was spent playing poker at the student center."

"Actually it was Blackjack. I had to pay for our tuition somehow, and just didn't have time for all that reading," Carl admitted. "In class I listened and took good notes. It was enough to get by."

"But then you seemed to turn over a new leaf at the end of your junior year. Why was that?"

"It's personal," Carl stated.

"Yes, very personal. Your best friend, other than your wife, died in a humanitarian operation in the Middle East. Don't look surprised. I said I know everything about you."

Carl briefly appeared shaken, but quickly regained his composure. "Jason stepped on one unexploded landmine while trying to defuse another. They both went off. It was quick and painless. Enough said."

"At any rate, his death changed your thinking. Suddenly you went from a mediocre student to one almost fanatically driven. I ask again. Why?"

"Jason had great potential. He was a brilliant artist. A real humanitarian. He thought he could heal the world. Always talking about what he could do to make the world a better place. That's why he got the training to remove unexploded land mines. There are millions of them scattered about in dozens of countries leftover from one brutal war after another. If Jason had lived a full life, he would have made a real contribution to the human race. After his death—I know this doesn't make sense—I felt I had to live for two people."

Denech turned to Mary. "Is that how you see it?"

"Carl turned his grief into a positive. It was part of his healing process."

"A very logical deduction, Mrs. Walker."

"You have still not answered Carl's question. Why us? Why not gifted scientists with years of research and experience?"

"To be frank. Most are too old for our use. Past thirty."

"Thirty is too old?"

"Yes, and most are committed to their pet projects and therefore lack a broader perspective. We need people completely open to new and potentially bizarre ideas."

"In other words, you want people who can still be molded into a form you, no doubt, have chosen," Mary stated.

"Yes, there's truth to that," Denech admitted. "Going even farther, it's the same reason the military picks young people to be soldiers. While they lack real life experience—in fact real life experience would be a handicap from the military point of view—their personalities can be altered and redefined with the military mindset. We have no plans to destroy your personalities—in fact it would be counterproductive—but make no mistake we could. You are yet young enough to be idealistic, adaptable, and even tolerant. These qualities tend to dissipate with age."

"So what else do you know about us?" Carl continued.

"I can give you much more personal data. First sexual experience, your intimate habits, and the like, but it would serve no purpose here. Suffice it to say that the work you will be doing absolutely requires an unbreakable physical commitment to one and only one other person. Neither of you have strayed from your relationship, though each has had many opportunities."

Carl stood to relieve the stiffness he felt in muscles tensed by mental stress, and paced toward a window. "So that was the first criteria? That we've been faithful to each other? Just how many other criteria are there?"

"There are over two hundred standards you had to meet. We began with a database of thousands of couples and have reduced that to just over a hundred. You really don't know how unique you are."

Carl's voice remained level, but grew considerably deeper, as he returned to his chair. His knuckles grew white as his fingers dug into the armrests. "Let me say as calmly as I can that right now I'm beyond angry, bordering on furious. What right do you have to intrude into our private lives, even into our most private affairs? Just what could you learn from our personal relationship, or was it just the workings of a sick mind?"

"Very good question. All together, we learned a lot. You, and I mean both of you, have the confidence to act upon your convictions. You attach very little importance to materialism. You tend to be impatient, as are most young adults, but, as evidenced here, you are the master of your emotions, and yet realize that emotions are part of the human experience and not to be ignored. We also know that you are looking for something indefinable out of life, some connection to something, that at this point has eluded you."

"And just how would you know all that? Half the time I don't even know that."

Denech deferred to Randolf Haays who had stood silently by as an observer. An unspoken message passed between them. "The particulars of our methods do not have to be announced here," Haays began. "From your comments, however, I see now we've done a poor job by way of explanation. I'm stepping beyond where we had intended, but I will give you this one more bit of information. While your wife, Mary, has clearly a greater mental capacity; you, Mr. Walker, have something even more endearing to this project. Besides your geology degree, you have a keen interest in exobiology, which means you study not so much what is known to be, but what might be possible based on what is known. That requires a great leap of imagination. It also means you have accepted without question the proposition that there could be life forms beyond the confines of earth."

Carl fixed his gaze on Haays. "So what are you saying? We're going to be studying little green men?"

"Hardly, or at least highly unlikely. In fact, you may never use your education in this project at all. But your perspective is part of the mix that I need to facilitate the success of Tranquility."

"You keep talking about 'the project.' Just what is Tranquility?"

"Again I am straying ahead, but I will tell you this. If all the parameters of Tranquility were known, there is a ninety percent chance the world of men would completely collapse within forty-eight hours and modern civilization would implode. While this may well be inevitable in any case, it is imperative that it be staved off for as long as possible."

"Assuming this is not a delusional trip down the rabbit hole, what time frame are we talking about?"

"A rabbit hole," Haays stated and glanced at Denech. "Interesting choice of words. But to answer your question, ideally, one year. After that, a big question mark."

"One year?" Carl exclaimed. "That's not much time to do anything in science."

Denech laughed and resumed his part in the conversation. "Tranquility, plan A, B, and C, and even F, began as a mere computer simulation several years ago. You're coming in at the very end."

"So Tranquility is a computer simulation?"

"Something like that. Suffice it to say we fed certain variables into a complex prediction program and got an unexpected and unsettling result. Over the intervening years we have continually updated and refined the program as more accurate information became available."

"And?" Carl pressed.

"And things have gone from bad to worse. *Everything* that Tranquility predicted is unfolding. And that's what's so frightening. Originally, we thought there might be some deviation, some moderation, but instead there has only been a steady reinforcement of what was originally mere speculation."

"What are you talking about really? Climate change? Alien contact? World war? Some devastating plague? Terrorists?"

Denech shrugged. "Don't let your imagination run wild. However, one man's terrorist is another man's freedom fighter. To the English, George Washington was a terrorist. Of course one can never rule out the possibility of a plague. Or mass starvation. Or geologic upheaval. And be prepared. The symmetry is already broken. The bomb is exploding. This is something far more important than little green men, I assure you."

"What then?" Carl asked.

"Our place in history. Humanity's place in history."

"Of course. Now I get it. We save the world."

"I'm afraid that's completely impossible."

"Impossible? Why?"

"What was once a positive is now a negative. But we may save humanity. Yet one of the questions you may be put in a position to answer is: *Should we?*"

Carl abruptly stood. "Then you have the wrong man. I'm not a philosopher, or even religious. What you seem to be asking is way outside my training."

"Don't you see? Your training, your mindset, confirms it. You believe in life outside the bounds of earth. That takes imagination, yes, but it also requires a certain degree of faith. That you are not affiliated with any organized congregation is completely irrelevant."

"My belief in extraterrestrial life is based on fact and reason, not myths and wishful thinking. Religion is way too violent for my tastes. I'll take an honest atheist to a religious fanatic any day. Just about every side of every war has always claimed to have a just and compassionate god on their side."

"I know. Now please sit down. You mentioned religion. I didn't. Don't confuse religion with faith."

"There's a difference?"

"Most definitely."

Carl's skeptical expression prompted Denech to explain.

"Religion is the bureaucracy that inevitably grows around any good idea. And like any bureaucracy, it is ultimately corrupted by self-serving individuals, and becomes rancid and cancerous. However, in its simplest form, faith is simply trust."

"I'm not following," Carl admitted.

Denech placed his pen back in his shirt pocket, taking the moment to contemplate his next statement. "Do you check up on your wife when she's at work?" He asked.

"What? Of course not," Carl answered.

"She's a very attractive and desirable woman. Aren't you worried some testosterone driven male may try to—as you young people say—hit on her?"

"I'm sure some do, but it doesn't bother me."

"Why?"

"Because I trust her."

"Precisely. You don't need proof. You have faith in her."

"That's way different than faith in prehistoric dogma or some hypothetical god."

"Maybe. Maybe not. You have been schooled in science. Analyze this from that point of view. But rest assured that as Tranquility unfolds faith will play a critical role, and yours may well be put to the test."

For several moments, no one spoke. Then Denech seemed to come to a decision and extracted a brown manila envelope from the desk drawer and handed it to Mary. "This is a generic list of your duties and some required training. Nothing you can't learn in a few minutes. Sorry if it's still pretty vague. Read it. Then tear it up and throw it away. At this point that's for your own protection. Included also are your two credit cards. Try them out. Spend a few days in Hawaii. But be back in Duluth in five days. We will contact you with your first assignment. Everything will happen very quickly now. Time is running out."

"I have one question before we accept these," Mary said.

"Go ahead."

"Is anything we would be doing illegal?"

"Absolutely nothing you will be doing is against any set of just rules or protocols."

"What about unethical, or that might compromise our future academic plans?"

"At this point I can give you an emphatic 'no', but I cannot predict for certain where this will lead you."

"So. No guarantees."

"No guarantees, except that it will be, well, interesting is the best I can say. The Tranquility program has laid out a definite future, but it is not necessarily specific to individuals. The future, as they say, is not for us to see. I am hopeful for a positive outcome."

"What about dangerous?" Carl cut in.

Denech nodded slightly. "We are talking about a potentially great change, and any departure from the status quo entails risks. Here I must be completely candid. Yes, there is the possibility of danger, certainly great risk, but also the possibility of great accomplishments."

"What great accomplishments?" Carl asked.

"In due time. In due time. Use the card. Go now to someplace nice. But be at your apartment in five days to begin phase one."

"What if we want to contact you sooner? Maybe to tell you to forget the whole thing."

"We won't be here. With others watching we cannot remain in one place too long or risk exposing our unique plans to competitors. Every evidence of our presence here—connections, computers, phones, everything—will be destroyed. The house, sterilized. And we will vanish. I know that seems suspicious or even sinister. You'll just have to trust me."

For several moments, Carl Walker studied the big man, and then looked to his wife, whose expression did not reveal the slightest hint of her thoughts. However, reading the unspoken message in her eyes, Carl nodded, and turned back to Denech. "Okay. You've aroused our curiosity. We'll play along for now."

"Excellent! Now just wait for a contact, and thanks. The codeword will be Flossy. Trust only the person who speaks that word."

"Flossy? Got it."

Denech nodded, and continued. "You are all we could have hoped for. Just remember. This is a once in a lifetime opportunity. This is a corporate secret, you might say, so you will discuss this offer with each other but no one else. You will dissect it, you will research it, and you will weigh each and every bit of information you have gleaned here. Don't worry. We expect that."

Peter Denech stood and moved around the desk as Carl and Mary Walker rose from their chairs. The big man placed his massive arms around the two like long lost children, surprising both with the display of affection. There was genuine emotion in his voice as he spoke, and tiny tears in the corners of his eyes. "I know you two as if I'd raised you myself. And I know you will be part of this. Remember. The future hangs in the balance."

Chapter 2

Randolf Haays, the diminutive man with dark rimmed glasses and thinning white hair, entered the room through a side door and set a neat stack of papers on the desk before Peter Denech. Silver hair tied back in a tight round ball, a middle-aged woman followed. With hands placed firmly in the side pockets of her white lab coat, she remained silent as the two men began examining the printouts, arranging them in different piles. Unlike the two men, the woman wore a nametag clipped to the collar of her coat. It identified her as Amanda Korneth, but gave no position or title.

"I can save you a great deal of time. Go directly to the summation," she suggested, and sat down on the seat recently occupied by Mary Walker. "The monitors told me the story, but I'm curious to hear your opinions."

The big man located the summary papers and began skimming through them with Randolf Haays looking over his shoulder. After a few minutes, Denech looked back at Korneth.

"Interesting. No sign of intentional deception in either. Some elevated physiological responses in Carl as expected. Some notable spikes in heart rate and respiration. Mary seems to have handled it all like a rock. All seems to coincide with what we already knew."

"As was expected. What's your projection for phase one?" Korneth continued.

"Mary should have no trouble whatsoever, and Carl—I believe he'll also survive."

Korneth nodded, then turned her attention to Haays who had so far not offered any comment. "Your expression leads me to believe you have doubts."

"Frankly, I disagree with Peter's assessment of both."

"Continue."

"Peter aptly described Mary as a rock with very little variation in emotional responses—even when Carl was noticeably upset—frankly almost as if she was bored with the entire process. Nothing seems to have fazed her."

"And you think that's bad because?"

"Rocks are hard to crack but when they do its usually with violent, and quite frankly unpredictable consequences."

"So you think she'll crack?" Korneth pressed.

"Not during the first phase. That I'll concede. However, at some future time—a far more critical time—she may."

"I totally disagree," Denech stated with poorly disguised irritation. "In fact, I would pick her for the leadership role. We're looking for stable, reasonable, intelligent, and adaptable people. She couldn't fit those parameters better—certainly better than others—and her background—"

"And what about Carl," Korneth interrupted, returning her attention to Haays.

"He won't survive the first week of phase one."

"You think he's corruptible?"

"He won't see it as seduction," Haays stated.

"All his indicators point to an ethical young man," Denech reminded him.

"But he is still a young man with all the normal impulses, and his ethics could be used against him. Bottom line. He'll fold within the first week."

"Again I vigorously disagree," Denech stressed, and let it go at that.

Amanda Korneth remained silent for a few moments before continuing.

"Carl and Mary seem to be ideal for our use. I'd certainly not want to break up the set. Their diverse genetic backgrounds alone make them a unique find. Carl is a good mix, and comes from long-lived stock. And Mary's bloodline has representative DNA from every major race. Not only that she has all the good stuff without any genetic markers for disease or impairment. Under ordinary circumstances she could very easily live to be a hundred."

Denech nodded in agreement. "Given what we know, it is doubtful Mary would continue without Carl, or Carl without Mary for that matter."

"So. Recommendations?" Korneth said.

"Proceed to phase one," Denech stated emphatically. "There is always going to be a chance of error."

"With this project, there can be *no* chance of error," Haays said slapping his hand forcefully down on the desk, and focused his attention squarely on Korneth to make his point.

"Your position is duly noted, Randolf. However, we have to be realistic, too. We have to accept the fact that even if everything goes off perfectly, there is still only the smallest chance that Plan C will succeed."

Denech grew pensive. "Well, heaven help us if we fail. I suppose we'd at least have the satisfaction of knowing we tried."

"Small comfort for those who don't have a clue what is about to happen," Korneth said.

"I hate to be the perennial pessimist," Haays continued. "But maybe we need to take a closer look at Plan F, and just let Nature sort it all out."

For the first time Korneth smiled, exposing perfect white teeth, and her tone lightened. "Interesting observation coming from a good Catholic."

"Fate or God. Take your pick. But in the end it will be in His hands."

"My money," Denech volunteered, "is on the two who just walked out that door."

"Frankly, Gentlemen," Korneth stated, "I believe the God-factor was removed from this equation long ago. The Tranquility program has no way to incorporate miracles."

"Nor should it," Haays stated, taking her comments seriously. "However, in the end that may be all we're left."

"You cling to your delusions," Denech interjected with no attempt to conceal his sarcasm. "Nature gave us a brain for a reason. Now if only we'd use it. If there's going to be a miracle, we're going to have to make it ourselves."

Several moments of tense silence followed and then Korneth continued, directing her comments at Denech. "Given your intimate knowledge of the Walkers, do you think they'll really spend the next week in Hawaii?"

"Not a chance. They'll go somewhere secluded, and try to sort through all this."

"And your assessment, Randolf?"

"On that, I agree. But I'd keep the link to their credit line open just in case we're wrong, and monitor their movements. Put Red on it. I don't like surprises."

Denech sat back and reflected. "So it has begun. This terrible, horrible thing we do has begun."

"You understand that what we are about to attempt is against everything I believe in," Haays said.

"Yet here you are. Why?"

"Maybe because deep down I don't think it will work."

"Yet you stay."

"I was there for the beginning and I'll be there for the end. As your friend, I owe you that much."

"You owe me nothing, Randolf. It is I who owe you. I just hope someday I can repay the debt." Denech abruptly rose. "Okay, then. We have thirty minutes. Let's make it happen."

* * * *

Neither of the Walkers spoke as Carl maneuvered the rental car back onto Maple Avenue through the continuous traffic, turned west until Main Street, and pulled into the first gas station on the right side of the road. Mary slid out of her side, and entered the convenience store as Carl put ten dollars worth of gas into the vehicle. Given the vehicle was a hybrid, the added fuel was more than enough to get back to O'Hare, but he had no intention of breaking down in the vast sea of humanity, which was Chicago and all her satellite children. The expenditure was really a chance to test out his recently acquired credit card from Peter Denech. If all of this was an elaborate hoax, better to have it cost him ten dollars than the cost of airline tickets to Hawaii. He was in the process of securing his receipt when Mary returned.

"Well?" she asked.

"Looks like the card is valid." He placed the receipt in her outstretched hand. "Here's the paper to prove it."

"Mine too," she added. "Bought some mixed nuts and grape juice for a snack, but—"

"But what?"

"But this is all so bizarre. We don't know anything about these people, and yet we are ready to dive into whatever they have going as if it were merely a dip in the pool."

"The credit cards prove at least that part of their story is true."

"It isn't them. It's *us*."

"Us?"

"Are we so desperate for excitement or money that we throw caution to the wind and charge blindly into something—something—"

"You said it. Bizarre. Are you having second thoughts?"

"It's strange. I felt so calm back there in the house. Like I was in complete control. Like I was *supposed* to be there. Now, the left side of my brain, the logical side, says everything is kosher, but the right side, the emotional side, is screaming at me to run from this as fast as we can. Do you realize how backwards that is for me?"

Carl grinned. "Something must be wrong. You hardly ever let the emotional side out to play."

"But when I do?"

"I am greatly appreciative," Carl admitted, placing his arms around her waist and playfully drawing her close. He moved her slowly away, and looked into her eyes. "This is scary. You're trembling."

"Sorry. It's those damn emotions."

"Look. I care about only you. If you think we should abort, then we abort. We're only a few minutes from Denech."

"I'm thinking it may be the wise thing to do. I just have this terribly bad feeling about this all of a sudden."

"Okay. We return the credit cards, give him twenty bucks to cover what we've spent, and say thanks but no thanks."

"We'd be giving up a lot of money," Mary reflected. "Money we could use to start a family, or get into graduate school. That's the other thing to consider."

"We'll find a way without Denech."

Mary relaxed in Carl's arms. "Thanks. I love you, you know."

"And all this time I thought you were just hanging around for my money," Carl teased. "Well, let's go give Denech the bad news."

* * * *

The return trip from the gas station to the meeting house took less than fifteen minutes and their total absence could not have been more than an hour, but Carl Walker circled several blocks in search of a plain dilapidated red brick home in need of demolition. He retrieved the slip of paper with the address, handed it to Mary, and together they searched for 2012 Washington Street. Finally, Carl slowed to a stop along the curb, and pointed to the number on a rambler style home. "2010. We have to be close." He idled the car slowly forward along the curb, and nearly passed the neatly trimmed low hedges that framed a manicured lawn. A child scampered about on the green grass, circling playfully around a polished copper birdbath with the water dish resting on the outstretched tongue of a lion. The home, made of shiny red bricks, seemed snug and inviting.

"This can't be it," Mary stated, and the recognition that it was sent a shiver up and down her spine. "What happened to this place? It's like we've gone back in time fifty years to when it was brand new."

"Either that or we've witnessed the fastest remodeling job in the history of carpentry," Carl added. "What the hell is going on here?"

Mary sat back and reflected. "Remember this morning when you asked me about those little hairs on the back of my neck."

"Yes."

"Well, they're all standing straight up at attention. This is beyond bizarre."

The little girl—about eight years old in blue denim bib overalls and long dark hair in braids—came within three feet of the car and stared at Mary. She held tightly to a tattered doll with golden hair, holding it against her chest.

"I can see you," she said in a shy sweet voice. "Can you see me?"

Mary and Carl nodded. "Yes, you are very pretty and we see you just fine," Mary said. "Is your mother or father home?"

"They are now."

"May we speak to them?"

The child giggled. "Of course, silly."

The child didn't seem to understand, and Mary continued on a different track. "Do you know Peter Denech?"

"Of course, but he's not here right now."

"Will you be seeing him anytime soon?"

"Yes. Soon."

From behind the steering wheel, Carl looked past his wife and into the eyes of the child. "Tell Peter we've changed our minds. We've decided not to be part of his organization."

The child's face grew sad. "But what will I do without Mother and Father?"

"I'm sure your mother and father love you very much."

"Yes, they will."

"How long have you lived here?" Mary asked, noting the child's anxiety, and anxious to change the subject.

"Always."

Mary smiled warmly. "Thank you for your help. We have to go now."

"Good, bye," she said. "Next time you come, we can play with my doll. Her name is Flossy."

Chapter 3

▼

All the man-made pieces of suburbia—homes and roads, warehouses and stoplights, old tenement buildings and pavement—flashed by the window of the commuter car as it entered deeper into metropolitan Chicago.

Carl and Mary Walker had several hours to fill before their flight left from O'Hare and it had been a spur of the moment decision to catch the commuter train in Downers Grove and ride into the downtown Chicago Loop. They sat together on the padded bench seat, almost as one, heads resting against each other, arms entwined, but silent in individual thoughts. The car was nearly empty with only one old man near the other end, and a middle-aged couple. Covered with a long black raincoat and wide brimmed hat, the white bearded senior was slouched over reading a newspaper. The middle-aged couple had their hands full trying to placate a fussing baby.

There was something about the smooth, subtle power that propelled trains along that resonated in the depths of Mary's consciousness. Air travel was fast, but train travel seemed more secure, more relaxing from the inner vibrations of the tons and tons of iron and steel moving without resistance. It was almost hypnotizing.

Carl suggested they catch a cab at Central Station and take in the Museum of Natural History and the Planetarium that rested on the shore of Lake Michigan. Maybe, if the May showers held off, they'd forgo the cab and hike the many blocks from the station instead. The time would not be devoted to being a tourist, however. It would provide them with the opportunity to dissect the recent events, and analyze just what they'd gotten themselves into.

At the meeting place, Mary had recognized Peter Denech immediately thanks to her ability to place a name on the face of every person she'd ever had more than fleeting contact. Several years before, while she was still in college, Denech came to the University in Minneapolis where she and Carl were attending school and presented the astronomy department with a gift of one hundred thousand dollars. Her academic advisor had strongly encouraged her, as well as most other students in the math and science fields, to attend the presentation ceremony as a "show of appreciation" as he put it. She had reluctantly gone, but Peter Denech had made an impression on her.

However, Peter Denech back then looked different. He had been quite a bit thinner, and much younger looking with considerably more hair. The few intervening years, it seemed, had not been particularly kind to him. However, their recent acquaintance was the same man, or an awfully good impersonator. The one thing that hadn't changed was his distinctive deep voice. Denech's financial gift to the University, she recalled, was to be used by Professor Edward Micals, head of the astronomy department, who was involved in the search for Near Earth Objects, or NEO's as the asteroids were called. He had found three, one of which passed within the orbit of the moon some years before. It had been a "near miss" reportedly coming within twenty thousand miles of earth. While a direct hit would not have caused a worldwide catastrophic event, it certainly could have ruined a perfectly good day for anyone within fifty miles of impact.

She remembered the news release at the time. It was a substantial asteroid about the size of a small mountain. There had been some widely scattered trailing debris, nothing larger than a basketball and a lot of sand and dust-sized particles, some of which entered the earth's atmosphere creating a rather spectacular meteor display. Some of the meteorites that made it to earth fell along a swath from South Dakota to Montana and even up into Canada, and there had been frenzied activity for a time as amateur geologists descended on the area hoping to find some of the space relics. The official reports were that none were found, however, having burned up in the atmosphere, and much to the chagrin of the prospectors, who were hoping for valuable minerals like gold or platinum. Any tiny piece would have been valuable to astronomers, however, because meteorites were often left over pieces of the building blocks of the planets, and billions of years old.

Peter Denech's presentation address to students and faculty had been somewhat anti-climactic. He said all the normal uplifting things that go in one ear and out the other. He noted that there was no such thing as good people or evil people. Only flawed people, and that flaws were often a matter of perspective and circumstance. In time the alarmist might become the prophet, the radical the visionary, the terrorist the freedom fighter. All things were relative, but there were basic propositions all humans needed to strive for: The ability to see through another's set of eyes, to look past the personal immediate and project into the human future, and the desire to be part of the solution and not the problem. He spoke for only a few minutes, made the ceremonial presentation of the check that measured two feet by four feet, shook hands with the university President and Professor Micals, and then disappeared from the podium. But before he left, Denech had done something then that stuck with her, and no doubt everyone who had been present. He removed a shoe and struck the podium in a comical imitation of what a former communist leader had once done at the United Nations General Assembly in total seriousness. She remembered Denech's words.

"You will remember this day not because of anything earthshaking that I have said, but because a weird guy took off his shoe and beat his prepared notes with it. And because you will remember the shoe, you will remember me. And because you remember me, you will remember this: Our time on earth is short. Make the most of it. This is the only chance we'll get to make things right."

Mary Walker remembered. Thinking about it the speech sounded more like the final words of a commencement address with a parting bit of wisdom. She remembered, even with perhaps five hundred people in the auditorium, how he seemed to single her out and how his gaze seemed to linger on her face. Now she wondered, given what Denech had said back in the dilapidated house, if he had been talking to her directly that day years before. That already the Tranquility project had begun. She wondered if on that day he had already begun his investigation into the lives of Carl and Mary Walker.

*　　*　　*　　*

"I know what you're thinking. I recognized him too," Carl Walker stated, and waved his hand in front of Mary's glazed over eyes. She awoke from her thoughts and smiled.

"I'm surprised you do. Even though you were sitting right next to me, you were somewhat distracted. You kept tickling my knee."

"What can I say? You were irresistible even then."

"More like you were in a sexual fever."

"Hey. Don't knock it. We're still together aren't we?"

"I hope there's more to our relationship than sex."

"Let me think. Was that a trick question?" Carl grew serious. "Okay. There's a logical explanation for all this," Carl stated, but his voice lacked conviction. "There has to be."

"Sure. We're offered big bucks because we're younger than thirty, a run down house magically transforms into a cozy cottage, and two men disappear into hyperspace. And a little girl, a total stranger in that same house, just happens to have a doll whose name is the code word for this entire operation. This is not coincidence. But for the life of me I can't make any sense of it. Except that now it looks like we're part of something that we can't get out of."

"Go some place and hide comes to mind," Carl stated, but his ear-to-ear grin betrayed his lack of seriousness. "Okay. One thing at a time. Why would they want young adults instead of seasoned scientists?"

"It's apparently the age factor. It has to be critical for some reason. Maybe because young people are generally in better physical condition," Mary guessed. She considered for a moment. "Or maybe it's just the obvious. Young people have more years ahead of them than behind."

"That implies a long term commitment of some sort. But Denech said that there was only a one year time frame."

"Well, from a universal perspective, time is relative," Mary observed.

"For whatever reason, brawn is just as important as brains in their Tranquility program. We're both in good shape."

"Well, what about the house?" Mary asked. "Is it possible to transform it like that in an hour?"

"Maybe, if you had a big crew. We could go back and talk to the neighbors. See if there was a lot of activity there after we left. I suppose, if you had the right people, it could be done."

"So, nothing magical about it. The question is: Why?"

"Denech did say that all evidence of their presence would be destroyed," Carl reflected.

"Yes. Because he didn't want their competitors to know what was going on."

"At any rate there was one thing that didn't get fixed."

"The cracked window pane. I noticed it too," Mary stated. "What about the little girl living there?" Mary pressed.

"Maybe just a good actor."

"And the name of the little girl's doll. The codeword. Flossy. That seems way beyond coincidence."

"True. But coincidences do happen. Though I agree there is almost certainly some connection."

"There was something else," Mary said. "But I'm reluctant to bring it up. It goes back to those emotions, and it's far from logical."

"What?"

"My brain is genetically wired to remember faces. I can't help it. It's crazy and impossible, but I *knew* that little girl."

"Knew? How?"

"From a long time ago, I think. But I can't for the life of me remember her name."

"How long ago?" Carl asked.

"It seems like forever, but of course it must have been relatively recent, since the girl couldn't have been more than eight or nine. But I don't remember her as a baby or a toddler. I remember her as she looks now."

Carl hesitated before continuing, knowing of Mary's own troubled childhood.

"Maybe," he began cautiously, "you are somehow mixing up your own past with the young girl. A psychological mirror. She did have a similarity to you."

"That is possible. Or more likely a barely remembered dream. But that still doesn't explain the doll named Flossy."

"True. There is another thing that occurred to me. Denech's short speech at the University when he presented the check. Remember?"

"How could I forget him beating his shoe on the podium?"

"You're the one with the near photographic memory. Remember his parting words?'

"Sure. 'Our time on earth is short. Make the most of it. This is the only chance we'll get to make things right.' What about it?"

"Maybe he was being literal."

"What do you mean?"

"Maybe he wasn't talking about just those that were there. Maybe he was talking about all of mankind."

Mary reflected. "So he was giving a warning to everyone on earth?"

"Makes sense, given our recent conversation with him. Remember, he said Tranquility was about saving humanity."

"But not the world," Mary completed. "He also said you might be put into a position to decide if you should. As if humanity was or wasn't worth saving."

"No pressure there, but since you and I are a part of humanity and I'm rather fond of living, I can see only one logical answer to that."

"There is one part of Denech's parting comments that day about making things right that truly does bother me."

"Which is?"

"That this would be the only chance we'd get."

A sudden flash of lightning followed almost immediately by exploding thunder drew their attention to the weather. A steady driving rain began beating against the windows, obscuring from view all beyond the pane of glass. The predicted May showers had arrived, and a change of plans was now in order. A dreary day spent in downtown Chicago with raw northeast winds rolling in off Lake Michigan was not the recipe for an enjoyable afternoon.

From just within his peripheral vision, Carl noticed the old man who had been reading the newspaper get slowly up and exit into the next car, leaving only the middle aged couple and their child. The youngster now grew quiet, as if a switch had been turned off. The crying child had not bothered Carl, however, as he was able to tune out most distractions, and, he reflected with a smile, the child was not his. The couple rose and began walking towards them along the center isle, and the thought crossed Carl's mind that it was not wise to leave a baby unattended. Now, as the couple approached, he noticed their attention was directed towards him and Mary, and suddenly nothing about the present circumstances seemed right, and, more critically, safe. Carl gently nudged Mary and she glanced at him, and then at the two that now stood staring down at them.

They were casually dressed. The clean-shaven man was unremarkable looking except that his eyes were piercing and focused, and the woman had the hardened look of an ex-con. After all the cooing and coaxing with the child, the transformation to their true intent was worthy of an academy award.

"Carl and Mary Walker?" the man began, and both man and woman removed identification badges from their pockets that identified them as FBI. "I'm agent Smith and this is Agent Johnson."

"What's up?" Carl asked conversationally, but his muscles tensed and he could feel Mary's grip on his arm grow considerably tighter.

"Just answer the question," the woman countered.

"I'm Mary Walker," Mary interjected, "and this is my husband, Carl. Is there something we can do for you?"

Smith stated firmly, "You will accompany us to a safe facility."

Carl remembered Denech's admonishment to trust only those who knew the code. "Is there some word you'd like to say to convince us of your good intentions?"

The agents exchanged glances, and Smith continued. "We are federal agents. We are under orders to place you into protective custody."

"Protective custody? From whom?"

"We are not at liberty to say."

"Then thanks but no thanks," Carl stated. "We can take care of ourselves."

The agents glanced at each other, and the man continued.

"Then we will place you under arrest."

"For what?" Carl asked.

"Un-American activities."

"This *is* America," Mary cut in. "And as Americans, we have the right to know just what it is we're being accused of, access to our attorney, and—"

"Not really," Agent Johnson interrupted. "Not if you're a suspected member of a terrorist organization."

"What are you talking about?" Carl asked incredulously.

Again the man and woman exchanged glances.

"On orders of the President, you are being detained indefinitely as suspected members of a terrorist organization. As such you are not entitled to any of the benefits and privileges of decent, hard working Americans. Habeas corpus does not apply. You are suspected enemies of the State and will be treated as such." The woman drew a breath and then continued in harsh tones. "Is that clear enough for you?"

To make her point clear, she drew a semi-automatic 8mm pistol from a hidden holster and pointed it directly at them.

"Please do not resist," she stated. "I assure you one or the other of you, or both, will die right here if you make any hostile move."

"This is crazy," Carl said, stunned. "We're not political. There has to be some mistake."

"The mistake was yours to get involved in subversive activities. Now please extend your wrists so Agent Smith can place the necessary restraints."

"I think not," Carl stated, and a hot blood rush of anger reddened his face.

Agent Smith drew his own weapon. "There is no use in resistance. We have orders to shoot to kill if need be."

"We are unarmed," Mary stated. "Killing us would be an act of murder."

"Not murder. Just doing our job. Killing what needs killing," Smith said. "When it comes to keeping America safe, people like you don't count. Now extend your wrists, or the train folks are going to have an awful mess to clean up."

Carl and Mary Walker did not move, the overwhelming absurdity of the situation keeping them frozen in place. The prospect of being separated only strengthened their grip on one another. If there was a way—any way—for Carl to lunge at the two, he would have and gladly taken a bullet to protect Mary. But the attempt would be futile, he knew. So instead they did nothing, no overt aggression but no compliance either. Just quiet passive resistance. The next move would be up to the agents.

However, the next move came from an unexpected source. Two tiny muffled puffs of sound filled the quiet of the commuter car, and Agent Smith and Johnson wilted to the deck.

"Quickly, now." The voice came from beneath the brim of a hat. "Help me get these two into a seat before we pick up more passengers."

Carl and Mary Walker remained frozen in place, and stared at the person who now holstered a weapon under her left arm, and removed the wide brimmed hat. From under it, reddish brown hair fell upon graceful shoulders. Removing the costume beard, the woman winced as adhesive pulled at her face. She looked directly at the Walkers and smiled a comforting smile. "My friends call me Red. Come on! Come on! Help me here," she urged, and began struggling with one of the bodies. "Trust me. They're not dead. Just down for the count. I assume you've figured out the 'baby' was a recording."

Carl and Mary quickly stood and helped the red haired woman prop up the two agents in an adjacent bench seat. When they were in place, Red stood with hands planted firmly on ample hips and looked approvingly at the sleeping forms. "Good. Like sleeping babies." She turned to the Walkers, who were just emerging from their state of shock.

"What—what in the world is going on here?" Carl stuttered. "And is that really you, or are you going to pull off another mask and turn into an elderly man again."

Red laughed, and her eyes flashed as she pointed to herself. "This is me."

"I can see how you got your name, but how did you happen to be here?" Mary asked skeptically.

"Not by accident, if that's what you're getting at. The Old Man said keep an eye on you in case things went south. Given our sleeping guests, I'd say it was a hell of a good thing he did."

"But FBI agents? We're not terrorists." Carl said.

"The only deviation from our normal lives was the meeting—" Mary began, but cut the comment short when she remembered

Denech's instructions not to divulge any aspect of project Tranquility to anyone unless he or she gave the code word.

Red smiled, and her deep blue eyes sparkled. "You still don't get it do you?"

"Get what?"

"Who you are, or more correctly who you might end up being."

"I hate riddles," Carl stated. "What are you talking about?'

"My god, the Old Man really did a number on you two. Like two babes in the woods."

"Old Man?'

"Denech, of course. I hate to break it to you, but—"

"But what?" Carl pressed.

"Best not spill the beans. Guess the Old Man had his reasons. Not my place to say more than has been said."

"You—somebody owes us an explanation," Mary said.

"Maybe so," Red reflected. "We didn't expect this so soon," and she gestured toward the agents. "This means our communications have been compromised. Radio frequencies will have to be changed. Code words altered." She extracted a cell phone from the inside pocket of her light blue windbreaker and punched in a number. After a few seconds, she said "Code Yellow", listened a few seconds to the response, and then returned the device to its place. "Sit down," she said. "We don't have much time but I'll tell you what I think I can without getting into trouble with Denech. You're right. You do have a right to know."

Carl looked at the two slumped over agents. "I don't like being here right now. We have to get off."

"We will," Red assured him, "but it will be an unscheduled exit. I've jammed the security cameras in the car here so all they see on the outside right now is a blank screen. That will buy us some time, but when the train slows, you must follow me and you must be prepared to run. Do I make myself clear?"

"But maybe this is just a mix up of some sort," Carl continued hopefully. "How do we know that you, Denech, and the rest *aren't* terrorists?"

"You don't," Red admitted. "But do you want to take the risk of spending the rest of you lives behind prison bars that no one will admit exist, or do you want to come with me and remain free?"

"May I look behind door number three?"

"There is no door number three. Stay here or go with me. Those are your only options." Red glanced at her wristwatch. "You have just under five minutes to decide. Would it help if I mentioned a doll named Flossy?"

* * * *

"I have to tell you right off the top that we went back to the meeting house to tell Denech to forget the whole thing," Carl Walker began, when the three were settled back in their seats. He gestured toward the two sleeping agents and his voice rose as he spoke. "Denech said nothing we would be doing was illegal, and yet those two were more than willing to blow us both away for being terrorists! The meeting with Denech was the only deviation from our normal lives. Mary is the one with the logical mind but to me that implies Denech is a terrorist!"

"Just shout it so all the world can hear!" Red countered, but then quickly regained her composure. "The FBI runs in packs. Where there are two, there's bound to be more. But these people are not normal FBI. The FBI is on our side, or at least I hope when the time comes they will be."

"Impersonators?" Mary asked.

"Not exactly. They're part of a special unit assigned to investigate domestic terrorism. The members come from the special ops and rogue mercenary groups. They operate under the radar."

"Under the radar?"

"They have their own set of rules, which really means no rules. They don't officially exist. They pretty much do as they please when they please. They answer only to the President."

"Only the President?"

"God! Do I have to draw you a picture?" Red said, and drew closer. "Okay. As their world crumbles, people get scared, then trade away their constitutional rights for what they believe is safety. This has been gradually happening for a hundred years, and greatly accelerated during recent times. People get paranoid. Everyone becomes a potential threat. Everything goes underground, secret. The good guys *and* the bad guys. But after a while, President or not, you can't tell who's good and who's not, because both groups use the same tactics. We call it black ops. Fear, intimidation, even murder. All this just makes the world crumble faster. Like throwing gas on a fire. Get it?"

"Like I said, we aren't political."

"This goes beyond politics, except that politicians are part of the problem and not the solution. Cars run on gas. Campaigns, especially Presidential campaigns, run on fear. Fear of terrorism. Fear of losing jobs. Fear of a faltering economy. Fear of changing. Fear of not changing. Fear of whatever happens to be on Joe Blow's mind. Fear gets people elected."

"So you and Denech are part of a secret underground," Mary stated. "Why?"

"That part I cannot say. I'm gagged to silence for the same reason you are. But I can say you have passed the first test, which came a lot earlier than expected."

"What first test?" Carl asked.

"You gave up no information, and only relayed back to me what information I had given you. You kept the promise you made to Denech."

"Denech left out a few important details," Carl said. "Like the prospect of getting shot within hours of our meeting. Whatever happened to that leisurely trip to Hawaii he mentioned? Phase one, whatever that was supposed to be, wasn't going to start for five days."

"There have been unforeseen complications," Red admitted.

"From where I sit, more like a massive Charlie Foxtrot," Carl countered. "Maybe you do this type thing everyday for fun, but having a gun barrel shoved in my face scared the hell out of me. Is this going to happen on a regular basis now?"

Red didn't immediately answer, but then nodded and said. "Nope. It's probably going to get worse."

"Well, so much for easy money. After this, those megabuck credit cards in our pockets are probably worthless."

"They have not been compromised. And if they ever were, we'd just issue new ones. Trust me. But it is not safe for you to go back to any of your familiar places. The plane ride back to Duluth is out. But you can take heart that you've saved a hundred lives."

"And how did we do that?"

"By not being on the plane. If you get on that flight, it may well get shot right out of the sky."

"This just keeps getting better," Carl moaned. "May we just go back twenty-four hours and start again?"

"Yes, things are coming unraveled, and a lot is riding on your part in this. But *everything* is riding on one thing: trust. At this point you have to have blind faith in me and Denech and the organization. It is the rock on which the success of Tranquility rests. In less than one minute the train will slow down. You can stay on board and face the music at the next station, or leave with me. It isn't our way to force anyone to do anything. The decision has to be yours. But know that it is my self-sworn duty to protect you and I will even if it means my own death."

"Where—?"

"We're slowing," Red stated, and looked expectantly at Carl and Mary Walker.

The train slowed to ten miles per hour, and then a lurch forward in movement indicated it was again regaining speed. Three persons, one after another, jumped from the end car in pouring rain, ran across several sets of tracks, and disappeared behind the rusty metal door of an abandoned warehouse.

Chapter 4

▼

With a burst of acceleration, Carl and Mary Walker and a woman named Red left the abandoned warehouse in an old white Chevy Blazer that still had the outmoded gasoline powered motor. Even in the current year, 2011, at least half of the automobiles had not been converted to the more efficient hybrids and fully electric vehicles, though these older vehicles were grossly inefficient. This was due in part to the escalating up-front costs of the eco-friendly transportation, and also to the emergence of much cheaper gas-only mini-cars from China and India that got gas mileage as high as 60mpg. Even with the high price of fuel, in the long term and because of the extremely low purchase price, the mini-cars, which had come to be called Throwaways, were a more cost effective option. Many were only two-passenger, but some held four people reasonably well.

Carl had no idea where they were headed, but Red, who drove like a wild woman, was intent on the signs and eventually entered the fast flowing stream of traffic on the expressway, headed northwest. She had expressed confidence that their departure would go without incident, since those who would be seeking them would be looking for an old man with a grey beard, and not an attractive redhead. It was also doubtful that the secret operation to which Agents Smith and Johnson belonged would blow cover and seek the assistance of the local authorities. But they might, and that thought kept Red from driving any crazier than the rest on the freeway.

Mary sat next to Carl in the back seat, and remained silent as Red weaved confidently and aggressively in and around the congested traffic, though question after question surfaced in her mind. She kept coming back to one overpowering thought: What had they gotten themselves into? Quiet and introspective by nature, her logical mind searched through the recent events for some bit of logic, but came up empty. Recent events, she concluded, defied logic.

For his part, Carl was looking for an exit plan. Given the current circumstances and despite Red's assurances, it was not clear who the good guys were and who the bad guys were. But a graceful exit, or any exit, might eventually entail a life on the run and not a clear knowledge of just whom they might be running from. He looked at Mary who returned a faint smile. Her silent expression was one of reassurance, but also an acknowledgement that she, too, was having similar thoughts. But without more information, Carl knew any attempt to strike out on their own might well have fatal consequences.

From his position on the right side of the rear seat, Carl leaned forward and touched Red's shoulder to get her attention. "Your driving skills are—are exceptional but don't you think a little more caution would be advised? I mean we don't want to draw attention to ourselves." He noted everyone was going a minimum of twenty miles over the speed limit.

"Are you saying I drive like a maniac?"

"Well, it beats a roller-coaster ride."

"Thanks for the compliment. Out here, it's self-defense. Everyone drives like madmen."

"What about the highway patrol?"

"You think any cop is going to be crazy enough to try to stop anyone in this mess? It'd be suicide. The only time you'll see them is if there's an accident."

"So where to now?" Carl asked.

Red smiled. "Be honest. What you really want to know is will getting out now somehow save your ass?"

"Something like that."

"We're going to the closest place I know is safe."

"Which you, no doubt, prefer not to tell us."

"Something like that," Red stated, and smiled her warm smile.

"Will Denech be there? And the other guy we met. Randolf Haays?"

"Probably. And one more."

"Well, here's something for you to consider. You, all of you, keep harping on this trust and faith business. Denech said it, Haays said it, now you've said it. Frankly, as a skeptic, I have little use for blind faith. I like my reality up front where I can grab hold of it. But because all of you have made such a big deal out of it, I'll—we'll—add our own twist. How about you start trusting us? How about we do absolutely nothing until you level with us? Trust works both ways."

Red sat silently and nodded, and then seemed to speak into empty air. "What do you think?"

From the empty air came an immediate response. The voice was that of Peter Denech. "Carl has a valid point. Bring them in. We'll begin phase one as soon as you arrive."

Red turned to face Carl, momentarily taking her attention from her driving.

"Satisfied?"

Carl said nothing and slumped back in the seat. Denech was ever-present, even when he wasn't. Mary nudged him gently. "We should be careful what we wish for, because sometimes we get it."

Carl suddenly realized what he'd inadvertently done. Their innocence and ignorance had guaranteed them a certain degree of immunity, since they could be released without putting Tranquility in danger. But as soon as they were told the particulars, they could be locked in for the duration. Whatever side, good or bad, Denech was on would then be their side.

"Oh crap," Carl said under his breath when he had thought the situation through.

"A bluff only works if you have the balls to carry it through," Red added knowingly from the front. She glanced at the two in the rear view mirror. "You'll get what you asked for. I hope you can handle it."

* * * *

Mary couldn't be sure exactly where they finally stopped hours later, but she was certain it was somewhere in Southeastern Minnesota. They had gotten off the main highway and proceeded west, crossed the Mississippi river, and then angled north again. The rolling hills of mostly cropland erupting in straight rows of emerging corn had given way to limestone bluffs and the green leaves of hardwoods. They had passed a sign welcoming people to Whitewater State Park. Finally, after following a narrow and winding gravel road, Red stopped the Blazer in a secluded valley at the edge of a clear stream and in front of a huge waterwheel. The building that supported the waterwheel was old with grey boards and missing wooden shingles, and the working mechanism of the grain milling equipment had apparently broken down or was absent, because the wheel was locked in place, unmoving, as the fast current of the stream splashed at its base. The entire structure was built up against the side of a solid limestone outcrop, where saplings and green vines clung to weathered crevices. There was little evidence of human activity, but a rusty Ford pickup, which had been painted maroon at one time, was parked in the shade of a black walnut tree. It effectively passed for junk, except Mary noted all the tires were properly inflated.

The evening air smelled clean and fresh with a distinctive aquatic fragrance as the three left the SUV and stood looking up at the early twentieth century grain mill. Mary could easily visualize the giant water wheel turning under the force of the water, which in turn rotated the grinding stones within, where shelled corn, wheat, oats and other grains were once reduced to fine flour. No toxic waste, no petroleum powered engines, no carbon footprint at all, just the free and clean power of gravity directing the flow of this stream down hill. Without any other human presence and the faint gurgling of the moving water and the sound of songbirds high above in the treetops, the place had a mystical and peaceful quality that elicited thoughts of gratitude. In a world of exploding population and environmental degradation, there were still places like this.

Red led the Walkers through a weathered door behind the water wheel, up a short flight of well-worn stairs, and into a large room that had at one time held all the grinding machinery. It was empty now except for the dust-covered cobwebs filling every corner, and dozens of tiny spiders suspended at the ends of long thin silver strings. The evening sun shone through a lone window above and filtered through the cracks between the exterior vertical boards, creating long straight parallel lines of light on the wooden floor.

Red turned to face Carl and Mary. "You wanted trust. You have it." She moved to the far wall, looked into a knothole in the interior planking. They heard an audible click and a narrow door way opened into what should have been solid rock, but was instead a dimly lit passageway into the depths of the limestone hillside.

"We're home," Red said as she gestured the two into the opening. "After you. Make sure you wipe your feet on the rug."

* * * *

There was no rug to wipe their feet, but Carl and Mary Walker could not have been more confused by what greeted them as they emerged from the passageway into a brightly lit room carved out of solid rock. Having taken many cave tours, Carl found the comfortable interior temperature abnormal, and noted a lack of the usual dripping moisture and condensation. The room had all the usual furnishings of a living room—sofa and chairs, end table and lamp, magazines and carpeting—with three dark passageways leading away from it. Just at the level of audible, a low hum or vibration filled the chamber.

For some reason, maybe after seeing too many science fiction movies, Carl expected rows and rows of computers humming away, screens flashing lines of code and images, and all powered by a tangle of wires reminiscent of a plate of spaghetti. Instead there was one old laptop computer on a small table against the innermost wall. The active feeds from security cameras featured a screen split into four quadrants. Beginning with quadrant one and progressing in a clockwise direction, they showed static pictures of the main room of the grain mill, the small parking area, a shot of the stream, and an empty dirt road.

A stocky bald man dressed in rumpled clothing sat on a padded office chair with his back to them. He hunched over the working computer, powering it down.

Peter Denech closed the laptop. He rose from the chair and turned to face his guests, the huge smile ever present on his face. "Welcome to the Rabbit Hole," he said, and moved forward like a tank, causing both Mary and Carl to retreat a step. He laughed and the great booming sound echoed throughout the chamber and down the passageways. One massive arm went around each, like a hug for long lost friends suddenly found, and then Denech stepped back and nodded approvingly. "I have to admit, I've been expecting you, though not this early. That's good. It advances a tight time frame, and will give me additional leverage with Haays and Korneth."

Carl and Mary exchanged glances.

"We're totally in the dark here," Carl stated. "Frankly we haven't a clue what this is all about, why we're here, who those thugs were who tried to arrest us—"

Denech held up his hand to signal a time out. "I know. I know. And since you made it to this stage—you're the only couple to make it this far which I knew would be the case—I will give you the next round of information."

"The next round?" Mary asked. "We are entitled to—"

Again Denech held up his hand, and reflected for a few moments. "You're a teacher, correct?"

"I have a math degree, but not a teaching license."

"But you teach Algebra."

"Officially, I'm an assistant, though I have complete control over my classroom decisions. If I had the paperwork, you could call me a teacher I suppose, and I would also be getting paid a lot more than fifteen dollars an hour."

"And your students?"

"Mostly eighteen and nineteen year olds that want to go to college, but didn't get or avoided Algebra in high school, and suddenly found out that it's a requirement for nearly all college degrees."

"And?"

"And most have convinced themselves they are hopeless, at least as far as learning Algebra goes."

"So the challenge for you is to do what?"

"I have to get them to realize they can do what they think they can't."

"Ah, yes. Not that much different than any true leader. Are you successful?"

"For the most part, yes. Algebra is not that difficult, but does require a shift in thinking."

"How's that?"

"Arithmetic is memorizing facts. Algebra is about learning processes and problem solving patterns. It utilizes a different part of the brain. Sometimes a specific answer is less important than how you arrive at it."

"And just how do you go about convincing these young people they can make this mental shift?"

"Break it down into small pieces. One concept at a time. Slowly and methodically build an abstract structure, and get them to see its relevance in the real world."

"Why not just throw the whole thing at them at once? Let them sink or swim."

"Because I'd lose them. They would be overwhelmed by all the information—" Mary hesitated, and nodded, making the connection.

"Precisely," Denech said. "All the information at once would be too much to handle, but piece by piece—"

"I don't scare them off," Mary finished.

Several moments of silence followed, and then Carl continued.

"That was a nice analogy, but our particular situation involves life or death consequences, not whether or not we pass first year college Algebra."

"True," Denech admitted. "But the concept is the same. And you haven't been scared off. Yet, at least. Are you ready for the next phase?"

"At this point, do we have a choice?"

"There is always a choice. There are no chains holding you here. The magnetic locks on the doors prevent people from getting in, not out. The question is do you have the mindset to continue?"

"Then we leave," Carl asserted confidently, but Mary, smiling her faint smile, grasped his hand with hers to get his full attention, and then shook her head slightly.

"We continue," Mary stated, redirecting her attention back to Denech. "Given what we've been through and seen, we have no other option."

"Good. First, there is one part of the analogy that I must impress upon you," Denech said. "Algebra, if I am not mistaken, is like a ladder. Each step is predicated on the steps before."

"That's true," Mary said. "You can't skip steps and expect to be successful."

Denech smiled. "Well then, there you have it. Red will show you to your quarters. Kick back and relax for a couple hours. Do whatever you'd normally do when you're alone. We'll have an evening snack around nine, at which time Haays will join us and another person you haven't met. After you rest, Red will give you a tour of the entire Rabbit Hole, and then later, when we meet back here, we'll continue this discussion. Fill in a few more of the pieces, and answer a few of your questions if we can."

Carl nodded, and automatically began a mental list of all the questions that flooded his mind. He had a couple questions for Mary as well.

Red moved toward a passageway, and led them to a tiny cavern with one narrow bunk, a metal file cabinet for personal items, and a single padded grey folding chair. There was no door, but the entrance curved sharply to the right blocking the view to the interior thus providing some privacy.

With three people in the room there was standing room only and Red gestured to the accommodations. "Not exactly a luxury suite, but then, as you've probably guessed by now, this isn't a vacation. The community bathroom is the next room on the right. If you'll look in the cabinet, you'll see the Old Man took the liberty of getting you some new clothes."

"Denech really was expecting us," Carl stated.

"Oh, yeah. You'll soon learn it's hard to get anything past the Old Man. Remember. I'm here to help and do whatever I can to make this work." Her gaze fell upon Carl and she smiled her warm and inviting smile. "Remember. If there's *anything*, personal needs or otherwise, all you need to do is ask. You'll find I have training in a vast number of different specialties."

"I'm sure," Mary cut in. "And the rest of the—the Rabbit Hole?"

Red's official reply, directed at Mary, lacked emotion. "I'll take you on that tour just before the evening meal," she stated, and left the two alone.

Carl and Mary Walker lay on their sides facing each other on the narrow bunk, with barely the thickness of a hand between their eyes. They spoke quietly, each politely waiting for the other to finish a thought. Going by tone alone, it could have been an intimate exchange between two lovers but was, in fact, in their own way a major disagreement. But there was no shouting or any other of the normal characteristics of an argument.

"You vetoed a chance to walk out of here," Carl was saying. "You should have discussed that decision with me."

"You also spoke for both of us when you decided to leave. There is no difference."

"You were the one who said that we should run from this. I thought you'd welcome the chance."

"You're right. I've done an about face."

"Why? Despite what you told Denech, you and I know there is no logical reason why we should stay. Yes, we have defensive skills, but we're groping in the dark here. This is all way beyond our—our—"

"Experience?" Mary offered.

"Yes, and a lot of other things. Face it. We have little real world knowledge. At least the kind of knowledge we need to deal with whatever is going on. Contrasted to this, we've led pretty sheltered lives."

"True."

"And, frankly, I don't like getting guns pointed at my face, and particularly your face."

Mary nodded, and recited from memory the words Red had spoken. "The Old Man really did a number on you. Like two babes in the woods."

"And yet you nixed my exit plan. What's going on in that head of yours? What happened to the logic center?"

Mary shrugged. "Still there, I hope. But somehow Denech got to me. Maybe because he reminds me of a father I'd like to have had. He seems to genuinely care. I don't know what's going to happen, but I do trust Denech. I *feel* we are safe here."

"But—"

"Carl, you have to trust *me* on this."

"You know I do. That isn't the problem."

"What then?"

"I'm beginning to wonder if I can trust myself."

Mary placed her arms around her husband and drew their bodies together. "Do whatever you normally do when you're alone," she said, parroting Denech's words.

"Sounds like a plan I can live with," Carl said with a sly smile, and pulled the blanket over them. But despite other intentions, within a few minutes both were sound asleep.

Chapter 5

At eight-thirty PM in the outside world it was still light, as the lengthening summer days held off the darkness until after nine o'clock. But inside the Rabbit Hole, without the artificial lighting, it would always be pitch black.

Peter Denech removed a cracked cup from a hook that was embedded in the solid limestone wall, retrieved a pot of coffee from a hotplate, and moved to one side of a small square table in a cubby hole that passed for the kitchen. Already seated on the other three sides were Randolf Haays, Amanda Korneth, and Rowanna Doran, otherwise known as Red. Denech refilled cups still half full, filled his own, and then seated himself at his place.

"Our guests?" Haays said, directing the question at Red.

"Sleeping like babies the last time I checked." She had changed into a black tank top and blue jeans, but still retained the weapon in the holster under her left arm. "Should I wake them?"

"No need," Denech stated. "Saw them on the monitor. They're awake and on their way. Intercept, give them the tour, and then bring them here."

Red nodded, left the kitchen, and found Carl and Mary Walker standing in the main cavern. Carl acknowledged her approach with a half-hearted wave.

"Ready for your tour, or headed out the door?" Red asked.

"The thought crossed my mind," Carl admitted and smiled, beginning to get a sense of her humor. "But it seems my wife has made up my mind for me."

Red disguised a wink exclusively for him. "Well, wives are good for a few things, are they not?"

Carl couldn't help but notice how Red's eyes played with his own, and he had to glance away, almost embarrassed by her lingering look.

Back to the business at hand, Red motioned toward the passageways that left the main cavern. "Very simple, really. Follow the one on left and you come to the three sleeping rooms on the left side and a community bathroom on the right. It's the only room in the place that has a door. Please close it when you enter and leave it open when you leave. The middle passageway opens into the guts of the place. The electronics hub, heat pump, ventilation, main computer and communications access, and so on. We call it the War Room. It is vital. If it goes down, we go down. I just came from the passageway on the right. That contains a tiny kitchen, but also a large food storage cavern. Also some weaponry, and other items that need not concern you at this time."

"Self-sustaining." Mary noted.

"Not quite, but there are enough resources for a couple people to survive down here for a month or longer if they had to. There's a minimum of twenty feet of solid rock above us, so we're also shielded from radiation and the prying electronic eyes of others."

"Like a fortress," Carl said.

"Pretty much, and not by accident."

"It's abnormally dry in here for a cave. Must be a dry cave, like the Mammoth Caves in Kentucky."

"True. It sits well above the water table and inside a limestone ridge. The part where we're standing is a natural cavern. Some of the rest was carved out during the prohibition days, when the mill outside was also the front for an illegal moonshine operation. The rest Denech and his people added a few years ago."

"But only one exit?" Mary asked. "That seems rather—"

"Actually there is another exit," Red interrupted. "The back door. All three passageways meet back there. From that point, there is a tunnel with a ladder to the surface. The manhole on the outside is camouflaged to look like bedrock. Last fall during deer season hunters walked right over the top of it and never noticed."

"An escape route," Carl guessed.

"An emergency escape route that we've never had to use."

"And hopefully never will," Carl added.

"What about power?" Mary asked.

"What about it?" Red countered.

"The lights, the electronics, the heating, all take electricity. Where does it come from?"

"We borrow it," Peter Denech answered, joining the group.

Mary turned to Denech. "Borrow?"

"There's a major transmission line about a half mile east of here. We tap into the flow of electrons just enough to meet our needs."

"That seems a bit risky. It must create a drain that would be detectable somewhere. 'Borrow' means steal, I take it," Carl added.

"There is a normal drop in current flow through the wires under the best of conditions. We stay below that which would be considered suspicious. Our needs are quite modest, and our usage will not put any power company out of business."

"What happens when and if there's a power failure?" Mary wondered.

"We have backup batteries that would last a few days without recharging. Under much reduced use, of course. We have a diesel-powered generator. Also only for emergency use. And solar panels, but they are stored away. A solar array or a diesel engine running outside would draw too much attention to our little shelter."

"And water? Plumbing?" Mary continued.

"We draw water from the stream and run it through a sterile filtering system," Denech continued, "and feed all waste liquids back into the stream through a similar system. We also use a chemical-electric toilet."

"Eco-friendly," Mary observed.

"So when are the atomic bombs supposed to drop?" Carl asked. "This is a survival fallout shelter if I've ever seen one."

"The bomb, as you put it, has already dropped. We're hoping, however, that the Rabbit Hole will never have to be used like that. But we must be prepared for all possible contingencies." Denech paused, then continued. "Now take your tour and then get something to eat. After that, we can continue this question and answer time."

* * * *

Rowanna Doran, with bright red hair falling casually to her shoulders, led Carl and Mary Walker back down the left passageway, past the sleeping quarters and bathroom, then a few yards more where the other two passageways joined it. A string of low watt, energy-saver light bulbs about ten feet apart lighted the entire passage way. Motion controlled, they blinked on as they approached and then off again after they passed out of view. Red pointed out the ladder and exit hole, and the side tunnel that led to the rear entrance to the 'guts,' the War Room. She then continued on to the storage cavern. About the size of a single car garage, it was dimly lit, but light enough for rows of canned goods and other essentials reaching to the roof to be visible. From there it was just a couple steps to the tiny kitchen area. The kitchen entrance then opened back into the living room, completing the entire circuit.

Peter Denech was in the kitchen waiting and officially introduced Carl and Mary to Rowanna Doran, whom they had come to know as Red. He then introduced Amanda Korneth, her silver hair tied back in a tight round ball. She wore a white lab coat, and as she returned the greeting, not a flicker of emotion registered on her blank face. Carl noted no smile lines, no crow's feet, in fact no outward evidence of emotion on her middle-aged face. The one exception was two deep crevices between her eyes. Despite outward appearances, this woman, Carl reflected, had a lot on her mind.

*   *   *   *

The rest of the occupants of the shelter made themselves scarce as Carl and Mary finished eating warmed up stew from a can and sipped hot green tea. A hand printed note stuck to the rock wall, apparently applicable to everyone, said, *"No maids here. Clean up your own mess."* Carl noted the time on his wristwatch, 9:45PM, as they made their way back through the tunnel, past the emergency exit, past their sleeping quarters and the bathroom, and back into the living room. It was the long way around, but also a chance to familiarize themselves with the twists and turns of the tunnel, and also to get a closer look at the backdoor exit if they should ever need to use it.

*   *   *   *

With a massive hand, Peter Denech gestured the Walkers toward the sofa, and pulled up a padded folding chair for himself. He sat down on the reversed seat and rested his arms on the backrest. Amanda Korneth, hands buried deep in the pockets of her white lab coat, took possession of the one comfortable living room chair. Randolf Haays also found a folding chair, but Rowanna Doran remained standing, somewhat distant and aloof, leaning against the rock wall. Her arms were crossed upon her chest, and her right hand resting on the pistol grip.

Despite his loyalty to his wife, Carl couldn't help but be attracted to the redhead. This in spite of the fact that in almost every way Rowanna Doran was the exact opposite of Mary. Where Mary was quiet and reserved, Red was blunt and outspoken. Mary tended to be demure and subtle, but there was nothing subtle about Red's smoldering sexuality. Her sparkling deep blue eyes and ample curves danced in his thoughts, and he couldn't help but wonder, against everything that made decent sense, what an "older woman" would feel like in his arms. After all, Rowanna Doran was at least thirty years old.

As if to counter his fanciful betrayal, Mary took his right hand and cupped it between hers. He looked at her, and she smiled her slight and knowing smile, and something like guilt crept into his mind. Mary squeezed his hand softly, and then glanced fleetingly at Red in silent confirmation of the fact that she was not naive. Carl managed a weak and wilted look and shrugged. He knew that Mary and he knew each other too well. In a way that disturbed him. There would be no more intimate surprises, no more exciting revelations. Where there had once been two, now there was one. What was left of each, he wondered? He knew he loved Mary more than anything or anyone, but he candidly wondered if love was enough to keep the lid on pure animal lust.

* * * *

Peter Denech's deep and steady voice rattled up against the walls of the main cavern, and echoed around the passageways. Carl expected a complete explanation for all the cloak and dagger activities, but it was not to be forthcoming.

"It is time for trust," Denech began. "From here on out we will take it for granted. There can be no second-guessing. We sink or swim on faith in one another." He looked directly at Carl and then Mary. "By way of explanation, I will begin with a question. Do you know of the significance of the year 2012?"

With all eyes focused on them, Carl nodded, but Mary filled in the blank. "Next year, 2012, and according to the Mayan people of South America, the present age will end. Also the Nostradamus predictions indicate major worldwide disruptions about that time."

"That sounds rather disturbing. The Mayan predictions," Denech said. "How does that work?"

"It's based on one of their time keeping methods called the Long Count, which is composed of one million eight hundred seventy two thousand days. That time period comes to an end in 2012."

"Sounds rather mystical," Haays cut in.

"Nothing mystical at all," Mary stated. "It's very sophisticated mathematics with a number system founded on base-20."

"Base-20?"

"Our number system uses ten symbols, zero through nine. That's base-10. The Maya counted out time in the Long Count by using twenty symbols. Thus, base-20. Not too shabby for people who hadn't discovered a practical use for the wheel. But somehow," Mary reflected, "I have the feeling you knew all that."

Denech nodded. "More or less. However, we are more concerned with the possible truth to the predictions."

"What predictions?" Carl interjected.

"For example, there has been some suggestion that the solar system will pass through a space barrier next year that might have a profound effect on earth."

"You're talking about the galactic plane," Carl confirmed.

"So there is something to that prediction."

"Yes, the solar system does oscillate back and forth through the galactic plane about every thirty-five million years. This interval of time does seem to coincide with mass extinctions on earth." Carl noted. "However, passing through the plane of the galaxy is not like passing through a sheet of paper. Yes, there may be some unforeseen gravitational effects. There may be increased radiation. But the 'sheet of paper' will take the sun and the planets forty years to get through at a velocity of about 6 million miles per day. Some very smart astronomers argue it would take a thousand years. But even if that forty-year time period is accurate, which it almost certainly is not, that means we started this transit in 1992 and will exit in 2032. In any case, from a cosmic perspective, there is nothing particularly special about the year 2012. You have to remember that space is an awfully big place."

"Interesting, and from your explanation, not very frightening," Denech stated.

"And figuring out just where the sun is in respect to the galactic plane is not exactly an exact science. Yes, there are those who say we are getting close, but they could be off by thousands of years."

"Be that as it may, I've been advised that the earth could see some major upheavals. Magnetic pole reversal, for instance, leaving all living things on earth exposed to lethal radiation. Violent fluctuations in the sun's heat and light output. Frequent and destructive storms. Bizarre weather patterns. Earthquakes. Increased volcanic activity. Solar instability with possible fatal consequences for earth. Even an earth changing asteroid or comet strike. Any truth to any of that?"

"Given vast amounts of time, all of that is possible."

"But not all at once?"

"You think—"

"I'm just asking. You and Mary have the degrees. What about the sun itself?"

"It is true that next year the sun will most likely reach the solar maximum, the peak period of its eleven year cycle," Carl said, relieved to talk about something he knew something about. He noted Amanda Korneth sitting quietly taking it all in, and Red shift position occasionally, but overall uninterested. Her disinterest in what he found fascinating was something of a blow to his ego. "This increased activity is the increasing sunspot activity," Carl continued. "You can think of sunspots as huge solar storms. You see, the sun pulsates on an eleven year cycle and—"

"Any danger there? I mean to earth," Denech cut in.

"Well, yes. A lot of extra solar radiation is generated around sunspots. This extra radiation heats up the outer layers of the earth's atmosphere more than normal. There is increased electrical activity, which may interfere with satellite communication, radio transmissions, and even electrical transmissions. If the radiation is severe enough."

"Anything else?" Denech prodded.

Carl nodded. "Because the atmosphere heats up, it also expands outward. Because of added friction, the expanding atmosphere could slow the orbital velocities of low earth satellites—"

"Whoa!" Denech said. "Remember, you're talking to a bunch of bureaucrats."

"As their velocity, their speed, slows, their orbits could shrink. In a severe case, they could spiral into the earth."

Red was suddenly interested. "You mean like crash? How many are you talking about?"

"There are dozens of communication satellites in low earth orbit. Probably dozens of spy satellites as well. But that is just a worst-case scenario. The chances are slim that it would happen, and even if we did lose some satellites, they'd mostly burn up in the atmosphere upon reentry. The chance of someone getting hit by a piece of one is just about zero."

"But not quite zero," Denech suggested. "You've mentioned a lot of possible things, all of which might be survivable. But, like I said, what if they all happened at once?"

"What do you mean?"

"I mean all of it. The radiation, the storms, the earthquakes, the comet strike. All of it. All at once."

Carl remained silent, as the light bulb went on in his head. He'd heard of groups like the one he now faced. Doomsday prognosticators. Survivalists. Living in caves, waiting for the end of the world that, of course, never comes. He glanced at Mary who still held his right hand ever so tightly. These people were certifiably nuts, and somehow he and Mary had gotten sucked into their dementia. Yet, they didn't seem dangerous. Certainly not to the level of a terrorist that Agents Smith and Johnson had alluded. They all sat silently watching him, waiting for some bit of information to reinforce and confirm their own delusions. Well, humor them he would, and then, in the middle of the night, he'd take Mary, dragging her if he had to, out the emergency exit, and get as far away as he could from these people.

"Well," Carl continued as seriously as he could. "That would pose a very serious threat for sure. If it happened, I'd like to be right here. Can't think of a safer place."

Amanda Korneth was not fooled. "But you really think it's all bullshit," she said forcefully, entering the conversation for the first time.

"No. No. Not really," Carl struggled. "I mean it could happen. Anything's possible."

Korneth looked at Peter Denech. "This isn't going to work. *They* aren't going to work. Too much information too soon. They can't handle it." She turned to Rowanna Doran. "It was a mistake to bring them here. This changes everything."

Randolf Haays nodded in agreement. "I hate to say it, Peter, but I told you so."

"I'm not ready to give up on them just yet," Denech stated. "I will continue."

Korneth shrugged. "Okay, you're the boss, but I'm going to get a cup of coffee, and check the updates from the organization in the War Room. Make your pitch. Later, we should meet in conference. Tranquility C may be dead."

Chapter 6

▼

Carl Walker, having decided to give reason another chance, stared at Peter Denech, trying to find a place to insert some logic into the discussion. He would have gladly deferred to his wife, Mary, but she remained silent, though from the impressions she'd no doubt leave on his hand from her iron grip, he knew that she, too, was equally apprehensive. The word "dead" kept reverberating in his thoughts, and its connection to Plan C was discomforting to say the least.

The trouble with logic, however, as Mary had pointed out to him on many occasions, is that it does not guarantee a 'truth.' It is merely a rigid thinking process of getting from a set of assumptions to a reasoned conclusion. If the original set of assumptions is not valid, then the final conclusion is likely to be, as Korneth had bluntly stated, bullshit as well.

Logic can't change a manure pie into a cherry pie, but it can, if allowed to work, point out the difference. So the challenge was to find some common ground from which to begin. Something that everyone could agree upon that was reasonable enough and frequent enough to be recognized as fact. But in the end, Carl merely plunged in, and hoped the truth would somehow float to the surface.

"My training—that is what I believe—I mean things are not always like we expect—" Carl began, and soon lost his way. Red left her post by the solid rock wall and took over the chair recently vacated by Amanda Korneth. She flashed Carl a quick smile, but it was all acting, and lacked the sparkling and playful eyes. Then with lips drawn tight, she sat with her right hand resting on the pistol under her left arm, and it was clear her part in this was not to be a part of the discussion, but a part of the containment.

"You're right," Denech agreed, and looked up at Carl. He'd had his face buried in his hands for the minute or two that Korneth had been absent. "Amanda is right. Haays is right. We drag two reasonable people into this and what do we expect? We expect them to abandon all reason! But it's a chance I was willing to take, and I'm not about to abandon Plan C just yet."

Before Carl could invent a response, Mary came to his rescue. "If I understand correctly, you have gone through all this trouble because of a Mayan prediction that an age is about to end?"

Denech was noncommittal. "Yes and no. But let me ask you something. Do you believe in prophecy? Not any specific prophecy, necessarily, but prophecy in general. I'm not talking about the notion of divine intervention or any of that. Just the idea that there are things that happen that could have been, or even were, predictable and foreseen."

"Science is based on the ability to predict outcomes when certain facts are known," Mary continued. "So yes, given the right variables and equations, I can predict the future. Given some initial conditions, I can tell you if a rocket will or won't make it into space, or where a particular planet will be in its orbit in three months. I can give you a rough idea of the weather next January and the probable planting dates for corn and soybeans next spring. With modern computer power, predictions—like weather forecasting for instance that require thousands of inputs—are possible."

"How about human beings? Would it be possible to create a computer program so precise it could predict our future?"

"Not impossible, but way beyond anything we can do now."

"Why?"

"There are just too many variables. Too many random events that could change the outcome. We don't have the ability to find them all, to measure them all, much less determine what effect they might have."

"I see."

"The problem is that extremely minute variations, things that we at our level of technology can't even detect, might have profound consequences."

"For example?"

Carl entered the conversation, encouraged to see Denech seemed to be taking a reasonable track. "Well, take this simple example. Suppose you wanted to go to the nearest star system. Alpha Centuri. After figuring out the proper course and so forth, you set off from earth, but one of your trajectories was off by a billionth of a degree. Not much of a problem going from here to New York, or from here to the moon, or even here to Mars, but that error would result in missing Alpha Centuri by millions of miles."

Denech nodded. "So, if I'm hearing you right, part of the problem is our accuracy of measurement. Another part is really our ignorance of all the variables. And finally no clear idea of just what consequences all the variables would have."

"That pretty much sums it up," Carl stated. "For now at least, the kind of prophecy for us, for humans, that you're talking about is not possible."

Mary nodded and continued. "So going back to your question, if you mean prophecy concerning the evolution of human beings and specific individuals in particular, then, no, I don't believe in prophecy, other than the obvious biological inevitabilities."

"The obvious? What inevitabilities?"

"Humanity cannot continue as we have in the past. We have become like the locusts, eating and consuming ourselves out of house and home."

"That is prophecy of a sort," Denech said.

"Not prophecy. Science and mathematics. An organism can only survive so long as there are the necessary resources for its survival. When those resources are gone, when the locusts have eaten everything, they do the only thing they can do. They die. We can easily see this happening with a swarm of locusts because it happens very rapidly. We cannot see it happening to ourselves because it is a much longer process. Wars and famine reduce our numbers, but agricultural advances increase food production so more survive. We believe it is our right to have children, disregarding the larger concern of overpopulation. Medicine prolongs life. All these factors only delay the inevitable end, and the end begins slowly, but it will be greatly accelerated just before the final collapse. In mathematics we refer to this as a geometric progression. In Nature, it's called the fast road to sudden extinction." Mary reflected for a moment and then continued. "The real problem is this: We just can't accept that we could do that to ourselves."

"Rather a fatalistic assessment for such a young person," Denech noted, and glanced at Haays, who suddenly became very interested.

"True," Mary replied. "But a positive outcome would require a critical mass of reasonable people who have the capacity to influence vast numbers of others. With the entire world choosing sides and embroiled in conflicts over resources, that possibility is unlikely."

"Can there be a happy ending?"

"Of sorts. Even some of the locust population survives to begin again. But that's not prophecy. That's just biology. A fact of Nature."

Denech unconsciously reached for a pen from his shirt pocket, and out of nervous habit began to rotate it between his fingers. After several seconds, he put it back.

"Okay. Fair enough. I see your point. Let's consider a different angle. Carl, when we first met, you mentioned a friend of yours who died trying to defuse a land mine."

"Yes. His name was Jason."

"You said that Jason was a great humanitarian. That he thought he could heal the world, I believe you said."

"That's right."

"Do you know the origin of the name Jason? What it means?"

"No."

"It comes from ancient Greek. It means 'healer.' Do you think that's a coincidence?"

"Yes. Probably."

"Well, how about your name. Carl. Do you know what it means? You once implied that your independence, other than Mary, was your greatest concern, or did I misinterpret?"

"No, that's true."

"In the archaic Germanic, Carl comes from a word that means 'free man.' Do you think *that's* a coincidence?"

Carl shrugged, but remained silent.

"And your lovely and intelligent wife, Mary, a name that she has elected to use rather than her full first name, which is Marianna. Do you want to know what Marianna means? I'll tell you what it means. It comes from Spanish and means 'quiet and thoughtful.' Or possibly from the Latin for 'beloved' and 'graceful.' Does that sound like your Mary to you? Are you starting to see a pattern here? Can this all be coincidence?"

"What are you saying?" Carl said, finally locating his tongue. "That our names predict our future?"

But Denech merely continued. "And how about Red. Rowanna Doran. Would you like to know what her name means?"

"I suppose—"

"Rowanna comes from an ancient Gaelic dialect. It refers to the color red, or a tree with red berries, or little red one. You've no doubt noticed her beautiful red hair. And, with Red's permission, we can take this a step farther." Red nodded, and Denech continued. "Red's last name, Doran, comes from the same Gaelic tongue and means 'exiled person.' She can explain the significance of that at some later time. Do you think all of that is coincidence, or is there the possibility that there is some underlying connection here?'

"Honestly," Carl stated. "I have to believe there is another explanation but I admit I don't know what it could be. What about your name? Peter. What does it mean?"

"Peter comes from ancient Greek. It means 'a rock' or 'stone'. Whether by choice or design, I have become the anchor point for Tranquility. The 'rock, as it were.'"

"And Mr. Haays?" Carl asked, nodding at the bespeckled man who had said almost nothing through the entire discussion.

"The name Randolf comes from the Germanic. It means 'shield wolf.' Mr. Haays has sworn an oath to protect me at all costs, even his life. Let's proceed now—" Denech continued, but Carl interrupted.

"What about Amanda Korneth? What does Amanda mean? Let me guess. Given her disposition, I'd say 'sour puss' or something similar."

For the first time Denech seemed to falter, and looked to Haays who merely shrugged. "You started this discussion, and it's an honest question," Haays said.

Reluctantly, Denech continued. "Amanda comes from Latin. It means 'lovable.' Well, hey, there's an exception to every rule."

There was a protracted moment of silence, and then Carl began to snicker, which was rapidly followed by full-blown laughter. At first Peter Denech was taken aback, but then began to laugh as well. The infection spread to Haays, then Rowanna Doran, and finally even Mary's face registered a wide smile.

"Well, they can't all be gems," Denech said finally, after the last giggle died away. "But who knows. Her life isn't over yet. There's still time for change."

"You've convinced me of one thing," Carl admitted. "You're not all crazy lunatics."

"That's a start. That's a good start."

Mary was thoughtful. "I have a related question. You said Randolf means 'shield wolf.' The name Adolph comes to mind, as in Adolph Hitler. Is there a similar connection?"

Peter Denech grew serious. "Yes, and since there can be no secrets between those of us here, I will tell you that Adolph is also from the Germanic tongue and means 'noble wolf' or 'noble ruler.' This raises an interesting question. If a person, knowing what his name means which I'm sure Hitler did, tries to live up to that name, and goes down in flames when those expectations are not achieved, what does that mean? Maybe there are underlying influences—random eddies in the stream of life—those unknown variables you mentioned—that cause what might have been a great man to turn into a terrible man. This I don't know. But I do know that these things happen enough times to convince me that there is something going on here that we can't explain. Not a miracle, as my good friend Randolf would believe, but some underlying natural connection to all events—past, present, and future. Laugh if you will, but I feel that we were brought together for a reason, and that reason might be to accept that which we *can* do to ourselves, and then do something about it."

Mary relaxed her grip on Carl's hand, released a long held in breath of air, and addressed Peter Denech. "Okay. Let's begin again. You said honesty and trust were the essentials here. I agree, therefore I admit I am still confused, though somewhat less apprehensive. But I think now I'm beginning to understand. You're not going to serve us the information. We have to hunt it down ourselves."

"Well put. And yes, that is the essence of Tranquility. Part of that is planned by us, but part is not planned because we don't know all the answers ourselves. The thing we are really trying to prevent is information overload. We don't want you to get to the point that you cannot process the information as it comes in. That was the thought behind Amanda's parting comment. Too much, too soon will definitely kill Plan C, and, indeed, all of Tranquility."

"We started out talking about the Mayans," Mary reflected. "Do you honestly think there is something to the dire predictions?"

"Truthfully, I can't say, and I admit a lot of it is probably overblown. But consider this. There is a lot of room for error but just suppose the time frames are even marginally accurate. Is it coincidence that the earth will be firmly embedded in the galactic plane at just about the time, 2012, the Mayan Long Count calendar reaches the end of its cycle? And that same year, the sun reaches its most violent outbursts in years? Maybe decades. Maybe centuries? What are the odds of these things happening all at once, as they may be? And here's one for you. How would those Mayan people, who had no knowledge of a simple wheel as you accurately stated, be able to devise a calendar where the end of a nearly two million day cycle—that's over five thousand years—coincides with events of literally cosmic proportions?"

"As far as the wheel goes, it comes down to a matter of need," Mary reflected. "Humans have always been good at inventing things, whether ideas or objects, when necessity demanded. The ancient Mayan people lived in very mountainous terrain. A wheel and corresponding inventions—carts, wheelbarrows, and so forth—would not be particularly useful under those conditions. Pack animals and human slaves served their needs quite well."

"So what was the need that drove their advanced astronomy, their mathematics, their calendars; the complexity of which is way beyond ninety-nine percent of people living today?" Denech asked.

"Accurate predictions of the changing seasons. Agriculture, maybe," Mary speculated. "I don't know."

"Or maybe it was something carried over from *before* the Mayan civilization. Knowledge they adopted from their predecessors for their own use," Denech added.

"Like what?" Mary asked.

"Knowledge is a very powerful thing. The ability to predict celestial events, like the return of comets or lunar and solar eclipses, would place those with that knowledge in a position of great awe by the rest of the ignorant masses."

"Which probably gave rise to the privileged and ruling class," Mary guessed. "But someone had to have learned this knowledge at some point in the past. Where did those people go?"

Denech smiled broadly. "Now that is the question, isn't it?"

"But all that aside and as strange as it may be," Mary reflected, "It still doesn't mean that the world is going to go berserk. There has to be more to what you're getting at."

"There is, of course."

"What?"

"In due time. In due time. It's after midnight. We begin again at eight in the morning. It'll be a tight fit, but we'll meet in the kitchen. May I count on you being here for the morning coffee, or will there be a late night departure out the emergency exit?"

They rose up together and Carl smiled. Nothing much did get past Peter Denech. "I've already received orders from my wife, though I think for a minute there she was having second thoughts. See you in the morning."

"Excellent! As was hoped." Denech exclaimed. "I know you better than you know yourselves. This will work. I have to believe that. Now this old man has other duties to attend to."

* * * *

Peter Denech and Randolf Haays left the Living Room, departing into the middle passageway and into the War Room, the cavern that held the electronic and mechanical guts of the operation. Carl and Mary Walker made for the left passageway and their sleeping quarters, but Red's voice caused them to turn to face her.

Mary suspected the others had departed for what would be a late night conference on all that had just transpired. The shared laughter had been a great tension release for all, and set the stage for the candid discussion that followed.

Carl noted Red's face radiated natural warmth again, her slightly parted full lips inviting, and the thought occurred to him that she had little control over her emotions, and that her moods were automatically and unconsciously reflected in her facial expressions. Maybe, he thought, her dancing and playful eyes represented not acting or deception at all, but indicated her true interest in him. That thought brought forth a confusing flood of emotions, but he couldn't deny the one overpowering emotion. Under different circumstances, things would be, well, different.

"You did good," Red began, rising from the chair and walking slowly towards them. "It started out pretty damn ugly, but you did good. Both of you. That will be my evaluation of things."

"Thanks, I think," Carl answered.

Mary, whose analytical mind was fully engaged again, picked up on something. "I assume Korneth has her own sleeping quarters. Mr. Haays and Mr. Denech probably share a room. Carl and I have the third."

"So?" Red asked.

"So, I can assume Carl and I have taken over your room. There are only three."

Red shrugged. "First, I'd hardly call the sleeping quarters rooms. More like closets. Amanda did volunteer to share her quarters but I said no thanks. I like my space. The couch here is comfortable. I don't mind. Besides, this way I can guard the main door in case you make a run for it."

"We don't intend—" Mary began.

"Hey. Just kidding."

Carl pointed to the pistol grip. "What about that pea shooter you so lovingly carry?"

"It's what I do here. Call it security. That's what I did back in— well, never mind."

"Tranquillizer darts, I take it," Carl continued.

Red removed the pistol, flipping it casually, expertly, even fondly from hand to hand to show its very light composite construction. "No metal components," she explained. "Invisible to x-rays, and virtually all forms of security except a full body search. The weapon holds ten projectiles in a clip, and fires like a semi-automatic.

The safety is in the trigger, so you basically point and shoot. And I carry two extra clips. The clips enable me to reload in about three seconds, two if I'm in a hurry. Not much firepower for sure, but then it's a stealth weapon, not an assault weapon."

"The agents in the train dropped like flies. How does that work?"

Red was in her element, and continued, as might an instructor. "A neural stimulator overloads the nervous system to create nearly instantaneous unconsciousness, and then a slower acting narcotic keeps the target down for up to four hours. There's usually quite a bit of memory loss. Some hallucinations. It takes about twelve hours to fully recover."

Carl reflected. "But not lethal."

"Well, it could be if the hit was in an eye or temple, but not likely."

"How accurate?"

"Depends upon the shooter like any weapon. The propellant has a maximum range of about fifty yards, but accuracy diminishes rapidly after twenty-five. But this thing is not for shooting deer. Most targets have been only a few feet away."

"So you've used this before. Before the agents in the train?"

"A few," Red conceded. "I am very good at what I do," and the statement was accentuated by a playful smile, as she returned the weapon to its holster.

"Getting back to taking over your room," Mary persisted. "I still don't like the idea of—"

"If giving up my bunk is the least of my sacrifices for this outfit, then I will consider myself lucky." She glanced at Carl and for a moment the playful sparkle returned. "Besides, I wouldn't want to come between a husband and wife."

Yet, immediately after Red spoke the words, her shoulders slumped and face saddened, as if her confident exterior had been suddenly canceled by some interior doubt or dark memory. For the first time since they'd met, Carl noted Red seemed less assertive, almost vulnerable, as her eyes clouded over with a thin mist.

Red's voice faltered. "You're both very lucky to have someone to go through life with. Someone you can trust. I couldn't help but notice the firm grip you had on each other's hand."

"I'm sure someone will come along for you," Mary began, but Red cut her off.

"More than one have, but none worked out. At any rate, it's too late now."

"But you're still young. And very beautiful," Mary reluctantly added.

"I'm afraid youth has nothing to do with it," Red stated, and then her mood lightened a bit. "But I do have a family. Peter, Randolf, even Amanda. And give Amanda a little slack. You might not see it but she does have deep feelings. She's just very good at keeping her defenses up. We all, I think, have strong emotions. If we didn't, none of us would be willing to make the sacrifice. We've been together doing our part for a long time."

"Mary and I don't have any families," Carl stated. "Other than my adopted Uncle and each other. You might say we're the last of our kind."

"Or the first," Red ventured. "You never know."

"Hopefully, someday," Carl said. "But I guess we have to get through this first. Mary and I talk about it a lot. Having children, I mean. Do we want to bring a child into a world that already has too many people? Have a child that will die someday in any case. What fate awaits her or him? Somehow it just doesn't seem fair, or maybe futile is a better word, and yet there is the desire to carry on, to leave something of ourselves when we leave for good."

"I think those thoughts are pretty much universal. Personally, I try not to think about having children of my own," Red reflected. "I know it will never happen, and so it would only be painful to dwell on it."

Red was about to say something else, but reconsidered, and the thin film of moisture in her eyes contracted into two tears, which broke free and trickled down her cheeks. Still she stood rooted in place, head held proudly, and looked in turn at each, eye to eye. There was a long awkward silence, and then, haltingly, she confronted Mary, and quickly embraced her with her arms. Then she moved to Carl and hugged him as well, lingering a bit longer, as his strong arms held her. Quickly she pushed away, wiping the tears from her face.

"Good night," she said. "Just hang in there with us. Peter has tremendous faith in you. And that's enough for me."

*   *   *   *

"They have turned in for the night," Red said, as she joined her three companions in the War Room. "I checked the monitor. They're both out like a light."

"Anything unusual to report?" Korneth asked.

"Nothing unusual for two sexually active adults."

"You watched?" Korneth continued.

"The beginning and the end."

"Well, at least you gave them *some* privacy," Denech cut in.

"Not really. A rapidly accelerating piece of discarded clothing flew over the concealed camera. When it slid off a bit later, both were buried under the blankets, and I assume sound asleep, because all was quiet."

Korneth nodded. "Okay, seal the hatch."

Red pushed a button and two metal doors, one on each end of the War Room, slid from the side effectively sealing the room. The War Room was, in effect, a cave within a cave. The statement she had made to the Walkers that the only door in the Rabbit Hole was on the bathroom was, of course, a lie.

The sound of the heat pump and small air-handling ventilation fan, as well as the cooling fans of the older laptops, produced a low hum that echoed faintly throughout the cavern. Undisturbed and sealed from the outside, the cavern temperature, under natural conditions, would never vary much from forty degrees, which was the temperature of the subsoil and bedrock come winter or summer. Early pioneers, and even some modern folks, built root cellars—essentially man-made caves—to keep food from freezing solid in the winter and refrigerator cool in the summer. The heat pump, which extracted heat directly from groundwater, raised the temperature to a steady sixty-eight degrees.

The underlying bedrock of Southeastern Minnesota consists of a vast layer of limestone, laid down in a shallow ocean millions of years before when dinosaurs still roamed the high ground, and is composed mostly of billions upon billions of the shells of tiny extinct sea creatures, made primarily of calcium carbonate. Rainwater trickling down through a large crack in the stone combined with carbonate to form weak carbonic acid. Though extremely dilute, over the millions of intervening years and along the crack, the acid dissolved the limestone, slowly but steadily creating the main cavern, the living room. With a shifting water table, the cave eventually dried up, and the natural building process ceased.

However, the stream that had at one time powered the waterwheel at the base of the valley kept flowing, and its cold water was also a direct result of the limestone deposits. On its way to the Mississippi river to the east, the stream filtered in and out of cracks and springs in the porous rock, cooling the water considerably and producing the ideal habitat for trout. Unfortunately, modern agricultural practices had all but eliminated the once abundant native fish.

Though it seemed like ages ago, Peter Denech had once been an avid fisherman, and he often wondered how the stream would have looked two hundreds years before when it was still unspoiled by human activities. To cast out a lure onto the pure water and have a trout lunge at it from under the protection of a submerged log was a dream that would never be fulfilled, but he knew also that without dreams man is merely a robot, an automaton, and without the potential to ever extend himself.

"Anything new?" Denech asked Rowanna Doran. "After I left?"

"Nothing," the redhead replied, and sat down heavily on one of the padded folding chairs.

"I know it's late. We're all tired. But we need your assessment of the progress of the second phase," Korneth stated without emotion. "In particular your part in it. So something more than a mere 'nothing' would be appreciated."

"They expressed concern about taking over my quarters. I told them it was no big deal. They were curious about the weapon. I gave them a general idea how it worked. They expressed some concern about bringing children into the world. I said that was entirely normal. They said good night. I said good night. I believe I have their trust. Is that what you wanted to hear?"

"Do you see their concern about bringing children into the world as a problem?"

"None at all. They are committed to each other, and under the appropriate conditions—"

"Would you say, then, that you have had no influence over Carl? I mean of a seductive or sexual nature?"

"If you mean do I think he wants to have sex with me, I can tell you the answer is yes."

"How do you come to this conclusion?"

"Because he's a normal man, and I'm a sexually mature and reasonably desirable woman. Because of the way he looks at me, and the way I look at him. That's how. There's nothing complicated about it. It's called instinct or lust or whatever. But wanting and doing are two separate things."

"And your feelings toward him?"

"Irrelevant."

Korneth considered. "Then you won't mind sharing them with us."

Red thought of refusing but instead spoke the truth. "Carl is—is unkempt," is all she could manage to say.

"Unkempt? What exactly does that mean?"

"Unruly hair, shirt tail half in and half out, a couple days worth of whisker growth."

"You mean sloppy?"

"Not sloppy. It's just that his personal appearance is an afterthought, which means he finds other things, like his wife or some other interests, more important. He has confidence in his abilities and doesn't have to rely on making a good impression."

"But the question was what are your feelings towards him? Not a critique on his personal dress code."

"I am not un-attracted to him," Red admitted.

Korneth stiffened. "Interesting double-talk coming from a straight shooter like yourself. Get un-attracted. The question is: Do you think you can take him all the way down?"

"Sure, but look. I'm not about to break up—"

Amanda Korneth interrupted violently. "This is *not* the time to get emotionally involved. Too much is riding on this. If he's corruptible, seducible, we have to know now. At some other time, a far more critical time, it will be too late."

"But they are people—idealist—"

"Oh shit!" Amanda exploded, and her carefully controlled placid face erupted into multiple furrows and ridges. "Just when things get hard, you go and fold on us. If you didn't think you could go through with this, you should have said something before it went this far. We could have found a stand-in."

"I thought I could. But that was when Carl was just a name on a piece of paper. But when you get to know someone, when you begin to understand someone—"

Korneth collected her composure, and then abruptly turned her back to Red, and faced Peter Denech.

"I just got word from the Organization. Plans A and B may have been compromised. The schedules have been moved ahead, but could easily fail. Plan A will be implemented as soon as possible. But they may have been targeted. Worst-case scenario: All we might have is Plan C, and from what I can see it's all going to hell as well. I'm not about to see all the years of planning go down the toilet." She turned back to face Red. "So get a grip on yourself. I've seen you in action. You're a true professional. Get your emotions under control. And tomorrow you get back in there and you seduce Carl Walker any way you can. And I mean *any way*. I don't care if you have to crawl up to him on your hands and knees buck-naked. We have to know if he's corruptible. We have to have enough time to bring in the next couple in line if the Walkers fold on us."

Rowanna Doran thought long and hard and then nodded. "Okay. Tomorrow it is. Carl and Mary are practically joined at the hip. We need to get the two separated. Some diversion. But I have a question for you."

"What?" Korneth retorted.

"How many couples are you willing to go through? How many men before one comes along that doesn't find me in the least desirable? And what would it prove anyway?"

Korneth remained silent, but Randolf Haays answered for her. "As many as it takes. And then when we run out of time, which is likely to be very soon and as I stated back in the dilapidated house in Downers Grove, Illinois, we fall back on Plan F. We step aside graciously and let Nature and God sort it all out."

Head downcast, Peter Denech stood to one side, barely listening. His vision was fading. The certainty that Carl and Mary Walker would be all that he had hoped and expected was now an unknown. From the first time he saw Mary sitting with her husband Carl in a vast sea of faces in an audience with over five-hundred mostly young adults, he knew he had found the person he had been looking for. The subsequent investigation into her background, and then Carl's, had only confirmed what he felt when their eyes had met. But now he wondered if he had only been deluding himself. The Walkers had done their part, and now it was up to him to do the rest. Randolf, Amanda, and Red were still mumbling in quiet conversation, but he would put this to rest now once and for all. Because if the Organization failed him or crashed, including Plan C, heaven help them all.

"All right," Denech cut in, and his low voice commanded attention. "We do this part your way. But if Carl comes through this tomorrow, there will be no more second guessing, no more backstabbing, and no more speeches from Randolf about miracles and Plan F."

"We let Nature—" Haays began, but Denech cut him off.

"Since when were human beings excommunicated from Nature? How do we know that Plan C is or isn't, in fact, Nature's plan? If Carl gets through this, we put personal opinion and prejudice aside and work as a team to make this work."

"Of course, Peter," Randolf stated, almost with sympathy. "But you and I both know what the outcome will be. Carl will fail the test, not because he's a bad person, but because he is a man. Corruptible, seducible, and replaceable."

Denech shook his head from side to side. "I keep asking myself, Randolf, just why you volunteered to be part of Plan C? From the beginning you never thought it had a chance. Always predicting failure."

"For one simple reason," Haays responded. "To prove to you that there are some things best left to God. To see you on your knees when the end comes, begging the God you don't believe in now to save you."

"My God! Randolf. You honestly *want* Plan C to fail. You are hoping, probably praying it will fail. Why?"

"To save your soul, my friend. But rest assured I will continue to do my part in this. I will fight right alongside you until the end. And in the end I will die with you if that is our fate."

"Why?"

"So that when the end comes you will know that it was God that saved us and there was nothing we could do to alter the destiny He had chosen."

"What about the others? All the millions of others?"

"Each will deal with it in their own way."

Denech turned to Amanda Korneth. "Did you know how Randolf felt about all this?"

"Yes."

"And you never told me. We could have replaced him months ago with someone more committed, more—more optimistic."

"He's here for that very reason," Korneth stated. "To make you strive harder. To harden your own commitment to the two young people sleeping in Red's quarters. To drive from your mind any doubt that we have chosen poorly."

Denech was silent, but Haays continued. "And it all comes down to Red tomorrow. I suggest we think now on Red's advice. To devise a diversion to physically separate the two." He turned to face Red directly. "Then it will all be up to you. I hope you realize that the fate of Plan C, not to mention the fate of an entire species, rests squarely in your lap."

* * * *

The morning sun rose bright and beautiful on the northeastern horizon, and flooded the hardwood forest and the solid limestone ridge with waves of heat and light. Robins called early, announcing the dawn. Meadowlarks and redwing blackbirds added their songs. And the great imitator, a catbird, called forth a wide assortment of chips and calls, and a longer drawn out wail that might, with a considerable degree of imagination, be misconstrued as a mournful cat.

On a bed of deep leaves that they had covered with a blanket and from under a second blanket, the bodies stirred. With bare arms and legs entangled, the two lay as one beneath the cover, and face-to-face. Clothing lay in a pile next to them. The young woman reached for a patch of unruly hair on her companion and attempted to smooth it down with her fingers, but it almost immediately popped back up again. He reached for his watch that rested on a patch of baron rock, and squinted to get his eyes to focus. The woman ran her fingers over his bristly face.

"You need to shave," she said. "If you want me to kiss you that is. Your face is getting like sandpaper."

"I'll expect the same from you when you start to get up in years," he joked.

"Please do. Time?" Mary asked, and glanced around at their surroundings.

"Almost seven. Better get up."

"Considering it was pitch black when we came up here, it appears we picked a good spot," Mary noted. "But I don't want to get up just yet."

Carl smiled. "Apprehensive?"

"You know me. Control freak." She encircled his nude waist with her arms and drew him close.

"We have the advantage, now," Carl said. "Let them come to us."

"And then?"

"We go with the flow and see what floats our way."

Mary nodded and breathed deeply. "The air in the cave smells old and used. But the air out here is so fresh and clean. Like after a rain. New."

"Spring is Nature's rebirth," Carl added. "A time when living things get another chance."

Mary frowned slightly. "Are you not the least bit worried?"

"Not now. If we handle this right."

"So much is riding on your shoulders," Mary added. "And I—"

"I can handle it," Carl said with a confidence he didn't completely feel.

"Even though I know what's coming, I feel unprepared," Mary admitted.

Carl gazed at his wife, and stroked her dark hair. "No one ever knows what's coming for sure. But remember. We have a friend on the inside, as you rightly believed all along. We just need to get him to prove it."

Chapter 7

▼

Rowanna Doran strode purposefully into the Kitchen where Peter Denech, Randolf Haays, and Amanda Korneth were already seated at the small square table drinking coffee. Amanda glanced up, and then did a double take as she noted the expression of concern on Red's face.

"What?" she asked.

"They're gone. Carl and Mary. They're not in their quarters."

"Did you search—?"

"Yes, of course. Every inch of the Rabbit Hole."

"Which means—"

"They're outside somewhere. Must have left during the night."

Amanda used her preferred explicative. "Shit!"

Denech took control. "Okay, don't panic yet. Let's get to the security feeds."

All four filed quickly into the War Room, and took up stations at four monitors. Each monitor screen was divided into four sections and represented four different security cameras each, or sixteen total. Computer controlled, each individual camera was controlled by a joystick, and could pan a wide area of the outside. One monitor covered the front of the grain mill and tiny parking area, one each for the left and right flank, and one monitor focused on the top of the ridge and the emergency exit. Within minutes, Randolf Haays, who worked the ridge cameras, noted two people sitting side by side in full sun on a section of the barren ridge, and looking out over the green valley below.

"Got them," he announced. "Sitting outside right above us on the ridge."

Korneth turned to Red. "Get them. And impress upon them the importance of remaining inside."

"I'll go too," Peter stated, noting Red checking her weapon. "Better to have them walk in under their own power than carrying in limp bodies."

* * * *

Shielding her eyes with her left hand from the sudden bright light of day, Rowanna Doran quickly scanned the ridge top as soon as she emerged from the emergency exit. Out of habit her right hand rested on the grip of the weapon under her left shoulder. Peter Denech quickly followed her out and closed the hatch behind him. A greeting of hello sounded from twenty yards away, and a lone figure waved. Red and Peter jogged over and found Carl sitting on the ridge, his feet dangling over the edge of the sloping limestone cliff. Seventy feet below, the blue stream appeared to wind its way through the green tops of stunted hardwoods. He waved his arm in a wide arc indicating the scenery beyond.

Carl smiled widely. "Good morning. Isn't this beautiful? Nothing but natural beauty for as far as the eye can see."

Red glanced around, ignoring the scenery. "Where's Mary?"

Carl noted that Red's emotional side was totally absent, having been replaced by the stark detachment of a combat soldier.

"We had a bit of a disagreement. She climbed down to the stream. Said she wanted to wade in the cold water and clear her head, whatever the hell that means. Then she was going back to the parking area to get a better look at the old grain mill."

Red relaxed a bit, and turned to Peter. "Go back in and check out the front. I'll take care of this end."

Peter nodded, and left the two alone.

Red sat down on the edge of the cliff next to Carl, and gave him a playful punch in the shoulder.

"You gave us quite a scare. Thought you might have deserted us after all."

Carl returned her warm smile. "Well, there were problems, but I'm sure you don't want to hear all the gory details."

"Problems? You mean between you and Mary?"

"You have to understand. Mary has to have all the answers, if you know what I mean."

Red placed her warm hand gently on his shoulder. "Not really, but if you want to tell me about it, I can be a good listener."

"She's a control freak," Carl stated. "And here she's not in control. Too many unknowns. She wanted to pull out."

"Please continue. I'm listening."

"After we left you last night, we had, well, words."

"A fight?" Red continued, and inched closer to Carl, pressing her body against his.

"Most people wouldn't recognize it as a fight if they happened to be watching. We don't shout at each other. It's all very civil and logical, and frankly I'm getting a little sick of it."

"So what happened?"

"When she gets frustrated, she ends up throwing things around, clothes and that. Really out of character. I did what I usually do when she gets into one of her moods. I turned my back to her, covered my head, and went to sleep. Later, when I woke up just around dawn, she was gone. I came up here looking for her. That had to be around six and found her up here."

"And?"

"And we continued where we left off."

Red slipped her arm around Carl's waist and snuggled closer. "Brrrr," she said. "Kind of a nip in the air this morning. Hope you don't mind."

Carl returned her wide smile, and looked into her deep blue eyes. But the playful sparkle that had been there before was absent. There were none of the lines and creases that represented true pleasure. As Carl had noted before, Red's emotions registered unconsciously on her face. It would always tell the truth, and the truth was what he had expected. Still, he continued.

"I don't mind at all. After the cold shoulder I got from Mary, it feels very nice."

"So what was the argument about?"

"I think you know," Carl stated.

Red pretended ignorance. "Not really."

"You, of course."

"Me?" Red said exaggerating surprise.

"She'd never admit it but she's jealous of you."

"But she's so smart, so pretty."

"Let's face it. Mary's afraid of her own shadow, and you're, well, exciting and brave. All the things Mary will never be."

Red's smile widened, and Carl noted the playful eyes had returned. From here on in, he realized, Red would not be making anything up. Whatever was about to happen would be an honest expression of her true feelings.

Red nodded. "Thank you for the compliment. You know I wish things could be different between us."

"Me too," Carl stated. "I'm not completely blind, you know. You're probably the most attractive woman I've ever known."

"I know I should keep my distance, but I'd be lying if I said I wasn't attracted to you."

Carl suddenly rose up and walked several paces to where he and Mary had spent the night in the pocket of windblown leaves. He stood leaning up against a misshapen oak that had managed to take a foothold in the cracks. Red came quietly next to him, then pulled him gently around to face her.

"We are human beings," she began, in a low seductive voice. "We have feelings. Needs. It's foolish to try to deny that. We are not perfect."

Carl struggled. "I know all that but—"

Red silenced him with gentle fingers to his lips. "It seems to me there is a simple solution to this. I have no doubt that you love your wife and I'd never want to take that away from you. But I need you too. I think I knew that from the first time I saw you."

Carl managed a weak shy smile. "I wanted you, too. I couldn't help it."

Red settled to the leaves, and drew Carl down next to her. She began running her fingers through his unruly hair. He reached over and kissed her tenderly on the neck.

"I've wanted this so badly," Red said softly.

"Me too," Carl repeated, and he lay upon her in the soft bed of leaves.

* * * *

Mary Walker reached the stream just as she saw Carl's company, Peter Denech and Rowanna Doran, arriving above. Hastily, she moved under the cover of the green oak and willow leaves, and continued downstream towards the old grain mill. To get past the water wheel, she had to ford the stream and the cold water soaked her slacks to just above her knees. Continuing on past the water wheel, she again crossed the stream. This put her back in the tiny parking area. The white Blazer was still parked where they had left it, and the rusty pickup had not been moved. Someone would be coming along soon, she knew. Logically and hopefully, it would be Peter Denech. The old war adage came to mind: Divide and conquer. Carl and she were now separated, and it did indeed feel strange to be away from someone who had become an integral part of her very existence. She found a comfortable place to sit on a huge moss-covered log overlooking the stream. All she could do now was wait.

*   *   *   *

Mary Walker didn't have to wait long. Though she didn't turn her head, in her peripheral vision she could see Peter Denech come through the door behind the water wheel. He stopped and his bald head turned this way and that, searching, and then settled on her location. She did not move as he approached. When he was within ten paces, she could no longer ignore his approach and turned to face him. His rumpled clothes, a white shirt and grey pants, seemed a bit more rumpled than usual, and she absently wondered if he had slept in them all night and not bothered to change in the morning. His face lacked his usual optimism, and deep lines of concern rippled across his forehead and between his eyes.

"Good morning, Peter," she said. This was the first time she could recall that she called him by his first name. "Come to join me? It's such a beautiful morning."

"You had me worried sick, young lady. I thought—"

"That we would have deserted you? Surely not. We did say we'd be here in the morning. Did you not say that we had to trust each other?"

"Well, yes. Of course. I just meant, well, I wouldn't want anything to happen to you. I would really like you to come back inside."

"Honestly, now, what could happen out here? It seems there isn't another human for miles." She hesitated, and then continued. "Come. Sit down. Enjoy the fresh air."

Peter Denech glanced back towards the mill and ridge, but then came forward and leaned up against the fallen trunk. Looking over his right shoulder, he continued the conversation.

"Yes, it is rather nice out here. I forget sometimes." He looked out over the stream. "I used to fish you know."

Mary nodded. "We still do. Speaking of fishing, there's something I'd like to ask you."

"Fire away."

"This is May, 2011. Yet everything I've seen around here is old technology. The Blazer still has the outmoded inefficient gasoline motor; all the electronics—the laptops and so forth—are at least eight years old. The old rusty pickup sitting over there is even more ancient, if it even runs. With your vast resources, surely you could have all the latest gadgets."

"The pickup runs. And yes there is a reason for what you are asking."

"A deep dark secret?"

"No. It's for security reasons," Denech said, and hoped the subject would end there but Mary persisted.

"Security?"

Denech hesitated, but then plowed ahead. "All new vehicles have embedded chips."

"I know that. To automatically record your mileage. The information is beamed via satellite directly to the appropriate state agencies for tax purposes. They did that when the high mileage Chinese and Indian imports started to flood the market, as well as the efficient hybrids. The states started to lose too much in gas tax so went to a mileage tax instead."

"All true. However, the chip can also be used to find any vehicle anywhere. That's one of the selling features for all new cars these days. Prevent theft and so on."

Mary nodded. "I see. These old vehicles wouldn't have any of that, except that even the older vehicles were supposed to be upgraded with the mileage chip."

"Oops. I guess we forgot," Denech said, and a smile lightened a cloudy face.

"And the old laptops?"

"Basically the same reason. On the open market there is no such thing as security anymore. All modern communication electronics have built in monitoring chips by the powers that be. 24/7. Anywhere on earth. Every word spoken, every keystroke or verbal command, every internet connection, is monitored by the NSA or some other anti-terrorist agency."

"That's old news."

"But did you know that virtually *all products* involving any electronics have specific identification chips. This includes digital cameras, the talking toys of children, even the newer wristwatches. *Anything* that uses any of the new electronics hardware comes standard with these ID chips. And each chip is specific to the item it happens to be in."

"Like a finger print?"

"Exactly. Only these fingerprints leave an electronic signal that, with the right detection equipment, can be located anywhere. In addition to that, people now insert a chip into their pets and even their children. Anything that they deem valuable."

"I remember reading about this, but I guess I never gave it much thought."

"The justification for the chips, of course, was to prevent theft, or in case there was a theft, say your car or your new electronic toaster, it could be located by the authorities."

"But a thief could easily remove the chip."

"Not so easily as you might think. At first the chips were simply glued on somewhere, but the second line of products began integrating the chip directly into the construction of the product."

"Hidden in the material itself."

"Yes. And you have to remember we're talking about a piece of technology about the size of the head of a pin. Not something that is going to jump out at you."

"Have they worked? I mean have thefts gone down?"

"At first, but there are ways to render the chips useless. Exposing them to an intense magnetic field for instance."

"Like an EMP. An electromagnetic pulse."

"Yes. As long as there are smart crooks, there will always be a way to get around the technology. And as long as there are smart crooks, ways will be found to confound them. The newest generation ID chips have shielding to protect against the effects of magnetic interference."

"So what does all this have to do with us?"

"What you may not know is anything that has these ID chips—from computers, to cell phones, from the talking baby toy to your toaster—can be specifically targeted."

"Targeted?"

"Suppose someone with political power believes you're a threat of some sort. Maybe it's political. Maybe it's economic. Maybe he just doesn't like you. You happen to be on your new cell phone or computer or just minding your own business shaving in the morning. Within a millisecond of your activation of that device, a small but deadly projectile is launched, and within mere minutes, sometimes seconds, you are dead."

"I don't ever remember reading about this type of technology."

Denech smiled. "And you never will, because it is, of course, just too preposterous to believe."

Mary reflected. "There was the flap about the woman in New York who supposedly exploded in broad daylight. I wrote it off as on par with a UFO sighting."

"Now you know better. In it's first incarnation, the technology was known as 'smart bullets.' But the technology has evolved into a much deadlier and much more accurate version. They are something like a cruise missile, only about two feet long."

"You mentioned these 'smart bullets' are launched? From where?"

"Orbiting satellites. Pilotless drones. Ground stations. Mobile launch sites. Even commercial aircraft. Whatever would happen to be closest to your location."

"Commercial aircraft?"

"The threat of terrorism has carried a high price. Almost all major corporations, especially those in communications and transportation, are working with Big Brother."

"But there are laws. People have rights."

"A scared person is an irrational person. A scared government is an irrational government. The tangle of anti-terrorism laws have become so jumbled that what's legal or not becomes anyone's guess. Laws are enacted secretly or after the fact to cover one illegal activity after another. And powerful people ignore the laws altogether."

"And your operation?"

"We operate with old junk that happens to still work and remain under the radar as much as possible. By the current government definition, that does make us terrorists."

Denech expected Mary to be shocked, but she merely considered. "Is that why I didn't notice a dish anywhere for communications?"

"We use them when we're out in public, but not here, and only in microbursts to keep our location secret."

"Microbursts?"

"Essentially a bundle of encrypted energy released in a split-second's time. If you come inside, Randolf can explain all the technical stuff."

Mary didn't move. "So what about here?"

"We use an omni-directional trans-ciever. It's here but well hidden at a higher location. It's left over technology from aircraft navigation and decades old. Completely obsolete now because of modern GPS, but perfect for our use."

"And that's how you keep in contact with the rest your organization?"

"We communicate on little used frequencies which are changed on a regular basis. We can also piggyback our signal on other carriers. We can even channel a signal through the electrical transmission lines to the east of us. Just as a precaution, our communications are usually limited to ten second bursts. They had never been compromised before this. I guess we got too confident."

"The two agents," Mary guessed.

"Somehow they found out about you and Carl. We changed everything—communication frequencies and code words—immediately after Red called in with a Code Yellow."

"Back in the train," Mary said.

"Yes."

"She was following us."

"Yes. For your own protection."

"Good thing she was there. But have you considered the other option?"

"What other option?"

"That the problem wasn't that someone intercepted your communications. That the problem might be that there is someone in your organization that is working for the other side."

"A spy. Yes, the thought has been considered."

"Well?"

"It's just too devastating to contemplate. Everything we've built is on trust and loyalty. Most of our people throughout the entire organization have been with us since the beginning years ago. All except you and Carl of course."

"So, no chance of that at all?'

"All have been tested by fire, as the saying goes. If someone has turned, if there is a traitor, then we might as well quit now."

"The good news," Mary stated, in a positive tone, "is that you're still here, and though I gather there are other problems, there has been no massive failure of whatever it is you're trying to accomplish."

Denech smiled. "That's true. And yes. That's what keeps us going."

Both sat quietly for nearly a minute. Denech pulled pieces of moss from the log and tossed them toward the river. He removed a pen from his shirt pocket and went through the same nervous ritualistic rolling between his fingers, and then put it back. Twice, he glanced back towards the top of the ridge. Finally, Mary began again.

"There is something else that tugs at the left side of my brain."

"And what is that?"

Mary chose her words carefully. "On this beautiful morning, you haven't asked me the most obvious question of all."

Denech was genuinely puzzled, and rubbed his right hand over his bald head. "You got me. What obvious question?"

"Where's my husband. Where's Carl?"

"I just thought—" Denech began, but then stopped.

"Knowing Carl and I like you do, you would of course think it odd that Carl is not with me. Perhaps you have not asked the question because you know precisely where he is and what you and the others have planned for him."

Because of the way each faced both had been speaking in opposite directions and never looking at the other, but now Mary turned to face Peter Denech directly, who merely shook his head in defeat. When she spoke, Mary's voice was no longer friendly, soft, or demure. "You lied to us, Peter Denech. About a lot of things. There is no trust here. Only paranoia. Red is borderline psychotic, fondling her weapon at every opportunity. Randolf is an end-times religious fanatic. Amanda appears to be locked in her own private hell. You remind me of the little Dutch boy with his finger in the dike trying to stop a tidal wave. And that's just the people we know. Is everyone else in your secret society as far away from reality as you four appear to be?"

"Please. Yes. No. Let me explain."

"No! No more lies or deceit. Until last night, I trusted you fully. Against all logic, I was willing to follow you."

Denech was confused. "But after our meeting last night, I thought we were on the same page. You agreed—"

"That's not the meeting I'm talking about. It's the one we weren't invited to. In the War Room."

"Okay, yes, we had a meeting after you and Carl were asleep. I admit—"

"We weren't asleep."

"But Red saw—"

"We found the hidden camera, and did a little acting to cover it up. With the few minutes we had, we padded the bunk to make it look like we were still there. Then we set out on some investigating of our own."

"I see."

"We couldn't help but notice the soundproof doors on the War Room. For an organization built on trust, they represent something of a contradiction wouldn't you say?"

"They're more than just soundproof and there's a reason—"

"I admit we couldn't make out much through the doors. It was extremely faint and muffled at best. But we did manage to figure out it was your intention to separate us. And Red was to be the wedge you'd drive between us."

"That was not my idea, I assure you."

Mary's voice did not change. "So, you see, you got us fairly angry at about the only thing that could get us angry. Now we intend to dissect your little operation one piece at a time, and then, if all the pieces don't fit, we go to the authorities."

Chapter 8

Randolf Haays and Amanda Korneth huddled together in front of a laptop screen watching events unfold on the ridge. Randolf occasionally adjusted the camera angle with a joystick, but a stunted oak tree and low shrubs blocked most of the view. Carl and Red were mostly out of sight of any of the cameras, but their legs were visible and in the prone position. Randolf smiled. It would be as he suspected. Carl Walker would fold, and humanity would be one more step toward the only outcome that one could reasonably expect. Amanda spoke quietly, though it was impossible for anyone outside to hear.

"We'll need a witness to the final act, since none of the cameras can get a clear shot. Get ready."

* * * *

Carl Walker moved his hand along Rowanna Doran's warm bare back beneath her blouse, as their lips locked in a passionate embrace. Her arms circled his neck holding him tightly, and together they rolled over onto their sides. Something hard poked Carl in the ribs, and he pulled pack slightly, a wide and hungry smile playing across his lips.

"Something's come between us," he teased. "Maybe you can part with the pea shooter, or do you intend to tranquilize me into submission."

Red laughed. "You wouldn't be much good to me unconscious. Give me a second."

She sat up and reached behind her back to unhook the holster, and then set the weapon next to them on the ground. Even in his passionate state, Carl noted she kept it within arms reach, with the grip fully accessible. Clearly this woman was taking no chances.

"Anything else you'd like me to unhook back there?" Red asked seductively, and willingly reached behind anticipating the obvious answer. But it was not to be.

With cat like quickness, Carl grabbed the weapon from the holster, and leaped backwards to his feet, leaving a confused woman on the ground. He backed ten feet away, pointing the pistol directly at her. Immediately, Red was on her feet, and there was no disguising the anger that flashed in her eyes.

Her tender voice a thing of the past, she now spat out words, and inched her way towards Carl. "You foolish boy. This you'll regret."

Carl did not flinch, and discharged one projectile into the ground between her feet. "I believe I have nine more," he stated. "But the next one will cut you down if you take one more step."

"You used me," Red sputtered through clenched teeth, but stopped her forward advance. "Now what do you intend to do, or hadn't you thought that far ahead?"

Red's eyes moved slightly from his and focused ever so briefly on something behind. Carl turned, fired at a target, and retrained the weapon on Red in a second's time. Behind him he could hear Randolf Haays wilt to the ground.

"One down. Three to go," Carl said. "And I have the only weapon. Do you have a preference for a place to get shot, or should I just use my imagination?"

Despite her predicament, Red noticeably relaxed, and slowly raised her hands above her head in submission. "Okay. You passed. You can set the weapon aside. Now you have to get inside."

"Passed? Passed what? And what's the rush to drive me back into the Rabbit Hole?"

"We believe Plan A was activated last night. Within a few hours nothing that isn't isolated from the atmosphere will escape."

"Right. Doomsday 101. What is it this time? Martians or a giant octopus?"

"You're not paying attention. We have to get back inside."

"We'll stay right here. By now Amanda is on her way up. No doubt she's been watching on the monitors. We'll just wait."

Carl still had his back to the emergency exit, and Red saw that as a weakness. She'd be ready the next time. When Carl was again distracted, probably by Amanda's appearance, she'd make her move. She was fully aware, however, that Carl held the weapon as if he'd had a lot of practice with a pistol. He didn't seem the least bit concerned that his back would be to Amanda when and if she arrived. "When she does come, she'll be a little more careful than Randolf," Red warned.

"Hopefully, she'll be a little more cooperative. I'll give her a chance, if she's polite and announces herself. Otherwise, well, a man could get jumpy, what with people sneaking up on him."

"How did you know Randolf—"

"Was about to bushwhack me? You told me."

"I never said a word."

"You didn't have to. You said it with—"

Again Carl whirled about, this time a smooth 360-degree rotation, firing at the approaching target, then sweeping around back to face Red who seized upon the opportunity to charge as soon as he moved. Carl fired again as Red lunged toward him, and her forward motion knocked him flat on his back. Groaning from the impact with solid rock, he pushed the dead weight of Rowanna Doran aside, and stood.

"Your eyes," he finished, as he looked down upon her sprawling body. "Three down, one to go."

* * * *

When Peter Denech saw Carl Walker emerge though the narrow weathered doorway behind the water wheel of the old grain mill, he knew that the plan had failed, or succeeded depending on how one looked at it, and that his three comrades were likely unconscious or worse. It was obvious now that Carl and Mary had learned just enough to believe there had been a secret plot to separate the two. It would now be impossible to convince them of his sincerity. In a way, however, his faith in the Walkers had been completely vindicated. They were all he could have hoped for: Intelligent, resourceful, dedicated, and young enough to be perfect for the mission. To try to convince them now that Red's advances had been nothing more than a test of their loyalty to one another would be impossible. Yet, he was going to try. Because if they all didn't get back inside the cavern and sealed in, it would make no difference, and more than seven years of work would be for nothing.

Maybe Randolf was right after all, Denech considered. Maybe it was best to let Nature sort it all out. But if Plan A had truly been activated, there was no going back. The only way to know was to get back into the War Room and check the updates from the organization. But first he had to convince Carl not to shoot him where he stood.

* * * *

As soon as Carl came through the doorway, Mary left her place on the moss-covered log and ran over to greet him. "Everything all right?" she asked, taking his left hand firmly with her right.

"Fine," Carl answered, and together they walked the few paces back to where Peter Denech stood quietly looking out over the placid stream. He stood slump shouldered, a man defeated, but turned as they drew near. Carl carried Red's weapon casually in his right hand at his side.

Peter's first thought was of his comrades. "How are they?"

"Sleeping. Explain to me why you shouldn't be doing the same."

"I have not betrayed you. No one here has betrayed you. But I know that I cannot convince you of that."

"No, you can't," Carl agreed. "But just for the sake of conversation, try."

"Not that it probably matters, but you are now full members of the organization, if you choose to stay. You had already passed every requirement but one. The one we had been calling Phase One."

"And just how did we do that?" Carl asked.

"Not we. You."

"Okay. How did I do that?"

"Think back to our first meeting in the old house. What was the first condition that put you on our list?"

"That we were faithful to each other," Mary answered.

"We had every reason to believe you were, but we had to know for sure. We had to know if one or the other might be tempted to stray."

"Red," Carl realized.

"Frankly, we were never worried about Mary. The thought of her having an extra-marital affair was ludicrous. However, men in general are a different story."

"So I was considered the weak link," Carl guessed.

"Not by me, though you might not believe that. But, yes, the others—to varying degree—felt you would fold, as Randolf was fond of saying."

"What exactly did go down in the War Room last night?"

"You were being set up," Denech said simply. "We had devised a plan to separate you and Mary, and Red was to use her seductive charms to tempt you into an act of unfaithfulness. You heard some of that but not enough to understand our true intent. You were able to use the information you did hear to turn the tables on us. And, it seems, you have done just that very efficiently."

"Divide and conquer," Carl said with a wide smile.

Peter nodded. "Mary kept me occupied here, while you dealt with the others."

"I figured you're the brains of the outfit," Carl said. "So Mary and I had an equal task. One question. What would have happened if I had—well, failed the test?"

"Both of you would have been drugged as my comrades are now, and you would have regained consciousness back at your apartment in Duluth. Federal agents would have shown up at your door and taken you away to a secret prison designed solely for suspected terrorists. Every tactic imaginable, and many that you can't imagine, would have been used on you to extract any bit of information you might know about this organization. But you would give up nothing, because we would have excised from your memory everything that has occurred in the last two days. And most likely you would have remained in prison separated from each other for the foreseeable future as enemies of the state, but never having the foggiest notion why."

"Cheerful thought. So much for the Bill of Rights."

"The Organization would have written you off as lab animals in an experiment that didn't work."

"Thanks. I like the way you sugar coat everything."

Denech smiled. "I am being as blunt and forthcoming as I know how, because I know that that is the only way to regain your trust."

"Well, here's something to consider," Carl continued. "Your test, this Phase One as you call it, never really was fulfilled."

"What do you mean?"

"I mean I was never tested in the way you wanted. I knew that Red's advances were phony."

"I'm still not following," Denech admitted.

"Simply this. You still don't know what I would have done if I'd been unaware of your plan. I still may be the weak link."

Denech glanced at Mary who remained noncommittal, and then at the weapon Carl carried at his side. "At this point, Carl, I'm willing to take you on your word."

A protracted silence followed and then Carl began again.

"What's Plan A?"

"The reason we urgently need to get back inside. All of us, but you and Mary most importantly. It's difficult to explain, but I can show you on the monitors."

Carl glanced at Mary, who nodded slightly. "Okay. We'll play along for now," Carl stated, and immediately remembered those were the same words he'd spoken back at the old house in Illinois.

* * * *

Working together without speaking—Carl above and Mary and Peter below—the three lowered three bodies into the emergency exit of the Rabbit Hole. From there they were moved into the living room and laid out side by side on the carpeted floor of solid rock. Denech assured Carl that the narcotic would last a full four hours, after which they would begin to exhibit the characteristics of REM sleep, followed by a slow awakening into consciousness. It was likely they would not remember anything about recent events at first and there would be several hours of confusion, but steadily over a twelve-hour period they would return to normal and most, if not all, of their memories would return. Denech assured them that the entire process was non-violent and was likened to a long period of awakening from a deep sleep.

Once Red, Amanda, and Randolf were taken care of, Peter Denech led Carl and Mary into the War Room, where he had promised a thorough briefing on Plan A. Carl had retrieved the holster from the rock ridge and now kept the weapon under his own left shoulder. Denech invited them to sit, logged into a specific program, and began to lock the place down. So as not to raise further suspicion, he explained each action to the Walkers. The facility, Carl realized, was being systematically sealed from the outside air. The air handling system, which had drawn air from the outside, now re-circulated the inside air only. Denech assured them that the natural oxygen supply in the cave together with a stored supply was sufficient to last up to two weeks, with six adults. But, if all went as planned, they would be back out into fresh air within a week.

Peter Denech had not elaborated on just why it was so pressing to get below ground, and why it was so important for Mary and Carl Walker in particular. But with the facility secure and interior electronics and machinery functioning, Denech was noticeably more relaxed. He maneuvered around several questions, requesting patience from the young couple. With the facility secure, he switched to a different laptop, and tapped into a private and encrypted data stream. Viewing over his shoulder, Mary watched as the words *package sent* appeared in the upper left hand corner. Then *system on-line*, and finally *all systems functional*. The screen suddenly went blank, and then the word *release* pulsated on and off repeatedly.

A video recording suddenly brightened the monitor, picturing a scene with about a dozen people gathered in a group. Some were sitting, others standing, some were hugging, and all seemed subdued, as one might expect at a funeral. Desks and chairs and electronics sat empty and idle. Mary noted Peter Denech was entirely engrossed in the sequence of events, and from the startled expression on his face it was clear this was all new to him. A man's face suddenly filled the entire view, as if he were taking video of himself. Distorted by the close proximity of the camera, his nose looked disproportionately huge, and the image jumped about. There was the quiet murmur of the people in the background, but nothing understandable until the man's voice drowned out everything. "Incoming. This is an official Code Red." There was a brief pause as he glanced back at the room where the others had gathered. He again looked at the camera, and stated in a very calm and resolute voice. "We did our best. Outcome unknown. Facility destroyed." For several seconds the man continued to speak, but the message was too broken to understand. But through the interference, a few words came through clearly. "*... Integrity compromised ... possible traitor ... message sent to alternate site for continuous replay.*" The signal abruptly terminated, leaving Peter Denech with his mouth open and staring in disbelief at a blank screen.

It only took a moment for Denech to react. His stubby fingers flew over the old keyboard and moments later the homepage of a twenty-four hour news site, NEWS 24/7, appeared. He selected "Breaking News" from the list of options. The screen changed immediately to a long distance video shot of a huge towering fireball. An attractive blonde reporter was narrating in the foreground. Obviously highly agitated, her voice could not mask the emotion she felt.

"*—and as you can see from our location here in Great Falls—we're actually standing along Highway 87 on the eastern outskirts of the city—the clouds created by the explosion continue to rise up into the sky.*" She broke away momentarily, listening to communications in her earpiece. She nodded. "*Got it. Got it.*" Then continued speaking into the camera. "*We have an unconfirmed report that it was an atomic explosion, which detonated approximately one hundred miles due east of Great Falls in a remote area of the state. We have been advised it was and I quote, 'A low yield device' about one tenth the power of the Hiroshima bomb. We have learned through an unidentified source, who was not authorized to speak to the public, that it was, in fact, a planned test by the military. We'll keep you updated as more information comes in.*"

The woman reporter disappeared, replaced by the male news anchor. "*For those of you who have just joined us, that was Leasa Anderson reporting from our local affiliate in Great Falls, Montana, earlier this morning. To recap, at 6:09AM Mountain Time in a remote area of central Montana, an intense fireball was clearly visible from a hundred miles away. Early reports said it was caused by the impact of a meteor or comet. We learn now that it might have been, in fact, an unannounced test of the military's new low yield bunker-busting atomic bombs. Above ground testing is, of course, banned by international treaty. I must stress this has not been confirmed by any official source. I repeat this has not been confirmed. We can, however, say for sure, as you've seen from the video, that there was indeed a huge explosion in Montana earlier this morning. As Leasa said, we will continue to keep you updated as more information becomes available."*

The news site automatically reset to the homepage. Denech had the option of replaying the news feed, but instead shut down the computer and then proceeded to sever all electronics from both electrical and communication connections. He then rose slowly from his chair, and turned to face Carl and Mary Walker. His eyes overflowing with tears and breath coming in gasps, Peter Denech's knees buckled, and he collapsed onto the rock underfoot.

Chapter 9

▼

The first thing Mary Walker did was to make sure Peter Denech was not dead. Given his size and age, there was the immediate fear of a heart attack, and it occurred to her that she had no idea where emergency medicines were stored if there were any at all. His pulse, however, appeared to be strong and steady, and it became apparent that he had merely fainted from the overwhelming shock of the news feed. Both Mary and Carl were in good physical condition, but it was still a struggle to get the big man back to the couch in the main cavern. Carl got a glass of water, and pressed a sip to Denech's lips as he regained consciousness. He waved off any further liquid, and slowly sat up, swinging his feet back onto the floor. Mary remained next to him, her hand on his shoulder, while Carl stood close by with arms folded across his chest. Eyes red and distraught, Denech looked at Mary.

"Your earlier observation was apparently correct. We have a traitor in our midst. A mole."

Mary nodded, but Carl continued. "The explosion?"

"Where you might have been. Our facility in Montana. Our people there. All gone."

"It wasn't a meteor, I take it."

"No. It was an assassination."

"Why?"

"It was the command center for Plan A. Fifteen full time comrades who have been with us since the beginning. Now—gone—" The thought was too much for Denech, and his face sunk into his hands.

"Who?" Mary asked. And then another thought occurred. "What about us? Here? Are we next?"

Denech looked up and regained a degree of control. "No. If they knew about this location, we'd already be reduced to atoms. We're safe for now. We'll stay put. There is still a chance that Plan A was initiated." He looked at Mary and Carl in turn. "And you are both too important to take a chance on exposure to the outside."

"Because of the radiation?"

Denech shook his head. "The radiation from the nuclear blast would be minimal at our location. We are in no danger even above ground."

"So I guess I'm still confused," Carl admitted. "Just why are we buried here under twenty feet of solid rock?"

"From the substance that Plan A—from the substance that we—have deliberately released into the atmosphere."

Carl and Mary exchanged startled glances.

"Something dangerous? A poison? What?" Carl said finally. "And why?" he added.

Denech didn't seem to hear, and nodded toward the three on the floor who continued their deep sleep. "How am I going to tell them about Montana? That our people are dead. How am I going to tell them that years of preparation may have been wasted?"

Mary's thoughts were restless and she knew why. Her ordered mind relied on facts, that was what kept her disposition on an even keel, and at this point there were few. She glanced at Carl, who understood her well enough to know that now she would take control of the conversation. She would, like a surgeon looking for an elusive tumor, begin an exploratory procedure to make some sense of recent events.

Mary began by resting her hand on Peter Denech's arm. "It is time," she said. "It is time for an explanation. I have to have some order, some logical approach, so please, just answer my questions. Don't elaborate. Don't wander off into tangential events."

Denech nodded. "You deserve that much, but you have to understand you're part—"

Mary glanced away, cutting Denech's statement short.

"Sorry," he stated. "I do get long winded at times."

"First of all you said that your friends in Montana were assassinated. By whom?"

"At this point I can't be positive, but probably by a rogue agency. We don't know for sure exactly who. We *believe* it is the same group that answers directly to the President. A special force that acts like the CIA might act in a foreign and hostile country. These people use the same clandestine tactics but against American citizens. Because they officially don't exist, U.S. law does not bind them. There is no moral conscience. They answer to no one. They operate as a completely independent force. Almost like a secret foreign pre-invasion force from another country. We have come to refer to them as the Agency or Wolf."

"Wolf? Sounds rather sinister," Mary observed.

"They are, as you've seen. A few months ago, Randolf noted they were like a pack of wolves. The name stuck."

"But a nuclear device is hard to believe. One does not simply carry around an atomic bomb in the back of a pickup."

"Believe me there are ways. If Wolf is behind it, we can assume it was a planned attack with authorization from the highest levels of government."

"What about the agents on the train."

"Yes, they're part of Wolf. But they are merely foot-soldiers following orders."

"You mentioned once that in the view of the government, you and your organization are considered terrorists. From a certain point of view, that might explain the destruction of your facility. Why exactly would the government believe you are terrorists? Mary asked.

"Because we are a secret society."

"There are many secret societies."

"Not on this scale. We have tremendous financial reserves. We are mostly scientists. We do not report our financial transactions to the IRS, or any government anywhere. We operate under the radar of modern electronics and surveillance techniques. What we do is known to us and us only."

"But apparently not under the radar any longer."

"Apparently not. Later I must go back on-line and see how many of our facilities have been compromised. Assess the damage. But there is now a time frame I must follow. A Code Red really means dig yourself a hole and stay there until the storm passes."

"How many facilities? How many people are we talking about?"

"Twenty-eight sites in twelve countries worldwide. One hundred fifty people total, though probably fifteen less with the loss of the Montana site."

"You operate a worldwide organization with just one hundred fifty people?"

"Those in the know, yes. However, we employ something like a thousand more. The go-fers as it were, who know nothing of the organization but who help support it. Deliveries, repairs, lab assistants."

"Well, obviously someone thinks you're a danger to something."

"Yes. Obviously."

"Why?"

"Because we are," Denech said, without hesitation. "Most people, the average Joe and Jane, would certainly lock us up if they knew what we've planned, and what may have already occurred."

"So now we get down to the nitty-gritty," Carl cut in. "Just what have you got planned? What is Plan A? And what did you release into the atmosphere?"

Peter Denech sat back against the couch and sighed. "With all due respect to Mary, here I must digress. I know you each well enough to know that you know who I am. We met, or at least our eyes did, years ago when you were both still at the University."

Mary nodded. "Yes, we recognized you. You presented the astronomy department with a rather large gift of money. A half million dollars, if I recall."

"Merely a token, really. For Professor Micals' work in searching for NEO's. Asteroids that might be a threat to earth."

"He found one, as I recall," Carl said.

"Actually he'd found three by that time, and one more since. But it was for one in particular that we were especially grateful."

"Yes. I remember," Mary continued. "The one that came within the orbit of the moon. About ten thousand miles closer, and it might have done some real damage. It could have taken out a major city. But not big enough to cause—"

"It was bigger. A lot bigger," Denech interrupted.

"But the official reports," Carl stated. "There were a lot of articles in several science magazines with pretty definite information about its size and shape. I know. I read them all. I don't recall anything catastrophic about it."

Denech smiled. "And you believe all you read, right?"

"Not usually, no, but then science—"

"All the information, all the articles, came from only one source. That source was Professor Micals, who did all the telemetry and compositional studies."

"What about other astronomers from other countries?"

"The asteroid came so fast and unexpected that few could get good data on it. Except Micals who got lucky. His telescope happened to be pointed in the right direction at the right time."

"You're saying Professor Micals gave out false information about the true nature of the asteroid?"

"Let's just say that we obtained exclusive rights to the information Micals had on it, and the information he released to the public was, well, somewhat less than accurate."

"You bought his silence with a check for a half million dollars," Mary concluded.

"Professor Micals is a member of the organization in very good standing," Denech corrected. "He is our eyes and ears within the rest of the scientific community. I give up this information freely to you for two reasons. One, in my mind, you are equal members of this group and deserve to know. And two at some future time, if unforeseen events demand it, you may seek out Professor Micals and know he is someone you can trust."

"But why did Micals give out false information?"

"Because the true nature of the asteroid was, shall we say, inconsistent with known facts about such objects."

Carl was intensely interested, and moved closer. "Inconsistent? How?"

Instead of answering, Denech responded with a question of his own. "You're the budding astronomer. How do we find these objects in the first place?"

"Essentially, through a telescope we take repeated digital pictures of the night sky over a period of time."

"And then?"

"A computer program analyzes the pictures looking for a point of light that has moved against the background stars."

"Which indicates what?"

"That there could be an object relatively close. Once we find it and track it's position over a few nights, we can get an idea of its orbit, and how close it might come to earth."

"Where does the light from the object come from?"

"It's reflected light from the sun."

"So what you're telling me is it's the light it reflects that gives it away."

"Yes. That's true."

"What if it doesn't reflect any light, or very little light?"

"Then we would have no way of detecting it before—"

"—it was too late," Denech finished.

"What are you saying?"

Denech hesitated, but then continued. "No one saw the Micals' asteroid coming because it is almost completely black, and its reflection signature was extremely faint. Micals can't be sure but he believes it's made of mostly carbon and silicon, or more likely some exotic compound that we don't know about. That would explain its dark surface. Micals got lucky, and so did this planet."

"How so?"

"According to our analysis, the object was fifteen to twenty miles in diameter, and passed within a thousand miles of earth. A virtual hair's breath away."

"Twenty miles in diameter?"

"Somewhat startling, wouldn't you say, since the asteroid is probably twice the size of the asteroid that wiped out the dinosaurs along with about seventy percent of all life on earth about sixty five million years ago?"

"But it missed," Carl emphasized.

"This time," Denech stated, and the stark knowledge hit Carl like slap in the face.

"That close approach altered the asteroid's orbit," Carl realized. "Gravitational capture. Next time, when it comes back around—"

"Next time it may not miss," Denech finished. "And even if by some miracle it does miss next time, it is certain to hit within a very few passes. That's Micals' view. However, I know precisely when it will hit, if it hits."

"That's a bit of a confusing statement," Carl noted. "'When it will hit, if it hits?'"

"Not at all confusing from my point of view."

"When is next time?" Mary asked. "When will its orbit return it to earth?"

"Micals can't be precise. The asteroid's rotation has kept him for the most part literally in the black. One side is almost totally non-reflective, with only a very small amount of reflectivity on the other. We thought about applying for time on the Space Telescope, but realized that would almost certainly lead to questions we are not prepared to answer. Yet, we believe we can say with reasonable certainty that its orbit will return it to earth—"

"Next year. In 2012," Mary finished.

"Very astute," Denech said. "Next May, to be more precise. I can even tell you where it will hit."

"Where?" Carl asked. "Let me guess. Las Vegas."

Denech smiled. "No, but good guess. It will hit in the Atlantic just off Brazil."

"Creating a tidal wave—"

"Oh, about a mile high. Probably higher. It will sweep clean the western coasts of Africa, Europe, and the eastern side of both North and South America. Florida will be washed into the Gulf of Mexico. But you and I know that that is the least of our concerns."

"The explosive discharge would darken the planet for years," Carl continued. "Vegetation would die. A prolonged winter on the scale of an Ice Age would likely encompass the entire planet. No vegetation means plant eaters would soon follow. No plant eaters, no predators."

"I'm afraid that magnitude impact would leave nothing but the smallest, most hardy organisms alive," Denech concluded. "It would literally be the end."

"But it hasn't happened yet," Carl stressed. "And it may not."

"True. It might not. But do you see now how this ties into the Mayan Long Count Calendar we were talking about? The end of an age. An asteroid impact of that size and magnitude would certainly do the trick. Couple that with the solar system's passage through the galactic plane, and the resurgent sun spot activity, and one begins to get a sense that something earth-shaking—if you'll pardon the choice of words—is imminent."

"I do see how it ties in," Carl stated. "I just can't believe it. This sounds like—"

"Science fiction?" Denech finished. "Well, I'm afraid you've heard just the prologue. And I assure you, it doesn't get any better."

* * * *

Carl had learned one thing. There was certainly such a thing as information overload. It was time for a break. Mary did a quick check of Amanda Korneth, Randolf Haays, and Rowanna Doran, who, by all appearances, were sleeping peacefully on the floor, and then joined Carl and Peter in the tiny kitchen. Amanda and Red, Mary noted, were beginning to exhibit the rapid eye movement typical of REM sleep, and would probably be the first to recover.

Peter Denech opened a can of fruit. With half of a peach stuck to the end of a fork, he pointed to the stock of food on the open shelves.

"Coffee and peaches for me but help yourself. Have to keep my strength up."

Carl sipped at a cup of cold tea laden with sugar, while Mary settled for some soda crackers and a glass of water. No one was particularly hungry, except for information. Once they were all seated at the small square table, Carl continued the questioning.

"So we have a secret society—you and your organization—that is aware of a possible impending asteroid strike. There's a secret government agency, Wolf, intent on destroying said secret society."

"Not destroying," Denech corrected. "Wolf wants to shut us down, yes, but we possess information that is priceless, at least from their point of view."

"So shut you down, but don't kill everyone," Carl summarized. "What information? Not the possible asteroid strike."

"No, not that. No one knows anything about that except a very select few within the organization itself."

"But if what you say is true, shouldn't you sound an alarm to the rest of the world?" Mary asked.

Denech shook his head. "What possible good would it do? Despite all the Hollywood science that would have us blowing the thing up with bombs, you know and I know that that is pure fantasy. We simply do not have the means to deflect something that large with the available technology. And even if by some miracle we did manage to blow it up, the pieces would still follow the same general orbit and instead of getting hit by a single bullet, we'd get hit by an equally powerful spread of buckshot."

"True, but—" Carl began.

"Let's make this personal," Denech said leaning forward. "If your death was absolutely certain on a certain day and a certain time, would you want to know about it? Or would you rather just continue living your life in a state of total ignorance until the very end?"

"Maybe I would and maybe I wouldn't."

"If you're like ninety percent of the population, you wouldn't. We know. One of the first things we did was conduct a scientific poll to find out. Of course, the wording of the questionnaire was such that our motives were not made public."

"Okay, backtracking a bit, if not the possible asteroid strike, what does Wolf want?"

"They want something else. Something a lot closer to home. They want me."

"Why you?" Carl asked. "Because of your leadership role in the organization?"

Peter Denech nodded. "That's part of it. I am the one person with intimate knowledge of all aspects of the organization. But we have a very loose organization here as far as leadership goes. We have team leaders, yes, but with a heavy emphasis on 'team.' For instance, I am in charge of this facility, but Amanda usually takes over when we're out in the field. A strict set of rules and protocols doesn't work with free-thinking scientific types, as you well know. Much like an artist, they have to have the mental space to encourage the creative process. So no.

I am not the leader as such. I am more like the top coordinator, duties I share with both Randolf and Amanda."

"But you could say that where we are right here is the headquarters."

"More like the operations center. From here we monitor all the various sites worldwide, and disperse the necessary information back to them. We—myself, Randolf, and Amanda, too—are, as I told you during our first meeting, the despised bureaucrats that make or break an organization."

"But there is something that doesn't add up," Mary interjected.

Denech looked across the table at her. "What?"

"If in fact the secret government agency, Wolf, did blow up your facility in Montana, they were taking an awful risk."

"You mean using an atomic weapon? The truth of that will never be known. It will all get hidden away in a top secret file called National Security."

"No, not that. The fact that they could have easily blown you up as well if you'd been there, which, if they consider you so valuable, they never would have risked."

Denech sat back in astonishment. "My God, you're right. Somehow they must have known I wasn't there."

Carl considered. "How many people, within the organization I mean, would have known your exact whereabouts last night?"

"Not many. I don't advertise my location to the world, as you might expect. Of course the fifteen in Montana would have known, Professor Micals knew, possibly a few at our Arizona facility. That's about it."

Mary shook her head. "Not quite. There's also the three of us at the table, and the three lying on the floor in the living room."

"And we will never know how many actual victims there were in the explosion. Maybe one of them provided the information and slipped away before the bomb went off," Carl suggested. "The video might provide an answer there. There were quite a few people in the background."

Denech agreed. "Good point. The recording might tell us something. But, honestly, I think there must be some other explanation. I know everyone in the organization personally, and I can't imagine any one of them that would deliberately be responsible for the deaths of any of the others. It just isn't in any of them. Unless—" Denech considered, but left the thought unsaid.

"Hopefully, you're right," Mary said, "Because if there is a mole, no one is safe."

Denech sat back in thought. "There is another explanation."

"What?" Mary asked.

"Something too terrible to contemplate. But something I must keep to myself right now."

Carl got up and announced a trip to the bathroom was in order. It was not an urgent call of Nature, however, that necessitated his departure. It was the overpowering feeling that if he didn't get up and pace, he'd explode in a ball of nervous energy. Unlike his wife, Mary, who seemed always calm and steady, his personality demanded movement. The trip to the bathroom was simply a chance to stretch stiff muscles. And most of the time, movement was the medicine that cleared his thoughts.

When Carl returned, he led off with the first question to Denech. "You said your leadership role was only part of the reason Wolf wanted you. What was the other part?"

"Ah, yes. Now we get into it," Denech said. "The final piece to this puzzle. I'm afraid I have a bit of a confession to make. I wasn't always a bureaucrat. There was a time when I was something respectable. A scientist of sorts and an engineer."

"It doesn't surprise me," Carl stated. "Why did you give it up?"

Denech grinned. "There is a saying in the corporate world. 'Screw up. Move up.' For me that was literally true. I screwed up and got promoted."

"I've heard that expression."

"It's all internal politics, really. If you're really good at your job, management would like to keep you right where you are. If you've been with a company for a while, and then mess up somehow or fall outside their accepted 'vision', they have to make a choice. Do they want to cut you loose with all the trade secrets that you might take to another company, or do they want to tuck you away somewhere in middle management where you can do the least damage?"

"Somehow, I think you probably fall into a third category," Mary decided. "You really are good at what you do."

"Thanks. But I miss the nuts and bolts stuff I used to do."

"Which was?" Carl asked, bringing the conversation back to the topic at hand.

"I did a lot of things for a lot of different corporations. Trouble shooting or free-lancing you might call it. But I always came back to the new kid on the block. Nanotechnology. Heard of it?"

"Of course. It's designing and making extremely small machines, nanites they're called, essentially atom by atom."

"And what would be the point of making microscopic machines?"

"Lots of potential uses," Carl stated. "Internal medicine, detoxification of industrial pollution."

"And dozens more, I might add. Well, that's what I always came back to. When I started back in the eighties and nineties it was mostly all theory, and the hardware was not yet perfected to transform theory into reality. Then in the first few years of the new century a few research facilities began to experiment with atomic compilers and made a few prototypes, machines on the order of a hundred nanometers or so."

"Not too shabby, considering a human hair is about a hundred thousand nanometers wide," Mary added.

"True. And today, of course, there are dozens of scientific teams working on various aspects of nanotechnology. In the early days, I was part of the 'brain trust' of one such team. But I had some major differences of opinion with management over the direction in which they were taking the research. When I fulfilled my contract, I decided to leave the company. In fairness to them, they gave me the option of moving into middle management. Instead, I went solo, and with the help of some very good and brilliant people, began to experiment with some of my ideas. To make a long story short, we discovered a few things that were both disturbing and wonderful at the same time."

"How does all this tie into us being here in the Rabbit Hole?" Carl asked.

"And how does it connect to a nuclear explosion in the middle of Montana?" Mary added.

"Because those brilliant people I mentioned that were with me from the start no longer exist."

"What happened to them?" Carl asked.

Denech's eyes filled with tears again, and his voice cracked. "They were all vaporized this morning in that explosion. Our Montana facility. That's where we did the nanite research. And that's how it all ties together."

*　　*　　*　　*

"I need a stiff drink," Carl admitted. "Either that or a bigger brain so I can get all this straight. There are just too many tangles to this. It's like trying to sort out all the loops in a wheelbarrow full of spaghetti."

Denech nodded. "I said it was a lot to digest. Pardon the pun."

Mary studied the face of Peter Denech. "The connection is obvious," she stated. "When you first logged in to your secure data stream, several words appeared on the screen. First *'package sent'*, then *'system on-line'*, then *'all systems functional'*, and then *'release'*, which repeated over and over. Then just before the Montana facility was destroyed, the man in the video first gave a warning. *'Incoming'* he said, so they must have known that the end was near. Then '*We did our best. Outcome unknown. Facility destroyed.*'"

"Yes, that's what happened pretty much word for word," Denech agreed.

"It's obvious then that since that was your nanite research facility, it must be nanites that you released into the atmosphere."

Denech's face grew grim. "Yes. That was the intent. That was the end goal of Plan A. But as you can see, whether we did or didn't is uncertain at this point."

"Well, even I can figure out the next question here," Carl said. "Just what in the hell would setting loose a bunch of microscopic machines into the atmosphere accomplish?"

Denech was direct. "It would depend on what they were engineered to do, wouldn't it?"

"What kind of operation—" Carl began, but Denech cut him short.

"Call it a seeding operation," Denech answered.

"And just what was it you were intending to grow?"

"Hope," Denech concluded. "Just a patch of hope."

Chapter 10

The two women, Amanda Korneth and Rowanna Doran, were the first to show signs of awakening. By noon, both were lucid enough to move about, but Peter, fussing over them like a mother hen, said they needed to rest in the sleeping rooms. They didn't protest, and were, in fact, quite amiable. For the first time, Carl noted a genuine smile on Amanda's normally sour face, but it was a smile that fit better on someone who was about half way to being falling-down drunk. Then right in the middle of a childish giggle, she started to cry, and asked Mary if she'd seen her doll. Suddenly, she ran to the corner of the room and picked up something that only her imagination could see, and began hugging the invisible companion.

While Mary and Peter helped Amanda to a sleeping room, it fell to Carl to deal with Rowanna Doran. She, too, exhibited the symptoms of alcohol intoxication, which by this time Carl recognized as a normal aspect of the recovery stage of the drug. With his arms around her and supporting her body, he began working his way toward the sleeping area, yet Red had other ideas. She began to lick his neck, and pepper his check with tiny kisses. It was then that Mary reappeared.

Mary watched for a few seconds, and then had a single comment. "Interesting," she said. "The drug has freed them of their inhibitions.

Their actions now probably represent repressed desires. In other words, their true nature."

"That's just what I wanted to hear," Carl grinned. "Good thing you can't hear what she keeps whispering in my ear."

"Probably that you ought to wash your neck," Mary shot back. "Or get a shave."

"I'll never tell," Carl teased. "Well, just don't stand there. Help me get her to a room."

Mary didn't budge. "It's more fun to watch."

"I'll get you for this," Carl threatened.

"Promises. Promises."

* * * *

Randolf Haays was unconscious a half-hour longer than either of the ladies. Denech said it was probably because he was such a short and slight man, outweighed by both of the women. Pound for pound, the smaller amount of body tissue had to absorb more of the narcotic. Eventually, however, he began to regain consciousness, but did not experience the same amiable drunken behavior as the women. Instead, he became cross and confrontational, though not physically violent. Agreeing sympathetically with every cross word, Denech led him away to the sleeping room that Carl and Mary had used. Just temporary, Denech assured them, as by later in the evening all three should be back to normal.

Carl wondered if it would be as Denech said, that they would most likely regain their full memory, and if Red would act upon the anger he had seen in her eyes when he had left her lying on the ground, and worse yet, taken her weapon. He had expressed his concern to Denech, but Denech assured him that all would be well, and that there would be no hard feelings over it. He and Mary were part of the organization now, and that demanded a high level of civility to one another. Still, Carl couldn't help but remember the old adage that there was no angry crocodile like a woman scorned, or something like that. Or don't get mad, get even. Or she's small, but so is a stick of dynamite. At any rate, he was glad he still had the weapon.

* * * *

More than anything at the moment, Carl Walker wanted to know what the nanites that the organization had released into the atmosphere were supposed to do. Many times smaller than the typical bacteria and roughly the size of an influenza virus, they would be easily carried away by the wind currents and distributed throughout the atmosphere. If the other sites in the other countries around the world had also released the tiny machines, within a few days every living thing on the planet could be breathing them in. But that would require the release of billions upon billions, and that seemed too remote a possibility to believe. Denech had said the six of them must remain isolated from the atmosphere for a week as protection against the affects of the tiny machines, but that seemed to contradict his statement that the intent of the release was to create 'a patch of hope', as he put it. Further, Denech refused to divulge just what they had engineered the nanites to do, despite his assurances that everyone present was now an equal member of project Tranquility. He kept dodging around the question by insisting that in a week's time they'd know, and if the project had failed, it would be best if both he and Mary didn't know any of the particulars. What you don't know, you can't tell others, Denech had emphasized, even under torture.

When he thought about it, Denech had still not revealed anything concrete about what the intent of the Organization might be. He had, however, provided a lot of information. But despite the fact that Denech seemed willing to answer just about any question put to him, the answers always seemed to fall just short of full disclosure. Adding to his uneasiness was the fact that only a day had passed in the Rabbit Hole and already he could feel the walls closing in on him. The artificial lighting seemed to grow fainter, and it was the clock on the wall and not the sun that indicated when it was time for rest. The inside air already smelled stale, and he considered sneaking outside for even a single breath of clean spring air. What could it hurt? He stood now staring at the front entrance that led into the abandoned grain mill. Mary and Peter Denech were in the kitchen. The others were still resting. Maybe he put a foot forward, or maybe it was just his imagination, but the large hand that suddenly rested on his shoulder was certainly real.

Denech stepped in front of him. "Don't."

"Don't what?"

"Ruin your future."

"It would help if you'd tell me what's so dangerous out there."

"I promise. When our time of seclusion is over and if Plan A is successful, you will know. If not, as I stated before, it's best you don't know. You'll just have to have—"

"Trust. I know. Where have I heard that before?"

"I was wondering. Maybe you'd like to review the recording of the last few seconds from the Montana facility with me?"

"Sincerely, or just as a diversion to get me away from the front door?"

Denech laughed, but then grew serious. "Both, actually. Friends died today. I might not be as objective as I should be when viewing the recordings."

Carl nodded. "Sure. Why not? Let's see if there's anything we might have missed."

* * * *

There was nothing new on the recordings, except that Carl and Peter Denech were able to positively identify fourteen different people in the background group when the project leader was recording his final words, thus accounting for everyone. From a frozen frame of the recording and one after another, Peter named them off, at first unemotional like reading a grocery list, but ending up in sobs that could not have been faked by the most brilliant actor. Despite all his doubts, Carl had come to agree with Mary's assessment of the man. He was someone that inspired trust, but then again so were any number of mass murderers. Carl recognized this residual doubt as a good thing. It would keep him alert to the possibility of deception. And though everything seemed straightforward enough, there was something about the recording of the last moments of the Montana video that troubled him. It seemed clear and graphic, yet there was something that just didn't seem—he searched for the right word—authentic, maybe. Denech's emotional reaction, however, was certainly genuine.

* * * *

By eight o'clock in the evening, Red, Amanda, and Randolf were back to normal. One by one they had filed in and out of the kitchen to get something to eat, and avoided contact with the others, especially Carl. Only once had Red and Carl inadvertently met in the passageway by the bathroom. They made very brief eye contact, there was a mumbled acknowledgement of each other's presence, and then both continued on their way. The avoidance behavior was not lost on Peter Denech, and at nine o'clock he announced an evening conference in the living room. He said it was to discuss the fine-tuning of the environmental controls, which didn't fool anyone. At the designated time, one after another filed in. Each displayed an exaggerated politeness that would have made any expert in proper etiquette sick. Denech came in last. Everyone was still standing, no one wanting to be the first to sit down. That might imply weakness, or even compromise. So Denech did what any first grade teacher would do. He assigned seats.

"Ladies, please take the couch. Randolf, the padded chair. Carl, get a couple folding chairs from the War Room for you and me."

Silently, each took their place, and Denech turned his chair backwards as was his habit and folded his arms upon the backrest. Carl sat a bit distant from the others, arms folded across his chest, and had resolved not to say anything unless directly addressed. But glancing at Red changed his mind. Where there had been extreme confidence before, now there was only insecurity. The proud way in which she had held her head and shoulders was replaced with a deflated and defeated demeanor. Her deep blue eyes had been playful and challenging, but now seemed dull and tame. She glanced up at him and managed a weak smile. The thought occurred to him that he was indeed a fool, probably all men were, and the question was what kind of fool would he turn out to be? There was the trusting fool, and the arrogant fool. He decided on the former.

Denech opened his mouth to speak, but Carl beat him to the punch. "I'm not all that good at—what I mean to say, especially to Red is I'm sorry for—" and that was as far as he got. Immediately, there was an overflowing of apologies from each, and each claiming responsibility for, as Denech pointed out, "the failure to communicate." After a few minutes, the babble of voices ceased, and Denech began.

"Thanks, Carl. You just said everything I wanted to say. In the last twenty-four hours we have all done what we felt we had to do. And it is a testament to us all that, despite some difficult events, we can all sit here together and not want to throttle each other. Carl and Mary are now equal members of the organization. There will be no more testing." He looked pointedly at Randolf and Amanda. "From now on we will operate on trust, on faith in one another. I don't know what we will find outside this safe haven when we leave. And somewhere in the organization there may be a traitor, but I am confident that person is not here among you. We sink or swim together." He paused, and then began again. "Now about those environmental controls—" A crumpled up piece of paper hit him in the forehead. "On that note," he concluded. "Class dismissed."

The others filed back into the kitchen but Red hung back, not sure of just where she should go. If the choice were available, she'd have gone for a quiet walk somewhere by herself. But here there was nowhere to hike or hide. Mary noticed, and pulled Carl aside. She gestured towards the redhead. "Stay. I'll be okay." She quickly kissed his whiskered cheek, and then joined the others, leaving Red at one end of the living room and Carl at the other. Carl turned, and noted Red suddenly very interested in studying the carpeting on the floor. Why, he wondered, did men have to do everything to break the ice, and all women had to do was stand there and look vulnerable, or sexy, or whatever.

"Hey," he said when no other word would come to mind, "Got a minute?"

Red looked up immediately. "Sure. Well, I suppose. What's up?"

"I was about to ask you the same thing?"

"What do you mean?"

"I was wondering where that fiery redhead went that used to hang around here."

Red smiled briefly, and moved forward. She slipped back onto the couch, and Carl pulled up a folding chair and sat down, Denech style, before her.

"Here's the thing," Red struggled, eyes downcast, and with her hands clenched in her lap. "God, I hate to admit it. I'm useless."

"What? Where did you ever get that idea?"

"Look around. Everyone has something important to do here except me. My only job was to provide a measure of security, which was never needed until now. And when a job came along that I could do, I failed at that. You read me like a book, and I'm the one who's supposed to have the experience."

"What can I say? You have an honest face."

"What?"

"Your emotions are reflected in your facial expressions. Something you can't fake. Didn't anyone ever tell you that?"

"No. What are you saying?'

"You can't lie. Your face will always tell the truth."

Red looked away as her face flushed red.

"See," Carl laughed. "Now you're embarrassed."

"Am not," Red shot back.

"Are, too." Carl returned.

Red grew serious. "There is one thing that might not have registered with you."

"What's that?"

"That maybe it's only you who can read my emotions like you do."

It was Carl's turn to turn a rosy pink.

"Now *you're* embarrassed," Red laughed.

"Well, now that we've embarrassed each other, I'd like to have the redhead I used to know come back."

"Really?"

"Really. And if she does, I have a gift for her."

"What's that?"

Carl unhooked the holster that he carried, wrapped up the weapon in the straps, and handed the bundle to Red. "A pea shooter."

Red was temporarily stunned. "You'd give me back the weapon? How do you know I wouldn't turn around and use it on you?"

Carl smiled broadly. "Because, I have faith in you. And besides, you look kind of funny without it."

Chapter 11

The next four days passed slowly. To minimize their electronic signature, only briefly would Denech, Amanda, and Randolf go into the War Room and check the updates from the outside. The doors to that special room were never closed, and any of the others were free to come in and observe if they so desired. Despite his obvious sorrow over the loss of his friends at the Montana facility, Denech was much relieved that the other sites, and his comrades, remained intact. There was no actual communication, but the words, *systems check*, were the code words to indicate they were still functioning.

The inhabitants of the cave passed time playing cards, dominoes, and word games, but Denech had warned against any of the thousands of computer games that were available to prevent an electronic signal from reaching prying eyes and ears. The chance of a leak was exceedingly remote, he admitted, but at this point too much was riding on the outcome of Plan A to take the chance. Without the electronic games, Randolf had complained that they were being forced to live in the Dark Ages, a statement that, though spoken in jest, also carried with it a ring of sincerity.

Peter Denech noted that the group had broken up in a manner common in human societies: By age. While he, Amanda, and Randolf spent most of their time monitoring the software and hardware in the

Rabbit Hole and would otherwise be in the kitchen engaged in discussion over cups of coffee, Carl, Mary, and Red spent most of their time in the living room alternating between the cards, dominos, and word games. Ever the student of human behavior, Denech noted that the three avoided games such as chess that required just two people. Always, it seemed, it was Mary who would insist that whatever diversion they might select, it would be one that would include all three. Denech also noted that there had been a subtle change in Mary. Always the logical and serious one, she nonetheless seemed even more introspective, and her shoulders seemed to slump just a little, as if she carried some burden. He was tempted to pry into those hidden thoughts, but reconsidered. If there was something bothering her, she would no doubt tell Carl and they would deal with it as they always had. It was entirely possible that it was simply her, or even his own, reaction to being cooped up without sunlight or fresh air for five days.

Peter Denech's main concern, however, was for the effective implementation of Plan A. Yet, at this point there was no way to know if it had been successful. Confirming data would begin to trickle in very slowly, yet that data would increase rapidly, almost exponentially, eventually reaching a point of such overwhelming certainty that every physically mature person on the planet would have to accept it. There would be that final run on the medical profession, those desperate last few who would need individual proof, rather than accept what the numbers that do not lie would show. And that would be the test: How would humanity react? As individuals. As nations. As one of Nature's organisms. How would people react to living out a life without the prospect of a biological future? These things were yet to be seen. And the answers to those questions would then determine the implementation, or not, of Plan B. And if not Plan B, then Plan C: Mary and Carl Walker. And if not Mary and Carl, then all that was left was Randolf's perennial favorite: Plan F. Nature would have to sort it all out, and there was no doubt it would.

At any rate, Denech thought, all was well within their little cocoon. There were no threats here. All systems; electrical, electronic, the air handling system, the plumbing; all were working just as they were designed. At least that was one thing he didn't have to worry about. But then came Day Six.

* * * *

In a cave there is no day or night. People trapped in such places of total darkness experience a distortion in time. Without the sun to regulate their internal clocks, people tend to go to sleep earlier. Their day effectively shortens. It was not dark in the Rabbit Hole but the meager artificial light did not have the same affect as the sun. Even imitating the day-night cycle by turning the lights off at 'night' and on during the 'day' was not enough to fool Nature. To varying degree all began to suffer the same regression of time as if they were in total darkness. The effect was increased mental fatigue, and also physical fatigue even though they could rest or even sleep whenever they chose. But sleep was often fitful. All knew this, but the knowledge of the effect did not prevent the effect. Denech was thankful there were only two more days to go, and he knew he spoke for everyone.

* * * *

At eight o'clock PM, which seemed more like midnight, on the evening of Day 5, Carl and Mary Walker bid the rest good-night and returned to their sleeping room. The hidden camera was long since removed. Mary noted the normal protocols involving modesty had become relaxed. In the morning lineup for the bathroom, no one covered their eyes if another happened to come running from their sleeping room in their underwear, and they were allotted 'heads' in the line without question or comment. They were becoming, she realized, like a family or maybe disciples, and she couldn't help but wonder if that was what Denech had planned all along. Despite the close quarters, there had not been one argument, and she wondered if Carl's conciliatory comments to Red at that earlier evening meeting might have set the tone for the rest of them.

They slipped from their clothing and lay down together, fitting together, Mary in front, Carl in back, like two spoons, as the saying goes. Mary could feel Carl's breath on her neck, and also his prickly whiskers that she had not yet convinced him to remove. She thought of the rest of the 'family'. Of Denech, the old mother hen. Of Amanda, stern yet competent. Of Randolf, who seemed to have sunk into himself and said little, and seemed even smaller in stature. And of Red. And it was on Red that her thoughts dwelled. Carl's even breathing told her he was nearly asleep, but with the end so close it was time to talk about something. It was something that she had been postponing ever since she saw the face of a little girl in a yard by a house that had miraculously transformed from a dilapidated hovel to a neat and cozy cottage. That little girl with the long dark braids, the one with the golden haired doll named Flossy, had been in her dreams every night since, and it was time that Carl knew the truth.

Mary turned to face her husband. Nose-to-nose and buried deep beneath the covers, she gently moved an unruly patch of hair that had fallen over his face.

Carl opened his eyes. "What?"

"I was just thinking."

"Now that's a shock. Is there a time when you don't?"

"Do you remember the child with the doll?"

"Of course. Cute kid. Reminded me of a much younger you."

"I've had dreams about her. Actually, the same re-occurring dream almost every night since then."

"Yes?"

"I'm back by that house standing on the sidewalk. It's a beautiful day. The sun is shining and I can feel the warmth of the rays on my shoulders. I can smell the newly mown deep green grass. There are birds splashing in the birdbath. The smiling child comes from the house dressed in her blue denim overalls and floats up to me and takes my hand. 'Do you want to play a game?' she says. She leads me back to the house and opens the door."

"And then?" Carl asked.

"The inside of the house is pitch black. Like the darkest night. So black it seems like a liquid barrier. And she leads me in, disappearing behind that barrier. Last to go in is her hand, which is pulling me in behind her. I don't fight it. The blackness engulfs me, and I am at peace."

"It was a dream. Don't make too much of it. You and I know that dreams are mostly bits and pieces of—"

"I know the psychology and physiology. But—"

"It's this cave. It's starting to get to you. Hell, it's a wonder we're still sane. The walls have been squeezing me from the first day. I have to believe the air probably smells like rancid gym socks in here, but we've gotten used to it so we don't notice. I for one will get down on my hands and knees and kiss the ground when we get out of here."

"And what will we find out there?"

"Well, Denech has assured me that there shouldn't be bodies stacked up like cordwood, so that's the good news."

"You know me better than anyone ever has, or ever will. I am not prone to mystical or wishful thinking. I am a skeptic."

"But?"

"But now I have had these feelings. Like an awakening in me to some part I never knew I had."

"What feelings?"

"Feelings of dread, but of excitement at the same time. This is going to sound like I'm crazy, but I can almost see the future, or maybe it's the past. I don't know. It's like solving an equation. It's all there right in front of me, but one variable is missing, so the answer is just beyond reach."

"And the little girl has something to do with that?"

"I have the feeling that the little girl is me, or if not me, than some part of me."

"There's just one thing wrong with your theory. Back at that house, I saw the little girl, too. She wasn't part of a dream. She was real. Unless we were both having the same dream."

Mary smiled her faint smile. "Not possible," she agreed, but then. "At least, not probable."

Carl pulled her tightly to him. "Don't worry about it. In two days when we get out of this hole and you breathe in some actual air, you'll feel like a different person."

"Logically, you're right, of course. But I want you to know something."

"What?"

"If anything should happen to me—"

"Hold it. Nothing is going to happen to you."

"If anything should happen to me, I want you and Red—"

"So let me get this straight. You're setting me up with another woman after—"

"It would be for the best. Red loves you."

"What am I supposed to say to that?"

"And you love her."

Carl did not immediately answer. Truth was the basis of their relationship, and he'd not deviate now. "My place is right here with you, and it will always be. Nothing or no one will ever change that."

"I know. But the future is—uncertain. I think—I feel—I see events, images of things—horrible things."

"Just two more days. Then we will be out of here. Hang in there."

Chapter 12

▼

The morning of Day 6 would not dawn in the cave as it usually did. The timer on the interior lighting in the Rabbit Hole was set for seven AM, and a few of the passageway lights and the bathroom light stayed on continuously, but when Peter Denech stirred for his nightly three AM trip to the bathroom, he knew immediately something was wrong. Even on the darkest night there was some light, but inside the cave all was black, and eerily quiet. The low hum from the heat pump and air handling systems was absent, and the rock walls reflected back only stone cold silence. Fumbling for his slippers, he stood and immediately hit his head on the rock ceiling, eliciting a series of mumbled profanities. Feeling along the wall through the blackness, he moved out into the passageway, followed it around to the emergency exit, but then turned right into the War Room. Though he knew exactly what to look for and where to find it, it still took considerable trial and error fumbling in the darkness to locate the control that switched the cavern from the external electrical power source to the battery reserve. Immediately, all the nighttime interior lighting came on, as well as the heat pump and air circulation fans.

Peter Denech glanced at his watch. 3:42 AM. Dressed in nearly knee length white undershorts and his slippers, he backtracked through the sleeping area awakening each of the others. One by one, in underwear and bathrobes, they filed into the Living Room, where Rowanna Doran still slept soundly on the couch. Her consciousness aroused by the stirring of the others, her eyes fluttered, and then opened. Still half asleep and like zombies, the others stood in a group in front of her. She pulled the blanket around her body, and swung her bare legs onto the floor. This, she realized, was not a normal conference call. Out of habit she reached for the weapon. It was not under her left arm, but remained wrapped up in the straps of the holster on the folding chair where she'd left it. Denech appeared in the doorway to the War Room and motioned them all in. Despite his concern over the use of electronic devices, this would be the exception to the rule.

"Main power's out," he said. "I don't know why. I've switched to the battery backup."

"You think our secret is out?" Randolf asked.

"Maybe there was a storm that knocked out the power grid," Mary suggested.

"First things first," Denech said. "The battery backup will only last about four hours on full use. That includes things like the heat pump, the lighting, the circulation fans, the kitchen hot plate, and the chemical-electric toilet."

"If we shut everything off but the lighting, then how long?" Carl asked.

"Two days at least."

"And what about heat," Red asked.

"It shouldn't be a problem," Randolf volunteered. "The background heat in the rock is fairly steady at around forty degrees. Plus the exposed rock has absorbed a considerable amount of heat from the increased temperature from the heat pump. Probably there is enough residual heat in here to keep away the chill for at least another day. Maybe two."

"And the toilet."

"It will not work properly without electricity, but it won't overflow either in two days time," Amanda said. "Unless," she added, "someone has a severe problem we don't know about."

"And water," Carl asked.

"The reserve tank holds thirty gallons. More than enough to keep us going but showers are out," Denech said.

Amanda Korneth sat down slowly on a folding chair, and Denech gestured for each to find a place to sit. He placed himself before the laptop that was used exclusively for outside connection to the Internet.

"Then I suggest we shut everything down but the lighting," Amanda said, "and only the lighting we absolutely need to get around without running into the rock walls. We should be fine. Inconvenienced maybe, but not crippled."

"Or we could simply leave the cave," Carl suggested. "At this point I'm not sure any of us are thinking all that clearly. We're losing our natural night-day rhythm. The reduced oxygen level is starting to have an affect. Humans did not evolve living in holes in the ground."

"We can't do that," Denech stressed. "Not at this critical time."

The others watched as Randolf moved over to an electrical panel mounted against the solid rock, and flipped a series of switches to off positions. With the task completed, he nodded to Denech. "Everything's off but the lighting in here and power for the laptop, or do you want to just rely on its own power source?"

"No. We'll save the reserve in the laptop battery. Nice to have that as a fall-back."

Denech immediately went to the news site he trusted, NEWS 24/7, and waited. Carl noticed that he had his fingers crossed. Superstitions, even benign ones, were hard to let go. For several seconds the screen remained blank, but then the familiar web page appeared, and Denech noticeably relaxed. He clicked on 'Breaking News' but immediately the image was replaced with the message, SITE TEMPORARILY OFF LINE FOR UPGRADES. Instead of going to another news site, he immediately disconnected and shut the computer down.

"Try another site," Randolf advised. "There are hundreds to choose from."

"I won't risk it. There may be a feedback loop. Later in the day, maybe." Denech turned to Carl. "Your suggestion to leave deserves a response."

"It's just that when even my own wife, the most rational person I know, starts to have problems sleeping—"

Denech turned to Mary. "What problems?"

"Just dreams. Keeps me from getting a good night's sleep."

"Would you mind sharing them with us?"

Her candid answer came as a shock. "I see my own death," she stated simply.

Denech glanced at Carl for confirmation. "We are, all of us, starting to lose it. I think it's more than just this confined space, or the diminished oxygen supply, or the lack of sunlight. There is something else going on, but I can't quite get hold of it. I felt it when we were looking at the video of the last few seconds at the Montana facility. Last night Mary told me the same thing. She described it as an equation that explains everything but with a critical part missing."

"Everyone views reality through their own window," Denech said. "Mary has the mathematical mind, so that is how reality is presented to her. But I stress again. We cannot go outside."

"Why?" Carl asked.

Denech didn't immediately answer, and turned to Mary. "It's because of geometric progression."

"You're losing me," Red cut in. "Remember, all I'm trained to do is shoot people. I don't have a science degree."

"It's the penny problem," Mary stated.

"Okay. I'm totally lost," Red admitted.

"It's a brain teaser, a test of mathematical perception, really," Mary began. "A test to see how well our 'common sense' matches with a mathematical reality."

"Count me out," Red continued. "I have difficulty with basic math."

"So did Einstein," Amanda cut in, "but it didn't stop him from being the greatest physicist of all time."

"Please continue, Mary," Denech prodded.

"The problem is usually presented something like this. Your new employer offers you a choice of payment for thirty days work. Either you can take a hundred thousand dollars up front, or you can take one penny the first day, two pennies the second day, four pennies the third day, eight pennies the fourth day, 16 pennies the fifth day, 32 pennies the sixth day and so on for thirty days. Each day your payment is twice what you received the day before. Your earnings for the first six days would total 63 cents. After ten days you'd have $10.23 total. Not very much considering one third of the month is already gone."

"That hundred thousand dollar up front deal is looking better all the time," Red said.

"True. Yet if you were to make a graph of your income, there would be something about it that should get your attention. It is not a straight line. Though its pretty straight for the first few days, it rapidly curves upward by the end of the month. Without getting into the detailed math behind it, this increasingly upward trend is called exponential growth or a geometric progression. When it starts to go up, it goes up in a big hurry."

"Okay. I knew I should have taken the pennies. How much?"

"Well, not to belabor the point, after thirty days you would have several million dollars."

"I knew that," Red responded, and laughed at her own joke.

Denech cut in. "Exponential growth starts out very slow and it is only at the very end that tremendous gains are made. Many things, other than money, have this type of growth. The bacteria on your skin after a warm bath. A fire with an unlimited fuel source. Even the escalating human population follows a similar trend."

"And how is this connected to why we can't go outside?" Carl asked.

"Because what we released into the atmosphere, those tiny machines, those nanites, experience that rate of growth, and outside, right now, they are on that rapidly expanding upward curve."

"If they're there at all," Randolf reminded him. "With the explosion in Montana, we can't be certain that Plan A even got off the ground."

"With the other sites in a lockdown mode, we won't know until we can be sure of secure communications, but we must proceed as if Plan A went off as scheduled. So close to the end, it would be foolhardy not to continue."

Carl looked at the other faces in the group, and when no one spoke up, he dove into the obvious. "Nanites are microscopic machines. They are manufactured. They are not living organisms. They are as dead as a rock. Therefore, there shouldn't be any more floating around in the air today then there were on the first day. Nanites could theoretically be designed to self-replicate but they can't reproduce in the manner of a living organism."

Denech glanced at Amanda and then Randolf before turning his attention back to Carl. "Our nanites can."

* * * *

Carl sat by himself in the living room on the stuffed chair. Most everyone else, even Mary, had drifted off back to bed, as there was nothing that anyone could do. Red disappeared into the kitchen for something to munch on. Lighting was reduced to just the bathroom light, the kitchen light, two small overhead bulbs in the passageway, and the one above his head. It was evident that Amanda was correct. With a little common sense usage, there would be no problem stretching out the batteries for just two more days. Nothing to worry about, except why they'd lost external power. Did it have something to do with the nanites, or had there been a storm-related electrical failure? Or worst case, had Wolf finally discovered Denech's well kept secret? Just when Carl had decided to join Mary, Peter Denech returned and sat down heavily on the sofa. Without looking at Carl directly, he said what Carl least wanted to hear. "We have a problem," Denech admitted.

"But not life threatening," Carl returned.

"I'm afraid it goes beyond our current situation."

"What problem?"

"After we leave here, we're going to have to separate. We can't take the chance of all being together if we encounter Wolf."

"We won't be staying here, I take it."

"The risk is too great. My presence with you creates a danger that is too great."

"So what's the plan? That we disappear into society? I'm assuming there still will be a society."

Denech smiled. "Yes, for a while at least, everything will still go on as normal. We may give you an older PCD that will be safe for Internet communications. But only if it is safe. Take no chances."

"Mary and I will be on our own again?"

"Not quite. Red will be with you. She'll help you and Mary with a disguise."

"A disguise?"

"The incident on the train indicates your identity is known to Wolf. We may have to change your identity."

"Then what?" Carl asked.

"Contact Professor Micals at the University. Red knows where to go. You'll be under his protection from then on. As we move into June, everything may begin to happen more quickly. And events will then be beyond my control. We have thrown a log across a stream and one cannot be certain if the dam will hold or simply make things worse."

"How long with Professor Micals?"

"You'll know," Denech assured him.

"And you? Amanda? Randolf?"

"We'll be okay. This is old hat for us. If electronic communications are completely compromised, we rely on old-fashioned newsprint. It's still good for something."

"How will that work?"

"We'll run a specific ad in the Personals section of the printed version of NEWS 24/7."

"How will I know it's you?"

"Let's just say you'll be able to read between the lines."

"Be careful. Remember, there could still be someone within your organization that may turn on you.

Denech nodded, and then led the conversation in a different direction.

"You know how long it took us to get this place up to specifications? Two years. The problem was the cracks. The natural fissures in the rock. We had to make it air tight, so naturally those cracks had to be sealed. The front door had to seal air tight, as well as the escape hatch out the back. But in the end after all the testing, we got it done."

"It certainly could pass for a bomb shelter."

"Some of our people asked why build it here? Why not in the Rocky Mountains somewhere, or hidden away in Alaska?"

"Earthquakes," Carl stated.

"Why yes."

"I have a degree in geology, remember. You'd want to pick a place that was geologically stable. Hard to find a better place than Southeastern Minnesota, though even here they occasionally get very minor tremors."

"We actually considered Ontario for a while, rock solid sitting on the North American Plate, but it's just too much hassle crossing in and out of Canada these days, which we'd have to do. And the tough winters were an added concern. We also considered Upper Michigan, and a few places around Mt. Katadan in Maine. The caves in Kentucky. All had their pluses and minuses."

"There was the Montana site and you mentioned the site in Arizona. Any others in the U.S.?"

"Nothing permanent. But a few mobile two person sites. And a few free-lancers like Professor Micals."

"You have people out there right now unprotected from your nanites?"

"Of course. You have to understand the only people in the world now completely protected are the six of us right here and the four women astronauts presently up in the Space Station. Maybe a few scuba divers, but that wouldn't be for long. There may also be a few isolated eddies in the normal atmospheric circulation patterns that might protect a few people on the ground. *Everyone* else that is breathing air from the atmosphere is exposed. We chose our release sites to maximize wind dispersal patterns and atmospheric circulation. The only other people on earth that could escape it for certain are not breathing."

"And only nanites that could reproduce would work?"

Denech nodded. "It would be virtually impossible to manufacture enough ordinary nanites to get the needed concentration in the atmosphere in the time frame we had."

"Knowing you I can't believe whatever you've done is fatal. But just what—"

"Don't go there," Denech interrupted. "We'll find out soon enough. But I can tell you it's not some foolishness to try to make everyone love one another. That would require a drug way beyond anything I could devise."

"Can you tell me how you managed to create nanites that reproduce?"

"Nothing specific, again for your own protection. However, I will tell you this. We were able to integrate nano-strands of synthetic reproductive bacterial DNA into the nanite compiler."

"Sounds pretty specific to me."

"Without knowing the chemical structure of the required catalyst, that information is useless."

Carl was amazed. "In other words you've created a hybrid entity that is both machine and alive."

"My nanites are no longer inanimate entities. They are a compete life form and totally artificial."

"A Nobel Prize for sure," Carl stated.

"Except that the specifics will never be known. All the research, all the experimentation data went up in smoke when the bomb went off. The Montana facility was the place where we designed, created, and constructed the nanites. As I said, the other facilities around the world are merely distribution sites for the final release. The Montana site is gone now, so the knowledge will die with me."

"But eventually some other brilliant scientist will come along and rediscover it."

"Probably. But in the meantime, I've bought humanity some time."

"But time for what?"

"To grow up."

Carl noted that Peter Denech had turned to face him. His close scrutiny was at first unsettling, but then he realized the big man was not staring at him so much as he was staring off into abstract space. Finally, his eyes came into focus. "They want me alive, Carl. Not because of what my nanites have done, but because of what they could do. I discovered the literal Pandora's box, but thankfully I believe the lid is back on."

"You will at some time in the future explain that to me."

"I promise, when the time is right, and if I am still alive, I will give you a full accounting of the effects, but not the construction. No one should have to bear that burden."

"I'd appreciate that. Because I'd really like to see how your nanites tie into a possible asteroid strike next year, and the ancient Mayan Long Count Calendar."

Denech smiled. "Of course you would. Mary, too. That's one reason I picked you. And with that I better say goodnight, or good morning I suppose would be more accurate. Go now. Lay next to your wife. Take very good care of her. Later, I'll attempt a communications access again, and maybe we'll learn something about the outside world."

Denech stood, and noted Mary leaning up against the passageway entrance.

"Sorry," she said. "I couldn't sleep without Carl. I overheard most of what you were talking about."

"That's perfectly alright, young lady. We were just wrapping up for the night."

"If you don't mind, there is one question I have."

"Fire away."

"When we leave here in two days, what's to protect us from the nanites? If they have reproduced exponentially as you say, we will be leaving at their most concentrated level."

"Very astute. But not to worry. In two days, the atmosphere will be clear of them."

"How?"

"They are not immortal. We engineered into them what we called a DLS. A Diminishing Life Span. They reproduce asexually, by division of course, and incredibly fast. They eat, I guess you could say, the necessary elements right out of their environment, but each successive generation lives a shorter period of time. The very last divisions will live only a few seconds. And finally, too short a time to complete the division process. In essence, they will all die of old age."

"I see," Mary said. "It's a fail safe. And I assume that their DLS comes to an end very soon."

"In about twenty hours, to be exact. At the end of Day 6. Today. We tacked on the extra day, Day 7, just to be safe. We've allotted plenty of time for all the human infections to occur."

"Infections?"

"Sorry. Poor choice of words. I mean to say that by then the nanites will have done their job, and no longer be needed."

Carl shook his head, as a thought registered. "They'll all be dead. All the nanites, I mean."

"Yes, that's true."

"You created a life form to exist for a week, but in that time to reach a population in the trillions, and then ensured that it would forever be extinct."

"Yes, sadly that's correct."

"Well, how does it feel to be God?"

Denech did not take offence at Carl's honest conclusion. "Not God. I don't have the gift of foresight. I'm merely gambling that in the end the sacrifice will—" Denech's voice trailed off.

"Be worth it?" Carl finished.

"I was going to say 'not have been in vain.' In a few hours, we'll know. Now I really must rest."

Chapter 13

Under the blanket of boredom, Day 6 passed slowly. Few words were spoken as the minutes fell one by one into the past. Inactivity, Mary came to realize, could be far more tiring than a strenuous workout. At 6:00PM, cave time, Red and Carl were in the living room and making a game of staring at the clock, and seeing which could hold their breath the longest. Mary had been invited, but she said "This is silly," and wandered into the kitchen for cold cereal and reconstituted powered milk, not her typical evening meal. Denech and Randolf were in the storage room checking out the leftover supplies, while Amanda Korneth was doing a routine check of the electrical connections. If the outside power came back on, a red light bulb would light up to announce the flow, but it had remained consistently dark.

Peter Denech came into the War Room through the rear entrance and announced he was going to attempt another connection to the outside world. The rest filed in, lastly Mary, cereal bowl in hand. All grouped around Denech, but gave him enough room to work. With surprising agility, his large fingers flitted over the old keyboard. Again, he located the NEWS 24/7 website, which promptly filled the screen. There he hesitated.

"This is as far as we got last time. What should I try?"

The others read the options over his shoulder and Randolf suggested they stick with 'Breaking News.'

"But it wouldn't be breaking any more," Amanda said, in her stern voice. "Go down to the specific stories."

Denech arrowed down and a list of headlines came into view.

"At least we still have headlines," Carl said, reading through the list. "But nothing about a power outage around here. And nothing about a massive outbreak of tiny little machine creatures either." Mary poked him in the ribs to remind him it wasn't funny.

"It's still too early," Randolf said. "Give it a week or two. No one would notice nanites anymore than they'd notice the mold spores in the air. We'll have to test one of our own people."

"Your own guinea pig *out there*," Carl guessed.

Denech interrupted. "Wait a minute. Here's something. *Freak explosion takes out substation.*"

The video stream began. *"Early this morning, an explosion at a substation along a major electrical transmission line temporarily knocked out power to over fifty thousand customers in Southeastern Minnesota and Northeastern Iowa. The utility, Central States Power, could not determine the cause of the explosion but had not ruled out a lightning strike, or the work of vandals...*.

"That explains it," Haays said. "At least ..."

Carl interrupted. "Wait. Wait. There's more."

"... made immediate repairs and customers were without power for only a couple hours."

"Yet here we sit in the dark," Carl noted, and then noticed another headline. He pointed it out to Denech and read the words aloud. *"Man sought for questioning in bomb blast in Montana."* Denech selected the headline and the video recording of the anchorman automatically began. A static picture of a younger version of Peter Denech filled the entire right side of the screen.

"Authorities at the highest level are looking for this man, Peter Denech, in connection with the as yet unexplained explosion in Montana that pro-

duced a crater five hundred feet in diameter and two hundred feet deep. There were no known fatalities, but sources close to the investigation, who spoke on condition of anonymity because they were not authorized to release the information, have stated the massive explosion was the work of a secret terrorist organization working within the borders of the United States. Authorities have not made clear what the purpose of the explosion might have been, but a possible test or warning might have been the reason. Authorities would give no reason for their interest in Mr. Denech except to say that he might have information valuable to the ongoing investigation. You are urged to contact your local FBI office if you think you may have seen him."

All remained silent after the news site automatically reset to the homepage. Peter Denech was the first to speak. "Well, at least they used a picture of me when I still had hair."

Mary realized something. "You still do, don't you?"

Denech smiled. "Oops. Guess my secret's out."

Carl was confused. "What secret?"

"He's in disguise," Mary stated.

"Not a disguise really," Red cut in. "He's the same man that's in the picture. I shaved his head, and he's put on about twenty pounds. He also has a nice week's growth of whiskers. It doesn't take a lot of major changes to make a person look totally different."

"So, as you see," Denech continued. "I'm pretty safe. This proves there are no updated pictures of me yet in the electronic soup. I'm really rather relieved to see I made the headlines. Everyone will be looking for *that* man and not me."

"However, from what you've told us, the information that's out there is not accurate," Mary continued. "No one, the Agency or the military, has taken responsibility for the explosion. No mention of a nuclear explosion either, and that would be impossible to keep under wraps."

"I hope you didn't expect them to come clean on this. And we have no way of knowing the exact nature of the explosion. The original broadcast suggested it might have been nuclear, but that assessment may have changed. None of this changes anything. We continue as planned."

Against his better judgment, Denech turned back to the laptop and selected 'Breaking News.' Again, the screen went blank, and SITE TEMPORARILY OFF LINE FOR UPGRADES appeared on the scene. Immediately, that was replaced with an ear-piercing squeal, and then *"I know you're out there Peter. Do the right thing. For God, for your country, for your friends, turn yourself in now."*

"No picture with the transmission," Randolf stated in a controlled voice, and immediately took control of the laptop. "Audio streaming only. Do a packet back-trace?"

Denech considered for only a second. "Yes."

Haays fingers raced over the old laptop keyboard. Lines of code flashed on and off the screen. Within a minute, he nodded to Denech. "Got him."

With a calm voice, Denech spoke into the microphone, "Please specify."

"You know me as Wolf," came the immediate reply.

With a swiftness that belied his size, Peter Denech ripped the power cord from the laptop, and powered it down.

Slowly, he turned to the others. "They're on to us."

"Now what do we do?" Red asked. "Make a run for it?"

Denech nodded. "Maybe that's what they're hoping for."

Mary considered. "If they knew precisely where we were, they'd already be knocking down the doors."

"Right," Carl agreed.

"They expect us to take off like scared rabbits. Give away our exact location," Red stated. "How fitting. We named this place the Rabbit Hole."

Mary had a thought, and faced Peter. "That man who just spoke. He called you by your first name as if he knew you personally."

"He does. His name is Barry Blacmann. We were friends a long time ago. In college."

"But not any more?"

Denech shook his head. "Afraid not. He went the political route and I went into engineering. We used to get together from time to time. At least now we can put a face on the wolf."

"Is Blacmann military?" Carl asked.

"No. CIA. At least at one time. Then NSA. But he's gone beyond that now. And I'm afraid he's not the typical flatfoot. He has a doctorate in abnormal psychology, specifically the criminal mind."

"In other words, we're in deep shit," Carl stated.

"That would be my assessment, as well," Haays stated.

"Except we're not criminals," Mary said.

"Right," Korneth agreed. "To get out of this, we have to remember that."

"As far as Barry is concerned, we are," Denech continued. "It's all about percentages. He'd normally proceed with what the statistics predict we'll do next. It's all very scientific, and done with a sophisticated computer program. However, he also knows me, and he's not so naïve as to ignore the human factor."

"Run like hell still sounds like a good plan," Carl said.

Denech reflected. "Exactly, so that's exactly what we *will* do."

"A double fake only works in football," Randolf reminded him.

Silence followed as Denech looked at his watch. "The very earliest we can leave is in four more hours. Midnight."

"And that assumes that the nanites performed exactly as engineered," Korneth said. "You and I both know that that is not a realistic assumption. That's why we factored in the extra day."

"I know. I know," Denech agreed. "Somehow, we have to get through another eight hours. And I'd prefer twelve."

Carl considered. "How likely is it that Blacmann would find us before then?"

"Anyone's guess," Denech said. "Apparently, they have triangulated our general location. But we have a slight advantage, because we now know exactly where Blacmann is, thanks to Randolf's quick thinking."

"You located his position," Mary guessed.

"A signal goes both ways," Randolf stated. "I have the coordinates of his transmission. That's the good news."

"And the bad?" Carl asked.

"He's very close."

"Oh, is that all."

"And we have no way of knowing if he is at a stationary or mobile location."

"Then I vote we leave now," Carl stated.

"We cannot do that!" Denech shouted, and the deep emotional voice startled everyone. "If Plan A and Plan B fail, you and Mary are all we have left." He turned to face Randolf Haays. "And if you start preaching, so help me I'll—I'll—"

Haays placed a hand on Denech's massive shoulder. "At this point, Plan F is irrelevant, my friend. We are talking about lives now. Give them at least that."

Denech sat defeated. "You're right. At least they'd have each other."

Carl and Mary exchanged glances, realizing the 'they' were themselves.

"I'm not following the thought, here," Carl admitted.

"The nanites are in no way lethal to any existing life form," Denech said. "Exposure will not kill you."

"I realize that. However, you did mention the word 'infection' before."

"Yes, they have an effect. It's just not fatal."

"So do we all turn into giant tadpoles or what?" Carl asked, with a considerable degree of sarcasm.

Denech ignored the comment and Mary continued, her mind in overdrive. "And it's the effect that you have decided not to share with us. But at this point what would it matter?"

"It doesn't, I suppose. For Amanda, Randolf, and me it never mattered."

"Me either," Red interjected.

For a brief moment Korneth's face relaxed with compassion. "You have been with us from nearly the beginning, Rowanna. But some things even you don't know."

"If you mean the effects of the nanites, I don't care. I never wanted to know. It wasn't my concern. After what happened to my cousin in New York, my only concern was in getting revenge against the government, and that meant protecting you. And I will or die trying."

For nearly a minute no one spoke. There was nothing to say. The only sane action was to follow Carl's suggestion and leave, probably on foot through the woods, and head east following the stream towards the Mississippi river. When far enough away, Randolf could signal for assistance, and someone from the organization would arrange to pick them up. From there it would be back into hiding again. Denech realized they might all live for a little longer, but the approaching asteroid would likely seal their fate in any case. His grand three-prong plan was about to go up in flames, and he realized if they stayed at their present location much longer that might be literally true. He remembered the images of the fireball in Montana that marked the end of the nanite facility and his friends. They were fighting forces that were just too overwhelming.

Randolf again spoke. "Peter, we were incredibly fortunate to get this far. No one tried harder than you to make this work. But we can't hide in here forever."

"It's just that we're so damned close. To fail now would be—be tragic."

"We've been lucky, but—"

Denech's face brightened. "You know, Randolf, you're absolutely right. We have been incredibly lucky. And what the hell. If we're going to die anyway, let's at least give them a moving target. Hell, why not just go right into the lion's den?"

Randolf nodded, understanding his intention. "What the hell. Why not two moving targets."

Korneth shook her head. "Randolf and Peter have taken up swearing. The oxygen in here must really be getting low. But I agree. Let's get to it now before we change our minds."

* * * *

The light from two powerful battery powered lanterns licked up against the rock walls of the cavern and reflected off the faces of the inhabitants. The passageways were black holes in the stone. The tiniest sound echoed around the chamber. And the ritual of parting was over. For some it was a stoic handshake, others tears and hugs, and yet others a mere tilt of the head in acknowledgement of a final good-by. All stood now in their final place before movement would take them down different paths.

"This is absolutely crazy," Carl stated, "and I just won't do it. Where's all that 'we have to work together' stuff."

"Funny," Peter said. "I don't recall ever saying that."

"Well, you implied it, then."

"This is the only way. We've worked out the escape route. Hopefully, Barry knows me well enough to think I wouldn't panic. We have to spread a little confusion in their ranks. Therefore, we have to make it look like we are panicking."

"Which in fact we are," Carl said.

"But a controlled panic."

"If there's a difference, I fail to see it," Carl continued.

"Don't worry. We'll be fine."

"Liar. You're apt to be hamburger or burnt toast within the hour."

Denech smiled. "Oh, ye of little faith, but if you can see a better way, I'm all ears."

Mary took Carl by the arm. "I have to agree with Peter. But I don't like the idea any more than you."

"If the nanites won't kill us, then I don't see why we can't all leave together," Carl insisted.

"You might not realize it now but you'll soon learn there are far worse things. Admit it. You're just jealous because I get to go outside before you," Denech said with a wide smile.

"One hundred percent guilty. I've forgotten what the sun even looks like."

"I told you before, Carl, we had to separate. I admit I didn't want it to be under these conditions but we have no choice."

"We understand that."

Denech continued. "I've powered everything down. We'll take the laptops and wireless and everything else that could leave a traceable electronic signature. You'll be safe. I don't think Blacmann would risk dropping a bomb on the place even if they did find it. Not with major cities like Rochester and La Crosse close by. But get out in ten hours. Six at the very least and only if you absolutely have to. Forget the PCD. Avoid the electronic net at all costs. Use only the necessary battery power in here for minimal lighting. Stay under the radar. You'll be cutting it close with the nanites, but if I've done my homework, they'll be gone by then."

"You plan on being the bait," Carl realized. "To lead them away from here."

Denech gestured to Amanda and Randolf. "The three of us are old fogies. We've put in our time. Right now you carry the seed, so to speak. Don't worry. We still have a few tricks up our sleeves."

"I should be going with you," Red insisted, but Denech shook his head. For a moment he remained rooted in place, but then wrapped his massive arms around the redhead. "You've been a great aid to the organization, and me in particular. But now it is Carl and Mary you have to keep an eye on. We'll be taking both vehicles, so you'll be hiking out of here. Follow the river. Keep to the woods. You know the area well enough to know where you'll end up. Avoid people. Remember. Get to Professor Micals. He'll set things up from there."

"What kind of man is Professor Micals?" Carl asked. "I never had him for an instructor at the U, though I did hear some rumors."

"What rumors?" Denech asked.

"Students liked him because he wasn't boring."

Denech nodded. "No, Edward is anything but boring. One might even say a bit radical. He refers to himself as an evangelical atheist."

"Oh."

"Truthfully, I have no idea what Edward's religious beliefs are. But I do know he loves to shock people. Get them thinking. Put them on the spot."

"How so?"

"He'll find out how a person believes on a certain issue, and then commence to pick the reasoning apart. He and Randolf have gone around and around a time or two."

"On what?"

"On religion, of course. On the proper way to light a Bunsen burner. On the possibility of extra-terrestrial life. On the best way to catch a walleye pike. On the final fate of humanity. You name it. Edward's argued it."

"A cantankerous sort," Carl decided.

"Not really. It's all done very politely and above board. It's his way of understanding people. To figure out where they're coming from. What motivates them."

"Sounds like just agreeing with him is the best way to avoid an interrogation."

Denech laughed. "That won't work. He'll just take the opposite side of whatever you bring up."

"Like I said, cantankerous. But how—?"

"He baits people. Take the existence of God. If you say you believe, he'll systematically tear every bit of your reasoning down to sawdust. If you say you don't believe, he'll proceed to build a plausible case for the possible existence of such an entity."

"In other words, you can't win," Mary observed.

"Ah, ha! Now you get to it. With Micals there is no such thing as winning or losing. It's all about the discussion, the exchange of ideas. If you happen to get into a discussion with him, just remember while you're trying to win your point, he's already gotten what he wants."

"Which is?"

"To get you to defend your position. Because he knows that a reasonable and intelligent person, if he or she is honest, will eventually recognize the flaws in their own thinking."

"And if he thinks we're unreasonable?"

"He'll dismiss you as a mere annoyance. He'll brush you off like the dust on your refrigerator."

"Yet he calls himself an evangelical atheist."

"As I stated, shock value mostly. He's an extremely complex man. If he has a religion, I'd say it was blunt honesty, or maybe science."

Carl shrugged. "Sounds like someone we could get along with."

Denech laughed. "For about a day. Then you'll have to come up for air."

"I'm guessing he's not married," Mary said.

"You'd guess wrong," Denech corrected. "He and his wife are rock solid."

"Bet they don't talk much."

"All the time, and plenty of time disagree. But it's always kept on an intellectual level. Never personal. And they had three kids, so they must have found time for other, more personal, interaction."

"I have another question," Mary continued.

Denech responded immediately. "Of course."

"The nanites are Plan A. Carl and I are part of Plan C. What about Plan B?"

"Plan B is temporarily on hold, until we have time to ascertain the success or failure of Plan A."

"How long? Someone mentioned two weeks."

"At a minimum. Yes, we could begin to see results in late June. However, I would estimate more like two months. Maybe even longer."

"Longer?"

"Yes, longer. However, when the effects begin to manifest themselves, there will be a very rapid domino effect, much like a geometric progression. At first the effect will be a mere curiosity on a few local news stations. But from that point it will rapidly escalate to worldwide headlines."

"And after that?"

Denech did not immediately answer, but then said, "After that will be the test, and I cannot predict what will happen."

"But if you can't predict what the effects of your nanites will be, it seems somewhat foolish to have released them in the first place."

Again Denech seemed lost in thought. "We had no choice. The decision was made for us."

"But—" Mary began but Denech cut her off.

"Time will tell. Time will tell."

Some moments of silence followed, and Carl recognized it was time for the final parting. "And what about you three? Where will you go?"

"Mum's the word on that. Remember. Read the Personals in NEWS 24/7. If we make it, we'll leave a message. *And stay under the radar.*"

With that Denech backed out of the War Room, leaving Carl and Mary Walker, and Rowanna Doran inside with one of the lanterns. He watched as the doors moved slowly shut, sealing them inside. There was a suctioning sound as the pneumatic seals set in place. Denech put his ear to the door, and heard three soft knocks on the inside, which indicated the War Room was now sealed and isolated from the rest of the Rabbit Hole. He returned the signal and without hesitation turned to face Amanda Korneth and Randolf Haays who waited by the front exit. Denech glanced at his watch: 8:09PM. Evening, but still there would be sunlight. It would be best to wait at the old mill for the cover of darkness. He nodded to Haays, who unlocked the door to the outside. A rush of sweet wind caressed their faces. Denech took a deep breath of the delicious fresh air and realized he probably inhaled thousands of microscopic artificial life forms. Living machines that would now begin to do their work in his own body. Do what he had designed them to do. For Amanda, Randolf, and himself, it didn't matter. But for billions of others worldwide, it would mark the end, or a new beginning. How would they react when there was no longer any doubt? That was the million-dollar question.

The nanites, the tiny bits of life, were his children, Denech realized. Children of one man, like the children of men, offered now for sacrifice, like the spilling of innocent blood on a sanctimonious religious altar. He brought his children into existence for only one purpose: To try to stop the inevitable.

Chapter 14

▼

Barry Blacmann spun around in his padded swivel chair and looked back towards the inside rear of the silver colored motor home, or at least that's what the vehicle looked like from the outside. The inside did have sleeping accommodations for four, a kitchenette, and a bathroom, but a bank of electronic equipment and monitors and several office-type chairs occupied the rest of the space. He had to marvel how surveillance had changed just in the last decade. What they used to haul around in truckloads and required dozens of technicians and flatfoots, now fit comfortably in the palm of his hand. With a single hand held device nicknamed the UFO, the Universal Information Observer, he could observe the world, send and receive information, translate in and out of hundreds of languages and dialects, tap into audio and video streams, monitor surveillance satellites and zero in on nearly anyone in real time, and if need be talk directly to the President, listen to a relaxing symphony, or diagnose his own stomach ache. Information about *everybody* and *everything* was a word away. No one was exempt from his scrutiny except his superior. As for the President himself, his boss had stated flatly, "The President doesn't know anything. That's by design. Ignorance is bliss."

Of course, that was the law. It was called the American Freedom Act, and it authorized the establishment of the Agency, which it came to be called, to operate under the jurisdiction of the presidency 'to more effectively and efficiently' protect the American people. It further stated 'the actions of no single individual or entity shall endanger the health, wealth, or security of the society at large.' And 'when said agency finds such actions as obviously corrosive to said society, said agency may take all reasonable and necessary steps to eliminate said activity.' Whether intended or not, the Agency swiftly evolved into judge, jury, and executioner, and everyone's life became an open book. But then if a person had done nothing to disrupt the fabric of society, kept their more radical opinions to themselves, they'd have nothing to hide and certainly nothing to fear.

Blacmann held the palm-sized screen in his hand. It was like holding the world in his hand. He wondered if that's how God himself felt. With that one device, he had the power of life or death. He could launch an ITP—an Individually Targeted Projectile—from the agency stash and selectively eliminate those that had come to be called 'Unamericans,' those people who, though not necessarily domestic terrorists, were obviously headed irreversibly in that direction. These were the people who took their causes a step beyond Letters to the Editor, or a street corner protest. They assembled into secret groups with unknown and potentially disruptive agendas, and as the Director had personally told him, "Best not to take chances. Just make sure you take out more sinners than saints."

The American Freedom Act and the resulting agency soon became heralded in certain circles as one of the most effective pieces of anti-domestic terrorism legislation. A TV camera crew in New York covering an unrelated event accidentally got good video of an ITP in action. A suspected domestic terrorist literally exploded in Central Park when an ITP targeted her cell phone. There were protests by the Constitution Party, and later there was evidence that the woman had been innocently using someone else's cell phone, but the point had been made. The new technology would save lives by selectively dissecting the evil components from the American population, and once that was accomplished: The world. Blacmann also knew that the technology was being perfected so that in addition to targeting an electronic device, it could target a specific DNA pattern, in essence a specific individual—eliminating the danger of the unfortunate sacrifice that had occurred in Central Park.

Blacmann turned back to his desk and set the monitor aside. He withdrew a brown envelope from the top drawer and slid the printouts out onto an enlarged map of Southeastern Minnesota, which was spread out on the metallic surface. The prints represented a new challenge. One pictured a young couple, Carl and Mary Walker, who could have been just your average underachieving slackers except for their close association with the man in the second print. Blacmann looked closely at the big man with barrel chest, and graying hair. The eyes looked directly at him, and he thought there was a mocking tone to them, as if to say 'come and get me if you can.' He noted Peter Denech had never been much of a ladies man when he knew him in college and, in fact, never married. He glanced at his own reflection in a side window. He and Denech were the same age, early sixties, and both above average in height, but he still retained a full head of slick silver hair, and a lean, clean-cut face.

But Peter Denech would be a prize catch in other ways. Through an informant from within Denech's secret group, Blacmann had learned of a potential technology so destructive as to make atomic weapons seem like b-b guns. There had come to his ears a rumor that an experiment might already be underway. But he did not deal personally with the informant, and had no idea who it might be. The informant dealt directly with his superior, and so the information was second hand. Blacmann suspected the head of the Agency knew a lot more. The impression was that the information Denech possessed could be used to create the utopian society, eliminating all the misfits and malcontents, or on the other hand could wipe the slate clean of everyone. This was pure bullshit as far as he was concerned. There would always be good people and evil people. Still, apprehending Denech would be a feather in his cap. Blacmann again stared at the picture of Peter Denech. "I know you're close. Where are you hiding?"

The side door opened and a woman entered the motor home. Dressed in a grey suit that looked more like a man's, her plain face had the hard and blank look of an ex-con. Brown hair cut short added to the manly appearance. Blacmann motioned for her to view the printouts.

"Just came through. See anyone you recognize?"

Agent Johnson nodded. "The Walkers, of course. And I've seen an entire album on Denech."

"He probably has more of his group with him. Intel says a woman about his age but no description."

"In other words, we have no idea."

"Unfortunately, we have no positive ID on any others, except, of course, the Walkers, and they may have split up already. The few that we knew about went up in smoke in Montana."

"Not much to go on."

"Just the communication intercepts and the word of the informant. Anything from anyone in the field?"

"Nothing yet, but tech support says they now have them within a twenty mile radius."

Blacmann considered. "Twenty mile radius. That's still over a thousand square miles."

"True. But we have aerial intercepts standing by. We have a dedicated satellite in synchronous earth orbit directly above us. We can monitor the feed from here. If they so much as twitch, we'll know it."

"The 'twitch' will have to be from a communications. Or if they run for it, the white blazer will stick out like a sore thumb."

"You think Denech will hang tight?" Johnson asked.

"I do. But he can't remain in his hole forever. Sooner or later he's going to go on line again. We intercepted two of his communications so far, and we now have his electronic signature. One or two more and we'll be able to drop into his back yard for a beer." Blacmann moved the prints aside and looked at the map. "Show me the ground logistics. I want to be sure every highway, every country road, hell, every animal trail through the woods is covered just in case he makes a run for it."

Johnson began tracing her finger over the map, explaining as it moved along.

"We're here at St. Charles along Highway 14. We have teams west at Lewiston and east at Dover. You'll note Highway 74 runs north and south. We have teams as far north as Elba and south to Troy. We have several squads from the highway patrol as well. We can phone-fax the photos to everyone involved."

"Good. We have them inside a circle. Like a noose."

"Looks that way."

Blacmann pointed to an area in the northern part of the search area. "What's this green and brown coloring up here?"

"Whitewater State Park and wildlife management area."

"Anyone in there?"

"Park Rangers. They've been advised of the situation, but—"

"But what?" Blacmann interrupted.

"Park Rangers hardly qualify as hardened law enforcement people. Unless you count giving out tickets for littering, or setting up your tent in the wrong spot."

"Denich isn't likely to be up that far anyway." His eyes swept the rest of the map. "It looks like a small area, but there really is a lot of ground to cover."

"Yes, a lot. Also you'll note Interstate 90 runs east and west just south of here. We have the state patrol on the lookout there, too."

Blacmann nodded approvingly. "Looks good."

"However, the blazer doesn't register an electronic signature," Johnson advised.

"Which means it has no identification chip. So we can't track him electronically. We'll have to rely on human eyes."

"Another problem. Tech support has combed every square centimeter of the satellite images but couldn't find a white Blazer. Is the vehicle information even reliable?"

"Came right from Director, who got it from the informant. But right now it's probably stashed in a building or under a tree. Anything else?"

Johnson nodded. "This is primarily farm country interspersed with large patches of heavily forested and some fairly rugged terrain. You'll note that the farm fields are often very irregularly shaped. That's because they sit mostly on workable land wherever the farmers could find it. Otherwise the ground is cut up by the deeply eroded valleys. The streams in those valleys merge into the Whitewater River, which flows to the Mississippi River to the northeast. Lots of places to hide if they're on foot, but the weak link for us are all these county roads that criss-cross the area."

"The local county sheriff should handle those."

"He should," Johnson agreed. "However, he's not very enthusiastic about pulling his squads from their regular patrols."

"How many?"

"He said ten units altogether would be on standby."

Blacmann nodded. "Should be sufficient."

"I should think so, if they try to drive away."

"One other thing. The Walkers, along with Denech's people, are expendable. But the boss wants Denech alive. If he should die, even accidentally, we, all of us, could end up being on the wrong end of an ITP."

"You think he'd go that far?"

Blacmann nodded. "I wouldn't bet against it. And since everyone in the Agency has an imbedded ID chip in their skull, I'd say that success in this mission is mandatory."

"Good point."

"If the Director gets his way with the cowards in Washington, soon *everyone* will have the ID chip. It would streamline this society and make things a lot easier for us."

"You think it will happen? I mean everyone?"

"Of course. Think what it would mean. You'd just walk out of a store with your purchases and a scanner would automatically ID your implanted chip and you'd get the amount deducted from your income. Simple. It would eliminate the need for money, and save the government billions in lost taxes that now disappear into the underground cash society."

"And those people who refused to get the implanted chip?" Johnson questioned.

"I don't know. Eat grass or starve, I suppose. But I doubt that people will have a choice in the matter. The effort would identify the true patriotic God-fearing Americans, and the rest could all go to hell, as far as I'm concerned."

"Best case scenario?" Johnson asked. "I mean about this present operation."

"We get them all alive, or failure to do that, we get at least Denech alive."

"What if the situation comes down to all dead or none?"

"Then we take none, and wait for the next time."

Johnson considered. "Why is Denech so valuable?"

"Ours is not to reason why," Blacmann stated. "But apparently Denech is tied to something major. The Director told me he's been moved to the top of every most wanted list in the country."

Johnson hesitated a moment and then continued. "You know I have a personal stake in this."

"I know."

"After what happened in the train, I may be inclined to shoot on sight."

"I know, and my sympathies are with you." But then Blacmann's voice grew hard. "But remember, if you screw up, you pull us all down.

If you don't think you can—if *I* didn't think you could—I'd pull you off this right now."

"I can handle it."

"Patience is the key word here. Denech is smart as a fox. But he's fighting a high-tech battle with obsolete junk, like a musket against a tank. There's no way he can win. Sooner or later he'll expose his weak side, and that's when we'll nail him." Blacmann again looked at the picture of Carl and Mary Walker. "And these two, I believe, will turn out to be his Achilles' Heel."

Johnson nodded. "I want to be there when it happens."

Blacmann noted the time. "It's 8:15PM. Patch the satellite feed into the larger monitors. You'll coordinate communications with tech support and ground. I want to be ready."

"It'll be dark soon. That could complicate things."

Blacmann shook his head. "He's close. Very close. I can *feel* it."

* * * *

In the gathering darkness, Peter Denech stood with his two comrades outside the old grain mill. He couldn't believe how utterly fantastic the fresh breeze felt brushing up against his face, and flowing into his lungs. It barely registered that the air was now contaminated with an artificial life form. Totally out of character, Amanda had spread her arms like a small child and spun around in an almost playful manner. Randolf Haays had knelt down, picked up a handful of earth, and let the dry dust filter down through his fingers.

But that was the extent of the celebration upon leaving the Rabbit Hole. They had two major problems to solve. One was the disposal of the white blazer. He couldn't simply leave it there. As far as he knew, the location of the facility was still a secret, and the white blazer would be like a red flag announcing its presence. But the white coloration would stand out on the road, even at night, and so the first order of business was to repaint it. The main problem with that was, of course, that they had no paint. The other problem was one of strategy. When one gets pursuers going one way, it's best if one is heading in the opposite direction. The laptop was the obvious answer. It was apparent Blacmann knew its electronic signature and would likely zero in on it as soon as it was activated. Under cover of darkness, it would not be all that difficult to place it onto someone else's vehicle, at a gas station or convenience store. But that would just shift the danger from them to some innocent bystander, who might end up in small pieces from an ITP. Was Blacmann willing to take such extreme measures? Or was Peter Denech worth more to them alive than dead? These were factors he could only guess at. However, there had been assurances made that his life was of premium value. In the end, he'd have to gamble that was indeed the case.

The problem of the white blazer was being solved as he spoke. Amanda and Randolf were in the process of smearing it with a coating of muck from the rich dark soil by the riverbank, transforming it to a shiny black. In broad daylight it wouldn't fool anyone but in the cover of darkness with no moonlight it might just buy them some time. Once the blazer and all electronics were disposed of, the three could transfer into the Ford pickup, a safe vehicle that was completely in compliance with a mileage chip, and properly registered to, as Denech liked to say with his wide smile, "a distant cousin, thrice removed." Korneth and Haays completed their task and came back to stand next to him.

Denech nodded toward the vehicle. "I'll take the blazer, and take the direct route to point one. You two follow about a mile behind with the pickup. We have to assume that Blacmann's people are literally everywhere, and have the local authorities ready to pounce as well."

"I don't like this," Haays stated. "You're taking a terrible risk. My place is with you."

Denech continued as if he hadn't heard. "I have confidence in our new outfits, compliments of Red. But if anything happens to me, you two know what to do."

"Protect the Walkers and go immediately to Plan B," Amanda said.

"But—"

"No buts. You have to carry this forward."

Amanda smiled, a rare occurrence. "That's not what I meant Peter. I was going to say nothing is going to happen to you."

"I like your optimism."

"My concern," she corrected. "We've been together for too long not to have built—well, you know, a bond—that is."

Denech looked at his closest friends. "We do make quite the team, don't we? An agnostic, a devout Catholic, and yours truly, just too confused to figure any of it out."

"People who have doubts are generally the most reasonable," Korneth reminded him. "Their minds are still open to differing views. It's those people who are absolute in their convictions that tend to be the most dangerous."

Denech nodded, and then began moving toward the mud-covered vehicle. "We can continue this discussion at some other, more secure time. But now we have a mission to fulfill."

Chapter 15

Although he had no way of knowing, Carl Walker figured it had to be dark outside. It was now past ten o'clock. If Peter Denech had figured correctly, the nanites in the atmosphere were now reaching their ferocious peak, on the order of billions upon billions of replications per cycle. If he had indeed selected key dispersion sites around the world, no place on earth except possibly a few rare isolated pockets of stagnant air or maybe the polar regions would have places that were yet clear of them. Yet no one would ever know, since the artificial life forms were as invisible as the influenza virus that swept the earth immediately after World War I, killing millions. Yet Peter had stressed no one would die as a result of his creations, but that there would be a profound change nonetheless.

Despite all that had transpired, and Peter Denech's very convincing rhetoric, Carl still retained the underlying suspicion that this was all an elaborate hoax. About the only thing that was verifiable was the existence of the Mayan Long Count Calendar, and that by itself didn't predict the end of the world. The end of it was something like a milestone, like the year 2000. The world didn't end in the year 2000. It just clicked over into 2001. It was obvious, however, that Red believed in whatever Denech was into. When Carl thought about it, that was the deciding factor as far as he was concerned. If Red believed, then there must be something to it. According to Denech, in a few weeks the secret would be out, and he found himself feeling the same anticipation he'd felt as a child waiting the last month before Christmas. But what manner of gift would this be?

Since Peter, Amanda, and Randolf had left, the others had made themselves as comfortable as possible in the War Room. The entire cave had been confining enough, and their new sealed quarters would have guaranteed anyone with even a smidgeon of claustrophobic tendencies a panic attack. Carl couldn't help but expect a colony of bats to suddenly take wing from the low ceiling above. Just one small light kept at least some of the pitch-blackness at bay. With the chairs folded and set to one side, each lay now on the rock floor on the padding from the sleeping cots, which they had secured before the room was sealed. Whether consciously or subconsciously, Mary had selected the mattress between Carl and Rowanna Doran. Yet sleep was an elusive quantity, and none of the three could do more than rest their eyelids.

There had been some initial conversation between them immediately after the others left, but for the last hour none had said anything. The quiet was absolute—like a coffin, Carl suspected—buried deep underground. Yet he could clearly hear the tiniest sounds: His own heartbeat in his ears, Mary's faint breathing, Red's restless movement, the tiny hiss of oxygen slowly escaping from the last reserve tank, even the tick of his own wristwatch. The entire world above them could have disappeared and they wouldn't have known it. For a brief moment he wondered what would happen if the pneumatically sealed doors should malfunction and they were stuck there forever. Would madness get them before starvation? Would suicide be preferable to a slow agonizing death? Would someone in the distant future find nothing but white bones and the marks on the doors where they had tried in vain to scratch their way out? He shivered violently and sat up, but Mary caught him by the arm. In the dim light, he noted her calm face.

"It's hard. Very hard," he said. "Never did like to be cooped up."

Red, who had been lying on her side facing away from them, rolled over and also rose to a sitting position. Her red hair was in tangles, and Carl realized that they all had let personal hygiene slide the last few days. Probably, they all looked and smelled somewhat less than what was socially acceptable, but since they all smelled that way, they didn't notice. They were trapped in a cave, but, Carl realized, at least there was a light at the end of the tunnel. In a few hours, they would be leaving the Rabbit Hole. He hoped it would be for good. The thought occurred to him that the people who had been at the Montana facility had not been so fortunate. The video of the group played back in his mind. He remembered how they had all been subdued just before the explosion, like mourners at a funeral. And then there was something else, something that hadn't made sense, a contradiction. Something that seemed very wrong, something obvious, but unseen.

"Can't see the forest for the trees," Carl muttered to himself.

Mary sat up also and pushed herself up against the rock wall.

"What trees?" Red asked. Carl noted the present situation had not dimmed the fire in her eyes.

"I was thinking about the people who died in Montana, and how something about the video was obviously wrong, but I can't nail it down." He turned to Mary, who absently stroked the long black hair she had pulled over her right shoulder. "Am I nuts, or was there something odd about it?"

"They knew they were about to die. It is reasonable to assume they were in a state of shock."

Red shook her head. "Not the way I'd gone out."

"No?" Mary asked.

"Nope. I'm not sure what I'd been doing, but my own philosophy is to keep fighting until there ain't no more fight in me."

Mary nodded. "You would. However, not everyone is as driven."

Carl considered. "Remember when Peter asked me if I really would want to know the exact time and place of my death? Remember how he said that the organization had actually done a survey, a scientific poll, to determine what the response of most people would be?"

"I do," Mary stated. "The vast majority of people would not want to know. Just keep on living right up to the last moment in a state of total ignorance."

"Why?" Carl asked.

"Because life is generally preferable to death. Because death is such an inescapably final thing. Because it is better to share a lifetime with people you care about even if it is only a few minutes. All these reasons and others I'm sure."

"I don't agree at all," Carl stated. "At least for myself, I think that's backwards."

"Explain." Mary prompted, but Red answered.

"I have to agree with Carl," Red stated. "I'd want to know. And maybe if we all knew the end was near, we'd find a lot of the petty shit that goes down between people was just plain stupid. Maybe we'd realize how precious life really is and take the remaining time to get straight with people we care about but have drifted away from."

"Interesting notion," Mary replied, "but not realistic. The logical outcome would be mass panic, and a total breakdown of social structure. A live-for-the-moment philosophy would take control. Some would weep, some would party, some would jump off the nearest tall building. Every last inhibition would dissipate. Every last desire would be fulfilled, or at least attempted. There would be total chaos. Many people, possibly most people, would be dead long before the end came."

"Some of that is probably true," Red agreed. "But I think a lot of people would take the opposite track. Spend the last bit of time in peace doing the simple things that make them happy, or even helping others. Not everyone has perverse tendencies. Not everyone is hedonistic. Not everyone is so self-centered. I have to believe, for many and in spite of everything, it could be a peaceful time."

"It is true," Mary said, "that there have been few scientific simulations to get any reliable probability figures on this, and no firm data from real world occurrences. It's probably safe to say that the response would be as varied as people are themselves."

Carl stood up suddenly as the realization struck.

"Exactly! That's it! That's exactly it! I know now what was wrong. Now I can see the forest!"

* * * *

By the shortest route, Highway 74, Denech knew it was less than fifteen miles south to the location of Blacmann's transmission. From the old paper maps, they had been able to put a name to that place. The crosshairs of the coordinates came down on the eastern edge of the community of St. Charles along Highway 14. If Blacmann was personally overseeing the operation, it was at least reasonable to assume he'd place himself in a centrally located position. If that reasoning was sound, then the rest of the net might be expected to radiate out from around him. That meant that the mud covered blazer and an old Ford pickup were now headed directly into the center of hostile territory. But for their plan to work, they'd have to get a lot closer. A lot, lot closer.

Two miles north of St. Charles, Denech turned east on a county road, proceeded for two miles, then turned south again, thus bypassing the bright lights of the small town. At the late hour there were few other vehicles on the country roads. He stopped at the intersection with Highway 14, where a scattered but continuous stream of vehicles passed by, and briefly considered. By turning east, he could flee the danger area altogether, and hope that the mud paint job would fool any and all law enforcement personnel he might pass. But if Haays had done his homework, Blacmann was less than two miles in the opposite direction somewhere along the highway just outside of town. That assumed, of course, that he was in the same location. Either direction was a gamble, and in the end Denech went with the plan and chose the direction that made the least amount of sense.

Peter Denech pointed the blazer west, and began looking for an operations center. He knew it wouldn't be blazingly obvious, as Blacmann's group shunned the spotlight, but he also knew, given Blacmann's fondness for the finer things, it would be something larger and more comfortable than a mini-van. Within a mile and sitting well off the highway on a grass covered access trail, Denech found what he was looking for: A sleek new silver motor home parked in the shadows of the first of the community's streetlights. There was a plain sedan parked behind it, but no official vehicles of any sort. There were none of the usual satellite dishes, or antennas that would indicate domestic use. Blacmann was, Denech realized, made obvious by attempting not to be.

* * * *

"Sit down before you bang your head on the rocks and hurt yourself," Red suggested, and pulled Carl back down to reality. "What are you talking about?"

"You're both right. Think about this. There's a group of people. They've just discovered a bomb is heading their way and will hit within seconds. Would they all, every last one, react in exactly the same way? Which was to just mope around like they were attending a wake, or sheep waiting to get slaughtered."

Mary nodded. "You're suggesting there should have been more emotion."

"Hell. I'm suggesting there should have been at least *some* emotion in *someone*. Wouldn't at least one person be crying, or throwing a fit, or beating fists on the wall? Wouldn't at least one person be attempting to get out of the place, even if it was a futile effort? You're the one with the fool-proof memory. Remember what the man said in the video?"

"Of course. At first, 'Incoming. This is an official Code Red.'"

"Then?" Carl prompted.

"Then 'We did our best. Outcome unknown. Facility destroyed.'"

"And then?" Carl pressed.

"There was a lot of interference and then something like 'Integrity compromised, possible traitor, message sent to alternate site for continuous replay.' Or something similar."

"Do you remember the people in the background?"

"Yes, vaguely."

"What were they doing and saying?"

"They were just sitting or standing around talking quietly."

"Exactly," Carl stated, and couldn't contain his excitement. "A bomb is about to reduce them to dust and they're just standing around talking quietly. Not just some of them. All of them. How realistic is that?"

"Not very," Mary agreed.

Red added. "Even the man who was speaking didn't seem all that excited. He sounded more like a bored newscaster. And as you said, no one was trying to get out or get to cover as I certainly would have been."

"So what does it all mean?" Mary asked.

Carl shrugged. "I haven't a clue. I just knew that it didn't add up. I'll leave it to you two to figure it out from here."

Mary took him seriously and turned to Red. "Drugged, you think?"

"I don't think so. Too alert. And no signs of slurred speech, disorientation, or poor balance that I can recall. Now that I think about it, their actions remind me of the final stage of grieving," Red volunteered. "I know. I've been there."

"How so?'

"Like when a loved one dies or when a person is told they are going to die. Or a bad divorce, or some other traumatic thing. We go through all the different stages. Though it may not seem so at the time, it's a normal process."

"Yes?" Carl said.

"First there's a certain amount of confusion and emotional upset, and denial that it could be happening at all. Then there are the deals we try to make with—for lack of a better word—God."

"Deals?"

"You know. If you'll just grant me this one wish, I'll be good forever, or I'll give all my money to the poor. Lies like that."

"Of course that doesn't work."

"No, so then anger sets in. God gets cussed out a lot at this stage. Depression follows that."

"Not good for one's health."

"But afterwards, in most people, there is a slow acceptance, and often a peaceful feeling settles in, and they get on with their lives."

"Time is the great healer," Mary acknowledged.

"And how long, start to finish?" Carl continued.

"No set answer there. Some people, a few weeks. Others, years. And some people get stuck in a particular stage and never get out. Usually anger or depression."

"A life wasted," Mary noted.

"And how does this tie into the people in Montana?" Carl asked.

"Well, either they were in the denial stage or in the acceptance stage. Given they were a smart bunch of folks, I'd have to say the acceptance stage," Red said.

"Sounds like they went though—" Carl began, but Red interrupted.

"You were going to let Mary and me figure it out from here, remember?" Red stated firmly, but flashed a grin.

Carl nodded in acknowledgement but continued anyway. "Looks like they went through all the stages in about sixty seconds. Not a reasonable conclusion."

Mary agreed. "There is only one reasonable conclusion. And it ties in with something that I didn't pick up on before."

"What? You missed something? How is that possible?"

"I'm not perfect," Mary responded seriously.

"But close. What did you miss?"

"The last two letters of a two word phrase."

"Yes?"

"The man in the video said 'Facility destroyed.'"

"So? Ah. I see," Carl said. "It's in the past tense."

Red nodded. "How could the place have been destroyed, and them with it, if they were still talking?"

"Maybe they weren't there at all," Mary suggested.

"They were there. I recognized the inside of the facility," Red confirmed.

"Or maybe," Carl said, "they had a lot more time to prepare for what they knew was coming, which, of course, begs the question: Why then stay there and get blown up? At any rate, I think there is someone who knows the answers to these questions."

"Peter Denech," Mary stated.

"Yes."

"You think Peter was holding something back?" Red asked.

"I do."

"What makes you think so?"

"Because nothing much gets past the man. If we picked up on this inconsistency, you can bet he did too."

"Peter is probably the only person I completely trust," Red stated defensively. "If there was some bit of information about the explosion he didn't tell us, he must have had a good reason."

"I do know this," Carl continued. "I was right next to him when we saw the video. There was no faking the tears I saw. Whatever he might have known certainly didn't cancel his grief." Carl squinted in the dim light to read the hands on his watch. "It's now after midnight. The very earliest Peter said we could leave. I vote we stay another four hours and get out just before daylight."

Red's thoughts were still on Montana. "Well, thanks, Carl. Because of you, what I thought I had figured out before no longer makes any sense at all."

"It makes perfect sense," Mary noted. "We just haven't found all the pieces to the equation."

The three fell into silence, and again lay back on the matting. At four in the morning, Carl intended for them to leave under the cover of darkness. He and Mary would then place their faith in Rowanna Doran, and eventually, if events went as planned, in Professor Edward Micals. But then what? It seemed like just yesterday he and Mary had been drifting through their predictable lives in ignorant happiness. Peter Denech and his secret, and by one definition terroristic, group had suddenly thrust them into dangerous waters from which there seemed to be no safe exit.

Chapter 16

▼

Barry Blacmann was beginning to get a smidgeon nervous. It was now after midnight, and there'd been no contact at all with Denech. More and more he was beginning to believe his first assessment was the correct one; that Peter and his crew would stay put, hiding out in a deserted barn, farmhouse, or root cellar. The blatant communication with him had been a gamble. He had unzipped his fly so to speak and exposed himself, letting Denech know he was in the area. But the reasoning was sound because the computer models predicted with an 80% certainty that the action would panic Denech into flight. Once flushed from cover, the probability of capture became a near certainty. But Denech was the one person who broke all the models. If there was a certainty, it was that the man's actions were based on a randomly generated set of outcomes.

Denech had come to the attention of the Agency in the same way many other domestic terrorists did. He batted a thousand, as the techs liked to say. The core of the Agency was not manpower or even law, but a bank of processors in Maryland in an underground warehouse the size of a football field. The Electronic Monitoring of domestic Intelligence for National Defense, or E-MIND, was the heart and soul of the Agency. The single-minded purpose of the installation was to monitor every bit of electronic communication within and to and from

America. All the various forms of phone conversations, wide band and narrow band radio communication, short wave traffic, all text messaging, all email messages—literally everything, was filtered through the electric mind. The Director had stated flatly: "If a pigeon farts in a hayshed in Maine, I want to know about it." However, the control center, or the Hub as it was called, did not reside in Maryland with the processors. For security reasons, it was buried in solid granite somewhere around the Great Lakes, or at least that was the propaganda that was deliberately leaked out. The exact location was known to few, and he was not one of the select few. It was home to the Director and a close circle of confidants.

E-MIND intercepted and filtered through the billions upon billions of bits of personal information, searching for key words and phrases that could represent potential subversive activity. Part of E-MIND ground away continuously at breaking codes and recognizing inferences in speech patterns, even though no obvious inflammatory wording by persons was being used.

Every American alive who had even once used an electronic communication device in the past ten years was in the database, as well as millions of others, and each had a scorecard. Each time someone used a word that represented suspicious activity they received points based on a rating system. Due to the huge volume of incoming data, the excess was regularly dumped, unless a conversation was of such extreme nature as to be considered worth saving. Of course, many of the points represented innocent conversation, or the words of a blowhard shooting off his mouth, thus the one thousand point threshold. But once someone reached one thousand points they ceased to be a U.S. citizen and became a target of interest, a TOI, which was pronounced TOY. A target of interest, a TOY, automatically lost all the privileges of decent law abiding Americans. The Bill of Rights and the right to a trial were suspended upon orders of the President alone. Suspects opened their doors, willingly or not, to a team of agents from the Agency and explained in great detail just why they should not be considered enemies of the state. When convenient, the obviously disruptive influences were selectively eliminated with an ITP. "A nice savings for the taxpayer," the Director liked to emphasize when addressing senior members of congress. "And a small price to pay for making America safe."

In 2009, Denech had made the B-team, as potential domestic terrorists were called. When an informant began providing information a short time later, the Director promoted him immediately to the A-team, and subject to apprehension or elimination. But then Denech disappeared, reverting back to ancient late nineties hardware and microbursts of encrypted communications that were difficult, but not impossible, to intercept. Denech's secret activities, alone, were against current anti-terrorism law, and grounds for immediate arrest. Denech was elusive, however, and it had been a game of cat and mouse ever since. He seemed to be able to anticipate every action by The Agency, or was extremely lucky. However, there was never any doubt that the new technology would prevail over his old junk. It was the new technology, and the possible help of an informant, that had pinpointed Denech's location to within a twenty-mile radius. Blacmann remained confident he'd meet his old college buddy very soon.

* * * *

All had been quiet for some time, and again Carl fought off the claustrophobic effects of the confined space. He'd always enjoyed visiting caves before, but this was something different. The caves he'd visited always had an entrance and an exit. He could feel his mind slipping back into the morbid thoughts that provoked his earlier attack, though he'd never admit his sudden rise to a sitting position had actually been a fit of the willies. This time he wouldn't let it get that far, and went back to his earlier defense: Conversation.

"You two sleeping?" he asked quietly.

"Not any more," Red answered immediately, and it was clear she had not been. She turned to Mary who lay on her back with eyes wide open. "Is Carl always this talkative?"

Mary answered honestly. "Only when he's nervous."

"Not nervous," Carl stated.

"Are too," Red shot back.

"Okay. Maybe a little jumpy. But I have something else to talk about that should help pass at least five more minutes."

"Which is?"

"Who's the traitor in Denech's organization?"

Red shrugged. "Why don't you ask me something hard? It could be anyone."

"Not *any*one," Mary countered. "I've been giving it a lot of thought. If we make certain assumptions, there are actually very few people who it *could* be."

"What assumptions?"

"That Wolf wants Peter alive, and wouldn't risk bombing a facility if he might be there. That everyone died at the Montana facility, and the traitor doesn't particularly want to die."

"Therefore, the traitor couldn't have been there, and is still a threat," Carl said.

"That all seems reasonable to me," Red agreed.

"Then who are we left with?" Carl asked.

"There are a few others that might have known in advance—" Red began.

Mary interrupted. "Forget those that could have known where Peter was. Let's stick with those that knew for sure."

"That does narrow it down."

"So who?" Carl asked, anxious to keep everyone talking.

"The only ones who knew for sure are the five of us with Peter in the cave, and Professor Micals at the university in Minneapolis."

"You sure?"

"Peter as much as told me so himself."

"Then let's begin the process of elimination," Mary stated.

"Seriously?" Red countered.

"Seriously. One at a time. We need to answer two basic questions. Possible motive and opportunity."

"Sounds like you've had some training in this," Red decided.

A brief smile flickered across Mary's face. "Not really. But I've seen enough movies to know at least that much. How about Professor Micals?"

Red shook her head. "No way. He's been Peter's friend for years. They're practically like brothers. He'd have plenty of opportunity, but no possible motive."

"But from what I gather, he's a rather obstinate person."

"Not really. He's very easy to talk to. It's just that after a while he'll start pricking you with little embarrassing questions. Picking your statements apart. But he'd never do anything to harm another living thing, man or beast."

"How can you be so sure?" Mary pressed.

"Well, for one thing he's a vegetarian. He doesn't believe in killing any animals, and so I would imagine that includes people."

Mary nodded. "Good point. What about Amanda?"

Red smiled. "You mean you haven't figured that out yet?"

"What?" Mary asked, genuinely confused.

"She's in love with Peter."

"You're joking," Carl cut in. "Since when?"

"Forever, I think. She'd never do anything that would cause him pain. And the death of his friends in Montana would definitely cause pain."

"How does Peter feel about it?"

"If he knows, if he feels the same way, he's kept it well hidden. I don't think at this stage of the game he'd allow himself the luxury of a personal relationship."

"That brings us to Randolf," Mary continued.

"Now we might have something there," Carl said. "He has as much as admitted that he was against the plan from the start."

"His reasoning process does seem to be somewhat limited by his primitive religious beliefs," Mary added.

Again Red shook her head. "You have to understand where Randolf is coming from. In his own way, he loves Peter as much as Amanda. To Randolf, Peter is like the wayward son, even though they're about the same age. Peter is someone to save and bring into the flock."

"Maybe it's Randolf who's gone astray," Carl suggested.

"Randolf fully intends to die fighting right alongside Peter one day. Not the sort of person you'd expect to betray you."

"What about you?" Mary asked, and her expression did not change.

For a moment, Red seemed taken back but then answered. "I would be dead if not for Peter Denech. I would betray my own mother before I'd betray him." Red smiled slightly. "But then my own mother was an abusive alcoholic so maybe that isn't saying much."

Mary seemed satisfied with that. "That only leaves the two of us. Mary and Carl Walker."

"Nope," Red concluded. "Not unless you've been secretly working for the other side for the last five or so years. And Peter has vouched for you from the start, and as we all know—"

"Nothing much gets past Peter Denech," Carl concluded. "So we're back to square one. The good news is that this discussion burned up another fifteen minutes. What else can we talk about?"

"I have a better idea," Red decided.

"What's that?"

"Shut up and *go to sleep*."

Chapter 17

▼

Blacmann stared at the monitors, expecting some change, some news about Peter Denech. This was the part he hated. The waiting. Agent Johnson sat at the desk before him, and seemed unaffected by the boredom. Her blank face, the hard set to her jaw never changed. She sat there with arms crossed and also stared at the monitor. Blacmann suddenly straightened from looking over her shoulder and began to pace. Six paces toward the tiny bathroom, then turned sharply military style, then six paces toward the kitchenette, all the while hands clasped together behind his back. Blacmann's nervousness was nothing new to Johnson, and she already knew what his next symptom would be.

"There's a pack of smokes in my car," she advised. "Want me to get them?'

Blacmann considered her offer, but then shook his head. "No. You watch the screens. I need a breather anyway. But yell if something comes up." With that, he stepped out into the shadows and moved around behind the motor home to where Johnson had parked the government issued sedan. He retrieved the cigarettes and lighter from the glove box, lit up, and leaning up against the side door sucked in deeply. The end of the cigarette glowed red. It was a nasty habit, and one he'd given up multiple times. But it was the one thing that seemed to calm his nerves when things weren't going as planned. Despite what he preached to his underlings, patience, he reflected, was not his strong suit.

Blacmann looked out toward the highway, which was now virtually devoid of traffic. In the distance he could see the lights of St. Charles, and maybe fifty yards away the first street light, though it was well out into the country. Its meager output barely cancelled the total darkness, but cast long and ugly shadows. Behind Johnson's car a narrow patch of woods partially blocked the view to a newly planted field of soybeans, and beyond that the yard light from a farmhouse shone in the distance. He realized the grass approach where he had parked provided access to the field, and his eyes absently searched the darkness for traces of ruts. For a moment, his eyes lingered on what appeared to be a large black box at the edge of the field, and the thought occurred that it was where the farmer had parked his tractor. But then there appeared to be movement around it, and Blacmann grew curious. With the cigarette dangling from the corner of his mouth, he began walking toward the grey shape. If nothing else, it would provide a secluded place to relieve himself.

Within a minute, Blacmann stood in front of a vehicle. Someone had parked it on the edge of the field next to the woods line. It was a dark color, some brand of SUV. He absently ran his finger along the front fender, painting a white line as he did so.

A voice from the darkness caused an immediate urinary accident. "Hello, Barry."

There was a brief moment of mental void, like the split second of time when a scaffold collapses underfoot and the body hangs suspended in mid air before the laws of Nature demand attention. Gravity took hold, and Blacmann went limp.

* * * *

"If you move, I will shoot you dead where you stand," Peter Denech said, deliberately ratcheting his voice down to a low growl. "Remain very still."

Blacmann could only see the rough outline of the man, but the barrel of a weapon was clearly visible. "Look, you caught me—" Blacmann stuttered.

"Take care of business and then keep your hands where I can see them."

Blacmann regained a bit of control, as Denech stepped from the darkness in front of him. He had a black stocking cap pulled down over his head to the level of his eyebrows, and appeared unshaven and unkempt. Blacmann attempted a feeble bluff. "Might as well give up, Peter. The area is crawling with my people." He noted the weapon in the other man's hand, but didn't recognize the model. Denech looked a lot bigger than he remembered him, and in a struggle there would be no question whom the victor would be.

"I've been here for some time, watching you and your partner. Never try to kid a kidder."

"So what now. You going to shoot me?"

"Most probably."

Blacmann began a stall for time. "Well, don't you want to ask me questions?"

"Can't think of any," Denech said, and noted beads of perspiration on Blacmann's forehead.

"Not even how we found you?"

"Superior electronics. Someone in my organization, I've been told."

"Yes, that's true," Barry said regaining confidence. "A name might be worth something to you, I suspect."

"Like what?"

"Well, my life for starters."

"Are you afraid to die, Barry?"

"Well, no. Yes. No. I just don't want to die for something stupid like this."

"I'm listening." Denech's voice remained low and steady.

"It was one of your people in Montana."

"And you are a liar. They were all friends and dedicated comrades. But why don't you tell me more about Montana?"

"Look, I had nothing to do with that, I swear."

"Right, and I'm supposed to believe that, too. What about the rest of the Agency? What about Wolf?"

"If the Director had something else going, he didn't tell me anything."

"What names do you have?"

"Just yours. Except—"

"Except what?"

"They have you on hold. They want you alive."

Denech slowly raised the weapon. "No others?"

"None. I swear."

"Sorry. I don't believe—"

"Wait! Wait! The Walkers. We know about the Walkers."

"What do you know?"

"Nothing except you've adopted them."

"Who's been targeted?" Denech demanded.

"What do you mean?"

"You know damn well what I mean. Who's on the ITP list to be eliminated?"

"No one. Yes, you were but—"

"And the Walkers?"

"Yes, they're still on the list."

"Why?"

"Because—"

"Because why?" Denech pressed, and took a step closer.

"Because they're linked to you. That's why. You put them on the list. Everyone you know will be on the list."

"The Walkers are old business," Denech lied. "They didn't work out. They know nothing. I cut them loose a week ago."

"Doesn't matter. You know that. I get my orders from the Director, and he gets them from the President."

Denech shook his head. "You and I know that the President is a non-entity in all this. A political rubber stamp for whatever the Director flashes across his desk."

"National security must be maintained."

"And what threat am I? Do you even know?"

"I know that the Director considers you to be the number one terrorist in the country. And that makes any of your associates targets as well."

"You can tell him to take the Walkers off his list. They are not part of anything."

"You know I can't do that. The decision has been made. If you know where they are, tell them to give themselves up to the authorities."

"So what? So they can disappear into one of your detention centers never to be heard from again."

"At least they'd be alive," Blacmann said.

"If you call that living."

"So where are they?" Blacmann asked.

"You mean you don't know. With all your new electronic gadgets you don't know?"

"We—we lost track of them in Chicago."

"I see. So did I."

Blacmann sweated profusely, realizing the end of the conversation was near. "So now what?"

Denech considered. "Run this by the Director. My life in exchange for the Walkers."

"What?"

"You heard me. A trade. He gets me alive, and agrees to leave them alone. They're just a couple innocent kids with their whole lives ahead of them."

Blacmann couldn't contain a brief snicker. "Sure. Why not? Can't hurt to ask."

"But you never will, will you?"

"Face it, Peter. You can't compete with modern technology. Within a very short time, you'll be in custody and the Walkers will be dead."

"Then maybe I'll have to seek a higher power. Go above your heads."

"There is no higher power unless you mean God."

"I was thinking more along the lines of the People."

This time Blacmann's snicker erupted into full-blown laughter. "The people? They're cattle. As long as they can eat and sleep and breed, they're happy. They're ignorant and they like it that way."

Denech remained silent for a few moments, and then relaxed his tone. "I have something of a problem here, Barry. I'm torn between shooting you right here, or taking you somewhere else and shooting you there." Barry Blacmann's laughter came to an abrupt halt. He suddenly remembered he had a loud voice, and opened his mouth to use it, but all that come out was a gurgling sound as he wilted to the ground.

* * * *

"How much time do we have?" Randolf Haays asked, as Peter Denech slid into the pickup. Amanda Korneth crowded a little closer to Haays to make room for the big man. "And which way do we go?"

"Four hours before Blacmann comes out of it. I removed the dart so it might take a while for them to figure out why he's unconscious. But I wouldn't bet on it."

"The best cover is north. The last safe house," Korneth advised.

"Then north it is, because all hell is going to break loose here as soon as Blacmann's companion realizes he's not coming back anytime soon."

"Where did you leave him?"

"In the Blazer, where else?"

Amanda grinned ever so slightly. "You really do like to rub their noses in it, don't you? And the electronics?"

"Destroyed, except for the decoy. That will send them off to LA for a while. Should buy us some time to get set up again."

Haays was thoughtful. "We'll need to monitor the news. See if Plan A went off as planned or not."

"We might know in couple weeks or a couple months."

"We'll need—" Haays began.

Denech understood, and continued. "We'll have to make a quick stop at Micals' and pick up another safe laptop. Let him know about Carl, Mary, and Red. That's an hour and a half away, but we'll make it well before the morning rush hour."

* * * *

In St. Charles, Haays turned north again on Highway 74. At well past midnight only the bar traffic occupied the streets, and Haays drove without incident out of the small town. But when they were a few miles north, a screaming procession of flashing lights and sirens flashed past, ignoring the old Ford pickup.

"Guess my four hour window was a little off," Denech said.

"At least they're all going one way and we're going the other. Like you planned it that way."

Amanda couldn't help but give Peter a nudge with her elbow. "Somehow, you got us out of that one."

Denech was thoughtful. "I just hope Carl, Mary, and Red fare as well."

* * * *

Mary Walker did not want to sleep, even though the regular breathing of Carl and Red provided strong evidence that they both slept soundly. Carl had gone out first, and then a few minutes later Red had followed suit. But, as had happened for the previous consecutive nights, as soon as her own eyelids dropped, unimaginable visions and sounds filled her head. A few days earlier she had to be sound asleep for them to appear, but now it was as though the visions were coming to life, creeping ever closer to her conscious state. Instead of buried deep, they lurked just behind her eyelids, waiting to commandeer her subconscious mind. It was now only sheer will that kept them at bay.

But she knew it was a struggle she could not win. A person has to sleep, or they will quite literally go mad. It was a losing battle either way. She also knew that Carl was aware of her mental slide. He blamed it on the Rabbit Hole, on the close and claustrophobic quarters, on the air that became more rancid and toxic with every breath. She knew all that was true, but the thoughts that sprang up like a jack-in-box were something different. They popped in and out of existence like virtual sub-atomic particles, but through intense concentration she could slow them down. She could slow everything down to the point where the world around her moved in slow motion. She knew that some people, when they believe death is imminent, experience the same distortion of time. This, together with the re-occurring dream of the little girl in the blue denim overalls, convinced her that her own death was very near. It wasn't logical, it didn't make sense, but there it was.

Yet, her more lucid thoughts were not of herself. Death did not frighten her. It would be like a sound sleep from which there was no awakening. Her concern was with her husband, with Carl, and how he would handle her demise. Red was the obvious answer, as there was no denying the attraction between them. She did not feel jealousy, and pushed them ever so slowly together even as she withdrew. She lay now between them, only because that was the acceptable arrangement that would arouse the least suspicion. All this, she realized, was not normal. A woman protects her turf, especially when it comes to her mate. And yet, considering everything, it was the logical thing to do. She didn't know why. She just knew it was.

Despite her resistance, sleep finally came to Mary. In her dreams, the same little girl with long dark braids came to her, leading her into the dark void. Like always, she didn't resist, and the darkness became swirling images of strange but beautiful beings and fantastic machines, of silver tipped mountains and wide green valleys, and a warmth engulfed her that felt something like love or maybe acceptance. There were voices also, speaking in a strange tongue, but almost understandable, and she felt that if she concentrated just a little harder she'd know what they were saying, and what they were trying to tell her. Then the little girl in the blue denim overalls and long dark braids let go of her hand and left her alone. And it was sadness, not fear, that overwhelmed her, and she collapsed in tears to the ground. The quiet sobs, so uncharacteristic for Mary Walker, woke her husband, and he gently shook her shoulder to stir her from the troubled sleep. Her eyes opened, and without hesitation she flung her arms around him.

Carl attempted to console her. "It's okay, Mary. It's okay. It was just a dream. You're awake now."

"You don't understand," Mary cried. "It's getting harder and harder to wake up."

"I don't understand. Why?"

"Because I don't want to. I just want to stay in that place. More and more it's like I belong there."

Red swung around and rose swiftly to her feet. "Okay. I've heard enough. Nanites or no nanites. We're getting the hell out of here now."

Chapter 18

A drop of moisture crackled suddenly into steam and the tiny explosion sent a flurry of sparks up against the inside of the glass doors of the fireplace. Flames licked under and around the three birch logs that provided heat and flickering light to the cave-like room. Surrounded on three sides by walls filled with books, an old oak desk rested with additional volumes stacked several deep. Two padded armchairs, light brown in color, sat facing the warmth of the early morning fire. In them, two men conversed in hushed and somber tones, as if hypnotized by the dancing flames.

As if it might help clear his thoughts, Peter Denech leaned forward and rubbed the palm of one hand with the thumb of his other.

His companion, a man with dark brown hair graying at the temples, continued. "The air samples came back with mixed results, but I'm reasonably sure the concentration was adequate."

"And when did the nanites expire?"

"Around two o'clock AM there was a rapid fall off. By four o'clock the air samples came back negative."

"In a couple weeks we'll need to test a specific subject for each sex," Denech said.

"I will. My wife also volunteered. She's forty-two and pre-menopausal. It won't be conclusive proof but it will be at least indicative."

"The good news is, according to Blacmann, no one besides me and the Walkers in the organization has been positively identified. The bad news is we're still under the communications black out so that cannot be verified."

"That would be good news. But can you be sure Blacmann was on the level?"

"No, but at the time he had a great incentive to be candid."

Professor Edward Micals smiled. "Yes, indeed. But then the Walkers are now in critical danger."

"Red is with them. No better bodyguard around, and if they avoid the electronic net, they should be safe. That is not the concern."

"So it is happening as we speak."

"Yes. Much faster in Mary than even I anticipated."

"Carl?"

"Not yet. But then Mary was quite thirsty and drank a good bit. Carl, only a mouthful to be polite, I suspect."

"But enough?"

"In time, yes. No doubt, enough."

"And there is no chance the change could be the nanite infection?" Micals asked.

"None. It began well before—right after we administered the dosage. And the seals on the Rabbit Hole were never breached. With the utmost confidence, I can say she is beginning the transformation."

"And psychologically, how are they taking it?'

"Confused, which is to be expected. Mary believes she is dying. Carl thinks the effects of prolonged confinement are having a psychological effect. I've told them no different."

"That was wise. For now at least. All the information at once would no doubt tip them over the edge."

"But eventually they'll have to be told," Denech concluded.

"Maybe not. Maybe the progression will unfold on its own, the cycle complete. Like growing up. Little by little and then one day you realize you're no longer a child."

"That would be a best case scenario, but somehow I don't think we'll be that fortunate."

Briefly, both sat in silence and then Denech continued. "And things on your end. Anything new?"

"Not good, I'm afraid. We lost track of the object. Gave us its dark side. We'll continue to monitor where we expect it should be in its orbit."

"Any change in trajectory?"

"Merely a refinement of our last calculations. We still predict it will hit in the Atlantic off the coast of Brazil."

"And just a little under one year from now."

"Three hundred sixty days, eight hours." Micals looked at his watch. "And thirty seven minutes."

"Chance of error?"

"There is a chance, but a very slim one. Unless it runs into something else we don't know about, about one in a hundred. Newton's laws of motion don't leave much wiggle room."

"Okay then, my friend," Denech said. "I do the handoff. From this point on the Walkers will be in your good and capable hands."

"Randolf? Amanda?"

"They're survivors. They'll be fine."

"And you?" Micals asked.

"I must recede, as the saying goes, so that others might advance."

Micals again smiled. "Why do I find that difficult to believe? You got this going and never once looked back."

"There is something else that's got my blood pumping," Denech admitted.

"What?"

"I have a fix on Wolf's location."

"You mean the Hub?"

"Yes, and I think you'd find it quite poetic. Not the easiest to get to, but a strike there would be worth something, don't you think?"

Micals considered. "You don't fool me, old friend. You're thinking of going out in one brilliant flash to protect Carl and Mary. No doubt you're going to try something stupid and get yourself killed."

"No, killing myself is not on my to-do list. True, I did try to cut a deal with Blacmann, but he brushed me off, so, of course, I had to shoot him. Non-fatal, of course, but I think I made my point."

"So, now what?'

Denech leaned forward as he was prone to do when making a point. "I'm tired of running, Ed. I'm tired of being the rabbit. For once, I'd like to be the fox."

"Or wolf? To quote you, 'have a little patience'. In a few weeks, we'll be in a much better position to know."

"I'm afraid we may not have a few weeks. Their electronics are getting more sophisticated each day. Blacmann may be right. Soon every person on earth will have a distinctive electronic signature, either by an implanted chip or unique DNA, or both. There will be nothing left of freedom or individuality. We will be part of the hive-collective, individually expendable for the 'greater good.'"

Micals reflected. "Perhaps that is the inevitable end of over-population coupled with technology. With everyone in a database, everyone's actions can be monitored. And the undesirables—those that don't conform to someone's idea of civilization or a moral code—selectively eliminated with the ITPs."

"That, of course, is the ultimate goal," Denech agreed. "All in the name of National Security and preserving the peace. The Constitution Party was our last hope, but they have folded through intimidation and fear."

"We give up our individuality, our creativity, for the illusion of safety. Many will find that appealing."

"But you and I know it wouldn't work. The rebellious gene runs deep in the human genome."

Micals smiled broadly. "Yes. I do know. I'm sitting right next to a case in point."

Denech nodded. "And I as well. And the Walkers. And many others who prefer to make their own way in the world without the shackles of established dogma, whether political or religious."

"Oops. Don't let Randolf hear you talk that way."

"Randolf is cognitively confused, and, I think, there is a lot of internal doubt, but he is a good man with good ideals."

Again a period of silence separated the two. Then Micals began again. "Have you given any thought to the potential traitor?"

"I have. I know and trust every one of the intimates. I cannot bring myself to believe the problem comes from within."

"Would you like me to make inquiries?"

"No. I will pursue this on my own. Your task now is simply to monitor the space object and protect Carl and Mary at all costs. And I mean *all* costs."

Micals nodded. "Are you going to share your new information with me? I mean the location of the nerve center for Wolf?"

"I will at the right time. To be safe, I'll communicate in the usual way. I've spoken to Carl about our primitive method as well."

Peter rose from the chair and Micals followed suit. A handshake confirmed their commitment. Then Peter Denech left the comfort of one fire for the heat of another.

* * * *

The sun was just peeking over the eastern horizon when three haggard looking humans, one male and two female, emerged from a weathered door partially hidden behind the water wheel of an old grain mill. One ran jubilantly to the stream and splashed refreshingly cold water on her face, one bowed in reverence to the rising sun, and one fell down on his hands and knees and kissed the soil.

The stream, Red noted, was considerably higher and evidence that a storm had passed through while they were underground. Maybe it had been a lightning strike after all that had taken out their power. After a week spent in the drabness of the cave, the outdoor colors seemed exceptionally vivid and bright. The odors pungent. The sounds of birds and insects crystal clear. And she noticed an almost immediate change in her own disposition, and the others too. It was like emerging from a dark time into enlightenment. Mary and Carl joined her by the stream, and all looked back toward the old grain mill.

"Now I know how bears feel when they come out of hibernation and leave their dens," Carl joked, and a smile stretched his face from ear to ear. "I don't care if I ever go into a cave again. Did you notice the smell out here? Did real air ever smell so good?"

Red nodded. "It does smell delicious. By the way you still have dirt on your face from kissing the ground." Carl wiped his mouth with his shirtsleeve, but nothing could remove the smile. Red continued. "Unfortunately, I have to go back in one more time. To get a few supplies, and the other peashooter just in case unpleasant things happen. I want to be prepared."

Mary looked at the others. "I suggest we take a minute and wash up and change clothes before we leave."

"In other words you're saying we're a little ripe," Red quipped.

"Well, I'm not going back in that hole to shower," Carl stated. "As cold as the water is, I'm going for a swim. In fact," he said, with a wicked grin, "I think we all should." With that he swept Mary off her feet and dropped her neatly over the riverbank into the flowing stream. He looked back at Red, who waved him off. "Oh, no you don't" she said, and plunged in on her own. Lastly, Carl did a grand belly flop and joined them.

"This water is freezing!" Red complained, her teeth chattering, but splashed Carl playfully in the waist deep water.

"What a wimp. The last couple years we went to my uncle's cabin up north after the ice went out, usually around the middle of April, and dove right in."

"You weren't in long, I bet."

"True. It was an in and out thing for bragging rights, but then the water was barely above freezing. This water must be at least forty-five degrees."

"Oh, that warm, huh."

With beads of water running down her long dark hair, Mary merely smiled at the two. They reminded her of children. Then her expression grew serious. Time was slipping by and soon she would be too.

*   *   *   *

An hour later in dry clothes and drenched in the bright morning sunlight, Rowanna Doran pulled a short cord and immediately a package of black rubber transformed into an inflatable raft about six feet long and four feet wide. She attached the wooden rudder to the back, threw in two paddles and a pack with some supplies, and gestured for the others to get in. Within minutes, the trio was floating down the quiet stream. Hardwoods grew along the bank and their branches reached up and arched over the ribbon of water, forming a green and winding tunnel. Red sat in the back steering and looked ahead, but Mary and Carl looked the other way, watching the old grain mill disappear behind a curtain of green leaves.

Carl had a thought. "You think we'll ever come back here?"

Red shook her head. "Very doubtful. But as far as we know, the place hasn't been compromised, so maybe."

"Funny. Now that we're leaving, I almost miss the place."

Mary nodded. "We cling to what is familiar. We go now to something unknown. Change is always accompanied by apprehension."

Carl picked up a paddle and began aiding the current's push on the raft. "So what's next, Red?"

"This is a tributary of the Whitewater River."

"Sounds like fun. Whitewater rafting."

"Nothing like the Colorado River I'm afraid. One thing. In a while, we're going to start seeing people. There are hiking trails throughout parts of the area. Campsites. A road roughly parallels the river, so we may occasionally see vehicles in the distance. We're going to be drifting by so they will see us too."

"No one is going to recognize us."

"That's probably true. But they might be able to identify you later on. I'd hoped to do a little makeup job on you two, but—"

"So best to lay low," Carl finished.

"Just pretend you're newlyweds making out in the bottom of the boat, and I'm your guide."

Carl turned to Mary. "Sounds like fun."

Mary merely nodded, and lay down passively on her side on the bottom of the raft. The glazed look in her eyes gave Red cause for concern, and she exchanged glances with Carl.

"We have to get her to Professor Micals," Red advised. "We're losing her."

Carl gently shook Mary by the shoulder but got no response. He beat down an immediate wave of panic. "What's happening to Mary? Is there something you're not telling me?"

Red looked away, and did not answer. Carl grabbed her free hand and squeezed hard to get her attention. "This has nothing to do with the cave, does it? What is happening to Mary!"

Red looked at him directly, and her voice was sincere. "If I knew, I'd tell you. All I know is we have to get her to Micals."

All the forewarning comments Mary had made came back to Carl. All the dreams she'd mentioned, the premonitions. He had dismissed it all as the effects of confinement, low oxygen, and boredom. But this was something different. It couldn't be the effects of whatever Denech had added to the atmosphere because it started well before. But when exactly had it started? It had started, he realized, right after their first meeting with Peter Denech in the old house in a suburb of Chicago. Or right after their visit with the little girl immediately afterwards. The chances of that being a mere coincidence were remote. Carl placed his fingers against Mary's neck and felt a strong pulse, and noted the gentle rise and fall of her chest. Except for the fact that she would not wake up, she was, by all symptoms, merely sleeping peacefully.

* * * *

Rowanna Doran had not intended to float all the way to the Mississippi River. Straight across country it was less than ten miles away, but following the meandering stream would triple that distance. She had hoped to abandon the raft when a few miles from the old grain mill, but Mary's condition had not changed, and there was no way she was going to walk out on her own. The only alternative was to stay on the river, which, thanks to the recent rain, was relatively easy to navigate. Eventually the river would pass under Highway 61 and then into Maloney Lake, a nearly four-mile widening of the Mississippi River. If the current strategy had collapsed, it was there she would have to make a major decision: Either wait at the bridge for emergency transportation that might never come, or continue on across the lake to a chain of isolated islands in the middle of the river and nearly two miles from shore. Neither plan was the game plan, but with Mary's deteriorating condition, the playbook had gone out the window. Carl had taken a breather from paddling and lay next to her in the bottom of the raft, stroked her forehead gently and continued to speak quietly to her, but without effect. Lines of concern rippled across his face. Getting Mary to a doctor seemed a prudent course of action. But that would announce their presence to Wolf, and so Carl had agreed to a wait-and-see strategy. After all, to his knowledge Mary had never been sick a day in her life.

For the fifth time, Red asked the same question. "How's she doing?" Without Carl paddling, the current seemed a snail's pace.

"The same. A slight fever maybe, but everything else seems fine, except that she won't wake up. But she's been mumbling faintly in her sleep."

"I should think that's a good sign."

"Except most of it I can't make out."

"You mean like gibberish?"

"No, like a foreign language. Only no foreign language I've ever heard."

"Anything at all that makes sense?"

"Not much, except something about a buffalo, or maybe a word that just sounds like the word buffalo."

"We'll soon be coming to a widening in the river and easy access to a forestry road. If the entire plan hasn't gone to hell, we should have a friend waiting for us there. The only problem is we were supposed to be walking out. The raft has slowed us down."

"What are you saying?"

"I'm saying we're a couple hours late, and our friend may not be there. He might have gotten spooked and left."

"In which case, what do we do?"

"I don't want to think about it. Man the paddle again and hope our friend has patience."

Thirty minutes later Red steered the raft to the north side of the river. Her stomach told her it was well past noon. Unfortunately, they weren't alone. They had occasionally seen hikers along the riverbank, but at the point where the river nearly touched the forestry road, a small group had assembled. They looked innocent enough, with backpacks and bottled water and several rambunctious children, and so Red decided to take a chance and land the boat a short distance away. Carl kept his head down, not looking directly at anyone, and shielded Mary's face as well.

Then a man's voice rose above the murmur of conversation.

"Has anyone here seen my poodle? She answers to the name Flossy."

"I have," Red called out. "And such a cute little dog she is."

CHAPTER 19

▼

The hikers had moved on, leaving Carl free to carry Mary to the waiting van unseen. The back rows of seats were absent making room for a medical gurney, as if, Carl suspected, someone knew it would be needed. Clearly, someone had anticipated Mary's condition and that someone could only be Peter Denech. Something else Denech had neglected to tell him, but then Denech had said that they'd have to fish for answers. Sitting beside Mary, who now rested quietly, he was beginning to believe his first instinct had been the right one when he'd gotten up to leave during the interview in Illinois. Still it had been Mary who gently pulled him back down.

And now Mary lay before him apparently sleeping with no sign of stress or pain on her face. She looked peaceful, or the thought occurred, like someone in a coma. But there had been fleeting moments of mumbled one-way communication, unintelligible for the most part, but still a sign that something was going on inside her head.

Reds "friend" turned out to be Professor Edward Micals. She had taken over driving the van leaving Micals, with Carl's permission, to attach several patches on Mary's head and right arm. Micals was, Carl realized, monitoring her vital signs, and they registered on narrow horizontal screens on a mobile diagnostic unit. He recognized heart rate, blood pressure, blood oxygen, but several others were unknown to him.

Professor Micals was not at all like Carl remembered. With a rugged face, muscular arms, and a fit compact body, he hardly fit the stereotypical mold of a pale-skinned academic. Dressed in a white T shirt, faded blue jeans, and well-worn hiking boots, he looked to be in his late forties, still with a good crop of dark brown hair graying at the temples. Large brown eyes gave the impression of intelligence, and to a degree, innocence. His jaw had a determined set, and he went about the business of setting up the monitoring equipment with the skill and confidence of an experienced para-medic, nurse, or doctor. When all was in place, he sat back on his heels, and extended his hand to Carl.

"Officially, I'm Ed Micals," he began. "Peter has gotten you into quite a mess here."

"How's Mary? Right now that's all I care about."

Micals glanced at the diagnostic screens. "Right now looks good. Everything within normal parameters."

"Peter once told me that if we didn't work out, we'd end up back in Duluth in our apartment with all memory of this nightmare erased. I'm beginning to like that option more and more."

"Sorry. I'm afraid we're well past that."

"Figures." Carl turned his attention to the diagnostic graphs. "I recognize the heart and blood related stuff, but what are those other read-outs?"

"We're monitoring the electrical activity in her brain."

"And?"

"And as you can see there's plenty of it. Extremely active in fact."

"So why isn't she doing a jig or something?"

Micals hesitated. "I don't know. But long term, there shouldn't be any danger. Plan C is still intact."

Carl felt his temper rising. "Plan C? Do you know how little I really care about Plan C?" Carl pointed to Mary. "*This* is because of Denech and the rest of your terrorist group. If I had any brains at all, I'd flag down the next cop and turn you all in."

"You have to give us a little more time—"

"To what? To make sure Mary turns into a vegetable? To carry on your little crusade against the establishment? To what end? I can't think of anything you could say that would be worth more than Mary's life to me. But I'll give you about ten seconds to give it your best shot."

"What we did was the only chance we had to save her life."

"You see. That's what I'm talking about. That double talk just doesn't do it anymore. You're going to have to lay it all out right now, or so help me, I'll turn into the worst enemy you ever had."

Micals glanced up and caught Red's glance in the rear view mirror.

"He does have a way with words," she said. "I told him nothing. Peter told him only the bare minimum. It's up to you."

"She would have died in any case," Micals said finally.

"Who are you trying to kid? Mary's never been sick a day in her life."

"Peter did tell you about the object we discovered in space? How it has a destiny with earth?"

"Yes. But right now I'm inclined to disbelieve you."

"Interesting choice of words. 'Inclined to disbelieve.' Not part of your usual vocabulary I suspect."

"The words seem more than adequate to reflect my feelings. How would you feel if your own wife was lying here?"

Micals smiled. "It's happening. It really is. Old man Denech was right. And how would I feel if my wife was lying there? I only wish she were."

"What is happening? Why is Mary in this vegetative state?"

Micals sighed. "By no means vegetative. In fact, just the opposite. Mary, for lack of a better word, is being transformed. So are you."

"Transformed? Into what?"

"More like into whom? We don't know for sure, but we believe they're humanoid in nature. Quite probably bona fide human beings."

Carl's jaw dropped. "You believe—humanoid in nature—just what are you talking about?"

Micals steered the conversation in a different direction. "Do you remember the little girl at the house in Illinois?"

"Sure. The one that Mary keeps seeing in her dreams."

"Well, for all but a very few, she doesn't exist. She's an illusion."

"We both saw her. And the house was transformed."

"Yes, transformed, but only in your mind," Micals emphasized. "The shared illusion was the first indication the transformation was in its initial stages. Eventually that illusion will take solid form."

Carl shook his head. "Impossible."

"Did you know that there is a natural drug derived from a type of fungi that elicits the exact same hallucination in every person who is injected with it?"

"No, but then mushroom toxins are not my specialty. What illusion?"

"Everyone, I mean *everyone*, sees eight little elf-like creatures dancing in a circle around a dark pit."

"You're saying Mary and I were drugged?"

"In a way."

"The water," Carl realized. "Denech offered us water and we both drank some."

"Denech said Mary drank quite a bit. You drank only a few sips. But the effect will be the same."

"So in a while I'll be laying there with Mary being transformed into an alien?"

"Yes, transformed. But no, not an alien. We're fairly confident of that."

"That's a relief. You're *fairly* confident. Well, I'm *fairly* confident you're all crazy. What other possibility is there?"

"You're upset. I understand that. When we get back to the lab, I'll show you the proof, or at least what we believe is proof. You have to realize we've given you and Mary a shot at life, and maybe a lot more.

And no, it isn't a totally unselfish thing we've done, because if you survive, you'll be giving the rest of us a shot at life as well."

"We're guinea pigs," Carl realized. "Or maybe rats in a lab experiment."

Micals nodded slightly. "At this point, Carl, we all are."

* * * *

With Mary apparently stable, Carl decided to adopt a wait and see approach. They had entered the fast and heavy flow of traffic on Interstate 35E, proceeded through downtown St. Paul, and continued north of the metropolitan area. For some reason, Carl knew their destination would not be in the metro area, and then it dawned on him that both the light and air pollution of a major city made for poor sky gazing. Professor Micals was, after all, an astronomer. They had continued north on the Interstate for several miles and then turned west at the North Branch exit, eventually winding their way through a forested area on a rural road and up a gradual incline. At the rounded and treeless hilltop, a single story rambler style home welcomed them with an open garage door. Red backed into the meticulously clean space, and the door automatically closed. Carl watched as Red and Micals removed Mary on the medical gurney, with the diagnostic equipment, and within minutes she appeared to be resting comfortably in what Micals said was the guest bedroom. The monitors continued to indicate all was well, though Carl began to wonder about food and water, not for himself but for Mary. He wondered if the next thing that he'd see would be an IV cart and a bag of saline solution, and within seconds of the thought, Micals came in pushing one. The professor noted Carl's concern. "Just in case we need it," he assured him. "Her vitals will tell the story."

"She won't," Carl said, and then wondered why he was so sure.

"Red will stay with your Mary in case there is any change. Come with me to the lab, and maybe some of this will begin to make sense."

* * * *

Carl Walker followed Professor Edward Micals through the main portion of his austere home and then into attached quarters that Micals called his laboratory. In contrast to the spotless garage, the room could only be termed a mess. There was a modest telescope of the amateur variety pointed out the east-facing windows. Several brown padded folding chairs leaned up against a long metal table along one wall, and one was tucked under a desk with a laptop computer and an antique TV/VCR combo sitting on top. Micals went directly to a haphazard pile of tapes, selected one, and inserted it into the machine.

"This is a copy of the video we took of what we have come to call Object Tranquility. It is the only copy. The original recordings and all of the original documentation have been destroyed. We use the old technology because—"

"It cannot be intercepted or traced," Carl finished. "Denech called his operation Tranquility."

"Not a coincidence. It all began with this space object. Without knowing the related vectors, this won't tell you much, but you will at least see that there is something out there. That we haven't made it up."

Micals pressed the 'play' button and within seconds a flash of light emanated from a screen that appeared to be a black sheet of paper with holes punched in it. Behind the paper a bright light shone and the holes became pinpoints of light. Carl knew the black sheet was really the blackness of space and the pin points of light were background stars.

Micals pointed to one of the brighter points of light. "Keep your eye on this one right here." Carl watched and very slowly the light moved, and grew faintly brighter. There appeared to be a secondary flash, and then slowly the light grew dim, until it finally disappeared altogether. The entire sequence lasted no more than a few minutes.

"Not much," Micals conceded. "Understand that the object didn't fade from view because it moved beyond our range. It faded from view because it turned its back on us, and the back reflected no light. But since then it's given us a peek now and then, so we can get a handle on its orbital dynamics."

"Size?" Carl asked.

"We estimate fifteen to twenty miles in diameter."

"Closest approach?"

"Within a thousand miles."

"Denech said it is now in a capture orbit."

"Yes."

"And is due back in a year."

"Yes."

"And will strike somewhere in the Atlantic off the South American coast."

"Unfortunately, yes."

"Another mass extinction," Carl said.

"We calculate no living organism on earth larger than a bacterium will survive the impact. It will have more destructive power than all the nuclear bombs on earth going off at the same time and the same place."

"Composition?"

"We believe it to be a dark composite made up of mostly compressed carbon with some other trace minerals, and with possibly an iron-nickel core."

"So, not a dead comet."

"No, for a couple reasons. One, it appeared to come out of nowhere, which implies it may be a pristine object from outside the orbit of Jupiter."

Carl nodded. "But a first time comet would still have all the volatiles, the frozen gases, and would be bright and shiny, not dark. It also would have announced its presence long before it ever reached here. And reason number two?"

"Based on the analysis of a piece of it we found in Montana, at least some of it didn't come from outer space at all."

"I'm confused," Carl admitted. "Where else could it have come from?"

"From Earth."

"How is that possible?"

Professor Edward Micals grew pensive. "That is what we're hoping you, or your wife, will tell us,"

"You're the professor, and have been at this for years. I don't even have enough credits to have a degree in astronomy. That tells me you're barking up the wrong tree."

"Possibly, but—"

"Sorry to interrupt my elder, but I have a couple more questions, or maybe concerns would be a better way to put it."

"Yes?"

"You're trying to tell me you just happened to be out stargazing one night and just happened to look up and see this doomsday asteroid and then just happened to destroy all the evidence but this video and you did it all essentially on your own and with no witnesses or colleagues or graduate assistants. Just you and the telescope and a camera and an asteroid."

"You find that unlikely?"

"I find that impossible. And even now you say you've been tracking it. How? Through a set of Boy Scout binoculars on your back porch? Even I know that at the object's current distance and low reflectivity it would take something like Palomar or Keck to even find it. And those machines don't run on their own."

"I have my own telescope," Micals said, and gestured toward the observation piece.

Carl almost laughed. "That? The way you have that thing pointed it could be focused in on your neighbor lady's bedroom window."

"You're very observant," Micals said.

"I'm just tired of being jerked around."

Micals reflected. "Perhaps you were not the right pick for this endeavor after all. This is a side of you that did not register on your personality profile."

"Maybe that's because I wasn't mad as hell back then. Maybe that's because my wife wasn't in a coma back then. Maybe that's because I hadn't gotten suckered into believing someone would actually pay the two of us a couple hundred thousand dollars for doing nothing."

"I had hoped you'd be reasonable."

"Reasonable? If I'd been reasonable, I would have taken my wife and gone skydiving or bungee jumping or maybe hunting rattlesnakes with our bare hands. That would have been reasonable. This is idiotic."

"Anything else that bothers you?'

"Look, you know and I know there is no way in hell you could have kept something this big under wraps. There are too many people, amateurs and professionals, trying to find NEOs to get their names on a piece of space rock for all eternity. What you've managed to convince me of is that this video is probably a hoax, a fake, pure and simple, and that whatever the truth is, if there even is a truth, it's something you've decided to withhold from me. And so the charade goes on."

"Okay. You're right. I have been less than forthcoming. How did you know? A variation of this video was good enough to fool a good many astronomers."

"It wasn't the recording."

"What was it then?"

"It was you. The moment you picked up that recording, your color changed."

"My color? What color?"

"The one that tells me you weren't telling me the truth. You are a poor liar, Professor Micals. I suggest you stick to the truth, because that is what you do best."

"Part of the recording is 'enhanced' as they say, but part is genuine. We had to do that to mask the true facts. To convince the scientific community that this thing was never coming back."

"Maybe, but you've omitted critical information. Lying by omission. And just who is 'we'? Others had to have been part of the discovery."

"Yes, there were a few others, as you suspected."

"What happened to them?"

"Peter and I convinced them to accept a rather large bonus and live happily ever after on an island in the South Pacific. The University has telescope time on a couple different refractors, and they don't monitor my activities. There are logs, of course, but my entries are somewhat less than accurate. That's how I keep tabs on the object."

"I see. So you bought the others off."

"They saw it more like early retirement. Plus, they knew full well the gravity of the situation. They're professionals—"

"Who no doubt have a fondness for girls in grass skirts."

"No doubt, but if Tranquility doesn't succeed, what possible difference can it make?"

"You tell me."

"I really—"

"Now, if you're done, I think I'd like to go lay with my wife."

"Yes. Of course. I'll consider what you've said and—"

Professor Edward Micals was at a loss for words. By all appearances Carl could have been just another green graduate student with little experience or insight. Instead Carl had turned the tables, and made the professor the student. He underestimated the young man, and he wondered now if it was pure Carl Walker or if it was part of the transformation process. Whatever the reason, he'd have to change his approach. It was clear Carl was perceptive enough to detect deception. He'd have to choose his words carefully now and attempt to repair the damage he'd done.

* * * *

Carl returned to the bedroom where Mary lay sleeping. Without removing his shoes, he lay down beside her. He slid one arm under her pillow and placed the other over her breast, drawing her close. With his head resting against her's, he breathed in and out a great deep breath and immediately fell into a deep slumber. Red watched from a distance and then closed the bedroom door and let them sleep.

* * * *

When they were standing alone together in the hallway, Rowanna Doran gave in to her curiosity. "How did it go?"

Edward Micals shook his head. "Not well, I'm afraid. Carl caught me off guard, and I rather blew it."

"Off guard?"

Micals chuckled in spite of the situation. "He turned my usual tactics back at me. Very perceptive young man."

"So damage control?"

"There'll be another chance. I'll be ready next time."

"And the transformation process? For my own information, I'd like to know just what will eventually come out of that room. Will Carl still be, you know, a man?"

"Tranquility does not specify what the end result will be."

"How about the nanites?"

"Gone now, all dead."

"You're still walking, and driving up through St. Paul everyone still looked normal to me."

"Peter never told you what to expect, did he?"

"No. I really didn't want to know," Red admitted.

"I sometimes wish I didn't."

Chapter 20

There was very little chance that what Peter Denech was about to do would normally make any difference in the long term, but then, given the current situation, long term was purely a matter of individual circumstance. For those people carrying on with their lives in complete ignorance of anything other than what was for supper, or the latest baseball scores, or which Hollywood actress committed the most outrageous act on national television, it probably was best that they remained in a state of ignorance. The vast majority of people lived only along the surface of life, never daring or even wanting to look any deeper than their comfortable illusions. Looking deeper was reserved for those few who possessed the genetics that drove them to lay awake at night, their minds racing in a thousand directions, wondering: Why this? Or what would happen if? Or why is there anything at all? Or thousands of other philosophical questions about existence and morality and intellect and why? Those who thought the deeper thoughts were often the most uncertain about such things as 'truth' or 'justice' or 'knowledge' or 'reality'. Their thoughts took them far a-field into actions and reactions well beyond the here and now. Rest was often a conscious decision that said, "All you little voices. Go to sleep now." Madness, maybe, but also creativity and genius. And often the line between them was paper thin.

Those who bought into the accepted dogma, whether religious, political, cultural, or economic, became ever more rigid and unyielding. They chose up sides each hiding within their own invented version of God, each declaring the sanctity of their own set of truths, each vilifying all others who thought differently. And the inevitable outcome, of course, came together in a place called the Holy Battlefield, where the men-children, the pawns, were ripped apart by the armaments of the collective ignorance. Nature had made a mistake, Denech thought, giving rise to an organism with no natural enemies, and so, to be fair about it, it turned man upon himself.

Such a strange word was 'war', Denech thought. Only three letters, a single syllable, and yet representing the deaths of millions upon millions of human beings, a mass suicide, an unholy testament to the base nature of man, of the undeniable proof that man was ninety-nine percent savage and one percent intellect. No wonder intellect was doomed to be forever left rotting in a ditch alongside the war road, as mindless automatons marched on by.

It wasn't that people didn't know better. The problem was that people always looked for the *other* person to change, the *other* person to make the sacrifice, the *other* person to take the first step. And with everyone expecting the *other* person to carry the burden, or to be 'enlightened', or to accept conversion, no one did.

The intricate set of natural tendencies called Nature carried one overriding mandate to all the diverse children: Adapt or die. The tragedy was that human beings were the only creatures ever to figure out that bedrock principle, and yet never fully realize that it applied to themselves as well.

Peter Denech had stumbled upon a way, perhaps the only way, to give all of humanity a chance to stop and take its breath along what he considered to be the mad race for the cliff's edge. He believed that the intractable philosophies of religion, politics, and economics would never sit down at the same table and reach a peaceful, let alone sane, conclusion. Each was locked into their own 'truths', and for those who have truth firmly locked up, it is never a debatable proposition. The only way to deflect the inevitable spears and the arrows was to provide a greater or more obvious truth, a circumstance or set of conditions more immediate and compelling, a circumstance or set of conditions that gave them pause to ponder and even reconcile.

Peter Denech decided long before that humanity required something like the electrical jolts sometimes used to re-set a dysfunctional brain; massive shock therapy to reset everyone to a natural and uniform default position, something that everyone—no matter where on earth they lived—could clearly identify with. Project Tranquility was just such a jolt. It came literally out of the blue one day several years before, like a prayer answered, if he believed in such things. And from that improbable sequence of events together with the right comrades and with the right technology and at the right time in human history, there was again a glimmer of hope. And though he didn't believe in much of anything, he did believe in hope. Or more correctly, he had faith in hope. It drove him out of bed each morning, like hunger for the first meal of the day, and it carried him off to sleep at night.

But the jolt to humanity would not be so easily accomplished as an electric impulse sent surging through a malfunctioning brain. The Tranquility program confirmed it would have to be broken down into three complicated parts, which he began to call Plans A, B, and C. For optimum success all three would have to work. Plans A and B could fail and there might still be hope, but Plan C, Carl and Mary Walker, was critical. If they failed, it was, as his father used to say, all over but the crying. Randolf Haays had added Plan F, which, as far as Denech was concerned, amounted to total failure. It would be the same as resetting the evolutionary clock back hundreds of millions of years when bacteria were the dominant life forms on earth.

And so Peter Denech's thoughts came back to Carl and Mary. He'd left them with his close friend and confidant, Professor Edward Micals, to oversee and to monitor their part in his three-prong plan. The Tranquility Program provided a framework but with no specific timeline, and only a vague and hazy inference like one might say "when spring comes", or "in that day". When he put it all together and considered all the possible things that could go wrong, it was easy to visualize hope sliding away and Plan F succeeding. His biggest concern, however, was the entity called Wolf. If Mary and Carl successfully emerged from the transformation process only to be eliminated by Blacmann or the Director before they could complete their part in Tranquility, all the rest would be meaningless. His game plan, therefore, switched from defensive to offensive. He would no longer be the rabbit. He would now be the fox, and do what the Director would least expect: Turn himself in. The ancient saying came back to him: "Keep your friends close, but keep your enemies very, very close."

The first order of business was the removal of Randolf and Amanda. They'd stopped at a wayside rest area along the interstate and walked to a secluded picnic table well away from the prying eyes of onlookers, and while Amanda was in the rest room, he'd shot Randolf Haays just as Haays was in the process of sitting down. When Amanda returned, she noted only that Randolf was resting his head on the picnic table, but one look in Peter's eyes told her what he'd done. She stood rooted in place, staring at the weapon she most feared, and shook her head and cried out in despair even as Denech pulled the trigger.

Now, Peter Denech noted the tears on Amanda's cheeks, as he sat her next to Randolf on the bench seat. He could not tell her that he loved her, too, and that is why he did what he did. Both his friends would sleep soundly now, and when they woke up, they'd be able to start a new life somewhere for however much time was left. Their part in Tranquility was over, but his part would now carry him into the very heart of an establishment so cold and mechanical as to be mere gears that meshed in a certain order and pattern, never varying, never compromising, just unbending steel grinding steel. But if he were fortunate, he might be able to disrupt those gears long enough to buy some time, even if the price was his own life. A pilot friend who narrowly escaped a fatal crash once told him, "Never trade even a little good luck for skill." Denech smiled. So far luck had been his friend.

*　　*　　*　　*

Since Red had left Carl and Mary alone in the bedroom, four hours had passed and it was now coming up on six o'clock. However, at that northern latitude and that time of the year, there were still four hours of daylight left. Red stood outside the back door of the Micals' home and breathed in the sweet smell of drying hay. Down below in the shallow valley, she could see a farmer on a red tractor pulling a machine that rolled up the long light green windrows into large round bales. Off to the west, a dark cloud loomed and a long narrow streak of jagged light reached all the way to the ground. As the distant thunder reached her ears, she wondered if the farmer was aware of the approaching thunderstorm.

How convenient it would be, she decided, if one could be warned ahead of time for all the storms that come into one's life. Or even if one could choose, before birth, this life or that life, depending upon which had the most favorable outcome. Of course, some people believed that the essence of one's being, soul for lack of a better word, did return again and again, each time trying to improve upon a past, and likely poor, performance. Her own life had started out bad and for the most part gone down hill from there. If not for Peter Denech, she would have died somewhere on the streets of New York, or maybe Boston, or LA. With a flip of her red hair, she forced the memories aside, and her thoughts turned to Carl and Mary. But mostly Carl.

Red remembered hearing how very rarely there come together by chance two people who mesh together completely, fulfill each other, understand each other, support each other, love each other. For such 'soul mates', as they were called, there developed an unspoken language, more subliminal than verbal, more existential than corporeal. It was all so much B.S. to her and with a capitol B—a fairytale, mere delusions of an overactive romantic writer's imagination. In the real world, things like that just didn't happen. People were flawed and in a relationship it was the flaws that were the cracks that eventually broke and split and disintegrated what was once whole. But now she wasn't so sure. Every time her eyes met Carl's something that could only be described as a thrill passed between them. She knew they *belonged* together. She also knew that it would never happen. Her job was to protect both Mary and Carl in the coming turbulent times. Mary had shared dark premonitions, but she had kept hers to herself. They were not dark. They were filled with warmth and love and laughter, and she knew they were a protective illusion she had constructed long before when, as a child, her mother—in fits of alcohol induced anger—would strike her with the back of her hand, or whatever was handy. Eventually, she learned to escape into her fantasy so completely as to not even feel the pain. This pain was different, however. It was the pain of loving someone who could not love you back, and she dared not leave her fantasy for fear of doing or saying something that would place Plan C at risk. She owed Peter Denech at least that much.

Rowanna Doran's thoughts came back to the farmer on the red tractor, and she wondered if there was a way to warn him of the approaching storm. Maybe he had Weather Alert inside the tractor cab and was already aware of it, and now raced as fast as he dared to get his hay crop into the protection of the round bales, which would shed the moisture. No doubt such things were of utmost importance to him, but were insignificant in the larger scheme of things. Or were they? Or were the actions of one reflected in the entirety of all? She shook her head to clear her mind. Such thoughts were best left to poets and philosophers. Her eyes strayed to a dirt road that paralleled the hayfield, and she noted two people in the distance walking hand in hand for a leisurely evening stroll. She could see the woman had long black hair, and the man—the man was Carl Walker.

* * * *

Without waiting to tell Edward Micals where she was headed, Rowanna Doran raced down the embankment, then wove around the trunks of oak, finally reaching the dusty access trail to the farmer's field. She'd noted from above that the trail entered the woods again on the far side, and then circled around behind. The quickest way to intercept the couple was straight across the field, a path that would take her directly past the farmer. Without hesitation, she raced for the other side, perhaps a quarter of a mile away, but as she passed the farmer, he stopped and gazed out at her. The confused look on his face indicted he didn't know the reason for her appearance, but as Red raced by she yelled out above the roar of the tractor, "Storm coming!" and pointed to the west. He straightened and follower her finger. He nodded, and mouthed a reply, "Thanks." Red continued on past, and the farmer continued with greater urgency. Were the actions of one reflected in all? Red thought again. It would seem so.

* * * *

A much-fatigued redhead gasping for air and holding her side that racked in pain stumbled from the forest into the path of Carl and Mary, and collapsed onto the dirt. Both briefly looked surprised, but their expressions quickly changed to that of concern.

"Are you okay?" Mary asked as they helped Red to her feet.

"In a minute," she gasped. "Give me a minute to catch my breath." Bent over with hands on her knees, Red slowly recovered, and then, when she was breathing almost normally, asked the obvious.

"Just where do you two think you're going?"

"Not sure yet," Carl said, "but we're thinking of maybe Uncle's cabin."

"And you were going to walk all the way to Northern Minnesota?"

"Not to worry. Something will come up."

"Well, you can't just leave. Not now," Red insisted.

Carl and Mary exchanged glances. "Why not?" Carl asked.

"Because you're too important. Because—"

"To whom?" Mary asked.

"To me, to Peter, to everyone."

"I don't think so," Carl stated. "Look at us. Whatever the transformation process was supposed to do, it didn't work."

"What do you mean it didn't work?"

"Mary woke up feeling fine. No change, and the strange dreams are not so unsettling. I didn't grow antennae or turn green. We don't have any super powers to fly off and battle evil and corruption or blast the asteroid out of the sky. We're the same. Sorry."

"It can't be," Red exclaimed. "*Something* must have happened."

"Other than waking up hungry and thirsty, I feel no different than I always have."

"We're of no use to the organization," Mary added. "Right now we're a liability. A target. Anyone associated with us is in danger, and that includes you."

"So, I'm supposed to let you both just walk away? I can't do that. I made a promise to Peter. I can't go back on my word."

"I guess you could use your peashooter on us and drag us back," Carl said, only half joking. "But unless you then intend to keep us locked up or in chains, we'll simply walk away again."

"What about Blacmann? What about the fact that there's a couple ITPs with your names on them?"

Carl grinned. "Then if I were you, I wouldn't get too close."

"Okay. if you won't come back, I'm going with you."

"I don't know—"

Red looked directly at Mary. "I promise to remain outside of your—your relationship. You won't even know I'm around."

Carl laughed, and extended his hand, which Red accepted. "Now *that* I don't believe. And what fun would you be anyway. Come on. The three of us. We're off to see the wizard."

"What about Professor Micals? Shouldn't we tell him where we're going?"

Carl shrugged, and grew serious. "Not really. I'm not sure he can be trusted anyway."

* * * *

Rowanna Doran had advised against it, but Carl declared he didn't intend to walk the next two hundred miles to his uncle's cabin. The credit card Peter Denech had given him worked well enough to rent a used off-white pickup in North Branch. Red noted he seemed unconcerned about wandering around in public view, and in the end she had to herd him into the relative protection of the pickup cab. Carl drove, Mary sat in the middle, and Red sat on the passenger side. She had a pretty good idea of where they were headed, north, and as they got underway back on Interstate 35, the interior of the cab grew comfortably warm. She hadn't had a good night's sleep in days, and her eyelids seemed to have lead weights pulling them down. She rested her head against the window, but jerked awake when another thought registered.

"If I happened to fall asleep, I wouldn't wake up along the road somewhere, would I?"

Carl looked at Mary and a smile passed between them. "Hadn't even thought of it," Carl stated. "But now that you brought that option to my attention—"

"No," Mary interjected. "We wouldn't. You have a part in this. A very important part, so you'll remain under our protection."

"Your protection? I hate to break it to you girl, but I'm the one with the peashooter."

"Of course."

"So where are we going, anyway?"

"Near a town called Orr. It'll be dark when we get there. Might as well catch a few winks." Carl looked over at Red and grinned. "I won't ever dump you. Promise."

For a moment Red wondered if the comment had more than one meaning, and looked back at Carl. Their eyes met, but it was impossible to tell what he was thinking. He smiled wider, and she knew her own eyes were more revealing. Then she lay her head against the window, closed her eyes, and rested.

Chapter 21

Just how she got there she didn't know but the first thing that broke through Rowanna Doran's slumber was the smell of brewing coffee. She opened her eyes, noting she lay on a sleeping bag before a rustic field stone fireplace. Immediately, she checked for the weapon, which was still secure under her left arm. Rough dark brown logs indicated the cabin's construction. Through a large window next to the fireplace she could see the fiercely bright rays of the morning sun shining around evergreen branches.

Red rose and knew immediately she was in the home of a bachelor. It was clean, but lacked the appearance of organization, and there were no curtains on the windows. No unnecessary frills. Just the Spartan necessities. The rustic room in which she had slept was the basic living space for everything: Kitchen, living room, dining room, all rolled into one. Fastened to the wall by the exterior door, an old style blackboard four feet square had a few grocery items written in white chalk, and a drawing of a structure or contrivance, the object of which eluded her. Two interior doors led, she suspected, to a bedroom and bathroom, and an open stairway, built of logs cut in half, led to an open loft above. Moving closer to the window, she looked out upon a rock-filled stream within a stone's throw from the log cabin. Green cedar, spruce, and balsam trees grew along the water's edge, forming a partial canopy over it. Like giant living columns holding up the sky, several great white pine trees, over two feet in diameter, occupied the space between.

"Uncle calls it the Holy River," Carl said, coming up behind her and placing his hand on her shoulder.

"Very beautiful," she acknowledged but her eyes remained steadfastly ahead. All she could feel was the warmth of his hand through her thin blouse. She moved away a safe distance and then turned to face him.

"Where's Mary? And your uncle?'

"Mary's still sleeping, and Uncle Raul went down to the stream to catch breakfast. It's just you and me kid."

Mary maneuvered around behind a round hardwood table, and in front of the old schoolhouse blackboard. "So where are I, I mean we?"

"About ten miles east of Orr. Very few permanent residents. Some summer cabins scattered around. Tens of thousands of acres of forested land with scattered lakes and streams. Holy country, Uncle calls it. Pull up a chair. I'll get the coffee."

When two cups of steaming coffee were set on the table and each occupied an opposite side, Red drew her mind away from personal thoughts.

"We have to do something about the rental. It has the mileage chip. If the people back at the car lot should recognize you—"

"They didn't."

"How do you know?"

"I just do."

"But eventually, when you don't bring it back, they'll come looking for it. They'll plug into the satellite system, and bring the authorities right here."

"It wouldn't be here. Uncle Raul will return it eventually. Not to worry. We'll 'modify' it to make it invisible to electronic eyes. When the time comes, we'll use his vehicle, and it's a safe vehicle."

"And right now your Uncle Raul is catching a fish for breakfast?"

"Something like that. He has his own private stock."

"Like a fish farm?"

"No. More like a fish trap. Somewhat more reliable than a hook and line."

"Is that legal?"

"It can be, depending upon what fish you catch. However, Uncle Raul is not that particular."

"You once said that neither you nor Mary have any family. How is it, then, you have an Uncle?"

"It's an honorary title, and the honor is mine." Red jumped. The deep voice came from directly behind her, and she quickly turned to see a lone figure standing in the morning shadows. Farmer-style blue bib overalls and a blue plaid shirt covered a stout and muscular body. Black hair streaked with a very few strands of silver grey ran through a beard that reached from his face to just below his neck. The similarly colored hair of his head, tied together behind, reached past his shoulders. In his hand he held a skillet with four large fish filets. He wiped his right hand on his pant leg and extended it towards Red. "How do, ma'am. Name's Raul Beck but folks around here just call me Mako."

"Hello. I'm Rowanna Doran." Red returned the handshake greeting, and felt the powerful grip of a heavily callused hand. She instantly realized this man could have squeezed her fingers to mush if he was so inclined. "But most folks call me Red."

Mary slipped down the stairs from the loft and came up quietly behind Raul Beck, taking custody of the skillet of fish. "You three talk. I'll cook," she directed.

Uncle Raul turned a chair backwards and sat down, reminiscent, Carl noted, of how Peter Denech liked to sit.

"So you and Carl are not related," Red continued.

"Well, we share a common father I suppose," he said, "But you'd have to go back twenty or thirty thousand years. I don't think that counts."

"And people around here call you Mako?"

"Yeah, there's a story behind that."

"Just how old are you anyway?"

"I turned forty this year. I guess that means I'm no longer a kid."

Red was curious. "If you don't mind my asking, how long have you been alone here?" Carl frowned and shook his head slightly, an unspoken message, Red realized, of don't go there. "I didn't mean—" she quickly added.

"Don't mind Carl. He's always lookin' out for my feelings. I don't run from my feelings. Never run from your feelings. Without feelings we're no different than a hollow log. Truth is I only loved two women in my whole life. The woods and my Rose. Up until five years ago, we lived in Minneapolis because she was a city girl and that made her happy."

Noting the past tense of Raul's statement, Red knew what was coming and regretted ever bringing it up. He smiled through tears, but plowed ahead.

"She died, you know. But I was lucky 'cause I had this other love. Nature, some call her. I had someone else to go to. And I've been with her ever since."

"Look, I'm so sorry. I have a big mouth sometimes."

The man brushed the tears away that had fallen into his black whiskers. "My wife had hair just like yours, you know. Bright red as the rose, it was. And sometimes yet I see her face when the sun goes down just right and the western sky lights up in a blazing ball of flame and orange. She just looks back at me and I can hear her voice telling me, 'I'm still here, looking after you.'"

Long moments followed, and an emotional lump welled up in Red's throat. How extraordinary it must be to have that kind of devotion to someone. But it was also tragic because without her this man had reverted to a mere hermit living out his years alone and isolated from the rest of his kind.

As much to change the direction of the conversation as her real concern, Red turned her attention back to Carl. "We shouldn't be here,

Carl. We're putting this man at risk. It's a foregone conclusion that Wolf knows about Mr. Beck. His cabin will be one of the first places they'll check in their search for you."

Uncle Raul Beck smiled. "Not likely. You see I'm also dead."

* * * *

The confused expression on Red's face caused Raul Beck to continue. He smiled, but because of the whiskers the only way one could tell was the pure white teeth that suddenly emerged from behind the dense growth. "Well, I'm only dead. Not dead, dead."

"There's a difference?" Red asked. "Isn't being a little bit dead something like being a little bit pregnant?"

"As far as the world knows, the man I used to be died five years ago." He glanced at Carl. "That was right about the time Carl and I got acquainted."

"You changed your identity," Red assumed. "Raul Beck is not your real name."

"It is now. In modern slang, I'm off-line, or off the grid. No electricity. No electronics. Mainly wood for cooking and heating. Hand pumped water from a well in the bathroom and kitchen. About the only thing I have that comes close to modern is the old jalopy, and the clothes on my back."

"Even so, you must pay taxes. The government must have a file on you."

"There is no file, and my taxes do get paid."

"How?"

"Same as how I buy a few groceries now and again. From an anonymous trust fund. A blind trust, we call it. Blind to the government, that is."

Carl excused himself, left the two alone, and went to help Mary finish preparing breakfast. Red was fascinated with her host and continued.

"You invented your new name. It sounds mysterious."

Again Beck laughed, a loud, honest laugh that verified his belief in giving his emotions a free rein.

"No, not mysterious. And I did have a choice. One of the elders from the local Ojibway tribe named me Mako Missaube."

"The name has some meaning, I take it."

"In the Ojibway language, Mako means bear, and Missaube means something like a big stout man. So a big stout bear-man."

"It fits."

"The old Indians had a thing about names. They're supposed to fit."

"But you didn't take him up on it."

"I declined his offer but he still stops in once in awhile and still calls me Mako. Found out later that when I first started building here five years ago, the elder had a different name for me. Roughly translated into English it meant 'Crazy-As-A-Loon Man.' So I guess Mako Missaube was an improvement."

Red laughed. "Raul Beck is probably more in line with convention. Not likely to draw too much attention. I won't ask what your name was before."

"Thanks, because I wouldn't tell you in any case. Even Carl and Mary don't know. Best that way."

Red nodded, and wondered just what this man had done for a living before he decided to give it all up for a life of solitude. She glanced at the old schoolhouse blackboard. A teacher, maybe. She knew that she couldn't make the same sacrifice. People often rubbed her the wrong way—they could be arrogant and stupid and petty and cruel—but she still needed the connection. To sever all bonds was an act of extraordinary courage, or extraordinary desperation. Looking at Raul, she wondered if maybe it was a little of both.

Carl and Mary appeared with the morning meal. Fresh pike, coffee, and hot cornbread muffins. Red could not remember when anything had ever tasted so good.

"You said that an elder from the local Ojibway tribe visits from time to time," Red continued through bites of fresh fish. "Is he apt to come back anytime soon? I mean while we're here?"

"Not this summer. He's gone to Wisconsin for a time of spiritual healing, he called it."

"Spiritual healing?"

"A few years ago on a Wisconsin farm a white buffalo was born."

"And?"

Raul Beck continued. "It's a Native prophecy. Native Americans call this present time, The-Time-Of-The-White-Buffalo. To them a white buffalo is a sacred animal. The odds of a white buffalo calf being born are about six hundred million to one, so it is a rarity. They believe it is an omen."

"An omen of what?" Red asked.

"Of change. Of a time of the return of the White Buffalo Woman. Someone that might bring back spiritual balance to human kind."

"This is going to happen when?"

Raul Beck laughed, but then grew serious. "Don't hold your breath. Not to disparage their beliefs, but people have been looking for a savior since day one, hoping there are better times ahead. Hoping someone will do for them what they should be doing for themselves."

"A little optimism can't hurt."

"I was there once. Then they took my Rose from me. If believing that makes you all fluffy and warm, I guess it can't hurt, but it's a ship that don't ever come in."

Red considered. "So what does this Indian prophecy predict?"

"The legend says that the first time the White Buffalo Woman appeared to the Indian people, she brought the knowing of things and guidance on how to live. She taught them how to survive."

"And this time?"

"Isn't it obvious?" Carl said entering the conversation. "The same thing."

Chapter 22

▼

Weeks passed. On the bright sunny summer days when the native biting insects lightened up a bit, Carl and Mary took to hiking forest trails. One day soon after they arrived, they hiked all the way to Orr, bought some needed clothes in the general store for themselves and Red, and then hiked the ten miles back. There was wild fruit in abundance. First wild strawberries and June berries. Then later in the season blueberries and raspberries. With fish from the stream and a few staples from the grocery in Orr to add a bit of diversity to their diet, they ate simply but well. Raul Beck puttered about in his shop working on hand carved wildlife, mostly replicas of wood ducks and blue birds. Red worked at physical training in an almost obsessive fashion. She didn't exactly avoid Carl, but kept a respectful and safe distance. She found a strenuous workout helped keep her mind off of other things. Though she'd never admit it, she was bored almost to tears. Not that the country wasn't beautiful but after you've seen one tree, or the same group of trees, over and over again they just didn't do it anymore. Daily, sometimes alone and sometimes with Carl or Mary or both, she hiked the mile out to the mailbox to pick up an occasional newspaper, though on many days the box was empty. There was never any junk mail or personal correspondence, and that seemed to verify Beck's statement that he was 'dead' to the rest of the world. When NEWS 24/

7 arrived twice weekly, they'd come together after dinner with its pages spread out on the round oak table, reading and re-reading every word, even the advertisements. Carl explained to Uncle Raul something of their past ordeal, what little he knew for sure about the possible nanite infection, and his, as well as Mary's, strange dreams. The older man listened intently, but offered little comment other than to say that if it was even partly true, something serious was about to come down. Carl did not, however, mention the approaching asteroid. He remembered Peter Denech's comment. Most people would just not want to know.

But other than the usual suicide bombings, economic woes, and celebrity drivel, there was nothing to indicate that anything unusually dramatic was in the works. The 'Personals' section was filled with things like "Hot lover seeks hot body," or "Are you my soul mate?" and nothing that could be interpreted as a message from Peter Denech or anyone else in the organization. Carl and Mary were in the dark, but there was little they could do. Carl remembered Peter's words: Things will start to unravel. Maybe in a couple weeks. Maybe in a couple months. It had now been a little over two months. The time was at hand.

Chapter 23

Peter Denech knew it would be as easy as a phone call, and that was his intent. The question was: When? And to whom? Timing was critical. Act too soon, and his value would not yet have been proven. Act too late, and his efforts might have collapsed humanity into something unsalvageable, and the Agency might put him on public trial out of pure spite. Yet it was doubtful a trial would happen at all. First, there would be no direct proof, only circumstantial evidence unless someone from the organization turned against him. There were only a handful in the U.S. who knew enough to testify, and those scattered facilities around the world had most likely disbanded, the members assimilating into the general populations. The Director, however, with or without solid proof, would know of his connection and so the outcome might well be cement shoes and a date with the bottom of Lake Superior. At well over a thousand feet deep, it would provide the perfect disposal location. On the other hand, he could stall with tidbits of information until such time as a strike on the Hub might do the most damage. The question was: How? An explosion in a sensitive area would create the most havoc, but walking through the main door with a box of explosives under each arm would not get past anyone. Still, there was a way. Sometimes it takes just one simple act to disrupt an entire army.

Since leaving Amanda and Randolf, Peter Denech kept to the backwaters of society with the homeless in Chicago for a time. In the eyes of civilized folks, the homeless were non-people, faceless and nameless. The arrogant well-to-do stepped over them like soiled rags, and the bleeding hearts heaped pity on them but the end result was the same: Nothing. They came from all parts of society. Alcoholics and druggies, bankrupt businessmen and prostitutes, war torn veterans and the insane. And many were multiple combinations thereof. They lived like the scavengers and animals the good people thought them to be. No one really ever looked at them. For Denech they represented a safe haven, because as one of them he became faceless and nameless.

But as the summer marched on, the blistering heat drove him north to Milwaukee, then west to Minneapolis, and finally north again to Duluth. His beard was full now, and the stocking cap rarely left his head, always pulled down to just above his eyebrows. He kept his head shaved for those times when his cap was removed, accidentally or on purpose, and he adopted different names as his location changed.

It was now nearing September—over two months since the nanite release—and still there was nothing in the papers to indicate that Plan A had succeeded. He thought about attempting a direct communication with Ed Micals, but decided against it. Their alternate means of communication, the personals section in the weekly printed edition of NEWS 24/7, had been silent. Something would have to develop soon, or he'd have to accept that Randolf's perennial favorite, Plan F, was now in full swing. There was another way to find out, however: Go to the press. Announce to the world what the organization had done. There would be immediate testing, and then, one way or the other, he'd know. No government cover-up could contain that information. The question now was who to contact? The national media had de-evolved into little more than the propaganda arm of the federal government. Nothing made the news until it had gone through what was called the corporate "filter." It amounted to a very simple formula: If a news story was likely to turn listeners off, it was 'creatively sculptured', sanitized and edited to make it palatable to the viewership, or simply ignored altogether. The few independent or public news outlets made a great show of courageous journalism, but skirted the controversial topics for fear of losing government funding.

But it was hard to keep a good man down. And there were several good men and women who pirated time on the Net with altered log-ins and identities. Getting on was actually the easy part. Avoiding the Agency was the hard part. But still, where there's a will there's a way, and so an underground and worldwide audience got the truth through what came to be called the Shadow Net. Denech suspected, however, that the Agency had infiltrated that group as well, slowly and methodically getting names and locations, until one day there would be a series of unfortunate accidents world wide. For the safety of all, dissenting voices must be silenced. Terrorists, they would be called, and good riddance. The thought occurred to Denech that those who pulled the strings on the puppet politicians might already know, and had made sure the information was censored from all of mainstream media. It was the general public, however, who would be the deciding factor, and when the time came, the puppet masters would be totally irrelevant.

But just what was the best way to introduce the knowledge? Through the lens of science seemed the most logical, but then since most people were scientifically illiterate that method would surely fail. There was the prospect of going through the various elected and self-appointed leaders, the Sadducees and Pharisees as it were, but they were lost to the self-righteous comfort of their safe places. That left the option of the ghetto where mainstream humanity had forced the sick and the decrepit, the leftovers of society. But ironically these fallen souls were also symptomatic of the insidious decay of institutions of men. No self-respecting man or woman would soil their hands with such people, and so it was the perfect place to begin.

* * * *

Through the unseen spaces between and around atoms and molecules and the exchange of electrons and minuscule bits of energy, the message crept around the earth, infecting first those who dared enter the Shadow Net. But even there the message was initially dismissed as the ramblings of a lunatic, a man with the Jesus-complex, mentally disturbed and pathetic. Yet a few who had been trying began to wonder. A few who read between the lines began to take the necessary steps to check the preposterous suggestion of the hobo with a dark beard and stocking cap pulled low above his eyes, the man who appeared distorted and faded in the on-line image. And with each confirmation the rumor took on greater force, and the tiny ripple became a great wave that circled the earth. And shock and disbelief turned into anger. And the ninety percent of the earth's population who believe in a divine presence could not explain or understand why God would do such a thing.

* * * *

Peter Denech had decided to reach the masses in the only way the majority would understand: The message of divine intervention. When a tragedy happens—a great earthquake or tsunami killing thousands—even educated people look for some reason, some divine purpose for such a horrible event. It never occurs to them that natural events happen, and humans in harms way get swept away, and Nature does not distinguish between the human prejudice of good and evil. The rain, as it is written, falls on the just and unjust alike. The earth's crust shifts and buckles and cracks and throws up geysers of molten rock. That's its destiny, because the earth is not a dead thing but a living entity, constantly changing, constantly evolving, and Providence gave humans the only defense it could: The intelligence to learn to stay out of

Nature's way. But possessing intelligence and using it are two different things. And the common fallback position is to ask "Why?" even when, from a moral perspective, there is no 'why'.

*   *   *   *

Parked in a wayside rest area along Interstate 74 in central Illinois just east of Bloomington, Barry Blacmann and his several aides sat huddled around the monitor in the mobile operations center, reviewing the recorded message that was now being confirmed around the world. The distorted image did not look like the person he knew as Peter Denech and the voice was digitally altered, but Blacmann was seventy-five percent certain it was his old college friend. That he could be behind what was unfolding seemed preposterous—the entire thing seemed preposterous—but the Director was convinced and had sent a special assistant to help sort it all out.

Following the incident in Minnesota, Blacmann expected harsh retribution from his superior, but instead received a mandate: Locate and capture Peter Denech or find a dark hole to hide in for the rest of your life. He'd been stripped of his god-like power. He no longer had possession of the UFO, the Universal Information Observer, and the power to launch ITPs. Without that power, he felt impotent and reduced to the same pathetic level as the gullible masses.

From the blurred background, it was impossible to tell with any degree of certainty where the recording had been made, but the distinct sound of a foghorn of a cargo ship narrowed it down to a port city. That still left the possibility of dozens, and that part of the investigation was now in the hands of the techs at E-MIND who would scrutinize every pixel of the picture and every nano-second of sound. But it was the content of the message itself that now concerned Blacmann. A small but significant piece of his mind wondered if the person was not Denech at all, and if the prophecy were true, as it appeared to be, could this be in fact a warning or even a curse from God? He motioned to Agent Johnson, who sat before the monitor.

"Replay from the beginning."

She nodded and directed the cursor to the replay mode, and the message began. The black-bearded man in the image sat on cement steps and behind him others, who appeared to be homeless reprobates, moved in and out of the frame. He held up his right hand, palm facing outward, as a sign of greeting.

"My troubled children. Peace be with you. I taught thee to nurture love to its blossoming, but you let your garden fill with the weeds of hate. I taught thee the sweet fruits of tolerance, but you prefer the bitter taste of prejudice and deceit. I taught you rebirth, but you have withered like sour grapes on the vine that die at season's end. I came as a teacher of peace and kindness, but you have abandoned the lessons and made me into a vengeful god in your own image. Yet the living shall not be punished through pestilence or plague. But I will deny you that which is the most precious to you. I will set this period of time a certain length, and it will be during that time the suffering will be carried from the old to the young by the unseen, and the coming times will be known forever as the Long Time of Sorrow. It will serve as the final lesson to all who live, and will eventually live, that though the Father and Mother remain at times silent, they still walk among you. But they will no longer move mountains or bring down fiery ashes from the heavens. For now and henceforth your destiny will be in your own hands and no other. You have all that is necessary. All the lessons have been taught. The signs are in the heavens and the earth. Let you now set your own path to enlightenment or destruction. In the name of all that is as it could be, let the New Age begin."

Agent Johnson ended the recording and shook her head. "What a nutcase. And you think that's Denech?"

"I'm reasonably certain," Blacmann stated.

"Denech is in his sixties. That man's beard doesn't have a hint of grey."

"Easily dyed."

"And the voice patterns don't match."

"Digitally altered."

"But his general appearance—"

"It's not his appearance. It's the content of his little speech."

"All pretty vague typical doomsday crap to me," Johnson said.

Blacmann considered. "How old are you?"

"Thirty eight," Johnson stated, "but what does that have to do with anything?"

"Have you been tested?"

"No. What? You believe the hysteria that's sweeping the world?"

"Just suppose it's true. I want you to get tested. Consider that an order." Blacmann reached over and drew another person into the conversation. "Mr. Haays. You're the resident expert on these nanite things, and brought in by the Director himself, who seems to have inside information on this. Is any of this related or even possible?"

The short man with thinning grey hair and dark rimmed glasses shrugged. "You'll have to be more specific."

"I have a hard time saying it, let alone giving the idea credence. Is what *might* be happening even possible?"

"Surely, it's possible. The potential for these microscopic machines, these nanites, is quite extensive."

"But to infect humans and only humans in such a targeted way seems, quite frankly, impossible."

"Researchers have now built nanites with dimensions similar to a virus that can selectively target and destroy cancer cells."

Blacmann laughed. "Even if what you say is true, the cure will never make it into public use. There's way too much money to be made in the cancer business and a simple cure would mysteriously disappear into bought up patents and bribes."

"Maybe," Haays conceded. "There is also theoretical work in nanite design that could even reverse the effects of aging. If that is possible, then it is also possible to design these machines to selectively target any family of cells in the human body, including those from the nervous system, skeletal, or the reproductive. So, yes, what you are suggesting is indeed possible."

"But not probable."

"Given enough time, very probable."

"But not now."

"The machinery required, electron microscopes and atomic compilers and so on, are proven technology. All it would take is a major breakthrough, probably a specific chemical catalyst, to make it all so."

Blacmann shook his head. "But it would take a major research team with millions of dollars of investment to pull it off. Correct?"

"Yes, but from what you've told me, this Peter Denech has unlimited resources and probably numerous contacts within the scientific community."

"Some within the Agency suspect that he might have had something going in Montana."

"Yes. The Director was aware of it."

"There was an explosion."

"Yes. Very unfortunate," Haays said. "Because a facility was destroyed, vaporized really, and we will never know its true purpose."

"So he could have done it. Manufactured these nanite things, I mean."

"That possibility exists."

"But to cause the kind of damage these things *might* have caused would have required staggering numbers of them, and a vast network of people to release them."

"It would seem so."

Blacmann considered. "In your expert opinion, Mr. Haays, what is the probability of such a thing actually happening?"

Randolf Haays didn't hesitate. "In light of recent evidence, I'd say a substantial probability. The question is: What is the extent of the damage?"

"Damage?"

"The infection rate. What percentage of the population has been infected?"

"What would be your guess?"

"I would have no way of knowing," Haays admitted. "But part of your effort, now, should be to determine how much of a concern this really is. Because, if the reports coming in worldwide are any indication, it is not something to be taken lightly."

"It just all seems so unbelievable."

"The naked truth often is. Your earlier suggestion to Agent Johnson to get tested was a good one. I'd further suggest that all of you do the same. However, there is a problem."

"Which is?"

"You may discover the effect but not the cause."

"I'm not following."

"It is quite likely that all of the nanites have been flushed from the body through the normal waste removal systems. The liver might hold some bit of residue, but you won't see it unless you have access to an electron microscope. The effects, however, if they are real, would be detectable by any competent fertility lab."

"You understand, Mr. Haays, that if what you're saying is true, if all this is really happening, Peter Denech will easily become the most effective and deadly terrorist of all times."

"There's a legal question there. He's killed no one."

"But he's—"

"You can't murder someone that hasn't yet come into existence. There is no clear law here to guide us. There is the legal opinion of something along the lines of physical assault, however. If indeed this turns out to be true."

"Assault, yes, on several billion people."

Haays nodded. "Yes. Again, it would seem so. But if I might add. To what end?"

"I'm not following."

"What was his reason? His motivation?"

"Does a terrorist need motivation, other than a sick mind?"

"The typical terrorist is not insane. He is fanatically driven, yes, but not insane."

"Driven by what?"

"By something far more deadly than bullets or bombs."

"And that would be?"

"A cause. The unshakable belief that he or she is battling evil forces for the greater good. Like the guerrilla warfare of our own founding fathers against the British."

"It would seem, then, Mr. Haays, that Denech's enemy is all of humanity. That he wants to kill everyone off."

"We might see it that way, but I'm sure in his own mind he's trying to save us."

Agent Johnson cut in. "Like I said. A certified nutcase."

"Examine his message closely. If we take him at his word and get past the religious overtones, then we note some interesting facts."

"If there's anything there but gobblygook, I've missed it," Johnson insisted.

"He's made several statements. The living will not be punished by pestilence or plague. So no disease epidemic. He said this Long Time of Sorrow, as he calls it, would last a certain length of time, so this will not go on forever."

"He also said this suffering would pass from the old to the young. That might imply this thing might be catchy," Blacmann added.

"Possibly. Or he might have meant it in a more philosophical sense. Like the sharing of unpleasant knowledge. And he said this would be a New Age from which we'd go on to enlightenment, or sink in destruction."

"Like that is anything new," Johnson retorted.

"And the last thing," Haays continued. "He's placed this firmly on our shoulders. There would no divine help, I assume referring to the miracles of Old Testament times."

"All that assumes this man is stable. I still go with whacko," Johnson said.

Haays considered. "Stable or unstable, if the Director's information is reliable, we are facing a worldwide traumatic event. Denech's most important statement, the one most telling is this: 'I will deny that which is most precious to you.' That statement ties in directly to what seems to be occurring worldwide. And there can be no doubt that this man, this Peter Denech, seems to be the focus of it all."

"Well, Haays, you're the Director's man," Blacmann said. "Now what?"

Haays smiled. "Continue what you have been doing. Monitor all communications. Capturing Peter Denech would seem to be of high priority since he is the one with the definitive answers. If the hysteria sweeping around the world is accurate, then we have to regroup and decide where we go from there."

"I can't see how it would change anything even if it is true."

"For us in this room, maybe nothing. But certainly there will be changes. The critical time will be roughly seven months from today. Probably February. That's when reality will set in. And if you think Denech is unstable, just wait until the rest of the world sees the final proof of his efforts."

Chapter 24

"Got it!" Carl Walker exclaimed, and immediately drew the others to read the personals ad over his shoulders. "This is it. I know it." While Mary, Red, and Uncle Raul looked on, Carl read aloud:

Lonely man seeks the company of a companion with healthy wolf with lazy eye. Send picture of wolf's eye to verify. I will be moving forward immediately so contact Lake Superior Wings for information on my location. Stay well. CM.

"That has to be it," Red agreed. "He said he'd make it obvious to us. But I have no clue what he's trying to say. I'm guessing, however, that 'Stay well. CM.' is a reference to you and Mary."

Face drawn in an expression of concentration, Mary slid onto a chair and studied the wording.

Carl continued. "Peter said it would be vague enough to not raise suspicion, but that we'd be able to understand it. No doubt every word or phrase has a double meaning. We just have to put our heads together and figure it out."

"I'll leave that puzzle to you," Raul admitted. "While you three do what you do, I'll wander over to the fish trap and grab supper."

With that, Raul Beck hurriedly left the others and exited the cabin. The outside air was damp and heavy and a light drizzle of rain soaked everything like a deep morning dew. He glanced back down the access trail and noted some distance away a lone figure standing without moving. She carried what appeared to be a small suitcase in her right hand. With quick steps he moved toward her, and she remained steadfastly in place. There was the quick hug of an embrace of friendship, and then they drew apart.

"How did you get here?"

"I thought it unwise to use the card to rent a vehicle, so I had to rely on my thumb and maybe a bit of bare leg. Not too shabby for someone in her fifties. Of course, when they get close, they see me for what I am, but by then out of pity for an old lady they have to stop."

Raul laughed. "Nice to see you're developing a sense of humor."

"After the last couple of months, believe me I needed one."

"We just got the message from the Old Man," Raul began. "Carl, Mary, and Red are in there now trying to figure out what it means."

The middle-aged woman nodded. "I'm thankful they made it. After the explosion in Montana, after the time in the cave, things have become—confused. Professor Micals is no longer reliable. Peter—Peter has gone solo, I believe."

"What happened to Micals?"

"No communication. Vanished off the face of the earth."

"What are you thinking?"

"Like I said. Confused. Maybe things got too hot and he went underground like the rest of us. I half way expected him to be here."

"Not here. And where's Randolf? He's supposed to be with you."

"Unknown. He slipped away without explanation right after Peter left us."

"Could he have turned?"

"Much as I think not, we have to accept that possibility. Same with Micals."

"But if they have turned, then this place would have been overrun by the Agency weeks ago. There must be some other explanation."

"Hopefully, yes, but we may also be under surveillance."

"Waiting for the big fish. Waiting for Peter."

"Yes, but Peter won't come here, so we may be safe for now even if we're under their microscope."

"And Plan A? There's been nothing in NEWS 24/7," Raul continued.

"Yes, indications are that it was at least partially successful, but nothing official from any government in the world, and no announcement from the U.N. But if you do have a message from Peter, that means that events are about to explode."

"I should tell you I've played dumb," Raul said. "The others are unaware of my knowledge of any of this. Red and I had never met. Carl, however, is extremely perceptive. It could be related to the transformation. How do you want to handle it?"

"If it is related, then there's only one way to handle it. Hold nothing back. Carl would be able to detect the 'aura of falsehood', as *they* called it."

"Agreed. Come on then. Walk with me to my fish trap. Time to get supper. That will give them some time to work on Peter's message. With any luck they'll have it figured out by the time we get back."

*   *   *   *

Red ran her fingers through her hair in frustration. "Carl, I think it's time to use your special powers. I have no idea what he's getting at." She had rewritten the message on the top of the blackboard with white chalk. Mary simply turned her chair around and continued to study it, but said nothing. Carl was rummaging through a drawer in the kitchen.

"This is all I can find," he said holding up a map of the contiguous states of America. "And sorry. There must be kryptonite in these logs. My super powers have left me."

"Let's break it apart," Mary suggested.

Red nodded. "You two do the thinking, I'll write it down."

"'Lonely man' must be Peter himself," Carl suggested.

"And indicates he is by himself," Mary finished.

"The next part, 'seeks the company of a companion with healthy wolf', must be in reference to the Agency. To Wolf.'

Red shook her head. "That would almost make it look like Peter is trying to get to Wolf. That doesn't make sense. That would be like walking into a rattlesnake pit."

"'I will be moving forward immediately' indicates whatever he's up to, he's doing it right now," Carl added.

"And Lake Superior Wings," Red continued. "What's that all about? He knows we can't contact anyone right now. Why would he say that?"

Carl wedged the top of the U.S. map between two logs next to the blackboard and let the rest unfold. "Obviously it has something to do with the Great Lakes. Maybe the 'wings' part indicates a threat from above. Or something in the water, maybe."

"Or a place," Mary suggested. "Lake Superior Wings might be an actual place."

"Or maybe it represents a person. But who?'

"And what would a wolf's eye, a lazy eye, have to do with anything?" Red persisted.

"Since Peter calls the Agency by the name Wolf, maybe the 'wolf's eye' represents the leader," Carl guessed. "Maybe he's talking about the Director himself."

"That would seem logical," Mary agreed. "So a working hypothesis would be that Peter is attempting to meet with the leader of Wolf. And at a place known to or as Lake Superior Wings."

"That still doesn't help us much. The big question is why?" Carl stated.

"And where?" Red added.

"Sometimes you have to stand back in order to appreciate your work," a woman's voice cut in, and all three turned to see Raul Beck and Amanda Korneth by the kitchen entrance. She walked the few paces to meet them, her usually reserved and stern nature absent, and greeted each with a warm handshake. "It's good to see you all well," she said, when the reunion was through.

"How did you know—?" Red began, but Amanda interrupted.

"We—Mr. Beck and I—will get to that in a minute. But first I believe I can furnish two pieces to your puzzle."

"Yes," Red prompted.

"First the question of why is simple if you understand Peter Denech. For the past several years he's made a career of staying just one step ahead of Wolf. Keeping the organization safe. Keeping Tranquility on course." She turned to face Carl and Mary directly. "You represent the keystone of this entire project, even if Plan A is or is not in effect. We will know shortly. But you two must now be kept safe at all costs. The asteroid is coming."

"I still haven't figured out how the nanites tie into the asteroid," Carl stated.

"You will. When the time comes, you will." Amanda's voice broke with emotion. "Understand that Peter is now ready to give—to give his life for you."

"But we're safe here," Carl insisted.

"Nowhere is safe. Our organization is in tatters. You and Mary, especially, must proceed with the utmost caution and vigilance. With the exception of the personals ads, we have lost all communication. Professor Micals and Randolf are unknowns. We have to at least consider the possibility that one or the other or both have gone over to the other side, or have been eliminated. The overseas facilities are silent.

Don't you see? We are crumbling. There could be a traitor. We no longer know who our friends are."

"But that still doesn't explain Peter's action," Carl said.

"He's tired of being the hunted. Always on the defensive. He's doing something they would least expect. He's taking the fight to them. And he's buying some time. That's all. Trying to deflect attention away from you and Mary. Trying to hold this all together until the asteroid returns next spring."

"And he's willing to get himself killed to do it?'

"Yes. The damn fool. A hundred times over if he could."

All were quiet, and then Mary continued. "And the question of where? I assume you mean where he's gone."

"Yes. Come with me for a short trip."

"A short trip?"

"Yes. Very short. Just over here to the kitchen. You too, Carl. You too, Red."

The three exchanged glances, but followed Amanda the short distance to the kitchen area.

"Now look back at your project on the blackboard and the wall."

"I admit, you lost me," Carl stated. "I see all our hen-scratching, but not much else."

"Kitchigami," Raul Beck explained. "The great water."

"The Ojibway word for Lake Superior," Carl realized. "It's right there on the map."

"Ever notice anything strange about the shape of Lake Superior?" Amanda asked.

Mary suddenly felt a tingle go up and down her spine. "Oh!" she said in uncharacteristic show of emotion. "It was there right in front of us all the time. The eye of the wolf."

"Yes," Amanda said. "Lake Superior has an uncanny resemblance to a wolf's head. And your eye, or rather Peter's reference to an eye, is clearly Isle Royale. The question is this: Is Peter's reference to it literal or merely symbolic of something else?"

* * * *

Mary shook her head. "I'm unconvinced that Peter Denech would be physically going to Isle Royal. For those who don't know anything about the place, the main island is about ten miles wide and fifty miles long. It's in the northwestern part of Lake Superior. There are also a lot of smaller islands around it. It's a federal park, undeveloped and completely forested, pretty rugged landscape, reserved primarily for backcountry hikers and campers. There's also several major shipwrecks in the adjacent waters, so a lot of recreational diving goes on as well."

Amanda was thoughtful. "So no place to hide the major Hub for the Agency?"

"Oh, there's plenty of places to hide such a facility, but it'd take a lot of work. There's lots of copper in the bedrock, and Native Americans beginning some three thousand years ago mined it. In the 1800's European mining companies blasted out deep mine shafts. There are over a thousand of them scattered around the island. There's also four pre-radio historic lighthouses, still intact."

"But no luxury accommodations that would be sufficient for a major operations center," Amanda continued.

"No and there's the problem of weather. The summer days are often foggy and nearly always cool. And winter temperatures may reach forty below zero, with even more brutal wind chills."

"So not exactly a south sea island."

"The weather factor alone could be a deciding factor against it. And furthermore it would be extremely difficult to keep such a place a secret. There are about a dozen park rangers that would have to be bought off one way or another. And even though it's a very primitive location, it still gets thousands of visitors each year. It wouldn't be impossible to keep it under wraps, I suppose, but unlikely."

"You seem to know a lot about this place," Red ventured.

"Carl and I spent a week there once hiking and camping."

"How do you get to it?"

"By boat or seaplane or helicopter. We took the ferry that runs from Grand Portage in the far northeastern corner of Minnesota."

"All of this is conjecture at any rate," Raul Beck interjected. "We may have misinterpreted Denech's message altogether. I think we may be letting our imaginations run wild here. There is also the possibility this message isn't even from Peter."

"It's from Peter," Amanda stated. "I know it is."

Mary noted a morsel of tension between the two, but then continued. "I think our initial assumption was the correct one. That Peter's reference to the 'eye of the wolf', the lazy eye, was the Director himself, or maybe a vital part of the Agency."

"If you take out a wolf's eye, he's then blind," Amanda added. "Peter's message could very well be interpreted that way."

Carl turned to face Beck. "One thing I didn't misinterpret is your apparent familiarity with Amanda. Mind telling me about that?"

Raul Beck nodded. "I've been with the organization almost from the start. This is what we call our Northern Safe House. I've worked with Peter and Ed Micals in Minneapolis ever since Micals discovered the asteroid. Ever since Tranquility began."

"So all the stuff about you moving up here to grieve over a lost wife. Was that merely more cover story?"

"No. It's true. My wife died. She was a casualty of the war we now wage with the Agency."

Carl studied Beck closely. There was no hint of falsehood.

"Okay," Carl continued. "I'll accept that for now. Getting back to Peter's message. Assuming we have the first part right, that Peter is setting up a meeting with the Director, how would he know where to go? How would he go about it? I assume the Director is not someone you can just call up and say 'Let's get together over a cup of tea.'"

"True," Amanda said. "Somehow Peter would have to have specific knowledge of the Director's location, or at least how to communicate with him."

"Which indicates Peter has had some previous contact with him," Mary added. "Some previous conversations."

"If he has, it's news to me," Amanda cut in, defensively. "And what about 'the eye of the wolf? If not Isle Royale, where?"

"The problem here is we aren't thinking big enough," Carl stated. "Wolf is all encompassing and here we sit in this little cabin. To figure this out we have to think like they do, with the kind of resources they have access to."

"That would be pretty much anything the Agency wants or needs," Amanda stated. "Hell, they could be up in the space station. The federal government is a bottomless pit of money, even if most of it is borrowed."

"The weather factor is the sticking point," Mary added. "They'd want a location with reasonably decent weather year round, with a clear sky access to satellites, but yet someplace out of the way, inconspicuous."

A thought occurred to Carl. "How about a boat?'

"What do you mean?" Beck asked.

"Think about it. A boat could go wherever there was a decent water access. It would be mobile, like a 'lazy eye.'"

"I assume you don't mean a rowboat," Red interjected.

"No, I mean a big boat, but not too big. Something that could be mobile enough to follow the weather, but—"

"Or a plane," Amanda interrupted. "A flying operations center would be the safest place. A converted commercial airliner, or even a cargo plane. That might also explain Peter's reference to 'Lake Superior Wings.'"

Mary shook her head. "But a plane would be too vulnerable, and have limited space. You could carry your own private army on a boat. And the more mobile helicopters if need be."

"You have a point," Amanda conceded.

"This is all getting too confusing," Raul declared. "We have no clear path here. Time to take a time out and let the information digest for awhile."

"One thing is certain," Red said. "If we can't figure this out, we don't have to worry about the Agency doing any better."

Mary was thoughtful. "You miss the point. They don't have to. Apparently Peter means to go to them. He has told us what he intends to do but not where. I wonder—"

"What?" Carl asked.

"Probably nothing, but I had a strange dream a couple nights ago—"

"Let's just stick to what we know is real," Raul interrupted.

"Peter doesn't want us there," Red realized. "He doesn't want us to know where he is. He probably thinks we'd try to help him in some way and place our own lives in danger."

"Now that's smart thinking," Raul said.

"But then why would he say to contact Lake Superior Wings for information on his location?" Amanda asked.

"I doubt Peter believes in such things, but maybe they're angel wings. Maybe it's a symbol for death. Maybe he's on a suicide mission," Carl decided. "He intends to blind the wolf or die trying."

* * * *

Raul Beck turned the white rental pickup around and headed down the rock and root-strewn trail that was the mile long entry point to his cabin, the Northern Safe House for Denech's organization. Amanda Korneth sat next to him in the middle and Carl Walker on the passenger side. The end of the trail intersected a narrow gravel county road and there his mailbox stood open and empty, and tilted to one side. Carl exited the passenger side, and came around to stand next to the driver side door. Uncle Raul Beck shut off the engine and rolled down his window. With his face now clean-shaven and hair neatly trimmed, he looked years younger, and as the hair on Carl's face seemed forever trimmed to a quarter of an inch, even younger then Carl.

"So what now?" Beck asked.

"We wait."

"Assuming Peter Denech's plan moves ahead. How long?"

"Until we hear. We'll continue to watch the personals section in NEWS 24/7, and the headlines."

"Amanda left the old laptop, so you have a link to the net as long as the battery holds. There's also the auto-plug adapter. It's probably safe."

"But I wouldn't use it unless you absolutely have to," Amanda added, "and then only if you intend to leave immediately afterwards. Chances are good it is safe, but—"

Carl nodded. "The world of today will begin to fall apart now."

"So it would seem," Amanda said. "The question is: Will it rebuild itself like the Phoenix or continue to decay?"

Carl looked past Beck at Amanda. "I know now what Peter has done. I understand the nanite infection. Mary, too. No one ever really explained it. We just know. It's very strange. Mary and I seem to be connecting on some deeper level."

"Do you understand why?" Amanda asked. "Do you understand why we took this action, which will be unilaterally condemned by every sane person on the planet?"

"Not entirely. I know it has something to do with the asteroid. I know—I feel enough to give you the benefit of the doubt."

Amanda nodded. "Denech—all of us—have gone beyond the end of a limb. There will be no mercy for us if we—or you—are captured. No doubt the nations of earth will gather together to decide the most heinous and tortuous way to end our lives. You understand that it's far from over. Even if Peter is successful in crippling Wolf, it is far from over."

"Yes. Mary has seen the possibilities in her dreams. But we know we were also joined with something—or someone—else."

"That part I can't help you with," Amanda stated, "because we don't understand it ourselves. I know—Peter felt you would grow stronger together, that you would feed off each other. Call it a force of some kind. No superhero type bullshit, but still something. All we can do now is wait. And whatever Peter is up to, I just hope he knows what he's doing."

"Me, too," Carl agreed.

"If Wolf were to find some way to get inside his mind and retrieve the knowledge that he possesses, I shudder to think what would happen."

"And you and Beck? Where will you go?"

Amanda smiled. "Somewhere. I have a lead on Micals so we'll seek him out first. Then continue to watch the personals. Keep up with the headlines. Just like you."

"Be careful." Carl hesitated, but then continued. "Sometimes I think I'm losing it, you know. I see things in my sleep. Not dreams really. Things that come true."

"What things?" Raul asked.

"Major things and simple little things. For example, I dreamt Mary accidentally dropped a book. At the very same time the book hit the floor in my dream, the real book hit the real floor. And I can tell when people aren't telling the truth. It's so obvious to me I'm embarrassed for them."

Amanda and Beck exchanged glances.

"You're not losing it," Amanda assured him.

"Is this the transformation process you were talking about?"

"Maybe. Or maybe you're just very good at reading people. What about Mary?"

"Her dreams are much more profound than mine. They are way out there, and I mean *way* out there, in time and space. They don't upset her anymore. She's found a way to separate herself from them. Like watching a movie."

Amanda reflected. "I have no answers for you, Carl. All I know is we did what we felt we had to do. Whether it was the right thing to do or not will be for posterity to decide. Stay here as long as you feel you must. Your credit cards are good wherever you might go. I won't give you advice because nothing I could say would be anything you don't already know. Except to say stay safe."

Carl nodded. "Thanks. You, too."

"Take care, man," Beck added.

Carl watched Raul and Amanda drive away. The tires of the white pickup kicked up a cloud of dust obscuring it from view, and he suddenly had the uncomfortable feeling that he'd just missed something important. But then perhaps it would come to him in a dream.

Chapter 25

▼

Twenty-four hours after Raul and Amanda left the northern safe house, Mary Walker disappeared. Carl had gone down to the fish trap for the traditional evening meal and then came running back when he felt a strange tearing in his chest. Not fifteen minutes had elapsed, but when he returned, Red was unconscious on the floor with blood gushing from a gash on the back of her head, and frantic unanswered calls indicated Mary was nowhere in the log cabin. He could feel her moving rapidly away, like an ethereal spirit or on eagle wings, and then she was gone, cut off from him by time and distance.

Carl's first instinct was to take off running, or get in Raul Beck's old dark sedan and chase after the lingering connection between himself and Mary. But an ever-increasing pool of blood around Red's head held him rooted firmly in place. Like a checklist inside his head, a dozen options flashed through his mind, and he settled on the one most pressing. He quickly secured a towel from the bathroom, and pressed down on the flowing wound. The white towel rapidly turned crimson, but slowly the copious flow reduced to a trickle and then ceased. With a second towel wrapped around her head, he secured the first in place. A flowing wound indicated the heart was still beating, and after checking for a pulse on her neck, he was relieved to feel the rhythmic surges beneath his fingertips. It was then he noticed her weapon, the peashooter as he called it, was still in its holster under her left arm. Whatever had happened had happened so fast she hadn't had time to put up a defense.

Slowly, he moved his arms under her limp body and moved her over onto a rolled out sleeping bag. He again checked her vitals and the makeshift bandage, and then went outside. There were dozens of strange boot prints in the soft soil, but no vehicle tracks, and the prints proceeded down the trail toward the county road. He jogged along after them, and a couple hundred yards away they disappeared, and impressions in the soil indicated where three vehicles had turned around. The tread marks were distinct. They were gone now, and they had taken Mary.

* * * *

On his knees beside the limp form of Rowanna Doran, Carl Walker gently dabbed the wound with a clean towel soaked in fresh cold well water. An opened bottle of disinfectant sat on the floor next to him. Most of the excess blood had gone onto the floor forming a large grotesque stain, but much had ended up running down the side of her face and soaking the front of her blouse. The wound itself was three inches long, a jagged tear down through her scalp, and tiny little drops of red blood, obvious against pink-white flesh, marked the coagulation points of now choked-off blood vessels. The skin had pulled apart about half an inch, and Carl knew the prudent thing to do would be to get her to a doctor. There was the possibility of a cracked cranium, internal bleeding on the brain, and certainly there should be some stitches to put her back together. Again, the various options clicked off, and the risk of being recognized was outweighed by his concern for her condition. He again slid his arms under her with the intent of carrying her to Raul's old sedan. But when he was standing with her draped limply in his arms, he felt movement. Red raised her head, rested it against his shoulder, and whispered something. He couldn't be sure, but it sounded something like an order.

"Put me down," Red repeated, this time slightly clearer.

"You have a nasty gash. You need a doctor. Stitches and an x-ray wouldn't hurt either."

"Stay safe," she managed to say. "Put me down. I'll live."

Carl hesitated. He knew full well that she was putting his welfare ahead of her own. Still if she was conscious, that was a good sign.

"Okay," he said finally. "Look at me."

"God, do I have to," she answered and managed a weak smile, but then opened her eyes.

"Truthfully, now. How many of me do you see?"

"Is this a trick question?"

"No bullshit now. You know as well as I that a severe concussion can cause double vision."

"One of you is bad enough, but two?"

"So?"

"My head is screaming in pain, but just one. Truthfully."

"Okay. I'm going to have to try to figure out a way to pull your scalp back where it's supposed to be. Raul has a pretty good medical kit. If he has a stitching needle, I'm going to try to put you back together. It's going to hurt."

"Do it. My head can't hurt any worse than it does right now."

"I'm also going to have to cut some of your hair down to the scalp around the gash. And your blouse is soaked with blood—"

"Fine. Do what you have to do. Just don't take advantage of me when I can't defend myself."

"Never crossed my mind."

"Right. Now are you going to hold me for the foreseeable future or are you going to let me rest?"

"Rest, I guess. But if you go and die, Mary will never forgive me."

"I let you both down," Red said faintly. "I should have been paying attention."

Carl shook his head. "We all should have been paying attention. Amanda warned me and I didn't listen. It's my fault, not yours. I got carried away with all this transformation talk. I actually started to believe it. And it's cost me Mary."

"We'll get her back. But I have to close my eyes now."

"Yes, we'll get her back. Somehow, we'll get her back."

Chapter 26

▼

It was obvious the Director was skeptical, but Peter Denech knew that his communication would not be simply filed away as another crank call. He had provided key information—information that only someone with intimate knowledge of the organization would know. He was also sure that there had been an immediate, if not automatic, voice print verification. The thought had first occurred to simply walk in through the main door, but given the tight security, some trigger happy guard would likely shoot first and ask questions later. So in the end he decided to provide his location and have them come and get him. This didn't guarantee a face-to-face meeting with the Director, but there was every reason to believe the knowledge he held in his head would be too much for the Director to pass up, once they verified his identity. He was counting on the weakness of people in that position, although they never see it as a weakness: The chance at absolute power.

Engrossed in a magazine, or so he hoped it would look to the casual observer, he stood, now, in the mystery section of the bookstore in the sprawling mall along Highway 53. New casual clothes and a clean-shaven face replaced the hobo persona. A forest green cap covered his bald head. From his vantage point he could see both the front and back doors, and watch dozens of people come and go. Like him, most were dressed casually, but he paid particular attention to several dressed in the typical uniform of federal agents—prim suits supporting a stiff posture. Finally, at the designated time, a tall and distinguished looking man came in. Silver hair graced his head, and he removed a pair of sunglasses and looked around to get the lay of the land. He tilted his head slightly, and spoke into a concealed microphone on his lapel, and Denech knew the end of one chapter of his own life was over. Within a few moments he'd know if the next chapter would end abruptly now.

* * * *

Barry Blacmann was convinced this was a waste of time, but orders were orders and his crew had left central Illinois the day before and drove straight through to Duluth. Since the information came from above in the chain of command, he had to treat it as fact. The informant had requested a face-to-face meeting with the Director and had arranged to give up in this very public location. No description was provided. Just the place, and the assurance that the informant would initiate contact. Perhaps the informant was finding things a little too hot with Denech and his crew and sought the protection of the Agency. It all seemed too pat, too orchestrated, but Blacmann went through the motions. All agents were in place, scattered around the bookstore. Agent Johnson had stationed herself by the rear exit. The Director's man, Randolf Haays, was en-route in his own transportation. Blacmann moved forward into the quiet of the interior of the bookstore, and casually picked a picture book off the discount table and thumbed through the child-level pages. This is what you get for screwing up, he thought. A stakeout for some low-level nobody, when there were lots bigger fish to catch.

Blacmann was only partially aware of the person who came up next to him, but he swung around immediately when the big man spoke.

"Hello, Barry. Interesting choice of reading material."

"You!"

"I'm afraid so."

Blacmann remained speechless for several seconds. Peter Denech stood just inches away, his hands concealed in the pockets of a blue windbreaker.

"Wait a minute, he said finally. "*You're* the informant?'

"Some might call me that." Denech removed his hands from the pockets and moved them forward, wrists together. "Anyway, here I am. Take me to your leader."

* * * *

Rowanna Doran sat up slowly on the couch and swung around to a sitting position. It was now late evening, and the sun was just above the treetops in the western sky. Gingerly, she reached behind and felt the bandage that covered the dressing over her head wound. The entire patch covered several square inches, and exposing a bit of vanity, she automatically drew some hair over it. She retrieved a hand mirror that lay next to her and inspected the damage. A bit of dried blood was still evident in her hairline, but her face was wiped clean, and her blouse had been replaced with a shirt she recognized as one of Carl's. A sound focused her attention behind—on someone on his hands and knees washing the floor. A bucket of red stained water was next to him. He glanced up, as she looked his way.

"Didn't want to scare you into thinking you'd lost all your blood, so thought I'd clean it up before you came to."

"It wasn't necessary."

"It's something to do until I figure out *wha*t to do."

Red merely nodded and Carl continued. "It isn't pretty but I put in about six stitches to hold your hide together. You're going to end up with one hell of a scar."

"Thanks, I think."

"I dumped a lot of peroxide on it, but we'll have to watch it for infection." He hesitated, and then continued. "Now that you can focus, what happened?'

"I don't remember much. I heard a noise by the kitchen door. I remember looking that way. The next thing I remember is coming to in your—in your arms."

"You didn't see anyone at all?'

"If I did, I don't remember it."

"There were several of them. Lots of boot tracks along the trail. They came in three separate vehicles."

Red nodded, and then continued. "Obviously our secret's out. The question is: Why did they take just Mary and not you too?"

"Maybe because I wasn't here, and they didn't realize I *was* still here—or maybe I'm just not considered important to them."

"Well, we both know Mary is the brains of the outfit," Red said in an attempt at humor, but it came out as a serious statement.

"The good news is they wanted her alive," Carl stated. "Otherwise they would have blasted this place off the map. That much, at least, is a relief."

Red nodded. "We have to consider something. How did they find this place? According to Amanda, this was always considered the Northern Safe House. I assumed 'safe' meant safe."

"Not so safe, it seems," Carl said.

"There's no question now. The Agency has to have someone in the organization working for them."

"Who even knew we were here?" Carl wondered.

"Not many. In fact, when I think about it, no one except the five of us, including Amanda and Raul. We never even told Micals where we were going."

"Denech probably would have realized we'd head this way. Possibly Randolf as well."

"I think we can forget about Peter or Randolf being the turncoat. So, to quote your wife, 'logically', either Raul, Amanda, or myself must be a traitor."

"Screw logic," Carl said. "I'm not ready to believe that one of my own friends would be behind this."

"That's a dangerous attitude. No one should be above suspicion. Which means we should be moving on."

"Unless—" Carl continued.

"Unless?'

"Right now they have no reason to believe there is anyone alive here. That blow you took could have easily killed you."

"Guess my hard-headed nature came in handy after all. So now what?"

"We have the old laptop and satellite access."

"But what are we looking for?"

"I don't know yet. Guess I'll just have to sleep on it."

Chapter 27

Peter Denech had been ushered into position and told to remain standing and still. Two guards had left, but one remained one step behind and off to his left. Handcuffs secured his hands, and black blinders covered his eyes. A bluish bruise appeared around the edges of the left patch, a parting gift from Barry Blacmann. Not all that much, all things considered. Between his meeting with Blacmann and where he now stood, there had been two hand-overs, which indicated two layers of authority between Blacmann and the Director. No doubt, with his capture, his college buddy would be moving up in the world.

Denech was effectively blind, but his other senses told him a great deal. The temperature was comfortable and controlled, the air smelled sanitized, and a murmur of voices indicated people in an adjacent room. In front, he could hear the rustle of papers, and he knew it was all part of psychological fear tactics to intimidate a captive, standard procedure just before they broke out the torture kit. None of this bothered Denech in the least, and he couldn't contain a knowing smile. Every step forward now was a measure of success. When one accepts one's death as inevitable, there is no longer much to be afraid of.

After five minutes of standing quietly in place, the swish of a door indicated another person had arrived. Denech could sense the newcomer standing a step behind and to his right. Then a male voice broke the almost perfect silence.

"Remove the blindfold, and take off those god-damned handcuffs."

There was a muttered, "Yes, sir," and then within moments Peter Denech could see.

The Director was not what he had expected. He had pictured a tough looking character on the order of a Russian general, maybe a bit overweight like himself, and with a ramrod posture and deep, threatening voice. On all those things, he'd been completely wrong. The gentle looking man with light brown hair that rose up from behind the curved office desk looked far too young, barely forty, and on the thin side of average. A light brown cotton shirt tucked haphazardly into light blue jeans looked well worn and faded. As he came around the desk, Denech noticed white golf shoes rather than the traditional black spit-polished standard issue. His lips turned up in a friendly smile, and he stretched out his right hand in greeting. Denech hesitated, but then returned the gesture. The Director nodded to the guard, and he left the three alone.

The Director motioned to a casual chair. "Come. Sit down. I'm glad you decided to drop in. Make yourself comfortable. We have much to discuss."

"What? No water torture," Denech asked, as he seated himself.

"No, that's illegal don't you know?" he said, but winked just the same. "Well, Peter—you don't mind if I call you Peter, do you?"

"Peter's fine, and you?'

"Sigo Markus. My name's a kind of contradiction really. My first name means a powerful peace, and the last means warlike. So I guess it fits really. I maintain a powerful peace by being warlike."

"As do all tyrants."

"Sometimes blood must be spilled for the greater good."

"Yes, but *whose* greater good?"

"In this case, good old U.S. of A. It's time we started eliminating the godless and the misfits. The hangers-on and, you know, those who have gone over to the other side, if you get my drift."

"Very clearly."

Sigo Markus looked closely at Denech's eye. "You have a nasty shiner. How'd that happen?'

"I fell on a door knob."

"Oh?"

"Its name was Barry Blacmann."

"I'll have a word with him. But you understand he's been under a lot of pressure lately." Markus began to laugh. "Ever since he soiled himself down by Rochester. He probably considered it something like payback."

"I'm sure."

"Well, Peter. You've really gone and done it this time."

"Well, I just thought I'd come in and we could have a chat. And talk about what—I don't know—ITPs, and blowing up people, and such."

Markus' smile never faltered. "Fair enough. You tell me all about your nanite project and I'll tell you all about—well, now that is something of a problem, isn't it? I'm not authorized to talk about much of anything."

"Come on. You can tell me your secrets. You and I both know I'll never get out of this facility with my life."

"Your life? That all depends on you. If we can reach a reasonable arrangement, you might just have a long and fruitful one. But sadly, no, you'll never leave this very nice place."

Denech considered. "So you know something about my little machines. How is that exactly?"

"Everyone of importance in the world knows of the effects at least. And though you won't read about it in the national press, it's caused quite a panic. I don't really care about that. You see I have a family. Of course my family thinks I'm an investment counselor, but that's another story. I'm not interested in the effects. I'm interested in the cause. For just about everyone but me, that's still a mystery. It could remain that way, you know. Just our little secret. And the rest of the world could keep believing it's an act of God, like your on-line propaganda bit. I have to hand it to you. That was very clever."

"More like a spur of the moment decision."

"I'm sure you never do anything spur of the moment."

"I used a method of communication that most people of the world would accept. We are still a very superstitious people."

"That we are. And ignorant and lazy and cowardly, and I could go on and on."

"I'm unsure just what you think I can share with you," Denech continued.

"Now that's the crux of it, isn't it? The unfortunate explosion of your facility in Montana in late May seems to have destroyed all information relative to your discovery. That only leaves one place to look. Inside your head. Almost like you planned it that way. So you see. Shutting down your mind in any way would be totally counterproductive."

"You would use the nanites for a weapon," Denech stated.

Sigo Markus laughed. "And you didn't? There's nothing I could do to match what you've done."

"I had my reasons."

"Good or bad, right or wrong. They won't matter to anyone. If I expose you, you'll be famous in the history books, a household name, right along side Hitler and Stalin. Me? I won't make a footnote, unless, of course, we come to an arrangement."

"And just what is it you think I've done?"

"Please. Don't' be coy. Admit it. You're the greatest terrorist of all time."

"I couldn't say. The future withholds its secrets until the last possible moment."

"And what moment is that?"

"It's called the present."

Sigo stood, and stretched his back. "Oh. Pardon me. May I get you something? A drink, maybe?"

"Nothing thanks."

"You sure? It might be your last chance for quite a while."

"No thanks. Rather than continue with this bit of theater, why not just tell me what you want."

"Right to the point. I like that. I want a few things actually. I want a weapon that I can use to target entire populations without putting a single American soldier at risk. I want to have the ability to create a race of super-intelligent, super athletic humans. God fearing Americans, of course. I want a weapon that is totally invisible, totally untraceable, and totally effective in eliminating those evil and ungodly people who continue to breed like rabbits. I know something about nanite technology. If you can design one to do what yours did, you could design one to do nearly anything."

"You don't want much, do you?"

"Just the chance to make the world a better place. No different, I suspect, than you."

"I'd have to look at your facilities. See what you have and what you need. Building a machine the size of a virus requires a bit more sophisticated hardware than a hammer and a set of vise-grips."

"If we don't have it, we'll get it. But there's something I need from you first."

"And that is?'

"Information. A formula or procedure for the manufacture of these things. Something that I can have my own team of experts check out to verify you're on the level."

"I'm sorry. You'll just have to trust me."

Markus laughed. "I'm afraid we don't operate on trust here. Trust is so—so unreliable. We employ other methods."

"Like fear?"

"Fear works. Payoffs work better. Having politicians in your back pocket works even better. But I take a kinder, gentler approach. Good old fashioned love."

Peter sat back. "Love? How exactly?"

"Not my love," Markus laughed. "*Your* love."

"I'm not following," Denech admitted.

"No doubt. But you soon will."

Peter Denech followed Sigo's gaze behind and for the first time noted the third person who had stood quietly during the entire conversation. "This is my new Number One, my right hand man, you might say. Meet Randolf Haays."

"Mr. Haays," Denech acknowledged after a startled recognition, and the slight man with thinning hair and glasses bowed slightly.

"Mr. Haays," Markus continued. "Will you ask the guards outside to bring in our guest?"

"Certainly, sir."

Within moments, the guards presented a second prisoner, who seemed almost in a drugged state. Peter Denech's heart fell, and he slumped back defeated in his seat. The smile on Markus' face grew wider. "Like I said, Peter. Love is a much more persuasive tool. Now, getting back to our conversation. I believe I had asked you to provide some specific blueprints so that we may begin our own nanite project."

Peter Denech remained silent. How could this have happened? How could the one person that might just hold the fate of everyone in her hands end up here? Why had Ed Micals let them all down?

*   *   *   *

"Do you believe in fate, Peter?" The Director asked.

"What?" Denech answered, only partly cognizant of what was going on. He continued to look at Mary Walker who stood without restraints but seemed lost to the real world, as if she were hypnotized or worse. He forced his eyes from her, and turned his attention back to Markus.

"Do you believe in fate?" Markus repeated. "You know. Providence or determinism, as you scientific types call it."

"The determinism—freewill debate continues to be ongoing in academic circles. On the scale of the very large, the Universe appears to work like an intricate piece of machinery. But on the scale of the very tiny, a random orderliness takes over, and things are not so cut and dried."

"You didn't answer my question. Do you, personally, believe that each of us has a certain destiny to fulfill, and that each of us has virtually nothing to say about it?"

"I am un-persuaded either way."

"Spoken like a true politician," Markus laughed. "Straddle the fence. I, however, have fallen off the fence in favor of fate. Take my new associate, Mr. Haays. I needed an expert on these nanite things and poof! Mr. Haays came knocking on my door. Well, not literally knocking, as there are extensive procedures and such, but there he was just the same."

"How very fortunate for you," Peter said, with a good bit of sarcasm.

"And then our retrieval of Ms. Walker. Planned well before your appearance here. We had simply intended to extract whatever information she had and dispose of her, but now, suddenly, she is so much more valuable. Do you see what I'm saying? Do you *see* what I'm saying? All of this is falling into place so nicely. One has to believe it was meant to be."

"Mrs. Walker doesn't know anything about anything. Let her continue on with her life. She is of no value to you."

"Oh, but she is. She is—what's the scientific term—the catalyst that will ensure the proper integration of all the variables of this endeavor. You most especially."

"She's part of a failed experiment, and of no use to me either."

"Deception is not your strong suit, Peter. I have inside information that this pretty young woman is like a daughter to you. That you would gladly give your own life for her."

Peter glanced at Randolf Haays who watched impassively and then again turned to look at Mary. She continued to stare off into her own private reality. "What have you done to her?"

"Me? Nothing."

"No drugs?"

"Of course not. We are not barbarians here, unless, of course, we have to be. She's been in this—in this state since we brought her in."

"And no others—"

"Sorry. We left no others alive."

"What! Why?" Peter Denech could not contain his grief and his chin fell to his chest as a quiet sob issued from deep within. The Director sat back and watched without emotion or comment. After a minute or two, Peter gained control.

"Then I do believe in fate," Denech said. "You have eliminated the only chance the human race had."

Curious, Sigo leaned forward. "And how's that?"

"Without Carl and Mary Walker, within one year's time no living thing larger than a bacterium will exist on this planet. And you, Sigo Markus, the Arrogant-Son-Of-A-Bitch, will surely supplant me as the greatest terrorist of all time."

Markus shook his head. "I've decided I don't like your attitude, Mr. Denech. I think it best we take a break. We're going to give you a room all to yourself. No light to hurt your eyes. No sound to disturb your thoughts. And maybe in a day or two you'll be able to think more clearly."

Chapter 28

Before midnight, Carl Walker knew exactly what he must do. Rowanna Doran didn't exhibit the typical symptoms of a concussion—double vision or nausea—and insisted she was ready to go where need be and do whatever needed to get done. Nonetheless, he'd spent a half hour on the antique laptop going from one web-site to the next, most of which made no sense at all to Red. The last one, a prenatal help group, also provided an extensive list of names an expectant couple might choose from for their child. When he seemed satisfied, he powered it down, removed the battery, and then flung it into the fireplace. Red came up beside him and together they watched as the machine dissolved before their eyes.

"Now what?" Red asked.

"Now we go."

"But where?"

"To get directions."

* * * *

Fifteen hours later in the middle of the afternoon and following a brief nap at a wayside rest area, Carl was again in familiar but strange territory. Momentarily shifting his attention away from the dense traffic, he looked across the bench seat of the dark sedan. Red rested with her head thrown back, eyes closed, and mouth half open. He reached over and nudged her gently. Immediately, she opened her eyes, yawned, and looked out the window at the mass of humanity, and all its trimmings.

"Chicago," she said, and blinked her eyes to get them to focus.

"Close. Just turned onto Washington Street. Downers Grove."

Within minutes, Carl parked the car along the curb of the red brick house. In the yard the unique birdbath sat shaped like a lion's head with the pan of water on its outstretched tongue."

"Ironic, isn't it? This is the place where it all started." Carl smiled and seemed in no hurry to get out of the car. "Tell me what you see."

Red shrugged. "I see a building that probably should have been torn down years ago. I see a lawn that needs mowing and a house that needs fixing."

"Not me. I see a very well kept and comfortable looking home."

Red looked at Carl's face for some sign of humor. "You're kidding."

"Not at all. Now imagine what we might find inside. Mary said it was like darkness so complete it reminded her of a black liquid. Let's go find out."

*　　*　　*　　*

The inside of the red brick house was not a thick blackness, but rather a dim and musty place with shafts of light that snuck in around the shaded windows. The unlocked door, the lack of furnishings, the crumbling and faded wallpaper all suggested to Rowanna Doran that the place was exactly as she first thought: Ready for the wrecking ball. But the slight smile on Carl's face as he ran his fingers along the walls indicated he was not seeing the same thing.

A strange feeling, more apprehension than fear, began to creep into Red's state of mind, and she did what was more habit than caution: She rested her right hand on the grip of the weapon beneath her left shoulder. Carl, however, seemed completely at home, and proceeded to a room that judging from the fading farm animals on the wallpaper must have been a child's bedroom at one time.

But Red noted Carl was not looking at the wallpaper. He appeared to be staring into one bare corner of the room at a place where a broad shaft of light illuminated a section of the cracked hardwood floor. He knelt down on one knee as if to get a better view of something, or as if he were about to converse with someone a lot shorter.

"Hello, Tranquility," he said to empty air. "How are you today?"

An unnerving feeling took firm hold in Red and she stepped back a pace. She watched with a mixture of fascination and anxiety as Carl continued to carry on a one sided conversation.

* * * *

Carl rounded the corner and saw what he had somehow suspected. A child of about eight years with blue bib overalls, and long dark hair in braids. She sat in the corner up against the wall, and held a ragged golden haired doll firmly to her chest. She looked up as soon as he spoke.

"Hello," she said. "Did you come back to play with me and Flossy?"

"Yes."

"I've been waiting for you."

"I know. What game would you like to play?"

"Whatever you want to play," she replied.

"How about hopscotch or pin the tail on the donkey?"

The child shook her head. "I don't know those games. How about the one you really want to play?"

"Which one do you think?"

"Hide and seek."

"Okay, do you want to hide first or should I?" Carl continued.

"Mommy, too?"

"Mother is already hiding," Carl said. "Do you think you can find her?"

"Of course. She's not hiding very well."

"Where is she?"

"On a boat, silly."

"What does the boat look like?"

"It's a very long boat with a house on each end."

"A cargo ship," Carl said more to himself than the little girl. "What else do you see?"

"There's white houses on a hillside."

"Duluth, maybe."

The little girl's face grew sad. "Mommy is not happy. We'll have to go get her. I don't think she likes this game."

"Yes, we will. Soon."

The child looked past Carl at Red. "She is afraid of me."

"Her name is Red. She really is a nice lady. I think she's just a little confused right now."

* * * *

Red watched as the bizarre spectacle unfolded. Carl was clearly convinced something or someone was directly in front of him. Briefly the thought occurred to her that he was suffering from a nervous breakdown, that the trauma of losing Mary had tipped him over the edge.

From his kneeling position, Carl looked back up at Red and extended his hand. Red pulled back slightly and shook her head.

"Carl, you're scaring me, and that ain't easy."

"Just take my hand and hold on. It's perfectly safe."

Red grasped his hand, and felt warmth and strength.

"Now kneel next to me," Carl continued.

Reluctantly, Red complied. "If this is a trick to get me on my knees, so help me I'll—"

"No trick. Just close your eyes, and extend your other hand. You'll begin to feel something."

"You're freaking me out here. What's going to happen?"

"For lack of a better explanation, you are about to get logged in."

With his other hand in the other reality, Carl grasped one hand of the child, and the child reached for Red with her other. Red felt an immediate rush through Carl's hand, a pleasant tingling sensation that seemed to engulf her entire body, and then flowed through her other hand into something else.

"Now open your eyes," Carl directed.

Rowanna Doran was held breathless. Where there had been empty space, a swirling mass of tiny points of light and energy formed the outline of a child, at first a translucent form with no specific features. The sight was so compelling that she instinctively jerked back, but Carl held tightly to her hand.

"What? Who?" she asked in confusion.

"You might add 'when' to that as well," Carl added.

"I don't understand. It's—she's so beautiful."

"Thank you. You're pretty, too," came the response, as the energy field coalesced into the solid form of a child.

"Where did you come from? How long have you been here?" Red asked when she could think clearly again.

"I came from here. I've always been here."

"So you just sit in this house? You must eat? Where's your family?"

The child turned to Carl. "Is this a new game?"

"Yes, if you want to play."

"Okay. I ate a long time ago, but I'm not hungry any more."

"And your family?"

"Right here, silly."

"Right where?"

"Right here, and on the boat. Daddy and Mommy."

"Your father and mother?" Red questioned.

"Sure. You know. Carl and Mary."

"Carl and Mary are your parents? Since when?"

"Since the beginning." The little girl looked at Carl. "We should go get Mommy now, don't you think?"

"Yes, I think so. Will you lead the way?"

"Of course. Should we fly?"

"I'm not ready for that just yet. How about a nice boat ride instead?"

* * * *

"You're bluffing," the Director decided. "There's no way you could accomplish the destruction of the entire planet." Peter Denech stood alone with two days worth of whisker growth darkening his face, and gazed directed at the floor. He clasped his hands before him, almost in a position of prayer. Methodically, he counted the one-foot square tiles on the floor. Twenty by twenty. Four hundred altogether. Sigo Markus sat behind a plain desk with an open laptop and waited for a response. Mary Walker had been brought in and sat on a straight-backed chair in one corner, a guard on either side. A white-robed technician and a mobile tray of syringes waited next to one of the guards. Mary appeared the same as before, lost in her own private reality. In the opposite corner, Randolf Haays stood watching impassively. Directly behind Denech, two more guards, fully armed, stood on either side of the door. The entire room was painted white and after nearly two days in total darkness, Denech's eyes burned in the bright light.

After nearly a minute, Denech raised his head, and looked directly at Sigo. "Not me, you fool. You. Your ignorance is going to get everyone killed."

The painted-on smile faded from Sigo's face. "I'm rapidly losing my sense of humor. And since I am *the* Director that is not a good thing, for you especially. Perhaps if we were to elicit a painful response from Ms. Walker, you'd refrain from talking in riddles."

"And perhaps if you had an ounce of decency you'd be an actual human being."

"Interesting response, but meaningless. I grow weary of this, so I will begin to ask specific questions. For every satisfactory answer, you'll get a pass to the next question. For every unsatisfactory answer, we will inject Ms. Walker with increasingly large doses of a popular hallucinogenic narcotic. Though not initially fatal, at some point the cumulative effects will result in violent seizures followed rapidly by a greatly accelerated heartbeat and death. To be clear, her heart will eventually quite literally beat itself to death. So that you fully understand our commitment here, you should know that we have already injected her with the first mild dose."

"I think I'd like to make my one phone call now," Denech said deadpan.

Markus smiled. "You're a terrorist, Mr. Denech. Under the special powers granted to the President, you have no rights, no recourse. You are a non-person. You are, in fact, atheistic scum. And it's my job to remove the ungodly scum from this society. A job, by the way, I take very seriously, and enjoy immensely."

Denech glanced over at Haays, who remained a silent observer and gave no hint of his intentions, and then back at the Director. "No doubt. But that doesn't change the facts."

"Well, let's begin there, shall we? Just what disaster has your imagination cooked up here?"

"An asteroid impact," Denech stated.

"Oh, the asteroid-hits-the-earth-and-kills-everything plot. Very Hollywood, but rather unimaginative on your part."

"Our best guess is the object will strike in the southern Atlantic off the coast of South America. It will be traveling twenty times faster than the fastest bullet. It will have many times the destructive power of all twenty thousand nuclear weapons on earth exploding simultaneously and at the same place. The sky will be blackened for decades, possibly centuries. Giant mile high tsunamis will splash around the planet wiping continents clean. It will trigger violent volcanic eruptions, and catastrophic earthquakes. The air will become deadly toxic to both plants and animals on the land and in the oceans. Shall I continue?"

"Be my guest."

"It will usher in a new Ice Age, but the term Ice Age doesn't do the conditions justice. Oceans will freeze solid. The only possible survivors will be microorganisms that dwell deep in the earth's crust, and maybe some other primitive bacteria. The evolutionary process of life on earth will be reset to its infant beginnings some two to three billion years ago. There is also the distinct possibility that the earth's rotation and orbital dynamics will be altered, leading to even greater disruption. If the asteroid should penetrate to the earth's mantle, then you can forget about even bacteria surviving. Are you getting enough facts, or would you like to hear more?"

"I haven't heard a peep about this supposed mystery asteroid, and I know *everything*."

"Few do. The information was kept secret to prevent a panic."

"Which few?"

"Myself. Those who died in Montana."

"So it's just your word we have to go on now. Convenient."

"Within a few months, some other independent research group is bound to discover it as well. But by then it may be too late."

"Too late for what?"

"To dissuade it from striking."

"Assuming any of that is even remotely true, how does this spaced out and pathetic person have anything to do with it?"

"Assuming you have in fact killed Carl Walker, we now must put all our hopes into this one woman. She's not like you or me. She is special."

Sigo Markus looked over at the dark-haired woman with the blank look. "Right. And I suppose she's going to don her super suit and fly up there and blast this asteroid right out of the sky."

"If you don't mind my saying so sir, you're an idiot. And as such there is nothing I could say to convince you."

"Perhaps you need to try harder, because I am unconvinced."

"Ask me anything. I will explain as truthfully as I am able. You have the technology. Hook me up to a lie detector."

"You're already 'hooked up.' I am getting the readouts on my screen as we speak. And frankly they are the only reason you and Ms. Walker are still alive."

"There you go. Told you so."

"Our lie detection is not perfectly one hundred percent accurate. There is the remote chance you are merely very good at lying."

"You just contradicted yourself."

"I don't see how that's possible."

"Two days ago you said deception was not my strong suit. Could it be that you're not quite as smart as you think you are?"

"My concern is with the big picture. I don't concern myself with the details."

"Yet here we are."

"Assuming, again, that there is some truth here, what part does Mary Walker play in this?"

"I can't say because I don't know."

"She's your personal savior, but you don't know how?"

"Yes, that's true."

"Well, I—" Markus began, but was interrupted by the intercom. "Yes, what is it?" The voice on the other end came back immediately. "We have a special envoy from the FBI field office in Minneapolis."

"Well, put him on hold or tell him to call back."

"It's a woman and she didn't call. She's here, sir."

"Stall then. Get her a cup of coffee. I'm busy right now."

"She said she has valuable information about some nanite thing. Said you'd know what it was all about. Said you'd want to see her right away."

The Director hesitated. "Okay. Let her through. But run her through the x-ray clean-sweep. If she has so much as a paper clip, I want it removed."

* * * *

At the cabin, Mary Walker had felt them coming and heard the hard boots hitting the soft dirt of the trail long before they arrived. And it was not fear that drove her from the cabin, but the curiosity of wondering if what she had felt so strongly was actually happening. She heard the door crack and splinter as the boots kicked it in, and she felt the force of the blow that sent Rowanna Doran unconscious to the floor. With rough and cold hands, they held her fast and led her away.

But there was a mental disconnect between perception and feeling, between reality and what would more accurately be described as a dream—a dream that she felt she could, with some effort, control. The dream took her to a place on a long low ship and to the odor of bathroom disinfectant and the murmuring sounds and deep vibrations. She was only vaguely aware of people moving about and of the distant floor under her feet that seemed miles away.

Her perception lifted above to some other place and reached out to something far beyond. Something in the black liquid of her dreams. There was a little girl there with blue bib overalls and long dark hair in braids. The child waved to her, and came running towards her. The thick ooze of darkness melted away as the child jumped into her arms and called her mommy. And Mary Walker collapsed to the floor.

Chapter 29

"Oh, Christ. Just what we need," The Director shouted. "Get her back in her chair. Strap her in if you have to." Her two guards and the technician lifted Mary back into the chair and she regained consciousness enough to remain sitting. The outside door opened and a woman swiftly and confidently strode in. An identification nametag dangled from a clip on the collar of her white blouse. A dark blue windbreaker—common to law enforcement personnel and with FBI in large letters on the back—was zipped up about half way. She glanced neither right nor left and strode immediately to the Director. Markus rose to greet her, and smiled faintly at the attractive woman.

"Yes? Agent—"

"Doran, Sir." The redhead glanced around. "Sorry to interrupt. But I'm on a tight schedule."

"You're always welcome. We have no secrets from the FBI," Sigo lied. "Actually, as fate would have it, you've come at an opportune time. We are presently processing the great Peter Denech. Something of a rogue domestic terrorist."

Agent Doran momentarily glanced back at the large man with the bald head and unshaved face. He grunted an acknowledgement and looked away.

"This man?"

"Yes."

"And what of the woman?" Doran continued, nodding toward Mary Walker.

"It's complicated. I won't bore you with all the details. Now about the information you said you had for me? As you can see, I'm rather busy."

"Ah, yes. A couple of things. The department has learned of a possible attempt at infiltrating your organization. Possibly even your floating headquarters here. I have to admit a converted ore carrier was a stroke of genius."

"I assure you there have been no breaches. We have several levels of security. In the summer, we purposely station ourselves in this backwater no-place to avoid the prying eyes of the major cities. We are incognito, as they say."

"I see. I guess we must have it wrong. Headquarters has always believed that this is the operations center, the Hub I believed they called it."

"It is. Lake Superior is close to the center of the continent. This central location allows us full access to anyplace in North America."

"Very impressive. Yet our sources are extremely reliable."

Sigo Markus began to laugh. "Okay, it's been fun but enough acting. Did you think you could just waltz in here and get away with it? We've had someone on the inside of Denech's group for a long time now, just waiting to pounce. I know who you are, and you're one of *them*."

"And I suggest you contact the FBI field office in Minneapolis, because you'll find I am also one of *them*. Yes, I've been in and out of Denech's group from time to time. It was my undercover assignment until your incompetent fools nearly killed me. If you want proof, take a look." Agent Doran turned her head and pushed red hair aside to expose the bandage to make the point.

"Of course we can check—"

"You have the laptop right in front of you so check, damn it, and quit wasting your time and mine."

"We will, I assure you. Now what was the other information you have for us? Something about the nanites?"

"Ah, yes. We believe it's a mass delusion, produced by something we call the 'ignorance factor.'"

"I realize that most people are stupid, but I have it on very good authority that these things are very real."

"Well then. I rest my case."

"What do—?" In his peripheral vision, Markus noted Mary Walker suddenly straighten and then lean forward. She began to speak, but it was not to anyone in the room.

"It's the hallucinogen we gave her," Markus said. "It's starting to have an effect. Let her rant to her imaginary friend. It'll wear off in a few minutes, unless we up the dosage."

* * * *

"How did you get here?" Mary asked. The others in the room fell silent, as she carried on the conversation with an empty place in the room.

"I came with Daddy in the boat. I brought Flossy with me. See?"

"Yes, I see. Where is father now?"

"Waiting. He'll be here soon. This game isn't any fun. You should come home now. Some of these people aren't nice."

"I know. I'd like to come home—it's hard to explain." Mary glanced up at the others who continued to stare at her. Red rubbed her left shoulder. Peter Denech smiled slightly. In the corner, Randolf Haays remained an impassive observer. Markus and his people were content to let her continue.

"Some of these other people don't see you like I do."

"I know. They are not part of the game."

"Can you tell me who does?"

"Sure. Peter and Red and Daddy, of course."

"These other people don't believe you're really here. Is there something you can do to let them know?"

"Like what? Would this be like a new game?"

"Yes. Make it something noisy."

"Okay. But then I'm going to get Daddy."

Markus shook his head, and turned to the technician. "Okay. I've heard enough of this nonsense. Shut her up with another shot." Suddenly, the tremendous roar of the foghorn echoed outside the room and its deep tone vibrated throughout the steel structure of the ship. With one smooth motion Rowanna Doran retrieved her weapon, whirled about and fired two projectiles within a split second of each other. Mary rose swiftly to her feet and the distraction caused her guards the momentary confusion needed for Red to dispatch the last two guards and the technician as well. It was all over within seconds, but a hard cold barrel pushed into Red's back brought the escape attempt to an equally fast end.

"No one move. The weapon I have jabbed into Red's back will leave a very large hole through her midsection should it go off." He reached around and took the weapon from Red's hand and pushed her forward. "Everyone. Move over by Mary where I can keep an eye on you."

Peter Denech was both shocked and bewildered. "Of all our people, it was you I trusted most of all. You were our safety net. You were the one we could always count on when everything else failed. Your wife gave her life for this project. I really felt you would honor her memory at all costs."

"You were always the one with the thing for names," Raul continued. "You should have taken the time to look up mine."

Denech nodded. "I did. Raul Beck means something like the wolf by the river."

"The wolf part should have given it away."

"Not if the wolf is on our side."

"Good. Good," the Director cut in and addressing Beck. "Keep them covered. I'll get help in here right now." He reached for the intercom but a huge spark of static electricity jumped from the desk to his fingertips. He yelped and jumped back in pain. "Go back out. Get help."

"There's no one out there. There's bells and whistles going off all over this ship, and your people are scrambling around like confused monkeys."

"Raul," Peter began, but Beck shook his head.

"This is where it ends. All the dirty little secrets are inside this room."

Denech took a step forward. "What are you getting at?"

"I just didn't have the heart to kill Amanda or Micals. I just couldn't look into their eyes and pull the trigger."

Denech took another small step. "What have you done? Where are they?"

"I left them in the Rabbit Hole. Jimmied the locks from the outside. They'll have each other for company when they die."

"But why?" Denech continued. "Your wife—"

"My wife was my life. You took her from me."

"We didn't kill her," Denech pressed.

"No? You *all* killed her. All of the greedy, arrogant, selfish people on earth."

"You can't mean that, Raul. People are worth saving. That was the entire point behind Tranquility."

"You once said there was no such thing as good people or bad people. Only flawed people."

"Yes. But as bad as things are in the world today, we can give them another chance."

"No more. No more chances. You and I know that in a hundred years they'll be right back at it again, murdering each other in the name of one bullshit cause or another. The strong will always make slaves of the weak. We are animals, Peter. Nothing but superstitious animals. You know it and I know it."

Denech's voice grew soft. "So. What do you intend to do?"

"I intend to die right here with all of you in a few minutes. Over the next few months, the asteroid will continue on its course. Probably some other research team will see it coming just before the end. Maybe there might even be enough time to launch a bunch of nuclear weapons toward it in a feeble effort to blow it up or knock it off course. We know that plan doesn't stand a snowball's chance in hell of working. It'd be like trying to deflect an elephant with a fly swatter. But the politicians will go ahead anyway and tell everyone everything will be just fine, and then they'll all die. Most will die within the first week or so. Some might linger on for a while in caves or in submarines. But as the atmosphere and the oceans die, so will mankind and just about everything else. And that is how it should be."

Again Denech inched forward. "Raul. You have to reconsider."

"Why? Everything I've just said you've said to me on more than one occasion."

"Those were hypotheticals. This is real. You've succumbed to an emotional response. You have to get past that."

"Emotional? Yes? That's the only way I survived my wife's death. I grieved, I cried, I ached until I thought I was done and then I started all over again. But after a while it didn't hurt quite so bad, and I knew I could never again deny my emotions. From that day forth I said I would *never* deny my emotions. That includes *all* emotions. And the one I feel right now is—"

"Hate?" Denech finished.

"I was going to say pity. Pity for all of us."

"But consider. It's taken natural forces four billion years to get to where we are today. Does it make sense to throw that all away now?"

"Maybe in the next four billion years the earth will get things right."

"You're a god-damned nutcase," Sigo Markus cut in. "Loonytoons. Completely fucked up. You'd see the world destroyed to avenge your goddamned wife. Probably a couple of godless kooks anyway."

Raul Beck smiled at Denech. "See? He just proved my point. It should be quick and relatively painless. I set a charge under the very center of the ship. This tub is eight hundred feet long. I know. I've been a guest here a few times. When the blast goes off, the center will buckle and we'll sink to the bottom in a matter of seconds. There's five hundred feet of water directly below us. And there's no way out except through the door behind me."

Mary stepped slowly over the body of the technician and came forward. "May I say something?" she began.

"Sure, but there's nothing you could say to convince me."

"We could have ended this, but we didn't. We wanted it to be your decision."

"Ended it? How? I'm in control here."

"Carl has been standing behind you for the last few minutes."

"What? No way." Raul was certain it was a bluff, but felt the hair on the back of his neck raise just the same.

"He's standing just out of sight outside the doorway. There's someone else here, too. You can't see her. Markus can't see her. But some of us can."

Raul looked about briefly, and then glanced toward Randolf. "What about you?"

Randolf cleared his throat. "I wasn't privy to that part of Tranquility."

"What part?"

"It was an attempt at direct communication. I drew the short straw so to speak. I was the failsafe in case things took a negative track."

Markus gave Haays a questioning look. "Just whose side are you on here?"

"I think it should be obvious by now."

Beck moved back slowly swinging the weapon back and forth to cover everyone, as Carl appeared in the doorway.

"It is like you said, and even worse. There is no denying that," Mary continued. "We have always been our own worst enemy. But I can show you what is possible. That people have been right here before and got past it. No, it's not for certain. Maybe not even likely, but it is possible."

"How?"

"Let me hold your hand. I give you my word I will not try to stop you from doing anything you want to do. Carl will not interfere. If we can't show just one person what is possible, then we all deserve to go down with this ship."

Raul hesitated. "Just my hand? And Carl will stay clear? You promise?"

"I promise."

"What about the rest? Denech and Red I trust, but Sigo—no way."

"I don't know about anyone else but I intend to yell my head off," Markus stated, and suddenly lunged forward. Haays raised his elbow at the opportune moment and caught Sigo Markus under the chin. His head snapped backwards, and he landed unconscious on his back. Calmly, Haays looked to the others. "I think we can continue now."

Mary extended her hand. Reluctantly and hesitantly, Beck reached for it and finally grasped it firmly in his. Mary looked to one side and reached out for another. Within seconds Beck's eyes grew wide as a swirling galaxy of dancing lights coalesced into the form of a child. Carl Walker came into the room and stood with his arm around the child's shoulders.

"Hello," the little girl said. "My name is Tranquility. This is my doll Flossy. Would you like to play a game?"

Chapter 30

Carl Walker was thankful, yet sad. It had ended as well as anyone could have hoped. Capitalizing on the mass confusion, Raul Beck had secured a life raft and gotten them safely aboard just as a powerful explosion rocked the ship. Considering the magnitude of the blast, there was very little noise, but almost immediately the center of the long ore carrier buckled, and tons of lake water flooded the hold. Despite vigorous protests from them all, Raul Beck refused to leave the ship. It was his time, he said, to be with his wife. There had been no time to argue and as they paddled frantically to get away from the dying vessel, they watched the two ends of the ship, the two 'houses' as Tranquility had called them, rise high in the air even as the center sank. Then like a great whale submerging, the bow and the stern disappeared beneath the waves, leaving men in red life preservers dotting the surface.

Once on land, they dropped Haays off at a car rental business in Superior, Wisconsin, and continued on to the only place that seemed like home: A log cabin in the woods.

* * * *

The fish trap was a homemade affair made of poultry wire, and covered an area the size of a kitchen table. On either end a conical shaped entrance enabled fish to get in, but once in, it was difficult for them to find their way out. Once the fish were in, the trapper could herd them into a narrow chute and getting fresh fish was as easy as reaching in and selecting the evening meal. In knee-deep water, Carl tugged at the four-foot wooden stakes that held the wire in place. Systematically, he moved from stake to stake until all were free of the sandy river bottom soil. On the shore, Rowanna Doran grabbed onto the loose wire and began heaving it up onto the bank.

"Next time we'll bring a rod and reel," Carl said from a sitting position on the bank. In turn, he removed his shoes and socks and emptied out the water.

"If there is a next time," Red said. "For you there may be."

"Heading back to headquarters?" Carl asked. "Doing your FBI duty and all that?"

"It may not seem like much to you, but it was Peter who encouraged me to sign on the dotted line. Because of my cousin, I did."

"Your cousin?"

"Years ago she came to stay with me in New York. She was a recently divorced mother of one. I was this young idealist who was going to make America a better place. Expose the establishment for the corrupt fraud that it is. It became like a thrilling game to me."

"And?"

"I was involved in every cause, every crusade imaginable. I *wanted* attention and I got it from those who considered me a disruptive nuisance. I *loved* rubbing their noses in their own hypocrisy. I know now I was the first to be targeted by the ITP technology. I was the test case to see if the projectiles would work."

"But here you are."

"Yes, here I am because I happened to lend my cell phone to my cousin that beautiful Sunday in April. She went to Central Park to feed the birds and call her mother."

"The Agency targeted your cell phone with an ITP."

"Yes. Witnesses say Marilyn literally exploded. There weren't enough pieces left to identify. It fell to DNA identification procedures to confirm her ID. Her death was listed as a bizarre accident."

"I am sorry for your loss."

"I suddenly realized these people are not playing a game. Among the big chip players, there are no rules or goals but domination and control. Individual life and citizen liberties are meaningless trivialities to them. Our guaranteed Constitutional rights are obsolete in their view. To them, a joke, really. By a stroke of luck—or fate—I came under Peter Denech's umbrella."

"So now you're leaving. That makes us—you know, the rest of us—what, chopped liver?"

"I have to leave, and you know it. I can't get too close. To forge a bond, and then have that bond broken is just too painful. Relationships are a luxury, and often a painful luxury at that."

"Have you talked to Mary about this?"

Red shrugged and then went off on a different tangent. "Raul Beck was a fool you know."

"How's that?"

"Emotions need to be controlled, not turned loose. In the end they killed him."

"I guess they did. But I guess it depends on which emotions we choose to turn loose. Is there something you're trying to tell me?" Carl pressed.

"You know damn well what I'm trying to tell you. I thought if I tried hard enough I could transform my—my feelings into something like a sister."

"But?" Carl pressed, and a wide smile betrayed his own feelings.

"So, it's best if I don't hang around."

"Sorry. You don't have my permission to leave."

"I am five years your senior. I don't need *your* permission to do anything."

"I don't know what is going to happen, but the four of us—Mary, you, me, and one little girl—are the beginning of something. The three of us were protected from the infection. Each of us has been touched by this small child from the past. We have been changed in some way."

"I'm not following."

"A living species doesn't suddenly shift en masse in a new evolutionary direction to avoid extinction. It begins with a single individual with a single rare positive mutation."

"What mutation?"

"Maybe something simple like a change of skin or hair color. Or something profound like the inherited ability to work in groups rather than as isolated individuals. Or just a different way of looking at life. Or even major changes in body shape. These changes help ensure the survival of the species. Over time that positive change is then passed on through offspring and gradually spreads out into the entire population."

"So you're saying that Tranquility is a mutation?"

"No. She is a real, living person. I'm saying that she produced a change in us that we might now transfer to our offspring. Something positive, I have to believe."

Red smiled and her eyes flashed. "That, Carl Walker, has to be the most lame, the most pathetic, the most disgustingly unromantic come-on I've ever heard. Just what would Mary say if she'd heard that little speech?"

"Actually, it's all very logical. And Mary is the one who put me up to it."

"And I suppose the thought never once crossed your mind."

Carl smiled, but then grew serious. "First things first. Let's get this fish trap out of the water, and then try to figure out how to stop a twenty-mile wide asteroid. I do know this. I want you and Mary by my side when everything starts to unravel."

Chapter 31

"The FBI has taken up the cause against the Agency," Rowanna Doran said, as she slid onto a chair by the solid oak table. She set a pot of coffee in the center and within everyone's reach. Directly across from her, Peter Denech poured himself a cup and then filled the cups for Carl and Mary. On a spread out sleeping bag on the hardwood floor of the log cabin and in front of the stone fireplace, a child with blue bib overalls and black hair in braids worked at her latest creation in a coloring book.

"I still can't believe you really are an FBI agent," Carl said.

"Afraid so," Red confirmed.

"Somehow, I feel—I don't know—violated. There goes the neighborhood."

"Believe it or not, there are still lots of dedicated people trying to do the right thing."

"Well, I know one for sure," Carl stated and looked directly into Red's eyes until her face flushed and she had to turn away.

"You're blushing," Carl stated.

"Am not."

"Are too."

"Mary. Break up your children," Denech advised.

"It's a phase they're going through. Eventually, they'll grow out of it," she predicted.

Denech held up his cup signaling a toast. "To coffee. If it didn't exist to keep generations of scientists awake, we'd all still be living in the Dark Ages."

"Amen to that," Red agreed. "Hear anything from Haays?'

"Received an e-mail this morning. Even though the Hub went down and for now the Agency is off-line, I still feel we should keep to the antique laptops and old technology. All the new toys and gadgets would be nice, but I would rather be safe than sorry."

"And Haays?" Carl prompted."

"He rescued Amanda and Micals. Physically, they came through the confinement in the Rabbit Hole fine, but their opposite personalities presented something of a problem."

"How so?"

"Well, when Randolf found them they'd divided the cave into 'his' and 'hers' and never the two shall meet."

"So much for dying in the company of a friend," Carl added.

"Any other tidbit from Randolf?"

"Just that he's using the window we have now before the Agency is up and running again to try to contact some of the rest of the organization around the world. Scattered reports so far. Micals and his wife went in for the test, and came back positive."

"Sad."

"Sad and terrible. But the alternative would have been worse."

"What are the projections?" Mary asked.

"Up to a fifty percent reduction in the human population over the next twenty to thirty year period."

"Yet, no one will die because of the nanites."

"The intent was never to kill anyone," Denech stressed.

"The blogs are filled with all sorts of explanations," Carl said. "Everything from Martians to the earth's passage through the galactic plane. Next year is 2012 you know."

"The end of an age, the ancient Mayan people would say."

"Or the beginning of a new one according to the Native American people," Mary added. "The return of the White Buffalo woman, who would bring understanding to her people and teach them how to survive."

"Ever think that might be you?" Denech asked seriously.

Mary turned to look at the child playing on the floor. "Not me, but maybe her."

"Given her probable ancestry, she certainly would fit," Carl agreed.

"In simple terms, explain Tranquility to me," Rowanna Doran asked.

"As best we can determine," Denech began. "Tranquility is a projection from the past. But she is more than a mere hologram. She is real. She is as alive as you or me. Even more so. But even more incredible is that she is *us*."

"Us?" Red questioned.

"Remember when you first saw her?" Carl continued. "You asked her where she was from."

"She said 'here'."

"Yes, here. Earth. But not of our time."

"But how did she get here?"

Denech entered the conversation. "When the asteroid swept past the first time, she, for lack of a better explanation, got off. I found a spherical shaped object in central Montana. I was holding it up to get a better look at some of the markings and this little girl appeared. We built the research facility around her."

"So the breakthrough on the nanites—"

"Didn't come entirely from my brain. Tranquility is like a walking encyclopedia of her people. A complete history of all that they were, all that they knew. The intellect, the hopes and dreams of a million people, and much more that we've only begun to tap. Yet all of it must be tapped through the avenue of a game. Like any child her age, that's a concept she understands. There are unimaginable things in her head, wonderful but also terrible things."

"What terrible things?" Red asked.

"Extermination. The ancients placed Tranquility on the asteroid and sent her out to come back at this time. They couldn't know what the human race would become. In this sense Tranquility is a probe. If certain conditions were not met, the asteroid would simply follow the laws of physics and do what it was intended to do: Reset the earth to day one."

"And that's where you came up with Plan A, B, and C," Carl guessed.

"No, I didn't come up with them. Tranquility came up with them. They were mandates from those people. If they weren't met, we would have been left with Randolf's perennial favorite."

"Plan F," Carl remembered.

"Just let the damn thing hit and the hell with the noise," Denech said.

"So Plan A is on course. Plan C was the symbiotic relationship between Tranquility and Mary and me," Carl surmised. "Whatever happened to Plan B. For that matter, what was Plan B?'

Denech smiled. "Better that you don't know."

Carl shook his head, and parroted Denech's favorite phrase. "You'll just have to trust me."

Denech laughed. "You're getting to be a mind reader, too. I'll tell you this. Plan B is in the hands of Japanese researchers because they were already heading in that direction."

"Which tells me nothing," Carl admitted.

Red reflected. "All that knowledge inside Tranquility and from only a million people?"

"That's what we think. Also that they were long lived. Maybe two hundred years or more."

"I wonder how they were able to get objects into space?" Carl asked.

"Not primitive rockets, I can tell you that," Denech said. "We think some form of reverse magnetic or gravity drive. Essentially using the earth's gravitational field to repel objects into space. But it also appears they were not space travelers. Just the opposite, actually. They were content to remain on earth, and took great pains to preserve it in its natural state."

"So how long ago are we talking about?"

"We believe they sent out the asteroid about a hundred thousand years ago. During the last Interglacial Warm Period."

"But apparently they died out along with their technology."

"No, they didn't die out. They evolved, or rather de-evolved, into us."

"I wonder why. They were obviously way ahead of us."

Denech nodded. "And here's another thought. Imagine where we as a human species would be—imagine what things we'd know now—if they had continued to advance, instead of degrading into the present human condition."

"Imagine where we'd be today if it weren't for our own Dark Ages," Carl added. "A thousand years wasted to human suffering and ignorance."

"There had to have been a reason those ancient people didn't make it," Mary continued. "Some flaw in their society maybe, or a radical change in environmental conditions. I'd really like to know."

"Eventually, we will know," Denech said. "I think we *have* to know. It's part of their test. Maybe to avoid what they couldn't."

"But why a child to represent them?" Red wondered. "Why not one of their great scientists, or a shaman?"

Mary smiled. "What better way to approach a strange and potentially hostile people than with a non-threatening child."

Denech continued. "After a few words of greeting, the very first thing I was able to discern from the initial contact was the word Tranquility. It means, of course, peace or calm."

"But she speaks in perfect English," Red observed. "That's certainly not her native tongue."

"How do we know for sure she is even speaking?" Denech said. "For all intents and purposes, she's a living energy field."

"As are we all," Carl reminded him.

"Yes, but we are chaotic. Hers is highly defined and—"

"Logical?" Mary added.

"Certainly highly evolved. We may simply be hearing her thoughts. I'm convinced now that when I first saw her on the barren hillside in Montana, she had somehow tapped into my mind. I had been thinking of an orphaned South American child that I'd seen in one of those appeals for financial help."

"Yes?" Carl pressed.

"Tranquility is the living image of the picture. Somehow, when I picked up the artifact—that she must have been part of—I triggered a mechanism that—I don't know—she adopted that form and that's what we all see now. But it's still beyond me."

"And there she is," Mary said. "Definitely more than a mirage."

"But not super-human. She didn't come bearing miracles. What she did bring was knowledge and chance for a change in course, but placed the burden on us. One thing is certain," Denech continued. "She is evolving, growing more solid for lack of a better word. Adapting to our environment. She's started eating."

"Do you think she has the capacity to grow?" Carl asked.

"I do. When she first appeared to me, she was more like pure energy, and for a short time I was part of that energy. You've experienced it. It is more ethereal than corporeal, but steadily becoming a part of our world."

"And yet she remains invisible to people until they go through a transformation."

"In that sense, she is like a computer program, and in order to access it, you have to log in. In other words, you have to want to—"

"Believe?" Red finished.

Denech nodded. "I suppose it could be put in those terms. We all have to have faith in something. What more could one ask for than the vast potential of an innocent child?"

Tranquility got up off the floor and climbed up onto Mary's lap. She placed her coloring book on the table before them. It was a picture of an elephant, and she'd colored it brown.

"How do you like it, Mommy," she asked.

"Very nice," Mary said.

"Mommy?"

"Yes?"

"Is this animal sick?"

"I don't think so. Why would you think so?"

"Because it doesn't have any hair."

Denech understood. "Remember, in her time and where she might have lived, elephants had hair. Today we know them as mammoths and mastodons."

Mary and Red left the table and returned with Tranquility to the spread out sleeping bag on the floor. Carl ran his finger around the edge of his coffee cup and stared off into abstract space.

"More coffee?" Denech offered.

Carl placed his hand over his cup. "No. No thanks. I'll be up all night. I was just wondering."

"Yes?"

"Not to be nosey, but you must have gone through a ton of money."

"You'd like to know where it came from."

"Unless it's a deep dark secret."

"No secret. One of the first things we got from Tranquility was detailed locations of earth's mineral deposits."

"Very handy."

"In a couple ways. Obviously, there was the limitless financial freedom, but something else much more important. We had suspected from the composition of the artifact that Tranquility had a terrestrial origin. The isotope ratios were a near perfect match with earth. However, it is my belief that the locations of the mineral deposits were provided as proof of where Tranquility had come from."

"Wealth and money probably had no real meaning or value in their lives."

"Exactly. Remember, there were only about a million of them with the resources of the entire planet to draw upon." Denech was silent for a few moments and then continued. "But something else is troubling you."

"Yes. The explosion in Montana. I can still sense an utter calm in those people when there should have been panic. I can still see their faces."

"As can I. And I always will."

"It wasn't the Agency that blew up the facility, was it?"

"No, not the Agency."

Carl remained silent waiting for a response.

"It was us," Denech said finally, and a tear broke from the corner of his eye.

"Us?"

"When we built the facility we included a self-destruct mechanism with a powerful explosive charge similar to a low yield nuclear device."

"For what reason?"

"We couldn't risk the knowledge falling into the wrong hands. Especially the Agency. When we found out about the possible informant, we knew our days were numbered."

"So you—"

"Not me. We discussed our options at length, and I came away from the meeting thinking we had several alternatives. What they decided to do was of their own making. Any one of those people—those good people—had invaluable knowledge and they knew it. So to keep Tranquility safe, they—they did what they thought they had to do."

"And Raul was the informant?"

"Yes, Raul, and one other."

"You," Carl realized.

"I was playing both ends against the middle as they say. I felt I needed to get a fix on the Hub's position. After some trial and error, I was eventually able to connect to Sigo Markus himself. I always ran my voice through a scrambler, and fed him bits and pieces of information that from the perspective of the whole were worthless. If all works perfectly, you know, it only takes a few contacts to be able to triangulate a position. Yet there was always error, I could never quite find his location, and I couldn't figure out why."

"His position wasn't static. The Hub was a huge mobile unit. The Lazy Eye."

"Precisely. It did finally dawn on me. And the last calls gave me a solid hit, and the rest is history."

Carl remained silent.

"I could call them—my friends in Montana I mean and Raul Beck, too—casualties of war, I suppose. Or I might take comfort in knowing I warned them in advance and explained the situation. They did have the alternative to escape. But they chose to stay and that is something I must deal with."

Carl nodded. "And what of the nanite infection? Are you simply going to let the people of the world keep thinking it was an act of God? Billions of people will go through this Long Time of Sorrow, as you call it, and believe that they have in some way offended their personal deity."

"Maybe it will force people to appreciate and take care of the few children there will be for the next twenty years or so. Maybe now none will starve or be murdered because they happened to be born a girl. Maybe it'll force people to give the seniors greater appreciation, rather than simply abandoning them. I honestly don't know what will happen. But it was part of the directive from Tranquility, and the alternative would have been a near certain date with a twenty-mile wide asteroid. And who knows? In the broader scheme of things, maybe it was an act of God or Nature or Providence or whatever one would like to call the things we don't understand."

"Randolf Haays should be here to hear you say that."

"Yes, my good Catholic friend. And who knows, maybe this was Plan F after all."

"It's still not over," Carl realized.

"No, not by a long shot. The asteroid is still coming. And there is another possibility that's been keeping me awake at night."

"What?"

"There is the remote chance—but one that must be considered—that Tranquility is not from this earth at all."

"What other possibility is there?"

"Consider this. We assumed—and I'm *almost* one hundred percent convinced—that Tranquility was from a different time, perhaps a hundred thousand years ago. If we accept that time is a forward arrow only, that is the logical conclusion."

"Because of the similar isotope ratios and her knowledge of the locations of the mineral deposits."

"Yes. They're almost a perfect match, but not quite."

"But are they within the limits of error?"

"Yes. Yes. Certainly, but what if there is some other explanation. As crazy as it sounds, maybe a parallel world. A sister world nearly identical to ours but in another dimension."

"And maybe she's an alien spy that wants to take over the planet," Carl added with undisguised sarcasm. "I think you're drifting off into conjecture and need to get more hours of sleep at night."

"But if she were from a parallel world, that might explain the slight discrepancies in atomic structure."

"In that case she wouldn't have to be from the past at all."

Denech nodded. "She could be from the past but wouldn't have to be. She could be from our own time and from a world overlapping with this very space, but out of phase so to speak. Similar to dark matter and energy. It's all around us but barely reacts with what we consider ordinary matter. This would also explain her invisibility."

"A characteristic she is steadily losing," Carl added. "If that line of thinking is correct, then this particular earth may not be the 'real' earth."

"Oh, it's real enough for us. It just might not be the one that makes it. We might be the sacrificial lamb offered up so the 'other' earth can continue."

"Or maybe," Carl reflected, "the people of her world have already experienced the end and placed all they were into this one being, who happened to appear to you as a child."

Denech nodded. "Either way, I guess it doesn't really matter. She could be our savior or our destructor depending upon how humanity reacts to this crisis."

"You do have a way of brightening one's mood," Carl said dryly. "And now you have me wondering."

"Wondering what?'

"Well, if Tranquility adapted to your thoughts of an innocent child, what would we be dealing with if you'd been thinking of an African safari? A lion or an elephant or maybe a rhino?"

"Somehow, I don't think that was ever a concern," Denech said seriously. "Remember, I believe there is an underlying connection to all this. She was meant to appear to us as a child, I'm certain. I just happened to pick her physical appearance."

"I have to agree."

"Hopefully, her concept of a game and the pictures she draws will continue to provide insight. We have less than one year to figure this out." Denech smiled. "The next part is really your part, or Mary's, or likely both. You are the ones, the chosen ones actually, with the symbiotic relationship with Tranquility. She has adopted you and Mary as her father and mother."

Carl glanced over and smiled at the child on the floor. "And we have grown very fond of her." The child looked up and smiled at Carl. "I love you, too, Daddy."

"It is pure conjecture at this point," Denech continued, "but we—but I believe that maybe somehow through communication with something left on the asteroid, that it might be deflected or maybe steered away."

"A lot of maybes," Carl stated, turning his attention back to Peter.

"And hopefully more than wishful thinking. Those people knew how to put it into a precise orbit. I assume they also knew how to change that orbit. I really don't know. I just know that for what I can tell, Plan C has been successful, at least so far. You and Mary are all that I could have hoped for, and I never had the least bit of doubt."

"Never?"

"Oh, well there was the time when you shot Amanda, Randolf, and Red, but, hey, we can forgive and forget. Right?"

"Wrong," Red said from the floor. "For that I still owe him one."

"That's what you get for hitting on a married man," Carl shot back.

"You're the one who gets all goggle-eyed every time you look at me."

"I just couldn't—"

"Couldn't what?" Red pressed.

"Nothing. Quit listening in on our conversations. It's men talk. Something you wouldn't understand."

"Oh, boy. Listen to him crow."

Carl glanced at Mary. She merely smiled her typical slight and knowing smile, and helped the child called Tranquility select the next crayon.

Epilogue

Mary and Carl Walker and the Tranquility child stood in the shadows of a great black walnut tree. Massive limbs a foot in diameter and twenty feet long reached out horizontally from the trunk, and Carl reached up and ran his fingers over the rough bark. In front of them a familiar water wheel remained still, even as the swift current splashed at its base. The weathered wooden structure of the abandoned grain mill remained exactly as they had left it. The cave behind would likely serve as home until the onset of winter forced a migration southward with Denech and Red.

With the temporary collapse of Wolf, Denech, Korneth, and Haays were in the process of drawing together the remains of the organization. Haays had proved his loyalty when, on his own, he had infiltrated the Agency. The Montana facility was gone, but the cause would continue. The affect of the nanites was still an open question, and an even more troubling concern was the psychological reaction the human population would have to the infection if it fully came to pass. That remained to be seen. Denech remained tight-lipped on Plan B, falling back on his standard line: "You'll just have to trust me." The symbiotic relationship between the Tranquility child and her adopted parents wouldn't be fully resolved until the following spring in 2012 when the earth had a potentially disastrous date with the huge piece of planetary debris.

Yet at the moment, none of that mattered to Carl. Despite all the arrows pointing in the wrong direction and despite the illogic, he felt nothing but a warm and peace-filled calm. He also knew that Mary did not completely share his serenity.

Together, they walked to the fallen tree by the cold stream where they had once discussed whether or not Peter Denech deserved a tranquilizer dart for his part in Red's fallacious romantic overtures. It seemed a long time ago, but only the length of a northern summer. Tranquility climbed up the fallen trunk and sat down between them. Mary looked kindly upon her innocent face, but suddenly the all too familiar wave of darkness swept through her.

"Don't be afraid," the child said.

"It's hard not to be," Mary admitted. "Events—my life—our lives are beyond my control."

Carl smiled at the child. "We won't let anything happen to her, will we Little One."

Tranquility nodded, but then thoughtfully added. "Others will begin to see me now. I won't be able to hide in the shadows."

Carl nodded. "You're growing. Every child has to grow up."

"Will I?" she asked.

"Will you what?"

"Grow up. Become as beautiful as Mommy?"

Mary lifted the child from her perch and held her tightly, and Carl circled his arms around them both.

"You will," Carl stated.

"Are you sure?"

"I'm sure. You'll just have to trust me."

And then Tranquility said a strange thing that did not come from the mind of a child. "Remember. What has been done, can, in time, be undone."

* * * *

Carl reflected. Life was a strange and often contradictory mixture of emotions and challenges and setbacks with a good bit of faith mixed in that all was not in vain—that life was more than a cruel joke played on unsuspecting sentient beings by unknown mischievous spirits. Yet human beings, himself included, were superstitious ape-men, really, with a primitive brain only recently and barely wrapped in the potential ability to be more than mere instinct.

Carl thought of the statement that few would want to know the time of the end of the world. That if all on earth knew, humanity would plummet into a morally rancid and violent time and few would even live to see the final end. Maybe so. It might yet come to that. But for himself, the knowledge that he might not live another year was in a strange way a gift. He'd try to give more, to love more, to live more, to *be* more.

What the hell, he concluded. It couldn't hurt.

978-0-595-51745-9
0-595-51745-5

```
BF       Perspectives on the
311      nature of
.P47     intellectual
2009     styles.
```

$75.00   35010000551943

DATE			

BAKER & TAYLOR

TSTI. *See* Thinking Styles in Teaching Inventory (TSTI) research tool
Twins, brain properties and, 236
Types I, II, III styles, 13–16, 64–65, 70–81, 175, 294, 295, 296
 business personnel, 79
 creativity and, 89, 91, 95, 100
 instructional style preferences and, 213–215, 218–219
 students', 70–71, 73–75, 77–81
 teachers', 71–72, 75–81
 Type I is adaptive and value-laden (empirical conclusion), 72–81
 See also Intellectual styles; Thinking styles; Three-fold model of intellectual styles

Unified structure, 116
Usefulness element of creativity, 147–150

VAK. *See* Visual, auditory, and kinesthetic learning
Valence, 127–129
 positive and negative, 9, 21–22
Value, theory-building and, 127–130
Value-differentiated styles, 294
Value-free system, 11, 15
Value-laden system, 15–16, 294, 296
 Type I as, 79–81
 vs. value-free, 13–14, 63–66, 214
Verbalizer-imagery style, 174, 176–177, 212–213, 295
Versatile style, 4, 15–19, 295
 See also Duplex model of cognitive style; Flexibility
Visual, auditory, and kinesthetic learning (VAK), 173
Vocational preferences, 272–274
Vocational purpose, Iowa Vocational Purpose Inventory, 71

Ways of thinking and practicing (WTPs), 51–53, 56–57
Wholist-analytic style, 4–5, 174, 176, 212–213, 295
Wholist cognitive approach, 39
Wholistic problem solving, 11
Wholistic thinking, 22, 30–32, 55–56, 67, 89
Work-based learning (on-the-job), 271
WTPs. *See* Ways of thinking and practicing

Zhang Cognitive Development Inventory, 71

Student voice, 200–201
Study strategies, Approaches to Study Skills Inventory for Students (ASSIST), 39–42
Supercomplexity, 57–58
Superconcepts, 152
    See also Paradigms
Superordinate style construct, 4, 107–108
Surface learning. See Shallow (surface) learning approach
Synthesizers, 13
System Checklist-90, 75

Tacit Knowledge Inventory for Managers, 19
Teacher beliefs/modeling and support, 197–198
Teacher-centered approach (knowledge-transmission approach), 72
Teacher-centered interpersonal behaviors, teaching styles and, 76
Teachers
    preferred styles of student/teacher interaction, 77–79
    research on thinking styles (Types I, II, III), 71–72, 75–79
    See also Initial teacher education (ITE); Personal learning styles pedagogy (PLSP); Preservice teachers (PSTs); Teaching styles
Teaching games, 226
Teaching-learning environments (TLEs), 46–49, 56–57
Teaching styles
    Approaches to Teaching Inventory (ATI), 72
    humor and, 76
    interpersonal behaviors toward students, 76
    occupational stress and, 76–77
    preferred styles of student/teacher interactions, 77–79
    student-centered (conceptual-change approach), 72
    teacher-centered (knowledge-transmission approach), 72
    See also Instructional style preferences
Team Role Preferences Inventory (BTRPI), 263–264

Teams, business and management, 263–265
Technology, teaching through, 221–223
Technology-based self-services, 261–262
Terminology
    addressing, 173–175
    problems with, 107–108
Theory-building and models of cognitive style, 111–113, 125–130
Thinking dispositions, 29–30, 34, 36–38
    ability, inclination, sensitivity triad, 37–38
    defined, 36
    mindfulness and, 36–37
    need for cognition, 36–37
    See also Disposition to understand for oneself
Thinking-feeling (TF) types, 262
Thinking styles
    achievement motivation study on Types, 74–75
    cognitive development and, 71
    computing and information technology (CIT) studies on Types, 74
    emotions study on Types, 74
    gifted students studies on Types, 75
    interdependent nature of, 5
    mental health study on Types, 75
    vocational purpose and, 71
    See also Intellectual styles; Mental self-government theory; Types I, II, III styles
Thinking Styles in Teaching Inventory (TSTI) research tool, 68–69, 75
Thinking Styles Inventory (TSI, TSI-R, TSI-R2) research tool, 68, 74
Three-fold model of intellectual styles, 213–215, 256, 293, 295
    amusement park theory (APT) and, 91, 95
    creativity and, 95, 100
    See also Intellectual styles; Thinking styles; Types I, II, and III
TLEs. See Teaching-learning environments
Torrance Tests for Creative Thinking, 101
Traits vs. states. See States vs. traits styles
TSI. See Thinking Styles Inventory (TSI, TSI-R, TSI-R2) research tool

Projects, 224–225
PSTs. *See* Preservice teachers
Psychiatric disorders, personality traits and, 240–241
Psychology. *See* Differential psychology
PsycINFO search engine, 87, 255
PTSLI. *See* Preferred Thinking Styles in Learning Inventory (PTSLI) research tool
PTSTI. *See* Preferred Thinking Styles in Teaching Inventory (PTSTI) research tool

Questionnaire on Teacher Interaction, 76

RASI. *See* Revised Approaches to Studying Inventory
Rational (analytical) system, 12
   See also Analytical (rational) model
Rational-actor models, 9
Rational Experiential Inventory (REI), 18, 257, 258, 259, 261, 262
Reasonable adventurers, 31
Recitation, 225
Relational thinking (wholistic), 55–56
Relativism, 33–34
Research methodology, 122–125, 127–130
   See also Theory-building and models of cognitive style
Research rubric, 123–125
Residual puzzles, 154–156
Revised Approaches to Studying Inventory (RASI), 269
Right-brain hemisphere, 30
Rote learning, 39

Sales and marketing, 260–263
   See also Business/management research and practice
School-wide enrichment triad model (SEM), 218–219
Science, normal science vs. science in crisis, 154–156
Self-concept, 108
Self-Esteem Inventory (Adult Form), 70
Self-managed work teams (SMWTs), 263
Self-regulated learning (SRL), 115
Self-reporting
   Approaches to Teaching Inventory (ATI), 72
   cognitive styles assessment and, 17–19
   creativity and, 95–97
SEM. *See* School-wide enrichment triad model
Sensing-feeling (SF) types, 262, 265–266
Sensing-intuition (SN) types, 262
Sensing-thinking (ST) types, 262, 264, 266, 278
Sensitivity to context, 36–38, 49, 57
   See also Disposition to understand for oneself; Learning processes
Sensitivity to understanding oneself, 49–51
Serialist style, 31–32, 55–56
Shallow (surface) learning approach, 39–40, 213
Sib-pair design, 240–241
Simulations, 223
Single-nucleotide polymorphisms (SNPs), 235
SMH. *See* Somatic marker hypothesis
SMWTs. *See* Self-managed work teams
SNPs. *See* Single-nucleotide polymorphisms
Social cognition research, 4
Somatic marker hypothesis (SMH), 9
Somatic phenomenal awareness, 22
Specialized level, 16
SRL. *See* Self-regulated learning
States vs. traits styles, 14, 63–65, 173, 214, 294
Stereotype development, 264
Stimulus-Response (S-R) chains, 151
Structure. *See* Paradox of structure
Structure of Scientific Revolutions, The (Kuhn), 152
Student-centered interpersonal behaviors, teaching styles and, 76
Student-centered teaching approach (conceptual-change approach), 72
Students
   preferred styles of student/teacher interactions, 77–79
   research on thinking styles (Types I, II, III), 70–71, 73–75, 77–79
   See also Learning styles

residual puzzles and counter instances, 154–156
role of, 152–153
structure and cognitive style and, 156–158
Paradigm shift, managing for developing new methodology, 122
Paradox of structure, 150–159
concepts and structure, 151–152
concepts to paradigms, 152–154
medieval astronomy example, 156
paradigms, structure, and cognitive style, 156–158
residual puzzles and counter instances, 154–156
See also Adaption-Innovation (A-I) theory
Patterns of learning, 173
Peer teaching, 225
PE models. *See* Person-environment (PE) fit models
Personality, genetic bases of, 239–242
Personality-centered theory of style, 112
Personality traits, Big Five, 36, 70, 73, 75
Personality types, 31–33, 56
Personal learning style (PLS), 169–171
application of cognitive styles models to practice, 197–203
See also Personal learning styles pedagogy (PLSP)
Personal learning styles pedagogy (PLSP), 169–208
application of cognitive styles models to practice, 197–202
cognitive experiential self theory (CEST) and, 199
Cognitive Styles Analysis (CSA) and, 170, 176–178, 199
Cognitive Styles Index (CSI) and, 170, 178–179, 199
creating optimal conditions for learning, 200
design of learning environments, 201–202
developing and adopting a, 179–202
in initial teacher education (ITE) context and setting, 169–172, 176, 178, 179–181, 198, 202–203
key themes, 181–196
selection and application of models, 198–199
student voice, 200–201

teacher beliefs/modeling and support, 197–198
terminology and conceptual issues, 173–175
Person-environment (PE) fit models, 272–274
PET, 5
PID. *See* Preference for Intuition and Deliberation
PLS. *See* Personal learning style
PLSP. *See* Personal learning styles pedagogy
Plungers (impulsive), 31
Positive valence, 9
Potential capacity, 139
Practice, intuition and, 20–21
Prediction/flexibility trade-off, 152–154
Predispositions, 13
Preference for Intuition and Deliberation (PID), 17–18
Preferences, 13, 16, 30
cognitive style and learned coping behavior and (Adaption-Innovation [A-I] theory), 138–143
intellectual styles, 63
personality and, 31–32
student/teacher interactions, 77–79
vocational, 272–274
See also Instructional style preferences
Preferred Thinking Styles in Learning Inventory (PTSLI) research tool, 69, 77
Preferred Thinking Styles in Teaching Inventory (PTSTI) research tool, 69, 77
Preservice teachers (PSTs), 169, 171–172
See also Personal learning styles pedagogy (PLSP)
Probability theories, 9
Problem solving
business and management, 265–268
as the key to life, 165–166
leadership and, 164–165
problem-solving level (unipolar concept) described, 137–138, 292, 293
problem-solving style (bipolar concept) described, 137–138, 292
See also Adaption-Innovation (A-I) theory

Management/organizational learning
    styles, 268–272
  course design, 270
  influence of styles on research
    supervision, 269
  learning performance, 269–270
  organizational learning, 271–272
  work-based learning, 271
  See also Business/management
    research and practice
Management research. *See* Business/
  management research and
  practice
Manifest capacity, 139
Marketing, 260–263
  See also Business/management
    research and practice
MBTI. *See* Myers-Briggs Type Indicator
Measurement
  for business and management, 257–259
  creativity and, 148–149
Meditation, 22
Memorization, 34, 39
Mental health
  genetics and, 240–242
  study on Types, 75
Mental self-government theory, 64,
    66–69, 88
  forms (monarchic, hierarchical,
    oligarchic, anarchic), 66–67
  functions (legislative, executive
    judicial), 66
  leanings (liberal, conservative), 67–68
  levels (local, global), 67
  Preferred Thinking Styles in
    Learning Inventory (PTSLI)
    research tool, 69
  Preferred Thinking Styles in
    Teaching Inventory (PTSTI)
    research tool, 69
  scopes (internal, external), 67
  Thinking Styles in Teaching Inventory
    (TSTI) research tool, 68–69
  Thinking Styles Inventory (TSI,
    TSI-R, TSI-R2) research tool, 68
  See also Intellectual styles
Metacognition, 34
Metacognitive skills training programs, 16
  See also Business/management
    research and practice
Metalearning, 34
Microdomains, 99–100

Mindfulness, 36–37, 56
Mindfulness meditation, 22
Monarchic thinking style, 66, 89
Monitoring understanding, 40–42
Moods, 21
Motivation, creativity and, 91
Myers-Briggs Type Indicator (MBTI),
    112, 258, 260, 262, 265, 269, 275

Narrative thought, 88, 103
NCS. *See* Need for cognitive structure
Need for closure (NFC), 267–268
Need for cognitive structure (NCS), 267
Negative valence, 9
NEO Five-Factor Inventory, 70, 73, 75
NEO Personality Inventory-Revised, 73
Neurons, 236–237
Neurosciences, 294
  intuition and, 5, 15, 19
  right/left brain hemispheres, 30
  See also Genes; Genetic etiology of
    intellectual styles
Neuroticism, genetic bases of, 240–241
NFC. *See* Need for closure
No Child Left Behind (U.S.), 169
Nonacademic settings, 64
  See also Business/management
    research and practice
Noncommitters (cautious), 31
Nurturing, 92

Occupational stress, teaching styles and,
    76–77
Occupational Stress Inventory, 76
Oligarchic thinking style, 66–67, 89
Onion model, 215, 255, 296
Ontology, 124
Operation learning, 31–32
Organizational learning styles.
    See Management/organizational
    learning styles; Business/
    management research and
    practice
Organized approach to studying, 39–42
Overlapping of styles across theories, 295

Paradigmatic thought, 88, 103
Paradigm dialogue, 115
Paradigms
  from concepts to, 152–154
  defined, 152
  limitations of, 153–154

IQ. *See* Intelligence quotient
ITE. *See* Initial teacher education

Job performance, 277–278
Journalists, 89
Judicial thinking style, 66, 88–89
Jungian style classifications, 266

KAI. *See* Kirton Adaption-Innovation inventory
KIRBA gene, 235
Kirton Adaption-Innovation inventory (KAI), 138, 140, 142–143, 258–264, 268
 See also Adaption-Innovation (A-I) theory
Knowledge, conceptions of, 33–34, 35
Knowledge-transmission approach (teacher-centered), 72

Leader-member exchange (LMX), 275
Leadership
 business and management, 274–276
 problem solving and, 164–165
 See also Business/management research and practice
Learner identities, disposition to understand for oneself and, 53–55
Learning
 approach to, 38–42
 conceptions of, 34, 35
Learning conditions, selecting optimal, 200
Learning environment design, 201–202
Learning processes, 29–42
 approaches to learning and study strategies, 38–42
 Approaches to Study Skills Inventory for Students (ASSIST), 39–42
 conceptions of knowledge, 33–34, 35
 conceptions of learning, 34, 35
 learning styles and thinking processes, 30–33
 sensitivity to context, 36–38
 thinking dispositions, 29, 34, 36–38
 See also Disposition to understand for oneself
Learning Skills Council review of learning styles, 113–114

Learning styles
 achievement motivation and, 74–75
 cognitive development and, 71
 computing and information technology (CIT) and, 73–74
 emotions and, 74
 gifted students and, 75
 instructional style preferences and, 210–212
 Learning Skills Council review of, 113–114
 management and organizational, 268–272
 mental health and, 75
 preferred styles of student/teacher interactions, 77–79
 vocational purpose and, 71
 See also Instructional style preferences; Personal learning styles pedagogy (PLSP); Students
Learning Styles Inventory (LSI-III), 218–228, 295
 1. direct instruction, 220–221
 2. teaching through technology, 221–223
 3. simulations, 223
 4. independent study, 223–224
 5. projects, 224–225
 6. peer teaching, 225
 7. drill and recitation, 225
 8. discussion, 225–226
 9. teaching games, 226
Left-brain hemisphere, 30
Legislative thinking style, 66, 88–89
Level-style distinction, 137–143, 292, 293
 See also Adaption-Innovation (A-I) theory
Liberal thinking style, 67, 89
Linear/Non-Linear Thinking Styles Profile (LNTSP), 257, 259
LMX. *See* Leader-member exchange
LNTSP. *See* Linear/Non-Linear Thinking Styles Profile
Local thinking style, 67, 89
Logic and detail (serialist) thinking, 55–56
LSI-III. *See* Learning Styles Inventory

Management of change, 159–165
 See also Adaption-Innovation (A-I) theory

High level element of creativity, 147–150
Humor, teaching styles and, 76
Humor Styles Questionnaire, 76
Hustlers (competitive), 31

IDQ. *See* Individual Difference Questionnaire
ILDs. *See* Individual learning differences
Improvidence (serialist style), 32
Inconsistency, creativity and, 149–150
Independent study, 223–224
Individual Difference Questionnaire (IDQ), 212
Individual learning differences (ILDs), 173
 See also Differential psychology
Individual learning performance model, 119–122
Initial teacher education (ITE), 169–172, 176, 178, 179–181, 198, 202–203
 See also Personal learning styles pedagogy (PLSP)
Innovation
 entrepreneurship and, 259–260
 overvaluation of, 143–150
 See also Adaption-Innovation (A-I) theory
Innovative creativity, 155–156
 See also Adaption-Innovation (A-I) theory
Instructional style preferences, 209–231
 cognitive and learning styles theories, 210–212
 Curry's onion model, 215
 intellectual styles theory (threefold model of intellectual styles), 213–215
 matching instruction to learning styles, 215–218
 Renzulli's learning styles inventory (LSI-III), 218–228, 295
  1. direct instruction, 220–221
  2. teaching through technology, 221–223
  3. simulations, 223
  4. independent study, 223–224
  5. projects, 224–225
  6. peer teaching, 225
  7. drill and recitation, 225
  8. discussion, 225–226
  9. teaching games, 226

 wholist-analytic and verbalizer-imager styles, 212–213
Integrated concept, 116–117
Intellectual styles
 conclusion: empirical evidence that styles are value-laden with Type I more adaptive, 79–81
 controversial issues, 63–64, 293–294
 definition and constructs of, 63
 earlier research on thinking styles (Types I, II, III)
  students, 70–71
  teachers, 71–72
 instructional style preferences and, 213–215
 new research on thinking styles (Types I, II, III)
  students, 73–75
  teachers, 75–77
 preferred styles: students and teachers in interaction, 77–79
 styles of business personnel, 79
 Type I described, 64–65
 Type II described, 64–65
 Type III described, 64–65
 See also Mental self-government theory; Thinking styles; Three-fold model of intellectual styles; Types I, II, III styles
Intelligence
 creativity and, 90–91
 genetic bases of, 234–239
Intelligence quotient (IQ), 234–239
Internal cues, 88
Internal thinking style, 67, 89
Interpersonal behaviors toward students, teaching styles and, 76
Interpersonal relationships, in business and management, 277
Intuition, in management, 19–22
Intuition-feeling (NF) types, 262, 264, 266, 278
Intuition-thinking (NT) types, 262, 265–266, 278
Intuitive (experiential) model, 3–22, 295
 See also Duplex model of cognitive style; Experiential (intuitive) system
Investment theory, 87
Iowa Managing Emotions Inventory, 74
Iowa Vocational Purpose Inventory, 71

styles-as-different-constructs vs. styles-as-similar-constructs, 14
styles-as-traits vs. states-as-states, 14
synthesizers, 13
Tacit Knowledge Inventory for Managers, 19
Types I, II, and III, 13–16
versatile style, 4, 15–19

EBSCO search engine, 255
Eclectics, 13
Educational applications. *See* Personal learning styles pedagogy (PLSP); Learning Styles Inventory (LSI-III)
Educational kinesiology, 173
EEG. *See* Electroencephalograph
Effort, organized, 39–42
EFT. *See* Embedded Figures Test
Electroencephalograph (EEG), 5
ELT. *See* Experiential learning theory
Embedded Figures Test (EFT), 7, 30
Emotions, 21
  study on Types, 74
Enhancing Teaching and Learning (ETL) project, 40, 47, 51–52
Entrepreneurship, innovation and, 259–260
Environment, creativity and, 91–92
Epistemology, 124
ESM. *See* Experience sampling method
Ethical judgments and reasoning, in business and management, 278
ETL. *See* Enhancing Teaching and Learning project
Every Child Matters (U.K.), 169
Exclusivity, creativity and, 148
Executive thinking style, 66, 88–89
Experience sampling method (ESM), 19
Experiential (intuitive) system, 11–12
  See also Duplex model of cognitive style; Intuitive (experiential) model
Experiential learning theory (ELT), 211
Explorers, 13
External cues, 88
External thinking style, 67, 89

Feedback, intuition and, 21
Field-dependence/field-independence, 30, 88, 214, 270
Fine artists, 89
Flexibility level, 16, 64
  See also Versatile style
Flexibility/prediction trade-off, 152–154
fMRI, 5, 19
Focusing, 22
Formal conversation (paradigm dialogue), 115

GEFT. *See* Group Embedded Figures Test
Gender differences, 34
General Symptomatic Index, 75
Genes
  apolipoprotein E (*APOE*), 237–238
  candidate, 235–236
  catechol-O-methyl transferase (*COMT*), 238–239
  neurotransmitters and genes related to their metabolism, 235
  related to developmental processes, 235–236
Genetic etiology of intellectual styles, 233–251
  brain structure, 236–237
  coping styles, 243–244
  genetic bases of intelligence, 234–239
  genetic bases of neuroticism, 240–241
  genetic bases of personality, 239–242
  See also Neurosciences
Genome-wide linkage and association studies (scans), 234–236, 240–242
Gifted students
  creativity and, 89
  studies on Types, 75
Globalized business world, 277
  See also Culture
Global thinking. *See* Wholistic thinking
Global thinking style, 67, 89
Globetrotting (wholist style), 32
Good style theory, 125–127
Group Embedded Figures Test (GEFT), 261, 262, 268
Groups, business and management, 263–265

Heuristic intuition, 6–7, 9
Heuristics, 4
Hierarchical structure of style, 4, 16, 89
Hierarchical thinking style, 66–67
Hierarchy, microdomains and, 100–101

Design of learning environments, 201–202
Different-constructs vs. similar constructs style, 14, 63–65
Differential psychology, 107–134, 293
  defining, 109–110
  defining style: a model of an individual's learning performance, 119–122
  good style theory: new, 126–127
  good style theory: traditional, 125–126
  knowledge creation and research methodology, 122–125
  Learning Skills Council review of learning styles, 113–114
  managing paradigm shift and developing new methodology for researching styles, 122
  need for a paradigm dialogue, 115
  need for reference to a unified structure in a person's psychological system, 116
  need for research theory enabling an integrated concept of the person, 116–117
  shift in thinking about individual differences, 110–111
  theory-building and models of cognitive style, 111–113, 127–130
Direct instruction, 220–221
Discontinuous thought element of creativity, 147–150
Discussion, 225–226
Dispositions
  defined, 36
  mindfulness and, 36–37
  See also Disposition to understand for oneself; Thinking dispositions
Disposition to understand for oneself, 42–58, 292–293
  approach to learning background, 38–39
  cultures of academic disciplines (ways of thinking and practicing [WTPs]) and, 51–53
  deep approach, 42–45
  learner identities and, 53–55
  students' sensitivity to opportunities for developing the, 49–51
  teaching-learning environments (TLEs) and, 46–49

Divergent thinking test, 101
Diverse styles accommodation, 81
DNA, 235
Domains of mind, 93
Domain theory, 87–106
  See also Amusement park theory (APT)
Drill and recitation, 225
DRM. *See* Day reconstruction method
DSS design. *See* Decision support system (DSS) design
Dual-process theories. *See* Duplex model of cognitive style
Duplex model of cognitive style, 3–28, 293, 294, 295, 296
  analytical (rational) model, 3–4, 7–9, 12, 16
  cognitive-experiential self-theory (CEST), 10–12
  cognitive mapping, 19
  cognitive style defined, 3
  Cognitive Style Index (CSI) and, 17, 18
  Cognitive Versatility Index (CVI) and, 18–19
  critical incident technique (CIT), 19
  day reconstruction method (DRM), 19
  eclectics, 13
  experience sampling method (ESM), 19
  explorers, 13
  fMRI application to intuition study, 19
  hierarchical structure of, 16
  intuition inclusion in business and management, 19–22
    awareness, 21–22
    feedback, 21
    practice, 20–21
  intuitive (experiential) model, 3–4, 6–10, 11, 16
  neuroscience and, 15, 19
  predispositions and, 13
  Preference for Intuition and Deliberation (PID), 17–18
  preferences and, 15
  Rational Experiential Inventory (REI), 18
  research issues for cognitive style, 4–5
  style as value-laden vs. value-free, 13–14, 15

instructional style preferences and, 210–212
paradigms and structure and, 156–158
preferences and learned coping behavior, 138–143
theory-building and models of cognitive style, 111–113, 127–130
translation into educational settings, 172–175
See also Duplex model of cognitive style; Personal learning styles pedagogy (PLSP)
Cognitive Style Index (CSI), 5, 17, 18, 257, 260, 269
Cognitive Style Indicator (CoSI), 112, 257
Cognitive Styles Analysis (CSA), 5, 170, 176–178
Cognitive Styles Index (CSI), 170, 178–179
Cognitive Versatility Index (CVI), 18–19
Comprehension learning, 31–32
Computing and information technology (CIT), studies on Types, 74
COMT gene. *See* Catechol-O-methyl transferase gene
Conceptions of knowledge, 33–34, 35
Conceptions of learning, 34, 35
Concepts
  to paradigms, 152–154
  structure and, 151–152
Conceptual-change approach (student-centered approach to teaching), 72
Conceptual issues, addressing, 173–175
Conceptual tempo, 211
Consensual Assessment Technique, 88
Conservative thinking style, 67, 89
Consumer behavior, 261–262
Consumer perception, 260–261
Context, sensitivity to, 36–38
Coping behavior, 142–143
  See also Adaption-Innovation (A-I) theory
Coping styles, genetics and, 243–244
Corpus callosum, 30
CoSI. *See* Cognitive Style Indicator
Counter instances, 154–156
Course design, management education, 270

Creative thinking, promoting through styles of thinking, 63
Creative writers, 89
Creativity, 87–106, 293
  creative domains, 101–103
  definition problems, 146–147
  field-dependence/field-independence, 88
  general thematic factors, 94–97
  investment theory, 87
  mental self-government theory, 88–89
  narrative and paradigmatic thought theory, 88
  overvaluation of innovation and, 143–150
  three-point descriptions (discontinuous thought, high level, usefulness) and weaknesses of, 147–150
  Types I, II, III theory, 89, 294
  variables essential to, 87
  See also Adaption-Innovation (A-I) theory; Amusement park theory (APT)
Creativity Achievement Questionnaire, 93
Critical incident technique (CIT), 19
CSA. *See* Cognitive Styles Analysis
CSI. *See* Cognitive Style Index
CSI. *See* Cognitive Styles Index
Culture
  of academic disciplines (ways of thinking and practicing [WTPs]) and, 51–53
  cross-cultural adaptation differences in business, 276–277
  cross-cultural cognitive style differences in business, 276
  need for more cross-cultural studies of styles, 297
Customer relations, 262–263
CVI. *See* Cognitive Versatility Index

Day reconstruction method (DRM), 19
Decision making, business and management, 265–268
Decision support system (DSS) design, 267
Deep approach to learning, 39–45, 213
Definitions, problems with, 107–108
Dendrites, 236–237

Apolipoprotein E (*APOE*) gene, 237–238
Applicative styles, 209
Approaches to learning and study strategies, 38–42
   See also Disposition to understand for oneself
Approaches to Study Skills Inventory for Students (ASSIST), 39–42
Approaches to Teaching Inventory (ATI), 72
APT. *See* Amusement park theory
Articulated (analytic) style, 30
ASSIST. *See* Approaches to Study Skills Inventory for Students
ATI. *See* Approaches to Teaching Inventory
Atomist cognitive approach, 39
Awareness, intuition and, 21–22

Behavior, coping behavior, 142–143
Behavior-genetic factors, 240–242
Big Five Personality Factors, 36, 70, 73, 75
Brain
   left and right hemispheres, 30
   structure of, 236–237
BTRPI. *See* Team Role Preferences Inventory
Business/management research and practice, 253–290, 292, 295–296
   cross-cultural differences in cognitive styles and adaptation, 276–277
   decision making and problem solving, 265–268
      decision support systems, 267
      general managerial decision making, 267–268
      strategic decision making, 265–266
   enhancing managers' intuitive awareness, 19–22
   ethical judgments and reasoning, 278
   future research implications, 278–282
   groups and teams, 263–265
   innovation and entrepreneurship, 259–260
   interpersonal relationships, 277
   issues for style researchers, 4–6
   job performance, 277–278
   leadership, 274–276
   management and organizational learning, 268–272
      course design, 270
      influence of styles on research supervision in management education, 269
      learning performance, 269–270
      organizational learning, 271–272
      work-based learning, 271
   person-environment (PE) fit models, careers, and vocational preference, 272–274
   review process, 254–255
   sales and marketing, 260–263
      consumer perception and information use, 260–261
      customer relations, 262–263
      individual differences in consumer behavior, 261–262
   theory and measurement, 256–259
   Type I and Type II thinking styles studies, 79

Candidate genes, 235–236
Catechol-O-methyl transferase (*COMT*) gene, 238–239
CEST. *See* Cognitive-experiential self-theory
Change
   agents of, 163–164
   leadership and, 164–165, 275–276
   style and, 161–163
   See also Adaption-Innovation (A-I) theory; Problem solving
Chromosomes, 235
CIT. *See* Critical incident technique
Cognition, need for, 36–37
Cognition-centered theory of style, 112
Cognitive development
   thinking styles and, 71
   Zhang Cognitive Development Inventory, 71
Cognitive-experiential self-theory (CEST), 10–12, 199
Cognitive gap, 159–160
Cognitive mapping, 19
Cognitive phenomenal awareness, 22
Cognitive style(s)
   addressing terminology and conceptual issues, 173–175
   application of models to practice, 197–202
   defined, 3, 108

Index

A-I theory. *See* Adaption-Innovation (A-I) theory
AACS. *See* Ability to achieve cognitive structure
Ability, 55
Ability, inclination, sensitivity triad, 37–38
Ability to achieve cognitive structure (AACS), 267
Achievement motivation, study on Types, 74–75
Achievement Motives Scale, 74
Achieving learning approach, 213
Activity-centered theory of style, 112
Adaptation, cross-cultural in business, 276–277
Adaption-Innovation (A-I) theory, 137–168
  agents of change, 163–164
  cognitive gaps, 159–160
  examples of, 144–145
  level-style distinction (cognitive style, preferences, and learned coping behavior), 138–143
  management of change and problem solving, 159–165
  overvaluation of innovation, 143–150
  problem solving as the key to life, 165–166
  problem-solving leadership, 164–165
  problem-solving level (unipolar concept) described, 137–138
  problem-solving style (bipolar concept) described, 137–138
  style and change, 161–163
  three-point description of creativity and problems with, 147–150
  See also Kirton Adaption-Innovation inventory (KAI); Paradox of structure

Adaptive creativity, 155–156
  See also Adaption-Innovation (A-I) theory
Adaptiveness, Type I thinking style and, 70–81
Advertising, 261
AERA. *See* American Educational Research Association
Affect, 9, 11
  defined, 21–22
Agents of change, 163–164
  See also Adaption-Innovation (A-I) theory
American Educational Research Association (AERA), 130
American Psychological Association, construct of intelligence, 114–115
Amusement park theory (APT), 90–103
  advantages of, 101–103
  creative domains, 94–97, 101–103
  domains, 97–99
  environment and, 91–92
  general thematic areas (domains), 92–97
  initial requirements, 90–92
  intelligence and, 90–91
  microdomains, 99–100
  motivation and, 91
  three-fold model of intellectual styles and, 91, 95
  See also Creativity; Domain theory
Analytical (rational) model, 3–22, 30, 295
  See also Duplex model of cognitive style
Analytic West-intuitive East dichotomy, 276
Anarchic thinking style, 66–67, 89
APOE gene. *See* Apolipoprotein E (*APOE*) gene

299

Riding, R. J., & Cheema, I. (1991). Cognitive styles—an overview and integration. *Educational Psychology, 11*(3 & 4), 193–215.
Snow, R. E., Corno, L., & Jackson, D. III (1996). Individual differences in affective and conative functions. In D. C. Berliner & R. C. Calfee (Eds.), *Handbook of educational psychology* (pp. 186–242). New York: Simon & Schuster Macmillan.
Sternberg, R. J. (2001). Epilogue: Another mysterious affair at styles. In R. J. Sternberg & L. F. Zhang (Eds.), *Perspectives on thinking, learning, and cognitive styles.* (pp. 249–252). Mahwah, NJ: Lawrence Erlbaum.
Sternberg, R. J., & Zhang, L. F. (Eds.). (2001). *Perspectives on thinking, learning, and cognitive styles.* Mahwah, NJ: Lawrence Erlbaum.
Tiedemann, J. (1989). Measures of cognitive styles: A critical review. *Educational Psychology, 24,* 261–275.
Witkin, H. A., Moore, C. A., Goodenough, D. R., & Cox, P. W. (1977). Field dependent and field independent cognitive styles and their educational implications. *Review of Educational Research, 47,* 1–64.
Zhang, L. F., & Sternberg, R. J. (2005). A threefold model of intellectual styles. *Educational Psychology Review, 17*(1), 1–53.
Zhang, L. F., & Sternberg, R. J. (2006). *The nature of intellectual styles.* Mahwah, NJ: Lawrence Erlbaum.

Fourth, the field of styles needs better links to other academic fields. Otherwise, it will continue to be isolated from and even disparaged by investigators in other fields in psychology and education.

Finally, the field needs more cross-cultural studies as well as cross-disciplinary and international collaborations. There is no such thing as a context- and/or meaning-free environment (LeVine, Miller, & West, 1988). We learn and make sense of our learning experiences within cultural contexts. Therefore, in studying the nature of intellectual styles, culture must be taken into account. Cross-disciplinary and international collaborations would play a pivotal role in further stimulating the field of intellectual styles to become more widely accepted.

REFERENCES

Armstrong, S. J. (1999). The influence of individual cognitive style on performance in management education. *Educational Psychology, 20*(3), 323–339.

Coffield, F. C. (2005, January 14). Kinaesthetic nonsense. *The Times Educational Supplement,* 17–18.

Coffield, F. C., Moseley, D. V. M., Hall, E., & Ecclestone, K. (2004a). *Learning styles and pedagogy in post-16 learning: Findings of a systematic and critical review of learning styles models.* London: Learning and Skills Research Centre.

Coffield, F. C., Moseley, D. V. M., Hall, E., & Ecclestone, K. (2004b). *Should we be using learning styles? What research has to say to practice.* London: Learning and Skills Research Centre.

Curry, L. (1983). An organization of learning styles theory and constructs. *ERIC Document, 235,* 185.

Epstein, S. (2008). Intuition from the perspective of cognitive-experiential self-theory. In H. Plessner, C. Betsch, & T. Betsch (Eds.), *Intuition in judgment and decision making* (pp. 23–37). New York: Lawrence Erlbaum Associates.

Freedman, R. D., & Stumpf, S. A. (1980). Learning style theory: Less than meets the eye. *Academy of Management Review, 5*(3), 445–447.

Grigorenko, E. L., & Sternberg, R. J. (1995). Thinking styles. In D. Saklofske & M. Zeidner (Eds.), *International handbook of personality and intelligence* (pp. 205–229). New York: Plenum.

LeVine, R., Miller, P., & West, M. (Eds.) (1988). *Parental behavior in diverse societies: Vol. 40. New directions for child development.* San Francisco: Jossey-Bass.

Messick, S. (1996). Bridging cognition and personality in education: The role of style in performance and development. *European Journal of Personality, 10,* 353–376.

Miller, A. (1987). Cognitive styles: An integrated model. *Educational Psychology, 7*(4), 251–268.

Perry, W. G. (1999). *Forms of intellectual and ethical development in the college years: A scheme.* (3rd ed.). San Francisco: Jossey-Bass.

Renzulli, J. S., Smith, L. H., & Rizza, M. G. (2002). *Learning Styles Inventory—Version III.* Mansfield, CT: Creative Learning Press.

Armstrong and Cools have provided an up-to-date and comprehensive review of some applications of styles to the business world. Finally, in relation to applications of styles, Sadler-Smith's chapter can be perceived to have cut across the educational and business worlds. Sadler-Smith proposes three ways in which his duplex model of cognitive style may be used in developing better intuitive judgment in management education and training: practice, feedback, and awareness.

One would naturally be wondering: What now? Where to next? What are some of the important directions one could take to further advance the field? Again, there could be many types of efforts that one could invest to enrich the field. We believe that the following five types of endeavors are critical for progress.

First, it is important that integrative models of styles be empirically tested. In the past two decades, a number of integrative models of styles have been postulated, the earliest of which was Curry's (1983) onion model of learning styles, and the latest of which is Sadler-Smith's duplex model of cognitive style, proposed in this volume (see Zhang & Sternberg, 2006, for a comprehensive review). Although each of these models seems to show great promise in unification, only Riding and Cheema's (1991) model has been extensively tested.

Second, although several chapters in this book articulate how styles can be used in school and at work, much of this discussion has been proposed merely at the theoretical level. Whether or not the proposed strategies can be implemented in the classroom and in the workplace and whether or not school and job performance would be enhanced as a result of this implementation remain to be seen.

Third, empirical research is needed to clarify the nature of intellectual styles, in particular, with regard to the issues of style value and style malleability. Take the issue of style value. Although contributors in this volume all take the same position that styles are not value-free and although, theoretically, Type I styles carry more positive value, there is a fundamental disagreement on the weight that Type I styles have in real life. For example, some authors (Jablokow and Kirton) argue that Type I styles tend to be overvalued, whereas others (Kaufman and Baer; Sadler-Smith; Zhang and Sternberg) maintain that Type I styles are undervalued. What do people really think about Type I styles? Are Type I styles really beneficial to their lives? To what degree are Type I styles constructive in people's success? Similarly, although it is generally agreed that styles are malleable, this discussion has, thus far, been conducted at a conceptual level rather than an empirical one.

modifiable. Similarly, Rayner and Peterson's stand on the malleability of styles is manifested through their assertion that "cognitive style should be viewed as a complex, dynamic structure defined as part of a person's psychological system" (p. 108 in this volume). The notion of style development also permeates the chapter by Entwistle and McCune. The investigators believe that the disposition to understand for oneself can be evoked and developed through one's interpretation of one's learning environments. From the perspective of etiology, Grigorenko argues that styles are at least in part socialized, although they may have some partial genetic basis. Nonetheless, Jablokow and Kirton maintain that styles are not modifiable.

There is general agreement that styles overlap highly across theories. For example, Evans and Waring acknowledge the overlapping nature of styles by discussing the notion of a hierarchy of interrelated cognitive style dimensions. Renzulli and Sullivan show overlap among styles by reviewing two of the most recent integrative style models: Riding and Cheema's (1991) wholist-analytic and verbal-imagery style dimensions, and Zhang and Sternberg's (2005) three types of intellectual styles. Rayner and Peterson allude to the overlapping nature of various styles by pointing out the confusion over definitions of and terminologies for styles. Endorsing the overlapping nature of styles, Kaufman and Baer argue for the strong association between Type I intellectual styles and creativity within the context of Zhang and Sternberg's three types of intellectual styles. As a final example, in proposing his duplex model of cognitive style, Sadler-Smith employs two modes (analytic and intuitive) and one style (versatile) to encapsulate a large array of previously proposed style labels.

The sixth and the final message is that styles can be applied to the business world as well as to education. In this volume, several chapters have demonstrated how the concept of styles can be applied to educational contexts. Evans and Waring detail how what they call "a personal learning styles pedagogy" can be created by integrating knowledge of styles into teacher education programs in higher education. Renzulli and Sullivan describe strategies that school teachers can take in using different instructional methods to accommodate students' stylistic preferences described in the Learning Style Inventory (LSI-III; Renzulli, Smith, & Rizza, 2002). Zhang and Sternberg discuss how research findings regarding people's valuing of styles can be effective in facilitating a better understanding of the possible discrepancy between what people say they want and what they do when it comes to rewarding Type I styles.

Although contributors in this book generally agree that styles are not value-free, that they are largely malleable, and that they overlap highly across theories, reaching a consensus on these issues seems unlikely.

Consider the general understanding that styles are value-laden. The common view shared by all contributors is that of styles' being value-differentiated. That is, context plays an important role in the effectiveness of a style—the same style that serves an individual in one situation could fail the same person in another situation. Yet, within this common understanding, contributors' views differ regarding which types of styles carry more positive value. For example, in discussing the relationship between Type I intellectual styles (i.e., creativity-generating styles; Zhang & Sternberg, 2005, 2006) and creativity, Kaufman and Baer have articulated the advantages of Type I styles over Type II styles (i.e., norm-favoring styles). Likewise, Zhang and Sternberg have cited numerous studies demonstrating that Type I styles are associated with a wide range of attributes deemed to be positive. Although these empirical findings suggest that Type I styles should be encouraged, in reality Type I styles are often stifled. Zhang and Sternberg have pointed out the discrepancy between what educators say they want (i.e., Type I styles from students) and what they often have done (i.e., encourage Type II styles among students, at least for most of the time). Similarly, Sadler-Smith has pointed out that much of education and training is directed more toward the development of the analytic mode (Type II style) than toward the intuitive mode (Type I style) of processing. He has argued that the intuitive mode should not be ignored. Contrary to this view, Jablokow and Kirton believe that too much importance has been placed on Type I styles.

Regarding the state-versus-trait dispute, the majority of contributors in this volume favor the notion that styles are malleable. For example, referring to his duplex model of cognitive style, Sadler-Smith has asserted that unless an individual's neural circuitry is damaged, he or she has access to both the analytic mode and the intuitive mode. Furthermore, both modes can be modified through learning and socialization. After an in-depth analysis of the complexities involved in the debate over the state-versus-trait issue, Evans and Waring point out that the development of a personal learning styles pedagogy is contingent on several key components, including explicit guidance, concrete and appropriate exemplars to contextualize the learning events, reinforcement and transfer of ideas to new contexts, and opportunities to observe different ways of seeing and doing. Clearly, Evans and Waring suggest that styles are

by Entwistle and McCune; "problem-solving level" by Jablokow and Kirton; "versatile style" by Sadler-Smith). Zhang and Sternberg's (2005, 2006) threefold model of intellectual styles has been used by a number of authors (e.g., Armstrong and Cools; Evans and Waring; Jablokow and Kirton; Kaufman and Baer; Rayner and Peterson; Renzulli and Sullivan; Zhang and Sternberg). Kaufman and Baer, for instance, have used the threefold model of intellectual styles as the guiding framework for illustrating the relationships between intellectual styles and creativity, both in general and specifically across domains. Sadler-Smith's duplex model of cognitive style also elucidates how some of the previously postulated style concepts in the field can be encapsulated by three overarching styles: intuitive, analytical, and versatile. Sadler-Smith also has taken a step further by drawing an analogy between the styles in his duplex model and those in Zhang and Sternberg's threefold model.

Fourth, it is possible to situate the styles literature within the larger context of psychological, educational, and business literatures. The field of styles is entwined with several fields of investigations. For example, Entwistle and McCune discuss at length how learning theories (e.g., conceptions of learning and knowledge), developmental psychology (e.g., Perry's [1999] theory of intellectual development), and personality theories (e.g., thinking disposition; Snow, Corno, & Jackson, 1996) can interact with intellectual styles to contribute to what they call "the disposition to understand for oneself." They further provide empirical evidence supporting the relationship between learner identity and the disposition to understand for oneself. Moreover, Jablokow and Kirton have adeptly integrated work in differential psychology (e.g., creativity) and organizational psychology with work on styles. Additionally, Kaufman and Baer have cogently presented their view on how styles are related to both people's general tendencies for creativity and their creativity across multiple specific domains. Rayner and Peterson also have successfully brought styles into the mainstream of differential psychology. Sadler-Smith has done something similar, constructing a duplex model of cognitive style based on Epstein's (2008) work on experiential and rational systems, which is itself rooted in a global theory of personality. Finally, in arguing for the position that styles are value-laden, Zhang and Sternberg have provided abundant empirical evidence indicating that intellectual styles are strongly associated with a wide range of constructs typically studied in the student-development literature.

Fifth, the three controversial issues mentioned in the preface (i.e., style value, style malleability, and style overlap) are still open to debate.

opinion of the state of research into cognitive styles has to be: there is no point in chasing a chimera!" (p. 273; see also Freedman & Stumpf, 1980). Some disagreed. For example, Armstrong (1999), Miller (1987), and Riding and Cheema (1991) traced the development of the styles literature. They acknowledged that the field of styles was not where it should be. Sternberg (2001) articulated some factors responsible for the premature decline of the field (see preface to this volume).

During the past two decades, the field of styles has regained some momentum. First, new theories better differentiate styles from abilities and make more contact with the psychological literature. Recent investigations are also, in many cases, more carefully conducted and their results more conclusive than those from some of the older research. More importantly, several scholars have attempted to integrate the existing literature under newly encompassing theoretical frameworks (e.g., Curry, 1983; Grigorenko & Sternberg, 1995; Miller, 1987; Riding & Cheema, 1991; Sternberg & Zhang, 2001; Zhang & Sternberg, 2005, 2006). Some, however, still reject the notion of styles (e.g., Coffield, 2005; Coffield, Moseley, Hall, & Ecclestone, 2004a, 2004b).

Here are six messages of this book: First, styles do matter! Styles make a difference in behavior and performance in diverse domains of our life, ranging from ways of learning and of solving problems to various aspects of development (such as affective development, cognitive development, career development, and identity development; e.g., Entwistle and McCune; Jablokow and Kirton; Renzulli and Sullivan; Zhang and Sternberg), and from academic achievement to job performance (e.g., Armstrong and Cools; Evans and Waring; Kaufman and Baer).

Second, as noted by Jablokow and Kirton, styles differ from abilities ("problem-solving level," to use the authors' terminology). For these authors, ability is unipolar and can be measured from high to low; it also has "a socially preferred end"; style, in contrast, is a bipolar concept that has "no socially preferred end." Although this distinction has been made by other authors elsewhere (Messick, 1996; Witkin, Moore, Goodenough, & Cox, 1977), Jablokow and Kirton newly elucidate relationships of creativity and problem solving to the level-style distinction.

Third, it is possible to build a common language, operating within a conceptual framework for styles. Some contributors to this volume have built an internal dialogue, in part by clearly stating what they meant by the style terms they adopt (e.g., Armstrong and Cools; Evans and Waring; Kaufman and Baer; Renzulli and Sullivan); other contributors have created their own terms (e.g., "the disposition to understand for oneself"

Epilogue—
Intellectual Styles:
Nehru Jacket or Solid Blue Blazer?

LI-FANG ZHANG AND ROBERT J. STERNBERG

Some kinds of clothing come into style, make a splash, and then are gone, almost as fast as they appeared. Indeed, most clothing is this way because clothing manufacturers need to keep selling new garments, just as scientists need to keep selling new ideas. For example, Nehru jackets came onto the scene, made a splash, and then were gone in a splash as well. In the same way, many paradigms in psychology and education come and go quickly. Today, for example, many psychologists may remember the name Würzburg School, but do not remember or never even learned what this once popular school of thought represented. Other kinds of clothing never go out of style but never make a strong fashion statement, because once you have one, it lasts an awfully long time and clothing manufacturers cannot easily encourage people to keep buying more of them. Blue blazers come to mind. They always work, but never put you at the top of the fashion pack.

We believe that intellectual styles are like blue blazers. They are never at the top of the fashion pack, but they have worn well, whatever their detractors may say. To many people, research on styles is as questionable as the stylishness of a blue blazer. Indeed, since the 1970s, the once flourishing field of styles of the middle of the 20th century has been subject to intermittent attacks from researchers who saw no point to studying styles. One critic, Tiedemann (1989), declared: "My personal

Tiedemann, J. (1989). Measures of cognitive styles: A critical review. *Educational Psychologist, 24*, 261–275.

Tierney, P., Farmer, S. M., & Graen, G. B. (1999). An examination of leadership and employee creativity: The relevance of traits and relationships. *Personnel Psychology, 52*, 591–620.

Tullett, A. D. (1995). The adaptive-innovative (A-I) cognitive styles of male and female project managers: Some implications for the management of change. *Journal of Occupational and Organizational Psychology, 68*, 359–365.

Tullett, A. D. (1997). Cognitive style: Not culture's consequence. *European Psychologist, 2*, 258–267.

Tullett, A. D., & Kirton, M. J. (1995). Further evidence for the independence of adaptive-innovative (A-I) cognitive style from national culture. *Personality and Individual Differences, 19*, 393–296.

Vance, C. M., Groves, K. S., Paik, Y., & Kindler, H. (2007). Understanding and measuring linear and non-linear thinking style for enhanced management education and professional practice. *Academy of Management Learning and Education, 6*, 167–185.

Van de Ven, A. H., & Johnson, P. E. (2006). Knowledge for theory and practice. *Academy of Management Review, 31*, 802–821.

Vermeulen, F. (2007). "I shall not remain insignificant": Adding a second loop to matter more. *Academy of Management Journal, 50*, 754–761.

Vroom, V. H. (1964). *Work and motivation.* New York: John Wiley & Sons.

Webster, D. M., & Kruglanski, A. W. (1994). Individual differences in need for cognitive closure. *Journal of Personality and Social Psychology, 67*, 1049–1062.

Whetten, D., Cameron, K., & Woods, M. (2000). *Developing management skills for Europe* (2nd ed.). Harlow, Essex, UK: Pearson Education.

White, J. C., Varadarajan, P. R., & Dacin, P. A. (2003). Market situation interpretation and response: The role of cognitive style, organizational culture, and information use. *Journal of Marketing, 67*, 63–79.

Wickham, P. A. (2004). *Strategic entrepreneurship* (3rd ed.). Harlow, Essex, UK: Pearson Education.

Witkin, H. A., Oltman, P. K., Raskin, E., & Karp, S. A. (1971). *A manual for the embedded figures tests.* Palo Alto, CA: Consulting Psychologists Press.

Yamazaki, Y., & Kayes, D. C. (2007). Expatriate learning: Exploring how Japanese managers adapt in the United States. *International Journal of Human Resource Management, 18*, 1373–1395.

Yiu, L., & Saner, R. (2000). Determining the impact of cognitive styles on the effectiveness of global managers: Propositions for further research. *Human Resource Development Quarterly, 11*, 319–324.

Yuen, C. C., & Lee, S. N. (1994). Learning styles and their implications for cross-cultural management in Singapore. *The Journal of Social Psychology, 134*, 593–600.

Zhang, L. F. (2004). Predicting cognitive development, intellectual styles, and personality traits from self-rated abilities. *Learning and Individual Differences, 15*, 67–88.

Zhang, L. F., & Sternberg, R. J. (2005). A three-fold model of intellectual styles. *Educational Psychology Review, 17*, 1–53.

Chapter 10 Cognitive Styles and Their Relevance for Business

Sadler-Smith, E., Allinson, C. W., & Hayes, J. (2000). Learning preferences and cognitive style: Some implications for continuing professional development. *Management Learning, 31,* 239–256.

Sadler-Smith, E., & Smith, P. J. (2004). Strategies for accommodating individuals' styles and preferences in flexible learning programmes. *British Journal of Educational Technology, 35,* 395–412.

Sadler-Smith, E., Spicer, D. P., & Tsang, F. (2000). Validity of the Cognitive Style Index: Replication and extension. *British Journal of Management, 11,* 175–181.

Sherman, J. W. (2001). The dynamic relationship between stereotype efficiency and mental representation. In G. B. Moskowitz (Ed.), *Cognitive social psychology: The Princeton Symposium on the Legacy and Future of Social Cognition* (pp. 177–190). Mahwah, NJ: Erlbaum.

Simon, H. A. (1976). *Administrative behaviour* (3rd ed.). New York: Free Press.

Simon, F., & Usunier, J. C. (2007). Cognitive, demographic, and situational determinants of service customer preference for personnel-in-contact over self-service technology. *International Journal of Research in Marketing, 24,* 163–173.

Singer, M. (2001). Individual differences in adaption-innovation and the escalation of commitment paradigm. *The Journal of Social Psychology, 130,* 561–563.

Singer, M. S., & Singer, A. E. (1986). Individual differences and the escalation of commitment paradigm. *The Journal of Social Psychology, 126,* 197–204.

Sojka, J. Z., & Giese, J. L. (2006). Communicating through pictures and words: Understanding the role of affect and cognition in processing visual and verbal information. *Psychology and Marketing, 23,* 995–1014.

Sparrow, P. R. (1999). Strategy and cognition: Understanding the role of management knowledge structures, organizational memory and information overload. *Creativity and Innovation Management, 8,* 140–148.

Spiro, R. L., & Weitz, B. A. (1990). Adaptive selling: Conceptualization, measurement, and nomological validity. *Journal of Marketing Research, 27,* 61–69.

Stepanek, M. (1999, December 13). Using the net for brainstorming. *Business Week.* Retrieved from http://www.businessweek.com/1999/99_50/b3659021.htm

Sternberg, R. J., & Grigorenko, E. L. (1997). Are cognitive styles still in style? *American Psychologist, 52,* 700–712.

Stratton, T. D., Witzke, D. B., Elam, C. L., & Cheever, T. R. (2005). Learning and career specialty preferences of medical school applicants. *Journal of Vocational Behavior, 67,* 35–50.

Stumpf, S. A., & Dunbar, L. M. (1991). The effects of personality type on choices made in strategic decision situations. *Decision Sciences, 22,* 1047–1072.

Sullivan, B. A., & Hansen, J. C. (2004). Mapping associations between interests and personality: Toward a conceptual understanding of individual differences in vocational behavior. *Journal of Counseling Psychology, 51,* 287–298.

Taylor, W. G. K. (1989). The Kirton Adaption-Innovation Inventory: Should the subscales be orthogonal? *Personality and Individual Differences, 9,* 921–929.

Tetlock, P. E. (2000). Cognitive biases and organizational correctives: Do both disease and cure depend on the politics of the beholder? *Administrative Science Quarterly, 45,* 293–326.

Thompson, D. V., & Hamilton, R. W. (2006). The effects of information processing mode on consumers' responses to comparative advertising. *Journal of Consumer Research, 32,* 530–540.

Priola, V., Smith, J. L., & Armstrong, S. J. (2004). Group work and cognitive style: A discursive investigation. *Small Group Research, 35*, 565–595.

Ramanathan, S., & Williams, P. (2007). Immediate and delayed emotional consequences of indulgence: The moderating influence of personality type on mixed emotions. *Journal of Consumer Research, 34*, 212–223.

Rao, H. R., Jacob, V. S., & Lin, F. (1992). Hemispheric specialization, cognitive differences, and their implications for the design of decision support systems. *MIS Quarterly, 16*, 145–151.

Rayner, S. (2006). What next? Developing global research and applied practice in the field of cognitive and learning styles. In L. Lassen, L. Bostrom & C. Evans (Eds.), *Enabling lifelong learning in education, training and development, 11th Annual Conference of the European Learning Styles Information Network* (CD-ROM). Oslo, Norway: University of Oslo.

Rayner, S.G. (2008). Are you researching in style? What about epistemology, paradigm shifts and the RIG? In E. Cools, H. Van den Broeck, C. Evans, & T. Redmond (Eds.), *Style and cultural differences: How can organisations, regions and countries take advantage of style differences? Proceedings of the 13th Annual Conference of the European Learning Styles Information Network* (pp. 95–114). Ghent, Belgium: Vlerick Leuven Gent Management School.

Reynolds, M. (1997). Learning styles: A critique. *Management Learning, 28*, 115–133.

Rhodes, J. D., & Thame, S. (1988). Accelerating innovation through real-time workshops. *Long Range Planning, 21*, 41–46.

Rickards, T., & Moger, S. T. (1994). Felix and Oscar revisited: An exploration of the dynamics of a real-life odd couple work relationship. *Journal of Applied Behavioural Science, 30*, 108–131.

Riding, R., & Cheema, I. (1991). Cognitive styles: An overview and integration. *Educational Psychology, 11*, 193–215.

Robey, D. (1992). Response to Rao et al.: More ado about cognitive style and DSS design. *MIS Quarterly, 16*, 151–153.

Robey, D., & Taggart, W. (1981). Measuring managers' minds: The assessment of style in human information processing. *Academy of Management Review, 6*, 375–383.

Robey, D., & Taggart, W. (1982). Human information processing in information and decision support systems. *MIS Quarterly, 6*, 62–73.

Rook, D. W., & Fisher, R. J. (1995). Normative influences on compulsive buying behavior. *Journal of Consumer Research, 22*, 301–313.

Ruiz, S., & Sicilia, M. (2004). The impact of cognitive style and/or affective processing styles on consumer response to advertising appeals. *Journal of Business Research, 57*, 657–664.

Sadler-Smith, E. (1998). Cognitive style: Some human resource implications for managers. *International Journal of Human Resource Management, 9*, 185–202.

Sadler-Smith, E. (1999). Intuition-analysis cognitive style and learning preferences of business and management students: A UK exploratory study. *Journal of Managerial Psychology, 14*, 26–38.

Sadler-Smith, E. (2001). A reply to Reynolds's critique of learning style. *Management Learning, 32*, 291–304.

Sadler-Smith, E. (2004). Cognitive style and the management of small and medium-sized enterprises. *Organization Studies, 25*, 155–181.

Kozhevnikov, M. (2007). Cognitive styles in the context of modern psychology: Toward an integrated framework of cognitive style. *Psychological Bulletin, 133,* 464–481.

Kubeš, M. (1998). Adaptors and innovators in Slovakia: Cognitive style and social culture. *European Journal of Personality, 12,* 187–198.

Lee, J. A. (1988). The effects of cognitive style on rating accuracy with an overall rating scale. *Human Performance, 1,* 261–271.

Leonard, D., & Straus, S. (1997). Putting your company's whole brain to work. *Harvard Business Review, 75,* 111–121.

Leong, F. T. L., Hardin, E. E., & Gaylor, M. (2005). Career specialty choice: A combined research-intervention project. *Journal of Vocational Behavior, 67,* 69–86.

Longenecker, C. O., & Simonetti, J. L. (2001). *Getting results.* San Francisco: Jossey-Bass.

Martin, R. (2007). How successful leaders think. *Harvard Business Review, 85,* 60–67.

Mazen, A. M. (1989). Testing an integration of Vroom's instrumentality theory and Holland's typology on working women. *Journal of Vocational Behavior, 35,* 327–341.

McIntyre, R. P., & Capen, M. M. (1993). A cognitive style perspective on ethical questions. *Journal of Business Ethics, 12,* 629–636.

McIntyre, R. P., Claxton, R. P., Anselmi, K., & Wheatley, E. W. (2000). Cognitive style as an antecedent to adaptiveness, customer orientation, and self-perceived selling performance. *Journal of Business and Psychology, 15,* 179–196.

McIntyre, R. P., & Meloche, M. S. (1995). Cognitive style and customer orientation. *Journal of Business and Psychology, 10,* 75–86.

Messick, S. (1996). Bridging cognition and personality in education: The role of style in performance and development. *European Journal of Personality, 10,* 353–376.

Miles, R. E., & Snow, C. C. (1978). *Organizational strategy, structure and process.* New York: McGraw-Hill.

Mitchell, R. K., Busenitz, L., Lant, T., McDougall, P. P., Morse, E. A., & Smith, H. B. (2002). Toward a theory of entrepreneurial cognition: Rethinking the people side of entrepreneurship research. *Entrepreneurship Theory and Practice, 27,* 93–104.

Murphy, H. J., Kelleher, W. E., Doucette, P. A., & Young, J. D. (1998). Test-retest reliability and construct validity of the Cognitive Style Index for business undergraduates. *Psychological Reports, 82,* 595–600.

Myers, I. B., McCaulley, M. H., Quenk, N. L., & Hammer, A. L. (2003). *MBTI manual: A guide to the development and use of the Myers-Briggs Type Indicator.* Palo Alto, CA: Consulting Psychologists Press.

Neuberg, S. L., Judice, T. N., & West, S. G. (1997). What the need for closure scale measures and what it does not: Toward differentiating among related epistemic motives. *Journal of Personality and Social Psychology, 72,* 1396–1412.

Nisbett, R. E., Peng, K., Choi, I., & Norenzayan, A. (2001). Culture and systems of thought: Holistic versus analytic cognition. *Psychological Review, 108,* 291–310.

Nutt, P. C. (1990). Strategic decisions made by top executives and middle managers with data and process dominant styles. *Journal of Management Studies, 27,* 173–194.

Ortenblad, A. (2005). Are the right persons involved in the creation of the learning organization? *Human Resource Development Quarterly, 16,* 281–283.

Park, D. C., Nisbett, R., & Hedden, T. (1999). Aging, culture and cognition. *Journal of Gerontology: Psychological Sciences, 54B,* P75–P84.

Ployhart, R. E. (2006). Staffing in the 21st century: New challenges and strategic opportunities. *Journal of Management, 32,* 868–897.

Hayes, J., Allinson, C. W., Hudson, R. S., & Keasey, K. (2003). Further reflections on the nature of intuition-analysis and the construct validity of the Cognitive Style Index. *Journal of Occupational and Organizational Psychology, 76,* 269–278.

Hayley, U. C. V., & Stumpf, S. A. (1989). Cognitive trails in strategic decision making: Linking theories of personalities and cognitions. *Journal of Management Studies, 26,* 477–497.

Hill, J., Puurula, A., Sitko-Lutek, A., & Rakowska, A. (2000). Cognitive style and socialisation: An exploration of learned sources of style in Finland, Poland and the UK. *Educational Psychology, 20,* 285–305.

Hmieleski, K. M., & Corbett, A. C. (2006). Proclivity for improvisation as a predictor of entrepreneurial intentions. *Journal of Small Business Management, 44,* 45–63.

Hodgkinson, G. P. (2003). The interface of cognitive and industrial, work and organizational psychology. *Journal of Occupational and Organizational Psychology, 76,* 1–25.

Hodgkinson, G. P., & Clarke, I. (2007). Exploring the cognitive significance of organizational strategizing: A dual process framework and research agenda. *Human Relations, 60,* 243–255.

Hodgkinson, G. P., Herriot, P., & Anderson, N. (2001). Re-aligning stakeholders in management research: Lessons from industrial, work and organizational psychology. *British Journal of Management, 12,* S41–S48.

Hodgkinson, G. P., & Sadler-Smith, E. (2003a). Complex or unitary? A critique and empirical re-assessment of the Allinson-Hayes Cognitive Style Index. *Journal of Occupational and Organizational Psychology, 76,* 243–268.

Hodgkinson, G. P., & Sadler-Smith, E. (2003b). Reflections on reflections . . . on the nature of intuition, analysis and the construct validity of the Cognitive Style Index. *Journal of Occupational and Organizational Psychology, 76,* 279–281.

Holland, J. (1985). *Making vocational choices* (2nd ed.). Odessa, FL: Psychological Assessment Resources.

Hough, J. R., & ogilvie, dt (2005). An empirical test of cognitive style and strategic decision outcomes. *Journal of Management Studies, 42,* 417–448.

Jansen, K. J., & Kristof-Brown, A. (2006). Toward a multidimensional theory of person-environment fit. *Journal of Managerial Issues, 18,* 193–212.

Jarzabkowski, P., & Searle, R. H. (2004). Harnessing diversity and collective action in the top management team. *Long Range Planning, 37,* 399–419.

Joniak, A. J., & Isaksen, S. G. (1988). The Gregorc style delineator: Internal consistency and its relationship to Kirton's adaptive-innovative distinction. *Educational and Psychological Measurement, 48,* 1043–1049.

Keller, P. A., & McGill, A. (1994). Differences in the relative influence of product attributes under alternative processing conditions: Attribute importance versus attribute ease of imagability. *Journal of Consumer Psychology, 3,* 29–49.

Kirton, M. J. (1976). Adaptors and innovators: A description and measure. *Journal of Applied Psychology, 61,* 622–669.

Kirton, M. J. (Ed.). (1994). *Adaptors and innovators: Styles of creativity and problem solving.* New York: Routledge.

Kirton, M. J. (2003). *Adaption-innovation in the context of diversity and change.* London: Routledge.

Kouzes, J. M., & Posner, B. Z. (2002). *The leadership challenge* (3rd ed.). San Francisco: Jossey-Bass.

Epstein, S. (1991). Cognitive-experiential self theory: An integrative theory of personality. In R. Curtis (Ed.), *The self with others: Convergences in psychoanalytic, social, and personality psychology* (pp. 111–137). New York: Guilford Press.

Epstein, S., Pacini, R., Denes-Raj, V., & Heier, H. (1996). Individual differences in intuitive-experiential and analytical-reasoning thinking styles. *Journal of Personality and Social Psychology, 71*, 390–405.

Fisher, S. G., Macrosson, W. D. K., & Wong, J. (1998). Cognitive style and team role preference. *Journal of Managerial Psychology, 13*, 544–557.

Fox, F. V., & Straw, B. M. (1979). The trapped administrator: Effects of job insecurity and policy resistance upon commitment to a course of action. *Administrative Science Quarterly, 24*, 449–471.

Foxall, G. (1994). Consumer initiators: Both adaptors and innovators. *British Journal of Management, 5*, 3–12.

Foxall, G. R., & Hackett, M. P. (1992). The factor structure and construct validity of the Kirton Adaption-Innovation Inventory. *Personality and Individual Differences, 13*, 967–975.

Foxall, G. R., & Hackett, M. P. (1994). Styles of managerial creativity: A comparison of adaption-innovation in the United Kingdom, Australia and the United States. *British Journal of Management, 5*, 85–100.

Foxall, G. R., & Payne, A. F. (1989). Adaptors and innovators in organizations: A cross-cultural study of the cognitive styles of managerial functions and subfunctions. *Human Relations, 42*, 639–649.

Furnham, A. (1995). The relationship of personality and intelligence to cognitive learning style and achievement. In D. H. Saklofske & M. Zeidner (Eds.), *International handbook of personality and intelligence* (pp. 397–413). New York: Plenum Press.

Gailbreath, R. D., Wagner, S. L., Moffett III, R. G., & Hein, M. B. (1997). Homogeneity in behavioral preference among U.S. army leaders. *Group Dynamics: Theory, Research, and Practice, 1*, 222–230.

Gallén, T. (2006). Managers and strategic decisions: Does the cognitive style matter? *Journal of Management Development, 25*, 118–133.

Garfield, M. J., Taylor, N. J., Dennis, A. R., & Satzinger, J. W. (2001). Research report: Modifying paradigms-individual differences, creativity techniques, and exposure to ideas in group idea generation. *Informational Systems Research, 12*, 322–333.

Ginn, C. W., & Sexton, D. L. (1990). A comparison of the personality type dimensions of the 1987 Inc. 500 company founders/CEOs with those of slower-growth firms. *Journal of Business Venturing, 5*, 313–326.

Goldstein, K. M., & Blackman, S. (1978). *Cognitive style.* New York: Wiley.

Guglielmino, P. J., & Roberts, D. G. (1992). A comparison of self-directed learning readiness in US and Hong Kong samples and the implications for job performance. *Human Resource Development Quarterly, 3*, 261–271.

Hayes, J., & Allinson, C. W. (1994). Cognitive style and its relevance for management practice. *British Journal of Management, 5*, 53–71.

Hayes, J., & Allinson, C. W. (1996). The implications of learning styles for training and development: A discussion of the matching hypothesis. *British Journal of Management, 7*, 63–73.

Hayes, J., & Allinson, C. W. (1998). Cognitive style and the theory and practice of individual and collective learning in organizations. *Human Relations, 51*, 847–871.

Brigham, K. H., De Castro, J. O., & Shepherd, D. A. (2007). A person-organization fit model of owner-managers' cognitive style and organizational demands. *Entrepreneurship Theory and Practice, 31*, 29–51.

Buckingham, M. (2005). What great managers. *Harvard Business Review, 83*, 70–79.

Buttner, E. H., & Gryskiewicz, N. (1993). Entrepreneurs' problem-solving styles: An empirical study using the Kirton adaption/innovation theory. *Journal of Small Business Management, 31*, 22–31.

Cassidy, S. (2004). Learning styles: An overview of theories, models, and measures. *Educational Psychology, 24*, 419–444.

Chan, D. (1996). Cognitive misfit of problem-solving style at work: A facet of person-organization fit. *Organizational Behavior and Human Decision Processes, 68*, 194–207.

Chilton, M. A., Hardgrave, B. C., & Armstrong, D. J. (2005). Person-job cognitive style fit for software developers: The effect on strain and performance. *Journal of Management Information Systems, 22*, 193–226.

Chow, K. A., & Esses, V. M. (2005). The development of group stereotypes from descriptions of group members: An individual differences approach. *Group Processes and Intergroup Relations, 8*, 429–445.

Clapham, M. M. (2000). Employee creativity: The role of leadership. *Academy of Management Executive, 14*, 138–139.

Cole, C. A., & Gaeth, G. J. (1990). Cognitive and age related differences in the ability to use nutritional information in a complex environment. *Journal of Marketing Research, 27*, 175–184.

Cools, E. (2008). *Cognitive styles and management behaviour: Theory, measurement, and application*. Saarbrücken, Germany: VDM Verlag Dr. Müller.

Cools, E., & Van den Broeck, H. (2007). Development and validation of the Cognitive Style Indicator. *The Journal of Psychology, 141*, 359–387.

Cooper, S. E., & Miller, J. A. (1991). MBTI learning style-teaching style discongruencies. *Educational and Psychological Measurement, 51*, 699–706.

Curry, L. (1983). An organization of learning style theory and constructs. In L. Curry (Ed.), *Learning style in continuing medical education* (pp. 115–123). Halifax, Nova Scotia, Canada: Dalhouse University.

D'Amato, A., & Zijlstra, F. R. H. (2008). Psychological climate and individual factors as antecedents of work outcomes. *European Journal of Work and Organizational Psychology, 17*, 33–54.

De Dreu, C. K. W., Koole, S. L., & Oldersma, S. (1999). On the seizing and freezing of negotiator inferences: Need for closure moderates the use of heuristics in negotiation. *Personality and Social Psychology Bulletin, 25*, 348–363.

Desmedt, E., & Valcke, M. (2004). Mapping the learning styles jungle: An overview of the literature based on citation analysis. *Educational Psychology, 24*, 445–464.

Dimov, D. (2007). From opportunity insight to opportunity intention: The importance of person-situation learning match. *Entrepreneurship Theory and Practice, 31*, 561–583.

Ehrhart, K. H., & Ziegert, J. C. (2005). Why are individuals attracted to organizations? *Journal of Management, 31*, 901–919.

Entwistle, N. J., & Tait, H. (1994). *The Revised Approaches to Studying Inventory*. Edinburgh: University of Edinburgh, Centre for Research on Learning and Instruction.

Armstrong, S. J. (2000). The influence of cognitive style on performance in management education. *Educational Psychology, 20*, 323–339.

Armstrong, S. J. (2004). The impact of supervisors' cognitive styles on the quality of research supervision in management education. *British Journal of Educational Psychology, 74*, 599–616.

Armstrong, S. J, Allinson, C. W., & Hayes, J. (1997). The implications of cognitive style for the management of student-supervisor relationships. *Educational Psychology, 17*, 209–217.

Armstrong, S. J, Allinson, C. W., & Hayes, J. (2002). Formal mentoring systems: An examination of the effects of mentor/protégé cognitive styles on the mentoring process. *Journal of Management Studies, 39*, 1111–1137.

Armstrong, S. J., Allinson, C. W., & Hayes, J. (2004). The effects of cognitive style on research supervision: A study of student-supervisor dyads in management education. *Academy of Management Learning and Education, 3*, 41–63.

Armstrong, S. J., & Priola, V. (2001). Individual differences in cognitive style and their effects on task and social orientations of self-managed work teams. *Small Group Research, 32*, 283–312.

Armstrong, S. J., & Rayner, S. G. (2002). Inquiry and style: Research verities and the development of a consensual theory? In M. Valcke, D. Gombeir, S. J. Armstrong, A. Francis, M. Graff, J. Hill, et al. (Eds.), *Learning styles: Reliability and validity* (pp. 25–36). Proceedings of the 7th Annual ELSIN Conference. Ghent, Belgium: Gent University, Department of Education.

Armstrong, S. J., & Sadler-Smith, E. (2006, August 11–16). *Cognitive style and its relevance for the management of careers.* Paper presented at the 66th Academy of Management Conference, Atlanta, GA.

Atwater, L. E., & Yammarino, F. J. (1993). Personal attributes as predictors of superiors and subordinates perceptions of military academic leadership. *Human Relations, 46*, 645–688.

Au, A. K. M. (1997). Cognitive style as a factor influencing performance of business students across various assessment techniques. *Journal of Managerial Psychology, 12*, 243–250.

Backhaus, K., & Liff, J. P. (2007). Cognitive styles and approaches to studying in management education. *Journal of Management Education, 31*, 445–466.

Baron, R. A. (2004). The cognitive perspective: A valuable tool answering entrepreneurship's basic "why" questions. *Journal of Business Venturing, 19*, 221–239.

Bar-Tal, Y. (1994). The effect on mundane decision making of the need and ability to achieve cognitive structure. *European Journal of Personality, 8*, 45–58.

Beckman, S. L., & Barry, M. (2007). Innovation as a learning process: Embedding design thinking. *California Management Review, 50*, 25–56.

Belbin, R. M. (1981). *Management teams: Why they succeed or fail.* London: Heinemann.

Berings, M. G. M. C., Poell, R. F., & Simons, P. R. (2005). Conceptualizing on-the-job learning styles. *Human Resource Development Review, 4*, 373–400.

Berr, S. A., Church, A. H., & Waclawski, J. (2000). The right personality is everything: Linking personality preferences to managerial behaviors. *Human Resource Development Quarterly, 11*, 133–157.

Blustein, D. L., & Phillips, S. D. (1988). Individual and contextual factors in career exploration. *Journal of Vocational Behavior, 33*, 203–216.

Finally, to give one last example, matching or mismatching cognitive styles may also be an important factor in social interaction that needs further empirical consideration, whether at the level of the dyad or the group. Despite the efforts of researchers over the past 30 years, the effects of matching or mismatching cognitive styles remain unclear. Evidence from the field of education has been inconsistent and, at times, contradictory. There remains a dearth of studies examining the matching hypothesis in relation to organization members working in an industrial context.

NOTE

1. The word *satisfice* is a portmanteau of satisfy and suffice. This is a term first used by Simon (1976) to describe the decision process where minimum acceptable requirements are met—a "good enough" solution based on limited information.

REFERENCES

Abdolmohammadi, M. J., Read, W. J., & Scarborough, D. P. (2003). Does selection-socialization help to explain accountants' weak ethical reasoning? *Journal of Business Ethics, 42,* 71–81.

Abramson, N. R., Lane, H. W., Nagai, H., & Takagi, H. (1993). A comparison of Canadian and Japanese cognitive styles: Implications for management interaction. *Journal of International Business Studies, 24,* 575–587.

Adkins, C. L. (2005). Staffing organizations: A comprehensive applied exercise. *Human Resource Management Review, 15,* 226–237.

Agor, W. H. (1984). *Intuitive management.* Englewood Cliffs, NJ: Prentice Hall.

Allinson, C. W., Armstrong, S. J., & Hayes, J. (2001). The effects of cognitive style on leader-member exchange: A study of manager-subordinate dyads. *Journal of Occupational and Organizational Psychology, 74,* 201–220.

Allinson, C. W., Chell, E., & Hayes, J. (2000). Intuition and entrepreneurial behaviour. *European Journal of Work and Organizational Psychology, 9,* 31–43.

Allinson, C. W., & Hayes, J. (1996). The Cognitive Style Index: A measure of intuition-analysis for organizational research. *Journal of Management Studies, 33,* 119–135.

Allinson, C. W., & Hayes, J. (2000). Cross-national differences in cognitive style: Implications for management. *International Journal of Human Resource Management, 11,* 161–170.

Allport, G. W. (1937). *Personality: A psychological interpretation.* New York: Holt & Co.

Antonietti, A., & Gioletta, M. A. (1995). Individual differences in analogical problem solving. *Personality and Individual Differences, 18,* 611–619.

Aritzeta, A., Senior, B., & Swailes, S. (2005). Team role preference and cognitive styles: A convergent validity study. *Small Group Research, 36,* 404–436.

Armstrong, S. J. (1999). *Cognitive style and dyadic interaction: A study of supervisors and subordinates engaged in working relationships.* Unpublished doctoral dissertation, University of Leeds, England.

Vermeulen (2007). Within the field of cognitive style, Armstrong and Rayner (2002) also called for a paradigm shift in order to bridge the relevance gap between theory and practice. In their perspective, this means that valence is an equally important element for the continuation of style research in addition to validity and reliability. Valence in their model means authenticity, credibility, and impact and refers to the extent to which the findings of a study are relevant to a particular context. Validity, reliability, and valence are three important elements (referred to as "verities" in their model) that need to be taken into account in the design of research and in the process of inquiry.

Organizations would, for instance, benefit from more research into the influence of cognitive styles on aspects of intrapersonal development and interpersonal relationships as a way of improving management practice in the workplace. Whetten, Cameron, and Woods (2000) emphasized the importance of intrapersonal self-awareness and thorough analyses of one's strengths and weaknesses as one way of improving management effectiveness. In this respect, understanding the interplay between stylistic preferences and day-to-day workplace behavior is known to be crucial for implementing effective individual development efforts (Berr, Church, & Waclawski, 2000).

Armed with higher levels of intrapersonal style awareness, organizations might then benefit from more research into ways in which this new knowledge can be put into the management practice through the development of more cohesive interpersonal relationships. The ability to work well with others and to enable others to act has become a critical differentiator between success and failure in executive ranks (Kouzes & Posner, 2002). Getting results as a manager requires a balance between effective task-oriented and people-oriented practices, with the latter being regarded as being most important (Longenecker & Simonetti, 2001). Understanding the implications of differences in cognitive style is thought to be a firm basis for fostering better interpersonal working relationships (Armstrong, 1999; Hayes & Allinson, 1994; Priola et al., 2004). Overlooking their impact can lead to interpersonal disagreements and conflict situations, as people with different cognitive styles may not understand or respect each other (Leonard & Straus, 1997). Respect for diversity is also important to enhance problem solving and creative thinking and may increase the organization's flexibility to respond to changing environments (Jarzabkowski & Searle, 2004). An awareness of the importance of cognitive differences is important here too. Again, further research in needed in these areas.

styles for management practice identified by Hayes and Allinson (1994). They highlighted the areas of task and learning performance, internal communication, career choice and vocational preference, career guidance and counseling, personnel selection and placement, team composition and team building, conflict management, training and development, PE fit, and decision making. If one considers the category of PE fit and careers and vocational preference alone, there has on average been less than one article per year devoted to this important area. This is despite the fact that cognitive style theory and research is known to have the potential to affect a significant number of career-relevant aspects, such as: selection; vocational choice and career success; group processes; diversity and conflict management; gender differences and careers; intuition and emotion in the workplace; education, training, and development; styles profiling and career management; and cross-cultural career management (Armstrong & Sadler-Smith, 2006). Furthermore, there are other major subdisciplines that would benefit from research in the field but that are hardly represented at all. These include international management; management consulting; organizational cognition; organizational development and change; technology management and design; gender and diversity management; operations management; and logistics to name but a few. There is clearly a need to promote more research in these areas.

One way of stimulating this might be through the idea of developing research communities (Rayner, 2006, 2008). The present authors believe that the cognitive styles field would gain significantly from international networks of scholars who adopt multidisciplinary perspectives in order to overcome the fragmented view of many studies in the field. Developing a joint research agenda across disciplines to produce a concise overview of what is already known about the impact of cognitive styles would enable us to identify important unexplored areas. This chapter may be seen as one small part of such a process.

From a practical viewpoint, for people in the context of business and management to derive relevant conclusions from empirical studies in the styles field, it is important to take a functional perspective that takes both practitioner awareness and applications of cognitive styles into account (Armstrong & Rayner, 2002; Rayner, 2006). In the field of management, Hodgkinson, Herriot, and Anderson (2001) addressed the need for a shift toward pragmatic science, which combines high theoretical rigor with high practical relevance for users, a view later endorsed by other notable scholars in the field such as Van de Ven and Johnson (2006) and

1997). In this chapter, we have attempted to highlight a number of key developments in the field over the past 20 years. From a theoretical perspective, several useful attempts to clarify the various concepts and identify appropriate taxonomies have been identified, together with developments of new instruments specifically designed for managerial and professional groups. From the perspective of practical applications of the theory and construct of cognitive style, there have been a number of important studies that have taken place in various subdisciplines as shown in Table 10.1.

However, the number of applied publications has to be considered to have remained relatively low. More than 100,000 articles were published over the past two decades in the 209 journals identified by this study as being potentially relevant for the field of business and management. Only about 0.8% of these (822 articles) were devoted to examining the influence of cognitive styles. Moreover, only 203 of these 822 identified articles (about 25%) were considered to be relevant in the context of business and management research. This is disappointing when one considers the range of potential implications of cognitive

Table 10.1

BREAKDOWN OF 203 ARTICLES REVIEWED BY SUB-DISCIPLINARY AREA

SUB-DISCIPLINE	ARTICLES	PER YEAR (ON AVERAGE)
Theory and measurement	20	1
Innovation and entrepreneurship	16	0.8
Sales and marketing	19	1
Groups and teams	10	0.5
Decision making and problem solving	29	1.5
Management and organizational learning	42	2
Person-environment fit, careers and vocational preference	18	0.9
Leadership	9	0.5
Culture	13	0.7
Other areas of business and management	27	1.4

self-directed learning and job performance ratings for employees in both the United States and Hong Kong. It was argued that this has important implications for businesses that are rapidly changing or require a high degree of problem-solving ability and creativity.

Finally, our review revealed some notable studies of the influence of cognitive styles on ethical judgments and reasoning. McIntyre and Capen (1993) tested the proposition that cognitive styles can influence one's perceptions of what is and is not a matter of ethics. Findings revealed that NF types were more likely to consider ethical questions than were either ST types or NT types. They concluded that NF types focus on morality, and should thus prove more comprehensive regarding what constitutes a question of ethics than would STs. In a study of ethical reasoning among accountants, Abdolmohammadi, Read, and Scarborough (2003) provided evidence that a selection-socialization effect exists in the accounting profession that results in recruiting accountants with disproportionately higher levels of the ST cognitive style. The study again found that ST types are associated with relatively low levels of ethical reasoning.

Clearly more research is needed in each of these areas, as all are considered by the present authors to be important for the general fields of business and management. Given the increased importance of interpersonal skills for effective management, more research on the influence of cognitive style differences on interpersonal cooperation would be highly desirable. Similarly, in the light of the continuing discussion on the link between styles and abilities—considered to be unrelated by some scholars and related by others—more research on style differences and job performance is needed. Finally, corporate governance and ethics are deemed to be exceedingly important for contemporary organizations, which justify the need for more studies on cognitive styles and ethical behavior.

CONCLUSIONS AND AREAS FOR FUTURE RESEARCH

The broad appeal of cognitive styles has the potential for considerable usefulness in the field of business and management, especially in light of increased attention on cognitive approaches to industrial, work, organizational psychology (Hodgkinson, 2003), and great promise for helping us understand some of the variation in job performance that cannot be accounted for by differences in abilities (Sternberg & Grigorenko,

Understanding the implications of style differences in a cross-cultural context is important in an increasingly globalized business world. However, the research on cross-cultural adaptation remains rather exploratory and mainly focuses on learning styles and learning/teaching approaches in particular expatriate contexts. Further research is needed in this area that looks at more and diverse cultural contexts and that also takes into account cognitive style differences. Moreover, the question still remains unanswered as to whether cognitive styles are biologically based, the result of early learning, lifelong learning, all of these, or none of these (Furnham, 1995). Answers to these questions will indicate the extent to which cognitive styles are likely to be influenced by external factors such as culture, education, and other social environments. More cross-cultural research is therefore needed to give us further insight into these relationships.

Other Areas of Business and Management

Our review identified a number of other articles in business and management-related areas that were less represented but may offer other interesting areas for future work. Subjects covered include interpersonal relationships, job performance, and ethical judgments and reasoning.

With regard to articles that were associated with the influence of cognitive styles on dyadic interpersonal relationships, Armstrong, Allinson, and Hayes (2002) found that the analysis-intuition dimension of cognitive style was partly responsible for shaping the overall effectiveness of mentoring relationships between mentor and protégé. Findings revealed that in dyads whose mentor is more analytic, congruence between the partners' cognitive styles enhances the quality of their mentoring relationships. Rickards and Moger (1994) also found that differing styles on the adaptor-innovator dimension (KAI) had significant effects on interpersonal relationships. They concluded that homogeneity of style may increase the likelihood of satisficing[1] behaviors, whereas heterogeneity reduces satisficing tendencies but with concomitant personal costs.

With regard to job performance, a study of the effects of cognitive styles on rating accuracy when evaluating job performance revealed that styles may significantly affect how accurate one is (Lee, 1988). Raters whose cognitive style was more articulated (i.e., field independents) rated job performance more accurately than raters whose cognitive style was more global (i.e., field dependents). A study by Guglielmino and Roberts (1992) revealed a positive relationship between readiness for

approaches to leadership; team leadership; culture and leadership; and gender in the context of leadership.

Culture

Our review revealed two major topics in this subcategory. The first is concerned with cross-cultural differences in cognitive styles, the second with the influence of style differences on cross-cultural adaptation.

Several studies examined cultural differences in cognitive style across different nations (e.g., Abramson, Lane, Nagai, & Takagi, 1993; Allinson & Hayes, 2000; Hill, Puurula, Sitko-Lutek, & Rakowska, 2000; Kubeš, 1998; Tullett & Kirton, 1995). Traditionally, cultural differences have been conceptualized as a dichotomy between the rational, analytic, left-brained West and the intuitive, wholistic, right-brained East (Allinson & Hayes, 2000; Nisbett, Peng, Choi, & Norenzayan, 2001; Park, Nisbett, & Hedden, 1999). There are, however, no conclusive results that confirm this dichotomy. Researchers using Kirton's (1976) KAI are firm in their belief that cognitive style is independent of culture. This is on the basis of similar results being obtained across various occupational groups in different nations (Kubeš, 1998; Tullett, 1997). They also believe that cognitive style is a stable cognitive process within adults that is largely uninfluenced by national culture. Other scholars, however, have reported clear differences between cultures, though results did not confirm the analytic West–intuitive East dichotomy. On the contrary, Allinson and Hayes (2000) found the reverse to be true and also argued for a more useful categorization of countries in terms of their stage of industrial development, rather than the simple East-West dichotomy. Reasons for these cross-cultural differences were not discussed by these authors. However, in a separate study of managers in Finland, Poland, and the United Kingdom, Hill et al. (2000), based on qualitative empirical evidence, attributed cultural differences in cognitive style to different learning processes, involving personal and cultural socialization.

A second topic of interest in this category focused on the effects of styles on cross-cultural and expatriate adaptation (e.g., Yamazaki & Kayes, 2007; Yiu & Saner, 2000; Yuen & Lee, 1994). Given the increased importance of doing business in a globalized context, these studies aimed to deliver a better understanding of how successful cross-cultural adaptation is dependent on people's cognitive and learning styles, skills, and abilities.

transformational and transactional leadership by both superiors and subordinates than were thinking types as defined by the MBTI. Those who process information via feelings as opposed to rational thinking are known to be more interpersonally oriented (Myers et al., 2003). Information processing that emphasizes the feelings of others may therefore be more conducive to leadership than a more rational emphasis. This notion was explored in a study of leader-member exchange (LMX) relationship by Armstrong (1999) and Allinson, Armstrong, and Hayes (2001). They found that intuitive leaders may be less dominating and more nurturing in LMX relationships than their analytic colleagues. Intuitive leaders were also more liked and respected by analytic members than analytic leaders were by intuitive members.

Clapham (2000) noted that the role of leadership is crucial in facilitating employee creativity and that individual characteristics such as cognitive styles as well as the relationship between employees and their leaders may be critical factors in determining the creative performance of employees. A study of leadership and employee creativity by Tierney, Farmer, and Graen (1999) revealed a clear link between employee cognitive style and supervisor ratings of creative performance that depended on the quality of the LMX relationship. Employees with innovative cognitive styles tended to have high creativity ratings regardless of leader-member relationships. However, employees with adaptive cognitive styles had higher creativity ratings when in positive leader-member relationships than when in less positive relationships.

Finally, a study by Tullett (1995) also revealed that cognitive styles are an important factor when leading change projects. The preferred cognitive style of leaders who are managing change processes is more innovative compared with managers in general. This finding was consistent with previous studies (Foxall & Hackett, 1994; Kirton, 1994) that found that those who occupy positions that operate across functional boundaries will have a tendency toward an innovative cognitive style.

Leadership is known to be critical for giving direction in times of organizational change, for developing a vision, sharing that vision, setting direction, and managing change by aligning, motivating, and inspiring others. While the studies outlined in this section provide incremental contributions, they represent only a small part of the overall subject area. Other areas that would benefit from research into the implication of cognitive styles include: skills-based approaches to leadership; leadership styles; situational leadership; contingency and transformational

is no longer sufficient. Future studies on cognitive misfit therefore need to embrace more complex models in which various individual and environmental factors are taken into account, involving multiple levels of analyses and longitudinal perspectives.

Leadership

Under this subcategory, our review revealed articles in the areas of effective leadership, leader-member exchange relationships, leadership and creativity, and leading and managing change. With regard to effective leadership, Martin (2007) was concerned with how successful leaders think. Drawing from interviews with more than 50 leaders with exemplary records, he identified a predisposition and capacity to hold in their heads two opposing ideas before creatively resolving the tension between those ideas by generating a new one that is superior to both. He termed this process of consideration and synthesis "integrative thinking" compared with more "conventional thinking." Integrative thinkers welcome complexity, whereas conventional thinkers seek simplicity. While he does not draw on specific cognitive style theory, these terms do resonate with those discussed by Agor (1984) and Kirton (1994). Drawing from adult learning theory, Buckingham (2005) refers to three predominant styles (i.e., analyzing, doing, watching) related to effective leadership and management and argues that these are not mutually exclusive. The analyzing style refers to someone who understands a task by taking it apart, examining its elements, and reconstructing it piece by piece. The most powerful learning moment for analyzers occurs prior to the performance. The doing style in contrast refers to someone whose most powerful learning moment occurs during the performance, where trial and error are integral to the learning process. Watchers are argued to learn a great deal when they are given the chance to see the total performance because they have a preference for viewing the complete picture. It is argued that great leaders do not try to change a person's style but recognize the differences and know that the most effective way to invest their time is to identify exactly how each employee is different and then to figure out how best to incorporate those enduring idiosyncrasies into his/her overall plan.

With regard to leader-subordinate relations, Atwater and Yammarino (1993) found that personal attributes accounted for a significant portion of variance in subordinates' ratings of transformational and transactional leaders. In particular, feeling type leaders were rated more highly on

Second, a number of studies have examined the interaction between individual difference characteristics and the work environment, believed to be central to person-environment (PE) fit models (D'Amato & Zijlstra, 2008). Chan (1996) introduced the concept of cognitive misfit, which refers to the degree of mismatch between an individual's cognitive style and the predominant style demands of the work context. Consistent with other PE fit studies, a fit between one's cognitive style and the job demands is expected to yield positive outcomes (e.g., job satisfaction, career success), while a mismatch is expected to lead to negative outcomes (e.g., increased turnover, higher levels of work-related stress). Chan (1996) concluded from his study with engineers that cognitive misfit was unrelated to employee performance but was significantly related to job turnover. In other occupational groups, Chilton, Hardgrave, and Armstrong (2005) found that performance decreased and stress levels increased as the gap between software developers' cognitive styles and the perceived demands of the work environment became wider. In their study of entrepreneurs, Brigham, De Castro, and Shepherd (2007) also found that cognitive misfit led to lower levels of satisfaction within the work environment, higher levels of intent to leave, as well as actual staff turnover.

Given the amount of investment in attracting, recruiting, selecting, and retaining high-quality employees, it is hardly surprising that there is considerable interest in the concept of PE fit to further our understanding of vocational behavior in order to develop effective human resource management strategies (Ehrhart & Ziegert, 2005; Ployhart, 2006). Knowing more about staff turnover and job satisfaction will potentially lead to improvements in selection and retention, resulting in substantial monetary savings. It is clear from the studies reviewed that understanding the link between cognitive styles, vocational preferences, and work environment fit remains a challenge. Each study investigates a particular aspect, but together these studies do not lead to unequivocal insights. Future research should take account of Chan's (1996) study that highlighted the possibility of underlying mediating variables and the multidimensional nature of PE fit. Both have implications for helping us further understand the impact of cognitive misfit. Other scholars have conceptualized PE fit as a multidimensional construct that evolves over time and that is composed of fit with the vocation, organization, job, group, and other people (Jansen & Kristof-Brown, 2006). Jansen and Kristof-Brown (2006) quite rightly argue that attempting to increase our understanding of single dimensions of fit in isolation of time and context

their self-awareness and metacognitive skills; how it can help determine whether and when to match or mismatch instruction to the learner; how it can influence the success of distance learning, Web-based instruction, and technology in the classroom; how it can influence diversity in the context of learning; and how it might influence how we assess students with widely differing styles.

Person-Environment Fit, Careers, and Vocational Preference

A number of articles have considered the usefulness of cognitive styles for selection, recruitment, job design, and workforce planning (e.g., Armstrong & Sadler-Smith, 2006; Hayes & Allinson, 1994; Sadler-Smith, 1998). Two major topics can be distilled within this subcategory: style differences and vocational preferences and cognitive styles and work environment fit.

First, a number of articles focus on the influence of style differences on vocational choice and career preferences (e.g., Blustein & Phillips, 1988; Sullivan & Hansen, 2004; Zhang, 2004). These studies sought insights into how individual differences affect career decision making and vocational development. An underlying assumption was that people self-select for jobs and careers in which the work demands are compatible with their preferred ways of perceiving and processing information and making decisions. Ways in which people differ in their occupational choices and the functions they choose to serve to match their preferences for task and job characteristics are typical areas of study. Hayes and Allinson (1998) suggested that, because of self-selection, people within many groups in organizations will share similar cognitive styles that are related to the information-processing requirements of their work. In this respect, Foxall and Payne (1989) examined the cognitive profiles of people in various managerial functions, and two other studies looked at vocational choice within medicine. Leong, Hardin, and Gaylor (2005) and Stratton, Witzke, Elam, and Cheever (2005) investigated the influence of cognitive and learning style differences on career specialty choice of medical students. Mazen (1989) tested Vroom's (1964) instrumentality theory, which distinguishes between preference and actual choice, and Holland's (1985) vocational interest typology among women, and, finally, Gailbreath, Wagner, Moffett, and Hein (1997) studied the assumed homogeneity in cognitive profiles among leaders in a military environment.

Work-Based Learning

Few studies have considered style in the context of work-based learning to inform training and development practice. In one theoretical article, Sadler-Smith and Smith (2004) identified challenges for instructional designers and facilitators engaged in the delivery of flexible learning in the workplace and suggested ways in which individual differences in styles may need to be accommodated. Another theoretical contribution (Berings, Poell, & Simons, 2005) combined theory from the educational psychology and workplace learning literatures, including personality types, cognitive style, thinking style, decision-making style, and learning styles, to gain insights into employees' on-the-job learning activities to help them improve their on-the-job learning by developing an adaptive flexibility in the use of the various strategies.

Organizational Learning

The importance of styles in the context of management learning has been extended to the concept of organizational learning. Hayes and Allinson (1998) reviewed two disparate literatures from adjacent fields of individual and organizational learning to identify implications for theory and practice. The article focused on the extent to which the individual level construct of cognitive style can be meaningfully applied to aid the understanding of learning at the level of the organization as well as at the level of the individual. Ways in which consideration of cognitive styles can improve the effectiveness of interventions designed to improve individual and organizational performance were also identified. Another article by Ortenblad (2005) considered the importance of individual cognitive styles in the sculpting of learning organizations, arguing for a heterogeneous mix of Jung's four personality types to ensure effective organizational learning.

While the preceding section on management and organizational learning has received most attention over the past 20 years compared with other categories, there remains enormous scope for future research. From a theoretical perspective, more needs to be known about the implications of cognitive styles for the management learning and knowledge transfer processes in the context of individual, collective, and collaborative learning. From the perspective of management education and development, more research is needed to help us understand how cognitive styles can be usefully employed to help learners develop

more students wanted to learn in a sensing style. The level of style congruency was positively related to academic performance. Witkin et al.'s (1971) field dependence/field independence has also been found to be an important factor influencing performance of business students across various assessment techniques. Au (1997) found that field-independent students perform better than field-dependent students in all forms of assessment, which included a multiple choice test, a written report, and a final examination. In a review article, Hayes and Allinson (1996) examined the effects of matching and mismatching learning activity with trainer and trainee style on learning achievement. While 13 out of 23 studies reviewed offered some support for the hypothesis that matching style with learning activity would have a positive effect on performance, their major conclusion was that—although matching may have a positive effect on trainees' attitudes toward their trainers—they do not believe there is significant evidence of the positive effects of such a match on learning. In a later study, Armstrong (1999) highlighted the need for a clearer and more systematic research program aimed at studying the matching hypothesis on the basis that its effect will always be mediated by the nature of the work context.

Course Design

A number of studies have implications for course design in formal management education and for training and development in organizational contexts. Sadler-Smith (1999) found support for the belief that learning preferences, defined as an individual's propensity to choose or express a liking for a particular teaching or learning technique, is a correlate of cognitive style. Using the CSI, he found that analysts expressed a preference for reflective and individually oriented methods of learning, whereas intuitive types were disinclined to use these methods. Later studies also found that style and gender interacted in their relationship with learning preferences for both business students (Sadler-Smith, 2001) and UK personnel practitioners (Sadler-Smith, Allinson, & Hayes, 2000). Adkins (2005) also considered the implications of cognitive styles and learning preferences on course design, drawing on Epstein's (1991) CEST. Using a learning course in human resource management, she highlights the importance of applied learning where methods of instruction such as a lecture are directed toward the rational system and applied approaches such as simulations are directed toward the experiential system of information processing.

Influence of Styles on Research Supervision in Management Education

Armstrong, Allinson, and Hayes (2004) examined the effects of differences and similarities in the analytic-intuitive dimensions of cognitive style on the research supervision process in management education. Findings suggested that analytic supervisors were perceived to be significantly more nurturing and less dominant than their more intuitive counterparts, indicating a higher degree of closeness in their relationships. This led to increased liking in the relationship and to significantly higher performance outcomes for the student. These effects were highest in dyads whose students and supervisors were more analytic. An earlier study by the same authors (Armstrong, Allinson, & Hayes, 1997) reported a relative lack of empathy being perceived by intuitive students allocated to intuitive supervisors. Armstrong (2004) also analyzed the impact of supervisors' cognitive styles on the quality of the research supervision process. Results revealed that students perceived the quality of supervision to increase significantly with the degree to which supervisors were analytic in their cognitive style. Students whose supervisors were more analytic also achieved significantly higher grades for their dissertations.

Learning Performance

A number of studies have examined the influence of cognitive styles on academic performance. Armstrong (2000) found that management students whose dominant cognitive styles were analytic attained higher grades in modules that focused on long-term solitary tasks involving careful planning and analysis of information. Contrary to expectations, tasks believed to be more suited to the intuitive style were also higher for analytic individuals, as was overall ability defined by final degree grades. Backhaus and Liff (2007) also examined the role of intuition and analysis as well as approaches to studying in management education using the CSI and the Revised Approaches to Studying Inventory (RASI; Entwistle & Tait, 1994). Results again revealed a relationship between analytical orientation and grade point average. There was also a correlation between academic performance and higher scores on the deep, strategic, metacognitive awareness, and academic self-confidence scales of the RASI. Using the MBTI, Cooper and Miller (1991) found that business professors were more likely to teach in an intuitive manner, whereas

and Oldersma (1999) also used the NFC scale to study its effect on negotiation in a decision-making setting. Negotiators with high NFC were more influenced by focal points when setting limits and making concessions than those with low NFC. Negotiators with high NFC were also more influenced by stereotypic information when making concessions than were negotiators with low NFC.

A number of investigations in this category involved the use of Kirton's (1976) KAI theory. For example, the tendency for a person to increase commitment to a previously chosen course of action when the outcome of one's previous decision is negative is referred to as escalation of commitment, a phenomenon that has significant implications for organizational decision making (Fox & Straw, 1979). Singer (2001) sought to determine whether there is a significant association between escalation and cognitive styles using the KAI. While previous studies of individual difference variables such as locus of control (Singer & Singer, 1986) have been found to be significantly associated with escalation, cognitive styles were not. Another study used both KAI and GEFT (Antonietti & Gioletta, 1995) to explore the implications of cognitive style for analogical problem solving. Their results showed that field-independent subjects were more likely to be analogical problem solvers than were field-dependent subjects, and rates of analogical solutions were higher in adaptors than in innovators.

This decision-making and problem-solving category contains the second highest number of research articles out of the 10 categories reviewed in this chapter. Despite this, there is still enormous scope for further studies in this important field. Examples include structured versus unstructured decision-making approaches, group and organizational decision making, rationality versus irrationality, decision behavior under conditions of uncertainty, skills development in decision making, risk taking, information use, problem definition, evaluation and choice, and analysis and interpretation techniques.

Management and Organizational Learning

This category has received most attention by researchers over the past two decades. Both theoretical and empirical studies are reported that consider the influence of styles on the process of research supervision in management education, learning performance, course design, work-based learning, and organizational learning.

Decision Support Systems

Rao, Jacob, and Lin (1992) formulated evidence against Robey and Taggart's (1982) use of the microscopic approach of neuroscience (analytic-intuitive hemispheric specialization) for providing theoretical foundations for decision support system (DSS) design. They did, however, concede that the psychological construct of cognitive styles has an important part to play in the DSS design process. By relating cognitive styles to decision-making situations, they suggest that a DSS would have the appropriate capabilities and tools to allow an analytic/intuitive decision maker to perform effectively. In a rebuttal of Rao and colleagues' article, Robey (1992) makes it clear that the most important feature of their earlier brain metaphor (Robey & Taggart, 1982) was the notion of integration of the intuitive and analytic styles, not their separation. Rather than thinking of individuals as either intuitive or analytic, they saw human decision makers as integrated processors capable of defining and solving problems using both intuitive and analytic processes. Researchers adopting an integrated, organic view of human information processing, in place of the analytic-intuitive dichotomy, should discover more challenges and more rewards in their efforts in DSS design according to Robey.

General Managerial Decision Making

Bar-Tal (1994) explored the influence of individuals' need for cognitive structure (NCS) and ability to achieve cognitive structure (AACS) when coping with uncertainty in decision-making situations. High NCS and low AACS individuals experience the greatest difficulties in their decision making; the more they perceived conflict in the situation, the more time they spent making the decision. Those with a high AACS and high NCS experienced least difficulty in the situation. Tetlock (2000) used cognitive style items adapted from Webster and Kruglanski's (1994) need for closure (NFC) scale to assess tolerance for ambiguity and strength of personal preference for simple comprehensive explanations of phenomena, for working on problems with clear-cut solutions, and for working in homogenous as opposed to heterogeneous social units. Cognitive styles emerged as a consistent predictor of the value spins that managers placed on decisions based on scenarios that depicted decision-making processes at micro, meso, and macro levels of analyses. De Dreu, Koole,

Intuitive managers were found to view the prospector or the analyzer strategy as the most viable future alternative for the firm, whereas the defender or analyzer strategy was preferred by sensing managers. Hayley and Stumpf (1989) revealed that different Jungian types habitually use distinct heuristics to gather data and then generate and evaluate alternatives in strategic decision-making processes. In a later study, Stumpf and Dunbar (1991) analyzed the effects of cognitive styles on the type and radicalness of choices made in strategic decision situations. Their results showed that individuals with different preferences (i.e., ST, NT, SF, NF) take patterns of actions that reflect specific biases (i.e., selective perception; positivity; social desirability; and reasoning by analogy, respectively). Nutt (1990) also drew on Jungian style classifications (ST, SF, NT, NF) to identify data- and process-dominant styles of strategic decision making. Decision styles were found to be a key factor in explaining the likelihood of taking strategic action and the risk seen in this action. Some managers applied intuitive processes with subjective data and heuristics. Others used a goal-directed process using logic and objective information. Still others were flexible in their approach, using both logic and intuition. Views of both adoption and risk were found to be influenced by decision style. The more judicial (SF) top executive was found to be more action oriented, the systematic (ST) top executive action averse, with the speculative and heuristic (NT and NF) top executives taking nearly identical and neutral positions.

Hodgkinson and Clarke (2007) outline an alternative two-dimensional framework to inform the investigation of the impact of cognitive styles on organizational strategizing. Development of their framework led to four broad types, depending on an individual's preference for analysis (low/high) or intuition (low/high). People occupying the low/low, low/high, high/low, and high/high preferences with regard to analysis and intuition respectively are labeled nondiscerning, detail conscious, big picture conscious, and cognitively versatile. These basic information-processing tendencies are believed by these authors to be fundamental to the ways in which strategists approach their work. While individuals normally favor certain styles, other evidence suggests that managers can make appropriate shifts in their style to fit the problem at hand (Robey & Taggart, 1981). Cognitively versatile individuals in Hodgkinson and Clarke's framework, for example, are more likely to switch between analytic and intuitive processing strategies according to the varying contingencies confronting them.

Once again, while the studies reviewed in this category have been useful for enhancing our understanding of some aspects of groups and teams in the workplace, there is significant scope for further studies. For example, cognitive styles will almost certainly have an impact on aspects of perception and communication in teams, membership formation, group norms and deviancy, individual versus group goals, team leadership, group problem solving and decision making, and group conflict. There is a dearth of studies in these areas.

Decision Making and Problem Solving

Cognitive styles may help explain why managers with similar skills and abilities make different decisions. The relevance of cognitive styles for decision making and problem solving has attracted significant interest among style researchers over the past 20 years. Areas investigated cover strategic decision making, decision support system design, and general managerial decision making.

Strategic Decision Making

Sparrow (1999) argues that managers cannot avoid having to deal with emotionality in today's complex world and that rational, strategic thought is often not appropriate in such a context. He highlights the need to consider cognitive styles, particularly intuitive skills and creativity, when considering aspects of strategic cognition. A number of studies have used the MBTI for exploring the effects of cognitive styles on strategic decision situations. In an examination of how cognitive styles affect strategic decision outcomes, Hough and Ogilvie (2005) found that NT managers used their intuition to make cognitive leaps based on objective information to craft more decisions of higher quality than other managers, whereas SF types used time to seek socially acceptable decisions, which led to a lower number of decisions and lower perceived effectiveness. Extravert managers were also perceived to be more effective than introverted managers even though extroverts were not more decisive than introverted managers. Gallén (2006) examined the effect of cognitive styles on managers' preferences for strategic decisions using the typology of Miles and Snow's (1978) three generic strategies of defender (stable products or services, compete on basis of value and cost), prospector (broad product market domain and often first to market), and analyzer (combined characteristics of prospector and defender).

a correlation matrix variously described as strong, weak, and negligible with each of the Kirton subscales (sufficiency versus proliferation of originality; efficiency; rule/group conformity) and the overall KAI score. Only 13 out of 24 subscale relationships were supported, revealing only a modest confirmation of the validity of the BTRPI construct. However, in a later study, Aritzeta, Senior, and Swailes (2005) demonstrated stronger convergent validity between the KAI and BTRPI. KAI subscale correlations were much more coherent than those reported by Fisher et al. (1998). Aritzeta et al. (2005) concluded that implementers, completer-finishers, team workers, and specialists will display an adaptive style; monitor evaluators and coordinators will act as bridges (moderating tensions occurring between high adaptors and innovators); and plants, shapers, and resource investigators will display an innovative cognitive style. A change in adaptor-innovator balance in any team must be brought about by changes in personnel in order to ensure the optimal team, which will of course be contingent on performance tasks and needs.

In the context of innovation and creativity, large companies are taking major initiatives involving teams in the hope of generating new paradigm-breaking ideas that can transform their products and services (Stepanek, 1999). Many are creating so-called ideas factories in which teams brainstorm using e-mail, Web-based groupware, and face-to-face meetings in the hope of generating ideas to spark changes to existing business paradigms. In relation to this, a study by Garfield, Taylor, Dennis, and Satzinger (2001) examined ways in which groupware-based creativity techniques, the ideas generated by other team members, and an individual's own creative style can influence creativity in terms of the types of ideas produced by the participants. Using the MBTI and KAI, they found that individuals who were NF types or KAI innovators generated more paradigm-modifying ideas than did MBTI ST types or KAI adaptors. KAI innovators also generated more novel ideas.

Finally, the concept of stereotypes has received attention from styles researchers to investigate factors that influence their development. Information-processing styles have been shown to play a major role (Sherman, 2001). Chow and Esses (2005) built on this work to investigate the relationship of personal need for structure (Neuberg, Judice, & West, 1997), need for closure (Webster & Kruglanski, 1994), and personal fear of invalidity (Neuberg et al., 1997) on stereotype development. Their findings revealed that personal fear of invalidity, personal need for structure, and need for closure all clearly affect stereotype development.

While the studies reviewed have made an important contribution, their application has been rather limited, focusing on aspects of behavior and relationships in the field of marketing, and information use in the area of sales. Areas of future research might also consider the implications of cognitive styles for market research and buying behavior, product concepts, branding and management, personal selling and sales behavior, advertising, publicity and sponsorship, and international marketing, to name but a few.

Groups and Teams

A number of articles have focused on the influence of cognitive styles on groups and teams. Areas of interest included behaviors of members of self-managed work teams, team role preferences, creativity and idea generation, and the development of stereotypes.

Armstrong and Priola (2001) sought to examine how differences and similarities in the analytic-intuitive dimension of cognitive styles affected the behavior of members of self-managed work teams (SMWTs) on task and emotionally expressive dimensions. As hypothesized, intuitive individuals and homogeneous intuitive SMWTs were found to initiate more social-emotional acts. Contrary to expectations, intuitive individuals and homogeneous intuitive teams engaged in more task-oriented behaviors too. This was thought to be due to the nature of the task facing the teams, which was relatively unstructured and organic. It was concluded that, had the task been more structured and mechanistic, the original hypotheses that analytics and homogenous analytic SMWTs would perform more task-oriented acts than social-emotional oriented acts may have been supported. This was later tested by Priola, Smith, and Armstrong (2004). In this study, it was found that because of the mechanistic and strictly defined problem, intuitive individuals could not relate to the task, nor could they find the right solution. They focused on maintaining the group cohesiveness and the group integrity against the external, hostile, and undecipherable setting (the exercise). The analytics comfortably and successfully implemented the logical thought process required by the kind of structured problem, which corresponded to their preferred problem-solving style.

Further studies explored the relationship between Belbin's (1981) Team Role Preferences Inventory (BTRPI) and Kirton's (1976) KAI. On the basis of a comparison between the theoretical underpinnings of the two theories, Fisher, Macrosson, and Wong (1998) hypothesized

a strong positive effect on the preference for technology-based self-services; persons scoring high on the experiential style prefer interactions with service personnel. Service complexity moderates the influence of cognitive styles on preference for service technology.

Ramanathan and Williams (2007) investigated emotional consequences of indulgence-impulsive consumption (e.g., credit card debt, obesity, binge drinking) and how impulsive personality traits affect emotional responses to indulgent choices. Impulsive versus prudent personality traits (Rook & Fisher, 1995) showed that consumers feel simultaneous mixtures of both positive and negative emotions in response to indulgences and that the specific components of those emotional mixtures vary, depending on differences in individual impulsivity.

Customer Relations

Altering sales behaviors during customer interactions based on perceived information about the nature of the selling situation is referred to as "adaptive selling" (Spiro & Weitz, 1990). Adaptiveness is seen as the key advantage of personal selling as a marketing tool. Using the MBTI, McIntyre, Claxton, Anselmi, and Wheatle (2000) found cognitive style to be an antecedent to adaptive selling behavior. Their study found that salespeople who prefer information intake by intuiting (rather than sensing) and prefer information processing by thinking (rather than feeling) were found to be more likely to practice adaptive selling. The more adaptive selling that was practiced, the greater customer orientation became. The greater the customer orientation, the better the self-perceived selling performance became. Another study by McIntyre and Meloche (1995) using the MBTI sought to determine whether cognitive style was an antecedent of salespeople's orientation toward the customer or the sale. The study found that sensing-thinking (ST) types were significantly less customer oriented than intuition-thinking (NT), sensing-feeling (SF), and intuition-feeling (NF) types on Myers-Briggs' thinking-feeling (TF) and sensing-intuition (SN) dimensions. Finally, Ruiz and Sicilia (2004) investigated the impact of cognitive style on consumer response to advertising appeals. They found that informational and informational-emotional advertising appeals that match consumers' processing styles (thinking and thinking-feeling processes respectively) generate more positive attitudes toward the brand, purchase information, and brand choice.

In summary, studies in the area of sales and marketing have made use of a variety of instruments, such as the MBTI, GEFT, REI, and KAI.

market situation, and they are more likely to appraise that situation as an opportunity.

With regard to information use in advertising, Cole and Gaeth (1990) studied the effects of cognitive style using the Group Embedded Figures Test (GEFT; Witkin, Oltman, Raskin, & Karp, 1971) on the use of information on consumer packaging. People with high field-dependence scores (i.e., more global information processors) took longer to dis-embed relevant information than did those with low field-dependence scores (i.e., more analytical information processors). Other studies (e.g., Keller & McGill, 1994; Thompson & Hamilton, 2006) examined the effects of information-processing mode on consumers' responses to comparative advertising (where explicit comparisons are made between two or more brands). Comparative advertisements were found to be more effective when consumers use analytical processing, whereas noncomparative advertisements were more effective when consumers use imagery processing. People's responses to visual and verbal stimuli in advertisements were evaluated by Sojka and Giese (2006). Drawing on Epstein's (1991) theory that affect and cognition work independently or together, they argued for four distinct processing styles of affective, cognitive, combined, or low motivated processors. Results revealed that high-affect individuals respond more favorably to a visual advertisement than do other groups. Individuals high on both affect and cognition respond more favorably to a combined visual/verbal advertisement.

Individual Differences in Consumer Behavior

First adopters of new products and brands are often referred to as consumer innovators, and researchers have sought to determine the role they play in the creation of markets. A study by Foxall (1994) discusses five empirical studies of innovative consumer behavior using the KAI. Three were concerned with the early adoption of new food products and brands (purchase innovativeness); two were concerned with consumers' use of personal computers to solve a range of problems (use innovativeness). There were no associations between consumer behavior and the innovator cognitive style. Innovators and adaptors were found among both groups.

Using Epstein et al.'s (1996) REI, Simon and Usunier (2007) investigated consumer differences in the use of technology-based self-services (e.g., ATMs or self-service fuel pumps) compared with personnel-in-contact services. Their study revealed that rational engagement has

cognitive style profiles) or whole-brain thinking for effective innovation at the organizational level. Individuals with a more intuitive or wholistic cognitive style are expected to be more effective in the initiation phase of the innovation process (i.e., the stage in which new ideas are generated), whereas individuals with a more analytical style may be better in the implementation phase (i.e., the stage in which ideas are put into practice).

While several studies have been conducted in the areas of entrepreneurship and innovation using various cognitive style models (e.g., KAI, CSI, MBTI), research has been somewhat limited. The recent focus on cognition as a way of enhancing our understanding of processes such as opportunity recognition, innovation, and entrepreneurial activity in small and medium-sized enterprises will hopefully stimulate more research into the influence of style differences. Areas of interest might include: the link between cognitive styles and the firm's entrepreneurial orientation; entrepreneurial teams and style differences; innovation and creativity in a team context; social entrepreneurship; and longitudinal studies on successful innovation, entrepreneurship, and intrapreneurship that also take contextual and situational aspects into account.

Sales and Marketing

Articles within this theme were found to fall into three subcategories. In the first subcategory, labeled "consumer perception and information use," two distinct areas of interest were discerned, relating to antecedents of people's interpretation of a market and information use in advertising. The second subcategory, labeled "individual differences in consumer behavior," focuses on consumer innovation, preference for technology, and indulgence. The final category we labeled "customer relations," and the studies here focused on the influence of cognitive styles on salespeople's behaviors and orientations toward the customers.

Consumer Perception and Information Use

White, Varadarajan, and Dacin (2003) sought to delineate antecedents of people's interpretation of a market situation. They found that managers with more extroverted, judging, intuiting, and thinking cognitive styles (compared with more introverted, perceiving, sensing, and feeling styles) tend to perceive situations as more controllable. Consequently, they are likely to perceive less risk when interpreting a given

Hammer, 2003). From the preceding review, it seems apparent that there may be a move away from the previously hypothesized unifactorial structure of cognitive style adopted by Allinson and Hayes (1996) and Kirton (1976) toward multidimensional concepts, such as the REI of Epstein et al. (1996), the LNTSP of Vance et al. (2007), and the CoSI of Cools and Van den Broeck (2007). Their uptake in the fields of business and management, however, is yet to be determined. Let us now turn our attention to the application of cognitive styles theory in the fields of business and management over the past two decades.

Innovation and Entrepreneurship

A number of articles were devoted to innovation and entrepreneurship. Given their importance for economic growth, wealth creation, business expansion, and technological progress, researchers sought to understand how innovations and opportunities are discovered, created and exploited, by whom, and with what consequences (Wickham, 2004).

Over the past decade, a more cognitive approach has been adopted to the study of entrepreneurship (Baron, 2004), providing an alternative lens through which the phenomenon may be explored. Studies have focused on detecting knowledge structures and mental models that entrepreneurs use to make assessments, judgments, or decisions involving opportunity evaluation, venture creation, and growth (Mitchell et al., 2002). In line with this new perspective, style differences have been studied in relation to the opportunity process to try to answer the question of why some people are able to discover and exploit particular entrepreneurial opportunities, while others are not (e.g., Dimov, 2007; Hmieleski & Corbett, 2006). Other studies have focused on the link between cognitive styles and firm growth and performance, making a comparison between the cognitive profiles of entrepreneurs from high performing and low performing firms (e.g., Ginn & Sexton, 1990; Sadler-Smith, 2004). Some scholars also compared entrepreneurs' cognitive styles with those of nonentrepreneurs (e.g., Allinson, Chell, & Hayes, 2000; Buttner & Gryskiewicz, 1993).

Innovation is also considered to represent an important competitive advantage for contemporary organizations (Beckman & Barry, 2007). Several authors have investigated how cognitive styles can be used to stimulate innovation in organizational processes (e.g., Beckman & Barry, 2007; Leonard & Straus, 1997; Rhodes & Thame, 1988). These studies emphasized the importance of style versatility (i.e., having a mixture of

and experiential. The rational system operates primarily at the conscious level and is intentional, analytic, and relatively affect free. The experiential system is assumed to be automatic, preconscious, wholistic, and intimately associated with affect. Based on this dual-process theory (CEST), a new self-report measure of individual differences in intuitive-experiential and analytic-rational thinking known as the REI was developed (Epstein et al., 1996).

Vance et al. (2007) also advocate multidimensional theories and measures of styles. Having failed to identify an instrument that measures an individual's composite picture of linear and nonlinear thinking, these authors elected to develop their own measure. They propose and test a multifaceted construct of thinking styles based on two primary dimensions: linear thinking (e.g., rationality, logic, analytical thinking) and nonlinear thinking (e.g., intuition, insight, creativity). A four-factor model emerges in their self-report diagnostic instrument, called the LNTSP.

Cools and Van den Broeck (2007) also recently developed a multidimensional instrument for use with professional and managerial groups. Known as the CoSI, the instrument assesses three dimensions, labeled knowing style, planning style, and creating style. People with a knowing style look for data, want to know exactly how things are, retain facts and details, and like complex problems that demand logical and rational solutions. People with a planning style have a need for structure and like to organize and control in a highly structured environment relying on preparation and planning. Those with a creating style like uncertainty and freedom and see problems as opportunities and challenges.

In addition to new instruments, there have been a number of reexamination/validation studies of earlier instruments used in the field of management too. The most notable is Kirton's (1976) Adaption-Innovation inventory (KAI). Studies of the KAI have supported the scales' internal consistency and reliability (Joniak & Isaksen, 1988). There have been other studies of the KAI, however, that have reexamined Kirton's claim for a three-factor model (Taylor, 1989), with suggestions that the sufficiency of originality subscale needs to be divided into subfactors, a view later supported by Foxall and Hackett (1992).

Summarizing, since its publication the CSI has been used most extensively in the fields of business and management, with nearly 300 studies being reported on its authors' user database. The KAI also remains a dominant theory. In the reviews that follow, the CSI and KAI are among the three most cited instruments, together with the longer standing Myers-Briggs Type Indicator (MBTI; Myers, McCaulley, Quenk, &

Chapter 10 Cognitive Styles and Their Relevance for Business

and learning style. While acknowledging its intuitive appeal, he points to contrary opinions of the theoretical and empirical validity from within the psychological field and argued for style differences and other forms of labeling to be discontinued. In a reply to this critique, Sadler-Smith (2001) provided a compelling argument to suggest that, while learning styles may suffer from over-usage and a weak theoretical base, there is growing empirical and psychological evidence to suggest that cognitive style is a valid concept that is not to be ignored.

Measurement

With regard to measurement, a number of new instruments have appeared over the past two decades along with a range of reliability and validation studies of those new instruments and of previous ones. The most notable new instruments for the field of management are the Cognitive Style Index (CSI; Allinson & Hayes, 1996) and the Rational-Experiential Inventory (REI; Epstein, Pacini, Denes-Raj, & Heier, 1996). More recently, the Linear/Non-Linear Thinking Styles Profile (LNTSP; Vance, Groves, Paik, & Kindler, 2007) and the Cognitive Style Indicator (CoSI; Cools & Van den Broeck, 2007) have appeared, but these are at an earlier stage of use and development.

The CSI assesses an individual's position on the generic analysis-intuition dimension of cognitive style. Answering the call of Allinson and Hayes (1996) for replication and extension, a number of early studies reported reliability and validity figures that were favorable (Armstrong, 1999; Murphy, Kelleher, Doucette, & Young, 1998; Sadler-Smith, Spicer, & Tsang, 2000). However, more recent studies have questioned the theoretical assumption that various facets of style can be subsumed under a single overarching dimension. Hodgkinson and Sadler-Smith (2003a) presented arguments as to why the previously hypothesized unifactorial structure of the CSI should be questioned. While these propositions were refuted by Hayes, Allinson, Hudson, and Keasey (2003) on the grounds of a lack of robustness in their theoretical or empirical arguments, Hodgkinson and Sadler-Smith (2003b) reasserted their challenge for an alternative two-dimensional conception of the CSI.

Others too have adopted this multidimensional theory approach. On the basis that people commonly experience differences between what they think (head) and feel (heart), Epstein (1991) developed the cognitive-experiential self-theory (CEST). CEST proposes that people process information by two parallel interactive systems labeled rational

and teams (10 articles); (e) decision making and problem solving (29 articles); (f) management and organizational learning (42 articles); (g) person-environment fit, careers, and vocational preference (18 articles); (h) leadership (9 articles); (i) culture (13 articles); and (j) other areas of business and management (27 articles).

Theory and Measurement

A number of important studies have focused on aspects of both theory and measurement of the cognitive style construct within the context of business and management, and these will be considered separately.

Theory

A theoretical study of Hayes and Allinson (1994) identified the most commonly cited dimensions of cognitive styles, examined ways in which they can be classified, and considered their relevance and implications for management practice in a variety of different areas. These authors identified a need to bring order to the literature by clarifying the various confusing and overlapping concepts and adopting appropriate taxonomies. One such taxonomy uses a threefold model with an umbrella term, called intellectual styles, to capture both cognitive and learning style labels (Zhang & Sternberg, 2005). The model, which divides all styles into three basic kinds, is not only a useful heuristic device but also provides a summary of empirical relationships. Other articles too have attempted to provide an overview of theories, models, and measures, but some have focused entirely on learning styles (e.g., Cassidy, 2004) with no clear distinction between the cognitive style and learning style bodies of literature. Desmedt and Valcke (2004), however, realizing that the two terms are often used synonymously (leading to confusion), used a citation analysis technique to develop an alternative organization of the two bodies of literature. Their article clarifies dominant theoretical orientations and serves as a useful road map for novices entering the cognitive style field.

Other review articles have been more critical, such as Tiedemann's (1989) that attempted to demonstrate severe limitations of the evidence in support of cognitive styles, arguing that while they are not rendered completely useless, a vast amount of empirical research needs to be reinterpreted. In a similar vein, Reynolds (1997) presented a damning critique of styles—but this again confused the two terms of cognitive style

ness, management, applied psychology, social psychology, psychology-multidisciplinary, educational psychology, and social sciences) within the Social Science Citation Index (SSCI), which led to a list of 173 journals. Additionally, we also screened the Academic Journal Quality List of the UK Association of Business Schools (http://www.the-ABS.org.uk) to identify other relevant journals, leading to a further 36 journals being identified and bringing our total to 209.

We used the EBSCO and PsycINFO search engines to locate articles published in the last two decades, which led us to identifying 822 articles. We used the following terms to guide our search: cognitive style; thinking style; intellectual style; personality style; and personality type. These terms all fit into the innermost layer of Curry's (1983) heuristic model that comprises three main strata resembling the layers of an onion. She used this model to differentiate between a variety of theories and constructs such as learning style, information processing style, instructional preference, and cognitive style. Curry labeled this innermost layer cognitive personality style, which she believed to be a relatively permanent personality dimension. Her definition of this layer matches our earlier definition of cognitive style—an umbrella term that will now be adopted for the remainder of this chapter and which was the most frequently cited term in our review.

We reduced the number of potential articles by excluding book reviews, comments, editorials, and articles that did not focus on the concept of cognitive style or that were not relevant to the management context. After this process we were left with 203 articles that were considered to be relevant for this chapter. These were then categorized according to different themes partly informed by previous reviews of the field (e.g., Armstrong & Sadler-Smith, 2006; Hayes & Allinson, 1994; Sadler-Smith, 1998) but more significantly from a detailed content analysis of the collected articles.

A REVIEW OF DEVELOPMENT IN THE FIELDS OF BUSINESS AND MANAGEMENT

Ten different categories within business and management were identified, including one that concerns aspects of theory and measurement. The order in which the 10 categories will be reviewed is as follows: (a) theory and measurement (20 articles); (b) innovation and entrepreneurship (16 articles); (c) sales and marketing (19 articles); (d) groups

publications grew rapidly (Riding & Cheema, 1991), demonstrating interest among practitioners to understand the influence of individual differences in cognition. Studies in the field of management grew because of an increased attention on cognitive approaches to industrial, work, and organizational psychology (Hodgkinson, 2003). Empirical studies have shown that cognitive styles can be a better predictor of people's performance in particular situations than can general abilities or situational factors and that differences in cognitive styles influence learning, problem solving, decision making, communication, interpersonal functioning, and creativity in multiple and important ways (Armstrong, 1999; Cools, 2008; Kirton, 2003; Sadler-Smith, 1998). According to Sternberg and Grigorenko (1997), styles will continue to provide a much needed interface between research on cognition and personality and show a great deal of promise for the future in helping us understand some of the variation in job performance that cannot be accounted for by individual differences in abilities.

Fifteen years ago, Hayes and Allinson (1994) reviewed what they considered to be a large and confusing body of literature relating to cognitive styles and addressed some of the potential implications of that research for managerial practice. Their review led to two major findings. First, despite the fact that the field of study is complex, with many confusing terms and overlapping definitions, it is possible to bring order to the literature by clarifying the various concepts and adopting appropriate taxonomies. Second, they highlighted considerable implications of this literature for the discipline of management and identified a range of important areas for future research. Since they reported these findings, there has been no systematic review of developments in the management field and therefore no way of knowing the extent to which these implications have been explored. The present authors feel that the time is now right to do this, and that is the overarching purpose of this chapter, where we conduct a detailed review of the field before drawing reasoned and authoritative conclusions as to where the literature is, where it should be going, and what the important questions are left to be asked.

REVIEW PROCESS

We chose to focus on articles in top-tier, peer-reviewed academic journals appearing over the past two decades. These were selected, primarily, on the basis of their impact factor (in 2006) in seven categories (i.e., busi-

10

Cognitive Styles and Their Relevance for Business and Management: A Review of Development Over the Past Two Decades

STEVEN J. ARMSTRONG AND EVA COOLS

Cognitive style relates to the characteristic way in which an individual processes and evaluates information, solves problems, and makes decisions (Goldstein & Blackman, 1978). According to Messick (1996), cognitive styles are conceptualized as stable attitudes, preferences, or habitual strategies determining a person's typical mode of perceiving, remembering, thinking, and problem solving. As such, their influence extends to almost all human activities that implicate cognition, including learning and social and interpersonal functioning. Although research into styles began in the early part of the previous century (e.g., Allport, 1937), activity didn't peak until a period between the 1940s and 1970s. Growing interests in cognitive styles during that period led to the development of a wide diversity of theories and instruments and this was immediately followed by a loss of appeal among cognitive scientists in the 1970s as identified by Kozhevnikov (2007):

> The field was left fragmented and incomplete, without a coherent and practically useful theory and with no understanding of how cognitive styles were related to other psychological constructs and to cognitive science theories. (p. 464)

Paradoxically, around the time that interest in the styles field declined among cognitive scientists, the number of applied styles

Tunbridge, E. M., Harrison, P. J., & Weinberger, D. R. (2006). Catechol-o-methyltransferase, cognition, and psychosis: Val158Met and beyond. *Bioliological Psychiatry, 60,* 141–151.

Vandenbergh, D. J., Zonderman, A. B., Wang, J., Uhl, G. R., & Costa, P. T. J. (1997). No association between novelty seeking and dopamine D4 receptor (D4DR) exon III seven repeat alleles in Baltimore Longitudinal Study of Aging participants. *Molecular Psychiatry, 2,* 417–419.

Wainwright, M. A., Wright, M. J., Luciano, M., Montgomery, G. W., Geffen, G. M., & Martin, N. G. (2006). A linkage study of academic skills defined by the Queensland Core Skills Test. *Behavior Genetics, 36,* 56–64.

Wang, X., Trivedi, R., Treiber, F., & Snieder, H. (2005). Genetic and environmental influences on anger expression, John Henryism, and stressful life events: The Georgia Cardiovascular Twin Study. *Psychosomatic Medicine, 67,* 16–23.

Winterer, G., & Goldman, D. (2003). Genetics of human prefrontal function. *Brain Research Reviews, 43,* 134–163.

Witkin, H. A., Oltman, P. K., Raskin, E., & Karp, S. A. (1971). *A manual for the Embedded Figures Test.* Palo Alto, CA: Consulting Psychologists Press.

Zhang, L. F., & Sternberg, R. J. (2006). *The nature of intellectual styles.* Mahwah, NJ: Lawrence Erlbaum Associates Publishers.

Posthuma, D., de Geus, E. J., Baare, W. F., Hulshoff Pol, H. E., Kahn, R. S., & Boomsma, D. I. (2002). The association between brain volume and intelligence is of genetic origin. *Nature Neuroscience, 5,* 83–84.

Posthuma, D., Luciano, M., Geus, E. J., Wright, M. J., Slagboom, P. E., Montgomery, G. W., et al. (2005). A genomewide scan for intelligence identifies quantitative trait loci on 2q and 6p. *American Journal of Human Genetics, 77,* 318–326.

Rapoport, M., Wolf, U., Herrmann, N., Kiss, A., Shammi, P., Reis, M., et al. (2008). Traumatic brain injury, Apolipoprotein E-epsilon4, and cognition in older adults: A two-year longitudinal study. *Journal of Neuropsychiatry and Clinical Neurosciences, 20,* 68–73.

Reuter, M., Peters, K., Schroeter, K., Koebke, W., Lenardon, D., Bloch, B., et al. (2005). The influence of the dopaminergic system on cognitive functioning: A molecular genetic approach. *Behavioural Brain Research, 164,* 93–99.

Salkind, N. J. (1979). *The development of norms for the Matching Familiar Figures Test.* Unpublished manuscript.

Scarmeas, N., & Stern, Y. (2006). Imaging studies and APOE genotype in persons at risk for Alzheimer's disease. *Current Psychiatry Reports, 8,* 11–17.

Schulman, P., Keith, D., & Seligman, M. E. P. (1993). Is optimism heritable? A study of twins. *Behaviour Research and Therapy, 31,* 569–574.

Shaw, P. (2007). Intelligence and the developing human brain. *Bioessays, 29,* 962–973.

Shaw, P., Lerch, J. P., Pruessner, J. C., Taylor, K. N., Rose, A. B., Greenstein, D., et al. (2007). Cortical morphology in children and adolescents with different apolipoprotein E gene polymorphisms: An observational study. *Lancet Neurology, 6,* 494–500.

Shifman, S., Bhomra, A., Smiley, S., Wray, N. R., James, M. R., Martin, N. G., et al. (2008). A whole genome association study of neuroticism using DNA pooling. *Molecular Psychiatry, 13,* 302–312.

Small, B. J., Rosnick, C. B., Fratiglioni, L., & Backman, L. (2004). Apolipoprotein E and cognitive performance: A meta-analysis. *Psychology and Aging, 14,* 592–600.

Smith, J. D. (2002). Apolipoproteins and aging: Emerging mechanisms. *Ageing Research Reviews, 1,* 345–365.

Stein, D. J., Newman, T. K., Savitz, J., & Ramesar, R. (2006). Warriors versus worriers: The role of COMT gene variants. *CNS Spectrums, 11,* 745–758.

Sternberg, R. J. (1996). *Successful intelligence.* New York: Simon & Schuster.

Sternberg, R. J. (1997). *Thinking styles.* New York: Cambridge University Press.

Sternberg, R. J., & Zhang, L. F. (Eds.). (2001). *Perspectives on thinking, learning, and cognitive styles.* Mahwah, NJ: Lawrence Erlbaum Associates Publishers.

Sundstrom, A., Nilsson, L. G., Cruts, M., Adolfsson, R., Van Broeckhoven, C., & Nyberg, L. (2007). Fatigue before and after mild traumatic brain injury: Pre-post-injury comparisons in relation to Apolipoprotein E. *Brain Injury, 21,* 1049–1054.

Teasdale, G. M., Murray, G. D., & Nicoll, J. A. (2005). The association between APOE epsilon4, age and outcome after head injury: A prospective cohort study. *Brain, 128,* 2556–2561.

Teter, B., & Ashford, J. W. (2002). Neuroplasticity in Alzheimer's disease. *Journal of Neuroscience Research, 70,* 402–437.

Tunbridge, E. M., Bannerman, D. M., Sharp, T., & Harrison, P. J. (2004). Catechol-O-methyltransferase inhibition improves setshifting performance and elevates stimulated dopamine release in the rat prefrontal cortex. *Journal of Neuroscience, 24,* 5331–5335.

Kendler, K. S., Kessler, R. C., Heath, A. C., Neale, M. C., & Eaves, L. J. (1991). Coping: A genetic epidemiological investigation. *Psychological Medicine, 21,* 337–346.

Kleim, J. A., Lussnig, E., Schwarz, E. R., Comery, T. A., & Greenough, W. T. (1996). Synaptogenesis and Fos expression in the motor cortex of the adult rat after motor skill learning. *Journal of Neuroscience, 16,* 4529–4535.

Kozak, B., Strelau, J., & Miles, J. N. V. (2005). Genetic determinants of individual differences in coping styles. *Anxiety, Stress and Coping: An International Journal, 18,* 1–15.

Kuo, P. H., Neale, M. C., Riley, B. P., Patterson, D. G., Walsh, D., Prescott, C. A., et al. (2007). A genome-wide linkage analysis for the personality trait neuroticism in the Irish affected sib-pair study of alcohol dependence. *American Journal of Medical Genetics. Part B, Neuropsychiatric Genetics, 144,* 463–468.

Lachman, H. M., Papolos, D. F., Saito, T., Yu, Y. M., Szumlanski, C. L., & Weinshilboum, R. M. (1996). Human catechol-O-methyltransferase pharmacogenetics: Description of a functional polymorphism and its potential application to neuropsychiatric disorders. *Pharmacogenetics, 6,* 243–250.

Lau, J. Y. F., Rijsdijk, F., & Eley, T. C. (2006). I think, therefore I am: A twin study of attributional style in adolescents. *Journal of Child Psychology and Psychiatry, 47,* 696–703.

Luciano, M., Wright, M. J., Duffy, D. L., Wainwright, M. A., Zhu, G., Evans, D. M., et al. (2006). Genome-wide scan of IQ finds significant linkage to a quantitative trait locus on 2q. *Behavior Genetics, 36,* 45–55.

Mellins, C. A., Gatz, M., & Baker, L. (1996). Children's methods of coping with stress: A twin study of genetic and environmental influences. *Journal of Child Psychology and Psychiatry and Allied Disciplines, 6,* 721–730.

Miller, G. F., & Penke, L. (2007). The evolution of human intelligence and the coefficient of additive genetic variance in human brain size. *Intelligence, 35,* 97–114.

Munafò, M. R., Clark, T. G., Moore, L. R., Payne, E., Walton, R., & Flint, J. (2003). Genetic polymorphisms and personality in healthy adults: a systematic review and meta-analysis. *Molecular Psychiatry, 8,* 471–484.

Nash, M. W., Huezo-Diaz, P., Williamson, R. J., Sterne, A., Purcell, S., Hoda, F., et al. (2004). Genome-wide linkage analysis of a composite index of neuroticism and mood-related scales in extreme selected sibships. *Human Molecular Genetics, 13,* 2173–2182.

Neale, B. M., Sullivan, P. F., & Kendler, K. S. (2005). A genome scan of neuroticism in nicotine dependent smokers. *American Journal of Medical Genetics. Part B, Neuropsychiatric Genetics, 132,* 65–69.

Palmatier, M. A., Pakstis, A. J., Speed, W., Paschou, P., Goldman, D., Odunsi, A., et al. (2004). COMT haplotypes suggest P2 promoter region relevance for schizophrenia. *Molecular Psychiatry, 9,* 859–870..

Papassotiropoulos, A., Stephan, D. A., Huentelman, M. J., Hoerndli, F. J., Craig, D. W., Pearson, J. V., et al. (2006). Common Kibra alleles are associated with human memory performance. *Science, 314,* 475–478.

Payton, A. (2006). Investigating cognitive genetics and its implications for the treatment of cognitive deficit. *Genes, Brain, and Behavior,* 5(Suppl. 1), 44–53.

Plomin, R., & Spinath, F. M. (2004). Intelligence: Genetics, genes, and genomics. *Journal of Personality and Social Psychology, 86,* 112–129.

Posthuma, D., & de Geus, E. J. C. (2006). Progress in the molecular-genetic study of intelligence. *Current Directions in Psychological Science, 15,* 151–155.

Cianciolo, A. T., & Sternberg, R. J. (2004). *A brief history of intelligence*. Malden, MA: Blackwell.

Cronbach, L. J., & Snow, R. E. (1977). *Aptitudes and instructional methods*. New York: Wiley.

Deary, I. J., Spinath, F. M., & Bates, T. C. (2006). Genetics of intelligence. *European Journal of Human Genetics, 14*, 690–700.

Deary, I. J., Whiteman, M. C., Pattie, A., Starr, J. M., Hayward, C., Wright, A. F., et al. (2002). Cognitive change and the APOE epsilon 4 allele. *Nature, 481*, 932.

Dick, D. M., Aliev, F., Bierut, L., Goate, A., Rice, J., Hinrichs, A., et al. (2006). Linkage analyses of IQ in the collaborative study on the genetics of alcoholism (COGA) sample. *Behavior Genetics, 36*, 77–86.

Ebstein, R. P., Novick, O., Umansky, R., Priel, B., Osher, Y., Blaine, D., et al. (1996). Dopamine D4 receptor (D4DR) exon III polymorphism associated with the human personality trait of novelty seeking. *Nature Genetics, 12*, 78–80.

Eley, T. C., Gregory, A. M., Lau, J. Y. F., McGuffin, P., Napolitano, M., Rijsdijk, F. V., et al. (2008). In the face of uncertainty: A twin study of ambiguous information, anxiety and depression in children. *Journal of Abnormal Child Psychology, 36*, 55–65.

Fanous, A., Gardner, C. O., Prescott, C. A., Cancro, R., & Kendler, K. S. (2002). Neuroticism, major depression and gender: A population-based twin study. *Psychological Medicine, 32*, 719–728.

Fullerton, J., Cubin, M., Tiwari, H., Wang, C., Bomhra, A., Davidson, S., et al. (2003). Linkage analysis of extremely discordant and concordant sibling pairs identifies quantitative-trait loci that influence variation in the human personality trait neuroticism. *American Journal of Human Genetics, 72*, 879–890.

Grigorenko, E. L., LaBuda, M. C., & Carter, A. S. (1992). Similarity in general cognitive ability, creativity, and cognitive styles in a sample of adolescent Russian twins. *Acta Geneticae Medicae et Gemellologiae, 41*, 65–72.

Harris, S. E., Wright, A. F., Hayward, C., Starr, J. M., Whalley, L. J., & Deary, I. J. (2005). The functional COMT polymorphism, Val 158 Met, is associated with logical memory and the personality trait intellect/imagination in a cohort of healthy 79 year olds. *Neuroscience Letters, 385*, 1–6.

Hulshoff Pol, H. E., Schnack, H. G., Posthuma, D., Mandl, R. C., Baare, W. F., van Oel, C., et al. (2004). Genetic contributions to human brain morphology and intelligence. *Journal of Neuroscience, 26*, 10235–10242.

Huttenlocher, P. R. (1991). Dendritic and synaptic pathology in mental retardation. *Pediatric Neurology, 7*, 79–85.

Jacobs, B., Schall, M., & Scheibel, A. B. (1993). A quantitative dendritic analysis of Wernicke's area in humans. II. Gender, hemispheric, and environmental factors. *Journal of Comparative Neurology, 327*, 97–111.

Jacobs, B., & Scheibel, A. B. (1993). A quantitative dendritic analysis of Wernicke's area in humans. I. Lifespan changes. *Journal of Comparative Neurology, 327*, 83–96.

John, O. P., & Srivastava, S. (1999). The Big Five trait taxonomy: History, measurement, and theoretical perspectives. In L. A. Pervin & O. P. John (Eds.), *Handbook of personality* (pp. 102–138). New York,: Guilford.

Kendler, K. S., Gatz, M., Garver, D. L., & Pedersen, N. L. (2006). Personality and major depression: A Swedish longitudinal, population-based twin study. *Archives of General Psychiatry, 63*, 1113–1120.

6. In other words, to minimize the costs of the analyses, these researchers combined DNA(s) from multiple individuals in one tube to cut down the number of reactions and compared the profiles of genetic variation in groups (tubes) of individuals with high and low neuroticism scores.

REFERENCES

Alloy, L. B., Abramson, L. Y., Metalsky, G. I., & Harlage, S. (1998). The hopelessness theory of depression: Attributional aspects. *British Journal of Clinical Psychology, 27,* 5–21.

Allport, G. W. (1937). *Personality, a psychological interpretation.* New York: Holt.

Barnett, J. H., Heron, J., Ring, S. M., Golding, J., Goldman, D., Xu, K., et al. (2007). Gender-specific effects of the catechol-O-methyltransferase Val(108)/(158)Met polymorphism on cognitive function in children. *American Journal of Psychiatry, 164,* 142–149.

Benjamin, J., Ebstein, R. P., & Belmaker, H. (2002). *Molecular genetics and the human personality.* Washington, DC: American Psychiatric Association.

Benjamin, J., Li, L., Patterson, C., Greenberg, B. D., Murphy, D. L., & Hamer, D. H. (1996). Population and familial association between the D4 dopamine receptor gene and measures of novelty seeking. *Nature Genetics, 12,* 81–84.

Bienvenu, O. J., Samuels, J. F., Costa, P. T., Reti, I. M., Eaton, W. W., & Nestadt, G. (2004). Anxiety and depressive disorders and the five-factor model of personality: A higher- and lower-order personality trait investigation in a community sample. *Depression and Anxiety, 20,* 92–97.

Blackman, J. A., Worley, G., & Strittmatter, W. J. (2005). Apolipoprotein E and brain injury: Implications for children. *Developmental Medicine and Child Neurology, 47,* 64–70.

Boomsma, D., Busjahn, A., & Peltonen, L. (2002). Classical twin studies and beyond. *Nature Reviews Genetics, 3,* 872–882.

Bouchard, T. J., & Loehlin, J. C. (2001). Genes, evolution, and personality. *Behavior Genetics, 31,* 243–273.

Boyce, P., Parker, G., Barnett, B., Cooney, M., & Smith, F. (1991). Personality as a vulnerability factor to depression. *British Journal of Psychiatry, 159,* 106–114.

Busjahn, A., Faulhaber, H. D., Freier, K., & Luft, F. C. (1999). Genetic and environmental influences on coping styles: A twin study. *Psychosomatic Medicine, 4,* 469–475.

Buttini, M., Orth, M., Bellosta, S., Akeefe, H., Pitas, R. E., Wyss-Coray, T., et al. (1999). Expression of human apolipoprotein E3 or E4 in the brains of Apoe-/- mice: Isoform-specific effects on neurodegeneration. *Journal of Neuroscience, 19,* 4867–4880.

Buyske, S., Bates, M. E., Gharani, N., Matise, T. C., Tischfield, J. A., & Manowitz, P. (2006). Cognitive traits link to human chromosomal regions. *Behavior Genetics, 36,* 65–76.

Caspi, A., Roberts, B. W., & Shiner, R. L. (2005). Personality development: Stability and change. *Annual Review of Psychology, 56,* 453–484.

Chklovskii, D. B., Mel, B. W., & Svoboda, K. (2004). Cortical rewiring and information storage. *Nature, 431,* 782–788.

genes and personality genes, are likely to be involved in the formation of individual differences in styles. And it is anticipated that the effects of these genes should be even smaller.

This is perhaps what makes the concept of styles so alluring—it appeals to researchers in both the fields of intelligence and personality, but it cannot be fully explained by either concept. Thus, styles remain popular and hold a tint of a mystery: stylish.

ACKNOWLEDGMENTS

Preparation of this chapter was supported by Grant No. P50 HD052120, as administered by the U.S. National Institutes of Health. Grantees undertaking such projects are encouraged to express freely their professional judgment. This article, therefore, does not necessarily represent the position of U.S. National Institutes of Health; no official endorsement should be inferred. I am grateful to Dr. Robert Plomin for his willingness to sift through his vast knowledge of the field of behavior genetics and confirm my educated suspicion that behavior- and molecular-genetic literature on styles is really small, ensuring that I did not miss the elephant in the room in this chapter. I also express my gratitude to Ms. Mei Tan for her editorial assistance.

NOTES

1. Heritability is a statistic that captures the proportion of a given trait's variation (i.e., phenotypic variation) in a population that is attributable to variation in genes. Higher heritability indicates higher levels of covariation between a variation in genes and a variation in the phenotype of interest; lower heritability indicates a higher level of covariation between a variation in environments and a variation in the phenotype.

2. A metaphoric image for this approach is early-morning scavenger activity at a public beach of, let's say, Hawaii, where the beach is screened for lost jewels by a person with a metal detector and, when the detector starts screeching loudly, the person starts digging, attempting to localize the precise placement of the object generating the signal.

3. For each gene, the number indicates the number of the chromosome, the following letter indicates the arm (p for short and q for long arms), and the final number indicates the chromosomal band.

4. A metaphoric image for this approach is looking for treasure with a treasure map. The general location of the treasure is delineated on the map, yet there is a certain degree of uncertainty: the treasure (statistical signal) might not be there after all, for a variety of reasons, including a wrong map or an inaccurate interpretation.

5. These 3 allelic variants differ at 2 single-base variations located in exon 4 at codon positions 112 and 158. The T and C alleles of *APOE* 112T>C (rs429358) and *APOE* 158C>T (rs7412) encode arginine and cysteine, respectively. The variants differ such that *ApoE2* has a T allele at both positions 112 and 158; *ApoE3* has T and C alleles at positions 112 and 158, respectively; and *ApoE4* has C at both positions.

factors may exert their influence and to what degree such influence will be enhanced or counter-acted by other nongenetic factors.

Such a degree of uncertainty seems to be even greater for intellectual styles. Indeed, although limited in number, when available, heritability estimates for styles are lower, on average, than those for either intelligence or personality (and ranging from 0% to ~30%). This can be explained by two considerations. First, definitions of intellectual styles, typically, include the factor of situations. Because, by definition, situations are not controlled by genes (they are by definition and nature environmentally based), the etiological contribution of situations to styles should diminish the impact of genetic factors and enhance the impact of nongenetic factors. Second, styles are derivative products of intelligence and personality, arising from a mixture of both within situations. As with any mixture, intellectual styles resemble to some extent their discrete ingredients and dilute the influence of any particular single ingredient. Thus, the influence of any genes contributing to intellectual styles by means of intelligence and personality gets weakened.

Of note also is that heritability estimates of both intelligence and personality appear to fluctuate throughout the course of development. For example, heritability of IQ is reported to be ~20% in infancy and early childhood, with an increase to around 40% in middle childhood, and a subsequent increase to 50% in adulthood, before a subsequent decrease in older age (Payton, 2006; Plomin & Spinath, 2004). Interesting age dynamics of temperament and personality within both constructs across the lifespan have been noted as well (Caspi et al., 2005). In the literature, these dynamics are attributed to presumed changes in gene expression. However, this hypothesis is difficult to verify since there is no comprehensive account of what genes might be involved and how they might be behind these changes. The presence of a developmental dynamic might be characteristic of the etiology of intellectual styles as well, although, at this point, there is no substantial corpus of data attesting to the validity of this hypothesis.

Clearly, the literatures reviewed here indicate a substantial amount of promise for the role of genes in the manifestation of individual differences in intelligence and personality, and, correspondingly, in intellectual styles. Yet, although there are many clues, there is no cohesive picture of how these genetic influences are expressed. One thing is rather clear, though: many genes of small effects appear to be involved in the formation of these individual differences. And, if the hypothesis presented here is plausible, even more genes, combined into groups of intelligence

were as follows: active coping (.21), defense (.52), emotional coping (.23), and substitution factor (.41).

In yet a different study (Kozak, Strelau, & Miles, 2005), coping styles were assessed as task-oriented, emotion-oriented, social diversion, and distraction; their corresponding heritability estimates were .35, .34, .33, and .39, respectively. Of interest is that in this study the researchers also estimated genetic and environmental correlations between styles and found that environmental correlations (.24) were substantially lower than genetic correlations (.52). Finally, in the most recent study of this type (Wang, Trivedi, Treiber, & Snieder, 2005), coping styles were defined as anger expression (subscales: anger-in, anger-out, and anger-control) and John Henryism (i.e., a strong behavioral disposition to actively handle psychosocial and environmental stresses of daily living). Heritability estimates for anger-in, anger-out, anger-control, the total scale of anger expression, and John Henryism were .0, .14, .34, .15, and .34, respectively.

Thus, in general, the landscape of published results on styles fit the hypothesis generated at the beginning of this chapter: although there is evidence for the presence of genetic influences on intellectual styles, these genetic influences appear to be of smaller magnitude than those characteristic of intelligence and personality.

COMMENTS AND CONCLUSIONS

Because the literature on the genetic bases of intellectual styles (or any styles, really) is quite limited, it is impossible to provide a comprehensive review of what is known about the etiological bases of styles. Traditionally, intellectual styles are viewed as emerging interactively; therefore when intelligence and personality are manifested in particular situations, it is hypothesized that, etiologically, intellectual styles should overlap with both intelligence and personality. Correspondingly, I reviewed the literature on the genetic bases of all three constructs: intelligence, personality, and styles.

In general, as is the case for most complex behavioral traits, the heritability estimates for both intelligence and personality linger at somewhere around 50%. In other words, although there is a substantial amount of evidence that both intelligence and personality are shaped by genetic factors, there is a tremendous amount (i.e., 50% or half the variance) of uncertainty and flexibility with regard to how these genetic

are smaller than those of intelligence and personality (e.g., Grigorenko, LaBuda, & Carter, 1992). Specifically, the only set of heritability estimates readily available in the literature is that on Witkin's field dependence-independence (Witkin, Oltman, Raskin, & Karp, 1971) and Salkind's reflection-impulsivity (Salkind, 1979). The heritability estimates of the former were ~11% and for the latter they were negative (i.e., correlations for monozygotic twins were higher than that for dizygotic twins). However, these correlations were not different from 0. It appears that this study is the only published, peer-reviewed, quantitative-genetic report of intellectual styles. It is possible, of course, that other reports are available either in chapters of books or in various theses, but they are not at the surface of the literature.

Yet there are studies of other *styles* that might substantiate the discussion here. For example, there have been a number of behavior-genetic studies on styles of coping. These styles are typically viewed as ways of dealing with stressful situations resulting from the interactions of these situations with the intelligence and personality traits of people in the environment of stress. There are different theoretical frameworks and, correspondingly, different assessment instruments used in these studies, and, thus, a direct comparison of the results is not possible. Yet forming a general profile of these findings might be of interest.

All these studies were carried out using twin methodologies. For example, in a study by Kendler and others (Kendler, Kessler, Heath, Neale, & Eaves, 1991), three coping styles were studied: turning to others, problem solving, and denial. The results indicated the presence of genetic influences on turning to others and problem solving, with heritability estimates at around 30%, and no evidence of genetic effect on denial. Yet another study (Mellins, Gatz, & Baker, 1996) used a different theoretical perspective on coping, which resulted in the assessment of seven coping scales. Findings from this study showed the presence of genetic influence on five of the seven scales. Specifically, heritability estimates were .99 for distraction, .55 for use of parents, .18 for use of peers, .53 for self-soothe, and .57 for problem focused; heritability estimates did not differ from 0 for the remaining two scales, problem solving and emotion-focused coping.

Similarly, in a study that utilized 19 coping styles (Busjahn, Faulhaber, Freier, & Luft, 1999), moderate heritabilities were established for some but not all styles. When first-order styles were summarized by four higher-order constructs, the heritability estimates for these constructs

genes (e.g., *COMT* and *MAOA*) have also been featured as candidate genes for intelligence and various components of cognition. A mosaic of positive and negative findings has been generated, but little can be said with high degrees of certainty. In fact, a recent meta-analysis of studies reporting data on associations between various candidate genes and personality traits concluded that there are few, if any, robustly replicable associations (Munafò et al., 2003). It appears that the early fascination with the idea of identifying the genetic forces acting on the manifestation of personality traits has given way to a more subdued appreciation of the indirect (Benjamin, Ebstein, & Belmaker, 2002) and, probably, small (Shifman et al., 2008) influences of the genome on personality.

Concluding this brief discussion of the literature on the genetic bases of personality, we ask what can be brought to bear on any hypotheses about the genetic bases of intellectual styles?

Similar to the relationships between intelligence and intellectual styles, the relationships between personality and intellectual styles are only partially overlapping. Yet this partial overlap is substantial enough to hypothesize that at least some of the genetic factors influencing the variation in personality might also be influencing the variation in intellectual styles. Again, similar to the now known mechanics of the genetic influence on intelligence, the mechanisms of genetic influences on personality are probably characterized by the orchestrated efforts of many genes of small effects. It is notable that there are candidate genes that appear to be influencing both intelligence and personality. It is then possible that these overlapping genes contribute to the genetic foundation of intellectual styles and can explain their connections to both intelligence and personality.

ASSOCIATED CONSTRUCTS

In situations where literature on the target construct is limited, one can venture into neighboring literatures, investigating constructs that are related to or overlapping with the construct of interest. Indeed, such an approach is found to be productive in understanding the etiology of intellectual styles.

There is a very limited number of behavior-genetic studies investigating the heritability of intellectual styles. Heritability estimates from these studies report the presence of significant (e.g., different from 0) genetic effects on the manifestation of styles, although their magnitudes

gestive linkage (i.e., an interesting signal, approaching but not crossing levels of significance) was shown at 11q. The second study, however, did not produce any findings at the genome-wide significance level (Nash et al., 2004). Yet it did report two regions with suggestive linkages, 1p and 6p, replicating previous findings.

Subsequently, Neale and colleagues (Neale et al., 2005) carried out a genome scan for neuroticism on a sample of sib-pair families, ascertained for concordance on nicotine dependence. Similar to the previous work, they pointed to regions on chromosomes 1p, 11p/q, and 12q as possibly linked to neuroticism. Furthermore, in a sib-pair sample from Ireland, evidence for linkage to neuroticism was found on chromosomes 11p, 12q, and 15q (Kuo et al., 2007). Finally, researchers (Shifman et al., 2008) performed a whole-genome association study with ~450,000 genetic markers of neuroticism using pooled DNA from 2,000 individuals from England selected from a very large sample of about 88,000 people on extremes (very high and very low) of neuroticism scores.[6] The results featured a polymorphism in the *PDE4D* (cAMP-specific 3',5"-cyclic phosphodiesterase 4D) gene located at 5q11. However, this gene accounted for no more than 1% of the genetic variance in neuroticism. Based on their own data and the data from the other four genome scans, the authors concluded that the heritability of neuroticism is possibly attributable to contributions from many genes each explaining much less than 1% (Shifman et al., 2008).

Similar to the field of genetic studies of intelligence, there have been numerous attempts to associate specific genes and their variants with various personality traits. For example, variation in the *DRD4* (dopamine receptor D4) gene, specifically a polymorphism in exon III of this gene, was associated with the trait of novelty seeking (Benjamin et al., 1996; Ebstein et al., 1996). Two comments are important to make in the context of the discussion of this finding. First, the original finding has not been consistently replicated (Vandenbergh, Zonderman, Wang, Uhl, & Costa, 1997). Second, since the 1996 report, this polymorphism in *DRD4* has been associated with several personality traits (e.g., adaptability and reward dependence) and neuropsychiatric conditions (e.g., attention deficit hyperactivity disorder, alcoholism, schizophrenia). Such a pattern of results is rather typical for genetic association studies of personality traits.

Hundreds of genes of potential interest (too numerous for a single list!), given their biological functions, have been investigated for associations with dozens of personality traits and/or psychiatric conditions that are related to personality traits. Of note is that a number of these

the three- or five-factor model of personality (John & Srivastava, 1999), supporting the traits of extraversion/positive emotionality, neuroticism/negative emotionality, and conscientiousness/constraint (for three-factor solutions), and, in addition, the traits of agreeableness and openness-to-experience (for five-factor solutions).

Of interest is that, regardless of what theoretical platform a particular behavior-genetic study (or a study of heritability) of personality utilized, the common conclusion in the behavior-genetic literature on personality is that the etiology of nearly all personality traits is characterized by the presence of moderate genetic influence, estimated at ~.50 (Boomsma, Busjahn, & Peltonen, 2002; Bouchard & Loehlin, 2001).

The literature is also replete with studies of correlations between personality traits and psychiatric disorders, such as major depression (Boyce, Parker, Barnett, Cooney, & Smith, 1991) and anxiety (Bienvenu et al., 2004). These correlations appear to be consistent and substantial. Of note also is that there is a rich literature correlating attributional *styles* to mental health (Alloy, Abramson, Metalsky, & Harlage, 1998).

In an attempt to understand these correlations, it has been hypothesized that they are likely to be explained by shared genetic factors (Fanous, Gardner, Prescott, Cancro, & Kendler, 2002; Kendler, Gatz, Garver, & Pedersen, 2006). Thus, the consensus in the literature is that both specific personality traits and attributional styles predispose for negative mental health outcomes, and the basis of this predisposition appears to be genetic. There are few studies examining etiological bases of attributional styles; they suggest the presence of genetic effects in the etiology of these styles (Lau, Rijsdijk, & Eley, 2006; Schulman, Keith, & Seligman, 1993). Similarly, there is evidence that cognitive biases (often called styles) in interpreting life events are also heritable (Eley et al., 2008).

Among personality factors, neuroticism/negative emotionality appears to be consistently associated with negative mental health outcomes. Correspondingly, there have been multiple attempts to map the genetic basis of neuroticism (Fullerton et al., 2003; Nash et al., 2004; Neale, Sullivan, & Kendler, 2005; Shifman et al., 2008).

Exploring the genetic foundation of neuroticism, two whole-genome studies used an extreme selected sib-pair design, subsampling from general population samples with the intent of increasing the resulting power to detect genetic signals of interest. One study reported the identification of five genetic loci that exceeded a 5% genome-wide significance threshold (Fullerton et al., 2003). Specifically, significant linkage was established to regions on chromosomes 1p, 4q, 7p, 12q, and 13q; sug-

(Winterer & Goldman, 2003) and thus higher IQ (Barnett et al., 2007; Tunbridge, Harrison, & Weinberger, 2006). Although, in general, the literature seems to be consistent in supporting this general hypothesis, it presents many complexities for the field's understanding of the role of this polymorphism in cognition. First, there are other polymorphisms in the *COMT* gene that affect the dopamine metabolism (e.g., Palmatier et al., 2004)]. Second, the *COMT* is not the only gene that affects this turnover (i.e., metabolism); in fact, there is evidence for the importance of gene-gene interactions in this turnover—for example, the role of polymorphisms in the *DRD2*, dopamine receptor D2, gene (Reuter et al., 2005). Third, there are interesting studies showing the differential (in some cases differentially advantageous, in others disadvantageous) impacts of Val and Met on a variety of psychological functions (Stein, Newman, Savitz, & Ramesar, 2006). And, fourth, there are mixed reports regarding the connection between the Met158Val polymorphisms and cognition across the lifespan (Harris et al., 2005).

How can all this information be related to the question of the etiology of intellectual styles? As per current views of the genetic etiology of intelligence, a substantial portion (~50%) of the population's variation in intelligence is controlled by variation in genes. It appears that many genes are involved in this control and, although collectively they account for a substantial amount of individual differences in intelligence, individually they appear to exert only small effects. There are multiple candidate genes that might be influencing intelligence, but their roles have not been convincingly and consistently verified.

What might we conclude from this summary that is relevant to the discussion in intellectual styles? First, because intellectual styles, at least partially, overlap with intelligence, it is likely that their etiology is also, at least partially, controlled by genes. Second, because there are no major genes of large effects for intelligence, it is unlikely that there are major genes of large effects for intellectual styles. Finally, it is possible that some of the genes that are considered candidate genes for intelligence might also contribute to the genetic foundation of intellectual styles.

GENETIC BASES OF PERSONALITY

Similar to the field of intelligence, studies of personality are characterized by a variety of different theories and approaches (e.g., for a review see Caspi, Roberts, & Shiner, 2005). However, lately, the literature has described the convergence of different theorists of personality on either

three variants of *APOE* that have been studied extensively: *ApoE2*, *ApoE3*, and *ApoE4*. These variants are responsible for the production of three different isoforms (Apo-ε2, Apo-ε3, and Apo-ε4) of the protein that differ only by single amino acid substitutions, but these substitutions have been shown to be associated with dramatic physiological outcomes.[5] Of these three isoforms, Apo-ε3 is associated with a normal protein, whereas Apo-ε2 and Apo-ε4 are related to abnormal proteins. In the context of this chapter, the *ApoE4* allele is of particular interest because it has been associated with atherosclerosis, AD, reduced neurite outgrowth, and impaired cognitive function. To illustrate, a meta-analysis of dozens of studies combining the data from ~20,000 individuals established that possession of the *ApoE4* allele in older people was associated with poorer performance on tests of global cognitive function, episodic memory, and executive function (Small, Rosnick, Fratiglioni, & Backman, 2004). Moreover, it has been shown that young healthy adults who carry the *ApoE4* allele demonstrate altered patterns of brain activity both at rest and during cognitive challenges (Scarmeas & Stern, 2006). In a pediatric cohort, carrying the *ApoE4* allele was related to having a thinned cortex in the region of the brain, the so-called entorhinal region, where the earliest AD-associated changes are typically registered (Shaw et al., 2007). There is also some evidence that the *ApoE2* allele may be protective; however, the mechanisms of this differential action of the variants in the *APOE* gene are not understood (Deary et al., 2002; Smith, 2002; Sundstrom et al., 2007). Yet the variation in this gene and its connection to variations in cognition and, subsequently, to the possible acquisition of AD, is of great interest to researchers in a variety of fields.

Similarly, the connection between the protein and its respective isoforms, the brain structure, and cognition is of great interest to researchers studying the gene for catechol-O-methyl transferase (COMT). Among polymorphisms in this gene, there is a single nucleotide substitution (G-to-A), which in turn leads to a valine-to-methionine substitution at codon 158. This polymorphism is typically signified in the literature as Met158Val variant. The function of this polymorphism is well studied: the Met158 allele results in a fourfold decrease in enzymatic activity in the prefrontal cortex (Lachman et al., 1996). This functional property of the Met158 allele results in slower inactivation of dopamine in prefrontal cortex (Tunbridge, Bannerman, Sharp, & Harrison, 2004; Winterer & Goldman, 2003). It has been hypothesized, based on a number of findings in the literature, that slower inactivation of dopamine in the prefrontal cortex and, correspondingly, the possession of the Met158 allele, may confer a greater efficiency in prefrontal cortical processing

strength of existing connections (Chklovskii, Mel, & Svoboda, 2004) and axonal remodeling and increased soma and nuclei of neurons (Kleim, Lussnig, Schwarz, Comery, & Greenough, 1996). These changes have been attributed to both genetic and environmental effects that are unfolding in a complex systemic fashion (Shaw, 2007). Although the causal hypothesis connecting brain maturation to the development of intelligence has been rooted in and supported primarily by animal literature, there are many correlational studies in humans that indirectly buttress this hypothesis. Specifically, postmortem studies indicate that the brains of individuals with higher IQ and higher levels of education are characterized by a greater number of dendrites and more dendritic branching (Jacobs, Schall, & Scheibel, 1993; Jacobs & Scheibel, 1993) compared to individuals with very low IQs (Huttenlocher, 1991). Yet recent evolutionary analyses of the covariation between brain size and intelligence indicate that there is an evolutionary preference for strong stabilizing (average-is-better) selection (Miller & Penke, 2007). Thus, although within a given population there is a tendency for intelligence and brain size to correlate, there is no evidence that evolution systematically promotes big brains and/or high levels of intelligence. One possible hypothesis here might be that this preoccupation with being average in terms of having more stable, biologically controlled traits (e.g., brain size and structure) might explain the greater flexibility and diversity in more dynamic traits such as style. For example, there is a lot of diversity in how people use their average cars (or their average TVs or vacuum cleaners), and those stylistic diversions might be what is encouraged by evolution (metaphorically speaking, of course).

There is some hope that these attempts to bring together genetic studies of the brain and cognition will lead to some insight into what underlies various forms of intellectual functioning, including its stylistic characteristics. To exemplify this line of work, here I present brief comments on research on two particular genes, *APOE* and *COMT*, which are clearly relevant to research on both brain structure and intelligence.

The apolipoprotein E gene (*APOE*) is located on chromosome 19q13 and is responsible for the production of an apoprotein that is essential for the normal catabolism of triglyceride-rich lipoprotein components. This gene has been long studied in the context of research of neuronal development and repair; this research, in turn, is directly related to work on Alzheimer's disease (AD) (Blackman, Worley, & Strittmatter, 2005; Buttini et al., 1999; Rapoport et al., 2008; Teasdale, Murray, & Nicoll, 2005; Teter & Ashford, 2002). The gene is polymorphic, and there are

dehydrogenase, *ALDH5A1* at 6p22; type-I membrane protein related to beta-glucosidases, *klotho* at 13q13; brain-derived neurotrophic factor, *BDNF*, at 11p14; muscle segment homeobox 1, *MSX1* at 4p16; synaptosomal-associated protein 25, *SNAP25*, at 20p12); and (c) genes of variable functions (e.g., heat shock 70kDa protein 8, *HSPA8* at 11q24; insulin-like growth factor 2 receptor, *IGF2R* at 6q25; prion protein, *PRNP* at 20p13; dystrobrevin binding protein 1, *DTNBP1* at 6p22; apolipoprotein E, *APOE* at 19q13; cystathionine-beta-synthase, *CBS* at 21q22; major histocompatibility complex, class II, DR, *HLA-DRB1* at 6p21). It is important to note, however, that in many of these studies of genes and cognition the behavioral variables of interest are defined beyond IQ. In fact, they encompass a whole gamut of characteristics of intelligence and even cognition (e.g., executive functioning, working memory, and IQ itself). And, although to many readers of this book these details might seem rather technical, establishing these specific associations between genes and intelligence (or cognition, however broadly defined) is a fundamental breakthrough, a switch from the hypothetical decomposition of variance that was characteristic of earlier heritability studies. The hope is that by understanding the functions of these genes and their interactive networks of their proteins, the field will gain some additional understanding of how the general biological (and the specific genetic) machinery of intelligence works.

Along these lines, one other relatively recent development in the literature connects the etiology of intelligence with the etiology of the brain structure. This common genetic basis has been suggested, in particular with regard to the observation that the correlation between the brain properties of monozygotic twins and their intelligence is higher than in dizygotic twins (Posthuma et al., 2002). Summative interpretations of the literatures on intelligence and the brain (e.g., Hulshoff Pol et al., 2004) point to the connection between IQ and the volume and density of the grey and white matter in the brain network that engages the regions of the right medial frontal, occipital and right parahippocampal (grey matter), and the regions of the superior occipito-frontal fascicile and corpus callosum (white matter connecting the corresponding grey matter regions).

Developmentally, increases in grey and white matter volume and density (i.e., increases in cortical thickness) are associated with brain (and, correspondingly, cognition) maturation. This maturation is the result of numerous morphological changes, including the formation of new neuronal connections by dendritic spine growth as well as changes in the

a large number of genetic markers that might be localized within a gene or in between-gene gaps of DNA. The point of such scans is to identify a particular region of the genome at which, based on specific statistics, there is an indication of the presence of putative candidate genes for the trait of interest. In other words, researchers start their search with the whole genome and then gradually, using statistical approaches, narrow their examination to specific regions of specific chromosomes, excluding the majority of the genome.[2] Once such regions are identified, they are mined for the genes located in them, so that a specific gene or a number of genes in that region, possibly contributing to the signal, can be detected.

Up till now, there have been six genome-wide scans for genes contributing to intelligence and cognition; the results of these scans coincided in regions on chromosomes 2q, 6p, and 14q as putatively harboring genes that could explain some of the variance in IQ (Buyske et al., 2006; Dick et al., 2006; Luciano et al., 2006; Posthuma et al., 2005; Wainwright et al., 2006). Note, however, that since the publication of these data, more high-resolution molecular methods have been developed. Specifically, one such method, a whole-genome association study with more than 500,000 single-nucleotide polymorphisms (SNPs), was applied in studies of human memory (Papassotiropoulos et al., 2006). The results revealed potential effects on cognition, in particular on memory, of an SNP in the *KIBRA* gene located at 5q35, which encodes a neuronal protein. Although the *KIBRA* association has not been replicated yet, it is fully anticipated that within a relatively short period of time, many more scans with dense genetic maps will be conducted.[3]

In candidate-gene investigations, the inquiry typically starts with a well-characterized candidate gene (or a set of genes) whose functions have led researchers to believe that it might have a role in forming the genetic foundation for individual differences in IQ.[4] There have been numerous studies of a variety of candidate genes (for reviews, see Deary, Spinath, & Bates, 2006; Payton, 2006; Posthuma & de Geus, 2006; Shaw, 2007). Among these genes are (a) neurotransmitters and genes related to their metabolism (e.g., catechol-O-methyl transferase, *COMT* located at 22q11; monoamine oxidase A gene, *MAOA* at Xp11; cholinergic muscarinic 2 receptor, *CHRM2* at 7q33; dopamine D2 receptor, *DRD2* at 11q23; serotonin receptor 2A, *HTR2A* at 13q13, metabotrophic glutamate receptor, *GRM3* at 7q21, and the adrenergic alpha 2A receptor gene, *ADRA2A* at 10q25); (b) genes related to developmental processes, broadly defined (e.g., cathepsin D, *CTSD* at 11p15; succinic semialdehyde

In this chapter, I attempt to do just that: Using the literatures on the etiologies of intelligence and personality and the very limited literature on the etiology of styles, I present some comments on the origins of individual differences in intellectual styles. I focus exclusively on the genetic etiology of intelligence, personality, and styles. There is, of course, a need to explore all sources of individual differences, whether primarily genetic or primarily environmental. Yet, here, the accent is made on the genes as sources of individual differences and, therefore, the chapter is not comprehensive. Nevertheless, such a move from genetic sources of variation in intelligence and personality to such sources of variation in intellectual styles can be informative. I argue, in the end, that it is the very fine texture of intellectual styles, the intertwined threads of intelligence and personality, and the merging elements of their etiologies into the etiology of styles that make intellectual styles so elusive, so "stylish." This elusiveness has been discussed by many, who have questioned the specificity of styles and their uniqueness from both intelligence (e.g., Cronbach & Snow, 1977) and personality (e.g., Allport, 1937). And yet the construct of styles keeps coming back, in different guises and forms, simply because there is something in intellectual styles that cannot be fully explained either by the concept of intelligence or the concept of personality. Regardless of the number of theories on intellectual styles and the voluminous literature on them, there is an underappreciation of the need of such constructs, as well as a lack of understanding of their etiology.

GENETIC BASES OF INTELLIGENCE

Despite its many flaws and limitations as a construct (e.g., Cianciolo & Sternberg, 2004; Sternberg, 1996), IQ has been widely used in studies aimed at exploring the etiology, especially the genetic etiology, of cognition. Results of dozens of heritability studies of IQ, when summarized in a review or meta-analyzed, suggest that IQ's heritability is ~.50 (Plomin & Spinath, 2004).[1]

Given this level of heritability, researchers have engaged in a search for the specific genes that are behind the genetic component of IQ's etiology. Such searches can unfold in two ways: by means of exploratory whole-genome investigations/screens and by means of hypothesis-driven studies of candidate genes. Both approaches have been used in studies of IQ.

In genome-wide linkage and association studies (often referred to as "scans"), the whole genome is covered, more or less equidistantly, with

9
What Is So Stylish About Styles? Comments on the Genetic Etiology of Intellectual Styles

ELENA L. GRIGORENKO

Intellectual style is a construct that is rooted in both the literatures on intelligence and personality and, at least partially, was intended to connect these two literatures. In individuals, the connection between intelligence and personality arises and unfolds as a person, possessing both, utilizes them in unique combinations in any given situation. Thus, styles are a type of psychological phenomenon, one that encapsulates the dynamics of the interactions between intelligence and personality in particular situations (for detailed reviews, see Sternberg, 1997; Sternberg & Zhang, 2001; Zhang & Sternberg, 2006).

This general definition of styles suggests that this construct might have both stable and dynamic features. Specifically, because both intelligence and personality form the foundation of styles, they establish the stable features of an individual's styles. However, because styles are manifested in many different situations, dynamic features are necessary for flexible and adaptive reactions to these situations.

Moreover, this general definition of styles also suggests that, etiologically, styles might arise by recruiting the etiological factors that contribute to intelligence and personality. In other words, a hypothesis can be formulated that, given that *styles* are constructs that are at least partially derived from intelligence and personality, some insights can be gained into the etiology of styles by looking into the etiologies of intelligence and personality.

Stewart, E. D. (1981). Learning styles among gifted/talented students: Instructional technique preferences. *Exceptional Children, 48,* 134–138.

Virvou, M., Katsionis, G., & Manos, K. (2005). Combining software games with education: Evaluation of its educational effectiveness. *Educational Technology and Society, 8,* 54–65.

Wenglinski, H. (1998). *Does it compute? The relationship between educational technology and student achievement in mathematics.* Princeton, NJ: ETS.

Witkin, H. A. (1972, November 8–10). *The role of cognitive style in academic performance and in teacher-student relations.* Paper presented at the symposium on Cognitive Styles, Creativity, and Higher Education, Montreal, Canada.

Witkin, H. A., Moore, C. A., Goodenough, D. R., & Cox, P. W. (1977). Field-dependent and field-independent cognitive styles and their educational implications. *Review of Educational Research, 47,* 1–64.

Woodward, J. (2006). Developing automaticity in multiplication facts: Integrating strategy instruction with timed practice drills. *Learning Disability Quarterly, 29,* 269–289.

Yen, W. M. (1978). Measuring individual differences with an information-processing model. *Journal of Educational Psychology, 70,* 72–86.

Zhang, L. F., & Sternberg, R. J. (2005). A threefold model of intellectual styles. *Educational Psychology Review, 17,* 1–53.

Oltman, P. K. (1975). Psychological differentiation as a factor in conflict resolution. *Journal of Personality and Social Psychology, 32,* 730–736.

Paivio, A. (1971). *Imagery and verbal processes.* New York: Holt, Rinehart & Winston.

Paivio, A., & Harshman, R. (1983). Factor analysis of a questionnaire on imagery and verbal habits and skills. *Canadian Journal of Psychology, 37,* 461–483.

Pask, G., & Scott, B. C. (1972). Learning strategies and individual competencies. *International Journal of Man-Machine Studies, 4,* 217–253.

Pettigrew, F. E., Bayless, M. A., Zakrajsek, D. B., & Goc-Karp, G. (1985). Compatibility of students' learning and teaching styles on their ratings of college teaching. *Perceptual and Motor Skills, 61,* 1215–1220.

Rayner, S., & Riding, R. J. (1997). Towards a categorization of cognitive styles and learning styles. *Educational Psychology, 17,* 5–27.

Renzulli, J.S. (1977). *The enrichment triad model: A guide for developing defensible programs for the gifted and talented.* Mansfield Center, CT: Creative Learning Press.

Renzulli, J. S., & Reis, S. M. (1985). *The schoolwide enrichment model: A comprehensive plan for educational excellence.* Mansfield Center, CT: Creative Learning Press.

Renzulli, J. S., & Reis, S. M. (1994). Research related to the schoolwide enrichment triad model. *Gifted Child Quarterly, 38,* 7–20.

Renzulli, J. S., & Smith, L. H. (1978). *Learning Styles Inventory: A measure of student preference for instruction techniques.* Mansfield Center, CT: Creative Learning Press.

Renzulli, J. S., Smith, L. H., & Rizza, M. G. (2002). *Learning Styles Inventory—Version III.* Mansfield, CT: Creative Learning Press.

Ricca, J. (1984). Learning styles and preferred instructional strategies of gifted students. *Gifted Child Quarterly, 28,* 121–126.

Rickards, J. P., Fajen, B. R., Sullivan, J. F., & Gillespie, G. (1997). Signaling, notetaking, and field independence-dependence in text comprehension and recall. *Journal of Educational Psychology, 89,* 508–517.

Riding, R. J., & Cheema, I. (1991). Cognitive styles—an overview and integration. *Educational Psychology, 11,* 193–215.

Riding, R., & Douglas, G. (1993). The effect of cognitive style and mode of presentation on learning performance. *British Journal of Educational Psychology, 63,* 297–307.

Riding, R. J., & Watts, M. (1997). The effect of cognitive style on the preferred format of instructional material. *Educational Psychology, 17,* 179–183.

Rohrbeck, C. A., Ginsburg-Block, M. D., Fantuzzo, J. W., & Miller, T. R. (2003). Peer-assisted learning interventions with elementary school students: A meta-analytic review. *Journal of Educational Psychology, 95,* 240–257.

Ruscio, A. M., & Amabile, T. M. (1999). Effects of instructional style on problem-solving creativity. *Creativity Research Journal, 12,* 251–266.

Saracho, O. N. (1990). The match and mismatch of teachers and students' cognitive styles. *Early Child Development and Care, 54,* 99–109.

Schiefele, U., Krapp, A., & Winteler, A. (1992). Interest as a predictor of academic achievement: A meta-analysis of research. In K. A. Renninger, S. Hidi, & A. Krapp (Eds.), *The role of interest in learning and development* (pp. 183–212). Hilsdale, NJ: Erlbaum.

Stahl, S. A., & Kuhn, M. R. (1995). Does whole language or instruction matched to learning styles help children learn to read? *School Psychology Review, 24,* 393–404.

Dunn, R., & Dunn, K. (1978). *Teaching students through their individual learning styles: A practical approach.* Reston, VA: Reston Publishing Division of Prentice Hall.

Dunn, R., Griggs, S.A., Olson, J., Beasley, M., & Gorman, B. S. (1995). A meta-analytic validation of the Dunn and Dunn model of learning-style preferences. *Journal of Educational Research, 88,* 353–362.

Fitzgibbon, A., Heywood, J., & Cameron, L.A. (1991). *Experience versus theory in teacher education.* Dublin, Ireland: Dublin University Press.

Foorman, B., Francis, D. J., Fletcher, J. M., Schatschneider, C., & Mehta, P. (1998). The role of instruction in learning to read: Preventing reading failure in at-risk children. *Journal of Educational Psychology, 90,* 37–55.

Ford, N., & Chen, S.Y. (2001) Matching/mismatching revisited: An empirical study of learning and teaching styles. *British Journal of Educational Technology 32,* 5–22.

Goodenough, D.A. (1976). The role of individual differences in field dependence as a factor in learning and memory. *Psychological Bulletin, 83,* 675–694.

Gregorc, A. F. (1984). Style as a symptom: A phenomenological perspective. *Theory Into Practice, 23,* 51–56.

Gregorc, A. F., & Ward, H. B. (1977). A new definition for individual. *NASSP Bulletin, 61,* 20–26.

Hansen, J., & Stansfield, C. (1981). The relationship of field-dependent-independent cognitive styles to foreign language achievement. *Language Learning, 31,* 349–367.

Kagan, J. (1966). Reflection-impulsivity: The generality and dynamics of conceptual tempo. *Journal of Abnormal Psychology, 71,* 17–24.

King, A. (1994). Guiding knowledge construction in the classroom: Effects of teaching children how to question and how to explain. *American Educational Research Journal, 31,* 338–368.

Klahrl, D., & Nigam, M. (2004). The equivalence of learning paths in early science instruction: Effects of direct instruction and discovery learning. *Psychological Science, 15,* 661–667.

Kolb, D.A. (1984). *Experiential learning: Experience as a source of learning and development.* London: Prentice Hall International.

Kolb, D.A. (1999). *Learning style inventory, version 3.* Boston, MA: Hay Group.

Kolb, A.Y., & Kolb, D. A. (2005). *The Kolb Learning Style Inventory—Version 3.1 2005 technical specifications.* Boston, MA: Hay Group, Hay Resources Direct.

Kozma, R. B. (2003). Technology and classroom practices: An international study. *Journal of Research on Technology in Education, 36,* 1–14.

Lesser, G. S. (1971). Matching instruction to student characteristics. In G.S. Lesser (Ed.), *Psychology and Educational Practice* (pp. 530–550). Glenview, IL: Scott, Foresman.

MacNeil, R. D. (1980). The relationship of cognitive style and instructional style to the learning performance of undergraduate students. *Journal of Educational Research, 73,* 354–359.

Mumtaz, S. (2001). Children's enjoyment and perception of computer use in the home and the school. *Computers and Education, 36,* 347–362.

Myers, I. B. (1962). *The Myers-Briggs Type Indicator.* Princeton, NJ: Educational Testing Service.

Oakland, T., Black, J. L., Stanford, G., Nussbaum, N. L., & Balise, R. R. (1998). An evaluation of the dyslexia training program: A multisensory method for promoting reading in students with reading disabilities. *Journal of Learning Disabilities, 31,* 140–147.

classroom activities—educators may be able to take what is needed from the idea of styles, without absorbing some of the more complex and troublesome aspects of style constructs. Moreover, by so doing, the focus may shift in education from the relative value of various styles to encouraging students to seek out environments that capitalize on their own styles, strengths, and interests.

REFERENCES

Aliya, S. K. (2002). The role of computer games in the development of theoretical analysis, flexibility and reflective thinking in children: A longitudinal study. *International Journal of Psychophysiology, 45,* 149.

Baron, B., Schwartz, D. L., Vye, N. J., Moore, A., Petrosino, A., Zech, L., et al. (1998). Doing with understanding: Lessons from research on problem- and project-based learning. *Journal of the Learning Sciences, 7,* 271–311.

Biggs, J. B. (1987). *Learning process questionnaire manual.* Hawthorn, Australia: Australian Council for Educational Research, Hawthorn.

Biggs, J. B. (1999). What the student does: Teaching for enhanced learning. *Higher Education Research and Development, 18,* 57–75.

Cassidy, S. (2004). Learning styles: An overview of theories, models, and measures. *Educational Psychology, 24,* 419–444.

Cook, D. A., Gelula, M. H., Dupras, D. M., & Schwartz, A. (2007). Instructional methods and cognitive and learning styles in Web-based learning: Report of two randomized trials. *Medical Education, 41,* 897–905.

Cronbach, L. J. (1967). How can instruction be adapted to individual differences? In R. M. Gagne (Ed.), *Learning and individual differences* (pp. 23–39). Columbus, OH: Merrill Books.

Curry, L. (1983). *An organization of learning styles theory and constructs.* Washington, DC: U.S. Department of Education. Office of Educational Research and Improvement.

Curry, L. (1990). *Learning styles in secondary schools: A review of instruments and implications for their use.* Washington, DC: Office of Educational Research and Improvement.

Davidson, G. (1990). Matching learning styles with teaching styles: Is it a useful concept in instruction? *Performance and Instruction, 29,* 36–38.

Dekkers, J., & Donath, S. (1981). The integration of research studies on the use of simulation as an instructional strategy. *Journal of Educational Research, 74,* 424–427.

Del Favero, L., Boscolo, P., Vidotto, G., & Vicentini, M. (2007). Classroom discussion and individual problem-solving in the teaching of history: Do different instructional approaches affect interest in different ways? *Learning and Instruction, 17,* 635–657.

Desmedt, E., & Valcke, M. (2004). Mapping the learning styles "jungle": An overview of the literature based on citation analysis. *Educational Psychology, 24,* 445–464.

DeVries, D. L., & Edwards, K. J. (1973). Learning games and student teams: Their effects on classroom process. *American Educational Research Journal, 10,* 307–318.

Dunn, R., DeBello, T., Brennan, P., Krimsky, J., & Murrain, P. (1981). Learning style researchers define differences differently. *Educational Leadership, 38,* 372–375.

CONCLUSION

As noted, the field of styles has a long, rich, and complex history that in some ways reflects the complexity of the various constructs falling under the styles label. We believe that styles can be tapped for educational purposes, and that classrooms where one or two styles are consistently favored fail to maximize students' learning potential. However, the very complexity of the styles literature and constructs may prevent educators from differentiating by style.

Enjoyable, engaged learning occurs when the instruction is varied and keyed to student preferences (Davidson, 1990; Fitzgibbon, Heywood, & Cameron, 1991; Saracho, 1990). Understanding the relationship between styles and learning efficiency is a necessary first step toward differentiated learning environments that result in actual classroom change (Stahl & Kuhn, 1995). Instruments such as the LSI-III can help teachers bypass the cognitive, personality, and information-processing preferences that underlie many style constructs, in favor of tapping directly into students' preferences for various types of classroom activities. This in turn may make differentiating for various styles more feasible and enjoyable for teachers.

Focusing on instructional styles may also allow educators to bypass difficult questions and value judgments prompted by other style constructs. For example, there may be comparatively little urgency in discerning whether instructional preferences are statelike or traitlike, as most students will respond to a variety of instructional formats, and, as discussed, students may embrace even less preferred instructional styles in service of a high-interest project or activity.

Moreover, while early educational settings may favor students with preferences for direct instruction, drill and recitation, and other highly structured activities, few assumptions are made about a person's intelligence or worth based on his or her preferences for one type of instruction over another. Different educational environments and activities favor different preferences. A talkative student who is frequently the object of ire in a classroom focused on teacher-directed activities may shine in a seminar environment or excel at peer tutoring. This flexible value system differs from the judgments surrounding some other style constructs—value judgments that may cause us to overlook students' very real abilities and cast an elitist pall over the very idea of styles. By placing emphasis firmly on the aspect of styles most relevant to the classroom—that is, diversity in preference and response to various

comparing and contrasting, judging sources, and recognizing the validity of others' opinions.

Discussion, by its very nature, is engaging. In one recent study (Del Favero, Boscolo, Vidotto, & Vicentini, 2007), students who were asked to solve historical problems through group discussions reported greater enjoyment and a deeper understanding of historical inquiry than did students in an independent learning cohort. Enjoyment alone, however, does not make for meaningful learning. Teacher input is required to ensure that discussion promotes understanding of key concepts. King (1994) found that, when compared to unguided student discussion or discussion focused solely on text, guided discussion in which students were trained to connect questions to concepts in text and personal experience promoted the highest level of conceptual discourse. Teachers using discussion with students in a differentiated classroom might group students based on shared or different experiences and interests or on ability level to achieve the greatest degree of student engagement.

Instructional Method 9: Teaching Games

Teaching games are games and contests that allow students to learn and/or show what they have learned. They are purposeful in nature and extend the curriculum in some way. Games are intuitively appealing; thus, it is not surprising that some researchers (e.g., DeVries & Edwards, 1973; Mumtaz, 2001) have urged educators to harness the power of games in teaching and learning. However, although research has suggested that some computer games can affect cognition in children (Aliya, 2002), there has been little research on the relative value of games as compared to other instructional models, or on how games may best be implemented in the classroom. Nonetheless, teaching games hold promise when well considered by educators. Virvou, Katsionis, and Manos (2005), for example, presented an interesting case study of a virtual reality geography game that produced both educational gains in elementary school students and a certain level of "fascination" on the part of students previously unmotivated by the topic (p. 63). Like any form of instruction, educational games may be one component of an effective collection of instructional strategies implemented in a classroom. Teachers may differentiate by allowing students to choose from among a variety of games involving different content and/or processes or by grouping students by ability level for games. Students can also be encouraged to design their own games that help them to learn and practice material.

the project, as measured by a traditional pen and paper test. Finally, they found that project participants almost universally described the project as an important part of their fifth-grade experience. These findings suggest that teachers can implement well-designed projects with students who prefer this style without sacrificing learning.

Instructional Method 6: Peer Teaching

As indicated by the name, peer teaching includes activities in which students work with peers to learn new information or review previously learned material. The main focus of these activities is the relationship between the students, which involves a reciprocal learning model.

Peer teaching has been shown to be an effective instructional technique for a variety of students. A recent meta-analysis (Rohrbeck, Ginsburg-Block, Fantuzzo, & Miller, 2003) of peer-assisted learning strategies found that these activities may be particularly useful for lower-elementary students and certain at-risk students, such as urban and minority students. Teachers can differentiate by pairing students who share a fascination with the same topic or by pairing students based on ability levels.

Instructional Method 7: Drill and Recitation

Drill and recitation activities include quizzes, response and answer sessions, and assignments that ask students for specific information. The drill component can take the form of oral or written work. While drill and recitation should not be the only instructional strategy in a teacher's toolbox, it can be an effective method for teaching information considered to be foundational to higher-level learning, such as math facts (Woodward, 2006). In addition, drill and recitation has been shown to be an effective component of reading instruction for students with learning disabilities, who may benefit from practice drills to compensate for deficits in short-term memory (Oakland, Black, Stanford, Nussbaum, & Balise, 1998).

Instructional Method 8: Discussion

Discussion involves activities that allow students to share their ideas and opinions. Ideally, educational discussions incorporate skills such as

self-directed learning. In fact, Yen found that most students performed better under drill/recitation conditions than under independent study conditions. Ideally, teachers would use an instrument such as the LSI-III (Renzulli et al., 2002) to determine which students might benefit from increased access to independent learning situations.

Instructional Method 5: Projects

Projects fit naturally into differentiated classrooms because they typically allow some level of choice in topic, process, and product style. Successful projects, however, require planning on the part of teachers, as well as knowledge of individual students. As noted by Baron et al. (1998), ill-defined and poorly planned projects can become "doing for the sake of doing," rather than legitimate learning experiences (p. 272). To avoid this outcome, Baron et al. recommended that teachers design project experiences with learning objectives in mind and a clear idea of how the activities undertaken by students will foster deep understanding of targeted concepts. They also noted the importance of scaffolding projects to ensure that these experiences do not become simple exercises in carrying out procedures. Examples of useful scaffolding noted by Baron et al. included reflection periods incorporated into activity periods and provision of informational resources that allowed students to solve problems as they arose during the life of the project. Assessing students' learning throughout and formally incorporating self-assessment may also allow teachers and students to identify what is being learned during a project. This in turn may encourage students to seek out resources on their own when restrictive conceptual or informational gaps become apparent, according to Baron et al. Finally, Baron et al. suggested using the power of social motivation to fuel learning through projects. They recommended making individual students in group learning experiences accountable for particular tasks or accomplishments, as well as allowing students to present projects to outside audiences. Each of these elements harnesses social reinforcement in service to learning.

After implementing a structural design project adhering to these guidelines, Baron et al. (1998) found that almost all fifth-grade students who had participated in the project could transfer learning to a new design task (i.e., drawing a blueprint for a chair). Moreover, blueprints were in almost every case objectively judged as superior to blueprints drawn prior to the project. The researchers also found that students increased their knowledge of standards-based geometry incorporated into

multimedia, audio, and text) can also help to accommodate various learning modalities.

Instructional Method 3: Simulations

Simulations are activities that involve role playing, acting, and engaging in real-world tasks. As the name implies, simulations require students to assume roles, make decisions, and face the consequences of their actions, all of which are mediated by the students' own experiences and personalities. Simulations provide a vehicle for concept attainment that can be altered according to students' interests and ability levels.

As is the case with other instructional methods, simulation has strengths and weaknesses. For example, a meta-analysis (Dekkers & Donath, 1981) exploring the impact of simulation activities on learning found that simulations were more effective than lecture when attempting to induce attitudinal change in students. However, the meta-analysis suggested that simulations were no more likely than lecture to increase cognitive development or retention of material over time. As noted by Dekkers and Donath, simulation could be a useful supplement to other teaching methods in a differentiated classroom. Teachers seeking to differentiate for students who enjoy simulation might include mock-trials, computer simulations, and other experiential activities that encourage students to take perspectives and engage in "as-if" experiences.

Instructional Method 4: Independent Study

Independent study activities are those in which a student works alone. Activities include studying, preparing projects, information gathering, and reading. Activities can be student or teacher initiated, but independent study requires students to structure their time and maintain attention during work periods.

Independent study is an example of an instructional method that should be applied selectively and judiciously. There is some evidence to suggest that students designated as gifted (as defined by standardized achievement or cognitive ability tests) may prefer working independently; whereas typical students prefer teacher-directed or group work (Ricca, 1984; Stewart, 1981). However, other research (Yen, 1978) has shown that while some students do indeed demonstrate higher achievement when allowed to study independently, there is not necessarily a direct correspondence between intelligence and an affinity for

information, and participate in interactive activities. Activities that involve the Internet and communicating via e-mail or in chat rooms are also included, as are more traditional technology methods implementing audio-visual equipment.

Technology lends itself quite naturally to the goals of differentiation, as students often work independently or in small groups with information technology, moving at their own pace. However, this does not mean that all uses of technology are beneficial in the classroom. Wenglinski (1998), for example, found a negative relationship between frequency of school computer use and student achievement. He noted that extremely high use of computers at schools might suggest use of technology for unproductive purposes, such as playing games without educational value. What was important, he noted, was how technology was used. Schools where higher-order skills were taught via technology showed higher achievement than schools that reported using technology primarily for activities such as drill and practice.

These findings were supported by Kozma (2003), who found that certain practices involving technology were likely to produce learning gains, while others were not. In an analysis of 174 case studies of classroom technology use from 28 different countries, studies that involved students who worked collaboratively and used technology for multiple purposes tended to report positive outcomes. Specific technology-related activities that resulted in learning gains when used in combination included searching for information, analyzing data, solving problems, publishing results, creating products, and evaluating others' work. These outcomes included increased knowledge of information technology and improved communication, collaboration, and problem-solving skills. In addition, many teachers involved in these studies reported the acquisition of new pedagogical skills. By comparison, cases in which technology was primarily used for drill and practice, or for e-mail communication, resulted in few teacher or student gains.

Teachers seeking to use technology to differentiate in the classroom might ask students to create a Webquest module or design a Web site using a project model that allows students to work through a concept at their own pace. Providing students with a choice of Web sites for finding information on a specific topic may allow them to make selections based on interest, a variety of style constructs, and ability. Likewise, the once unimaginable volume of information offered on the Internet makes finding resources for interest-based projects faster and easier than ever before. Using the variety of formats available via technology (i.e., video,

a lesson, explains new information, or presents various viewpoints. Other direct instruction activities include teacher-issued instructions and teacher-lead discussions.

Often, direct instruction is viewed as inferior to discovery learning or student-directed learning, but research suggests that this is not always the case. For example, in a study (Klahrl & Nigam, 2004) of more than 100 elementary school science students, children who received direct instruction in designing unconfounded experiments outperformed students who were allowed to design experiments after exploring and experimenting with designs on their own. In this case, direct instruction consisted of a teacher explaining why various experiments did or did not determine the impact of a specific variable on the outcome of the experiment. Seventy-seven percent of the students in the direct instruction cohort were then able to design multiple unconfounded experiments, as compared to 23% of the students in the discovery learning cohort. Students who had received direct instruction were also more successful in critiquing experiments described in science fair posters than were those in the discovery learning group. Another study demonstrated that direct instruction in letter-sound correspondence produced greater reading gains in at-risk first- and second-grade students than did implicit instruction through exposure to literature (Foorman, Francis, Fletcher, Schatschneider, & Mehta, 1998).

There are several issues that teachers might wish to consider when differentiating for students whose preferences include direct instruction. First, direct instruction is more than lecture. Relying heavily on lecture with elementary and middle school students is a poor use of direct instruction. Alternating between lecture and questions may help students to stay connected to the lesson. Infusing storytelling might increase interest in the topic at hand. In addition, the teacher may have students summarize information or react to information to promote active engagement. Concept attainment is another consideration for this style. Teachers should provide examples and nonexamples of the concepts being introduced. Asking students to do the same can engage the students in a meaningful manner. Finally, guest speakers may help provide students with alternate viewpoints as well as add expert depth to the material.

Instructional Method 2: Teaching Through Technology

Instruction through technology involves the use of computers and other forms of educational technology to learn new information, review

All of these experiences revolve around student preferences and motivation. We assume, as educators and researchers, that students working in their preferred styles of learning and in areas of keen interest are likely to do their best work. As noted by Curry (1990), learning styles may affect academic performance by increasing or maintaining motivation in students, which in turn may lead to greater task commitment and perseverance. A meta-analysis (Schiefele, Krapp, & Winteler, 1992) of studies from 18 different countries also provided support for the importance of motivation in achievement. Across studies, which included 121 independent samples, ranging from grade 5 to grade 12, the correlation between interest (an intrinsic motivator) and achievement was .40. Schiefele et al. noted that this finding, along with other findings related to interest, suggested that it may be a more powerful predictor of achievement than many other affective variables.

The LSI-III was designed to be a teacher-friendly tool for tapping into students' interests and motivations, by providing information about students' instructional preferences. The underlying assumption was that teachers, as a matter of course, seek to match instruction to student needs. However, traditional research has reported that teachers have often used informal methods such as observation to make instructional decisions (Cronbach, 1967; Lesser, 1971). This method of decision making leaves much to chance and can result in classrooms that favor very few instructional style preferences. Moreover, as previously noted, even the most vigilant and intuitive teachers may find themselves challenged when attempting to modify concrete instructional behaviors to fit style constructs grounded in cognitive or psychological theories. The LSI-III was designed to highlight students' preferred learning modes by allowing students to explicitly select instructional methods that meet their preferences.

There are two versions of the LSI-III: One for elementary school students (LSI-III/ES) and one for middle school students (LSI-III/MS). There are slight differences in these two versions to accommodate the different activities that take place in elementary school and middle school classrooms. The instructional preferences assessed by the LSI-III are listed in the following sections.

Instructional Method 1: Direct Instruction

Direct instruction refers to activities with direct teacher input. As implied by the name, direct instruction occurs any time the teacher presents

particular interest or talent in a given area to further explore the topic in a small group format. For example, students who demonstrate a particular interest in a presentation on pollution might work with an environmental scientist to learn more about pollution in their own region. Finally, Type III experiences are research or creative projects in which individual or small groups of students have the opportunity to act as practicing professionals in an area in which they have demonstrated substantial interest or achievement. An example of a Type III would be a sixth-grade student who, after expressing interest in literature and creative writing, undertook the task of writing and publishing a novel. Each type of enrichment is viewed as a component of a wholistic process that blends present or newly developed interests (Type I) and advanced-level thinking and research skills (Type II) with application situations based on the modus operandi of the first-hand inquirer (Type III).

SEM built on the triad model by making interest- and preference-based learning experiences available to all students. Rather than providing these experiences solely to students formally identified as gifted, SEM schools provide Type I and Type II enrichment to all students in the forms of broad exposure to a wide variety of high-interest activities such as field trips and presentations, as well as small group training experiences called enrichment clusters, in which interest is the primary qualifier for participation. SEM schools also support a talent pool of the top 15%–20% above-average/high-potential students. These students are identified through a variety of measures, including achievement tests, teacher nominations, assessment of potential for creativity and task commitment, as well as alternative pathways (self-nomination, parent nomination, etc.). High achievement test and IQ test scores automatically include students in the talent pool.

The talent pool concept was designed to ensure that students formally designated as gifted receive services, while leaving room for other students who demonstrate gifted responses to particular forms of instruction or learning experiences. By assuming that gifted behaviors, such as task commitment and creative productivity, occur in certain people at certain times and under certain conditions, Renzulli (1977) also assumed that instructional preferences were more statelike than traitlike. Under the right conditions—a high level of interest being one such condition—students may, and often do, respond favorably both to preferred instructional styles and to styles and activities for which they might have a low preference under typical classroom experiences.

A potential cause of the varied findings on learning styles and achievement is the complexity involved in attempting to ascertain how the psychological and cognitive qualities associated with various styles affect talent and affinity for instructional and learning practices. In other words, many style theories fall into the inner tiers of Curry's (1983) onion model, while instruction, by its very nature, lies in the outer tier. Thus, even when teachers make the effort to gather data about students' learning styles, they may not know how to modify instruction to best meet students' individual needs. Renzulli's work with instructional styles and the subsequent development of the Learning Style Inventory (LSI-III; Renzulli et al., 2002) was designed to overcome this hurdle by bypassing the psychological underpinnings of student preferences in favor of direct assessment of their preferred instructional styles and academic activities.

Preference-Based Learning and Renzulli's Learning Styles Inventory

The LSI-III (Renzulli et al., 2002) evolved from the idea that harnessing students' interests and preferences could lead to the highest levels of creative and academic excellence. This belief was formalized and operationalized in an educational theory called the enrichment triad model (Renzulli, 1977), which later gave rise to a more comprehensive and flexible educational model called the school-wide enrichment triad model (SEM; Renzulli & Reis, 1985, 1994). Both the triad model and SEM are in use in schools today and were designed to provide students with high-end, interest-based learning opportunities, with the goal of greatly increasing students' interest, enjoyment, and achievement in learning.

The triad model laid the foundation for SEM by advocating a three-step process for engaging high-achieving or gifted students. Under the triad model, student interest is initially captured by exposure to a broad array of creative and educational experiences, labeled Type I experiences. These include field trips, plays, concerts, guest speakers, and other creative/educational exposure opportunities. Type II enrichment includes instructional methods and materials purposefully designed to promote the development of thinking, feeling, research, communication, and methodological processes. Type II activities are designed to build on Type I experiences, by allowing students who have demonstrated

on their field-dependence or independence. Field-dependent students were considered matched to materials that provided breadth of information before depth of information. Field-independent students in matched conditions received materials that provided depth of information first. The proposed task was to build a Web page. Researchers found that matched students outperformed mismatched students on measures of conceptual knowledge gain. However, there were no significant differences between matched and mismatched students on a practical test of Web page design.

Riding and Douglas (1993) also had some success in matching students to conditions favoring their learning styles. They randomly assigned adolescents to one of two computer training modules designed to show how car brake systems work. In one condition, students received text-only computer instruction. In the other, they received text plus pictures. After completing training, participants were tested on their new knowledge. Their learning styles were then assessed on two dimensions: verbal-imagery and wholist-analytic. Researchers found that imagers outperformed verbalizers in the text-plus-pictures training conditions, while verbalizers outperformed imagers in the text-only condition, suggesting that in this case, matching had a positive impact on learning. In another study, Riding and Watts (1997) further tested the verbal-imagery/wholistic-analytic match by giving students three versions of a study-skills worksheet. One version provided information in paragraphs with headings (structured verbal). Another offered the information in paragraph form without headings (unstructured verbal). The third version offered information in paragraph form with pictures to illustrate the suggested study skills. Riding and Watts found that most verbalizers chose the structured verbal format, while most imagers chose the structured pictorial format. No students selected the unstructured verbal format. These results suggested that given choices, students would select materials that match their learning styles.

Finally, Dunn, Griggs, Olson, Beasley, and Gorman (1995) analyzed 36 studies of instruments designed to assess Dunn and Dunn's learning styles. The studies yielded a sample size of more than 3,181, with 65 different effect sizes. Findings suggested that the academic achievement of students whose learning styles were matched might be as much as three-quarters of a standard deviation higher than that of students whose learning styles were not matched. These findings were promising in light of criticisms suggesting that learning styles remained unproven as a construct affecting educational outcomes (Dunn et al., 1995).

will learn through whichever strategy the teacher prefers to use" (p. 372). For years, researchers have attempted to support this claim by exploring how teachers' presentation and assessment of information affect learners. Ruscio and Amabile (1999), for example, asked 82 college students to complete a structure-building task after receiving one of two types of video instruction. The first type of instruction explicitly taught building strategies in the context of creating a model that met the specifications of the experimental task. The second type of instruction also showed a model that met specifications but that demonstrated strategies heuristically. In this second video, instructors suggested loose groups of potentially helpful building strategies. Researchers found that the two groups were equally able to build structures meeting predetermined specifications. However, participants receiving step-by-step instruction were most successful when they closely copied the structure demonstrated during their instructional video. They were less successful when they tried to diverge from that model to build a novel structure using the techniques incorporated into the instructions. Participants in the heuristic instruction condition, on the other hand, were less successful when they tried to reproduce the structure in the video but more successful than participants in the step-by-step condition at producing novel structures that met building conditions. This type of research suggests that instructional styles do indeed affect students' learning outcomes in complex ways that are neither linear nor well-understood.

A more specific question, however, is whether matching instructional styles to individual students' learning styles improves academic outcomes or student attitudes toward their learning experiences. To date, findings have been mixed. Pettigrew, Bayless, Zakrajsek, and Goc-Karp (1985) found that strongly matching and strongly mismatching students and professors based on learning and teaching styles had no impact on students' ratings of professors. MacNeil (1980) tested two different instructional styles on field-dependent and field-independent students and found no differences in learning outcomes based on instruction or style. Cook, Gelula, Dupras, and Schwartz (2007) randomly assigned medical residents to Web-based courses that were either matched or mismatched to their active or reflective learning styles, as defined by Kolb (1984). Researchers found no significant differences in learning gains between matched and mismatched students (Cook et al., 2007).

Ford and Chen (2001) had more promising results. They matched or mismatched instructional materials to postgraduate students based

of even the most creative people often involve routine tasks and limited opportunities for independent thinking. How individuals with various intellectual styles adapt to changing expectations and cognitive requirements across environments and the lifespan are interesting questions for future research. However, regardless of the direction of value judgments in style constructs, the association of judgment with various styles poses problems for democratic ideals of education, where various learning styles are often proposed to be different but equally valid.

Curry's Onion Model

One of the most comprehensive and well-known systems for classifying styles literature was that proposed by Curry (1983, 1990). Using the metaphor of an onion, Curry suggested that style theories fall into one of three categories or layers, each concerned with successively more central personality and information-processing characteristics.

Theories falling in the innermost layer of the style onion, according to Curry (1983), address "cognitive personality style" (p. 8). Qualities addressed by these theories are relatively permanent and underlie learning processes rather than interacting directly with the environment. Theories in this stratum, according to Curry, include Myers and Briggs' personality theory (Myers, 1962) and Witkin's (Witkin, 1972; Witkin et al., 1977) cognitive style research. The second layer of learning style research dealt with what Curry (1983) called "information processing style" (p. 11). She saw this layer as dealing with relatively stable learning preferences that nonetheless could be modified by instruction or strategies. Theories in this stratum dealt with individuals' tactics for assimilating information. Curry cited the work of Kolb (1984, 1999) as an example of a theory fitting into this stratum. The third, outermost layer of the onion was "instructional preference" (Curry, 1983, p. 8). She saw this as the most observable layer, the least stable, and the most interactive with environment, including teacher expectations. Instructional preference refers to learners' relative affinity for specific learning environments. We propose that the work done by Renzulli and colleagues (Renzulli & Smith, 1978; Renzulli, Smith, & Rizza, 2002) on instructional styles falls into this third tier of style theories.

Matching Instruction to Learning Styles

More than 25 years ago, Dunn, DeBello, Brennan, Krimsky, and Murrain (1981) declared, "We can no longer afford to assume that all students

the issues of whether styles are states or traits and whether they are value-laden or value-free. According to Zhang and Sternberg, styles can be socialized and modified, and thus are more statelike than traitlike. They also suggested that style constructs are frequently value-laden. Specific examples provided by Zhang and Sternberg included Witkin's (1972) field-independence/dependence model and Kagan's (1966) reflective versus impulsive model. In both cases, the former is often considered superior to the latter, with research often implicitly supporting these positions.

For example, Witkin, Moore, Goodenough, and Cox (1977) described an unpublished study by Frances Harris in which participants were asked to create a shelf with two supports but were provided with only one nail and a pair of pliers. They noted that field-independent people were more likely than field-dependent people to see that the pliers could be used in a novel way as the second support for the shelf. Hansen and Stansfield (1981) found that field-independent foreign language learners in a Spanish class learned more effectively, as measured by achievement scores, than field-dependent learners. Rickards, Fajen, Sullivan, and Gillespie (1997) found that field-dependent, but not field-independent, learners benefited from signaling phrases when taking notes from a lecture. They hypothesized that these signal phrases acted like tags that helped field-dependent learners impose structure on the material they were hearing.

Zhang and Sternberg (2005) argued that not only is field-independence valued over field-dependence but that, in general, Type I styles are valued over Type II styles—although they noted that context plays a role in these judgments. In many societies, Type I characteristics such as creativity and an affinity for complexity have been seen as inherently superior to Type II characteristics such as concrete thinking and impulsive conceptual tempo.

If we accept these proposals, we are naturally led to consider how style-based value judgments may play out in schools. For example, in the United States, primary and elementary school classrooms often revolve around order, memorization, and regurgitation of facts. We do not know whether, in general, students favoring Type II or Type III styles perform better in these structured environments than those favoring Type I styles or whether it is possible that some young students favoring Type I styles may use their creativity to make necessary adaptations.

In the upper grades and in adult American society, complex thinking and creativity are highly valued. Nonetheless, the early career years

Interestingly, Riding and Cheema (1991) labeled as learning strategies several prominent theories that others have seen as style theories. These included the Myers-Briggs Type Indicator (MBTI; Myers, 1962), and the work of Kolb (Kolb, 1984; Kolb & Kolb, 2005) and Dunn (Dunn & Dunn, 1978).

Intellectual Styles

Zhang and Sternberg (2005) proposed a *threefold model of intellectual styles*. In this categorization system, three types of styles were identified: Type I, Type II, and Type III. Zhang and Sternberg suggested that individuals with a preference for Type I intellectual styles prefer tasks with limited structure and high degrees of complexity, creativity, and freedom. They characterized Type II intellectual styles as a preference for tasks with a high degree of structure, well-established ways of doing things, and relatively shallow processing of information and ideas. Finally, they proposed that Type III styles comprise an amalgam of the previous two, with fluctuations in style depending on the task demands and the level of engagement on the part of the learner.

An interesting facet of this system is that rather than slotting style theories into various categories, Zhang and Sternberg (2005) fit concepts relating to each theory into a new organizational system. For example, Biggs (1987, 1999) proposed three types of approaches to learning: deep (learning for intrinsic purposes, reading broadly, and relating material to previously learned ideas), surface (doing the bare minimum and focusing on memorization and reproduction), and achieving (doing what is necessary to achieve regardless of interest level). In the threefold model of intellectual styles, Zhang and Sternberg characterized the deep learning approach as a Type I orientation, the surface approach as a Type II orientation, and the achieving approach as a Type III orientation. In the case of Gregorc's (Gregorc, 1984; Gregorc & Ward, 1977) learning modes, Zhang and Sternberg classified concrete random (a preference for intuitive, experimental, and independent learning) as a Type I style and concrete sequential (a preference for hands-on, linear, and structured learning) as a Type II style. Abstract random (a preference for reflective, unstructured, and wholistic learning) and abstract sequential (a preference for symbols and images, rational, and sequential learning) were classified as Type III styles.

In addition to classifying various well-known style theories using the threefold model, Zhang and Sternberg (2005) took an explicit stand on

(Dunn & Dunn, 1978) was provided as an example of this orientation. Dunn and Dunn have been credited with adapting Kolb's work with adults to meet the needs of children in the classroom (Desmedt & Valcke, 2004). Myers (1962), who built on the work of Jung and identified 16 personality types, was another prominent researcher in this group.

Wholist-Analytic and Verbalizer-Imager Styles

Riding and Cheema (1991) argued that most style theories and models could be grouped into one of two style categories or, alternatively, labeled as "learning strategies." Riding and Cheema used the term "styles" to refer to relatively fixed, inborn characteristics (a traitlike interpretation), while the term "strategies" referred to malleable methods of tackling various tasks (a statelike interpretation). Riding and Cheema believed that unlike styles, strategies can be learned and can change over time or in response to task demands.

The first of Riding and Cheema's (1991) style categories was the wholist-analytic family of theories. Theories in this category address whether one tends to process information by taking in the big picture (wholist) or by adding up the parts (analytic). Interestingly, similarly to Desmedt and Valcke (2004), Riding and Cheema saw Witkin (1972) as the central theorist in this group of style researchers. Kagan (1966) was also included in this category, as were Pask and Scott (1972), who classified learners as serialists or holists. According to this theory, serialists learned by seeking specific data in a linear manner, while wholists looked for patterns in large quantities of data. Pask and Scott believed that despite this stylistic difference, serialists and holists were equally adept at learning.

Riding and Cheema's (1991) verbalizer/imager distinction referred to whether one preferred to mentally store and recall information as words or as pictures. Riding and Cheema saw Paivio (1971) as the central figure in this family of theorists. His Individual Difference Questionnaire (IDQ) was designed to measure individuals' habits as well as abilities in storing information. By exploring what people typically did as well as their strengths, Paivio (1971) was attempting to capture a fuller picture of storage and recall than other instruments available at that time (Paivio & Harshman, 1983). For example, in addition to a typical item probing a test-taker's ability to visualize moving objects, the IDQ included items such as "I often remember work I have studied by imagining the page on which it is written," and "I enjoy visual arts, such as paintings, more than reading" (Paivio & Harshman, 1983, p. 462).

heavily on visual context when perceiving and interpreting information. In contrast, field-independent people are able to perceive and interpret information with relative accuracy regardless of visual context. By analyzing co-citation among authors in the cognitive styles literature, Desmedt and Valcke (2004) found that not only was Witkin highly cited, but he was also central to the largest of six clusters of researchers who collaborated and influenced each other in the cognitive styles field. Other theorists in this dominant cluster included Kagan (1966), who explored what he called *conceptual tempo*—the idea that individuals are either reflective or impulsive in their decision-making styles. Goodenough (1976) and Oltman (1975) also belonged in this cluster, investigating the impact of field-independence/dependence on learning and memory (Desmedt & Valcke, 2004). While some of the authors in this cluster presented unique cognitive style models, Desmedt and Valcke suggested that they were bonded by a common focus on information processing and perception. Desmedt and Valcke also noted that a substantial number of the authors citing Witkin shared a theoretical position that cognitive styles were relatively stable modes of perceiving and organizing information. In other words, this group of researchers saw cognitive styles as more traitlike than statelike.

Returning to Desmedt and Valcke's (2004) analysis, Kolb (Kolb, 1999; Kolb & Kolb, 2005) was the most cited author in the learning styles camp, with 49% of articles using the keywords "learning styles" referencing his work. Kolb has been best known for his experiential learning theory (ELT), in which he suggested that learning was constructed through an exchange between an individual and the environment. Learning styles in this model were proposed as the outcome of two different modes of experiencing the world (concrete experiential and abstract conceptualization) and two different modes of grasping information (reflective observation and active experimentation). The interactions of these two dimensions resulted in four different learning styles, which Kolb identified as diverging, assimilating, converging, and accommodating.

Just as Witkin (1972) was central to the largest cognitive styles cluster, Kolb (Kolb, 1999; Kolb & Kolb, 2005) was central to the largest cluster of mutually referencing authors in the learning styles literature (Desmedt & Valcke, 2004). This cluster included Dunn (Dunn & Dunn, 1978), Myers (1962), Witkin, and Curry (1983, 1990), among others. Desmedt and Valcke suggested that many of the researchers in this cluster generally championed the ideas that learning styles are relatively fixed individual differences, that no one learning style is superior to any other, and that schools must take learning styles into account to maximize student performance (Desmedt & Valcke, 2004). The work of Dunn

issue of students' instructional style preferences, we hope to increase engagement, efficiency, and enjoyment in learning.

CLASSIFICATION SYSTEMS AND INFLUENTIAL THEORIES

As noted, styles theories abound, each with different constructs and many with different instruments for the measurement of those constructs. Inevitably, researchers seeking to create order out of chaos have created systems to categorize this literature. In this section, we will address some of these systems, as well as some of the prominent style theories they attempt to classify.

Cognitive Styles and Learning Styles

One of the most basic approaches to classifying literature on styles distinguishes between cognitive theories and learning theories (Cassidy, 2004; Desmedt & Valcke, 2004; Rayner & Riding, 1997; Riding & Cheema, 1991). As previously noted, there are no universally agreed-on definitions of these terms. Nonetheless, this was a distinction preferred by Rayner and Riding (1997), who argued that cognitive style research and learning style research represent divergent traditions. They noted that the former dates to the 1930s, with the latter entering the scene in the 1970s. Cassidy (2004) likewise discussed the broad categories of cognitive style versus learning style and suggested that cognitive preferences may be a component of learning preferences.

A recent citation analysis (Desmedt & Valcke, 2004) of the literature on styles supported the idea that learning style research and cognitive style research represent two distinct traditions. Using the keywords "cognitive style" and "learning style," Desmedt and Valcke searched the Institute for Scientific Information's Social Science Citation Index, dating back to 1972. In the more than 1,000 articles located by the search, Desmedt and Valcke found that researchers were consistently identified either as learning style theorists or as cognitive style theorists. Moreover, they found almost no academic collaboration between those studying cognitive styles and those studying learning styles. Of the 49 most-cited authors across the learning styles and cognitive styles literature, only 4 contributed significantly to both spheres of inquiry (Desmedt & Valcke, 2004).

Among cognitive style researchers, Witkin (1972) was the most cited, with 39% of literature in this category referencing his field-independence/dependence theory. Witkin proposed that field-dependent people rely

8

Learning Styles Applied: Harnessing Students' Instructional Style Preferences

JOSEPH S. RENZULLI AND ERIN E. SULLIVAN

Current literature on the topic of *styles* as they pertain to learning and instruction testifies to the wide range of interpretations of the construct. Various models address personality traits, information-processing preferences, decision-making approaches, and a broad array of additional understandings and conceptions. The terminology relating to these theories is also diverse, including the labels *learning styles, cognitive styles, thinking styles,* and more. As there are no agreed-on definitions of these terms, we will refer to theories by the terminology preferred by the authors we discuss in this chapter. We will use the term "styles" when speaking generally about theories in this body of literature.

In this chapter, we will explore various classification systems for organizing the styles literature, as well as some of the more influential theories in the field. Then we will look at research addressing attempts to match learning experiences to various student styles. Finally, we will present a theory that is concerned with what might be called *applicative styles*—that is, the issue of how styles are manifested in the classroom. Specifically, this model addresses students' preferences for various instructional techniques. These techniques range from direct instruction to independent study and include methods such as simulations and peer teaching. By encouraging researchers and educators to consider the

the 13th Annual Conference of the European Learning Styles Information Network (pp. 75–91). Ghent, Belgium: Vlerick Leuven Gent Management School.

Vermunt, J. D. (2007, June 12–14). *Student learning and teacher learning.* Keynote address at the European Learning Styles Information Network 12th Annual Conference: Exploring Style: Enhancing the Capacity to Learn, Trinity College, Dublin.

Vigentini, L. (2008). A matter of style? A preliminary report on the relationship between styles and the use of learning technologies. In E. Cools, H. Van den Broeck, C. Evans, & T. Redmond (Eds.), *Proceedings of the 13th Annual Conference of the European Learning Styles Information Network* (pp. 577–598). Ghent, Belgium: Vlerick Leuven Gent Management School.

Wang, A. H., Coleman, A. B., Coley, R. J., & Phelps, R. P. (2003). *Preparing teachers around the world.* Princeton, NJ: Educational Testing Service.

Waring, M., & Evans, C. (2005, September 14–17). *Things have to change: The necessary evolution of initial teacher training.* Presented at the British Educational Association 2005 Annual International Conference, University of Glamorgan, Treforest, Wales.

Williams, S. L., & Cervone, D. (1998). Social cognitive theories of personality. In D. F. Barone, M. Hersen, & V. B. Van Hasselt (Eds.), *Advanced personality* (pp. 173–208). New York: Plenum.

Witkin, H. A., Moore, C. A., Goodenough, D. R., & Cox, P. W. (1977). Field-dependent and field-independent cognitive styles and their educational implications. *Review of Educational Research, 47*(1), 1–64.

Yates, G. C. R. (2000). Applying learning style research in the classroom: Some cautions and the way ahead,. In R. J. Riding & S. G. Rayner (Eds.), *International perspectives on individual differences. Volume 1: Cognitive styles* (pp. 347–364). Stamford, CT: Ablex.

Zhang, L. F. (2004). Thinking styles: University students' preferred teaching styles and their conceptions of effective teachers. *Journal of Psychology, 138*(3), 233–252.

Zhang, L. F., & Sternberg, R. J. (2005). A threefold model of intellectual styles. *Educational Psychology Review, 17*(1), 1–53.

Zhang, L. F., & Sternberg, R. J. (2006). *The nature of intellectual styles.* Mahwah, NJ: Lawrence Erlbaum.

Riding, R. J. (2002). *School learning and cognitive style.* London: David Fulton.

Riding, R. (2005). Individual differences and educational performance. *Educational Psychology, 25*(6), 659–672.

Riding, R. J., & Cheema, I. (1991). Cognitive styles—an overview and integration. *Educational, Psychology, 11*(3–4), 193–214.

Riding, R., & Rayner, S. (1998). *Cognitive styles and learning strategies: Understanding style differences in learning and behaviour.* London: David Fulton.

Riding, R. J., & Rayner, S. (Eds.). (2000). *International perspectives on individual differences. Volume 1: Cognitive styles.* Stamford, CT: Ablex.

Rosenfeld, M., & Rosenfeld, S. (2007). Developing effective teacher beliefs about learners: The role of sensitising teachers to individual learning differences. In J. A. Redmond, A. Parkinson, C. Moore, C. A. Stenson, C. Evans, S. Rayner, et al. (Eds.), *Proceedings of the 12th Annual Conference of the European Learning Styles Information Network* (pp. 268–292). Dublin, Ireland: Trinity College.

Rosenfeld, M., & Rosenfeld, S. (2008). Developing effective teacher beliefs about students: Do teachers' own individual learning differences (ILDs) make a difference? *Educational Psychology, 28*(3), 245–272.

Sadler-Smith, E. (2008). Does cognitive styles research connect with relevant psychological theory? In E. Cools, H. Van den Broeck, C. Evans, & T. Redmond (Eds.), *Proceedings of the 13th Annual Conference of the European Learning Styles Information Network* (pp. 437–456). Ghent, Belgium: Vlerick Leuven Gent Management School.

Saracho, O. N. (2000). A framework for effective classroom teaching: Matching teachers' and students' cognitive styles. In R. J. Riding & S. G. Rayner (Eds.), *International perspectives on individual differences. Volume 1: Cognitive styles* (pp. 297–314). Stamford, CT: Ablex.

Schmeck, R. R. (Ed.). (1988). *Learning strategies and learning styles.* New York: Plenum Press.

Sharp, J. G., Bowker, R., & Byrne, J. (2008). VAK or VAK-ous? Towards the trivialisation of learning and the death of scholarship. *Research Papers in Education, 23*(3), 293–314.

Sternberg, R. J., & Grigorenko, E. L. (1997). Are cognitive styles still in style? *American Psychologist, 52*(7), 700–712.

Sternberg, R. J., & Zhang, L. F. (2001). *Perspectives on thinking, learning and cognitive styles.* London: Erlbaum.

Thies, A. (2003). Connections, neuropsychology, neuroscience, and learning style. In S. J. Armstrong, M. Graff, J. Hill, S. Rayner, E. Sadler-Smith, & D. Spicer (Eds.), *Bridging theory and practice: Proceedings of the Annual Conference of the European learning styles information network* (pp. 608–612). Hull, England: University of Hull.

Tomlinson, C. A. (2005, November 17–19). Differentiated instruction as a way to achieve equity and excellence in today's schools. *Building inclusive schools, a search for solutions conference report* (pp. 19–21). Canadian Teachers' Federation Conference, Ottawa, Ontario, Canada.

Vanthournout, G., Coertjens, L., Gijbels, D., & van Petegem, P. (2008). The development of approaches to learning of student teachers with different "study approach-profiles." In E. Cools, H. Van den Broeck, C. Evans, & T. Redmond (Eds.), *Proceedings of*

Kingston, E. (2006). Emotional competence and drop-out rates in higher education. *Education and Training, 50*(2), 128–139.

Kirton, M. J., & de Ciantis, S. M. (1994). Cognitive style in organisational climate. In M. J. Kirton (Ed.), *Adaptors and innovators: Styles of creativity and problem solving* (pp. 72–90). London: Routledge.

Konings, K. D., Brand-Gruwel, S., & van Merrienboer, J. J. G. (2006). Teachers' perceptions on innovations: Implications for educational design. *Teacher and Teacher Education, 23*(6), 985–997.

Kozhevnikov, M. (2007). Cognitive styles in the context of modern psychology: Toward an integrated framework of cognitive style. *Psychological Bulletin, 133*(3), 464–481.

Kulinna, P. H., & Cothran, D. J. (2003). Physical education teachers' self-reported use and perceptions of various teaching styles. *Learning and Instruction, 31*(6), 597–609.

Lawrence, M. V. M. (1997). Secondary school teachers and learning style preferences: Action or watching in the classroom? *Educational Psychology, 17*(1–2), 157–170.

Leonard, N. H., Schooll, R. W., & Kowalski, K. B. (1999). Information processing style and decision making. *Journal of Organisational Behaviour, 20*, 407–420.

Messick, S. (1984). The nature of cognitive styles: Problems and promise in educational practice. *Educational Psychologist, 19*, 59–74.

Messick, S. (1996). Cognitive styles and learning. In E. De Corte & F. Weinert (Eds.), *International encyclopaedia of developmental and instructional psychology* (pp. 638–641). Oxford: Elsevier Science.

Miller, A. (1991). Personality types, learning styles, and educational goals. *Educational Psychology, 11*, 217–238.

Nielson, T. (2008). Implementation of learning styles at the teacher level. *Education and Training, 50*(2), 167–182.

Noel, J. (2000). *Developing multicultural educators.* New York: Longman.

Nosal, C. S. (1990). *Psychologiczne modele umyslu* [Psychological models of mind]. Warsaw, Poland: PWN.

Oosterheert, I. E., Vermunt, J. D., & Denessen, E. (2002). Assessing orientations to learning to teach. *British Journal of Educational Psychology, 72*, 41–64.

Patrick, H., & Pintrich, P. R. (2001). Conceptual change in teachers' intuitive conceptions of learning, motivational instruction: The role of motivational and epistemological beliefs. In B. Torf & R. Sternberg (Eds.), *Understanding and teaching the intuitive mind: Student and teacher learning* (pp. 117–144). London: Lawrence Erlbaum.

Peterson, E. (2005, Winter). Are we on a quasi evangelical crusade to transform all levels of education? Some thoughts on the Coffield et al., learning style report. *European Learning Styles Information Network: An International Forum Newsletter*, 5–6.

Peterson, E. R., Deary, I. J., & Austin, E. J. (2003). On the assessment of cognitive style: Four red herrings. *Personality and Individual Differences, 34*(5), 899–904.

Pollard, A., & James, M. (2004). *Personalised learning.* Cambridge: Teaching and Learning Research Programme.

Reber, A. S. (1993). *Implicit learning and tacit knowledge: An essay on the cognitive unconscious.* New York: Oxford University Press.

Riding, R. J. (1991). *Cognitive styles analysis.* Birmingham, UK: Learning and Training Technology.

Riding, R. J. (1994). *Personal style awareness and personal development.* Birmingham, UK: Learning and Training Technology.

Evans, C. (2004). Exploring the relationship between cognitive style and teaching. *Educational Psychology, 24*(4), 509–531.
Evans, C., & Graff, M. (Eds.). (2008). Exploring style: Enhancing the capacity to learn? *Education and Training, 50*(2), 93–102.
Evans, C., & Sadler-Smith, E. (2006). Learning styles. *Education and Training* (Special Issue), *48*(2–3), 77–83.
Evans, C., & Waring, M. (2006a). Towards inclusive teacher education: Sensitising individuals to how they learn. *Educational Psychology, 6,* 499–518.
Evans, C., & Waring, M. (2006b, September 6–9). *The stability of cognitive style: Implications for teacher education.* Presented at British Educational Research Association 2006 Annual International Conference, Warwick University, Coventry, United Kingdom.
Evans, C., & Waring, M. (2007). Using the CSI in educational settings. In H. H. Knoop, L. M. Lassen, & L. Bostrum (Eds.), *Learning and learning styles: About niche and shared roads in pedagogy* (pp. 103–122). Virum, Denmark: Dansk Psykolgisk Forlag.
Evans, C., & Waring, M. (2008). Trainee teachers' cognitive styles and notions of differentiation. *Education and Training, 50*(2), 140–154.
Fuller, A., & Unwin, L. (2003). Learning as apprentices in the contemporary UK workplace: Creating and managing expansive and restrictive participation. *Journal of Education and Work, 16*(4), 407–426.
Geake, J. (2008). Neuromythologies in education. *Educational Research, 50*(2), 123–133.
Graff, M. (2006). Constructing and maintaining an effective hypertext-based learning environment: Web-based learning and cognitive style. *Education and Training, 2–3,* 143–155.
Hadfield, J. (2006). Teacher education and trainee learning style. *RELC Journal, 37,* 367–386.
Hayes, J., & Allinson, C. W. (1994). Cognitive style and its relevance for management practice. *British Journal of Management, 5,* 53–71.
Hayes, J., & Allinson, C. W. (1996). The implications of learning styles for training and development: A discussion of the matching hypothesis. *British Journal of Management, 7*(1), 63–73.
Hede, A. (2003). *A critical review of learning styles in higher education* (Faculty of Business Working paper series 03/02, 6(2), pp. 1–41). Maroochydore, Australia: University of the Sunshine Coast.
Heffler, B. (2001). Individual learning style and the learning style inventory. *Educational Studies, 27*(3), 307–316.
Hobson, A. J., Malderez, A., Tracey, L., Giannakaki, M., Pell, G., & Tomlinson, P. D. (2008). Student teachers' experiences of initial teacher preparation in England: Core themes and variation. *Research Papers in Education, 23*(4), 407–433.
Hodgkinson, G. P., & Sadler-Smith, E. (2003). Complex or unitary: A critique and empirical reassessment of the Cognitive Style Index. *Journal of Occupational and Organisational Psychology, 76,* 243–268.
Huber, G. L., & Roth, J. H. W. (1999). *To find or search? Teaching and learning in times of uncertainty.* Schwangau, Germany: Ingeborg Huber.
Kholodnaya, M. A. (2002). *Cognitive styles: On the nature of individual mind.* Moscow, Russia: PER SE.

(Eds.), *Proceedings of the 7th Annual Conference of the European Learning Styles Information Network* (pp. 13–24). Ghent, Belgium: Gent University.

Atkinson, T., & Claxton, G. (Eds.). (2000). The intuitive practitioner: A critical overview. In *The Intuitive Practitioner* (pp. 253–255). Maidenhead, UK: Open University Press.

Backhaus, K., & Liff, J. P. (2007). Cognitive Style Index: Further investigation of the factor structure with an American student sample. *Educational Psychology, 27*(1), 21–31.

Bokoros, M. A., Goldstein, M. B., & Sweeney, M. M. (1992). Common factors in five measures of cognitive style. *Current Psychology: Research and Reviews, 11*, 99–109.

Bolhuis, S., & Voeten, M. J. M. (2004). Teachers' conceptions of student learning and own learning. *Teachers and Teaching: Theory and Practice, 10*(1), 77–98.

Campbell, R. J., Kyriakides, L., Muijs, R. D., & Robinson, W. (2003). Differential teacher effectiveness: Towards a model for research and teacher appraisal. *Oxford Review of Education, 29*(3), 347–362.

Cassidy, S. (2008). Approaches to learning and competitive attitude in students in higher education. *The Psychology of Education Review: Special Issue: Cognitive Learning Style, 32*(1), 18–27.

Claxton, G. (2006, September 6–9). *Expanding the capacity to learn: A new end for education?* Keynote speech, British Educational Research Association Annual Conference, 2006, University of Warwick, United Kingdom.

Claxton, G. (2007). Expanding young people's capacity to learn. *British Journal of Educational Studies, 55*(2), 115–133.

Coffield, F., Moseley, D., Hall, E., & Ecclestone, K. (2004). *Learning styles and pedagogy in post-16 learning: A systematic and critical review*. London: Learning and Skills Research Centre, LSDA.

Curry, L. (1983, April 1–5). *An organisation of learning styles theory and constructs*. Paper presented at the Annual Meeting of the American Educational Research Association, Monteal, Quebec.

Diseth, A. (2008). Course experience and personality as predictors of students' approaches to learning and academic achievement. In E. Cools, H. Van den Broeck, C. Evans, & T. Redmond (Eds.), *Proceedings of the 13th Annual Conference of the European Learning Styles Information Network* (pp. 259–266). Ghent, Belgium: Vlerick Leuven Gent Management School.

Donche, V., & Van Petegem, P. (2008). Variability and consistency of learning patterns in teacher education. In E. Cools, H. Van den Broeck, C. Evans, & T. Redmond (Eds.), *Proceedings of the 13th Annual Conference of the European Learning Styles Information Network* (pp. 65–74).Ghent, Belgium: Vlerick Leuven Gent Management School.

Dunn, R., Griggs, S. A., Olson, J., Beasley, M., & Gorman, B. S. (1995). A meta-analytic validation of the Dunn and Dunn model of learning style preference. *Journal of Educational Research, 88*, 353–362.

Epstein, S. (1994). Integration of the cognitive and the psychodynamic unconscious. *American Psychologist, 49*, 709–724.

Epstein, S. (2004, February 19–22). *Intuition from the perspective of cognitive-experiential self-theory*. Presented at 5th Heidelberg Meeting on Judgment and Decision Processes "Intuition in Judgment and Decision Making." University of Heidelberg, Germany.

instead of a reductionist focus on style types, we advocate a focus on how cognitive constructs may have an impact on the learning process. Consequently, PSTs should be mindful of the fact that some learners may be more capable of style flexibility than others and that for some of them flexibility is not a necessary goal. Therefore, interventions with and by PSTs to promote flexibility of style need to develop rather than merely reinforce learning behaviors. Accommodation of styles through the development of strategies to cope in situations where style delivery is at odds with style preference is also important to assist in independent learning. The extent to which PST self-awareness, acquired through the adoption of metacognitive approaches, facilitates styles development is worthy of further exploration. So is the extent to which a PST's understanding of style correlates with the ability to modify style and/or to select the styles most appropriate to the contextual needs of a situation; in other words, is knowing sufficient to effect change? This leads on to a need to consider further what teaching and learning approaches are most effective in enabling PSTs to use appropriate styles and/or strategies, how such pedagogical interventions compete with existing norms of practice within HEI ITE contexts (and schools), and which may be appropriate to bring about the development of a PST. Whether changes in PSTs beliefs are sustained following preservice training interventions also requires further study, as does the matter of which interventions have the most impact. Consequently, there is a strong need for collaborative school-based research that bridges the HEI and school divide.

Finally, although the search for an overarching dimension of cognitive style may be unrealistic (given the diverse nature of cognitive styles), focused attention on developing a general theory of cognitive styles to include a hierarchy of cognitive styles and clarification of how different cognitive styles relate to one another in determining an individual's personal learning style would be highly valuable in advancing our understanding of the styles field. In clarifying such a hierarchy it may be possible to ascertain to what degree individuals have choice over the development of certain cognitive styles.

REFERENCES

Allinson, C. W., & Hayes, J. (1996). The Cognitive Styles Index: A measure of intuition-analysis for organisational research. *Journal of Management Studies, 33*(1), 119–135.

Armstrong, S. J. (2002). Effects of cognitive style on the quality of research supervision. In A. Francis, S. Armstrong, M. Graff, J. Hill, S. Rayner, E. Sadler-Smith, et al.

the specific needs of students, while at the same time training them in how to cope in situations where the organization of learning is not to their liking. It is not about designing multiple derivations of a lesson plan or resources for each student; it is more about accommodating the overarching dimensions of styles as identified by Zhang and Sternberg (2006). If the following are carefully considered individually and collectively, all PSTs should have access to learning, as well as fostering an appreciation of the learning needs of others: Suitability of resources reflecting different levels of detail, different ways of organizing, structuring, and presenting information; nature of assessment to promote the enhancement of both analytic and intuitive thinking; explicit modeling of less familiar teaching approaches and one-to-one support (peer and tutor) in developing these new skills; timing/availability of information/assessment to accommodate both incremental and consolidated learning approaches; attention to specific areas of weakness, with time built in to address and encourage self- and peer-reflection; and appropriate range of support mechanisms: peer and tutor support to match specific needs.

MOVING FORWARD WITH A PLSP IN ITE

A perspective on employing cognitive styles as part of a PLSP within a higher education ITE setting has been presented, and a number of key themes that permeate the development of a PLSP have been identified. These include: the importance of choice for learners; the centrality of the learner in the process; recognition of the unique starting points of learners; the importance of explicit guidance; the need for concrete and appropriate exemplars to contextualize learning events; the need for reinforcement and transference of ideas to new contexts; and opportunities to observe different ways of seeing and doing. Many PSTs may have had limited experience of a wide range of teaching styles and alternative learning strategies, so it is vital that they are exposed to a broad range of learning experiences to enable them to adopt and experiment with new ideas within their own contexts. Help with deconstructing learning episodes is an essential part of this if PSTs are to be able to make sense of the new learning experiences they are being exposed to and the ones they are creating. There is a real danger, however, of becoming too preoccupied with the concept of specific style types, especially considering that personal learning styles incorporate a range of different styles and that strength in one style does not preclude strength in another. So

for and choice of different approaches in the classroom. In addition, central to a 21st-century curriculum has to be the needs of the 21st-century Internet technology literate PST. The acknowledgement and harnessing of the skills that new teachers bring to the classroom is essential.

Design of Learning Environments

Within this context, design includes: (a) presentation of materials (range of presentation modes, nature of activities, range of assessment modes); (b) structuring of information (the use of organizers and summaries, the chunking and splitting of information, incremental vs. concentrated learning episodes); (c) delivery (nature of questioning [open vs. closed], degrees of interaction, types of activity [discovery vs. directed learning], wait time for responses to questions, sequential vs. tangential episodes, sequence [concrete to abstract vs. abstract to concrete]); (d) focus: curriculum content (attention to detail vs. concern for global effects; development of rational, sequential thinking vs. intuitive, tangential thinking; development of creativity; reward of impulsivity vs. reflectivity in learning); (e) control issues: formal versus informal (facilitator vs. director of learning), levels of autonomy of the learner (tightly controlled vs. loosely controlled learning environments), degrees of flexibility, degree of delegation, encouragement of style strengths versus style flexibility; (f) social interaction: degree of personal involvement with learners, frequency and nature of interactions, personal knowledge of students (seen as individuals vs. seen as a group); and (g) organization of the classroom: the nature of groupings (group, pair, and individual learning), face-to-face versus distance learning. By considering alternative approaches to learning, a PST would be enabled to approach learning tasks from both wholistic/analytic and intuitive/analytic perspectives depending on the requirements of that task. In a PLSP, various teaching styles would be employed to encourage dissonance in learning and development of style, accepting the mobility of style while not being overly concerned about matching teaching styles to every single learning style of the students (Zhang, 2004).

An understanding of cognitive styles should enable a teacher to maximize the opportunities for learning by considering in detail how the organization of learning may differentially affect learners (e.g., some preferring more incremental learning while others prefer concentrated phases of learning) and being able in their planning to accommodate

Creating Optimal Conditions for Learning

What we are advocating here is a constructivist approach to teaching, which focuses on the processes involved in learning, making explicit the many different ways in which solutions to questions can be arrived at. Connected to this is the requirement for expert subject knowledge development of PSTs, as without this, a teacher will not be able to engineer and make accessible to students alternative ways of doing and knowing. When attending to individual learning differences, a PLSP should be used to sensitively, constructively, and critically inform the learner so as to enable the pursuit of self-directed learning. Supporting our notion of a PLSP, Vermunt (2007) argues the need to adapt teaching to certain design principles in order to promote more favorable learning patterns in real settings. Consequently he advocates the customization of teaching and the importance of providing and gradually removing scaffolding of learning experiences to enable the learner to become more independent. It is essential to have considered discussions with students regarding their prior experiences and conceptions of learning if appropriate scaffolding is to be put in place as part of the development of their metacognitive skills. By offering choices in learning and by encouraging PSTs (and their students) to select the most appropriate strategies, a PLSP helps PSTs to be increasingly empowered to perform more effectively in various contexts. This is not solely about advocating the development of style flexibility; it is also about fostering the ability to know what to do when you don't know what to do.

Student Voice

In developing powerful learning environments, Evans and Graff (2008) argue the need for the development of the involvement of learners more centrally in the process of learning. Greater emphasis on the emotional aspects of learning is essential if relatively fixed attitudes to learning are to be modified (Patrick & Pintrich, 2001). One of the key considerations with this in mind is how to move a PST's thinking from awareness to action. A less-is-more approach, whereby PSTs engage in structured dialogue about teaching events, is advocated here. In addition to whole classroom teaching, which is currently the dominant mode of training in schools, more attention needs to be placed on quiet time used to deconstruct learning episodes through a variety of mediums such as video analysis and discussion among different PSTs regarding the justification

time in research and training will need to be tailored to the specific needs of the learners in relation to the context of learning and teaching. We argue the ability to be flexible in addressing analytic and intuitive aspects of style is an essential attribute of an effective teacher. If teachers are to be able to develop both analytic and intuitive capacity in their students, they need to be able to model this in the classroom and design learning tasks to stimulate the development of both areas. Being able to think on your feet in a classroom situation and adapt delivery as necessary is an essential part of being an effective learner and teacher (Hodgkinson & Sadler-Smith, 2003). A useful underpinning theory that may assist with this is Epstein's (1994, 2004) cognitive experiential self theory (CEST) as advocated by Sadler-Smith (2008) in enabling consideration of the multidimensional nature of this cognitive style. Such an understanding may facilitate a useful focus for classroom practice in relation to what forms of processing are being promoted or favored through the design of classroom activities, nature of delivery, and assessment. CEST considers the multidimensional nature of style by distinguishing between the two information-processing systems: the experiential system operating "automatically, pre-consciously, non-verbally, rapidly, effortlessly, and concretely," and the rational system, "an inferential logical system [operating] consciously, primarily verbally, slowly, and effort fully" (Sadler-Smith, 2008, p. 443). The experiential system is thus viewed as intuitive, associated with affect, whereas the rational system is analytic and affect free. This is especially pertinent given the current neglect of intuitive development in schools within England, where a rational, analytical model of teaching is predominant and identified in the highly analytic CSA and CSI scores of PSTs (Evans, 2004; Evans & Waring, 2006a, 2006b, 2007, 2008). Perhaps this testifies to the enculturation of students via the English educational system, supporting Atkinson and Claxton's (2000) assertion there is a tendency for academia to predispose teacher educators toward the scientific and objectively verifiable. The stability and relative dominance of one system over the other is contextualized as being dependent on previous and accustomed ways of working that may be self-perpetuating through the reliance on learned behaviors, as well as on the extent to which an individual is emotionally engaged in and committed to the task. Although the focus here has been on developing the analytic and intuitive capacity of PSTs, our approach actively encourages consideration of how such style constructs relate to other elements of a PLSP and therefore should definitely not be viewed in isolation from other interrelated variables such as gender, age, culture, intelligence, and personality, along with the classroom context.

2008; Kingston, 2006; Nielson, 2008). The key issue here is about sustaining interventions through carefully planned formal and informal training opportunities where ideas and experiences can be exchanged and tried out in the classroom with the support of knowledgeable others. Whether changes in teacher beliefs are sustained following preservice training interventions requires further study, as does the matter of which interventions have the most impact.

When examining one's own views on learning and approaches to teaching, it is vital to consider one's relative effectiveness with different individuals and groups of learners. A useful framework to assist in this is Campbell, Kyriakides, Muijs, and Robinson's (2003) five dimensions of differential teacher effectiveness. These encourage PSTs to consider where they are most and least effective in relation to: (a) differences in activity (roles of teacher); (b) differences in subjects and/or components of subjects (consistency of teacher performance across subject); (c) differences in pupils' background factors (differential teacher effectiveness with children of different ages, ability, gender, socioeconomic background, ethnicity, etc.); (d) differences in pupils' personal characteristics (differential effectiveness in promoting learning of pupils with differing personalities); and (e) cognitive learning styles, motivation, self-esteem, and differences in cultural and organizational context (differentially effective depending on type of school). Consideration of why PSTs are more effective with certain students and in certain contexts may facilitate greater self and whole-school examination of the strengths/biases in instruction, and in so doing enable them to be better placed to meet the needs of all students. Within the ITE context it is essential for teaching placement schools to consider which styles are promoted at the expense of others and why and how this may affect PSTs. The approach identified here, although a useful framework, should be used developmentally with PSTs at appropriate stages in their development as teachers. Particularly important in developing a PLSP is the opportunity for PSTs to explore diverse learning environments. For many students entering ITE programs in the United Kingdom they do not experience a wide variety of teaching styles while on teaching placement in schools (Evans & Waring, 2006a, 2007, 2008).

Careful Selection and Application of Models

In the context of teaching and learning, we have chosen to focus on developing analytic and intuitive capabilities of PSTs. A PSLP acknowledges the importance of a wholistic view of style. The specific focus at any one

and try out new ideas within their own contexts. Help with deconstructing learning episodes is essential if PSTs are to be able to make sense of the new learning experiences they are being exposed to.

Application of Cognitive Styles Models to Practice

Table 7.1 exemplifies how an understanding of cognitive styles as part of a PSLP can be integrated into an ITE program by identifying limited and expanded opportunities to do so. Five key interrelated areas to address to enable PSTs to be able to understand and apply styles ideas to the classroom to facilitate differentiated instruction have been highlighted in Table 7.1: (A) *Exploration of teacher beliefs/modeling and support* that is in relation to learning and creating opportunities to model ideas in practice; (B) *Careful selection and application of models* so as to suit needs of specific learners; (C) *Creating optimal conditions for learning;* (D) *Student voice* by having full involvement of learners in the process of learning; and (E) *Design of learning environments.* Ideally, a PLSP should permeate all aspects of learning and teaching in a systematic approach and not be viewed in terms of a bolt-on or stand-alone model. In order to incorporate a PLSP into an ITE program, a number of potential barriers need to be addressed, including PST potential intransigence to new ways of doing and engaging in a shared commitment to such an approach given the number of partners delivering the ITE program across a variety of school contexts and learning cultures.

Exploration of Teacher Beliefs/Modeling and Support

By examining teacher beliefs it is possible to explore how style differences in PSTs manifest themselves in their language, beliefs about students, and classroom practice. Such approaches, focusing on the process of learning, arm PSTs with an expanded vocabulary and repertoire of ideas subsequently facilitating the explication of factors affecting pedagogy that are often subconsciously hidden from the PSTs (Nielson, 2008). PSTs can be sensitized to personal learning styles and a PLSP, enabling them to have a better understanding of learner needs through instruction that adopts a metacognitive approach (Evans, 2004; Evans & Waring, 2006a; Nielson, 2008) that facilitates open exchange and development of ideas as afforded in effective communities of practice. In so doing PSTs are encouraged to analyze their own learning approaches in order to enhance their sensitivity to ILDs (Evans & Waring, 2006a,

Table 7.1

PERSPECTIVES ON THE USE OF PERSONAL LEARNING STYLES PEDAGOGY (PLSP) IN PRACTICE (*Continued*)

ISSUES	PEDAGOGY OF POVERTY	PEDAGOGY OF PLENTY	ASSOCIATED CONSIDERATIONS/QUESTIONS TO ASK
		learning styles where some aspects of style are more malleable than others. Consequently styles can be developed.	whether PST's have taken on board new learning; stage 4: embed new approaches through reflection and reinforcement activities. • Employ scenarios training to ascertain whether PSTs can select the appropriate styles for specific tasks—debrief and focused training.
7. Informed and responsible use of groupings to encourage development of styles.	Teaching and grouping to type: for example, specific singular cognitive style. Exclusive matching of teaching style to learning style—reinforcement over development of styles (Hadfield, 2006; Hede, 2003).	Informed use of mixed groupings and rotation of groupings. Matching and nonmatching to encourage challenge in learning and development of new approaches (Evans & Sadler-Smith, 2006).	How can PSTs be encouraged to understand and use style groupings responsibly? • By explicitly addressing the importance of matching the learning task to the organizational unit (individual, pair, or group) by the PST reflecting on collaborative planning activities with peers and mentor and why the organizational grouping is most appropriate for the learning task. The postlesson debrief and reflective journal employed to do this would include consideration of alternative groupings for learning tasks. • Providing PSTs with a tool kit of questions to examine how they use the grouping of pupils according to their style to enhance learning. Questions relate to: the value of grouping in a particular way; the basis on which the groupings are derived; the importance of varying groupings; avoidance of labeling that may limit rather than enhance learning opportunities; how groupings will be explained to students.

5. Use of technology to support learning.	Uncritical use of technologies ignoring individual learning differences, adding ICT without considering the needs of the learner and how it will enhance the learner's opportunity to access and engage with the learning objectives.	Critical and informed use of technologies, acknowledging individual differences to fully support learning (Evans & Sadler-Smith, 2006; Graff, 2006). Awareness of how the organization and use of ICT will affect individual learners in different ways. Using ICT after informed and critical consideration of its form and potential benefits in relation to the needs of the individual learner.	How should PSTs engage with ICT as part of a PLSP? • Demonstrate how technologies can both support and restrict learning as part of the ITE program. • Receive targeted specific training in how to use technologies based on ILDs. • Consideration of how a VLE can be designed to be accessible to different learners (how VLE designed/pathways to areas within site/size of images/interactive opportunities/organization of materials). • Consider the kind of pedagogy to encourage learners to engage in VLE—for example, design activities which require use of VLE and include explicit teaching sessions on this at the beginning of the course. • PST discusses with tutors and mentors their patterns of use of the VLE and whether their approaches are helpful or unhelpful learning pathologies.
6. Identification of types and awareness of labeling students.	Learners can be easily characterized into particular categories. Styles are fixed and cannot	Learners do not fit neatly into categories (Yates, 2000, p. 359). Individuals have personal	How can styles be developed around a PLSP? • Demonstrate through specific interventions how styles can change. Stage 1: observe PSTs tackle specific task; stage 2: training in alternative approaches; stage 3: set similar task in different context to ascertain

(*Continued*)

Table 7.1

PERSPECTIVES ON THE USE OF PERSONAL LEARNING STYLES PEDAGOGY (PLSP) IN PRACTICE (*Continued*)

ISSUES	PEDAGOGY OF POVERTY	PEDAGOGY OF PLENTY	ASSOCIATED CONSIDERATIONS/QUESTIONS TO ASK
	developing areas of relative weakness.	learning and to select appropriate strategies (Claxton, 2007; Evans & Sadler-Smith, 2006).	• Encourage PSTs to plan for the same learning outcomes using the same content but to deliver it in very different styles; interview pupils on the impact and conduct through debrief of experience with PST. • Provide additional support in the classroom and manage the retreat of support to enable PST to function independently.
3. Accommodating different styles.	No appreciation or understanding of the need to accommodate different styles in any learning context.	Understanding style differences to inform philosophy of teaching and design of curriculum, including assessment (Evans & Sadler-Smith, 2006) that is used to accommodate different styles in any learning context.	How can PSTs be encouraged to accommodate different styles? • By using a PLSP to consider overarching style dimensions such as degree of conformity, degree of authority, cognitive complexity, structure, and groupings of learners (Zhang & Sternberg, 2006). • Encourage PST to consider how the following factors may affect an individual's access to learning: volume of material to be delivered; modes of presentation; classroom organization (tight vs. loose); structured versus unstructured; variety and nature of resources used; pace, speed and nature of transitions; range of activities; discovery versus directed teaching; classroom design; management of power relations (facilitator vs. director of learning); design of learning sequences (tangential vs. sequential); nature of questioning (open vs. closed); impulsivity versus reflectivity; the use of groupings.

		their learning, eventually becoming codesigners of their own learning environments (Evans & Sadler-Smith, 2006; Evans & Waring 2006b, 2007, 2008).	other in the classroom; presentations and written work). • Through negotiated learning experiences with school-based mentor—for example, modification of PSTs training plan via discussion with HEI and school-based mentors to focus on specific needs including enrichment opportunities (e.g., developing new schemes of work using PLSP). • HEI and school recognizing and acting on PST feedback on their learning experiences in order to address PSTs needs within their training program.

E. Design of learning environments

1. Toleration of uncertainty.	Low toleration—inability of teacher to engage with open and collaborative learning (Huber & Roth, 1999).	High toleration—ability to create learning situations encouraging self-directed learning (Huber & Roth, 1999).	How can PSTs be prepared to be receptive to new and different learning contexts? • ITE courses encourage learners to be able to deal with both predictable and unpredictable situations through: design of varied learning situations; role play; scenarios; provision of diverse opportunities within schools and HEI settings highlighting alternative models of curriculum design and delivery.
2. Extending the learning challenge.	Encouraging security and non-risk-taking—teaching to an individual style and reinforcing strengths, but not	Expanding learning capacity by encouraging a metacognitive approach to enable individuals to understand their	How can PSTs be encouraged to use a wide range of styles and strategies in their teaching? • Promote responsible risk-taking through enhanced consideration of and discussion with the PSTs of the barriers to their learning, including the emotional aspects of learning.

(*Continued*)

Table 7.1

PERSPECTIVES ON THE USE OF PERSONAL LEARNING STYLES PEDAGOGY (PLSP) IN PRACTICE (*Continued*)

ISSUES	PEDAGOGY OF POVERTY	PEDAGOGY OF PLENTY	ASSOCIATED CONSIDERATIONS/QUESTIONS TO ASK
D. Student voice			
1. Metacognitive use of cognitive styles.	Cognitive styles instruments not used to encourage reflection and metacognition, nor inform classroom pedagogy (Coffield et al., 2004).	Use of cognitive styles instruments to identify unhelpful or pathological approaches to learning/teaching and identification of strategies to overcome this (Evans & Waring, 2006b, 2008; Nielson, 2008; Rosenfeld & Rosenfeld, 2007; Yates, 2000).	How do you get PSTs to think metacognitively using cognitive styles? • Having identified approaches to learning and style bias, actively encourage PSTs to consider alternative approaches by examining teaching episodes directly or via video; analyze lesson planning and through PST reflection on learning using critical incidents analysis. • Ask PSTs to trial new approaches with their peers and students to reinforce and develop newly acquired approaches to learning. • Through PST reflection on the benefits and limitations of different strategies and approaches to learning within specific contexts by using reflective journals/discussion boards (synchronous and asynchronous), through critique of their own and peer written work using assessment criteria devised in collaboration with their tutors and peers.
2. PSTs as codesigners of their learning experiences.	Learners' dependent on teacher to make decisions about their learning.	Learners encouraged to make informed choices and to self-regulate	How can PSTs become codesigners of their learning experiences as part of a PSLP? • Involve PSTs in assessment of their own and each others' work (peer assessment of each

| 4. Choices in learning. | Lack of flexibility in approaches and options for the learner. | Flexibility and informed choice for students (Evans & Sadler-Smith, 2006). | How can ITE programs accommodate choices in learning as part of a PLSP?

• Offer multiple/alternative forms of assessment (oral presentations, posters, written assignments, reports, debate) with various weightings to promote development of specific skills and promotion of flexible styles in the classroom.
• Provide multiple/alternative forms of presentation of materials and resources—for example, visual, audio, mixed mode in virtual and hardcopy form.
• Employ a blended learning approach that integrates information communications technology (ICT) into practice, rather than treating it as a stand-alone aspect.
• Facilitate collaborative and individual learning opportunities.
• Offer appropriate levels of support to reflect ILDs.
• Provide opportunities to work in varied groupings across and within subject areas along with exposure to as many varied styles/different environments as possible (relative to individual needs) in order to develop awareness.
• Provide opportunities to proceed through the course at appropriate pace for the individual: clear and alternate pathways identified.
• Provide opportunities to specialize or generalize within specific learning contexts. |

(*Continued*)

Table 7.1

PERSPECTIVES ON THE USE OF PERSONAL LEARNING STYLES PEDAGOGY (PLSP) IN PRACTICE (*Continued*)

ISSUES	PEDAGOGY OF POVERTY	PEDAGOGY OF PLENTY	ASSOCIATED CONSIDERATIONS/QUESTIONS TO ASK
	style fits all learners and contexts. Lack of discussion between mentor and mentee, tutor and mentee, tutor and mentor about individual learning needs. Focus on outcomes rather than process of learning. Little discussion of pedagogy with students. No variety in approaches with students or attempts made to explore their learning.	broadening styles and strategies (Evans & Sadler-Smith, 2006; Nielson, 2008; Rosenfeld & Rosenfeld, 2008). Adopts a constructivist approach in the classroom—open and explicit discussions between teacher and students about the process of learning. Using a variety of approaches with students to encourage exploration of their learning—for example, use of narratives and concept mapping (Claxton, 2006).	face and using reflective journals, discussion boards, e-portfolios (including microteaching excerpts and critiqued dialogue between PST, mentor, and tutor), tutorials, and seminars. • Explore learning histories/memories of previous learning episodes and the perceived impact these have had on the learner. • Explore attitudes toward and conceptions of learning using scenarios; role play/drama; narrative; concept mapping. • Explicitly model alternative ways of doing and identify strategies to overcome learning barriers—for example, through instruction that enables learners to remodel information into more accessible forms. • Encourage PSTs to model teaching approaches with each other and their students using microteaching.

	scaffolding. No developmental relationship between different assessments of the learning objectives of the program acknowledged or even considered.	the task is described (easy or difficult/open or closed questioning/response times to questions/whether risk-taking is actively encouraged and rewarded, and so forth. Discussion on the impact of emotions on working memory capacity and receptivity to new ideas.
• Promote the importance of risk-taking—that is, the trial of different approaches (along with teaching styles and strategies) within the classroom to facilitate learning.
• Provide guided support within classrooms by peers and mentors in order to facilitate the trying out of less familiar approaches with PSTs.
• Consider the design and nature of assessment and its potential to affect learning approaches—for example to promote a deep approach to learning and to consider whether a deep approach is always desirable within an ITE context.
• Consider various approaches to giving feedback (written, oral, demonstration); timing of feedback; involvement of PSTs in giving feedback (and the collaborative generation of assessment criteria by PST, their peers and tutor).
	stated goals and explicit guidance about requirements of assessment and their developmental relationship to each other and the learning outcomes of the program are presented and acknowledged in different online and hardcopy formats throughout the ITE program (Evans & Sadler-Smith, 2006; Vermunt, 2007).	
3. Sensitivity to the needs of the learner.	Lack of awareness of individual learner's needs—notion that one approach and one	Use of instruction sensitive to the needs of the learner, aimed at developing and	How do you sensitize the learning environment for the learner?
• Develop conversations with learners from the outset of the course around a PLSP. This takes place in both open and confidential forums virtually and face to

(*Continued*)

189

Table 7.1

PERSPECTIVES ON THE USE OF PERSONAL LEARNING STYLES PEDAGOGY (PLSP) IN PRACTICE (*Continued*)

ISSUES	PEDAGOGY OF POVERTY	PEDAGOGY OF PLENTY	ASSOCIATED CONSIDERATIONS/QUESTIONS TO ASK
			process, collaborative clusters of schools to share and develop pedagogy beyond school boundaries and as part of an integrative pedagogy (in addition to increased collaboration across HEIs and departments within HEIs).
			• PSTs consider how children operationalize learning across different contexts within and outside of a school context.
			• PSTs examine how different school cultures promote both similar and different approaches to learning—for example, by considering policies, teaching approaches, and CPD in relation to which cognitive styles they are promoting.
			• PSTs consider which type of working environment best supports their needs as learners and teachers.
2. Enabling a positive learning environment.	Lack of awareness of the importance of creating the conditions for learning—no explicit guidance provided for the learner, nor appropriate	Creation of a positive teaching environment, including attention to issues of delivery and feedback (these are key features of the student's course experiences), clearly	How can you create a positive learning environment in ITE programs?
			• Highlight the importance of cognitive and affective elements of learning specifically to include motivational aspects such as fear of failure, learned helplessness, and mastery orientations through demonstration activities that show how one can use educational psychology ideas in classroom contexts—for example, whether questions directed to group or individual/how

188

		strategies in their pursuit of knowing what to do when not knowing. PSTs encouraged to identify and explore successful coping strategies (including reminders and evidence of decisions made so they can reflect on them).
2008; Nielson, 2008; Rosenfeld & Rosenfeld, 2008).		

C. Optimizing conditions for learning

1. Approach to apprenticeship in ITE.	Restrictive and limited development opportunities for PSTs to engage in discussions about the process of teaching (Fuller & Unwin, 2003).	Multiple developmental opportunities for PSTs to share and exchange opinions and engage in discussions that are reflected on in an individually meaningful way as part of a fully mapped and integrated ITE program that highlights and enacts a wholistic view of organization to include the process of learning (Fuller & Unwin, 2003).	How do you maximize opportunities for learning using a PLSP? • ITE programs encourage and develop an enhanced understanding among PSTs of how subject knowledge and pedagogic knowledge are integrated and possible reinforcement effect of subject on cognitive style and vice versa. • Provide integrative pedagogies that transcend subject boundaries and encourage interdisciplinary collaboration. • Develop practice within partnership schools to ensure wider access to learning opportunities as part of an informed and innovative curricula structure and content, exposure to varied assessments (formal and informal), as well as PSTs team-teaching with their mentors; sharing planning and delivery with mentors and tutors; adopting different roles (e.g., class teacher, teaching assistant, coach). • HEIs encourage, through their ongoing mentor training (provided to those schools who are involved in their ITE partnership) and the organization of their placements

(*Continued*)

Table 7.1

PERSPECTIVES ON THE USE OF PERSONAL LEARNING STYLES PEDAGOGY (PLSP) IN PRACTICE (*Continued*)

ISSUES	PEDAGOGY OF POVERTY	PEDAGOGY OF PLENTY	ASSOCIATED CONSIDERATIONS/QUESTIONS TO ASK
	CSA, thinking styles (Sharp, Bowker, & Byrne, 2008).		• A PLSP encourages PSTs to reflect on how certain teaching styles have a variable impact on a learner's access to the specific learning context. • When exploring verbalizer-imager dimensions of style, the existence of different types of visualization style and also the unipolar nature of verbalizer-imager styles, as well as how it is possible to be both highly verbal and visual is acknowledged. • Consideration of how wholist and analytic (CSA) and intuitive and analytic thinking (CSI) can affect teaching styles.
3. Appropriate application of styles measures.	Instruments used to classify learners into types and to reinforce learning behaviors (Hadfield, 2006; Hede, 2003).	Instruments used as a metacognitive tool to enable learners to understand how they learn and to enable development of strategies to enhance learning (Evans & Waring 2006b, 2007,	How do you use styles instruments appropriately? • Instruments such as the CSA and CSI are used as starting points to engage and direct discussions about learning and the adoption of specific strategies to consider in particular: big picture versus detailed thinking and rational and sequential thought versus intuitive thinking on ones' feet. • ITE course design to encourage resourcefulness, resilience, and self-reflection through journals and identification of developmental targets and associated

	Models employed lack reliability and validity (Coffield et al., 2004).	school settings and through a needs analysis conducted at interview and subsequently through individual and group activities, analysis of performance on assessed tasks, as well as video analysis of teaching and coplanning during the ITE program. • Through review of how styles models have been successfully used before and in what contexts. • Consideration of reliability and validity issues. Weaker instruments (in relation to reliability and validity) may be used for pedagogic reasons to explore particular ideas about learning and to discuss potential limitations and misconceptions associated with such choices. • Selective judicious use of models to avoid meaningless overuse and lack of purposeful use in learning situations—being clear about their educational value. • A co-constructed rationale, whereby the reasons for using styles models is explored and shared with PSTs prior to (at introduction) and/or after testing (debriefing) depending on the nature of the test and research design. How can the use of models be integrated into the program? • A PLSP considers the wholistic nature of styles and explores the relationships between different measures of style—for example, considers relationships between cognitive style, gender, age, culture, and personality constructs; links between cognitive styles and learning strategies.
2. The inclusion of styles models.	Over-emphasis and uncritical adoption of a particular model VAKT to the exclusion of other cognitive styles models, e.g. CSI,	Integrated use of different models as part of a critically informed pedagogy (Evans & Sadler-Smith, 2006).

(*Continued*)

Table 7.1

PERSPECTIVES ON THE USE OF PERSONAL LEARNING STYLES PEDAGOGY (PLSP) IN PRACTICE (*Continued*)

ISSUES	PEDAGOGY OF POVERTY	PEDAGOGY OF PLENTY	ASSOCIATED CONSIDERATIONS/QUESTIONS TO ASK
			• Where cognitive/learning styles scores are interpreted and explained in a concrete way to assist PST understanding—for example, demonstrations of how learning behaviors relate to wholist and analytic, and intuitive and analytic thinking.
			• Where time is given to each PST to individually explore style concerns and understanding of styles.
			• Where new concepts are introduced and subsequently reinforced in follow up sessions—for example, new ideas demonstrated and PSTs asked to describe in alternative contexts.
			• Where PSTs are set up in cross-subject groups to research and feedback to their peers on key questions arising from the styles literature.
			• Where the university tutor/facilitator is accessible virtually and/or face to face, to follow up on questions within a specified and agreed on timescale.

B. Careful selection and application of models

1. Selection of personal learning styles models.	Lack of criticality in selection and use of models (Evans & Sadler-Smith, 2006).	Critically informed selection and use of robust models (Evans & Sadler-Smith, 2006).	How do you select styles models to support a PLSP?
			• The models used should reflect the identified learning needs of the specific group(s) of PSTs based on observation of learning behaviors in university and

difference central to design of learning environments (Evans & Waring, 2006b, 2008; Evans & Sadler-Smith, 2006; Nielson, 2008).

- Where incremental approaches and ones that consider the nature of materials and methods of delivery take account of not overloading PSTs early on in their training.
- Where delivery by the HEI is clear, explicit, and accessible using a range of teaching styles.
- Where direction to resources is clearly signposted and organized, for example, provision of advance resources—handbooks (hardcopy and in a dedicated ITE virtual learning environment that PST, tutor, and mentor can access).
- Where lectures are followed up with practical sessions and ideas demonstrated in relation to PST's own contexts.
- Where PSTs are exposed to both familiar and unfamiliar ways of working in relation to all aspects of the ITE program—for example, sequential versus tangential questioning; directive versus facilitative teaching approaches; individual versus various forms of grouping; individual versus group assessment.
- Where the written work of PSTs is used to identify favored approaches and then alternative ways of writing are explored early on in the ITE course.

(*Continued*)

Table 7.1

PERSPECTIVES ON THE USE OF PERSONAL LEARNING STYLES PEDAGOGY (PLSP) IN PRACTICE

ISSUES	PEDAGOGY OF POVERTY	PEDAGOGY OF PLENTY	ASSOCIATED CONSIDERATIONS/QUESTIONS TO ASK
A. Exploration of teacher beliefs/modeling and support			
1. Teacher's view on learning.	Teacher views learning as an individual process whereby learners develop themselves (Bolhuis & Voeten, 2004).	Teachers have a social view of learning whereby the importance of collaborative and social learning (CSL) is central to classroom pedagogy (Bolhuis & Voeten, 2004).	What are the issues to consider in developing CSL? • Ensuring ITE programs adopt a variety of approaches such as practical demonstrations of how different theories of learning can be applied to classroom contexts in order to assist PSTs in their translation of theory into practice. • Development of formal and informal peer support groups within and across phase and subject specialties. • Encouragement of PSTs to share and challenge their own and others' conceptions of learning through examination of the impact that wholist and analytic (CSA) and intuitive and analytic (CSI) thinking may have on an individual's views on CSL.
2. PST preparation—training to heighten sensitivity to learners needs.	Poorly informed training limiting application of ideas in real contexts (Hadfield, 2006; Hede, 2003; Sharp, Bowker, & Byrne, 2008).	Expert modeling of ideas and integration into everyday practice through careful design of training. Understanding of individual	In what situations is a PLSP most successful in sensitizing PSTs to different learner needs? • Where there is guided individual and group exploration of how ILDs affect student performance and how modifications in delivery by the PST can support pupil learning and how such an understanding of ILDs can assist in the planning of lessons.

- *Who should a PLSP be delivered by?* PLSP champions in the HEI should be identified who are both informed and able to translate/exemplify a PLSP in an accessible and practical manner for PSTs and school-based mentors. They would coordinate opportunities to share and develop learning resources within the HEI/course team through an ongoing program of continuing professional development (CPD) including workshops and collaborative preparation for sessions with PSTs. They would also coordinate aspects of CPD for school-based mentors, identifying approaches to inculcate a PLSP within existing practice. Such training would provide sustained and progressive opportunities as part of a formal developmental mentoring program.
- *To what extent does matching and mismatching play a part in the design of the PLSP, especially in relation to the mentoring of PSTs?* Advantages of matching mentor/mentee may include affective rewards in that a PST can feel more in tune with a mentor and therefore feel less threatened within a new learning situation. Consequently the PST may be more able to take on new ideas especially if, from a cognitive perspective, information and ideas are presented in a format that is readily accessible to the PST. The advantages of mismatching mentor and mentee include exposure to new ways of doing and greater opportunity to challenge existing beliefs and ways of working, which may facilitate the development of new strategies and broadening of style.
- *How is it best to build on PSTs' initial starting points without overloading them?* The needs of the PST would be identified through an initial thorough needs analysis to establish the priorities for development and strategies/learning challenges that are appropriate to achieve them over time.

As highlighted in Table 7.1, a number of key themes permeate the development of a PLSP. These include: the importance of choice for learners; the centrality of the learner in the process; recognition of the unique starting points of learners; the importance of explicit guidance; the need for concrete and appropriate exemplars to contextualize learning events; the need for reinforcement and transference of ideas to new contexts; and opportunities to observe different ways of seeing and doing. Given the fact that many PSTs may have had limited experience of alternative ways of doing, it is vital that they are exposed to a wide range of learning experiences in ways that enable them to take on board

180   Perspectives on the Nature of Intellectual Styles

Awareness of interaction of multiple factors affecting classroom climate and practice: Understanding of the complexities of styles and the interaction effect of cognitive styles with other variables that have been identified, namely, intelligence and gender (Kozhevnikov, 2007; Riding, 1991, 2002) and affective elements (Zhang & Sternberg, 2006).

Coherence v divergence of style measures: Style constructs measure different aspects of style as part of a learning profile (Kozhevnikov, 2007; Riding & Rayner, 2000).

Awareness of PLSP: Broader understanding of different style constructs and pedagogical potential (Evans & Sadler-Smith, 2006; Evans & Waring, 2008).

Knowledge and understanding of cognitive styles as part of a PLSP

Style or Styles? Acknowledgment that a preference for one type of processing does not automatically exclude an individual from another (Geake, 2008; Hodgkinson & Sadler-Smith, 2003).

The polarity fallacy: (Reber, 1993): Understanding of the complex and multidimensional nature of style: that is, it can be both highly intuitive and analytic at the same time (Hodgkinson & Sadler-Smith, 2003).

Origins of styles—an awareness of the role of culture in their conceptualization: Understanding the impact that cultural dimensions (home, school, and workplace) have on the development of styles (Kozhevnikov, 2007).

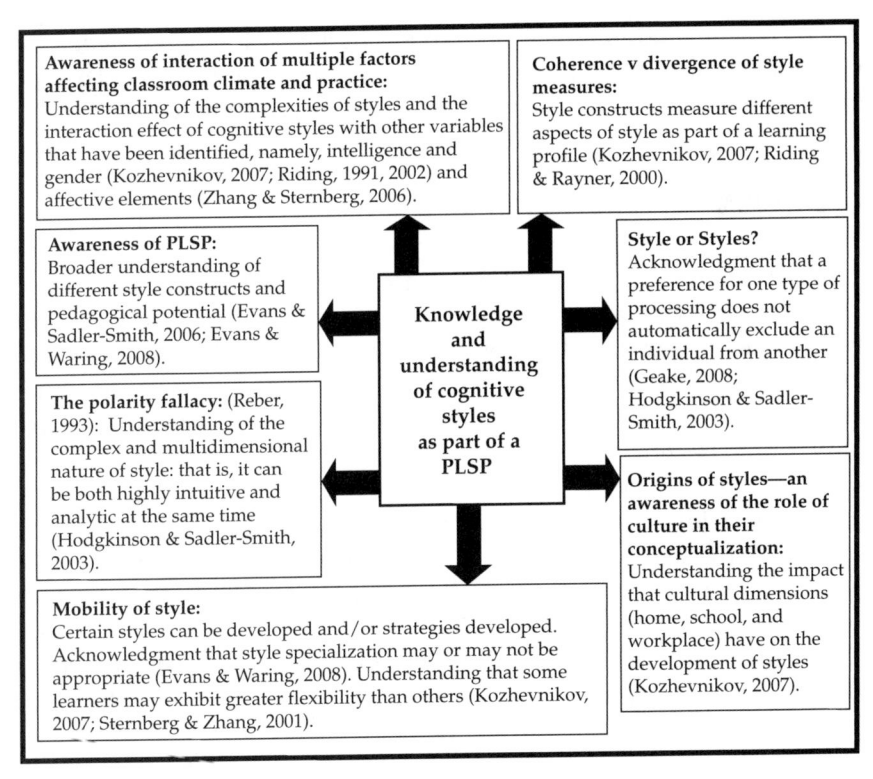

Mobility of style: Certain styles can be developed and/or strategies developed. Acknowledgment that style specialization may or may not be appropriate (Evans & Waring, 2008). Understanding that some learners may exhibit greater flexibility than others (Kozhevnikov, 2007; Sternberg & Zhang, 2001).

Figure 7.1 The knowledge and understanding of cognitive styles as part of a PLSP.

Developing Knowledge and Understanding of Cognitive and Learning Styles as Part of a PLSP

Intelligent and critical use of any cognitive style(s) instrument is essential when attempting to enhance an individual's understanding of his or her own learning (Evans & Waring, 2006a). Central to a PLSP is the importance of how to involve the learner beyond a research object (Rosenfeld & Rosenfeld, 2008). The learner should be challenged to experiment with a variety of approaches to learning rather than perpetuating learning behaviors that may not always be most appropriate to address the demands of the task. Key questions to ask when designing an ITE curriculum that incorporates a PLSP should therefore include:

- *How and when is a PLSP delivered throughout the year?* An enriched model of delivery would involve an integrated learning design with ongoing incremental opportunities for enhancement.

but intercorrelated, unipolar constructs (an analysis dimension *and* an intuition dimension) rather than as originally developed as a bipolar unitary conception of style measuring analysis versus intuition.

DEVELOPING AND ADOPTING A PLSP

To clarify, our conception of styles and associated PLSP acknowledges: (a) the existence of a hierarchy of cognitive styles rather than one unifying dimension of style (Kozhevnikov, 2007; Nosal, 1990); (b) the notion that cognitive styles are distinct from learning styles (Riding and Rayner, 1998); (c) the interaction of cognitive styles with other variables (e.g., personality, gender, affect, and environment depending on style constructs being considered) (Diseth, 2008; Kingston, 2006); (d) the multidimensional nature of cognitive styles (Hodgkinson & Sadler-Smith, 2003); (e) the value of dual-process theory in developing both analytic and intuitive thinking (Sadler-Smith, 2008); (f) the pejorative nature of style (Zhang & Sternberg, 2005); (g) the flexibility of style and notions of fixed and mobile individuals (Kholodnaya, 2002); and (h) the importance of overarching concepts of style (Zhang & Sternberg, 2005).

The centrality of the learner is fundamental in the development and co-construction of knowledge and understanding of cognitive styles as part of a PLSP. A PLSP is not about promoting the accommodation of each learner's predominant styles in each situation. It is about adopting a central philosophy that has at its core an understanding of individual difference. In order to make the move from a "pedagogy of poverty" to a "pedagogy of plenty" (Tomlinson, 2005, p. 20) while catering to the increasing diversity of student learning needs, PSTs will need to be aware of and use a variety of teaching styles (Kulinna & Cothran, 2003). To do this Nielson (2008) argues that more preservice training time should be devoted to how to utilize the information about styles in order to apply them more effectively to practice.

The development of a knowledge and understanding of cognitive styles and how such an understanding can inform pedagogy is a significant dimension of a PLSP. Figure 7.1 identifies those characteristics around the notion of a pedagogy of plenty that are associated with the kind of knowledge and understanding of cognitive styles that is conducive to incorporating a PLSP into ITE curricula design and pedagogy.

wholist does not in itself mean that one cannot process analytically; it is about relative strengths. In addition, given the fact that the CSA is based on the relative speed of response to questions to measure different aspects of cognitive style, an intermediate position on the wholist-analytic scale could be the result of very slow responses to questions on both analytic and wholist tests or equally a very fast response to both. The interpretation of the intermediate position of wholist-analytic dimension is often misguided in that the middle position along this continuum does not necessarily denote moderate preferences (Evans & Waring, 2006a). This relates to wider misconceptions in that extremes of style do not automatically denote extreme learning accommodation needs within the classroom as has often been interpreted in some research findings (e.g., Rosenfeld & Rosenfeld, 2008). In relation to the design of learning environments, emphasis on typical characteristics of certain styles with an emphasis on extreme types when most people do not have extreme styles (Evans, 2004) may limit good pedagogical practice as acknowledged by Hede (2003). The practice of categorizing style types must be done carefully and if/when used applied critically and sensitively. For example, instructors need to share with their PSTs how such categories have been deduced and how key style strengths do not preclude the development of other styles.

Another measure of style applicable to educational contexts is the CSI devised by Allinson and Hayes (1996), measuring a similarly named but different aspect of cognitive style compared with the CSA (Evans & Waring, 2006b; Riding and Rayner, 1998, 2000; Sadler-Smith, 2008). Analysis in this context relates to reflectivity, rational, sequential, and logical thinking with intuition representing impulsivity, creativity, and thinking on one's feet. The use of the CSI to identify and assist the development of both analytic and intuitive dimensions of style is particularly pertinent within the UK educational context, where current trends in education and educational leadership have stressed the relative importance of analytic over intuitive thinking, resulting in an impoverished model of teacher education (Evans, 2004). The CSI (Allinson & Hayes, 1996) in its modified form acknowledges the complex rather than unitary nature of style (Hodgkinson & Sadler-Smith, 2003) and has great relevance for ITE. Hodgkinson and Sadler-Smith (2003) convincingly argue the case for a complex conception of style, this multidimensional configuration is supported by Backhaus and Liff (2007) who agree that intuition-analysis cognitive style is better conceived of as two separate

of style open to serious question; specifically, there are issues with the nature of the content used in the CSA to measure this dimension of cognitive style as commented on by Peterson et al. (2003). Thus given the unreliability of the verbalizer-imager dimension of the instrument and associated conceptual problems (as to whether it is possible to separate verbal and nonverbal processing) we would question the use of the verbalizer-imager in this format. This is a view supported by the neuroscience literature, which identifies verbalizer-imager dimensions as integrated aspects of thinking (Geake, 2008; Kozhevnikov, 2007). However, the continued use of the wholist-analytic dimension can be justified given its greater reliability as acknowledged by Coffield et al. (2004) and Peterson (2005) and substantiated by Evans and Waring (2006b), especially if used as a tool to gain entry into discussions about how we organize learning rather than to purely typecast learners.

Style models, used appropriately, can be highly successful learning aids. Within educational contexts it is important that the emphasis, when using a PLSP, should be on how learners use relative style strengths, develop areas of *relative* weakness, learn what to do when one doesn't know what to do, and thus develop appropriate strategies to specific learning contexts that might involve the development of new skills and/or involve delegation of key tasks. For example, as a teacher and manager of learning it is important to know intuitively when to adapt one's strategies in the classroom rather than to pursue ineffective ones. In addition, knowing what to and when to delegate specific tasks to a more capable individual within a specific context requires a strong sense of self, demonstrating the interplay between cognitive style, metacognitive capacity, and affect.

Characteristically, styles models involve classification into types based on norms as identified by the author of the tool or based on score distributions (means/medians) within a specific sample group. At its most reductionist level, the classification of individuals into, in some cases, arbitrary types offers limited educational potential. The key issues here lie with how (a) the data sets are derived, (b) information is interpreted, and (c) such information is used with learners. In relation to the first of these issues, the CSA, for example, classifies individuals on the two binary dimensions of wholist-analytic and verbalizer-imager using ratios of response times for each dimension. Whether we are comparing like for like in terms of where cutoffs are placed is an issue that limits the generalizability of findings, as does the small-scale nature of much research (Hede, 2003). In terms of interpretation, to be identified as a

encoding of information to the conscious level involving decision-making processes, and that these will have an impact on which learning strategies are employed in any given learning situation (Kozhevnikov, 2007). In educational contexts, identification of the whys and hows in relation to the processing of information is critical. Cognitive styles influence the ability of the individual to adopt flexible learning styles as part of an overall PLSP. The ways in which cognitive styles interact with internal variables and are responsive to external controls will affect the learning approaches contributing to a PLSP in any given situation.

Within a PLSP it is possible to consider a whole raft of styles measures affecting learning. The nature of the relationship between different styles measures is an important consideration within this context. Attempts to consider relationships between cognitive styles and learning styles are dependent on the measures being used and cannot be generalized given the very specific nature of certain cognitive styles, which can be exemplified by the Cognitive Styles Analysis (CSA) (Riding, 1991), which measures wholist-analytic and verbalizer-imager dimensions of style whereby the wholist-analytic dimension of style is quite different from the intuitive-analytic dimensions of Allinson and Hayes (1996) Cognitive Styles Index (CSI). In the realms of ITE the two aforementioned models are particularly appropriate to consider given their potential impact on how students and teachers access information and make decisions in classroom situations.

Riding's CSA, introduced in 1991 in the form of a computerized test measuring two dimensions of style wholist-analytic (big picture vs. detailed thinking) and verbalizer-imager (words vs. imagery as dominant perceptual mode), has done much to raise the profile of the importance of how information is organized, presented, and delivered and how variations in this can have large and differential effects on student learning. The interaction of cognitive style, personality, intelligence, gender, and the environment in affecting an individual's personal learning styles profile is identified in a range of studies spanning over 30 years (Riding & Rayner, 1998).

In using such instruments with learners, it is important to be able to use them judiciously. Although the CSA is seen as an objective and valid test (Riding & Rayner, 1998) and has demonstrated high face validity (Evans & Waring, 2006b), reliability and validity issues relating to the model and especially to the verbalizer-imager dimension of style have been identified and substantiated (Coffield et al., 2004; Peterson, Deary, & Austin, 2003). This makes the use of the verbalizer-imager dimension

ing may not automatically exclude another. Complex rather than unitary conceptualizations of style allow for an individual to be both analytic and intuitive. Building on the work of Curry (1983) and Riding and Cheema (1991), a more recent attempt to unite the different cognitive styles under one umbrella, so as to identify common themes, is Riding and Rayner's (2000) concept of the learning profile of an individual. This comprises many different dimensions of style and has particular relevance in ITE (and educational training generally) by requiring educationalists to consider a range of parameters that combine to make up an individual's approaches to learning. In addition, Zhang and Sternberg's (2005) attempt to unify different intellectual styles and to focus attention on their use in learning contexts (Type I–III styles), highlights the importance of a number of central concepts: high degrees of structure versus low degrees of structure; cognitive simplicity versus cognitive complexity; conformity versus nonconformity; authority versus autonomy; and for group versus individual work. It is important therefore, for practitioners to consider the extent to which curriculum planning, design, delivery, and assessment reinforces the development of particular style attributes. For example, to what extent is scaffolding put in place to encourage learners favoring high degrees of structure to work effectively in less structured environments?

The identification of different levels of cognitive processing (in that cognitive styles operate at different levels of cognitive complexity and different types of mental processes (Kozhevnikov, 2007; Nosal, 1990) is important because certain higher-level styles may determine the flexibility with which an individual is able to choose the most appropriate lower-level style for certain situations. While the notion of a hierarchy of cognitive style dimensions is not new (Bokoros, Goldstein, & Sweeney, 1992; Leonard, Schooll, & Kowalski, 1999; Miller, 1991; Nosal, 1990) such findings testify to the fact that there is neither a single unifying dimension of style, nor the operation of certain styles in isolation of one another, but rather there is a "structural relation among them" (Kozhevnikov, 2007, p. 477). Our understanding of the relationship between distinct cognitive styles to each other is an area that needs further exploration.

USING STYLES INSTRUMENTS IN EDUCATIONAL SETTINGS: CONFRONTING THE ISSUES

In developing a PLSP, it is important to acknowledge that there are a range of cognitive styles that operate at varying levels, from the automatic

any change in cognitive styles, Donche and van Petegem (2008) question whether this is dependent on the learning patterns students exhibit on entering higher education. In the context of ITE this is especially pertinent given the relatively intransigent conceptions of learning identified among PSTs (Konings, Brand-Gruwel, & van Merrienboer 2006). Even though, as Vigentini (2008) would argue, "styles have state-like features which make them modifiable" (p. 4), the origins of cognitive style, often described as a mixture of innate and developed capacities, are increasingly seen as the result of "a range of variables [including] . . . intellectual abilities, previous experience, habits and personality traits" (Kozhevnikov, 2007, p. 477). The degree of conscious choice over the development of certain cognitive styles is an area requiring further investigation. In addition, the context-free assumption of many cognitive style theorists has also been challenged. For example, Williams and Cervone (1998) argue that "adopting context-free units [specific styles] sacrifices much important information and obscures the processes by which people flexibly and idiosyncratically adapt their behaviour to meet varying situational requirements" (p. 194). The nonpejorative nature of cognitive styles has also been questioned (Zhang & Sternberg, 2005). Cognitive styles do matter (Evans & Graff, 2008), and organizations do have preferred styles (Kirton & de Ciantis, 1994), and for specific tasks/ contexts, certain cognitive styles are indeed preferable. Evans and Graff (2008) have also pointed to the changing currency of specific cognitive styles both temporally and spatially. The nonpejorative nature of style is highly dependent on context. For example, it may well be better to be of a certain style to perform in a specific context, rather than having a balance of styles. The key issue therefore, lies in the ability of individuals to accurately adapt their approach to the demands of the situation and/ or to delegate effectively in situations where certain cognitive styles may be less favorable to the successful completion of a task.

Whether there are multiple cognitive styles or two key styles (i.e., Riding and Cheema's [1991] wholist-analyst and verbalizer-imager styles) remains open to debate, as not all cognitive styles claiming to measure the same dimension actually do (Riding & Rayner, 1998). The bipolar nature of style in relation to certain style measures has also been challenged by Hodgkinson and Sadler-Smith (2003) and Backhaus and Liff (2007), both seeing cognitive styles as multidimensional rather than unidimensional. Many would argue that unidimensional conceptions of the cognitive style construct oversimplify and undermine what is indeed a very complex area (Hodgkinson & Sadler-Smith, 2003). As Evans and Sadler-Smith (2006) have outlined, a preference for one type of process-

evident. Riding (2005) similarly acknowledges the indiscipline of cognitive styles researchers and a lack of integration of their work into that of other investigators, citing over 100 individual difference labels within the literature. However, he also highlights the tendency of researchers to have the simplistic expectation that a few variables will account for large differences in performance. These expectations, compounded by the ambiguity in nomenclature employed, have made the choice of appropriate measures by practitioners increasingly difficult (Evans & Sadler-Smith, 2006; Nielson, 2008).

What we are witnessing is the increasing proliferation of "pseudoscience, psychobabble and neurononsense" in English schools (Sharp, Bowker, & Byrne, 2008, p. 293) with the wide-scale adoption of visual, auditory, and kinesthetic learning (VAK) and educational kinesiology. Unfortunately, the use of such unreliable and untested instruments is increasingly compromising the educational experience of students by labeling them into types, where "teacher's ideas and beliefs about VAK are often second-hand, confused and misinformed" (Sharp et al., 2008, p. 311).

Addressing Terminology and Conceptual Issues

While a portion of the literature might assert the fixed nature of style characteristics, which are difficult to change in the context of education (Messick, 1996), increasingly reference is being made to terms such as *individual learning differences* (ILDs) when referring to cognitive and learning style constructs (Rosenfeld & Rosenfeld, 2007) and *patterns of learning* in relation to learning orientations (Vermunt, 2007). This represents a direct attempt to draw attention to the modifiability of certain types of styles as a direct consequence of instruction in specific learning environments. The state-or-trait nature of styles, as well as their complexity, continues to obfuscate the transfer of information about style applications into workplace and educational contexts (Evans & Graff, 2008; Zhang & Sternberg, 2006). This is compounded by a lack of longitudinal studies (Vanthournout et al., 2008) although developments indicate that in certain situations and for certain people, cognitive styles are modifiable (Cassidy, 2008; Evans & Waring, 2006a; Thies, 2003). The identification that some people may be more capable of style flexibility than others is also highlighted by Kozhevnikov (2007). However, the extent to which style flexibility is possible (Armstrong, 2002) and desirable (Evans & Sadler-Smith, 2006) remains debatable. When examining the nature of

Today's higher education ITE programs face the challenge of not only having to teach PSTs about a bulk of domain-specific frameworks and disciplinary insights but also having to foster the development of skills that will enable the PSTs to become knowledge workers and lifelong learners. To achieve these goals, ITE programs should make use of instructional methods and powerful learning environments that stimulate a deeper approach to learning in PSTs (Vanthournout, Coertjens, Gijbels, & Van Petegem, 2008). In so doing, they should attend "to the unique characteristics of the individual trainee" (Hobson et al., 2008, p. 17) through a "shift of attention towards the process of learning and specifically learning to learn" (Claxton, 2007, p. 121). This is a necessary prerequisite if we are to develop the metacognitive capacity of learners. In considering effective learning characteristics as identified by Claxton (2007) (flexibility and openness in learning situations; analysis and intuitive abilities; collaboration and independence; along with the importance of self-regulation and resilience in learning) a broader understanding of learning facilitated through a PLSP is important. Thus, the metacognitive potential of cognitive styles work in raising individual awareness of self and others' learning (Waring & Evans, 2005) in the pursuit of more positive learning environments for learners and teachers must be a key goal (Oosterheert, Vermunt, & Denessen, 2002). Therefore, although ITE programs globally may vary in terms of their emphasis and priorities (Wang, Coleman, Coley, & Phelps, 2003), we stress that a key element of them all should be the development of an understanding of how to learn.

TRANSLATION OF COGNITIVE STYLE IDEAS INTO EDUCATIONAL SETTINGS

Even though there is a growing body of evidence identifying the benefit to both learners and teachers of instructional interventions aimed at enhancing teacher awareness of their own cognitive styles and the ways in which such styles affect classroom practices (Coffield, Moseley, Hall, & Ecclestone, 2004; Dunn, Griggs, Olson, Beasley, & Gorman, 1995; Evans & Graff, 2008; Evans & Waring, 2006a, 2007; Heffler, 2001; Lawrence, 1997; Nielson, 2008), the overall impact on educational practice remains limited. Any lack of and often misguided translation into educational settings is hardly surprising given the bewildering library of style measures (over 71 theories of styles) (Coffield et al., 2004) that are

to an individual's habitual or typical way of perceiving, remembering, thinking, and problem solving. The justification for our focus on cognitive styles, as part of a PLS, is based on the significant role that cognitive styles can play in learning choices and behaviors. As acknowledged by Saracho (2000, p. 247), cognitive styles are intertwined with an individual's personality and interact with several "classroom factors and influence educational practice in how students learn, how teachers teach, how teachers and students interact, and how learners make educational choices" (Witkin, Moore, Goodenough, & Cox, 1977, p. 2).

Underpinning a PLSP, therefore, is a desire to improve the conditions for learning for all learners by acknowledging, accommodating, and developing difference. In order to best enact this in ITE, PSTs need to have a sound knowledge and understanding of the possibilities and limitations of styles research. In addition, they should focus on the process of learning that makes explicit alternative approaches to learning situations and that acknowledges and is sensitive to the differing ways in which individuals perceive and react to learning situations.

We know that there are robust differences in the way that individuals approach cognitive tasks (Kozhevnikov, 2007, p. 468) and that cognitive styles tools, when used appropriately, can allow for the exploration of such differences in the pursuit of a greater understanding of our own and each other's learning. There is widespread recognition of the potential for cognitive styles to affect learner performance specifically in relation to: the mode of learning; the structure and context of learning; the learning strategies that individuals adopt in particular contexts; knowledge acquisition; performance in public examinations; occupational stress; decision making; and the nature of social interactions in the learning process (Hayes & Allinson, 1994, 1996; Riding, 1994; Sternberg & Grigorenko, 1997). An enhanced understanding of cognitive styles may therefore enable both teacher and student to understand why individuals do better in certain educational settings and with certain approaches than others. Thus allowing for more consideration as to the extent to which HEI ITE (and schools), both directly and indirectly, shape the cognitive and learning styles of PSTs and students (Yates, 2000); educational organizations, therefore, need to carefully consider what patterns of thinking, believing, communication, and acting they are promoting (Noel, 2000). With this in mind, cognitive styles can be used, in an expansive (to analyze learning situations) rather than a restrictive way (focus on types), to consider a number of interrelated areas that affect individual access to learning.

chapter deals with those problems associated with the translation into educational settings of cognitive style ideas as part of a PLSP. This includes an outline of the awkward conceptualization of styles and ambiguity in the use of the associated terminology that currently exists. The focus of the chapter then shifts to confront issues around the selection and application of styles instruments in educational settings and within a PSLP, attending to the application of two models in particular: the Cognitive Styles Index and Cognitive Styles Analysis. The development and adoption of a PLSP is then outlined and explored in terms of those characteristics that are associated with the kind of knowledge and understanding of cognitive styles that is conducive to incorporating a PLSP into an ITE curricula, as well as key questions to ask when designing a curriculum that incorporates a PLSP. An exemplification of how an understanding of cognitive styles as part of a PLSP can be integrated into an ITE program is then presented around five key areas. The chapter concludes by reflecting on how to move forward with a PLSP in ITE.

A PLS involves the disposition to adopt specific strategies within a learning context. Within this definition, "strategy" refers to the implementation of a set of learning tactics/procedures for learning (Schmeck, 1988). A personal learning style includes a range of cognitive and learning styles as identified in Riding and Rayner's (2000) learning profile. Cognitive styles are perceived as higher order constructs/heuristics and are seen as consistent differences in the ways in which individuals organize and process information (Messick, 1984). Cognitive styles are thought to be affected by previous experience, habits, and socialization and are seen as interacting with personality, intelligence, gender, and other external variables to have an impact on learning behaviors (Kozhevnikov, 2007). An individual may use a number of cognitive styles as part of their PLS at a number of different levels from the simple perceptual level as to how one processes individual preferences to decision-making styles and decision-making behavior, which will have a differential impact on the choice of strategies/approaches adopted in particular learning situations. Learning styles have been seen as much broader constructs than cognitive styles and much more responsive to task and situational demands. Within the context of this chapter we consider a personal learning style to involve cognitive (thinking and knowing), motivational and affective (mood, feelings), and physiological behaviors and to be associated with preferred working environments, approaches to studying, and learning processes. We consider cognitive style(s) to refer specifically

7

The Place of Cognitive Style in Pedagogy: Realizing Potential in Practice

CAROL EVANS AND MICHAEL WARING

As educational researchers in higher education institutions (HEIs) involved in the organization and delivery of preservice teacher education programs, we are faced with the dilemma of how to challenge and disrupt current practice so as to enable preservice teachers to cope with and generate educational change that will enable them to provide solutions for the independent learners of the future. In the current era of personalized learning (Pollard & James, 2004) and the associated demands being made by current government educational policy (e.g., in the United States = No Child Left Behind; United Kingdom = Every Child Matters) on higher education teacher education (and schools), questions should be asked of the part cognitive styles can play in enhancing the individualization of the learning climate.

Informed by key research literature, this chapter provides a pragmatic perspective on employing cognitive styles as part of a personal learning styles pedagogy (PLSP) within a higher education initial teacher education (ITE) setting in an attempt to maximize teacher educators' and preservice teachers' (PSTs) understanding and potential for learning as they learn to teach. Having defined a personal learning style (PLS) and its relationship with cognitive and learning styles as key components of it, the chapter progresses by offering a justification for concentrating on cognitive styles within an ITE context. The next portion of the

Puccio, G. J., & Schwagler, N. (2008). Personality traits and the creative process: Examining relationships between the Jackson Personality Inventory and creative process preferences. *Proceedings of the International Conference on Creativity and Innovation Management, 2*, 164–175.

Selby, E. C., & Treffinger, D. (1993). Styles of adaptive and innovative creativity among 8th graders. *Learning Styles Network, 14*(3), 4–5.

Simonton, D. K. (1987). Genius: The lessons of historiometry. In S. G. Isaksen (Ed.), *Frontiers of creativity research: Beyond the basics* (pp. 66–87). New York: Bearly Limited.

Sood, A., & Tellis, G. J. (2005). Technological evolution and radical innovation. *Journal of Marketing, 69*(3), 152–168.

Sternberg, R. J., & Grigorenko, E. L. (2001). A capsule history of theory and research on styles. In Sternberg, R. J. & Zhang, L. F. (Eds.), *Perspectives on thinking, learning, and cognitive styles* (pp. 1–22). Mahwah, NJ: Lawrence Erlbaum Associates.

Tandon, R. (1987). *Study of the initial success for early investors in entrepreneurial new ventures.* Unpublished doctoral dissertation, Minneapolis, MN: University of Minnesota.

Taylor, J. (1994). The stability of schoolchildren's cognitive style—a longitudinal study of the Kirton Adaption-Innovation Inventory. *Psychological Reports, 74*, 1008–1010.

Tushman, M. L., & O'Reilly III, C. (2002). *Winning through innovation: A practical guide to leading organizational change and renewal.* Boston: Harvard Business School Press.

van der Molen, P. P. (1994). Adaption-innovation and changes in social structure: On the anatomy of catastrophe. In M. J. Kirton (Ed.), *Adaptors and innovators: Styles of creativity and problem solving* (pp. 137–172). London: International Thomson Press.

van Spronsen, J. W. (1969). *The periodic system of chemical elements.* Amsterdam: Elsevier.

Vehar, J. (2008). Creativity and innovation: A call for rigor in language. *Proceedings of the International Conference on Creativity and Innovation Management, 2*, 259–277.

Vicere, A. A. (1992). The strategic leadership imperative for executive development. *Human Resource Planning, 15*(1), 15–31.

Wallach, M. A., & Kogan, N. (1965). A new look at the creativity-intelligence distinction. *Journal of Personality, 33*, 348–369.

Zhang, L. F., & Sternberg, R. J. (2005). A threefold model of intellectual styles. *Educational Psychology Review, 17*(1), 1–53.

Zhang, L. F., & Sternberg, R. J. (2006). *The nature of intellectual styles.* Mahwah, NJ: Lawrence Erlbaum Associates.

Chapter 6 Problem Solving, Creativity, and the Level-Style Distinction

Davidson, M. (1982). *Occupational stress in female managers.* Unpublished doctoral dissertation, Department of Management Sciences, University of Manchester Institute of Science and Technology (UMIST).

Davidson, J., & Cooper, C. (1983). *Stress and the woman manager.* Oxford: Martin Robertson.

Driver, M. (2003). Diversity and learning in groups. *The Learning Organization, 10*(2/3), 149–166.

Drucker, P. F. (1969). Management's new role. *Harvard Business Review, 47,* 49–54.

Edgerton, D. (2006). *The shock of the old: Technology and global history since 1900.* Oxford: Oxford University Press.

Eysenck, H. J. (1967). *The biological basis of personality.* London: Springer.

Eysenck. H. J. (1970). *The structure of human personality* (3rd ed.). London: Methuen.

Getzels, J. W., & Jackson, P. W. (1962). *Creativity and intelligence: Explorations with gifted students.* New York: Wiley.

Golley, J. (1996). *Genesis of the jet: Frank Whittle and the invention of the jet engine.* Shrewsbury, UK: Airlife Publishing.

Guilford, J. P. (1950). Creativity. *American Psychologist, 5,* 444–454.

Jablokow, K. J. (2005). The catalytic nature of science: Implications for scientific problem solving in the 21st century. *Technology in Society, 27*(4), 531–549.

Jablokow, K. J. (2008). Developing problem solving leadership: A cognitive approach. *International Journal of Engineering Education, 24*(5), 936–954.

Jablokow, K. J., & Booth, D. E. (2006). The impact and management of cognitive gap in high performance product development organizations. *Journal of Engineering and Technology Management, 23,* 313–336.

Kanter, R. M. (2006). Innovation: The classic traps. *Harvard Business Review, 84*(11), 72–83.

Kelly, G. A. (1963). *Theory of personality* (Vol. 1). New York: Norton.

Kirton, M. J. (1976). Adaptors and innovators: A description and measure. *Journal of Applied Psychology, 61*(5), 622–629.

Kirton, M. J. (2003). *Adaption-innovation in the context of diversity and change.* London: Routledge.

Kotter, J. P. (1996). *Leading change.* Boston: Harvard Business School Press.

Krauss, L. (1994). *Fear of physics: A guide for the perplexed.* London: Jonathan Cape.

Kuhn, T. S. (1962). *The structure of scientific revolutions.* Chicago: The University of Chicago Press.

Lewis, A. V., Cosier, G., & Hughes, P. M. (2001). Dimensions of change—a better picture of disruption. *BT Technology Journal, 19*(4), 15–23.

Mawer, S. (2006). *Gregor Mendel: Planting the seeds of genetics.* New York: Abrams.

McCarthy, R. (1993). *The relationship of individual characteristics of women managers to the pressures experienced at work and choice of coping strategy.* Unpublished doctoral dissertation, University of Hertfordshire.

Orwell, G. (1946). *Animal farm.* Harcourt Brace Jovanovich.

Parkhurst, H. B. (1999). Confusion, lack of consensus, and the definition of creativity as a construct. *Journal of Creative Behavior, 33*(1), 1–21.

Popper, K. (2001). *All life is problem solving.* London: Routledge.

Puccio, G. J., & Grivas, C. (2008). Examining the relationship between behavioral traits and creativity styles. *Proceedings of the International Conference on Creativity and Innovation Management, 2,* 118–128.

principle holds for that most complex example of *all* the machinery we try to manage in our lives, the "engine" on which we *all* depend—the brain and its problem solving process.

NOTES

1. For example: lead is a useful element in the manufacture of electric batteries, but we cannot—as the alchemists discovered long ago—turn it into gold.

2. Gestalt theories brought creativity and problem solving closer together, since both emphasize the cognitive restructuring of concepts as the core activity. Concept is also a key term in early studies on creativity (e.g., those of Guilford [1950], which focused mostly on level—in particular, high level or genius). In this case, the complexity and number of concepts being handled was of interest. So we see the notion of a concept rising as an overlapping element for problem solving, creativity, and learning.

3. Note how this concept formation can be used to define cognitive style: cognitive style contains (inside the boundary) the elements *preferred, stable, manner* (of problem solving)—as distinct from (outside the boundary) *flexible, level/capacity* (of behavior). Then, to manage the seeming impasse between the stable and flexible characteristics, coping behavior is introduced (as another concept and learned skill).

4. Note our general use of the term "science" to include any generally recognized field of study.

5. Strictly speaking, it is more accurate to refer to individuals as "more adaptive" or "more innovative" (to reflect the continuous nature of A-I cognitive style); however, the terms "adaptors" and "innovators" are sometimes used (although cautiously) for linguistic convenience.

ACKNOWLEDGMENT

The authors would like to thank Diane Houle-Rutherford for her expertise and assistance in researching and reviewing this work.

REFERENCES

Amabile, T. M. (1983). The social psychology of creativity: A consensual assessment technique. *Journal of Personality and Social Psychology, 45,* 357–376.

Basadur, M. S., Graen, G. B., & Wakabayashi, M. (1990). Identifying individual differences in creative problem solving style. *Journal of Creative Behavior, 24*(2), 111–137.

Burke, J. (1985). *The day the universe changed.* Boston: Little, Brown and Company.

Buttner, E. H., & Gryskiewicz, N. (1993). Entrepreneurs' problem-solving styles: An empirical study using the Kirton Adaption-Innovation Theory. *Journal of Small Business Management, 31*(1), 22–31.

Cohen, F. J. (2005, January). Macro trends in pharmaceutical innovation. *Nature Reviews: Drug Discovery, 4,* 78–84.

Collins, J., & Porras, J. P. (1997). *Built to last.* New York: Harper Collins.

knowledge and insight related to Problem B. This new combination will allow a leader to help the team direct their combined energy efficiently toward the collective solving of Problem A, with as little disruption as possible from any potential Problem Bs (Kirton, 2003). So, now, it is the *team* that solves the problem, under knowledgeable leadership, given that "knowledgeable" has been broadened and redefined to include new key components.

PROBLEM SOLVING AS THE KEY TO LIFE

By adopting a broad functional model for human cognition, A-I theory links creativity, problem solving, and decision making together: the brain uses the same fundamental cognitive process (essentially, problem solving) for all of them. Since all humans utilize this process, we can assume that all humans are creative, solve problems, and make decisions, in one field or another, at one comfortable level or another, in one preferred style or another, in pursuit of one opportunity or another—all focused (ultimately) on our own survival.

Among these variations (i.e., this diversity), no style, level, or motive is better than any other *in general,* only more or less effective (appropriate and efficient) for finding the required solution to a *specific* problem and implementing it. Every style and level has advantages and disadvantages, in which the style and level of *the problem,* not one's preference, are the keys (Kirton, 2003). This is a vital element of Kirton's theory that moves us from allowing popular trends to determine the so-called "best" approach to problem solving (e.g., "Innovate or die!" or "Always go by the book!"), to the more reasonable approach of determining what the problem actually *requires* for its resolution (in terms of level, style, etc.)—regardless of what the latest trends say. In actual practice, a specific team member may not fit the latest trend, but he or she may be most helpful (given that person's particular level and style) with the present problem, at the present stage.

With these principal elements and assumptions in place, we have a model of cognitive diversity at the individual level that is both rigorous and useful. In problem solving, we must—at a minimum—manage this individual cognitive diversity in order to manage individual change; to manage wider change, we must manage wider social diversity (i.e., that of the group) as well. Engineers know that to get the best out of any engine—especially a complex one—we need to understand it; the same

by the more adaptive as being overly risky, peripheral to the problem, or "just plain silly" (confounding them once again). These different perceptions of change are yet another representation of cognitive gap, which—when understood and appreciated—can lead to valuable insights that aid in its management (i.e., a shift from "how annoying you are" to "how useful you might be if only I could collaborate with you better"). Much of leadership's task, then, is teaching—facilitating the understanding of Problem A, pointing out how each member of the team might contribute (level, style, or whatever else), which may lead to a reduced Problem B.

Leadership

And so we have come to leadership—in a general sense. In essence, all the elements described above represent the knowledge and insight required by a problem-solving leader in order to manage the efforts of a problem-solving team successfully. They also represent the knowledge (and insight) required by every member of that team in order to help a leader be successful; there are no ideal leaders who can "do it all." In the past (and sometimes still today), a great deal of time was spent searching for an ideal leader, with the definition of "ideal" shifting over time. This ideal leader was chosen (or took command) because he or she appeared to have expert knowledge of the problem domain—and this was assumed to be enough. This leader was then expected to dominate the problem-solving process, using whatever human and material resources were available, leading and commanding while others followed.

A-I theory rejects the notion of an ideal leader. Instead, a *problem-solving leader* is any person who assumes whatever leadership *role* it is (e.g., autocratic, democratic, monarchic, charismatic, transformational) that will facilitate (including teaching) the available team in solving a particular problem, over a specific time, with the currently available resources: we seek a pragmatic approach, not an unattainable ideal. To achieve this aim, a problem-solving leader needs a new set of attributes, composed of two general parts. First, he (or she) *still* needs knowledge of Problem A (the original problem)—not in order to dominate it completely, but enough to be able to hold his own as *an* expert (but not necessarily *the* expert) within the team.

In terms of Problem A, this is a more modest requirement than before, but it is only part of what is needed. The other part is an understanding of the problem-solving process and the problem solver—that is,

and these new conditions can create needs that the present team is not well equipped to handle.

In essence, every large and complex problem (at least) is a moving target (Kirton, 2003), and we must learn how best to track it. One solution is to identify competent, experienced people who, although currently at a disadvantage and seemingly out of favor in the present environment, will be needed at the appropriate time and stage to adjust and help control the change trajectory (avoiding the pendulum of change, seeking a spiral) in due course. In other words: leadership (particularly) needs to identify what will be needed when the current phase of problem solving has changed the operating conditions and what will be needed in the next phase of problem solving; it helps if the entire team shares in these insights and assists in the process. So, to manage change widely and well, a team needs to manage diversity (both of problems and of its own internal array) equally widely, wisely, and well (Jablokow, 2008).

Agents of Change

Within this model of change and its management, it is also useful to note Kirton's revision of the concept of *agents of change* (Kirton, 2003). Just as every person is creative and solves problems (at different levels and with different styles), so *every* person is an agent of change—also with different levels and styles. In fact, throughout the universe, there is no such state as "no change"; that means, also, that there are no generalized resistors to change, no universal agents *against* change (despite what the popular press often implies).

Instead, A-I theory suggests that a person is most likely to accept a change if it matches that individual's preferred style, current level, present attitudes, and so forth. In other words, a person will most readily accept those changes that he or she understands and with which he or she agrees, all done as quickly (or slowly) as that person considers appropriate. As Kelly (1963) noted, no healthy individual can accept a change that is so large or challenging that it threatens that person's understanding of self and reality.

With respect to structure, then, a person is more likely to accept changes that represent a degree of (or shift in) structure that matches that person's style preference (or, say, knowledge). So, for example: more adaptive solutions, ideas, or products may be dismissed by the more innovative as mere tinkering or "hardly creative" (confounding style and level), while more innovative solutions may be viewed warily

2008). Where are the points of greatest weakness within this developmental process—for both individuals *and* organizations? A-I theory asserts that they fall at the two extremes: first, in (more) flexible infancy, and second, in (more) well-defined old age—not forgetting that an individual's preferred cognitive style does not change (we end life as adaptive or as innovative as we began it; Kirton, 2003).

From an organizational perspective, companies reflect the climate set by their members. Given that fact, Buttner and Gryskiewicz (1993) (following Tandon [1987]) showed that start-up companies are more likely to be (although they are not always) set up by innovators; however, disproportionately more innovator-led entrepreneurial companies fail, while there are more overly adaptive companies that peter out in "old age". Survival depends on a *constant* aligning (and realigning) to the requirements of the problem, however the enterprise begins. More Adaption may be needed at the start (when early Innovation isn't *steady* enough) in order for an organization to *reach* its prime time, or more Innovation may be required (when early Adaption isn't *flexible* enough) in order to make it *past* that prime time. Experienced, healthy, "middle age" seems to be the safest state, if it can be reached and maintained.

From this, we can see a more balanced (and truly equitable) view of change and the respective roles of level and style emerging: for optimum problem solving and growth (i.e., an upward, catalytic *spiral of change*) we must shift—repeatedly and independent of any specific timeframe—to more or less (say) Adaption or Innovation and more (or less) domain knowledge and expertise (i.e., various forms of level, to varying degrees), depending on the (changing) situation. What we want to avoid are dramatic, precipitous shifts between (say) highly innovative and highly adaptive extremes, and/or between particular, disparate levels (say, engineering and sales); such a *pendulum of change* typically leads to little forward progress, considerable wasted effort, and much frustration.

Framed in the *paradox of structure*, Kirton has described the *management of change* done well as "managing structure, by adjustment and readjustment, so as to set just sufficient limits that will achieve maximum enabling" (Kirton, 2003, p. 287). How can we apply this notion in a practical way? As one strategy, consider the following: when teams are first formed, a good deal of time is spent assembling the best possible combination of people in style, talent, knowledge, motivation, and so forth, for the *current* problem in its *current* form. But any team, by virtue of its own success in solving the original problem, creates new conditions,

Style and Change

As we continue to develop our theme, we are coming closer to an understanding of the complex relationships that exist between the principal elements of problem solving (including level and style) and their combined impact on the progression of change and its management. In this context, we see that the management of cognitive gap is a building block for the management of diversity, which undergirds the management of change and effective problem solving.

There are many models of change and equally many scholars discussing its management (e.g., Kotter, 1996; Lewis, Cosier, & Hughes, 2001; Sood & Tellis, 2005; Tushman & O'Reilly, 2002; van der Molen, 1994; Vicere, 1992). These contributions come from diverse fields (although many are rooted in business) and address the notion of change in the form and function of ideas, artifacts, and organizations (Jablokow, 2008). Once again (recalling our discussion on the overvaluation of innovation), a fundamental weakness of some of these (e.g., van der Molen, 1994; Vicere, 1992) is their tendency to see growth solely as an outcome of Innovation (i.e., revolution, radical change), and catastrophe as an inevitable result of excess Adaption (i.e., evolution, incremental change). They fail to note the high death toll experienced by many innovative ventures (e.g., start-up companies) and the critical growth found in many adaptive efforts (e.g., pharmaceutical testing). In an interesting variation, some authors (e.g., Cohen, 2005; Tushman & O'Reilly, 2002) appear to recognize the value of both "types" of change (occasionally even making use of a continuum), but all too often, Innovation still seems to come out on top in the end (reminiscent of Orwell's *Animal Farm* [1946], in which all the animals were equal, but some were "more equal than others").

In contrast, Kirton (2003) and others (e.g., Collins & Porras, 1997; Edgerton, 2006; Lewis et al., 2001; Sood & Tellis, 2005) suggest that there are dangers *throughout* the change process, with more danger likely at *both* extreme ends, just as we see in biology. Consider our own human development, for example: we are born in a highly flexible (but also essentially helpless) state. As we age, our physical and mental abilities grow, reaching a "prime time" (middle age) during which we are highly productive and most secure. As we continue to age, we begin to lose our physical abilities, but this loss is balanced by gains in knowledge, wisdom, and insight, and, for a time, we can maintain our productivity. Eventually, however, both our physical and mental abilities wane (in old age), and we become as vulnerable as a baby once again (Jablokow,

as the cognitive differences between the individuals or groups themselves; these are referred to as person-problem gaps and person-person gaps, respectively (Jablokow & Booth, 2006; Kirton, 2003). The presence of cognitive gap is another example of the *paradox of structure*: that is, cognitive gaps (a psychological structure) both *enable* and *limit* the solution of problems. In particular, by bringing together the diverse problem solvers needed to minimize the person-problem gaps between the team and the current, complex problem, other gaps (between those same problem solvers) will be formed. These person-person gaps will require careful handling, or they will limit collaboration and its effectiveness through their potential to create Problem Bs within the team. As Driver (2003) noted, both too little and too much diversity can harm group performance.

In applying this notion, Jablokow and Booth (2006) explored the impact of cognitive gaps (of both level and style) and the paradoxical situation they create in the context of high-performance product development organizations. In that particular setting, cognitive gaps are created as a result of the problem-solving diversity needed to develop new products and bring them to market efficiently, but these gaps may (simultaneously) create disruptions in communication and threaten the good will required for collaboration.

In the end, understanding and clarifying the distinction between level and style appears to be one of the most effective ways to manage cognitive gaps (Jablokow & Booth, 2006; Kirton, 2003). When an individual learns about cognitive differences (their source, their value, their limitations, etc.), then relationships with others (even with those they consider problematic) can be understood better. In fact, everyone needs to understand better that diversity pays off *if* it can be managed. Differences between individuals can be recognized as desirable, as (for example) a particular difference in level or style may be exactly what is needed (at some stage in the problem-solving process) to resolve the current Problem A.

With this insight, the situation has been transformed from a battle into a mutual problem to be solved, with each team member learning how to focus on Problem A, working to avoid or minimize Problem B, and helping others in the team do so too. A person *can* be hostile, of course, but it is wise to be sure of this before counter-attacking. We all need to remember that the mismanagement of diversity (e.g., seeing it as hostile when it is merely different) can *arouse* hostility, which then also needs to be managed.

engineering discipline (at, say, a high level), and when must we move outside the discipline altogether (say, to nearby physics, or further away to marketing or psychology)? When does this particular high level need to change? Once more, it is the *problem* that should determine the "which" (discipline, degree of complexity, etc.), the "when," and (in this case) the "how much"—not our individual preferences.

THE MANAGEMENT OF DIVERSITY AND CHANGE

We can find examples of the paradox of structure and the interaction of style and level within the catalytic progression of change in every discipline (science, music, engineering, education, management, etc.). In each case, it is clear that multiple problem solvers are necessary to resolve the complex problems we find there—that is, we need individuals with different levels, styles, motives, views of change, and perceptions of opportunity. What is equally obvious is that this diversity (of problems *and* people) needs to be coordinated and facilitated; it will not generally take care of itself. The question is: how do we manage this multifaceted diversity, making best use of the power it offers while minimizing the complications it can introduce?

Kirton (2003) has described this very real challenge as follows: every time individuals collaborate, each person automatically acquires *two* problems. The first is Problem A—the original problem around which a team is formed (even if it is a team of only two and whatever is the problem); the second is Problem B—managing the collective diversity of the team. In the end, more energy should be spent on Problem A than on Problem B, or the effort (and the team) will eventually fail.

As one might imagine, there are many forms of Problem B; the potential differences between two individuals (much less, two or even two hundred would-be collaborating groups) in perceptions of opportunity, motive, style, and level are innumerable. In addition to these variations among people, the team must also manage the differences between its (human) problem-solving resources and the requirements of Problem A; this is another form of Problem B.

Kirton's notion of *cognitive gap* can help us understand and manage this challenge. In A-I theory, cognitive gap describes all the cognitive differences (of style, level, motive, etc.) that exist between individuals (working alone or in a team) and the problems they are tackling, as well

the innovators—although the adaptors may be more so. The bigger the paradigm, the more people are involved, the more fear, anxiety, and chaos are created, and the more resistance appears (i.e., the bigger the war). *Paradigm shifts* (as Kuhn originally defined them—here, again, is a term that is often misused) are typically *not* a pretty business.

The Paradox of Structure

Throughout this discussion, we have seen how important and challenging it is to balance flexibility and predictability in our management of structure (of every type and at every level): we must *all* solve this paradox of structure with every problem we face. A-I theory proposes that structure, like cognitive style, can be mapped on a continuum, ranging (theoretically) from total rigidity to total chaos. Humans cannot exist at either extreme (we cannot operate within total rigidity or total entropy); instead, we operate in a (relatively) narrow band in between, but with very significant differences among us based on our cognitive diversity.

Naturally, proponents of any particular structure or solution will play down its limiting side and play up its enabling side—whatever the nature of that structure might be. Here, we must be careful: within the business literature (and some scholarly works as well), breaking down or shedding structure (i.e., Kirton's Innovation) is considered better (i.e., "less structure is more creative")—which, from a cognitive perspective, confounds level and style once again by assuming that structure is always only limiting.

Clearly, A-I theory strictly rejects this notion. Adaption and Innovation (as general approaches to problem solving) are equal in fundamental value, as are those whose preferences lean in either direction—all this wrapped around the management of structure. Those who are more adaptive are more likely to see the advantages of a tighter structure, while the more innovative are more likely to see its limitations. Likewise, adaptors can work *with* the limits better than innovators in order to enable and succeed, and innovators can see *past* the limits better than adaptors in order to succeed. As we have seen in our examples (and recognize in principle as well): we need a diversity of problem solvers, using a diversity of problem-solving styles, to manage the vast diversity of problems we are faced with today.

In closing this section, it is critical to note that what we have applied here to style also applies to level. For example: while solving an engineering problem, when must we continue to stay completely in the

does one know when to *retain* the paradigm and when to *replace* it? Or, in other words: how do we know whether to tighten or loosen the structure of the paradigm in order to accommodate the new information? These *should* be objective questions, objectively answered—but are they?

The fact is, as we now recognize, different individuals will see different merit in retaining or replacing (tightening or loosening) the *same* paradigm, even in the face of the same information, depending on their individual cognitive preferences—that is, on their respective *cognitive styles*. This makes scientific progress all the more difficult (and interesting), particularly as our problems become more challenging and our dependence on others (our collaborators) becomes greater. Now we begin to see that there may be an advantage to having colleagues who are not like us, if we can manage them.

As a result of their differences in preference, those who are more adaptive and those who are more innovative will have different views of what constitutes *change* with respect to a paradigm. Every time novelty (new data) is resolved by a paradigm, the paradigm changes—no matter *how* that novelty is resolved. Therefore, Adaption produces change (what one might call *evolution*), even though innovators tend to ignore these changes (they are looking for *revolution*);[5] Innovation also produces change, even though adaptors tend to reject these changes as irrelevant or sometimes even ridiculous. Viewed another way, adaptive problem solvers more readily recognize the efficiency of a paradigm's structure, while innovative problem solvers often need to be reminded of its value. On the other hand, innovative problem solvers are more willing to shed the paradigm's structure when it has become obsolete, while their more adaptive counterparts may need more encouragement before they are willing to do so.

In general, though, all individuals (whatever their preferred style) recognize that paradigms need to be changed: more adaptive problem solvers tend to change the paradigm just enough to make it better, while more innovative problem solvers are more likely to replace it completely. Either approach, ranging from strong Adaption to strong Innovation, may prove to be the right one in a *particular* situation, but *neither* will be right *all* the time; the best choice depends on the current problem. In the end, evolution will continue to work as long as it solves the present problem(s), but if it moves too slowly, it sets itself up for revolution. When this happens (i.e., when a paradigm is threatened), there is disorganization, fear, and great anxiety; everyone is threatened—including

A Brief Example From Medieval Astronomy

To illustrate the preceding discussion, let's consider how a typical paradigm works, using an example from medieval astronomy: the development of a model for our universe (Burke, 1985). Under the leadership of Aristotle, the ancient Greeks first modeled the universe as geocentric (Earth-centered), with the sun, moon, other planets, and stars all orbiting the Earth on concentric, crystal spheres. This model (paradigm) served them well, and for some time it was able to accommodate any new data they collected while watching the heavens.

Eventually, however, as new developments in the technology of star gazing began to accumulate, the data gathered agreed less and less with the prevailing paradigm's predictions, and over time, the paradigm was changed repeatedly as a result. In some cases, new data were treated as *residual puzzles:* for example, Ptolemy (one of the Greek, ruling, elite savants in Egypt) added smaller circular orbits called "epicycles" on the edges of the circular planetary paths (called "deferents") in order to account for retrograde motion (among other variations). In this case, the geocentric nature of the model was maintained, along with the circular shape of all the orbits—both of which were central tenets of the prevailing paradigm. The addition of epicycles *adaptively* refined these key assumptions in a way that brought the paradigm into closer accord with observation, and this adjusted model remained in use for over 1,000 years.

In other stages of the model's development, new data were treated as *counter instances,* eventually leading scientists to replace the geocentric model with a heliocentric (sun-centered) system, although *not*—initially—with the elliptical orbits that we know today. This more radical restructuring of the prevailing paradigm (moving the sun to the center and downgrading the Earth to a mere planet, while retaining circular orbits) represents a more *innovative* change, which—while a step in the right direction (we can tell ourselves *now*)—required a significant amount of *adaptive* fine-tuning before it was acceptably accurate.

Paradigms, Structure, and Cognitive Style

We have been looking at how humans (working alone or together) organize and develop their knowledge using concepts and paradigms. Within this context, the individual practitioner of a particular paradigm is left with a recurring problem: in the face of some new piece of data, how

in cycles, with periods of what Kuhn called "normal science" alternating with periods of "science in crisis" (Kuhn, 1962). In *normal science* (where we spend much of our time), the prevailing paradigm is explored, refined, modified, improved, and adjusted. Data seen as new (novelty) are treated as residual puzzles, which can be resolved *within* the context of the paradigm. In accommodating these new data, the paradigm is—inevitably—changed, and these changes *retain and improve* (i.e., tighten) the paradigm during the time in which it dominates. Practitioners in the field are generally content with these changes, since more modification does not seem needed. These predominantly adaptive times of paradigm extension (i.e., *evolution* of a paradigm) are an excellent representation of *adaptive creativity*.

When the paradigm can no longer accommodate the new data, the scientific community has moved into a period of what Kuhn called *science in crisis*. Here, evidence accumulates to suggest that the prevailing paradigm can no longer explain all that is happening. The residual puzzles—if central enough—are now seen as counter instances, perceived proof that the current paradigm does *not* work, rather than special cases that might still be explained using the current paradigm (with minor modifications). An alternative paradigm is needed (i.e., the current paradigm must be replaced or modified extensively), based on radical scientific achievement that will loosen the structure currently in place. These times of science in crisis (i.e., *revolution*) are splendid examples of *innovative creativity*.

It is important to note that any suggested alternative paradigm must accommodate the new troublesome data, but it must also support—or at least explain—*all* of the old. Thus, new scientific theories do not completely eradicate the old; instead, they are dependent upon them, even if they serve primarily as a springboard. As Krauss (a physicist) noted: "Popular wisdom might have you believe that new discoveries in science always center on radically new ideas. In fact, most often the opposite is true. The old ideas not only survive but almost always remain seminal" (Krauss, 1994, p. 57). Here we begin to glimpse an important insight: a science cannot progress without both the adaptive *and* the innovative contributions; the key is to know which style of contribution will be most effective at any particular time in any particular place within the process. We also note that the application of A-I theory to the progression of Kuhn's paradigms suggests that residual puzzles and counter instances are not strictly two, distinct alternatives, but lie on a common continuum instead.

as well as *predictable,* so they can be extended and changed to deal with relevant new problems and data (i.e., appropriate novelty).

The Progression of Paradigms: Normal Science Versus Science in Crisis

To understand the growth and extension of paradigms, we need to consider two more useful terms introduced by Kuhn: *residual puzzles* and *counter instances* (Kuhn, 1962). First, let's set the stage: as practitioners of a science go about their daily work, new data are uncovered that must be squared with the prevailing paradigm—that is, the practitioners must decide whether the new data (and any new conclusions they foster) fall inside or outside the boundary of the paradigm; if they (data and/or conclusions) *do* fall inside the boundary, their relationship with the existing elements of the paradigm must be determined.

In making this determination, Kuhn proposed that one of two things occurs. In the first case, practitioners are able to incorporate the new data and/or conclusions into the prevailing paradigm, either by inserting them directly into the existing structure or by adjusting the structure incrementally—that is, in such a way that the paradigm retains its currently understood form but with adjustments to its boundary and/or internal (elemental) structure that make it (the paradigm) more accurate and efficient. Data that can be incorporated into a paradigm in this way are called *residual puzzles,* that is, residual details of a stable framework of understanding that are plugged into place as they become known.

Counter instances are quite different. In this case, practitioners are *not* able to incorporate the new data and/or conclusions into the prevailing paradigm, even with incremental adjustments to its boundary and/or internal elemental structure. In other words, the new data cannot be made to fall inside the boundary of the prevailing paradigm, no matter how hard the practitioners try. Counter instances, then, by their very nature, call the validity of the prevailing paradigm into question, creating the need to investigate more radical changes to its structure—perhaps even its complete replacement.

With residual puzzles and counter instances defined, now we can consider how the underlying structure of a science (i.e., its corresponding paradigm) changes and progresses over time. According to Kuhn, any science (be it engineering, education, or entomology) progresses

determines which elements are to be included and excluded—just as a concept defines the domain of an idea. For example, the paradigm determines which *data* are relevant or irrelevant, which *problems* are to be tackled and the way those problems are to be perceived, the kinds of *solutions* to be sought and the ways and means appropriate for seeking them (including both theoretical frameworks and supporting technologies), and the *criteria* for proof or falsification. In other words, the paradigm determines what a science *is*, what that science *does*, and *how* that science is carried out.

As an example, let's consider the paradigm of 21st-century medicine. Within this paradigm, we know that data related to all human body functions are included, but data related to crop growth or engine design are not. In terms of relevant problems, medical doctors are expected to tackle human health-related issues of all kinds (within a hierarchy of severity), but we do not expect them to deal with animal grooming or precision manufacturing. Doctors and nurses are also expected to develop their solutions to problems based on empirical evidence and sound reasoning; crystal balls and magical spells are not considered appropriate means. And so it goes on—the expectations established by a particular scientific community (medicine, in this case) form the internal structure of the paradigm and draw a boundary around it, giving everyone a predictable sense of what its practitioners know and do.

Paradigms, then, are *efficient* by imposing order on the problems within them; the effectiveness of this order is judged by its past success (is it useful?) and by its promise of future success (will it continue to be useful?). Paradigms are also enabling in their establishment of the accepted training and knowledge requirements for the practitioners of the paradigm; taken together, this training and knowledge define the practitioner or professional of the given field, which benefits both the practitioners themselves and those who want to use their (now mutually recognized) expertise.

But paradigms are not perfect—they have their *limitations* as well. For example: paradigms provide very few immediate solutions to *specific* problems; that is, our models (paradigms) only promise answers *in general*, which we must then seek and find *in particular*. More importantly, perhaps, paradigms are always incomplete, since we cannot know when relevant new information will become available that was not considered when the paradigm was originally formed. Paradigms are designed to handle only the problems and data that we *expect* they will need to handle. Fortunately, paradigms (like concepts) must be *flexible*

the other hand, if the structure *never* changes, then we won't be able to update our concepts with new information, and our learning will suffer.

As we learn and solve problems, we are constantly faced with this trade-off between *prediction* and *flexibility* in our thinking: when the structure is tight, we have high predictability, but with fewer options and less flexibility. When the structure is loose, we have high flexibility, but with more options (perhaps generated exponentially at an increasing rate until it all becomes more than we can handle) and less predictability. In the end, we need both prediction *and* flexibility in proper balance to manage the current problem successfully. If there is too *much* structure (i.e., the structure is too tight), there will be too few options and increasingly limited problem solving. If there is too *little* structure (i.e., the structure is too loose), there will be too many options, resulting in indecision (through lack of focus) and again, no problem solving. The exact balance needed depends on the *problem*, not on what any one person prefers.

From Concepts to Paradigms

As the simplest form of cognitive structure, concepts can be created by an individual and held by that individual alone (i.e., concepts are not *necessarily* shared). When cognitive structures become larger and more complex, and when they are developed with and by the consensus of others, we often give them other names: as models or theories (in science and engineering), rules (in law), policies (in business), frames of reference (in psychology), and classifications (in biology), to name a few. However, the widest, most powerful, and most important example (that covers them all) is a *paradigm*.

The term *paradigm* became a household word when T.S. Kuhn published his landmark book, *The Structure of Scientific Revolutions,* in 1962. In this extended essay, Kuhn described the ways in which scientific frameworks and the technologies that support them change and develop over time. Within this broad perspective of scientific change, Kuhn used the term *paradigm* to describe an intellectual structure or body of knowledge that identifies the set of beliefs agreed upon by the practitioners of a science to *define* that science.[4] In effect, paradigms are shared superconcepts that have been formed by the practitioners of a particular field; an individual cannot develop or maintain a paradigm in isolation.

The role of paradigms is essential and fundamental. By defining the *domain* of a science, a paradigm sets a boundary around it and

The answer to which is best, flint or mud, depends on the problem and your skill in managing (processing) it.

When applied to structure in general (of any kind—physical, intellectual, social, etc.), Kirton refers to this phenomenon as the *paradox of structure* (Kirton, 2003), that is: *every* structure, by its very nature (including the human brain), is both enabling and limiting at the same time. In fact, a structure limits (i.e., focuses our efforts) *in order* to enable, but it must enable *more* than it limits, or it will impede our efforts. The challenge is to find a good balance in every circumstance; that is, we must find ways to minimize the limiting factors and maximize those that enable in order to optimize the benefits for all.

In fact, at times, we must actually *increase* the limits to get (more effectively) the enabling that we need, and at other times, we must *limit* the limits in the search for *different* enabling! To see how this might be done, let's consider how the brain uses structure to organize and manipulate information in the solution of problems, starting with the most basic intellectual structures (concepts), then expanding their size and complexity as we investigate the roles of level and style along the way.

Concepts and Structure

We begin in the field of learning theory (in which the study of problem solving originated), where we find (within both the behaviorist and the gestalt schools) the notion of a *concept,* that is, a nugget of knowledge or packet of information, composed of an ordered arrangement of chains and patterns (e.g., Stimulus-Response [S-R] chains), that operates as a basic unit of cognition.[2] Concepts are defined by a boundary that distinguishes what is in the concept (i.e., its content) from what is not; within the boundary, we find elements that are stable in number and order, giving a consistent meaning to the person holding the concept. If the location of the boundary (plus the content and its order) is agreed upon by more than one person, then the concept can be shared among those individuals, and communication of ideas (up to, e.g., the very language being used) and more complex collaboration become possible.[3]

So, within the notion of a concept, *structure* is implicit (i.e., boundary, elements with stable number and order, etc.). We need such structure in order to use and communicate concepts, and by doing so, we learn and collaborate. If there is *no* stable structure—that is, a concept changes continually—then we can't use it as knowledge; it loses its meaning. On

on Amabile's three-point description of creativity, Mendel was "not creative" while he was alive. However, several decades later (after Mendel's death), three botanists (Hugo de Vries, Carl Correns, and Erich von Tschermak) rediscovered his papers and realized the importance and value of Mendel's work; in fact, it became the foundation on which the theory of genetics was built (Mawer, 2006). Returning to the three-point description of creativity, are we now to conclude that Mendel *became* creative only *after* he died? It would seem that the "useful" criterion needs further refinement before it can be consistently and (forgive the pun) usefully applied.

Summary

The popular definition of creativity and that found in the formal literature are often in agreement. Both are biased toward a particular level (high) and a particular style (innovation), leaving us with a number of problems that include too few people being considered creative and inadequate measures of creativity that appear to confound level and style. All this helps explain the current overvaluation of innovation, and it also makes it clear that a better and more rigorous understanding of creativity is needed in order to restore a balanced view. In A-I theory, creativity is related to problem solving, as they are both products of the same fundamental cognitive function. Like problem solving, then, creativity can be measured in terms of style and level, as separate influences. This distinction will allow us to appreciate the contributions of the creativity literature without entertaining misconceptions about which elite owns creativity itself.

THE PARADOX OF STRUCTURE

Returning now to the variations of style and level discussed earlier, and recognizing their corresponding impact on and value in problem solving, we can begin to see a paradox: the style (preference for structure) and level (expertise, skill, knowledge) that enables problem solving in one instance may hinder it in another. For instance: just as any physical attribute (quality, substance, etc.) is useful in one setting, it may not be so useful in another. Stone Age man discovered that flint flakes could be used as tools, but flint is not as good a material when compared to soft stone or even baked mud for creating an image of the mother goddess.

against other creativity measures; the average of the correlations was around .25 (an unsatisfactory result if we hope to assess creativity in a reliable way). Likewise, when Getzels and Jackson (1962) compared creativity measures against intelligence measures, the average correlation was .28—again, a troubling result. If the creativity measures they had available were measuring the *level* of creativity, then they should have correlated much higher with intelligence (which is clearly a level measure). If the creativity measures were assessing some *other* independent dimension of creativity (e.g., style), then the correlations with intelligence should have been close to zero.

In reviewing their results, Wallach and Kogan (1965) came to this conclusion: many measures of creativity are poor, either because they have been poorly designed psychometrically or because they are technically invalid (i.e., they do not measure the same thing)—or both. In seeking an explanation for this in light of the three-point description of creativity, consider the following: if some creativity measures stress *usefulness*, while others have different ways of assessing *high level* and/or different definitions of *discontinuous thought*, is it any wonder they do not agree? Accurate measurement is impossible if you aren't clear about what you are measuring, no matter how skilled the technician.

Problem 3: Inconsistency

Finally, let's consider the "useful" criterion in light of an interesting example from biology (Mawer, 2006). Gregor Mendel was a clever friar who taught in a religious school in what is now the Czech Republic around 1900. Besides his senior brotherly duties, Mendel had a passion for both botany and mathematics, and he was put in charge of the greenhouse. He observed that there were a great variety of sweet peas (e.g., dark green peas, light green peas, smooth peas, wrinkled peas, etc.), and he became interested in seeing what happened if he bred these in various combinations (e.g., what happens if you breed smooth peas with wrinkled peas, etc.). So he set up a meticulous system for isolating and pollinating the plants, observing the results, drying and saving the peas, and repeating this exercise over many generations (i.e., thousands) of pea plants.

In publishing the results of his experiments, Mendel received polite interest, but no particular fanfare; his papers disappeared into the archives of his school, and he died without any special recognition for his work. Clearly, it was *not* considered useful to "self + one," and so, based

Problem 1: Exclusivity

Here, we have a general theoretical problem. The three-point description of creativity has led many people (practitioners and scholars alike) to conclude that there are a large number of people who are *not* creative. Specifically, consider the three points from above: first, what does "discontinuous thought" mean? If it refers to making a break, shifting a paradigm, or dismantling structure, then it sounds very much like Kirton's Innovation. In that case, only about 50% of the population would be comfortable doing it (Kirton, 2003).

Next: when it comes to "high level," an IQ of 120 is often used as the cutoff point (Simonton, 1987). If this criterion were accurate, then (in this context) only about 10% of the 50% would satisfy the first two criteria, further reducing the creative portion of the population to a humble 5%. Finally, in defining "useful," Amabile and others generally point to the consensual agreement of others (Amabile, 1983)—with a minimum of "self + 1"—which cuts the 5% in half, implying that, at best, a mere 2.5% of the world's population is creative.

In the end, if we subscribe to the three-point description, then creativity is rare indeed! But does such exclusivity really make sense? Psychologists rarely (if ever) describe individuals as noncreative or unintelligent; rather, they speak of an individual's *degree* of intelligence or *degree* of creativity. So, returning to Kirton's four principal elements of problem solving (opportunity, motive, level, and style), we should be able to measure the *level* of creativity, asking "how creative are you?" or "how creative was that particular act?"—given that the answer will never be zero. All human beings are creative within at least one domain (e.g., physics, art, horticulture) to *some* degree (level); that level is likely to be in proportion to one's intelligence (or, say, one's appropriate knowledge), even if the correspondence is not perfect. Likewise, we should also be able to assess the *style* of creativity, asking "in what *way* are you creative?" or "*how* are you creative?" This level-style distinction brings creativity back within the reach of all humankind—a claim long supported (despite any other confusion) by many (if not all) creativity scholars.

Problem 2: Measurement

Other problems with the three-point description have come about as various researchers have tried to assess creativity psychometrically. Wallach and Kogan (1965) correlated a selection of creativity measures

Chapter 6 Problem Solving, Creativity, and the Level-Style Distinction

Vehar, 2008), and, in fact, the two are closely linked (as we shall see). As early as 1960, scholars had identified over 50 different definitions for creativity in the extant literature, and the situation had not improved four decades later when other researchers revisited the task (Parkhurst, 1999). The situation is equally problematic today, as disagreements about the definition of novelty and the role it plays in creativity are further compounded with controversy over the relationship between creativity and divergent thinking.

In the popular press, creativity is frequently associated with a few, highly gifted (but misunderstood) individuals, whose rash and risky ideas are out-of-the-ordinary, unfinished (yet brilliant), and frequently rejected by the rest of society. Using Kirton's terms, the popular view of creativity closely resembles high level, high innovation. But how realistic is this view? If this view of creativity were accurate, it would mean that only a small fraction of the total population is creative (only the brilliant, high innovators)—and we would certainly have made little progress as a result. In truth, however, the progress we are making as humans is considerable (and in some cases, remarkable—we are, after all, the only organism so far that writes and reads books about creativity). So we must ask ourselves: do we misunderstand creativity, or are we considering only a small piece of it—or both?

Going to the formal literature, we find a similar situation: a plethora of definitions for creativity, many of them vague and confusing, as well as inconsistent (even scholars have difficulty defining and measuring it). Over the years, a number of researchers have tried to sort out the situation. Amabile (1983), a well-known scholar in the field of creativity, analyzed the collection of definitions she found and systematically reduced the number of characteristics used to describe creativity to those few that appeared most frequently in the literature. In 1984, at a conference focused on creativity, Amabile noted that the following three elements were mentioned by many authorities (Kirton, 2003):

- Discontinuous thought
- High level
- Useful

There are weaknesses in this three-point description (which still appears often today), and yet quite a number of creativity assessments and studies have been constructed on this basis. Let's explore some of the problems that arise with its use, including the overvaluation of innovation.

which sews the seeds of confusion and does not help the field flourish. I humbly submit that there is a need for rigor in our language, a need for us to be clear about what it is that we research, seek, teach, and facilitate."

This problem of definition is demonstrated by the many ways in which the term "innovation" is used—referring (in turn) to a style, a process, a product (the result of process)—and in the many (often inconsistent) ways in which these uses overlap. For example: in the business literature, "innovation" is frequently used to refer specifically to radical, breakthrough change—a meaning that (if applied in the context of a full continuum of change) resembles Kirton's definition of innovative style applied to the outcome of problem solving. In other cases, researchers and practitioners have recognized the need to differentiate between types of change, coining terms like "incremental innovation" and "discontinuous innovation" as a result (Cohen, 2005; Tushman & O'Reilly, 2002). While this latter insight is laudable, the proliferation of terms is less useful; Kirton's existing A-I continuum can be used to describe these variations in a context that is even more inclusive (representing, as it does, a full range of possibilities, rather than just two extremes).

Without delving further into an analysis of all these variations (such a study could comprise a chapter in itself), we note that in most cases, there is an element of the unorthodox or nontraditional assumed within the common definition of innovation, but this is not always spelled out clearly. What is interesting is the fact that the ill-defined nature of the term has not stood in the way of a general feeling that innovation is something particularly good and desirable. This bias towards innovation can be seen in many places today: in the popular (e.g., business) press, in the scholarly literature, and across many different fields and domains (e.g., engineering, education, the pharmaceutical industry). Of course, innovation has not always been the ideal—other long periods have been marked by an insistence that we need to remain within the current (classical, approved, proper, consensual, etc.) view held by accepted authority (acknowledged expert, standard, etc.). The terms used to define these seeming antagonists are numerous (e.g., evolution vs. revolution, tradition vs. a renaissance). Fortunately, human progress continues throughout, nevertheless.

The state of confusion surrounding the definition and role of innovation bears a striking resemblance to the long-standing confusion surrounding the definition of creativity (Kirton, 2003; Parkhurst, 1999;

Chapter 6 Problem Solving, Creativity, and the Level-Style Distinction   **145**

The springboard to complex problem solving (in terms of style) is not always an innovative one, as a second example shows us. In the late 18th and early 19th centuries, we find the chemists of the day struggling with the identification and classification of the elements (i.e., the basic substances of which our world is made)—an adaptive problem that required the development of precise and reliable structure. Their work represented the latest efforts in a long line of exploration that can be traced back to Aristotle and other ancient natural philosophers. By the 1820s, the need for a highly accurate tabulation of atomic weights had become critical—without it, no further progress could be made in classifying the elements in a systematic and reliable way. Cannizzaro finally provided the solution to this part of the problem in 1858, presenting his detailed list of atomic weights (for all the elements known at the time) to the greater scientific community (van Spronsen, 1969).

Once Cannizzaro had established this underlying structure, other chemists took on the job of rearranging and organizing the elements (using their atomic weights) into broader patterns (this included, e.g., the search for periodicity), a task that required the more innovative contributions of men like Meyer and Mendeleev (van Spronsen, 1969). Mendeleev's efforts (in particular) resulted in one of the most well-known (but not the only) forms of the periodic table—a superstructure into which the known elements could be placed. But Mendeleev's table also had "holes" in it—that is, gaps in which he correctly predicted as-yet-undiscovered substances would sit. These gaps would be filled later by further meticulous (adaptive) experimentation by scientists like Ramsay and Marie Curie—and so the alternating pattern of styles over time (and their equality of merit) is demonstrated here as well.

The Bias Toward Innovation

In both of the preceding examples, we see that it is the leveraging or management (used in the broadest sense) of *diverse* levels and styles that is needed, rather than the wholesale adoption of some particular alternative in every case. This view lies in contrast to those who promote a particular style over all others; a key example of this phenomenon is the current promotion of "innovation," the definition of which (outside A-I theory, at least) is often a problem in itself. As Vehar noted recently (Vehar, 2008, p. 260): "Yet in this age of Innovation, which is again the buzzword *du jour* (Kanter, 2006), many well-meaning practitioners use the words creative process, creativity, and innovation interchangeably,

styles are better or worse than others, or whether all styles are equal in merit. A-I theory is clear in this regard: there is *no* best or ideal style (or level, motive, perception of opportunity) *in general*. Viewed from the perspective of the specific problem at hand (rather than any one person's preference), *any* style (level, motive, etc.) may have an advantage within *that* problem at some particular time, with the advantage shifting to a different level and/or style at some later time. Within another problem, other levels and styles may have the advantage, in different sequence and priority—and so on.

The Equal Merit of Different Styles: Two Examples

Within engineering, for instance, we can see this phenomenon during the development of one of the 20th century's key transportation technologies: the jet engine (Golley, 1996). When Frank Whittle was designing the jet engine (as an alternative to the propeller-driven model) in 1929, he needed engineering knowledge at a high level. Once a full (and expensive) prototype was nearing production, however, the requirements of knowledge and expertise changed, both in *kind* (e.g., more management, finance, and marketing were needed) and *degree* (e.g., engineering knowledge was still required, but not, perhaps, at quite so high a level). By applying these different levels (both intellectual and physical), Whittle moved the problem-solving process forward to a point of success that changed the problem once again. Failure in any one of these domains (i.e., failure to cope by learning all that was needed) would have limited the success of the aspiring Whittle—just as it has done at one time or another for every one of us.

The same principle applied to style in Whittle's case as well. Whittle began with an innovative problem (how to design an engine that would lift airplanes—literally—to previously unknown heights in order to take advantage of less turbulent, but thinner, air), but most of what he needed to solve it was known and embedded in current practice. His specific contribution was to combine those elements in a way that was unorthodox (more innovative), and this proved to be a good start. But as the engine was developed further, it had to fit into the world in which it was to be used (including current manufacturing methods) and conform to that world's standards (e.g., safety regulations). So, gradually, Whittle's innovative solution was revised, tuned, and integrated into adaptive practice—getting better and more efficient all the while, until eventually, more Innovation was needed (again).

of work pressure (Davidson, 1982; Davidson & Cooper, 1983) with this result: the bigger the perceived gap, the higher the perceived pressure.

So, if coping comes at a cost, when (and why) is it worth it? It stretches us away from our cognitive comfort zone (i.e., preferred style and existing level) by a great enough amount and for the required time to solve the current problem (or some part of it)—but *only* for as long as the extra energy is available. We must find the motive that will provide the added energy in order to achieve the particular perceived reward (i.e., the return payment for our coping—called, in behaviorist terms, reinforcement). Alternatively, if we are not up to the task ourselves, we may seek the help of those *not like us* but who (we recognize) are valuable to solving our problem. This, however, is not as easy as working with people *like* us, and also requires knowledge, insight, and coping behavior (on our part *and* theirs). The payoff, again, needs to be commensurate to the effort—as leaders (in particular) would do well to recognize.

In summarizing this section, then, A-I theory offers precise definitions of level and style and rigorous distinctions between these and other key variables within a broad context of cognition that identifies creativity and problem solving as facets of the same fundamental cognitive process. Here, level and style are influences on (rather than defined by) this process, with Innovation and Adaption defined strictly as styles that fall along a continuum. In addition, A-I theory presumes preferred style to be fixed (non-malleable), as demonstrated by the stability of KAI scores over time, their uniformly high internal reliabilities (across cultures), the early onset of preference, and the large array of trait correlates of Adaption and Innovation tested in the literature (for more details on these supporting studies, see Kirton, 2003). The seeming impasse between the stability of preference and the obvious flexibility of one's behavior is explained through learned coping behavior, which enables us to behave outside our preferences without permanently changing them. Now, let's see how this framework can help us sort out another issue—the current overvaluation of innovation.

PROBLEMS WITH CREATIVITY AND THE OVERVALUATION OF INNOVATION

As pointed out by Zhang and Sternberg (2005, 2006), a much-debated and important issue in the investigation of style is whether particular

learning (level), and their combined progress toward a solution that is separate from both.

A-I theory helps sort out this confusion by distinguishing between process (a general, idealized template for problem solving) and technique (a specific learned method for making best use of our problem-solving faculties)—with both of these being separate (also) from level and style. Within a process (which is defined by its stages and the ideal order in which they are to be carried out), any style and any level can be applied independently in any stage, and any technique can be used as well.

This is not to say that all styles, levels, and techniques are equally appropriate in every stage of a particular process, but the stage itself does not define any of the three. So, for example, within Guilford's model of the thinking process (Guilford, 1950; Kirton, 2003), the divergent operation can be carried out at high to low level and more adaptively to more innovatively—and using any relevant technique as well. Likewise, Guilford's convergent operation can also be implemented using any combination of level, style, and technique. From this we see that there are no mutually exclusive groups of divergent thinkers and convergent thinkers—despite what many popular business and self-help books seem to suggest. All humans (all brains) both diverge *and* converge, with different degrees of aptitude and skill, and in a variety of characteristic ways.

Indeed, one of the great strengths of the human brain is its capacity to be flexible. How, then (as noted earlier in this section), do we get around (when necessary) these apparently deep-seated preferences for a particular style strategy and certain levels (e.g., aptitudes) with which we are more comfortable? A-I theory proposes (backed by sound research), that when we discover (sometimes belatedly) that our preferred level or style is inappropriate for a *particular* problem, we make an extra effort to behave in an accommodating way with respect to that problem—temporarily simulating a style (without changing our stable, underlying preference) that is different from the one we prefer and/or learning in an area in which we are less competent and less interested. This is called *coping behavior* (Kirton, 2003).

Coping behavior is learned and comes at an extra cost. In one of the earliest studies (McCarthy, 1993), a sample of women managers was sent two KAIs each: one to be completed describing self, and one to fill in describing "a typical colleague." The aim was to measure, indirectly, the climate style; the outcome was a measure of perceived gap between self and some significant other. This score (gap) was related to a measure

keep the system running smoothly in both the short and the long term. Their advantage lies in their preference for finding ways to enable and create change *within* a structure, making best use of its defining properties and resources, changing the structure *as an outcome* of solving a problem. Their disadvantage is their tendency to hold on to a structure too long—that is, even when its usefulness is being overshadowed by its faults (Jablokow, 2008).

Those who prefer (cognitively) the innovative strategy (strictly: those who are more innovative), on the other hand, often work more at the edges of the current structure, or they may even detach a problem from its customary frame of reference, searching for unorthodox solutions in unexpected places. The value of this approach is also clear: it can provide a more dramatic shift in structure when such a shift is required. It is also riskier—altering, from time to time, even the most fundamental elements of the structure *in order* to solve the problem. The advantage of the more innovative lies in their preference for manipulating boundaries and combining information in ways that their more adaptive peers may miss; their disadvantage is their tendency to cast off a structure too soon—that is, when it is still useful, despite its faults (Jablokow, 2008).

Kirton is not the only scholar to support a sharp distinction between level and style. In their review and synthesis of cognitive style theory over several decades, Sternberg and Grigorenko (2001) define styles (in general) as a set of preferences, explicitly distinct from abilities (i.e., level); this view is reflected by Zhang and Sternberg (2005, 2006) as well. In addition, there are numerous studies (all using the fully validated KAI and samples of appropriate size and composition) that show that level and style are insignificantly related (see, e.g., Kirton, 2003).

Yet there are others who confound the two—as Sternberg and Grigorenko go on to note: "both successes and failures that have been attributed to abilities are often due to styles" (Sternberg & Grigorenko, 2001, p. 4). For example, some creativity scholars (e.g., Basadur, Graen, & Wakabayashi, 1990; Puccio & Grivas, 2008; Puccio & Schwagler, 2008) put style in direct relation to a process (e.g., the Creative Problem Solving process), where they associate preferences with the stages of that process (e.g., problem clarification, idea generation, solution development, etc.) and refer to them as "creativity styles." In this view, every individual has a preference for a particular stage within the creative process, and so spends more time there, increasing his or her natural ability for it, as well as developing the thinking skills that are needed in that stage. Clearly, there is confusion here between preference (style), with research showing that (at least) it is set early (e.g., Selby & Treffinger, 1993; Taylor, 1994), and with hints (van der Molen, 1994) that there is a genetic link (as is supposed with all dimensions of personality (Eysenck, 1967, 1970). Behavior, on the other hand, must be assumed to be more flexible—enabling an individual temporarily to depart (in action) from his or her fixed preference when the need for such a change is perceived. However, operating outside one's preference is harder (more costly) to undertake and is likely only for as long as it is needed (i.e., preference reasserts itself when we perceive that the need to act differently has expired). This precise definition of style as fixed and distinct from behavior (which is flexible) is supported further by numerous studies done by Kirton and others (for details of these studies, see Kirton, 2003).

In general, cognitive style (like cognitive level) has multiple dimensions, which can be assessed by different means. As measured by KAI—the Kirton Adaption-Innovation inventory (Kirton, 1976)—cognitive style differences lie on a bipolar continuum that ranges from strong Adaption on one end to strong Innovation on the other. The main pattern that differentiates among these preferences (remembering that it is a continuum of style, not a dichotomy) is the characteristic way in which an individual manages structure. Individuals who are more adaptive prefer to solve problems using more structure, and with more of this (cognitive) structure consensually agreed. In contrast, more innovative individuals prefer to solve problems using less structure and are less concerned with gaining consensus around the (cognitive) structure they use. Of course, they do want their solution accepted—which means that it *becomes* the current structure! For further descriptions of the characteristics of Adaption and Innovation (in general, and as observed in various contexts), see Jablokow (2005) and Kirton (2003).

Moving from description alone to building a better understanding, one basic distinction between level and style could be that level is an operational element of cognition, and style is a strategic one. For example: it is a strategic decision (in this case, preference) to approach problems characteristically by aiming for a "better" or a "different" solution (using Drucker's [1969] terms)—particularly at a time when the problem may not yet be well understood. Those who prefer the adaptive strategy (strictly: those who are more adaptive) approach problems from within the given, accepted, frame of reference (i.e., model, standard, paradigm—all conceptual structures), looking for solutions that are more immediately effective, sound, and reliable. These individuals bring value through consistency, stability, and efficiency, all of which

affects problem solving. Yet, as noted above, there was this confounding of level and style, problematic at best or even quite harmful, especially when leading to the under- or overvaluation of particular styles and the alienation within a team of those whose preferences they represent. This mirrored a problem in terms of level, when teams who were trying to solve, say, an engineering problem, demeaned any other discipline.

A-I theory seeks to clarify and resolve these issues, beginning as follows: all organisms have needs and, therefore, must find ways to meet those needs (or die). In other words, all organisms solve problems (as Popper [2001] also noted), at however high or low a level and in whatever manner. To describe the problem-solving process at its simplest, the first step in meeting a need is to perceive an opportunity (this part of the process includes the search for opportunities). Next, we must have motive, that is, the allocation of energy (in sufficient amount, over sufficient time) to resolve the question of how to exploit the opportunity. With the problem and the will to solve it in hand, the means to do so are now required: both the right levels (which ones and to what degrees) and the appropriate styles (characteristic approaches). Both of these selected means are best determined by the nature of the problem—not, for example, by the current mode of trendy thinking, the organizational climate, or some dominating senior colleague.

In general, cognitive (problem-solving) level is defined and assessed in terms of an individual's inherent *potential capacity* (such as intelligence or talent) and *manifest capacity* (such as managerial competence, domain of expertise, or technical skill) (Kirton, 2003). We all seem to have some understanding of the role of level in problem solving. As Jablokow and Booth noted: "in assigning problem solvers to a particular task, we routinely consider their natural limits (potential level) and their current skills and abilities (manifest level)" (Jablokow & Booth, 2006, p. 321).

In addition, even the most conceited autocrat among us gets the message (sometimes) that the least senior and knowledgeable member of the team could have, at this moment, in this part of the problem, the *one* bit of knowledge that is needed to move the overall solution forward. So: the level required must be of the right sort, in the right amount, at the right time—as needed by the problem. Given this kind of level diversity, why do we have different styles, and when is any particular variation appropriate (or not) in the solution of a particular problem? This facet of problem solving has been less easy to appreciate.

Kirton (2003) has defined cognitive style as the "strategic, stable characteristic—the preferred way in which people respond to and seek to bring about change" (p. 43). This *preference* appears to be well set,

is, altering cognitive structure *as an outcome of solving the problem.* Drucker (1969) described these contrasting approaches as "doing things differently" or "doing things better," respectively. A-I theory argues that either option (more accurately, any position along the bipolar continuum of which they are a part) may be the right way, depending on the nature of the problem itself—*not* on a past or present trend.

A-I theory also asserts that level and style are independent influences on behavior—and that both are separate from process: we can work in any stage of a problem-solving process at any level within one style or with any style within one level. This is not the view of those who favor innovation, for although they may refer to innovation as a style, their bias turns style into a level—and a barely attainable one at that (e.g., only high innovators are creative and the rest of humanity is not). Studies using the fully validated KAI (Kirton's measure of Adaption-Innovation) clearly point to the level-style separation (Kirton, 2003); other studies are less clear. If we accept that the evidence demonstrates that style is *not* level yet is valuable in problem solving in its own right, how is the current confusion and bias toward innovation to be explained?

Furthermore, if both level (e.g., capacity) and style are key elements in problem solving, are there some common underlying principles linking the two that might also help us understand and manage cognitive gap (i.e., gaps between the attributes and resources needed to solve a particular problem and those that are currently available)? Can both level and style help us resolve the *paradox of structure* (Kirton, 2003), that is, the fact that every structure is simultaneously enabling and limiting (be it intellectual or physical)?[1] And, finally, how are level and style linked to the successful management of diversity (e.g., a diverse team of problem solvers) as a foundation to the management of change?

This chapter explores important differences and similarities between A-I theory and other views within the context of problem solving, creativity, and cognitive style. We begin (proceeding in clear progression) with the key underlying issues (such as those related to the level-style distinction and the overvaluation of innovation) and end with the placement of style and level within an integrated theory of problem solving as the key to life.

THE LEVEL-STYLE DISTINCTION

Kirton's work on cognitive style began with the observation, based on varied experience, that we all have a characteristic, preferred style that

6

Problem Solving, Creativity, and the Level-Style Distinction

KATHRYN W. JABLOKOW AND MICHAEL J. KIRTON

Adaption-Innovation (A-I) theory rests on the basic assumption that all forms of life must solve problems successfully or perish; different species do so in different ways and with different degrees of success. Humankind is so successful at it that most of our current problems are of our own making. In fact, so complex is our world now, even advanced knowledge within the most sophisticated technical disciplines is not enough. We all (not just a few experts) need to know more about the nature and process of problem solving itself in order to solve today's problems, using a brain that has changed little (if at all) since the Stone Age.

A-I theory also clearly distinguishes between two ways of describing and measuring our problem solving, namely: problem-solving level ("how well") and problem-solving style ("in what way"). Level is a unipolar concept that is measured low to high (with a socially preferred end), while style is an independent, bipolar concept (with no socially preferred end) that has, in this context, strong Adaption and strong Innovation as its two respective poles (Kirton, 2003).

Recently (when measured in decades), some scholars and many practitioners in the creativity field have taken a special fancy to innovation, that is, to solving problems by changing the current, consensually agreed, cognitive structure *in order to solve the problem*. Others recognize the value of solving problems by making use of the current structure—that

Applications

PART II

Zhang, L. F., & Sternberg, R. J. (2005). A threefold model of intellectual styles. *Educational Psychology Review, 17*(1), 1–53.

Zimmerman, B. J. (2008). Investigating self-regulation and motivation: Historical background, methodological developments, and future prospects. *American Educational Research Journal, 45*(1), 166–183.

Rayner, S. (2007b). *Managing special and inclusive education.* London: Sage.
Rayner, S. (2007c). What next? Developing global research and applied practice in the field of cognitive and learning styles. In L. Lassen, L. Bostrom, & H. K. Knoop (Eds.), *Laering og Laeringsstile. Om unikke of faelles veje I paedagogikken* [Learning and learning styles. A unique and inclusive approach to teaching] (pp. 165–183). Virum, Denmark: Dansk Psykologisk Forlag.
Rayner, S. G., & Riding, R. (1997). Towards a categorization of cognitive style and learning style. *Educational Psychology, 17*(1–2), 5–27.
Reynolds, M. (1997). Learning styles: A critique. *Management Learning, 28*(2), 115–133.
Riding, R. J. (1991). *Cognitive styles analysis.* Birmingham, UK: Learning and Training Technology.
Riding, R. J., & Cheema, I. (1991). Cognitive styles—an overview and integration. *Educational Psychology, 17*(3–4), 193–215.
Riding, R. J., & Rayner, S. G. (1998). *Cognitive styles and learning strategies.* London: David Fulton.
Ritter, L. (2007). Unfulfilled promises: How inventories, instruments and institutions subvert discourses of diversity and promote commonality. *Teaching in Higher Education, 12*(5–6), 569–579.
Scarr, S. (1994). Burt, Cyril L. In R. J. Sternberg (Ed.), *Encyclopedia of intelligence* (Vol. 1, pp. 231–234). New York: Macmillan.
Scott, D. (2000). *Realism and educational research.* London: Routledge Falmer Press.
Sternberg, R. J. (1988). Mental self-government: A theory of intellectual styles and their development. *Human Development, 31,* 197–224.
Sternberg, R. J. (1997). *Thinking styles.* Cambridge: Cambridge University Press.
Sternberg, R. J. (2001). Epilogue: Another mysterious affair at styles. In R. J. Sternberg & L. F. Zhang (Eds.), *Perspectives on thinking, learning and cognitive styles* (pp. 249–253). Mahwah, NJ: Lawrence Erlbaum.
Sternberg, R. (2008). Applying psychological theories to educational practice. *American Educational Research Journal, 45*(1), 150–165.
Storberg-Walker, J. (2006). From imagination to application: Making the case for the general method of theory-building research in applied disciplines. *Human Resource Development International, 9*(2), 227–259.
Thomas, G. (2007). *Theory and education: Strangers in paradigms.* Maidenhead, UK: McGraw Hill, Open University Press.
Thurstone, L. L. (1944). *A factorial study of perception* (Psychometric Monograph, No. 4). Chicago: University of Chicago Press.
Tiedemann, J. (1989). Measures of cognitive styles: A critical review. *Educational Psychologist, 24,* 261–275.
Torraco, R. J. (1997). Theory-building research methods. In R. A. Swanson & E. F. Holton III (Eds.), *Human resource development handbook: Linking research and practice* (pp. 114–137). San Francisco: Berrett-Koehler.
Vermunt, J. D. (1996). Metacognitive, cognitive and affective aspects of learning styles and strategies: A phenomenographic analysis. *Higher Education, 31,* 25–50.
Witkin, H. A. (1962). *Psychological differentiation: Studies of development.* New York: Wiley.

Kagan, J. (1966). Developmental studies in reflection and analysis. In A. H. Kidd & J. L. Rivoire (Eds.), *Perceptual development in children* (pp. 487–522). New York: International University Press.

Kozhevnikov, M. (2007). Cognitive styles in the context of modern psychology: Toward an integrated framework of cognitive style. *Psychological Bulletin, 133*(3), 464–481.

Kuhn, T. S. (1962). *The structure of scientific revolutions.* Chicago: University of Chicago Press.

Lohman, D. F. (2001). Issues in the definition and measurement of abilities. In J. M. Collis & S. Messick (Eds.), *Intelligence and personality: Bridging the gap in theory and measurement* (pp. 79–98). Mahwah, NJ: Lawrence Erlbaum Associates.

Lynham, S. A. (2002). The general method of theory-building research in applied disciplines. *Advances in Developing Human Resources, 4*(3), 221–241.

Marsh, H., Byrne, B., & Shavelson, R. (1988). A multi-faceted academic self-concept: Its hierarchical structure and its relation to academic achievement. *Journal of Educational Psychology, 80,* 366–380.

Messick, S. (1994). The matter of style: Manifestations of personality in cognition, learning and teaching. *Educational Psychologist, 29*(3), 121–136.

Myers, I. B., & McCaulley, M. H. (1988). *Manual: A guide to the development and use of the Myers-Briggs Type Indicator.* Palo Alto, CA: Consulting Psychologists.

Neisser, U., Boodoo, G., Bouchard, T. J., Jr., Boykin, A. W., Brody, B., Ceci, S. J., et al. (1996). Intelligence: Knowns and unknowns. *American Psychologist, 51*(2), 77–101.

Nesselroade, J. R. (2002). Elaborating the differential in differential psychology. *Multivariate Behavioral Research, 37*(4), 543–561.

Oosterwegel, A., & Oppenheimer, L. (1993). *The self-system: Developmental changes between and with-ion self-concepts.* London: Lawrence Erlbaum Associates.

Paul, J. L., & Marfo, K. (2001). Preparation of educational researchers in philosophical foundations of inquiry. *Review of Educational Research, 71*(4), 525–547.

Peterson, E. R., Rayner, S., & Armstrong, S. (2008). *Learning and individual differences.* Unpublished manuscript.

Petit, S. C., & Huault, I. (2008). From practice-based knowledge to the practice of research: Revisiting constructivist research works on knowledge. *Management Learning, 39*(1), 73–91.

Rayner, S. G. (2000). Re-constructing style differences in thinking and learning: Profiling learning performance. In R. J. Riding & S. Rayner (Eds.), *International perspectives in individual differences* (pp. 115–180). New Developments in Learning/Cognitive Style. Stamford, CT: Ablex.

Rayner, S. G. (2001a). Aspects of the self as learner: Perception, concept and esteem. In R. J. Riding & S. G. Rayner (Eds.), *International perspectives on individual differences* (pp. 25–52). New Developments in Self-Perception and Learning. Westport, CT: Ablex.

Rayner, S. G. (2001b). Cognitive styles and learning styles. In N. J. Smelser & P. B. Baltes (Eds.), *International encyclopaedia of the social and behavioural sciences* (pp. 2171–2175). Oxford: Elsevier.

Rayner, S. (2007a). A teaching elixir, learning chimera or just fool's gold? Do learning styles matter? *British Journal of Support for Learning, 22*(1), 24–31.

Coffield, F. C. (2005, January 14). Kinaesthetic nonsense. *The Times Educational Supplement*, 17–18.

Coffield, F. C., Moseley, D. V. M., Hall, E., & Ecclestone, K. (2004a). *Learning styles and pedagogy in post-16 learning: Findings of a systematic and critical review of learning styles models*. London: Learning and Skills Research Centre.

Coffield, F. C., Moseley, D. V. M., Hall, E., & Ecclestone, K. (2004b). *Should we be using learning styles? What research has to say to practice*. London: Learning and Skills Research Centre.

Collis, J. M., & Messick, S. (Eds.). (2001). *Intelligence and personality: Bridging the gap in theory and measurement*. Mahwah, NJ: Lawrence Erlbaum Associates.

Cronbach, L. J. (1957). The two disciplines of scientific psychology. *American Psychologist, 12*, 71–84.

Cunliffe, A. L. (2002). Reflexive dialogical practice in management learning. *Management Learning, 33*(1), 35–61.

Curry, L. (1987). *Integrating concepts of cognitive learning styles: A review with attention to psychometric standards*. Ottawa, Canada: Canadian College of Health Services Executives.

Deary, I. J. (2000). *Looking down on human intelligence*. Oxford: Oxford University Press.

Delanty, G. (1997). *Social science: Beyond constructivism and realism*. Buckingham, UK: Open University Press.

Edmondson, A., & McManus, S. E. (2007). Methodological fit in management field research. *Academy of Management Review, 32*(4), 1155–1179.

Entwistle, N., & Tait, H. (1996). Identifying students at risk through ineffective study strategies. *Higher Education, Individual Diversity in Effective Studying, 31*(1), 30–44.

Furnham, A. (2001). Test-taking style, personality traits and psychometric validity. In J. M. Collis & S. Messick (Eds.), *Intelligence and personality: Bridging the gap in theory and measurement* (pp. 289–304). Mahwah, NJ: Lawrence Erlbaum Associates.

Goddard. H. H. (1914). *Feeble mindedness: Its causes and consequence*. New York: Macmillan.

Gregorc, A. F. (1982). *Gregorc Style Delineator: Development, technical and administration manual*. Columbia, CT: Gregorc Associates.

Grigorenko, E. L., & Sternberg, R. J. (1995). Thinking styles. In D. H. Saklofske & M. Zeidner (Eds.), *International handbook of personality and intelligence* (pp. 205–230). New York: Plenum Press.

Grossman, P., & McDonald, M. (2008). Back to the future: Directions for research in teaching and teacher education. *American Educational Research Journal, 45*(1), 184–205.

Guba, E. G. (Ed.) (1990). *The paradigm dialog*. London: Sage Pubs.

Hammersley, M. (2002). *Educational research policymaking and practice*. London: Paul Chapman.

Hearnshaw, L. S. (1979). *Cyril Burt, psychologist*. Ithaca, NY: Cornell University Press.

Johnson, P., & Duberley, J. (2000). *Understanding management research*. London: Sage.

Jones, A. E. (1997). Reflection-impulsivity and wholist-analytic: Two fledglings? Or is R-I a cuckoo? *Educational Psychology, 17*(1–2), 65–77.

An agreement to pursue such an agenda is to facilitate a global aim for general theory building in the style research community. It will require increasing levels of international and interdisciplinary collaboration, combined with a readiness to consider multiple paradigms in research methodology. This will necessarily entail a deliberate attempt on the part of the research community to manage knowledge production and share in a common aspiration for the advancement of the field. A first step might be to model previous success in a related field and call for a series of symposia following the example of the paradigm dialogue and SRL symposia (Guba, 1990; Zimmerman, 2008). These events held at an American Education Research Association (AERA) annual meeting, realized consensus in theory building and the production of a common research rubric and a new research paradigm. It is this kind of event that enables a discourse that will help to focus the researching community and establish a shared movement toward a global paradigm in the field of cognitive style research. The way forward is one of reaffirming the style construct and working as a researcher community of practice that aims to relocate cognitive style or styles as a situated theory in the wider domain of differential psychology.

REFERENCES

Allport, G. G. (1981). The general and the unique in psychological science. In P. Reason & J. Rowan (Eds.), *Human inquiry: A sourcebook of new paradigm research* (pp. 83–92). Chichester, UK: John Wiley.

Anastasia, A. (2007). *Differential psychology: Individual and group differences in behavior.* New York: Anastasi Press.

Armstrong, S., & Rayner, S. (2002). Inquiry and style: Research verities and the development of a consensual theory? In M. Valk, D. Gombier, S. Armstrong, A. Francis, M. Graf, J. Hill, et al. (Eds.), *Proceedings of the 7th Annual Conference of the European Learning Styles Information Network* (pp. 25–36). Ghent, Belgium: University of Gent.

Biggs, J. B. (1993). What do inventories of students' learning processes really measure? A theoretical review and clarification. *British Journal of Educational Psychology, 63,* 219.

Burns, R. B. (1979). *The self-concept in theory, measurement, development and behaviour.* London: Longman.

Byrne, B. M. (1996). *Measuring self-concept across the life span.* Washington, DC: American Psychological Association.

Cattell, R. B. (1966). The data box: Its ordering of total resources in terms of possible relational systems. In R. B. Cattell (Ed.), *Handbook of multivariate experimental psychology* (1st ed., pp. 67–128). Chicago, IL: Rand McNally.

Cervone, D., & Pervin, L. A. (2008). *Personality: Theory and research* (10th ed.). New York: John Wiley & Son.

conviction that social science must essentially be conceived as an applied discipline. What is notably absent in traditional style research, as well as the wider domain of differential psychology, is any reference to the essential quality of meaning (*valence*), identified by Rayner (2007c), in developing an epistemology for the study of style differences in human performance. It is this quality in methodology above all others that might arguably serve as a catalyst in forming a meaningful interaction between domain-general and domain-specific theory.

Managing Theory Building by Utilizing Basic and Applied Research

The further consideration of value in theory-building research must be related to the issues of impact and application and the often asked "so what?" question. The inclusion and integration of an applied aspect to the theory-practice continuum in research is a very necessary step in building an integrated theory and relevant methodology for style research. The aim is not transformation but instead one of facilitating a step-wise paradigm shift that will enable the following:

- An inclusive research rubric for advancing diverse contexts and mixed methodologies making up the style research field.
- A theory-building research methodology suitable for advancing applied and academic research in a real-world context.
- An integration of style theory and its reconnection with a unifying conceptual framework reflecting personal and differential psychology.
- An attempt to reaffirm the structural definition of style variables in an individual's psychology making up human performance.
- Production of a quality-warranted collection of psychometric measures for use in further developing experimental research and practice (with careful review of reliance on self-report as a basis for assessment).
- New research projects integrating academic and applied research methodologies in the production of new knowledge about style and its effect in a diverse range of theoretical contexts (for example, social, emotional, and critical paradigms).
- Generation of practice-based evidence linked to domain-general theory utilizing a mix of research methodologies for further developing personalized education.

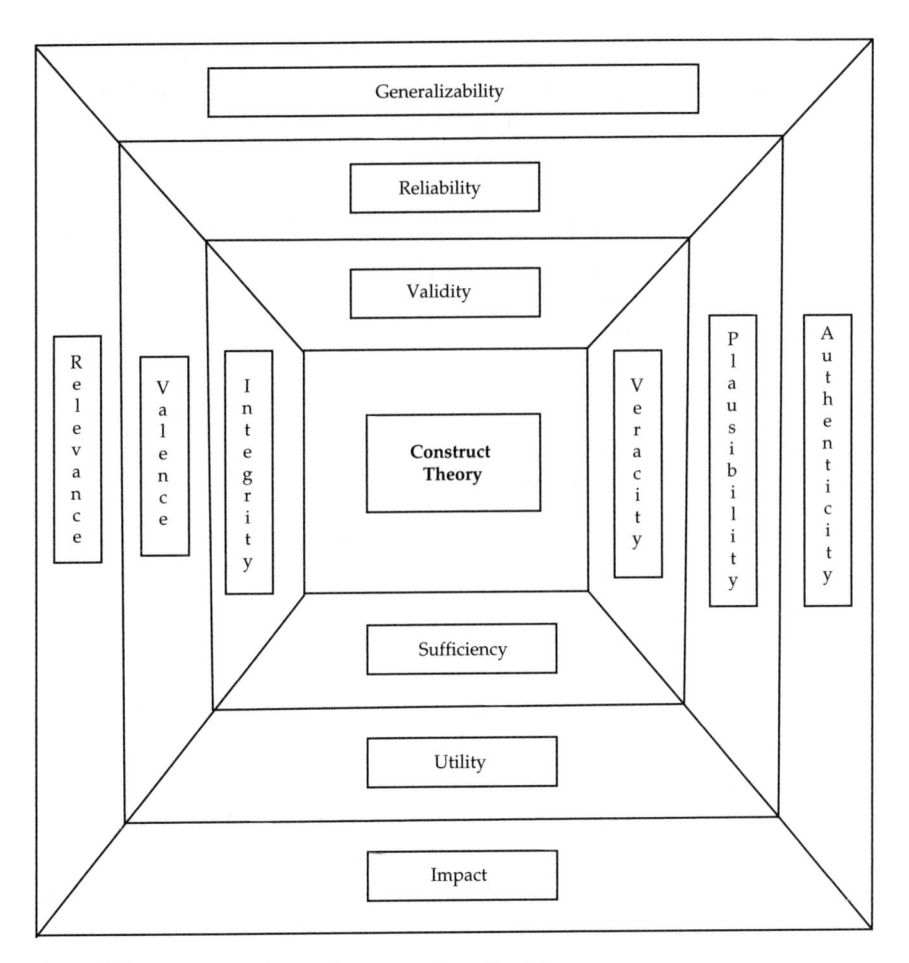

Figure 5.2 Building an integrative research methodology.

Labels in figure (pyramid faces):
- Top face: Generalizability, Reliability, Validity
- Center: Construct Theory
- Bottom face: Sufficiency, Utility, Impact
- Left side (vertical): Relevance, Valence, Integrity
- Right side (vertical): Veracity, Plausibility, Authenticity

All of these methods must include a consideration of the interface at each level in its construction. This means, for example, ensuring a consideration of *valence* linked to the complementary qualities of *authenticity*, *relevance,* and *impact*. Other levels of the construction reflect a similar integration of qualities required in an effective design. As action flows up or down and in and out of the pyramid, a second set of conceptual integration occurs, linking construct to context as represented at the base level of the pyramid. The emphasis on context in Figure 5.2 is represented as a basis for this structure and arguably as a reference to an applied perspective at every level of the pyramid, reflecting an ontological

used in two research projects investigating the effects of cognitive style on student supervision and self-perception as a learner (Armstrong & Rayner, 2002). This account, drawing on the notion of dialogic process (Cunliffe, 2002), explored how interleafing quantitative and qualitative paradigms in a research account might play a role in advancing the state of the science in researching cognitive style and human performance. It offered one way of incorporating paradigm dialogue and a research script for the kind of conversation and exchange of perspective previously identified as a requirement for paradigm shift.

Enabling Theory Building in Styles Research: Assuring Rigor and Value

A third approach involves reconsidering the research verities of rigor and value. The issue of value is a key criterion for applied research and in any subsequent evaluation of new method or methodology in basic research. In this regard, methodology should arguably reflect epistemology. This should certainly include a set of principles or attributes to ensure the value of the research. For example, such an epistemology would refer to the research attributes of *integrity*, *veracity*, and *valence*, as identified by Rayner (2007c). These are arguably deeply embedded features in any form of successful social science research but in particular constitute cardinal qualities for a pragmatic methodology in applied research (see Figure 5.2). To this end, these attributes help form a framework for an integrative methodology by ensuring that *validity*, *reliability*, and *generalizability* as qualities in nomothetic design, and *authenticity*, *plausibility*, and *veracity* as qualities in ideographic design, are integrated. Both these and other attributes such as *impact*, *sufficiency*, and *valence* are included in developing the construction of a research methodology illustrated in Figure 5.2 with an inside-out pyramid. The figure outlines a framework of attributes with which possible options for developing a blended methodology using mixed method designs or templates is considered to support research designs investigating style. For example, the construction of a theory-building research design may be framed in a number of different ways. It may be top-down, starting with theory or a construct (hypothetico-deductive template), or bottom-up, ending in a production of theory (inductive-grounded template), or side-to-side ascent or descent reaffirming theory (utilizing meta-analytic or multiple-method templates).

- The etiology of cognitive style and its definition through research investigating cause and effect;
- The amount of variance in factor analysis data afforded to style and the question of incremental validity;
- The nature or structure of the style variable—and its relationship with other key variables affecting learning performance in the individual. (p. 292)

While Furnham offers a starting point for further theory building, this is with a positivist template and offers a traditional approach to developing style theory. Sternberg (2001) argues that style as a construct and theory may not neatly fit into this traditional framework of factor analysis and nomothetic design. He furthermore suggests that a lack of unified theory perhaps exemplifies the very nature of styles and has perhaps inevitably led to the current state of the science in style research. We again argue that this is not necessarily the case, and even if, as is increasingly likely, style is proven to be a mediating variable and part of a more complex cognitive system as suggested by Kozhevnikov (2007), this in turn, should and can be redefined as part of a more coherent and unified psychology of the individual. As in the study of personality, however, following Cervone and Pervin (2008), we do acknowledge that a good cognitive style theory should ideally include data that are scientific (objective) and theory that is systematic (ideas are related in a logical and coherent way), testable (measurable), comprehensive (address a wide variety of psychologically significant aspects of a person), and applied (beneficial and useful applications). These goals can be seen as a useful set of criteria for framing and evaluating a global theory of cognitive style.

Extending a Good Style Theory: Using New Recipes, Scripts, and Templates

We also propose, however, a second approach to theory building for styles research. The construction of a more inclusive methodology includes an applied dimension that is referenced to a body of knowledge as well as a pragmatic epistemology. In research design of this kind, Lynham (2002) argues that special attention should be given to the core phases of theory building, that is, *"operationalization, confirmation* and *application"* (p. 231, emphasis added). One example of this kind of blended approach in the field of style research is a reflexive account of methods

a framework intended to support building theory, knowledge, and methodology are also important for the development of applied practice. In the final analysis, as Coffield et al. (2004a, 2004b) rightly point out in their appraisal of styles and pedagogy, if there is no coherence or agreement to what a cognitive style or learning styles are or are claimed to be—it is pointless to expect educationists or practitioners to accept any relevance of this knowledge either as an idea or for use in their own pedagogic practice. A careful integration of theoretical content, in the form of conceptual knowledge, with a fit-for-purpose process of inquiry (framed as a bespoke methodology in style research, and acting as a vehicle for paradigm shift), is a positive step forward in realizing theoretical advancement of cognitive style theory.

The Assay of Theory in Practice for Researching in Style

Taking this previous argument a step further—the yield from a gold strike is worth what is finally decided on the scales in an assay office. It is also the point at which an analysis of the ore will confirm whether the substance is really gold. The danger is of course that a prospector has discovered iron pyrite or fool's gold. Research, similarly, must aim to produce new knowledge yet remain cautious about its claims for theory and the application of knowledge to the world of practice (Rayner, 2007c; Zhang & Sternberg, 2005). The nature of styles has been the subject of many such claims of a gold strike, asserting new academic and applied knowledge. The project of affirming styles as a core construct in the field of differential psychology, however, should not necessarily set out to adopt a specific paradigm or singly pursue a definitive perspective on style differences in human performance. It is, rather, a project that aspires to create a deliberative, collaborative, comprehensive, and inclusive approach to the production of new knowledge. The assay of research output in such a project should deal in specific principles or qualities as applied to methodology. We suggest the following four complementary approaches to assuring this rigor.

Recognizing a Good Style Theory: Reusing Traditional Recipes, Scripts, and Templates

The first approach is psychometric. Furnham (2001), adopting a psychometric method, makes a case for facilitating consensual theory by confirming:

terms for describing and analyzing teaching, teachers, and teacher education. They argue that

> Such a framework for teaching would require a careful parsing of the domain, an effort to identify the underlying grammar of practice, and the development of a common language for naming its constituent parts. (p. 186)

In this respect there may be many ways to reestablish theoretical coherence in a disciplinary domain or enable the reaffirmation of domain-general theory. The goal of an agreed-on conceptual language, understandings, rubric, and epistemology is one that needs to be shared by a majority of members making up the researcher community. A critical mass, in this instance, is crucial to success in managing a paradigm shift. A second example of this approach is found in Torraco's account of managed theory building as a distinctive research methodology in human resource development. Torraco (1997) identified the following benefits in such an approach:

- A basis for the concerted production of new knowledge;
- An approach for applying problem-posing and solving as key drivers in the research process;
- A solutions-focused strategy for both academic and applied research;
- A means for meta-analysis and an evaluation and affirming the conceptual basis of accumulated knowledge;
- An opportunity for agreement of a research agenda to identify important new issues and prescribe the most critical research questions that need to be answered to maximize understanding of the issue;
- A means of providing members of a professional discipline with a common language and a frame of reference for defining boundaries of their profession;
- A means to guide and inform research so that it can, in turn, guide development efforts and improve professional practice. (p. 117–119)

A methodology rubric might comprise such a series of questions—for example—helping researchers become aware of their beliefs about the nature of the living world (ontology), the way and form in which they explain this world (epistemology), and an integrated methodology (how they should consider a multidisciplinary approach to research). The benefits of

aware of how their own beliefs and theories of knowledge influence research practice. In a discussion about seeking a paradigm shift, Storberg-Walker (2006) concludes:

> I suggest that . . . thinking through paradigmatic differences is fine, but deeper probing into the connection between paradigm, knowledge creation and action illuminates the influence of ontological and epistemological perspectives on . . . practice. What is real (ontology) and how we know what is real (epistemology) influence our decisions on which paradigm to "use" to do the work. (p. 231)

There are many ways of prospecting for gold: panning is the least efficient but probably most satisfying and eco-friendly, sluicing more efficient but harmful to the environment, strip mining deeply disturbing, and use of dynamite rather explosive and final. The metaphor invokes the idea of alternative options for the researcher prospecting for style or any other construct, theory, or knowledge in social science. Traditional approaches favor a positivist paradigm; less traditional approaches may reflect a qualitative or mixed method paradigm. More recent developments might include a more extended method mix, for example, one or more of the following: a systems paradigm, an action-orientated paradigm, a critical theory paradigm, a participatory paradigm, and a pragmatic paradigm. What actually provides for consistency of purpose and theory in research design is not reliance on a single paradigm but the internal match and alignment between methodology and procedure or tools that comprise the method adopted. To achieve coherent and relevant theory means ensuring appropriate principles are embedded in a wider approach underpinning research practice. In other words, research design requires an epistemology that will articulate and enable a fit for purpose methodology. It is an approach that emphasizes purpose and relevance in research design and the careful calibration of methodology and method to serve the research intention (see Edmondson & McManus, 2007)

The idea here is not to create a prescriptive approach but to establish a comprehensive but focused *research rubric* that will allow researchers to reflect on the selected methodology for a research project, and to provide a basis for understanding and meaning required in new theory building. Again, a precedent exists, in Grossman and McDonald's (2008) recent description of a need for an interdisciplinary approach to teacher education research. Grossman and McDonald (2008) explain that the field of teacher education lacks a framework with well-defined common

Kozhevnikov's argument, and our own attempt at illustrating a structure portraying an individual's learning performance, both address the criticism expressed by Coffield et al. (2004a, 2004b), that the style domain has become entirely separated from mainstream psychology. In this way, the question of connectedness is therefore without doubt as much about knowledge integration within the wider domain of differential and mainstream psychology as it is equally about developing an integrative methodology for research in the related fields of style differences and learning theory.

Managing Paradigm Shift and Developing New Methodology for Researching Styles

Paradigm shift in the social sciences is generally acknowledged to be different from that experienced in the natural sciences, which is more usually described as a revolution, explosively overturning or transforming an established orthodoxy (Kuhn, 1962). Instead, a paradigm shift in social science has been described by Paul and Marfo (2001) as

> a valid challenge to the foundations of science, more like a shifting of tectonic plates of seismic proportions than a volcano. It is not about a counterforce; it is more about the collapse of the intellectual framework of empiricist science. The issue is the normative understandings that guide the work of social scientists. The "new science" is not an add-on but rather a change in the way we think about, conduct, share, and defend research. (p. 527)

While a paradigm shift in the social sciences may not be as disruptive as that experienced in the natural sciences, the shift is likely to be a messier process, often proving to be slow and imprecise. The influences of prevailing orthodoxies rarely completely disappear but are eventually encompassed within a modified epistemology. Nonetheless, if we are seeking a paradigm shift in our thinking about researching and theorizing cognitive styles, this process of change needs to be deliberately stimulated as a way of creating new knowledge. It will not happen spontaneously or necessarily result in an instant transformation of knowledge.

Knowledge Creation and Research Methodology: Epistemology and Ontology

Storberg-Walker argues that in attempting to generate a paradigm shift researchers need to consider not only how knowledge is created but be

individual difference variables (intelligence, personality, as well as other individual differences related to social psychology such as gender and ethnicity). Cognitive style is also located at this level, working as a mediating and interactive factor. Cognitive style is therefore construed as a dynamic construct. It is also to be found at level 2. It is construed as a factor that interacts with other variables such as cognitive abilities, skills, and routines. It also forms the basis for personal style differences in learning and other related aspects of human performance (for example, leadership, management, social behavior). Cognitive style as presented here as a factor is therefore perhaps covert, less fixed, but nonetheless stable and operates at both levels 3 and 2 of the performance structure.

The foundation level located at the base of this model represents the origin of cellular building blocks in personal psychology. It consists of two core states, namely cognition (e.g., knowledge storage, information processing, beliefs, understanding, and recall) and affect (perception, insight, intuition, and empathy). While each level has been labeled separately, the strands that are core states run through the structure to determine surface behavior like a running thread of affect and cognition. Finally, each of these levels forms a heuristic spinning plate, and this is a reminder that style researchers need to refer to the wholistic structure of personal psychology, with its theory of multiple constructs and interacting influences on an individual's performance. The structure of an individual's learning performance is in this way understood to represent a psychological system that entails a series of processes and interactions flowing toward and in response to a demand in any specific context. Cognitive style is located as an intervening variable at a midpoint in this system. It is conceptualized as a mediating factor shaping and regulating other variables that are deeper aspects of a personal psychology (other differential and foundational constructs forming the basis for actual behaviors observed in the actual world of human performance).

This model, we suggest, is in keeping with the ideas of Kozhevnikov (2007), who recently proposed that

> Integrating the concept of cognitive style into research on intelligence, personality, cognitive science, education, and neuroscience may enhance the development of each field. Further study of the nature and mechanisms of cognitive styles and an attempt to solve the methodological problems that have beleaguered the field to date seem to be real and necessary steps forward in understanding the dynamics of an individual's cognitive development in the context of personal abilities, needs, motives, and environmental requirements. (p. 478)

The Learning Event
Context + Instruction + Action

Surface Level (1) Learning Performance
Skills+ Attitudes+ Feelings+ Behaviour

Mediating Level (2) Self-Referencing System
Learning Styles+ Self-Regulated Learning+ Self-perception

Differential Level (3) Individual Differences
Personality+ Intelligence+ Gender + Ethnicity + Cognitive Style

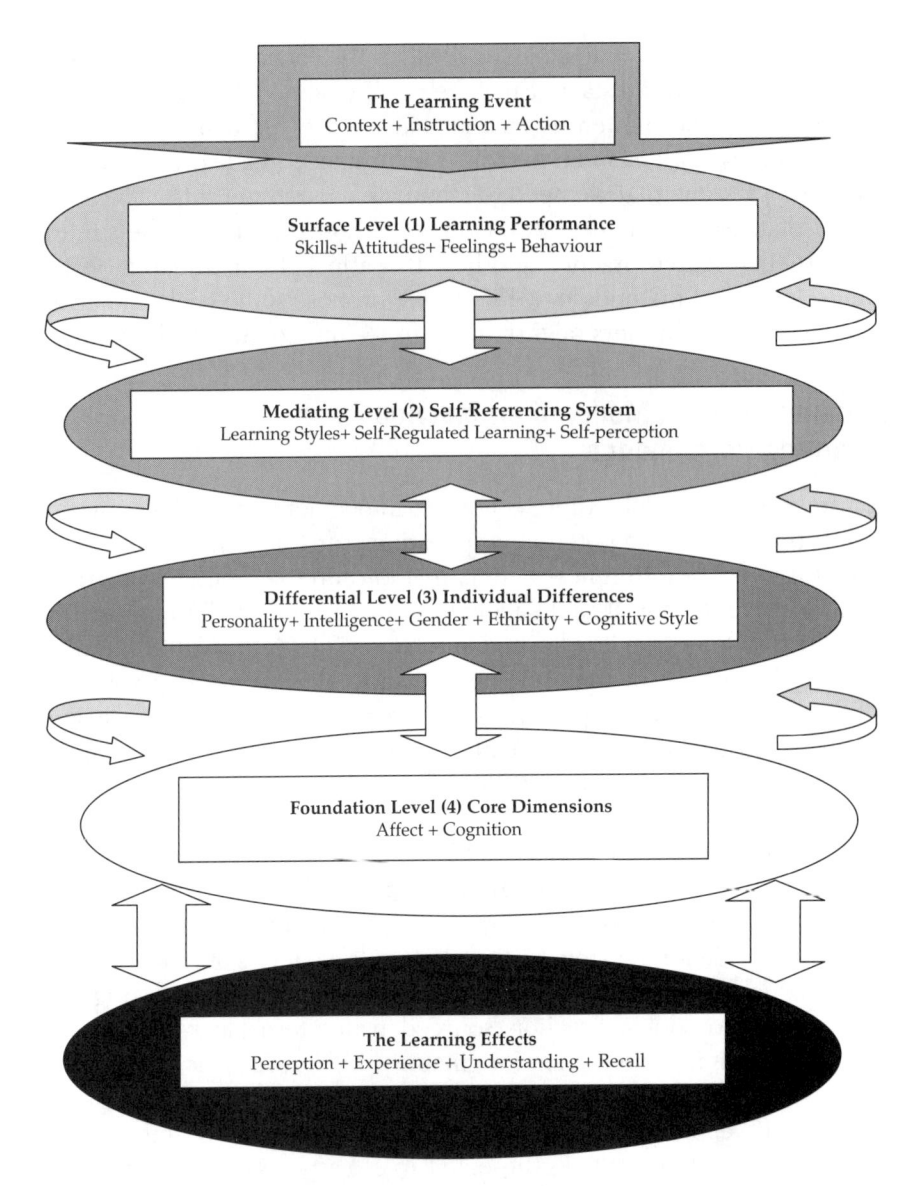

Foundation Level (4) Core Dimensions
Affect + Cognition

The Learning Effects
Perception + Experience + Understanding + Recall

Figure 5.1 An individual learning performance.

of performance. The mediating level (2) is what we define as an individual's personal learning style. This level includes aspects of a person's psychology that directly influence the way an individual approaches thinking and learning (cognitive style, motivation, and self-regulated learning). The deeper differential level (3) involves the functioning of more stable

new deposits of knowledge, having decided the conceptual terrain is still good for a worthwhile stake. First, we propose a model that might serve as a guide to the numerous factors that need to be considered when trying to fully understand a person's performance in a learning context. Second, we argue that we need to stimulate a paradigm shift. Third, we argue that researchers need to be aware of how their own beliefs influence their research practice and how this affects their research design and selection of methodology. Finally we propose some goals and criteria that style researchers might pursue in seeking to build style theory.

Defining Style: A Model of an Individual's Learning Performance

In prospecting for gold, there is need to know more about the nature of the substance and its potential applications (or for domain theory, the structure of style differences and its relationship to other key constructs in the domain), as well as its likely location in the broader context (for cognitive style, where it is located and how it integrates with the fundamental dimensions of cognition, affect, and behavior in the psychology of the learner). An attempt is made in Figure 5.1 to illustrate how cognitive style as an intervening variable in the psychology of the self might operate both as part of a person's self-referencing system (level 2) and as an individual difference (level 3) within the broader structure of the self-system (Rayner, 2000; Rayner, 2001b). The self-system in this model is therefore construed as a hierarchy comprising four interacting and dynamic levels of function. These are continuously and constantly interacting and provide for dynamic exchange at multiple levels of functioning as well as dual directional flow of information and sensory stimuli originating both in a top-down direction (sourced in an external learning context) as well as bottom-up direction (originating in learner's prior experience). The system in this way reflects a gestalt representing core aspects of differential psychology (for example, perception, personality, intelligence, abilities, motivation). It links these, in turn, to aspects of learning performance (behavior, understanding, attitudes, skills, and knowledge).

The surface level portraying an individual's behavior consists of the skills, attitudes, and knowledge that make up an individual's learning performance. This surface level is observable psychology. It is frequently a level of performance or behavior tested or assessed in educational settings. Other levels of functioning are not directly observable, but each contributes to and influences the behavior expressed at the surface level

management. The metaphoric mapping of a terrain related to the geography of knowledge is a powerful heuristic with which to chart and understand the purposes and actions of a community of researching practice (Armstrong & Rayner, 2002; Peterson, Rayner, & Armstrong, 2008; Rayner, 2007b). In a world of knowledge, paradigm, and perspective, the map is also a very useful tool for direction finding and navigating a pathway toward new knowledge creation. If we chart the present domain of differential psychology, it is a conceptual terrain that resembles a Diaspora rather than a single unified community. Lohman (2001) argues that what we have described here as a Diaspora of differential psychology is a divided domain too deeply entrenched in an extreme form of essentialist methodology. While the knowledge boundaries and borders of this domain shift over time, the present state of the field appears to be something like a worked-out gold field. There is therefore unsurprisingly an academic concern for its actual value, and particularly with respect to style, whether the field is worth any further prospecting. As Coffield et al. (2004a) commented:

> the complexity of the learning styles field and the lack of an overarching synthesis of the main models, or of dialogue between the leading proponents of individual models, lead to the impression of a research area that has become fragmented, isolated and ineffective. In the last 20 years, there has been only a single use of the term "learning styles" and three uses of the term "cognitive styles" in the *Annual Review of Psychology*. We have also noted that these terms are not included in the indexes in four widely used textbooks on cognitive and educational psychology. (p. 136)

This description of the field bears an uncanny resemblance to one of a worked-out knowledge Klondike. There is a need to re-map the ground, to stake out new areas of research and claims for establishing knowledge synthesis, and creation. Coffield et al. (2004a) reach a very negative conclusion with regard to this possibility. The challenge is like purposefully prospecting for deposits of new knowledge or gold as well as reworking older stakes in a difficult terrain. There is also undoubtedly a need to better navigate a way through the maze of old mine workings and knowledge stakes in the production of a new global research paradigm for style theory.

In the rest of this chapter, we will consider how a paradigm shift might be managed in order to generate new ways of prospecting for gold in the cognitive style field. We are, in other words, panning or digging for

continued to pursue the same questions, using the same methodology, perpetuating a theoretical tautology. What we argue is now needed is an extending base for pragmatic research methodology that will combine the nomothetic and ideographic dimensions identified by Allport (1981) in his call for establishing a morphogenic psychology. Nesselroade (2002), however, suggests an alternative but less radical perspective for psychologists committed to a positivist stance. He refers to a number of multivariate tools available for applying methods of statistical analysis to data that will better capture the process of change.

> Application of these very powerful tools extends the concept of structure to where it overarches patterns of change as well as the more traditional "stable" scores with which we are familiar. This, I believe is the multivariate experimental psychologist's key, at this point in our history, to coming to grips in a meaningful way with the concept of process. (p. 557)

Neither proposal, if considered as methodological revision, is an abandonment of an empirical approach. Indeed, traditional statistical techniques based on estimates of so-called true scores in multivariate experimental psychology (including use of tools such as canonical correlation, factor analysis, linear structural equation modeling) are extended. Nesselroade argues for these tools to be used in new ways for looking at old problems and as a consequence to greater effect. For example, he makes a case for not only measuring interindividual differences between groups or types of individual differences, but also intraindividual differences located at different periods of time with the same group. In this way, measuring rates of change requires a shift away from a focus only on structure to an equal or greater concern for complexity and measuring the dynamic of interaction, that is, process and change. Both researchers, finally, present a persuasive case for a scientific paradigm shift in research methodology.

A KNOWLEDGE DIASPORA: DOMAINS, DEFINITION, AND DIFFERENCE

An alternative but complementary approach to redeveloping research methodology and building domain-general theory in the field of cognitive style is to more directly adopt the perspective of knowledge

A Need for Reference to a Unified Structure in a Person's Psychological System

When focusing again on individual differences, we need to reintegrate cognitive style in the broader psychology of an individual as well as a learner's performance in a particular context. We believe that if researchers wish to advance a generalized style theory, they must reconnect working with theory to applied research methods and develop a greater understanding of how a cognitive style and styles interact with an individual's behavior. An early personality researcher, Gordon Allport (1981), advocated such an approach to the study of personality in a powerful review of the contemporary state of the field. Allport believed the ultimate role of psychology was to comprehend *"man's understanding of man"* (p. 63, emphasis added). He argued that

> the psychologist, as psychologist, can properly make two sorts of statement; he can say:
>
> ■ the problem of human personality concerns me deeply;
> ■ the problem of Bill's personality concerns me deeply.
>
> Although superficially similar the two statements are poles apart. In the second we are speaking of one and only one person; in the first we are extracting elusive properties from all of the three billion inhabitants of the Earth. Both statements are true: both appropriate; and both fall squarely in the domain of psychological science. (p. 63)

Allport concluded that an individual differences researcher should not only look at the generalized aspects of people's behavior (nomothetic approach) but also focus on the uniqueness of the individual (ideographic approach). Hence, arguably, an in-depth study of individuals will help researchers more generally understand people and deepen existing research predicated on larger-scale survey.

A Need for Research Theory Enabling an Integrated Concept of the Person

The lack of a unified or global theory for the psychology of the self has stifled knowledge building in the domain of differential psychology resulting in a paucity of innovatory or applied research. Consequently researchers, and particularly those concerned with cognitive style, have

politicized assertions and recriminations; it needs self-restraint, reflection, and a great deal more research. The questions that remain are socially as well as scientifically important. There is no reason to think them unanswerable, but finding the answers will require a shared and sustained effort as well as the commitment of substantial scientific resources. Just such a commitment is what we strongly recommend. (p. 97)

A more recent and equally relevant example of a successful researcher dialogue aimed at enabling a consensus of theory can be found in motivational psychology and the study of self-regulated learning (SRL). Zimmerman's account described how a community of researchers worked together to produce a new research rubric (methodology) and, as an outcome, built consistent and coherent new knowledge and applied theory (Zimmerman, 2008). The key to facilitating this kind of development is a readiness to review and revise fundamental methodologies or epistemology in a field of research. The inclusion of multiple perspectives or paradigms associated with both theoretical and applied research areas can help provide such an opportunity. To advance this kind of development in the field of styles research, we suggest that researchers meet the following needs.

A Need for a Paradigm Dialogue

We argue that a formal conversation or generalized discourse is necessary for any progression toward greater levels of consensual theory in an applied subject domain. An example of this type of conversation is nicely captured in the collection of essays described as a *paradigm dialogue* in the field of educational research in the United States (Guba, 1990). When applied to the domain of differential psychology, or perhaps more directly to style research, this endeavor is aimed at sustaining a deeper discourse and specifically includes reflective thinking as part of an actual *paradigm dialogue.* Another more specific example of this approach within the field was a conference organized in acknowledgement of the contribution of Spearman to differential psychology (Collis & Messick, 2001). Such academic dialogue, ideally, can help in reconnecting the *past* (theories of psychology) with the *present* (developing applied research methodologies and an understanding of style) and help move the field (community of researchers) to the *future* (new knowledge, theory, and informed application of style differences in human performance).

The report found that cognitive and learning styles was an area of knowledge characterized by incoherent theory and a research community demonstrating a questionable lack of integrity, frequently reinforced by messianic, commercialized, and largely unverifiable research polemic. Despite these criticisms and the publicity attached to this report in Europe, the concept of style has remained very popular among practitioners in both education and the workplace (Rayner, 2007a). It is often associated with an intuitive or tacit form of knowledge that makes common sense in the real world of human performance and so has an enduring appeal. However, a researcher visiting the subject of styles for the first time is faced with a bewildering mix of models, measures, and meaning. A Google search can return many thousands of hits, and more academic literature searches reveal a similar number of returns for the keywords, *cognitive styles* and *learning styles*. The recurring questions for both researchers and practitioners are typically what information and which knowledge or theory can be safely used when working with people? The field most certainly faces a challenge in providing a better fit with applied practice and a more clearly developed theory or explanation of the nature and phenomenon of style differences as they affect human performance. This cannot be realized without ensuring a domain theory is made more safe and secure. Drawing upon traditional research (experimental and psychometric), this must be joined by research that is applied and or contextualized in order that a method and output mediates between theory that is both domain-general and domain-specific.

Locating Cognitive Styles Within a Broader Psychological Theory

What is perhaps increasingly urgent, and we have made this point earlier, is the place for revision in the research methodology and epistemology of differential psychology. Indeed, there have been several recent examples of this kind of intervention taking place in the last decade. The American Psychological Association task force convened more than 12 years ago to review the contemporary state of knowledge surrounding the construct of intelligence (Neisser et al., 1996). This group stated

> In a field where so many issues are unresolved and so many questions unanswered, the confident tone that has characterized most of the debate on these topics is clearly out of place. The study of intelligence does not need

and practitioners in the style research field (Peterson, Rayner, & Armstrong, 2008). Zhang and Sternberg (2005) and Jones (1997) have also acknowledged this particular model working as a widely used stimulus for further developments in theorizing style and cognitive styles research.

These three attempts at theory building stand in stark contrast to a plethora of new tests of style emerging during the same period (see Messick, 1994, for an excellent summary of the cause and effects of this trend). It is important to note that all three attempts reflect a contemporary reliance on a traditional epistemology (a positivist paradigm located within classical psychology). This, in turn, has meant a continuing regard for traditional scientific principles such as validity and reliability in psychometric measurement and the identification of psychological variables or constructs correlated with observed behavior.

REAFFIRMING COGNITIVE STYLES AND MOVING TOWARD A GLOBAL THEORY?

Arguably, while these examples of theory building go some way to explain the concept of style and individual differences, none provide a full account of how styles fit within a coherent theory of differential and personal psychology. This lack of a global theory and failure on the part of researchers to situate cognitive styles within the wider areas of differential psychology, the psychology of the person or a social context, has been the subject of consistent and sometimes virulent criticism (see Reynolds, 1997; Ritter, 2007; Tiedemann, 1989). One recent and widely reported example of such research is a critical review of learning styles, commissioned by the Learning Skills Council, a body responsible for further and technical education in the United Kingdom. The review, carried out by Coffield et al. (2004a, 2004b), presented a very negative report on the field of style research. It was rejected as largely irrelevant to further education in the United Kingdom. Coffield (2005), reflecting on the outcomes of this review, stated that

> The field of learning styles suffers from almost fatal flaws of theoretical incoherence and conceptual confusion; for example, you can read about left-brainers versus right-brainers, pragmatists versus theorists, and globalists versus analysts. We collected 30 such pairings—the logo for the learning styles movement should be Dichotomies R Us. There is no agreed technical vocabulary and after 30 years of research, there is no consensus. (p. 19)

A second attempt at theory building was made by Sternberg (1997), stretching over a number of years with several different partners. Grigorenko and Sternberg (1995) identified three stages in the history of style differences, with each stage producing a wave of research and related theory. These were cognition-centered, personality-centered, and activity-centered theories of style. The cognition model was located in the domain of cognitive psychology and was closely related to the construct of ability. Influential models of style in this first wave included Witkin's (1962) theory of psychological differentiation (field-dependency) and Kagan's (1966) theory of reflection-impulsivity. The second wave involved a personality model linking the style construct to a study of individual differences such as personality, trait, and developmental psychology. Examples of influential models in this tradition were identified as the Myers-Briggs Type Indicator (MBTI; Myers & McCaulley, 1988) and Gregorc's Cognitive Style Indicator (Gregorc, 1982). Finally, the third stage saw the emergence of an activity model of style, focused on learning process. Work in this area assessed differences in orientations to study (Biggs, 1993; Entwistle & Tait, 1996; Vermunt, 1996). Building both on this review and other work, Sternberg (1988, 1997), using an extended metaphor of government, developed a comprehensive model of thinking styles. According to this theory, people exercise their thinking in terms of mental government, that is, by managing processes of function, form, level, scope, and learning. Zhang and Sternberg (2005, p. 10) summarize and provide an account of subsequent quasi-experimental research validating this theory comprising 13 thinking styles falling along five dimensions of mental self-government.

A third attempt at integrative theory building was made by Riding and colleagues over a 30-year period (see Riding & Cheema, 1991; Riding & Rayner, 1998). This work drew a distinction between the formation of skills and strategies (cognitive and learning) and personal style (cognitive). Rayner and Riding (1997) argued that many labels or models called learning styles actually described learning processes (orientations to study, preferences for environmental conditions, and learning strategies). This was linked to Riding's earlier work in the assessment of cognitive styles. Riding (1991) developed a model that posited two fundamental dimensions in the structure of an individual's cognitive style (wholistic-analytic and verbal-imagery). A theory of cognitive style and learning strategies was subsequently elaborated (see Riding & Rayner, 1998). This latter publication was recently identified as the most used by researchers of cognitive style in an international e-survey of researchers

This kind of separation or theory drift is particularly evident in the way in which several constructs associated with individual differences and differential psychology (for example, intelligence, personality, and style), have been the focus of rejection in the applied world of instruction and education (see Furnham, 2001; Neisser et al., 1996; Ritter, 2007).

We suggest that this state of the science points to a need for re-interrogating the psychology of individual differences, and reaffirming key concepts and constructs while developing new forms of knowledge. The challenge is to enable a reconnection between theory building and applied practice in research methodology. This is work that we argue will help pave the way toward a revaluing of differential psychology as a continuing, relevant, and valuable source of knowledge in the educational setting and workplace. It is also a necessary stage in prospecting for new knowledge and will be integral to reaffirming a theory of individual differences (and in particular style differences) as it is applied to human performance. As part of this revision, new forms of applied perspective and related methodology should also be considered and used in the development of style research. This approach in turn, we argue, can help redevelop a robust epistemology in the field of style differences in human performance.

Building Theory and Models of Cognitive Style

There have arguably been three significant attempts at building an integrative theory in the field of style research over the past 50 years. Each has tried to move the field forward by developing a more coherent account of the nature of style differences in cognition and learning. The first was made by Curry (1987), in a timely and extremely useful effort at reorganizing measures of cognitive and learning styles into a methodological heuristic she dubbed the "style onion." Curry, using this heuristic, inferred a basic psychological structure for style. The onion portrayed a hierarchy comprising several levels of psychological functioning. At its center, a more stable and traitlike core existed, graduating toward increasing instability as functions were located in areas nearer the surface skin of the onion. Curry argued that these outer style mechanisms were increasingly sensitive to environment and experience. In this way, the style onion models an internal to external leveling of cognition or affect (and by association, effect). Further, the model enabled psychologists to construe a relationship between style and other structures (e.g., personality, intelligence) that make up an individual's personal psychology.

This perspective of individual differences largely reflects a positivist epistemology and a classical form of empiricism. Consequently, the epistemology of differential psychology and its research methodology has been reliant upon psychometric testing, with statistical controls or techniques applied to data generated from groups of people. An excellent example is found in the early work of Thurstone (1944), who identified stylistic factors across individual perceptual performance. Indeed, Messick (1994, p. 126) described this research as the first succinct working formulation of the *cognitive-style thesis* in the field of differential psychology. This *differential* tradition of focusing on the process and structure of cognition is deeply embedded in style research (see Witkin, 1962).

A Shift in Thinking About Individual Differences

Nesselroade (2002) has dramatically suggested that differential psychology is bordering on a *mid-life crisis* due to a growing dissatisfaction with its theory and the threat of competing newer theories and methodologies. He argued that this change in the intellectual status of the field has largely been the result of methodological shifts in the wider community of social science research and a growing need to demonstrate its relevance to an applied context. This trend reflects a questioning of orthodoxy that is largely reliant on the experimental method and continuing psychometric practices (Delanty, 1997; Johnson & Duberley, 2000; Scott, 2000).

Alternative ways of conceptualizing research knowledge and methodology have been appraised by several writers interested in the relationship between the applied context and domain-focused knowledge creation (e.g., Hammersley, 2002; Petit & Huault, 2008; Thomas, 2007). A similar critique is directly applied to educational psychology by Sternberg (2008), who reverses the emphasis on applied research to argue that it has resulted in a fracturing of the relationship between theory and practice. He proposed that within educational psychology there is an urgent necessity to regenerate the theory of psychology in the actual world of education. This reflects two fundamental approaches to the application of psychology in education: the first is *domain general;* the second is *domain-specific.* Sternberg (2008) insists

> One of the greatest challenges facing modern research in learning and instruction is devising and then empirically testing domain-general theories. (p. 150)

THE PSYCHOLOGY OF INDIVIDUAL DIFFERENCES

A theory of individual differences, drawing on differential psychology, has been an important source of knowledge for educators interested in how the learner learns for more than a century. This domain of psychology has also held a long-standing but also controversial role in educational policy and related practices associated with the learner, assessment, and learning design. For example, Deary (2000) describes how Alfred Binet devised the first intelligence tests with the intention of helping to distinguish between children who were mentally subnormal and those who were capable of learning with extra help. Others subsequently suggested the use of intelligence tests for less philanthropic purposes as a way of weeding out so-called morons (Goddard, 1914). A second example of this continuing controversy, involving Cyril Burt, a leading educational psychologist in Great Britain (Hearnshaw, 1979; Scarr, 1994), is a story of alleged scientific malpractice. Burt stands accused of fictionalizing assessment data and faces censure for using controversial intelligence testing to legitimize systematic differentiation in the postwar British educational system. The controversy perfectly reflects a problematic application of the theory but also an insecure conceptual base within the subject domain.

The domain of differential psychology is described by Anastasia (2007) as the study of individual differences in behavior phenomena and social groupings of people. Differential psychologists are identified as researchers who typically focus on individuals, while studying groups, by identifying and isolating psychological dimensions or variables shared by all individuals (e.g., sociability) but upon which individuals differ (e.g., some people are shy, others are gregarious). The methods of differential psychology are associated with classical experimental psychology (Cattell, 1966; Cronbach, 1957). The approach also reflects a preoccupation with *structural* aspects of behavior, rather than the *process* in which that behavior manifests itself. As Nesselroade (2002) explains, differential psychology is about a concern for the following *differences* associated with the individual:

(a) comparisons among kinds of entities (e.g., qualitative differences);

(b) comparisons among entities of the same kind (inter-individual differences); and

(c) comparisons within the same entity over different occasions (intra-individual differences). (p. 544)

multiplex comprising many styles (usually defined as a series of processes or types of metacognitive strategies or skills of thinking). Consequently, a research focus and theoretical perspective slips from a core definition of style to one of styles, and in a reciprocal way, to process from structure and then often back again. The same theoretical slippage occurs in relation to other constructs used in education and psychology, for example, with a construct such as self-concept. Self-concept was originally construed as a unitary structure (Burns, 1979; Byrne, 1996), but has more recently been described as an open system of self-perception comprising a collection of dynamic self-percepts that together make up the self-referencing system (Marsh, Byrne, & Shavelson, 1988; Oosterwegel & Oppenheimer, 1993). Like the style construct, the unitary construct of self-concept has been replaced by models theorizing multiple constituents and processes operating in a more open structure. The different ways of conceptualizing these constructs is potentially confusing and often contradictory.

The chapter explores this controversy and a conceptual instability in style theory. At the broadest level, we question how style is investigated within the field of psychology and whether style research should be reconceptualized. We argue that a traditional individual differences approach to studying styles (which is positivist and generally psychometric) should be deliberately extended and its methodology made more pragmatic, inclusive, and dynamic. One way to do this is to directly focus on research methodology and theory building as knowledge management. As part of this consideration, and following Messick (1994), a first step in such a process is identified as paradigm shift. This will require a shared approach among researchers in rebuilding what Sternberg (2008) calls a "domain-general theory."

We suggest that cognitive style should be reexamined as a unified but not necessarily unitary construct. In other words, cognitive style should be viewed as a complex, dynamic structure defined as an integral part of a person's psychological system. Cognitive styles, therefore, describing individual differences in processes and strategies, should be more carefully and distinctively defined within this superordinate style construct as part of broader psychology of the self. An analogy we might use is to make the comparison between hardware and software found in the computer (see Riding & Rayner, 1998), albeit the reality is that an interaction between both style and styles is more dynamic and the structural interrelationship yet more complex.

5

Reaffirming Style as an Individual Difference: Toward a Global Paradigm or Knowledge Diaspora?

STEVE RAYNER AND ELIZABETH R. PETERSON

The study of style differences in human psychology is regarded by many academics as light-weight, problematic or even flawed (e.g., Coffield, 2005; Coffield, Moseley, Hall, & Ecclestone, 2004a; 2004b; Tiedemann, 1989). Its history, reflecting a huge growth in international research stretching over nearly a century, is a story of continuing difficulty in applying psychological theory. Cognitive style and learning styles, nonetheless, remain recognized topics in the study of individual differences and differential psychology (Curry, 1987; Messick, 1994; Rayner, 2001b; Riding & Rayner, 1998; Sternberg, 1997; Witkin, 1962). In this chapter, we focus on cognitive style. We define cognitive style as relatively stable individual differences in human psychology that are integrally linked to a person's cognitive system, influencing the way that person processes (perceives, organizes, and analyzes) information. We also propose a conceptual structure for the interrelationship between an individual's cognitive style and aspects of human performance, specifically learning.

The difficulty with a theory of cognitive style for a novice researcher begins almost immediately with a confusion of definition and terminology. This reflects a history of casual use of key terms or constructs such as "cognitive style," "cognitive styles," "learning style," and "learning styles." For example, the construct cognitive style is conceptualized by some researchers as a superordinate structure but by others as a

Grigorenko, & J. L. Singer (Eds.), *Creativity: From potential to realization* (pp. 153–167). Washington, DC: American Psychological Association.

Rawlings, D., & Locarnini, A. (2007). Validating the Creativity Scale for Diverse Domains using group of artists and scientists. *Empirical Studies of the Arts, 25,* 163–172.

Rowe, P. (1997, January). The science of self-report. *APS Observer, 10,* 35–38.

Rudowicz, E., & Hui, A. (1997). The creative personality: Hong Kong perspective. *Journal of Social Behavior and Personality, 12,* 139–157.

Rudowicz, E., & Yue, X. (2000). Concepts of creativity: Similarities and differences among Mainland, Hong Kong, and Taiwan Chinese. *Journal of Creative Behavior, 34,* 175–192.

Ruscio, J., Whitney, D. M., & Amabile, T. M. (1998). Looking inside the fishbowl of creativity: Verbal and behavioral predictors of creative performance. *Creativity Research Journal, 11,* 243–263.

Sternberg, R. J. (1985). Implicit theories of intelligence, creativity, and wisdom. *Journal of Personality and Social Psychology, 49,* 607–627.

Sternberg, R. J. (1988). A three-facet model of creativity. In R. J. Sternberg (Ed.), *The nature of creativity* (pp. 125–147). New York: Cambridge University Press.

Sternberg, R. J. (1997). *Thinking styles.* New York: Cambridge University Press.

Sternberg, R. J., Grigorenko, E. L., & Singer, J. L. (2004). *Creativity: From potential to realization.* Washington, DC: American Psychological Association.

Sternberg, R. J., & Lubart, T. I. (1995). *Defying the crowd.* New York: Free Press.

Sternberg, R. J., & Lubart, T. I. (1996). Investing in creativity. *American Psychologist, 51,* 677–688.

Torrance, E. P. (1974). *Torrance Tests of Creative Thinking: Directions manual and scoring guide. Verbal test booklet A.* Bensenville, IL: Scholastic Testing Service.

Witkin, H. A., & Goodenough, D. R. (1981). *Cognitive styles: Essence and origins, field dependence and field independence.* New York: International University Press.

Zhang, L. F., & Huang, J. (2001). Thinking styles and the five-factor model of personality. *European Journal of Personality, 15,* 465–476.

Zhang, L. F., & Sternberg, R. J. (2006). *The nature of intellectual styles.* Mahwah, NJ: Lawrence Erlbaum.

Grigorenko, E. L., & Sternberg, R. J. (1995). Thinking styles. In D. Saklofske & M. Zeidner (Eds.), *International handbook of personality and intelligence* (pp. 205–230). New York: Plenum Press.

Guilford, J. P. (1967). *The nature of human intelligence.* New York: McGraw-Hill.

Guilford, J. P. (1988). Some changes in the structure-of-intellect model. *Educational and Psychological Measurement, 48,* 1–4.

Hocevar, D. (1981). Measurement of creativity: Review and critique. *Journal of Personality Assessment, 45,* 450–464.

Holland, J. L. (1997). *Making vocational choices: A theory of vocational personalities and work environments* (3rd ed.). Odessa, FL: Psychological Assessment Resources.

Ivcevic, Z., & Mayer, J. D. (2007). Creative types and personality. *Imagination, Cognition, and Personality, 26,* 65–86.

Ivcevic, Z., & Mayer, J. D. (in press). Mapping dimensions of creativity. *Creativity Research Journal.*

Kaufman, J. C. (2002). Narrative and paradigmatic thinking styles in creative writing and journalism students. *Journal of Creative Behavior, 36,* 201–220.

Kaufman, J. C. (2003). The cost of the muse: Poets die young. *Death Studies, 27,* 813–822.

Kaufman, J. C. (2006). Self-reported differences in creativity by ethnicity and gender. *Applied Cognitive Psychology, 20,* 1065–1082.

Kaufman, J. C., & Baer, J. (2004). The amusement park theoretical (APT) model of creativity. *Korean Journal of Thinking and Problem Solving, 14,* 15–25.

Kaufman, J. C., & Baer, J. (Eds.). (2005). *Creativity across domains: Faces of the muse.* Hillsdale, NJ: Lawrence Erlbaum Associates.

Kaufman, J. C., & Baer, J. (2006). Intelligent testing with Torrance. *Creativity Research Journal, 18,* 99–102.

Kaufman, J. C., Cole, J. C., & Baer, J. (in press). The construct of creativity: Structural model for self-reported creativity ratings. *Journal of Creative Behavior.*

Kaufman, J. C., Evans, K. L., & Baer, J. (in press). The American Idol effect: Are students good judges of their creativity across domains? *Empirical Studies of the Arts.*

Kaufman, J. C., Plucker, J. A., & Baer, J. (2008). *Essentials of creativity assessment.* New York: Wiley.

Miller, A. L. (2007). Creativity and cognitive style: The relationship between field dependence-independence, expected evaluation, and creative performance. *Psychology of Aesthetics, Creativity, and the Arts, 1,* 243–246.

O'Hara, L. A., & Sternberg, R. J. (2001). It doesn't hurt to ask: Effects of instructions to be creative, practical, or analytical on essay-writing performance and their interaction with students' thinking styles. *Creativity Research Journal, 13,* 197–210.

Oral, G., Kaufman, J. C., & Agars, M. D. (2007). Examining creativity in Turkey: Do Western findings apply? *High Ability Studies, 18,* 235–246.

Park, S.-K., Park, K-H., & Choe, H-S. (2005). The relationship between thinking styles and scientific giftedness in Korea. *Journal of Secondary Gifted Education, 16,* 87–97.

Paulos, J. A. (1988). *Innumeracy: Mathematical illiteracy and its consequences.* New York: Vintage Books.

Plucker, J. A., & Beghetto, R. A. (2004). Why creativity is domain general, why it looks domain specific, and why the distinction does not matter. In R. J. Sternberg, E. L.

REFERENCES

Amabile, T. M. (1996). *Creativity in context: Update to the social psychology of creativity*. Boulder, CO: Westview.

Anderson, J. A., & Adams, M. (1992). Acknowledging the learning styles of diverse student populations: Implications for instructional design. *New Directions for Teaching and Learning, 49*, 19–33.

Azar, B. (1997). Poor recall Mars research and treatment. *APA Monitor, 28*, 1, 29.

Baer, J. (1993). *Creativity and divergent thinking: A task-specific approach*. Hillsdale, NJ: Lawrence Erlbaum Associates.

Baer, J. (1996). The effects of task-specific divergent-thinking training. *Journal of Creative Behavior, 30*, 183–187.

Baer, J., & Kaufman, J. C. (2005). Bridging generality and specificity: The Amusement Park Theoretical (APT) model of creativity. *Roeper Review, 27*, 158–163.

Beghetto, R. A., & Kaufman, J. C. (2007). Toward a broader conception of creativity: A case for "mini-c" creativity. *Psychology of Aesthetics, Creativity, and the Arts, 1*, 13–79.

Brophy, D. R. (2001). Comparing the attributes, activities, and performance of divergent, convergent, and combination thinkers. *Creativity Research Journal, 13*, 439–455.

Brown, R. T. (1989). Creativity: What are we to measure? In J. A. Glover, R. R. Ronning, & C. R. Reynolds (Eds.), *Handbook of creativity* (pp. 3–32). New York: Plenum.

Bruner, J. (1986). *Actual minds, possible worlds*. Cambridge, MA: Harvard University Press.

Carson, S., Peterson, J. B., & Higgins, D. M. (2005). Reliability, validity and factor structure of the creative achievement questionnaire. *Creativity Research Journal, 17*, 37–50.

Feist, G. J. (1998). A meta-analysis of personality in scientific and artistic creativity. *Personality and Social Psychology Review, 2*, 290–309.

Feist, G. J. (1999). The influence of personality on artistic and scientific creativity. In R. J. Sternberg (Ed.), *Handbook of human creativity* (pp. 273–296). New York: Cambridge University Press.

Feist, G. J. (2004). The evolved fluid specificity of human creative talent. In R. J. Sternberg, E. L. Grigorenko, & J. L. Singer (Eds.), *Creativity: From potential to realization* (pp. 57–82). Washington, DC: American Psychological Association.

Gallagher, A. M., De Lisi, R., Holst, P. C., McGillicuddy-De Lisi, A. V., Morely, M., & Cahalan, C. (2000). Gender differences in advanced mathematical problem solving. *Journal of Experimental Child Psychology, 75*, 165–190.

Gallagher, A. M., Levin, J., & Cahalan, C. (2002). *Cognitive patterns of gender differences on mathematics admissions tests* (GRE Board Research Rep. 96–17). Princeton, NJ: Educational Testing Service.

Gardner, H. (1993). *Creating minds: An anatomy of creativity seen through the lives of Freud, Einstein, Picasso, Stravinsky, Eliot, Graham, and Gandhi*. New York: Basic Books.

Gardner, H. (1999). *Intelligence reframed: Multiple intelligences for the 21st century*. New York: Basic Books.

Gridley, M. C. (2006). Preferred thinking styles of professional fine artists. *Creativity Research Journal, 18*, 247–248.

is likely that for many people such openness to experience is limited to one or two general thematic areas, or possibly limited to a single domain. For example, a musician might be open to many kinds of experiences related to sound but not be open to new experiences related to mathematical ideas or to ideas related to being an entrepreneur. And in fact this hypothetical domain-based difference in the importance of openness to experience has been demonstrated empirically in Feist's (1998) meta-analysis, in which he found that while openness to experience may be of only minor importance for mathematicians, it is crucially important for artists.

Another example of ways that levels of domain specificity might affect the relationship between creativity and intellectual styles can be seen in Kaufman's (2002) study of narrative and paradigmatic thinking in journalists and creative writers. One of his findings was that creative writers used more narrative thought than journalists. In addition, journalists tend to be more executive and less legislative in their thinking than poets. These are examples of ways that thinking styles can affect creativity differently in different domains—even in domains that are part of the same general thematic area. This parallels Baer's (1993, 1996) research, which has shown that somewhat different skills affect creativity in writing poetry and writing short fiction. It is also possible that a person might switch thinking styles for different kinds of tasks, just as people use different skills and knowledge bases for different purposes.

We have provided some examples of ways that different thinking styles might fit different levels of the APT hierarchy (and ways they might vary from area to area or domain to domain), but as yet there is no comprehensive theory of thinking styles that includes this level of specificity. Whether it uses the APT model or some other hierarchical model that integrates domain-general and domain-specific components of creativity, we believe that a complete understanding of how thinking styles influence creativity will need to include such a hierarchical, multilevel analysis. When pondering the question of how intellectual styles affect creativity, it may be best to first consider what level of creativity you wish to focus on.

ACKNOWLEDGMENT

The authors would like to thank Candice D. Davis for her helpful suggestions and assistance on an earlier draft of this chapter.

What can the APT model offer researchers and theorists who are trying to understand how intellectual styles influence creativity? Broadly speaking, the APT model argues for a multilevel conception of creativity, in which some components (initial requirements) speak to all types of creativity and other components (microdomains) refer to a very specific type of creativity. One way of considering intellectual styles' relationship to creativity is that it varies as the type of creativity varies. At broader levels, for example, Zhang and Sternberg's (2006) Type I style would likely be related to most types of creativity. At more specific levels, particular facets may be more important. Both judicial and legislative thought are part of Type I thinking, yet judicial thought would likely be associated with creativity in the law or English literature. Legislative thought might be related to poetry or theoretical physics, in which a strong desire to break new ground is more important.

Looking at the many factors that affect creativity, one can include a variety of skills, aptitudes, traits, knowledge bases, preferences, propensities, and motivations. None of these is a simple or single-dimensional attribute. As discussed previously, each of these might influence creativity at the most all-encompassing initial requirements level, or at the lower levels of general thematic area, domain, or microdomain. We mentioned, for example, that motivation can be very general—one can simply be motivated to do *something* creative—and such a general drive to create might facilitate creativity in many endeavors. But one might lack such a general all-purpose motivation to create and nonetheless find the math/science general thematic area of special interest and be motivated to do something in just that area. Or perhaps one's motivation is even more specific; it might extend only to doing work in the area of cosmology or (more specific still) be pretty much limited to an interest in galaxy formation. All of these are motivations that can be expected to influence creativity, but each works at a different level of specificity.

Intellectual styles must work in the same multilevel fashion. For example, we noted that Zhang and Huang (2001) had discovered a relationship between the personality factor openness to experience, an aspect of personality that many researchers have argued promotes creativity (e.g., Feist, 1998, 1999), and a particular blend of thinking styles (where openness to experience was positively associated with legislative, judicial, liberal, and external styles, and negatively associated with conservative styles). It is possible that some people may be open to new experiences across the board—at the most general, initial requirement level—but it

amusement parks based only on how good the popcorn is at the food court. Someone else may only go to cheap amusement parks (Big Nate's Generic Roadside Attraction). In a similar way, microdomains or domains may be selected for reasons that are less obvious. Dave may be a multitalented renaissance man, but he may be motivated to do things that will impress Aviva—and *only* do things that will impress Aviva. So Dave may learn how to be a creative filmmaker and make movies about how great Aviva is, and he may become a creative architect and build a monument to her beauty, or he may become a creative botanist and discover a new breed of rose that he calls the Aviva rose. Yet if you only looked at the microdomains that Dave pursued, the resulting data would be incoherent (unless, of course, Aviva had a whole host of similarly single-minded suitors).

ADVANTAGES OF THIS TYPE OF MODEL AND ITS RELEVANCE TO INTELLECTUAL STYLE RESEARCH AND THEORY

We are not arguing that the APT model is the only or best such model that integrates domain-specific and domain-general perspectives—indeed, the hybrid model discussed earlier does a great job as well (Plucker & Beghetto, 2004). There may be future models that integrate the domain-general and domain-specific viewpoints even more effectively than the APT model described here. The question of creative domains needs to be addressed, however, in any major conceptualization or assessment. Older assessments, such as the divergent thinking tests, tend to assume that creativity is domain general (such as the Torrance Tests for Creative Thinking; Torrance, 1974). There is a preponderance of evidence for some amount of domain specificity in creativity (Kaufman & Baer, 2005; Sternberg, Grigorenko, & Singer, 2004). Few researchers, even those who may lean toward the general side of the spectrum, would agree with the completely domain-general stance of divergent thinking tests. We believe that divergent-thinking tests' reliance on this singular concept is one reason that other creativity assessments have gained favor over the past decade. As Feist (2004) argued, the notion of complete domain generality "is a rather naïve and ultimately false position and that creative talent is in fact domain specific . . . There are some generalized mental strategies and heuristics that do cut across domains, but creativity and talent are usually not among the domain-general skills" (p. 57).

to know, and what one needs to know how to do, in order to be creative when undertaking different tasks in that domain. It's rather like the transition from undergraduate to graduate education. As an example, everyone in a graduate program in psychology may be preparing for a career as a psychologist, but future clinical psychologists, social psychologists, and cognitive psychologists likely take few of the same courses. Similarly, studying fruit flies intensively for 5 years may help one develop creative theories in one of biology's microdomains but be of little use in another, and practicing on a 12-string guitar may help one perform creatively in some microdomains of the music world but not others.

It is at this lowest level that the smallest differences in intellectual styles would be seen. Poets may differ from journalists in intellectual styles, but differences between different types of poets would be minimal. One could predict that Type II thinkers would be more likely to follow conventional rules of poetry and that Type I thinkers would be more likely to write thoughtful, emotional poetry, but such discussion is for now still just conjecture.

Strange Bedfellows

No theory can explain everything, and there are still a lot of weird connections that go on. On one hand, the nested hierarchy of microdomains grouped within domains grouped within general thematic areas feels nice and tidy. On the other hand, there are all sorts of things that are left unexplained. Just as there are important similarities among the differently themed roller coasters located in different theme parks, there may occasionally be connections among domains and microdomains in different general thematic areas that will surprise us. In studies with elementary and middle school children, for example, Baer (1993) found relatively small and generally statistically nonsignificant correlations among the creativity ratings given to different kinds of creative products (including poems, collages, mathematical word problems, equations, and stories), but there was a surprisingly consistent (but as yet unexplained) correlation between creativity in writing poetry and creativity in producing interesting mathematical word problems. These two tasks would seem to be comparatively unrelated—they come from different general thematic areas—yet there appears to be some kind of link somewhere.

In addition, there will also always be strange bedfellows that make sense only upon closer examination. Someone may decide to pick their

bases that are foundational for work in the social sciences, such as the differences between psychology and political science. This is also true of some skills needed for creative performance in different domains. Although in a general thematic area there will be many skills shared across all domains in that area, there are also some more domain-specific skills of importance only in some domains and not others, even within the same general thematic area. In the artistic-verbal domain, for example, many of the skills underlying creative performance in writing poetry appear to be quite different from the skills needed to write creative short stories (Baer, 1993, 1996). This trend is also present at the mini-c level of creativity, defined by Beghetto and Kaufman (2007) as the novel and personally meaningful interpretation of experiences, actions, and events.

Some personality traits may also be particularly useful in some domains. For example, being conscientious may be vitally important for scientists. However, it may be of little importance (or possibly even harmful) for those in other fields (such as, perhaps, artists). Similarly, some traits may prove to be related to creative performance in one domain in only a minor way, but at the same time be overwhelmingly important in another (i.e., although openness to experience is of some importance for mathematicians, it is *essential* for artists; see Feist, 1998). Environment and opportunity are also components here. As an example, some creative acts require a particular *kind* of nurturing background. A child who wants to play the violin (or take up horseback riding) may be out of luck if his or her family cannot afford lessons. If that child's sibling has an interest in poetry—which requires less of a financial investment to get started—then poverty may be less of an obstacle for him or her. And if one is working for Exxon, the working environment may be more conducive to creativity in the domain of geology than in the domain of pure math.

APT: Microdomains

Imagine that you have gone to a zoo, such as the world-famous Wild Animal Park. All the activities at the Wild Animal Park involve animals, but they still vary greatly. Maybe you want to spend time feeding leaves to long-necked giraffes. Maybe you want to look at the lions stretching and majestically sunning themselves. Or else you might not feel like walking around, so you take the monorail and see the animal preserve from the comfort of a slow-moving train.

Similarly, there are many commonalities among all the tasks that are part of a domain. Yet there are still big differences in what one needs

be many similarities between the two writers. Both will have strong verbal abilities and a love (or at least tolerance) of the written word.

Despite their similarities, creative writers and journalists work often under radically different conditions and with varying expectations—a top-notch journalist may have to crank out a piece in 10 minutes to make a deadline, whereas an equally respected novelist may be allowed 10 years to perfect a book. Creative writers such as novelists, poets, and, to a lesser extent, playwrights may be introverted or avoid social encounters; their success or failure depends on a product that may be created with little outside input. Journalists, in contrast, must thrive on such interactions, as much of their work typically involves gathering information and opinions from other people.

Indeed, journalists and poets show many individual differences. For example, journalists and other nonfiction writers outlive poets by approximately six years, although this is only true at the most eminent level (Kaufman, 2003). Many other differences are less readily apparent—journalists have been found to have different thinking styles than poets (Kaufman, 2002). In addition, as discussed, to journalists showing a more executive thinking style and creative writers showing a more legislative thinking style, there was also a difference on Bruner's theoretical distinctions. Creative writers scored significantly higher than journalists on narrative thought, but an interaction occurred on paradigmatic thought. Male journalists significantly outscored male creative writers, but a nonsignificant trend in the opposite direction was observed for females; these results stayed significant when personality and motivation factors were controlled. One reason for this interaction may be that women tend to not use visual-spatial solutions when confronted with problems they have not seen before (Gallagher et al., 2000; Gallagher, Levin, & Cahalan, 2002). One possibility is that they inherently use verbal solutions, meaning that female journalists and female creative writers would not necessarily treat the task differently.

If journalists and creative writers show such domain-based differences, one can only imagine that more distinct domains (such as chemistry and humor) would show even larger differences in thinking styles and other areas. In addition to thinking styles, knowledge plays a large role at the domain level. Let's explore domains that fall under the math/science area. Chemistry, physics, biology, and geology may all fall under the same area and may all involve a certain type of analytic and precise thought. However, the knowledge bases for these four natural-science subjects are strikingly different, with only modest overlap, as are the knowledge

flate or distort their responses, and especially no motivation to favor one kind of creativity over another.

Regardless of what the general thematic areas actually are, what do they mean for the APT model? Let's assume that you have enough brains and motivation and are in a suitable environment. The general thematic areas are the next step. Regardless of the number of general thematic areas of creativity, each of them requires different skills and traits, and likely different thinking styles. For example, there might be a certain profile of abilities and preferences that you might associate with someone interested in the musical/performance general thematic area. Some might be abilities (such as a sense of pitch), some might be more personality related (probably more extraverted, since it's hard to perform with stage fright), and some might relate more closely to thinking styles (perhaps evidencing a more legislative bent, although performance-oriented musicians might have a more executive style—but this is all speculative, awaiting future research results for confirmation). Someone more inclined to be creative in the mathematical/scientific general thematic area might have a completely different profile. We're still working on finding these patterns. But our theory doesn't end here.

APT: Domains

We've now spent considerable time discussing how many general thematic areas there are, but this question is only one piece of the puzzle. Indeed, once you have decided on a type of amusement park to visit, there are still many more decisions left. Even within one genre, there are many different parks to choose from. If you want roller coasters, do you choose Six Flags or Disneyland? If you've decided on an animal theme, do you pick the San Diego Zoo, Sea World, or the Wild Animal Park?

Similarly, within each of the general thematic areas are several more narrowly defined creativity domains. For example, the artistic-visual general thematic area might include such domains as drawing, painting, woodworking, pottery, sewing, scrapbooking, making collages, and many other things. And each of these domains may have a unique profile of related strengths and weaknesses, of skills and important knowledge bases, and of best-suited thinking styles and work preferences.

Let's compare, for example, a creative poet and a creative journalist. Both would fall in the general thematic area of artistic-verbal (or, following Feist or Gardner, linguistics or language). Indeed, there will likely

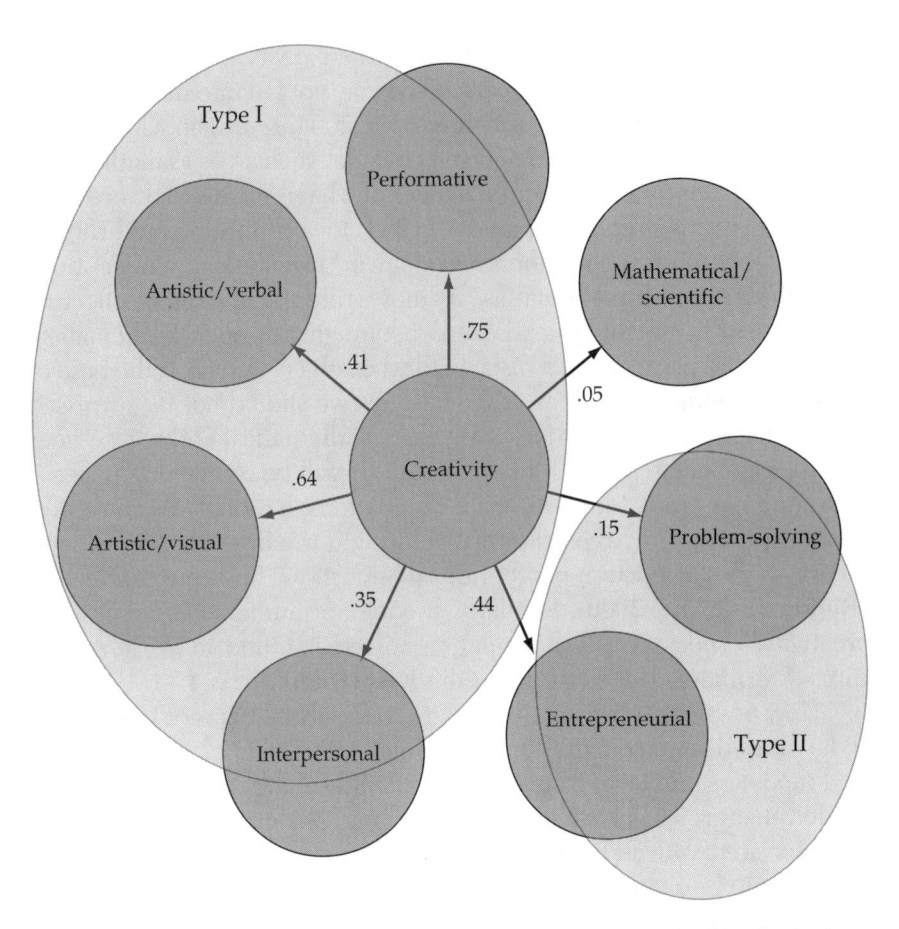

Figure 4.1 General thematic areas showing creativity and hypothesized intellectual styles.
Modified from "The Construct of Creativity: Structural Model for Self-Reported Creativity Ratings," by J. C. Kaufman, J. C. Cole, and J. Baer, in press. *Journal of Creative Behavior.*

talent" (p. 455), others have questioned the validity of self-report scales, both in creativity research and other areas (Azar, 1997; Brown, 1989; Rowe, 1997). Kaufman, Evans, & Baer (in press), for example, reported that fourth-grade students' self-assessments of their own creativity did not match the assessments of experts in any of the four domains tested (math, science, writing, and art). It is important to note that in the data gathered by Kaufman, Cole, et al. (in press), the 3,500-plus subjects had no stake in the outcome and thus no reason, at least consciously, to in-

math/science factor was the least related to creativity. One theory to explain this is that mathematics and science may not fall into many people's conceptions of creativity (Kaufman & Baer, 2004; Kaufman, Cole, et al., in press). The average person may not consider such areas as math or science as representing their mental images of what it means to be creative. This idea is consistent with Paulos's (1988) idea of innumeracy, the inability to accurately use numbers and chance. "Romantic misconceptions about the nature of mathematics," Paulos wrote, "lead to an intellectual environment hospitable to and even encouraging of poor mathematical education and psychological distaste for the subject and lie at the base of much innumeracy" (1988, p. 120). Perhaps we should not be surprised to find that a society that does not value mathematical ability also does not associate creativity with mathematics. It will be interesting to see if this same pattern is found in Asian populations; although Western perceptions of creativity typically revolve around the arts (e.g., Sternberg, 1985), studies of Eastern perceptions do not show this same connection (Rudowicz & Yue, 2000). Similarly, the idea of humor being related to creativity (especially interpersonal creativity) is found in Western cultures (Sternberg, 1985) but not in the East (Rudowicz & Hui, 1997).

How do these seven areas compare to the three types of intellectual styles? Based on the integration of Holland's (1997) model with the threefold model of intellectual styles (Zhang & Sternberg, 2006), it could be argued that artistic-verbal, artistic-visual, and performance areas would be associated with a Type I style and entrepreneur and interpersonal areas would be associated with a Type III style. Type II would likely not be associated with any domain of creativity, and problem-solving and math/science could be associated with either Type I or Type II.

Figure 4.1 shows the seven factors that Kaufman, Cole, et al. (in press) found and their relationship with (standardized loadings on) a general creativity factor. The relationship between creativity and intellectual styles is also included in this figure.

It should be emphasized that these seven factors only reflect people's *perceptions* of themselves, and there are many reasons why such perceptions might be inaccurate. After all, nearly all people believe they are above-average drivers. A quick jaunt on any major city freeway will clearly establish that not only is this discrepancy statistically impossible, but the opposite (and equally statistically impossible) option will at least seem to be true—*no one* is an above-average driver. Although some writers, like Hocevar (1981), have argued that such self-report data are "perhaps the most easily defensible way to identify creative

Another similar line of research has been conducted by Zorana Ivcevic and her colleagues, who have studied self-reported creative behaviors instead of self-ratings in different creative areas. Ivcevic and Mayer (in press) tested college students with open-ended questionnaires and group discussions, which then resulted in a comprehensive assessment of creativity across specific behaviors. Factor analysis of these behaviors resulted in three second-order dimensions: The first factor was dubbed the creative lifestyle (comparable to both the hands-on factor and the empathy/communication factor from Kaufman and Baer). This first factor included crafts, self-expressed creativity, interpersonal creativity, sophisticated media use, visual arts, and writing. The second factor was dubbed performance arts, and encompassed music, theatre, and dance, and is close to the hands-on factor from Kaufman and Baer (2004). The third factor, intellectual creativity, represented creativity in technology, science, and academic pursuits. This factor is akin to Kaufman and Baer's (2004) math/science factor. In a separate investigation, Ivcevic and Mayer (2007) used a creative activities checklist in combination with a personality inventory to derive five types: conventional, everyday creative individuals, artists, scholars, and Renaissance individuals.

The next study to build off of the work by Kaufman and Baer and Ivcevic and Mayer expanded the number of domains. This new study asked over 3,500 people to rate their own creativity across 56 different domains (Kaufman, 2006; Kaufman, Cole, & Baer, in press). We found seven general thematic area factors:

- Artistic-verbal
- Artistic-visual
- Entrepreneur
- Interpersonal
- Math/science
- Performance
- Problem-solving

These seven factors were found as hierarchical second-order factors—in other words, there is some type of c analogous to intelligence's g, but such a single construct is only part of the broader picture. It is interesting to note that some general thematic areas were strongly related to the c factor (i.e., overall creativity), while others were much less closely aligned with the higher-order general creativity factor. The performance and artistic/visual factors were strongly related, whereas the

general thematic areas are there? One? Ten? One hundred? Many different scholars have weighed in on this (broad) question. Feist (2004) uses the phrase "domains of mind" and has proposed seven such domains: psychology, physics, biology, linguistics, math, art, and music. Gardner (1999), famously, has proposed eight intelligences; although they are usually interpreted as aspects of intellectual ability, they serve just as well as areas of creative achievement (e.g., Gardner, 1993). His eight areas are interpersonal (i.e., dealing with other people), intrapersonal (dealing with yourself, so to speak), spatial, naturalistic, linguistic, logical-mathematical, bodily-kinesthetic (which could be dancing or playing baseball, for example), and musical. Holland's (1997) model of vocational interests could also apply to creative interests; his six categories are realistic, investigative, artistic, social, enterprising, and conventional.

Kaufman and Baer (2004) investigated how many general thematic areas there were by asking people to rate themselves on their own creativity across many domains. First, they asked 241 college students to rate their creativity in nine areas—science, interpersonal relationships, writing, art, interpersonal communication, solving personal problems, mathematics, crafts, and bodily/physical movement. They next did a factor analysis of their responses and found three factors from these nine domains: creativity in empathy/communication (creativity in the areas of interpersonal relationships, communication, solving personal problems, and writing); hands-on creativity (art, crafts, and bodily/physical creativity); and math/science creativity (creativity in math or science). Interestingly, these are close to three factors found in the area of student motivation—writing, art, and problem solving (Ruscio, Whitney, & Amabile, 1998). Rawlings and Locarnini (2007) replicated the factor structure, and found that professional artists scored higher on the hands-on factor and that professional scientists scored higher on the math/science factor.

A study of Turkish undergraduates found a slightly different factor structure, with an arts factor (art, writing, crafts), an empathy/communication factor (interpersonal relationships, communication, solving personal problems), and a math/science factor (math, science). Bodily/kinesthetic was not associated with any factor (Oral, Kaufman, & Agars, 2007).

Carson, Peterson, and Higgins (2005), in developing the Creativity Achievement Questionnaire, selected 10 domains, which loaded onto two factors: the arts (drama, writing, humor, music, visual arts, and dance) and science (invention, science, and culinary). The 10th domain, architecture, did not load on either factor.

thing for a woman living in Saudi Arabia or Pakistan as compared with a woman living in England or Portugal. And no matter what the country, a child growing up in an abusive household may have a more difficult time expressing novel ideas than may a child growing up in a nurturing family.

As with motivation, we mean environment here in a very general sense. There are also certainly specific environmental influences to be found at other levels of the model, such as a family that invites study or inquiry in one area (e.g., music), but not in another (e.g., engineering), or an environment that contains the tools and materials necessary to one kind of creativity but not another (e.g., if you grow up with an abundance of sports equipment but no musical instruments, then your environment is more conducive to athletic creativity than to musical creativity). But there is also a general, initial requirement-level aspect to both early and current working environments. Environments that encourage exploration, that nurture an openness to new ideas, that allow time for ideas to develop, that emphasize the intrinsic excitement of creative thinking more than the rewards or accolades that such thinking might garner, and that tolerate the ambiguity of not finding immediate answers are both (a) more likely to result in personality development that is conducive to creative thinking (in this case past environments will influence later creativity) and (b) more likely to produce creativity in the here and now (e.g., by setting up motivational constraints that lead to intrinsic motivation, which is an environment that promotes creativity; Amabile, 1996). People with Type III styles, who are the most influenced by context and social interactions (Zhang & Sternberg, 2006), will be most dependent on a nurturing environment.

APT: General Thematic Areas

Once you have decided to go to an amusement park, you must decide what kind of amusement park you wish to visit. Maybe you are in the mood to go to a water park and splash around. Or perhaps you are feeling more daring (or you don't like the way you look in a swimsuit), and you want to enjoy extreme roller coasters or those rides that plunge you into free fall. Maybe you want to see animals or fish, or you want to visit a theme park centered on a movie or a cartoon character.

Just as all of these different places fall into a larger category called "amusement parks," so can many different types of creativity fall into larger categories that are called "general thematic areas." How many

of intelligence is needed for any creativity activity; there's a reason why rocks don't compose sonatas (other than the fact that they don't have opposable thumbs). In looking at the three types of intellectual styles posited by Zhang and Sternberg (2006), different styles may be related to different types of intellectual abilities. Type II might be related to very academic and grade-related intellectual abilities, whereas Type III would likely be associated with more goal-driven intellectual abilities. Type I might be related to the most relevant intellectual abilities (such as divergent thinking) although less related to school performance.

Similarly, when we talk about motivation, we're not being specific about what things motivate people or what techniques they may use to motivate themselves. We're simply referring to the motivation to get up off the couch and do *something*. If someone is not motivated to do something (anything) for any reason, then that person isn't going to be creative. As an extreme case, someone who lies on the couch all day and doesn't have the motivation to initiate any activity will simply not be creative. And daydreaming isn't enough; a writer who never translates his or her ideas into words at the keyboard is not going to be a creative writer (or any type of writer). As Woody Allen famously said, "Eighty percent of success is showing up."

We should note that motivation isn't a simple or one-dimensional construct. There is motivation to do *something*, which is what we are talking about when we include motivation as an initial requirement. A person may be highly motivated to do something creative, or may have little of this kind of motivation. There is also motivation that takes the form of special interests. One may be very motivated to write poems but not at all motivated to balance one's checkbook. (This can be a problem, we've found, but that's another story.) This kind of domain-specific motivation is part of the APT model at a much lower level of the hierarchy. Intellectual styles intersect with motivation at the lower levels of the APT model—Type I styles are more related to intrinsic motivation—yet at the initial level, any of the three styles can theoretically yield a motivation to do something.

Another initial requirement takes the form of environments, which are important in both the past and present tenses. A person who grows up in a culture or in a family in which creative thoughts or actions are not encouraged (or are even punished) will have a harder time being creative. A person living or working in an environment that is supportive of original thought is more likely to be creative than a person in an environment that discourages such thought. Being creative is a different

THE AMUSEMENT PARK THEORY

We have developed the APT model of creativity to integrate generalist and domain-specific views of creativity. We are not the first to try to synthesize these ideas. Others, for example, have proposed a hybrid view in which creativity is primarily general but appears domain-specific in real world performance (Plucker & Beghetto, 2004). According to this theory, the level of specificity changes according to social context and matures as a person advances from childhood into adulthood.

The APT model uses the metaphor of an amusement park to explore the nature of creativity (Baer & Kaufman, 2005; Kaufman & Baer, 2005, 2006). We start with the initial requirements. What do you need to go to an amusement park? First, you need the time off to go. Amusement parks usually take up an entire day; trying to cram everything into one or two hours would just be silly. If you don't have a day to take off, you probably won't be going to an amusement park. But having the time is just the beginning. You need money to get in. You need a way of getting to the amusement park. You need the basic desire to go: If roller coasters terrify you, then you likely will not choose to go to a Six Flags park.

APT: Initial Requirements

Initial requirements are things that are necessary, but not by themselves sufficient, for any type of creative production. They include such things as intelligence, motivation, and suitable environments. Each of these factors is a prerequisite to creative achievement in any domain, and if someone lacks the requisite level of any of these initial requirements, then creative performance is at best unlikely. Higher levels of these initial requirements, in combination with other more domain-specific factors, predict higher levels of creative performance in general. It must be noted that although all of these initial requirements are necessary for creativity in any domain, the specific degrees of intelligence, motivation, and suitable environments needed to succeed in different areas of creative endeavors vary (just as the height requirements found at different rides may vary depending on the nature of the ride).

As an example of this, intelligence is an important contributor to creative performance in all domains, but it is much more highly correlated with creativity in certain domains than in others. Picturing a less-intelligent creative dancer or woodworker, for example, may be easier to do than picturing a less-intelligent creative physicist. But *some* degree

structure. Judicial thinkers like to judge and evaluate things. There are also four different forms: monarchic (focusing on one thing at a time), hierarchical (focusing attention on multiple tasks with a set priority), oligarchic (focusing attention on multiple tasks without a set priority), and anarchic (working on tasks with no system). There are two levels, local and global: local focuses on attention to details and global looks at the big picture (indeed, there are similarities between Sternberg's levels and Bruner's narrative-paradigmatic distinction). There are two scopes: internal is more geared to working independently, whereas external is linked with working with people. Finally, there are two leanings: liberal (preferring novelty and ambiguity) and conservative (following rules and procedures).

Unsurprisingly, there are some clear connections between creativity and these intellectual styles. Creative writers were more likely to use a legislative style, whereas journalists were more likely to use an executive thinking style (Kaufman, 2002). Fine artists preferred legislative and liberal thinking styles over executive and conservative styles (Gridley, 2006). Park, Park, and Choe (2005) investigated gifted Korean science students (who were noted for being creative) and compared them with nongifted students. Gifted students tended to have legislative, judicial, anarchic, global, external, and liberal styles. The nongifted students, in contrast, preferred executive, oligarchic, and conservative styles. Zhang and Huang (2001) found that the personality factor openness to experience (long associated with creativity; see Kaufman, Plucker, & Baer, 2008, for an overview) was positively associated with legislative, judicial, liberal, and external styles, and negatively associated with conservative styles. O'Hara and Sternberg (2001) also found that legislative thinkers were more creative than executive thinkers.

Clearly, there is a pattern of creative thinking styles here, and Zhang and Sternberg (2006) have integrated the mental self-government theory and a variety of other related theories (e.g., Guilford, 1967, 1988; Holland, 1997) into a threefold model of intellectual styles. Type I thinkers are the creative thinkers, with the pattern of legislative, judicial, global, and hierarchical (and field independent) styles. Type II thinkers are more conventional (executive, local, monarchic, and conservative), whereas Type III thinkers are more realistic (oligarchic, anarchic, internal, external).

How do intellectual styles relate to creativity by domain? One way of approaching this question is to use the Amusement Park Theoretical (APT) model.

In this chapter, we will first discuss the relationship between creativity and intellectual styles, surveying the available research literature. We will then integrate theory and research on intellectual styles into an existing theory of creativity that accounts for both domain-specific and general tendencies in creativity. Our goal is to use this theory as a framework for integrating creativity and intellectual styles, in the hope that such a chapter may inspire more empirical research. Although there are numerous theories of intellectual styles (including many articulated elsewhere in this book), we will primarily focus on the work by Zhang and Sternberg (2006) because of its encompassing, integrative nature. Some other styles will be briefly touched on because of their relationship to creativity research.

Much of the past research on creativity and intellectual styles has focused on the theory of field dependence versus independence (see Witkin & Goodenough, 1981, for an overview). People who rely on the context of a situation, or external cues, are called field dependent (or relational), while people who rely more on internal cues and focus on specific details are called field independent (or analytical; Anderson & Adams, 1992). One criticism of this theory claims that field independence is too similar to fluid intelligence, and should therefore be considered an ability, rather than a style (Grigorenko & Sternberg, 1995). Although there are still some studies that look at creativity and thinking styles using this model (e.g., Brophy, 2001; Miller, 2007), the theory has generally fallen out of fashion.

Another theory is Bruner's (1986) distinction between narrative and paradigmatic thought. Paradigmatic thought is logical and scientific, whereas narrative thought seeks connections and sees the world as a story. If paradigmatic thought is concerned with capturing *what is*, then narrative thought is focused more on *what may be*. Kaufman (2002) operationalized narrative and paradigmatic thinking by asking participants to write captions for photographs and then having the captions scored by trained raters. This technique is similar to Amabile's Consensual Assessment Technique (Amabile, 1996). Raters agreed on how much a caption represented a paradigmatic or narrative thinking style. To date, despite the potential of this technique, narrative and paradigmatic thought has not been empirically measured in other studies.

Sternberg's (1997) theory of mental self-government comprises three functions: executive, judicial, and legislative. Legislative thinkers prefer to create things and to be self-directed. Executive thinkers prefer to follow directions, to carry out orders, and to work under a great deal of

4

How Are Intellectual Styles Related to Creativity Across Multiple Domains?

JAMES C. KAUFMAN AND JOHN M. BAER

Both intellectual styles (also known as thinking styles) and creativity are constructs that have inspired passionate interest and pockets of empirical studies over the last few decades. Each topic has had its ups and downs, but both are starting to become more in fashion in recent years. As the groundswell of theory and research increases, the degrees of interrelationship between intellectual styles and creativity become more salient.

In the last 20 years, there have been several new theories of creativity that have been proposed and discussed. One of the most popular theories of creativity, Sternberg and Lubart's (1995, 1996; expanded from Sternberg, 1988) investment theory, argues that the key to being creative is to buy low and sell high in ideas. In this model, a creative person is like a successful Wall Street broker. Sternberg and Lubart list six variables as being essential to creativity: intelligence, knowledge, personality, environment, motivation, and thinking styles.

However, whereas research on creativity and most of the other variables in Sternberg and Lubart's theory are well-studied, the connection between thinking styles and creativity is comparatively unexplored. For example, a PsycINFO search found just 33 articles in peer-reviewed journals on creativity and thinking styles (and only seven for creativity and intellectual styles). A similar search produced 1,030 articles on creativity and intelligence and 3,540 articles on creativity and personality.

Zhang, L. F. (2008). Preferences for teaching styles matter in academic achievement: Scientific and practical implications. *Educational Psychology, 28*(6), 615–625.

Zhang, L. F. (in press). Thinking styles and emotions. *The Journal of Psychology.*

Zhang, L. F., Fu, H., Jiao, B. (2008). Accounting for Tibetan university students' and teachers' intellectual styles. *Educational Review, 60*(1), 21–37.

Zhang, L. F., & He, Y. F. (2003). Do thinking styles matter in the use of and attitudes toward computing and information technology among Hong Kong university students? *Journal of Educational Computing Research, 29*(4), 471–493.

Zhang, L. F., & Higgins, P. (2008). The predictive power of socialization variables for thinking styles among adults in the workplace. *Learning and Individual Differences, 18*(1), 11–18.

Zhang, L. F., & Huang, J. F. (2001). Thinking styles and the five-factor model of personality. *European Journal of Personality, 15,* 465–476.

Zhang, L. F., Huang, J. F., & Zhang, L. L. (2005). Preferences in teaching styles among Hong Kong and U.S. university students. *Personality and Individual Differences, 39,* 1319–1331.

Zhang, L. F., & Postiglione, G. A. (2001). Thinking styles, self-esteem, and socioeconomic status. *Personality and Individual Differences, 31,* 1333–1346.

Zhang, L. F., & Sachs, J. (1997). Assessing thinking styles in the theory of mental self-government: A Hong Kong validity study. *Psychological Reports, 81,* 915–928.

Zhang, L. F., & Sternberg, R. J. (1998). Thinking styles, abilities, and academic achievement among Hong Kong university students. *Educational Research Journal, 13*(1), 41–62.

Zhang, L. F., & Sternberg, R. J. (2002). Thinking styles and teacher characteristics. *International Journal of Psychology, 37*(1), 3–12.

Zhang, L. F., & Sternberg, R. J. (2005). A threefold model of intellectual styles. *Educational Psychology Review, 17*(1), 1–53.

Zhang, L. F., & Sternberg, R. J. (2006). *The nature of intellectual styles.* Mahwah, NJ: Lawrence Erlbaum.

Sternberg, R. J., Wagner, R. K., & Zhang, L. F. (2003). *Thinking Styles Inventory—Revised.* Unpublished test, Yale University.

Sternberg, R. J., Wagner, R. K., & Zhang, L. F. (2007). *Thinking Styles Inventory—Revised II.* Unpublished test, Tufts University.

Sternberg, R. J., & Zhang, L. F. (Eds.). (2001). *Perspectives on thinking, learning, and cognitive styles.* Mahwah, NJ: Lawrence Erlbaum.

Torrance, E. P. (1988). *SOLAT (style of learning and thinking) manual.* Bensenville, IL: Scholastic Testing Service.

Trigwell, K., & Prosser, M. (1996). Congruence between intention and strategy in science teachers' approaches to teaching. *Higher Education, 32,* 77–87.

Witkin, H. A. (1962). *Psychological differentiation; studies of development.* New York: Wiley.

Wubbels, T., Créton, H. A., & Hooymayers, H. P. (1985, April). *Discipline problems of beginning teachers.* Paper presented at the Annual Conference of The American Educational Research Association, Chicago. ERIC Document Reproduction Services No. ED 260040.

Yu, D. M. (2008). *Teachers' teaching styles and interpersonal behaviors.* Unpublished manuscript.

Zhang, L. F. (1997). *The Zhang Cognitive Development Inventory.* Unpublished test, the University of Hong Kong, Hong Kong.

Zhang, L. F. (2001). Do thinking styles contribute to academic achievement beyond abilities? *The Journal of Psychology, 135*(6), 621–637.

Zhang, L. F. (2002a). Measuring thinking styles in addition to measuring personality traits? *Personality and Individual Differences, 33,* 445–458.

Zhang, L. F. (2002b). Thinking styles and cognitive development. *The Journal of Genetic Psychology, 163*(2), 179–195.

Zhang, L. F. (2002c). Thinking styles and the Big Five personality traits. *Educational Psychology, 22*(1), 17–31.

Zhang, L. F. (2003). *The Preferred Thinking Styles in Teaching Inventory.* Unpublished test, the University of Hong Kong, Hong Kong.

Zhang, L. F. (2004a). Contributions of thinking styles to vocational purpose beyond self-rated abilities. *Psychological Reports, 94,* 697–714.

Zhang, L. F. (2004b). Thinking styles: University students' preferred teaching styles and their conceptions of effective teachers. *The Journal of Psychology, 138*(3), 233–252.

Zhang, L. F. (2005). Validating the theory of mental self-government in a non-academic setting. *Personality and Individual Differences, 38,* 1915–1925.

Zhang, L. F. (2006). Preferred teaching styles and modes of thinking among university students in mainland China. *Thinking Skills and Creativity, 1*(2), 95–107.

Zhang, L. F. (2007a). Do personality traits make a difference in teaching styles among Chinese high school teachers? *Personality and Individual Differences, 43,* 669–679.

Zhang, L. F. (2007b). *Preferred Thinking Styles in Learning Inventory.* Unpublished test, the University of Hong Kong, Hong Kong.

Zhang, L. F. (2007c). Revisiting thinking styles' contributions to the knowledge and use of and attitudes towards computing and information technology. *Learning and Individual Differences, 17,* 17–24.

Zhang, L. F. (2007d). Teaching styles and occupational stress among Chinese university faculty members. *Educational Psychology, 27*(6), 823–841.

Holland, J. L. (1973). *Making vocational choices: A theory of careers.* Englewood Cliffs, NJ: Prentice-Hall.

Hood, A. B., & Jackson, L. M. (1997). The Iowa Managing Emotions Inventory. In A. B. Hood (Ed.), *The Iowa student development inventories* (2nd ed., pp. 22–31). Iowa City, IA: HITECH Press.

Hood, A. B., & Zerwas, S. C. (1997). The Iowa Vocational Purpose Inventory. In A. B. Hood (Ed.), *The Iowa student development inventories* (2nd ed., pp. 93–108). Iowa City, IA: HITECH Press.

Jung, C. (1923). *Psychological types.* New York: Harcourt Brace.

Kagan, J. (1966). Developmental studies in reflection and analysis. In A. H. Kidd & J. L. Rivoire (Ed.), *Perceptual development in children* (pp. 487–522). New York: International University Press.

Kirton, M. J. (1976). Adaptors and innovators: A description and measure. *Journal of Applied Psychology, 61,* 622–629.

Klinger, T. H. (2006). Learning approach, thinking style and critical inquiry: The online community. *Korean Journal of Thinking and Problem Solving, 16*(1), 91–113.

Langer, E. (1997). *The power of mindful learning.* Cambridge, MA: Da Capo Press.

Lee, K. L. (2002). *Thinking styles and approaches in teaching among Hong Kong kindergarten teachers.* Unpublished manuscript. The University of Hong Kong.

Martin, R. A., Puhlik-Doris, P., Gray, J., & Weir, K. (2003). Individual differences in uses of humor and their relation to psychological well-being: Development of the Humor Styles Questionnaire. *Journal of Research in Personality, 37,* 48–75.

Mshelia, A. Y., & Lapidus, L. B. (1990). Depth picture perception in relation to cognitive style and training in non-Western children. *Journal of Cross-Cultural Psychology, 21*(4), 414–433.

Nachmias, R., & Shany, N. (2002). Learning in virtual courses and its relationship to thinking styles. *Journal of Educational Computing Research, 27*(3), 315–329.

Osipow, S. H. (1998). *Occupational Stress Inventory-Revised Edition (OSI-R): Professional manual.* Lutz, FL: Psychological Assessment Resources.

Park, S. K., Park, K. H., & Choe, H. S. (2005). Relationship between thinking styles and scientific giftedness in Korea. *Journal of Secondary Gifted Education, 16*(2–3), 87–97.

Perry, W. G. (1970). *Forms of intellectual and ethical development in the college years: A scheme* (2nd ed.). New York: Holt, Rinehart and Winston.

Perry, W. G. (1981). Cognitive and ethical growth: The making of meaning. In A. Chickering (Ed.), *The modern American college* (pp. 76–116). San Francisco: Jossey-Bass.

Piaget, J. (1952). *The origins of intelligence in children.* New York: International Universities Press.

Shokri, O., Kadivar, P., Farzad, V., Sangari, A. A., & Ghana-ei, Z. (2006). The role of personality traits and thinking styles in academic achievement: Introducing casual models. *Journal of Iranian Psychologists, 2*(7), n.p.

Sternberg, R. J. (1988). Mental self-government: A theory of intellectual styles and their development. *Human Development, 31,* 197–224.

Sternberg, R. J. (1997). *Thinking styles.* New York: Cambridge University Press.

Sternberg, R. J., & Wagner, R. K. (1992). *Thinking Styles Inventory.* Unpublished test, Yale University.

Betoret, F. D. (2007). The influence of students' and teachers' thinking styles on student course satisfaction and on their learning process. *Educational Psychology, 27*(2), 219–234.

Biggs, J. B. (1978). Individual and group differences in study processes. *British Journal of Educational Psychology, 48,* 266–279.

Brown, G., & Lawson, T. W. (1975). Sex differences in the stability of reflectivity/impulsivity in infant school pupils. *Educational Studies, 1*(2), 99–104.

Cano-Garcia, F., & Hughes, E. H. (2000). Learning and thinking styles: An analysis of their relationship and influence on academic achievement. *Educational Psychology, 20*(4), 413–430.

Chen, G. H. (2007). *University teachers' humor production in the classroom and student ratings of teaching effectiveness.* Unpublished dissertation, the University of Hong Kong.

Chen, G. H., & Zhang, L. F. (2008). *The role of thinking styles in mental health.* Unpublished manuscript.

Chickering, A. (1969). *Education and identity.* San Francisco: Jossey-Bass.

Chickering, A., & Reisser, L. (1993). *Education and identity* (2nd ed.). San Francisco: Jossey-Bass.

Coopersmith, S. (1981). *Self-esteem inventories.* Palo Alto, CA: Consulting Psychologists Press.

Costa, P. T., Jr., & McCrae, R. R. (1992/1995). *The NEO-PI: Professional manual.* Odessa, FL: Psychological Assessment Resources.

Derogatis, L. R., Rickels, K., & Rock, A. (1976). The SCL-90 and the MMPI: A step in the validation of a new self-report scale. *British Journal of Psychiatry, 128,* 280–289.

Fan, W. Q., & Zhang, L. F. (in press). Thinking styles and achievement motivations. *Learning and Individual Differences.*

Fer, S. (2005). Validity and reliability of the Thinking Styles Inventory/Düsünme Stilleri Envanterinin Geçerlik ve Güvenirlik Çalismasi. *EDAM Egitim Danismanligi Ve Arastirmalari Merkezi, 5*(1), 33–67.

Fjell, A. D., & Walhovd, K. B. (2004). Thinking styles in relation to personality traits: An investigation of the Thinking Styles Inventory and NEO-PI-R. *Scandinavian Journal of Psychology, 45*(4), 293–300.

Foxall, G. R., & Hackett, P. M. W. (1992). Cognitive style and extent of computer use in organizations: Relevance of sufficiency of originality, efficiency and rule-conformity. *Perceptual and Motor Skills, 74,* 491–497.

Giesme, T., & Nygard, R. (1970). *Achievement Motivation Scale.* University of Oslo.

Gregorc, A. F. (1985). *Inside styles: Beyond the basics.* Maynard, MA: Gabriel Systems.

Grigorenko, E. L., & Sternberg, R. J. (1993). *Thinking Styles in Teaching Inventory.* Unpublished test, Yale University.

Grigorenko, E. L., & Sternberg, R. J. (1995). Thinking styles. In D. Saklofske & M. Zeidner (Eds.), *International handbook of personality and intelligence* (pp. 205–229). New York: Plenum.

Grigorenko, E. L., & Sternberg, R. J. (1997). Styles of thinking, abilities, and academic performance. *Exceptional Children, 63*(3), 295–312.

Guilford, J. P. (1967). *The nature of human intelligence.* New York: McGraw-Hill.

Higgins, P., & Zhang, L. F. (2009). *Malleability and value of thinking styles in the workplace.* Unpublished manuscript.

foundation for us to reaffirm our position that intellectual styles are value-laden, with Type I styles more adaptive.

As mentioned at the beginning of the chapter, style value is an important issue. It is important also in part because this issue could help us observe some major discrepancies between what we say we value (and what styles are effective in real life as evidenced in the findings reviewed) and what we demonstrate we value in practice (such as what's rewarded at school and at work), discrepancies that we would not have otherwise observed. For example, people have diverse intellectual styles. Yet, in many organizations, academic and nonacademic, only a limited number of styles work well. Styles that do not fit into the immediate needs of an organization may not be tolerated because they are considered deviant. Although Type I styles are clearly more adaptive, Type II styles are often more encouraged. For example, in secondary school settings in Hong Kong and Israel and in university settings in Hong Kong, the Philippines, and Spain, students with Type II thinking styles tended to be higher academic achievers, whereas those who scored higher on Type I thinking styles tended to be lower academic achievers (Bernardo, Zhang, & Callueng, 2002; Cano-Garcia & Hughes, 2000; Nachmias & Shany, 2002; Zhang & Sternberg, 1998). Thus, findings reviewed in this chapter as well as the discrepancies revealed by these findings have significant implications. We point out two, one each for practice and for research.

At the practical level, we believe that we should honor our values— our value of diversity and of creative intellectual styles. To do so, we need to find ways to accommodate diverse styles and to reward and develop Type I styles (see Zhang & Sternberg, 2006, for some sample strategies). At the level of research, we contend that there is a pressing need for studies that probe into factors that prevent people from committing themselves to what they truly believe in.

REFERENCES

Alborzi, S., & Ostovar, S. (2007). Thinking styles of gifted and nongifted students in Iran. *Psychological Reports, 100,* 1076–1082.

Allinson, C. W., Armstrong, S. J., & Hayes, J. (2001). The effects of cognitive style on leader-member exchange: A study of manager-subordinate dyads. *Journal of Occupational and Organizational Psychology, 74*(2), 201–220.

Atkinson, J. W. (1964). *An introduction to motivation.* New York: Van Nostrand.

Bernardo, A. B., Zhang, L. F., & Callueng, C. M. (2002). Thinking styles and academic achievement among Filipino students. *Journal of Genetic Psychology, 163*(2), 149–163.

to work on Sternberg's (1997) theory of mental self-government, for at least six reasons, the conclusion being drawn is well grounded.

First, the research methods used in the majority of the studies reviewed are sound, with the possible confounding effects of such variables as age, gender, and abilities having been removed and with relatively stringent statistical procedures such as partial correlations and hierarchical multiple regressions (with Bonferroni Correction at times) being applied. Second, the conclusion is based on the study of the relationships of thinking styles to a great variety of variables, ranging from perceptions of work environments to mental health, from occupational stress to teaching behaviors, and from preferred teaching and learning styles to their effects on students' satisfaction with teachers' teaching. Third, the conclusion is rooted in research evidence gathered across school levels (secondary schools and universities), across cultures, and across different occupational groups. Fourth, the conclusion was reached based on convergent findings—findings that have been obtained through four different assessment tools that are anchored in the same theoretical framework. Fifth, the conclusion is convincing also because when some of the studies were replicated in different populations, identical results were obtained. For example, the relationships between thinking styles and the Big Five personality traits are practically identical for students and teachers, and for samples from Hong Kong, Iran, mainland China, Norway, and the United States.

Finally, the conclusion made in this chapter is well grounded also because the findings based on research on the theory of mental self-government are resonant with findings obtained from studies of other style constructs. Indeed, one could easily find evidence based on studies of other style constructs that would lead one to the same conclusion regarding intellectual styles. There are various ways to do so. For example, if one were to survey the particular styles that researchers usually aim at developing in their training programs, one would find that the target styles are normally Type I styles such as field independent, reflective, deep learning approach, divergent thinking, and wholistic mode of thinking (e.g., Brown & Lawson, 1975; Klinger, 2006; Mshelia & Lapidus, 1990). Also, for instance, if one were to review works on the relationships between styles and leadership behavior, one would conclude that, in general, Type I styles (e.g., field independent, innovative, and intuitive styles) are strongly associated with leadership behaviors that are more conducive to human development (e.g., Allinson, Armstrong, & Hayes, 2001; Foxall & Hackett, 1992). All this helps to establish a solid

A further question that one might have is whether or not people are positively affected by their perceptions that other people use Type I styles. In Spain, Betoret (2007) examined the relationship between perceptions of teaching styles and student course satisfaction among 102 university students registered in an instructional psychology course. The author concluded that, in general, students who perceived their teacher to be using Type I teaching styles expressed higher levels of satisfaction with the course.

Styles of Business Personnel

Until now, the majority of existing studies (the ones that were not reviewed in our 2006 styles book) relevant to the argument that Type I thinking styles are more adaptive than are Type II styles were conducted in the academic settings. Yet there are also studies that have been conducted in nonacademic settings. In a series of three studies, Zhang and her colleague (Higgins & Zhang, 2009; Zhang, 2005; Zhang & Higgins, 2008) investigated the relationships of working adults' thinking styles to a range of their perceptions about work environments. The first study (Zhang, 2005) involved 333 working adults from various business sectors in Guangzhou, People's Republic of China. The second study (Zhang & Higgins, 2008) was conducted among 117 managerial personnel working for three types of organizations (construction, manufacture, and service) in England. The third study (Higgins & Zhang, 2009) involved 149 adults in the workplace from three occupations (fire-fighting, volunteering, and human resource management), again in England.

In all three studies, it was consistently shown that positive perceptions of one's abilities and of one's work environments contributed to Type I thinking styles. In contrast, negative perceptions contributed to Type II styles, thus revealing once more the positive value carried by Type I styles.

CONCLUSIONS AND IMPLICATIONS

Based on the empirical evidence reviewed in this chapter, a major conclusion follows: intellectual styles are value-laden, with Type I styles generally more adaptive. Although the evidence we presented to argue for the adaptive value of Type I intellectual styles here is primarily restricted

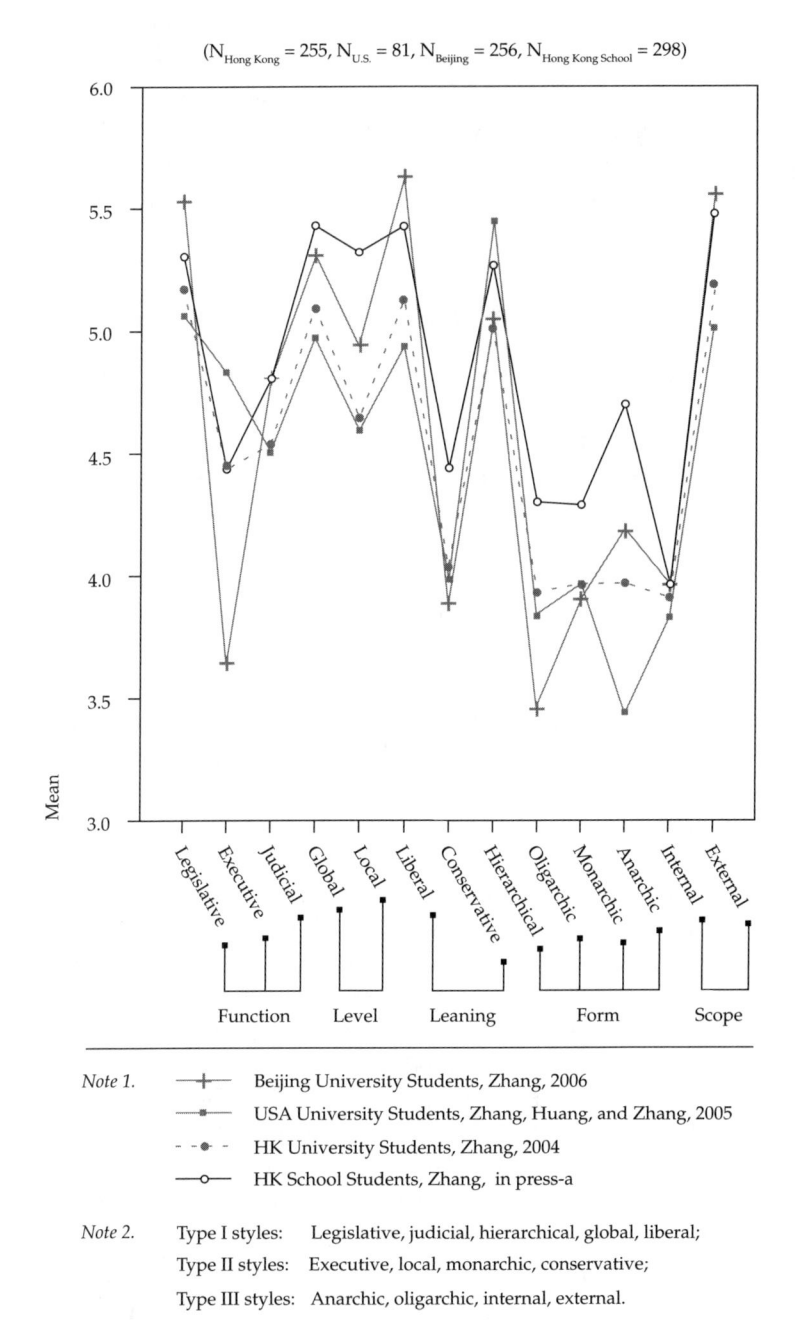

$(N_{\text{Hong Kong}} = 255, N_{\text{U.S.}} = 81, N_{\text{Beijing}} = 256, N_{\text{Hong Kong School}} = 298)$

Note 1.
- ──+── Beijing University Students, Zhang, 2006
- ┈┈■┈┈ USA University Students, Zhang, Huang, and Zhang, 2005
- ─ ─●─ ─ HK University Students, Zhang, 2004
- ──○── HK School Students, Zhang, in press-a

Note 2. Type I styles: Legislative, judicial, hierarchical, global, liberal;
Type II styles: Executive, local, monarchic, conservative;
Type III styles: Anarchic, oligarchic, internal, external.

Figure 3.1 Line chart for students' preferred teaching styles.

After self-rated abilities were taken into account, occupational stress remained to be a significant predictor for teaching styles. Whereas a stronger feeling of role overload and a more frequent use of the rational/cognitive coping strategy were conducive to the use of both Type I and Type II teaching styles, a stronger feeling of role insufficiency and that of psychological strain had a negative impact on the use of Type I teaching styles.

Preferred Styles: Students and Teachers in Interaction

To further explore the nature of thinking styles as they relate to the issue of style value, researchers also examined whether or not students and teachers explicitly express their preference for each other to use in Type I thinking styles in teaching or learning. To investigate students' preferences for their teachers' teaching styles, Zhang (2003) constructed the Preferred Thinking Styles in Teaching Inventory (PTSTI). A series of four studies have been conducted to identify the kind of teaching styles that students prefer among their teachers. The first study (Zhang, 2004b) involved 255 students from the University of Hong Kong; a second study (Zhang, Huang, & Zhang, 2005), 81 students from a large university in the United States; a third study (Zhang, 2006), 256 students from a large teacher education university in Beijing; and a fourth study (Zhang, 2008), 298 first-year students from a Catholic boys' secondary school in Hong Kong.

Across these studies, several variables were taken into account, including gender, age, students' thinking styles, their self-rated abilities, and their family background. Consistently, it was found that students indicated a much stronger preference for their teachers to teach in Type I teaching styles over Type II teaching styles (see Figure 3.1).

To understand teachers' preferences for their students' learning styles, Zhang (2007b) constructed the Preferred Thinking Styles in Learning Inventory (PTSLI). So far, the inventory has only been tested in one study. Zhang et al. (2008) administered the inventory to 175 faculty members in Tibet University in the Tibetan Autonomous Region and to 144 faculty members in Nanjing Normal University of mainland China. Although compared with the academics in Nanjing, the Tibetan academics indicated a stronger preference for their students to learn more conservatively, a stronger preference for Type I learning styles was clearly demonstrated within both groups when data were analyzed separately for each group.

157 teachers from two senior high schools in the People's Republic of China. Zhang (2007a) concluded that teachers' Type I teaching styles were positively related to conscientiousness and that Type II teaching styles were negatively associated with the openness personality trait.

In his doctoral dissertation, Chen (2007) tested teaching styles against humor styles among 388 university academics in Guangzhou. Humor styles were assessed by the Humor Styles Questionnaire (Martin, Puhlik-Doris, Gray, & Weir, 2003). Results indicated that while Type I teaching styles were strongly associated with beneficial humor styles (including the affiliative and self-enhancing styles); Type II teaching styles were strongly associated with detrimental humor styles (including the aggressive and self-defeating styles). In the same dissertation, Chen (2007) concluded that university teachers with Type I teaching styles received significantly better teaching evaluations from their students than did teachers who scored higher on Type II teaching styles.

In a further study, Yu (2008) investigated the relationship of teaching styles to teachers' interpersonal behaviors toward students among school teachers in Macau and Hong Kong. Teachers' interpersonal behaviors were measured by the Questionnaire on Teacher Interaction (Wubbels, Créton, & Hooymayers, 1985). Results suggested that teachers scoring higher on Type I teaching styles tended to report more student-centered interpersonal behaviors such as helping, understanding, and allowing students freedom, whereas teachers scoring higher on Type II teaching styles tended to report more teacher-centered interpersonal behaviors such as being strict, showing dissatisfaction, and expressing anger.

Finally, Zhang (2007d) investigated the relationships between teaching styles and occupational stress among 144 academics from a large university in mainland China. The participants, again, responded to the Thinking Styles in Teaching Inventory. In addition, they responded to four scales (i.e., role overload, role insufficiency, psychological strain, and rational/cognitive coping) from the Occupational Stress Inventory-Revised (Osipow, 1998). Role overload assesses the extent to which one perceives job demands as exceeding resources (personal and workplace) and the extent to which one reports that one is able to accomplish one's workloads. Role insufficiency assesses the extent to which one perceives one's training, education, skills, and experience as appropriate to the job requirements. Psychological strain measures the extent to which one perceives that one is experiencing psychological or emotional problems. Rational/cognitive coping measures the extent to which one reports that one possesses and uses cognitive skills in dealing with work-related stress.

the prediction that Type II thinking styles were negatively related to achievement motivation to approach success and that Type I styles were negatively correlated with achievement motivation to avoid failure.

In yet a recent study, Chen and Zhang (2008) examined the relationships of thinking styles to mental health as measured by a Chinese version of the System Checklist-90 (Derogatis, Rickels, & Rock, 1976). Participants were 250 university students majoring in management and business from Guangzhou University of Foreign Studies in Guangzhou, People's Republic of China. It was found that students scoring higher on Type I thinking styles (e.g., the hierarchical and liberal styles) tended to report better mental health, scoring lower on depression and hostility scales as well as lower on the General Symptomatic Index. By contrast, students scoring higher on Type II styles (e.g., local and monarchic) tended to score higher on such scales as phobic anxiety, obsessive-compulsive, and psychoticism.

Finally, within the context of studying students' thinking styles, researchers have also found that gifted students scored significantly higher on Type I thinking styles than did nongifted students. For example, Park et al. (2005) compared the thinking styles of 179 gifted students from two science high schools with those of 176 students from general high schools in Korea. The authors concluded that Korean gifted students preferred Type I (and Type III) thinking styles, whereas nongifted students demonstrated a stronger preference for Type II thinking styles.

In Iran, Alborzi and Ostovar (2007) compared the thinking styles of 91 gifted students with those of 109 nongifted students. Participants were from a junior high school. Results are identical with those obtained in Korea. That is, students who were identified as being gifted showed a stronger propensity for Type I (and Type III) thinking styles, whereas students who were classified as being nongifted tended to be predisposed to Type II thinking styles.

Styles of Teachers

As in research findings about students, research findings about teachers since the publication of our 2006 styles book also continued to demonstrate the superiority of Type I thinking styles over Type II styles. For example, Zhang (2007a) examined the relationship between the Big Five personality traits (as measured by the NEO Five-Factor Inventory; Costa & McCrae, 1992/1995) and teaching styles (as measured by the Thinking Styles in Teaching Inventory; Grigorenko & Sternberg, 1993) among

more positive attitude toward the use of computing and information technology (CIT) in education. Underlying this hypothesis is the assumption that being more open-minded to new ways of teaching as represented by using CIT is a manifestation of a positive attribute compared with being close-minded to it. Participants in the first study (Zhang & He, 2003) were 193 students from the University of Hong Kong, while those in the second study (Zhang, 2007c) were 105 students enrolled in a general psychology course from a large university in Texas. Students' knowledge about and attitude toward the use of CIT in education were understood through students' response to a comprehensive list of CIT operations (including basic operations such as Windows and RichWin, documentary operations such as Acrobat Reader and Ghost Script, graphic and media operations such as Video Capturing and MPEG Video Players, and Web and net operations such as PC-Pine and Web-authoring software) as well as through their expression of willingness to receive further training in CIT. The authors' hypothesis was fully confirmed. In both studies, Type I thinking styles positively predicted knowledge about CIT as well as a favorable attitude toward the use of CIT in education, whereas Type II thinking styles negatively did so.

In a further study, Zhang (in press) explored the relationships of thinking styles to emotions among 93 Hong Kong Chinese university students. Five types of emotions (happiness, attraction, anger, depression, and frustration) were assessed by the Iowa Managing Emotions Inventory (Hood & Jackson, 1997), which is grounded in Chickering's (1969) theory of psychosocial development. Results indicated that although Type II thinking styles were not significantly correlated with any of the emotion scales, Type I thinking styles (e.g., hierarchical, liberal, and judicial) were shown to be more conducive to the development of students' ability to deal with negative emotions and to the enhancement of positive emotions.

In yet another study, Fan and Zhang (in press) investigated if thinking styles would make a difference in students' achievement motivation. In addition to the Thinking Styles Inventory-Revised, 238 university students in Shanghai responded to the Achievement Motives Scale (Giesme & Nygard, 1970), based on Atkinson's (1964) achievement motivation theory. Results largely supported the hypothesis that Type I thinking styles were positively related to achievement motivation to approach success, an achievement motivation considered to be more positive, but negatively to achievement motivation to avoid failure, an achievement motivation deemed to be more negative. Results also partially supported

Styles of Students

Findings obtained from investigating students' thinking styles against a range variables have demonstrated the superiority of Type I thinking styles over Type II ones. These variables include personality traits, attitudes toward the use of computing and information technology in education, identity, emotions, achievement motivation, and mental health. Furthermore, comparative studies of gifted versus nongifted students have also shown that Type I thinking styles are more adaptive.

In a first study, Fjell and Walhovd (2004) from the University of Oslo examined the relationship of thinking styles to the Big Five personality traits (measured by the NEO Personality Inventory-Revised; Costa & McCrae, 1992/1995). Participants were 107 university students from the United States and a convenient sample of 114 people consisting of university students, employees from a local hospital, and players of a local football club in Norway. Results indicated that in general, openness and conscientiousness were significantly correlated with Type I thinking styles, whereas neuroticism was strongly associated with Type II thinking styles.

Similarly, when a group of Iranian scholars (Shokri, Kadivar, Farzad, Sangari, & Ghana-ei, 2006) investigated whether or not the Big Five personality traits (measured by the NEO Five-Factor Inventory) influenced the thinking styles of 419 college students in Iran, they obtained three key findings. First, openness and conscientiousness had a significantly positive effect on the judicial, global, and liberal styles (all being Type I). Second, neuroticism had a significantly positive impact on the executive, local, and conservative styles (all being Type II). Third, the openness personality trait had a significantly negative effect on the conservative thinking style. Thus, findings from recent studies carried out in Iran, Norway, and the United States supported the results from previous studies (e.g., Zhang & Huang, 2001) conducted in the Chinese context. All these studies suggest that Type I thinking styles were related to personality traits that are normally perceived to carry more positive value, such as openness and conscientiousness, and that Type II styles were correlated with neuroticism, a personality trait considered maladaptive in most cultural contexts.

In a series of two studies, Zhang and her colleague (Zhang, 2007c; Zhang & He, 2003) tested their hypothesis that students scoring higher on Type I thinking styles would be more knowledgeable about and have a

more work experience in addition to teaching in school settings, (b) report that they enjoyed adopting new teaching materials to a much larger degree, and (c) have received more professional training. Moreover, Type I teaching styles were also found to be related to teachers' positive perceptions of their work environments, including their career prospect, autonomy at work, and the quality of their students. Similar results were found among Hong Kong kindergarten teachers (Lee, 2002).

Another type of research evidence is from findings suggesting that teachers' teaching styles are significantly related to attributes perceived to be more adaptive. For example, Zhang (2001) examined how teachers' thinking styles in teaching are related to their teaching approaches. Teaching approaches were assessed by Trigwell and Prosser's (1996) Approaches to Teaching Inventory (ATI). The ATI is a self-report test. Containing 16 items, it assesses two different teaching approaches: student-centered (also known as the conceptual-change approach) and teacher-centered (also known as the knowledge-transmission approach).

Participants in this study were 76 in-service teachers from the Faculty of Education at the University of Hong Kong. Based on the definitions of the teaching styles defined in Sternberg's theory of mental self-government and on the two teaching approaches defined in Trigwell and Prosser's model, we predicted that teachers who reported using Type I teaching styles would score significantly higher on the conceptual-change teaching approach, whereas teachers reporting more frequent use of Type II teaching styles would score significantly higher on the knowledge-transmission teaching approach. Results fully supported this prediction. Moreover, this finding has been confirmed by Lee's (2002) study of kindergarten teachers in Hong Kong.

TYPE I THINKING STYLES ARE MORE ADAPTIVE: NEW EVIDENCE

Since the publication of our 2006 book on the nature of intellectual styles (Zhang & Sternberg, 2006), much more new empirical evidence has appeared in the literature, consistently suggesting that Type I thinking styles are more adaptive than are Type II ones. Such evidence can be found in studies of students, teachers, students and teachers in interaction, as well as in studies of business personnel.

Researchers also investigated whether or not students' thinking styles are related to their cognitive development. For example, Zhang (2002b) examined the relationship of thinking styles to cognitive development as measured by the Zhang Cognitive Development Inventory (Zhang, 1997), which is based on Perry's (1970, 1981) theory of ethical and intellectual development. Adopting an epistemological approach pioneered by Piaget (1952), Perry sought to trace the development of ways of reasoning among university students, moving from being dualistic and concrete to being more contingent and relativistic, and to being more committed. Research participants were 82 university students in Hong Kong. It was found that, in general, students who reasoned at higher levels of cognitive development tended to use a wider range of thinking styles, whereas students who reasoned at lower levels of cognitive development tended to be confined to a narrower range of thinking styles.

Another aspect against which thinking styles were tested was vocational purpose. Vocational purpose, according to Chickering (1969; Chickering & Reisser, 1993), is an important aspect of psychosocial development for university students. It refers to one's awareness of one's vocational interests and values and to one's conscious efforts of setting and working toward vocational goals. Zhang (2004a) examined the relationships between the thinking styles and vocational purpose as measured by the Iowa Vocational Purpose Inventory (Hood & Zerwas, 1997) among 233 students majoring in history and computer science from a large, research-oriented university in the People's Republic of China. It was concluded that Type I thinking styles contributed positively to students' vocational purpose and that Type II styles did so negatively.

Styles of Teachers

Not only students, but also teachers, prefer Type I thinking styles. In the process of studying teachers, we have gathered at least two types of research evidence demonstrating that Type I thinking styles in teaching (i.e., teaching styles) are more adaptive than are Type II styles. The first type of evidence comprises research findings obtained from studies of the relationships of teachers' teaching styles to a range of situational characteristics and a range of their perceptions of their teaching environments. For example, in their study of 119 Hong Kong secondary school teachers, Zhang and Sternberg (2002) found that teachers who reported more frequent use of Type I teaching styles tended to (a) have

TYPE I THINKING STYLES ARE MORE ADAPTIVE: A RECAPITULATION

Previously, we have argued from various perspectives that thinking styles are value-laden and that Type I thinking styles are, in general, more desirable than are Type II styles (Zhang & Sternberg, 2006). Among these various perspectives, examining the relationships of thinking styles to different human attributes has been the most telling. Many studies have been reviewed to demonstrate that Type I thinking styles are more adaptive because they have been consistently associated with positively valued human attributes. We recapitulate here the results of selected studies.

Styles of Students

Students' thinking styles have been tested against their levels of self-esteem. In a first Study, Zhang (2001) investigated the relationship of thinking styles to self-esteem among 794 university students from Hong Kong. Self-esteem was assessed by the Self-Esteem Inventory (Adult Form; Coopersmith, 1981). It was found that higher levels of self-esteem were significantly positively related to Type I thinking styles but moderately negatively related to Type II styles. In a second study of an independent sample of 694 university students from Hong Kong, Zhang and Postiglione (2001) obtained strikingly similar results.

In several studies, researchers addressed the question of whether or not Type I thinking styles are related to personality traits that are generally considered to be more desirable. Between 2001 and 2003, four such studies appeared in the literature, all examining the relationships between thinking styles and the Big Five personality traits as assessed by the NEO-Five Factor Inventory (Costa & McCrae, 1992/1995). In a first study (Zhang & Huang, 2001), research participants were 408 university students from Shanghai. The second study (Zhang, 2002a) involved 257 university students from Beijing. One hundred and fifty-four university students from Hong Kong participated in the third study (Zhang, 2002c), while 199 parents of secondary school students from Hangzhou, People's Republic of China were the participants in the fourth study (Zhang, 2003). Consistently, these studies indicated that Type I thinking styles were positively related to such adaptive personality traits as openness and conscientiousness, whereas Type II styles were positively related to neuroticism, a personality trait often regarded as undesirable.

style) and (b) "I prefer teaching the same subject and same class level every year" (conservative style).

The TSTI has been proved to be a reliable and valid inventory for assessing the teaching styles of both school teachers and university academics. It has been tested in Hong Kong (e.g., Lee, 2002; Zhang & Sternberg, 2002), mainland China (Zhang, 2007d), and in the United States (Grigorenko & Sternberg, 1995).

The Preferred Thinking Styles in Teaching Inventory (PTSTI; Zhang, 2003) is composed of 65 statements, with each set of 5 statements contributing to the measurement of students' preferences for one of the 13 thinking styles in teaching (i.e., teaching styles) described in the theory. For each statement, the participants rate themselves on a 7-point response scale, with 1 indicating that they absolutely disagree that the statement describes the way that they prefer that their teachers carry out tasks in their educational practice, and 7 denoting that they absolutely agree. Here are two sample statements: (a) "It is important that teachers allow students to develop their own ways of solving problems" (legislative style) and (b) "Teachers should encourage students to be more critical of what they read" (judicial style).

Satisfactory reliability and validity data of this inventory have been obtained in Hong Kong, mainland China, and the United States. Furthermore, such data have been obtained at both schools and universities (e.g., Zhang, 2004b, 2008; Zhang, Huang, & Zhang, 2005).

The Preferred Thinking Styles in Learning Inventory (PTSLI; Zhang, 2007b) is a 35-item self-report questionnaire. It measures teachers' preferences for the thinking styles that their students use in learning (i.e., learning styles). Like the TSTI, the PTSLI concerns seven styles described in Sternberg's theory: four Type I (legislative, judicial, global, and liberal) and three Type II (executive, local, and conservative) styles. For each item, the respondents rate themselves on a 7-point Likert scale, with 1 representing that they absolutely disagree that the statement describes the way that they prefer that their students carry out their learning tasks, and 7 suggesting that they absolutely agree so. Two sample items are: (a) "As a teacher, I like students who are mindful of checking and rating opposing points of view or conflicting ideas" (judicial style) and (b) "As a teacher, I like students who follow definite rules or directions when solving a problem or doing a task" (executive style).

Until now, the inventory has only been tested in Hong Kong and mainland China. It has proved to be reliable and valid in both sites (Zhang, Fu, & Jiao, 2008).

five dimensions, rather than along one. Second, the theory yields a profile of styles for each individual, rather than merely the identification of a single style. Based on both empirical data and conceptual arguments, we classified the 13 thinking styles into the three types (Zhang & Sternberg, 2005, 2006) shown in Table 3.1.

Main Research Tools Based on the Theory of Mental Self-Government

The Thinking Styles Inventory (TSI; Sternberg & Wagner, 1992) as well as its two revised versions (TSI-R and TSI-R2; Sternberg, Wagner, & Zhang, 2003, 2007) is a self-report test consisting of 65 statements. Each of the 13 thinking styles is assessed by 5 statements. For each statement, the participants rate themselves on a 7-point Likert scale, with 1 indicating that the statement does not at all describe the way they normally carry out tasks, and 7 denoting that the statement characterizes extremely well the way they normally carry out tasks. Here are two examples: (a) "When faced with a problem, I use my own ideas and strategies to solve it" (legislative style) and (b) "I like to figure out how to solve a problem following certain rules" (executive style).

This inventory is the most general one. It has been used with a variety of populations, including students, teachers, parents, and working adults from different walks of life. Furthermore, it has been validated in many studies conducted in different cultures, such as in the United States (e.g., Grigorenko & Sternberg, 1997), Spain (e.g., Cano-Garcia & Hughes, 2000), mainland China (Zhang & Sachs, 1997), and, more recently, in Korea (e.g., Park, Park, & Choe, 2005), Norway (e.g., Fjell & Walhovd, 2004), Turkey (e.g., Fer, 2005), and the United Kingdom (Zhang & Higgins, 2008).

The Thinking Styles in Teaching Inventory (TSTI; Grigorenko & Sternberg, 1993) is a 49-item self-report questionnaire in which teachers rate themselves on a 7-point response scale, with 1 denoting that the statement does not at all describe the way they normally carry out teaching tasks, and 7 denoting that the statement describes extremely well the way they normally carry out teaching tasks. The inventory assesses seven styles that fall into two types: Type I (legislative, judicial, global, and liberal) styles and Type II (executive, local, and conservative) styles. Each style is assessed by seven items. Two sample statements are (a) "I frequently assign students independent projects" (legislative

are prioritized. An individual with an *oligarchic* style also likes to work toward multiple objectives during the same period of time, but without setting clear priorities. Finally, an individual with an *anarchic* style enjoys working on tasks that require no system at all.

Levels

People's mental self-government takes place at two levels: local and global. An individual with a *local* style enjoys being engaged in tasks that require one to work with details. An individual with a *global* style pays more attention to the overall picture regarding an issue.

Scopes

There are two scopes of mental self-government: internal and external. An individual with an *internal* style enjoys being engaged in tasks that allow that individual to work independently. In contrast, an individual with an *external* style likes to be engaged in tasks that provide opportunities for developing interpersonal relationships.

Leanings

Finally, in mental self-government, there are two leanings: liberal and conservative. An individual with a *liberal* style enjoys being engaged in tasks that involve novelty and ambiguity, whereas a *conservative* person tends to adhere to existing rules and procedures in performing tasks.

Compared with other existing style models, the theory of mental self-government has several advantages, one of which is its breadth. The theory of mental self-government is a particularly general model of styles not only because the theory can be applied to various settings—academic and nonacademic—but also because it embraces all three traditions of the study of styles (Grigorenko & Sternberg, 1995). The styles in this theory are cognitive in their way of looking at things (e.g., judicial style, global style, and so forth) and correspond to preferences in the use of abilities. But the styles are typical performance rather than maximal performance. Therefore, they fall into the personality-centered tradition. Finally, the styles are part of the activity-centered tradition in that they can be measured in the context of activities.

Apart from being general, the theory of mental self-government also possesses two differentiating characteristics when compared with the majority of previous style models. First, the styles it specifies fall along

revealed from studies of the thinking styles proposed in Sternberg's (1997) theory of mental self-government.

The rest of this chapter is composed of four parts. The first introduces the theory of mental self-government and the main research tools for assessing thinking styles. The second recapitulates some of the research evidence provided in our earlier work. The third provides a detailed account of some of the research findings, most obtained after the publication of our 2006 styles book (Zhang & Sternberg, 2006). The final part draws conclusions from the empirical findings presented in the preceding two parts.

THE THEORY OF MENTAL SELF-GOVERNMENT AND ITS ASSESSMENT

The Theory of Mental Self-Government

Using the term "government" metaphorically, Sternberg (1988, 1997) contended that, just as there are many ways of governing a society, there are many ways of managing our activities, also known as thinking styles. According to Sternberg, there are 13 thinking styles that fall along five dimensions: functions, forms, levels, scopes, and leanings.

Functions

As in government, there are three functions in human beings' mental self-government: legislative, executive, and judicial. An individual with a *legislative* style enjoys being engaged in tasks that require creative strategies—that is, seeing or doing things in a new way. An individual with an *executive* style is more concerned with implementation of tasks with set guidelines—that is, getting things done in a way that is clearly specified for him or her. An individual with a *judicial* style focuses attention on evaluating others and the products of their activities.

Forms

Also as in government, a human being's mental self-government can take any of four different forms: monarchic, hierarchical, oligarchic, and anarchic. An individual with a *monarchic* style enjoys engaging in tasks that allow complete focus on one thing at a time. An individual with a *hierarchical* style prefers to distribute attention across several tasks that

Table 3.1

INTELLECTUAL STYLES

	STYLE TYPE	TYPE I	TYPE II	TYPE III
	Learning approach[a]	Deep	Surface	Achieving
	Career personality type[b]	Artistic	Conventional	Realistic, investigative, social, enterprising
	Mode of thinking[c]	Holistic	Analytic	Integrative
	Personality type[d]	Intuitive, perceiving	Sensing, judging	Thinking, feeling, introversion, extraversion
Style construct	Mind style[e]	Concrete random	Concrete sequential	Abstract random, abstract sequential
	Decision-making style[f]	Innovation	Adaptation	
	Conceptual tempo[g]	Reflectivity	Impulsivity	
	Structure of intellect[h]	Divergent thinking	Convergent thinking	
	Perceptual style[i]	Field independent	Field dependent	
	Thinking style[j]	Legislative, judicial, global, hierarchical, judicial	Executive, local, monarchic, conservative	Oligarchic, anarchic, internal, external

Note. Theoretical foundations: [a]Biggs's (1978) theory of student learning. [b]Holland's (1973) theory of career personality types. [c]Torrance's (1988) construct of brain dominance. [d]Jung's (1923) theory of personality types. [e]Gregorc's (1985) model of mind styles. [f]Kirton's (1976) model of decision-making styles. [g]Kagan's (1966) model of reflectivity-impulsivity conceptual tempo. [h]Guilford's (1967) model of structure of intellect. [i]Witkin's (1962) construct of field-dependence/independence. [j]Sternberg's (1988) theory of mental self-government.

different labels. Using our empirical investigations into the thinking styles proposed in Sternberg's (1988, 1997) theory of mental self-government as a starting point and drawing on other major works in the literature, we address these issues by proposing the threefold model of intellectual styles (Zhang & Sternberg, 2005, 2006). This model divides all styles into three basic kinds.

Specifically, the model classifies existing main style constructs into three broad types: Type I, Type II, and Type III styles. Type I intellectual styles denote preferences for tasks that provide low degrees of structure, that require individuals to process information in a more complex way, and that allow originality and high levels of freedom to do things in one's own way. Type II intellectual styles indicate preferences for tasks that are structured, that allow individuals to process information in a more straightforward way, and that require conformity to traditional ways of doing things as well as high levels of respect for authority. Type III styles may manifest the characteristics of either Type I or Type II styles, depending on the stylistic demands of a specific situation. We have organized 10 existing style models/constructs in terms of the threefold model of intellectual styles (see Table 3.1).

According to the model, styles have both traitlike and statelike aspects. For the most part, they are modifiable and hence more statelike; most styles are value-laden rather than value-free; and they overlap highly across theories. For each of these arguments, we provided empirical evidence (Zhang & Sternberg, 2005, 2006).

This chapter further pursues the issue of style value. Developing styles that can be used to respond effectively to one's environment is more important than ever before because the world is changing faster than ever before. Ideally, people should aim at acquiring high levels of flexibility in intellectual styles so that they can handle a variety of challenges.

One motivation for scholars to do research in the field of styles is to make suggestions, for example, to teachers and to students, regarding how they can develop more effective teaching and learning styles. The same aim applies to investigating people's intellectual styles in nonacademic settings. A question of broad import is whether there are particular styles that people should aim to develop. In previous publications (Zhang & Sternberg, 2005, 2006), we have argued that deliberately fostering Type I styles can be effective in preparing people to meet the challenges of a fast-changing world. The aim of this chapter is to amplify our previous argument that intellectual styles are value-laden (with Type I styles, on average, more adaptive), drawing on new research evidence

3

Revisiting the Value Issue in Intellectual Styles

LI-FANG ZHANG AND ROBERT J. STERNBERG

For the last two decades or so, developing creative thinking has been part of the mission statement of many educational institutions around the world. However, there is little evidence of many successes or even systematic efforts to develop creative thinking in educational institutions at any level (Langer, 1997). Such a discrepancy between what educators say they want and what they do reminds one of how much harder it is to develop creative thinking than to say one is doing it. We (Zhang & Sternberg, 2005, 2006) have recently argued that creative thinking can be developed through the promotion of certain styles of thinking.

An intellectual style refers to one's preferred way of processing information and dealing with tasks (Sternberg & Zhang, 2001; Zhang & Sternberg, 2005, 2006). The term "intellectual styles" is used in a general way to encompass the meanings of all major style constructs postulated in the past several decades, such as cognitive style, conceptual tempo, learning style, mind style, perceptual style, and thinking style. To varying degrees, an intellectual style is cognitive, affective, physiological, psychological, and sociological (see Zhang & Sternberg, 2005 for details).

The field of intellectual styles presents three particularly controversial issues: styles as value-laden versus value-free, styles as traits versus states, and styles as different constructs versus similar constructs with

Improving students as learners (pp. 262–271). Oxford, UK: Oxford Centre for Staff and Learning Development, Oxford Brookes University.

Teaching and Learning Research Programme. (2007). *Learning and teaching at university: The influence of subjects and settings* (Research Briefing 31, December 2007). Retrieved July 7, 2008, from http://www.tlrp.org

Tenenbaum, G., Naidu, S., Olugbemiro, J., & Austin, J. (2001). Constructivist pedagogy in conventional on-campus and distance learning practice: An exploratory investigation. *Learning and Instruction, 11,* 87–111.

Thomas, P. R., & Bain, J. D. (1984). Contextual dependence of learning approaches: The effects of assessments. *Human Learning, 3,* 227–240.

Trigwell, K., Prosser, M., & Waterhouse, F. (1999). Relations between teachers' approaches to teaching and students' approaches to learning. *Higher Education, 37,* 57–70.

Tynjälä, P. (1999). Towards expert knowledge? A comparison between a constructivist and a traditional learning environment in the university. *International Journal of Educational Research, 31,* 357–442.

Vermunt, J. D. (1998). The regulation of constructive learning processes. *British Journal of Educational Psychology, 68,* 149–171.

Vermunt, J. D., & Vermetten, Y. J. (2004). Patterns in student learning: Relationships between learning strategies, conceptions of learning, and learning orientations. *Educational Psychology Review, 16,* 359–384.

Weinstein, C. E., Husman, J., & Dierking, D. R. (2000). Self-regulation interventions with a focus on learning strategies. In M. Boekaerts, P. Pintrich, & M. Zeidner (Eds.), *Handbook of self-regulation* (pp. 727–747). London: Academic Press.

Wenger, E. (1998). *Communities of practice: Learning, meaning and identity.* Cambridge, UK: Cambridge University Press.

Westen, D. (1999). *Psychology: Mind, brain and culture.* New York: Wiley.

Wiske, M. S. (Ed.). (1998). *Teaching for understanding: Linking research with practice.* San Francisco: Jossey-Bass.

Witkin, H. A., Moore, C. A., Goodenough, D. R., & Cox, P. W. (1977). Field-dependent and field-independent cognitive styles and their educational implications. *Review of Educational Research, 47,* 1–64.

Witkin, H. A., Oltman, P. K., Raskin, E., & Karp, S. A. (1971). *Embedded Figures Test, Children's Embedded Figures Test, Group Embedded Figures Test.* Palo Alto, CA: Consulting Psychologists Press.

Zhang, L. F., & Sternberg, R. J. (2006). *The nature of intellectual styles.* Mahwah, NJ: Lawrence Erlbaum.

Chapter 2 The Disposition to Understand for Oneself at University and Beyond 61

Perkins, D. N., & Ritchhart, R. (2004). When is good thinking? In D. Yun Dai & R. J. Sternberg (Eds.), *Motivation, emotion and cognition: Integrative perspectives on intellectual functioning and development* (pp. 351–384). London: Lawrence Erlbaum Associates.

Perkins, D. N., & Tishman, S. (2001). Dispositional aspects of intelligence. In J. M. Collis & S. Messick (Eds.), *Intelligence and personality* (pp. 233–258). Mahwah, NJ: Lawrence Erlbaum.

Perkins, D. N., & Tishman, S. (2006). *Learning that matters: Toward a dispositional perspective on education and its research needs.* Unpublished paper, Harvard Graduate School of Education, Cambridge, MA.

Perry, W. G. Jr. (1970). *Forms of intellectual and ethical development in the college years: A scheme.* New York: Holt, Rinehart.

Perry, W. G. (1988). Different worlds in the same classroom. In P. Ramsden (Ed.), *Improving learning: New perspectives* (pp. 145–161). London: Kogan Page.

Pervin, L. A. (2001). Persons in context: Defining the issues, units, and processes. In J. M. Collis & S. Messick (Eds.), *Intelligence and personality* (pp. 307–318). Mahwah, NJ: Lawrence Erlbaum.

Piaget, J., & Inhelder, B. (1969). *The psychology of the child.* London: Routledge and Kegan Paul.

Prosser, M., & Trigwell, K. (1999). *Understanding learning and teaching: The experience in higher education.* Buckingham, UK: Society for Research into Higher Education and Open University Press.

Rezulli, J. S., & Dai, D. Y. (2001). Abilities, interests, and styles: a person-situation interaction. In R. J. Sternberg & L. F. Zhang (Eds.), *Perspectives on thinking, learning and cognitive styles* (pp. 23–46). Mahwah, NJ: Lawrence Erlbaum.

Riding, R., & Rayner, S. (1998). *Cognitive styles and learning strategies.* London: David Fulton.

Säljö, R. (1979). *Learning in the learner's perspective. I. Some common-sense conceptions* (Report 76). Gothenburg, Sweden: University of Gothenburg, Department of Education.

Säljö, R. (1982). *Learning and understanding: A study of differences in constructing meaning from a text* (Gothenburg Studies in Educational Sciences, 41). Gothenburg, Sweden: Acta Universitatis Gothoburgensis.

Scouller, K. (1998). The influence of assessment method on students' learning approaches: Multiple choice question examination versus assignment essay. *Higher Education, 35,* 453–452.

Shommer-Aikins, M. (2002). An evolving theoretical framework for an epistemological belief system. In B. K. Hofer & P. R. Pintrich (Eds.), *Personal epistemologies: The psychology of beliefs about knowledge and knowing* (pp. 103–118). Mahwah, NJ: Lawrence Erlbaum.

Snow, R. E., Corno, L., & Jackson, D. (1996). Individual differences in affective and conative functions. In D. C. Berliner & R. C. Calfee (Eds.), *Handbook of educational psychology* (pp. 186–242). New York: Simon & Schuster Macmillan.

Sperry, R. (1983). *Science and moral priority.* Oxford, UK: Blackwell.

Svensson, L. (1977). On qualitative differences in learning. III—Study skill and learning. *British Journal of Educational Psychology, 47,* 233–243.

Tait, H., Entwistle, N. J., & McCune, V. (1998). ASSIST: A re-conceptualisation of the Approaches to Studying Inventory. In C. Rust (Ed.), *Improving student learning:*

and university teaching (BJEP Monograph Series No. 2: Psychological Aspects of Education—Current Trends, pp. 91–111). Leicester, UK: British Psychological Society.

Hounsell, D., & McCune, V. (2002). *Teaching-learning environments in undergraduate biology: Initial perspectives and findings*. ETL Project Occasional Report 2. Edinburgh: Universities of Coventry, Durham, and Edinburgh.

Langer, E. (1989). *Mindfulness*. Reading, MA: Addison-Wesley.

Langer, E. (1997). *The power of mindful learning*. Cambridge, MA: Da Capo Press.

Lonka, K., & Lindblom-Ylänne, S. (1996). Epistemologies, conceptions of learning, and study practices in medicine and psychology. *Higher Education, 31,* 5–24.

Marton, F. (2007). Towards a pedagogical theory of learning. In N. J. Entwistle & P. D. Tomlinson (Eds.), *Student learning and university teaching* (British Journal of Educational Psychology Monograph Series II, No. 4, pp. 19–30). Leicester, UK: British Psychological Society.

Marton, F., & Säljö, R. (1976). On qualitative differences in learning: I. Outcome and process. *British Journal of Educational Psychology, 46,* 4–11.

Marton, F., & Säljö, R. (1997). Approaches to learning. In F. Marton, D. J. Hounsell, & N. J. Entwistle (Eds.), *The experience of learning* (2nd ed., pp. 39–58). Edinburgh: Scottish Academic Press.

Masui, C., & De Corte, E. (2005). Learning to reflect and to attribute constructively as basic components of self-regulated learning. *British Journal of Educational Psychology, 75,* 351–372.

McCune, V. (2000). *The development of first-year university students' approaches to studying*. Unpublished PhD thesis, University of Edinburgh.

McCune, V. (2007, August 28–September 1). *Final year biosciences students' willingness to engage: Teaching-learning environments, authentic learning experiences and identities*. Paper presented as part of the Invited Symposium of the Higher Education Special Interest Group at the 12th Biennial Conference of the European Association for Research on Learning and Instruction, Budapest, Hungary.

McCune, V. (in press). Final year biosciences students' willingness to engage: Teaching-learning environments, authentic learning experiences and identities. *Studies in Higher Education*.

McCune, V., & Hounsell, D. (2005). The development of students' ways of thinking and practising in three final-year biology courses. *Higher Education, 49,* 255–289.

Nieminen, J., Lindblom-Ylänne, S., & Lonka, K. (2004). The development of study orientations and study success in students of pharmacy. *Instructional Science, 32,* 387–417.

Northedge, A., & McArthur, J. (in press). Guiding students into a discipline: The significance of the teacher. In C. Kreber (Ed.), *The university and its disciplines: Teaching and learning within and beyond disciplinary boundaries*. London: Routledge.

Pask, G. (1976). Styles and strategies of learning. *British Journal of Educational Psychology, 46,* 128–148.

Pask, G. (1988). Learning strategies, teaching strategies and conceptual or learning style. In R. Schmeck (Ed.), *Learning strategies and learning styles* (pp. 83–100). New York: Plenum Press.

Perkins, D. N. (2008). Beyond understanding. In R. Land, J. H. F. Meyer, & J. Smith (Eds.), *Threshold concepts within the disciplines* (pp. 3–19). Rotterdam, Netherlands: Sense Publishers.

Entwistle, N. J. (1988). *Styles of learning and teaching*. London: David Fulton.
Entwistle, N. J. (1998). Motivation and approaches to learning: Motivating and conceptions of teaching. In S. Brown, S. Armstrong, & G. Thompson (Eds.), *Motivating students* (pp. 15–23). London: Kogan Page.
Entwistle, N. J. (2007). Research into student learning and university teaching. In N. J. Entwistle & P. D. Tomlinson (Eds.), *Student learning and university teaching* (British Journal of Educational Psychology Monograph Series II, No. 4, pp. 1–18). Leicester, UK: British Psychological Society.
Entwistle, N. J. (2008). *Taking stock: Teaching and learning research in higher education*. Review prepared for an international symposium on "Teaching and Learning Research in Higher Education," Guelph, Ontario, April 25–26.
Entwistle, N. J., & Entwistle, A. C. (1991). Contrasting forms of understanding for degree examinations: The student experience and its implications. *Higher Education, 22,* 205–227.
Entwistle, N. J., & Entwistle, A. C. (1997). Revision and the experience of understanding. In F. Marton, D. J. Housell, & N. J. Entwistle (Eds.), *The experience of learning* (2nd ed., pp. 145–158). Edinburgh, UK: Scottish Academic Press.
Entwistle, N. J., & Entwistle, D. M. (2003). Preparing for examinations: The interplay of memorising and understanding, and the development of knowledge objects. *Higher Education Research and Development, 22,* 19–42.
Entwistle, N. J., & McCune, V. (2004). The conceptual bases of study strategy inventories. *Educational Psychology Review, 16,* 325–346.
Entwistle, N. J., McCune, V., & Hounsell, J. (2003). Investigating ways of enhancing university teaching-learning environments: Measuring students' approaches to studying and perceptions of teaching. In E. De Corte, L. Verschaffel, N. Entwistle, & J. van Merriënboer (Eds.), *Powerful learning environments: Unravelling basic components and dimensions* (pp. 89–108). Oxford, UK: Elsevier Science.
Entwistle, N. J., & Ramsden, P. (1983). *Understanding student learning*. London: Croom Helm.
Entwistle, N. J., & Tait, H. (1990). Approaches to learning, evaluations of teaching, and preferences for contrasting academic environments. *Higher Education, 19,* 169–194.
Fyrenius, A., Silén, C., & Wirell, S. (2007). Students' conceptions of underlying principles in medical physiology: An interview study of medical students' understanding in a PBL curriculum. *Advances in Physiological Education, 31,* 364–369.
Fyrenius, A., Wirell, S., & Silén, C. (2007). Student approaches to achieving understanding—approaches to learning revisited. *Studies in Higher Education, 32,* 149–165.
Hattie, J., Biggs, J., & Purdie, N. (1996). Effects of learning skills interventions on student learning: A meta-analysis. *Review of Educational Research, 66,* 99–136.
Heath, R. (1964). *The reasonable adventurer*. Pittsburgh, PA: University of Pittsburgh Press.
Holland, D., Lachiotte, W. Jr., Skinner, D., & Cain, C. (1998). *Identity and agency in cultural worlds*. Cambridge, MA: Harvard University Press.
Hounsell, D., & Anderson, C. (2009). Ways of thinking and practicing in biology and history: Disciplinary aspects of teaching and learning environments. In C. Kreber (Ed.), *The university and its disciplines: Teaching and learning within and beyond disciplinary boundaries* (pp. 70–83). London: Routledge.
Hounsell, D., & Hounsell, J. (2007). Teaching-learning environments in contemporary mass higher education. In N. Entwistle & P. Tomlinson (Eds.), *Student learning*

climate change) will result in encounters with supercomplexity. Against this background, the importance and the challenges inherent in encouraging the disposition to understand for oneself become clear. To be effective in the world, students will need the sensitivity to context required to see how their understanding can be applied to complex problems and to be aware of ongoing opportunities to enhance their understanding in relation to a rapidly changing world. The challenges of maintaining the inclination component of the disposition to understand in the face of complex and supercomplex problems makes clear the importance of a higher education that supports students in developing a truly robust will to learn and the confidence to build and commit to personal perspectives on what is learned without becoming closed to others' viewpoints (Barnett, 2007; Perkins, 2008).

REFERENCES

Ausubel, D. P., Novak, J. D., & Hanesian, H. (1978). *Educational psychology: A cognitive view* (2nd ed.). New York: Holt, Rinehart & Winston.

Barnett, R. (2007). *A will to learn: Being a student in an age of uncertainty*. Berkshire, UK: Open University Press and Society for Research into Higher Education.

Baxter-Magolda, M. (in press). Educating students for self-authorship: Learning partnerships to achieve complex outcomes. In C. Kreber (Ed.), *The university and its disciplines: Teaching and learning within and beyond disciplinary boundaries*. London: Routledge.

Baxter-Magolda, M., & King, P. (Eds.). (2004). *Learning partnerships: Theory and models of practice to educate for self-authorship*. Sterling, VA: Stylus.

Belenky, M. F., Clinchy, B. M., Goldberger, N. R., & Tarule, J. M. (1986). *Women's ways of knowing*. New York: Harper Collins.

Biggs, J. B. (1987). *Student approaches to learning and studying*. Melbourne, Australia: Australian Council for Educational Research.

Biggs, J. B. (2003). *Teaching for quality learning at university* (2nd ed.). Buckingham, UK: SRHE & Open University Press.

Biggs, J. B. (2007). *Teaching for quality learning at university* (3rd ed.). Buckingham, UK: SRHE & Open University Press.

Cacioppo, J. T., Petty, R. E., Feinstein, J. A., & Jarvis, W. B. G. (1996). Dispositional differences in cognitive motivation: The life and times of individuals varying in need for cognition. *Psychological Bulletin, 119*(2), 197–253.

Craik, F. I. M., & Lockhart, R. S. (1972). Levels of processing: A framework for memory research. *Journal of Verbal Learning and Verbal Behavior, 11*, 671–684.

Crawford, K., Gordon, S., Nicholas, J., & Prosser, M. (1998). Qualitatively different experiences of learning mathematics at university. *Learning and Instruction, 8*(5), 455–468.

Eizenberg, N. (1988). Approaches to learning anatomy: Developing a programme for preclinical medical students. In P. Ramsden (Ed.), *Improving learning: New perspectives* (pp. 178–198). London: Kogan Page.

aligned with understanding aims (Wiske, 1998), and from interventions that focus on teaching the learning strategies in context and interview studies with individual students. However, these interviews also explain why it is difficult to develop the deep approach, and by extension the disposition to understand for oneself, simply by such interventions. Even when students have the necessary inclination, in the early stages of a degree they still lack the understanding of the WTPs in the discipline and the experience of differing ways of developing their understanding that will lead, later, to the sensitivity to context necessary to make their inclination effective. Teaching that helps students to see themselves as nascent professionals, and provides authentic contexts within which to think about real-life problems and situations, seems to be one important way of developing sensitivity to context.

The term "disposition" carries with the idea that all three elements—in our case, learning strategies, the will to learn, and sensitivity to context—act in consort, probably synergistically, to create understandings that are both academically stronger, and more practically useful, than would otherwise be the case. We have found all the elements of the disposition to understand for oneself in students at university, with evidence that each, separately, is likely to affect understanding performances. Having at least some level of each of these elements will be necessary to achieve flexible, transferable use of academic understanding, and it is logical that these pull together in improving the effectiveness of performance.

At this stage, first, we do have to consider whether it is worth introducing yet another concept into the formidable array of existing concepts already used to describe learning at university. Its strength lies in focusing the combined contributions of its troika of elements pulling toward the ways of thinking and practicing that graduates are expected to develop at university and to be able to use thereafter. And such a disposition, it can be argued, has become more important in the 21st century because of major changes in society that are affecting working contexts and everyday lives. In their working lives after graduation, students will have to tackle problems that are not just complex—in the sense of open-ended, real-life situations in which any attempt at a solution will have unforeseen effects—but also "supercomplex" in that the problems faced are fundamentally irresolvable, as competing proposed solutions spring from incompatible ideologies and value positions (Barnett, 2007). Even in the hard sciences, where there are large bodies of well-established knowledge, the application of that knowledge to real world issues (such as

seen to lie on the cusp of descriptions of personality, it was far from clear which aspects of personality they covered. Another research tradition from that same period explained performance in terms of an individual's needs, either for achievement or for cognition, keeping intellectual influences separate. Nevertheless, as we saw, the need for cognition was associated with openness, the most cognitive element of the big five personality traits, and also to conscientiousness, with its links to motivation.

The idea of mindfulness also stressed the importance of openness, in the sense of being open to information and to new ways of describing phenomena, but it also brought in the idea of reaching and drawing out information from the environment. Mindfulness was seen as a disposition that could be strengthened; in other words, while being consistent it was still amenable to change over time and with suitable experience. And this leads to the idea of a *thinking disposition* that explicitly links ability, motivation in the form of inclination, and sensitivity to context. To be able to deal effectively with problems and new situations, you must have the necessary intellectual and other capacities, you must want to use them, and you must also be sensitive to the opportunities for using the understandings accrued over time. Perkins (2008) describes this reaching out into the environment as going "beyond understanding."

Our notion of a *disposition to understand for oneself* is a particular kind of thinking disposition that reveals itself within university and other educational contexts. It appears to be a more consistent and stronger form of the intention to understand found in the deep approach to learning, seen as a continuing will to learn (Barnett, 2007), in the sense of wanting to reach the fullest and most satisfying understanding possible at a particular time. It includes learning strategies (ability), seen in the use, *in tandem,* of relating ideas (holist) and the critical use of evidence and attention to detail (serialist), and depends on reaching the sophisticated conception of learning associated with effective monitoring of learning processes and understanding. It also requires the student to have grasped the essence of knowledge and academic discourse within the disciplines or professional areas being studied. The disposition to understand for oneself leads to a continuing determination to use acquired knowledge and WTPs in new contexts, as well showing an alertness to possibilities for applying them. And there is clear evidence that the component aspects of this disposition are amenable to improvement, although often over time and with difficulty.

Evidence for a strengthening of the deep approach comes both from the work on the influences of the whole TLE when it is constructively

ing respect for students' current understandings while helping them to understand how new knowledge is developed (Baxter-Magolda, in press; Baxter-Magolda & King, 2004). This process is intended to aid them in reaching a position where they feel able to form their own viewpoints, while respecting contrasting viewpoints and being prepared to learn from others. The intention is to: show students explicitly how knowledge is constructed; to give them a role in creating their own understandings; and to help them, where relevant, to accept the provisional nature and uncertainty of the knowledge claims being made in the topic under study.

DISCUSSION

The focus of this book is on the nature of *intellectual styles,* and we need to consider our idea of a disposition to understand for oneself from that standpoint. Earlier, we mentioned several research approaches related to intellectual styles and dispositions, and, in such studies, we see a range of attempts to make sense of the varying influences on reaching a target level of understanding (Entwistle, 2007). The origins of these ideas can be traced to the discovery, by Witkin et al. (1977), that people differed in the ease with which they were able to distinguish figure from ground or an image from its context. That capability might now be seen as a sensitivity to context within the perceptual field that was lacking in those who had low scores on field-independence. Although the method of measurement led some researchers to see field independence as a perceptual *ability,* Witkin maintained that it was a cognitive *style,* with each pole being equally functional, although for different purposes. And that characteristic was carried forward into the subsequent idea of the more generalized forms of articulated and global thinking.

The distinctions within these broader styles appear to be similar to those drawn by Pask (1976) between broad, relational thinking (holistic) and the concern with logic and detail (serialist). But these polarized styles lose the complementarity seen in the deep approach, where the intention to understand draws on both relating ideas (holist) and use of evidence (serialist) to become a versatile style. Yet none of these categories contain any sense of the tendency to reach out, to find opportunities to develop and use understanding, which are involved in sensitivity to context and seemed to exist, perceptually, within field-independence.

The early research on cognitive styles saw them as being more or less fixed intellectual characteristics of the individual and, while they were

biosciences and their willingness to engage deeply with their studies. Their sensitivity to context was shaped by the search for relevance in relation to their future work and by their identification with particular subject areas:

> If you are very good at one subject then you have a special way of thinking about that subject, . . . so outside that subject you try to link it to this main subject . . . I'll always be thinking from a micro-biological point of view . . . So that it can help me direct my interest.
>
> I think the students have a lot more questions to ask because they have their own specific areas of interest now. And before I think, a lot of people have just been sitting there, asking simple questions and now they are really relating it to their actual real life experience, their actual projects. (McCune, 2007)

Close analysis of the data revealed that some of the students were describing a profound shift in their learner identities, which seemed to have a marked impact on the effort they subsequently put into their studies and their disposition to understand for themselves. The key shift seemed to be toward feeling genuinely able to engage critically with research findings, and this was associated with feeling like a scientist, rather than like a *student of* the sciences. The students also described certain authentic learning experiences that seemed to support this shift. These experiences were described by students variously as: similar to how they imagined scientists work in the real world; involving their engagement with open-ended research questions, contradictory findings, and contested interpretations; their social integration into research communities; and being trusted to approach tasks independently and responsibly.

Earlier in this chapter, we noted that changes in conceptions of learning and knowledge can see students experience a shift in which they come to see themselves as actively responsible for their own learning, rather than as passive recipients of knowledge from Authority. This represents a profound shift in students' learner identities. The more developed conceptions of learning and knowledge are related to the intention to understand, more active learning processes, and greater engagement in self-regulation of learning. Thus such shifts in students' conceptions would be expected to strengthen the disposition to understand.

Baxter-Magolda has written extensively on the nature of the learning experiences that may provoke development in students' conceptions and their sense of personal agency as learners. Emphasis is placed on show-

discipline will often struggle to make sense of definitions or arguments in that discipline because the basis for understanding these is the taken-for-granted approaches, values, and histories of debate, which are unknown to the student. Northedge and McArthur draw on the work of Bruner to emphasize the importance of students and teachers attaining *states of intersubjectivity* where mutual understanding becomes possible through teachers focusing students' attention on a common object on which shared framing assumptions may be brought to bear. What the teacher therefore has to do is create a context within which students can focus with the teacher on a mutually accessible example, such as a case study, and discuss this using language that has sufficient connection with students' current understandings for them to be able to connect with the teacher's perspectives. Over time this support can be withdrawn as the student gains an understanding of the tacit features of the discipline that allow them to make sense of more challenging material and to have the sensitivity to attend to what will support this developing understanding.

Learner Identities and the Disposition to Understand for Oneself

Learner identities can include several aspects, namely individuals' senses of who they are; their perceptions of their positions in networks of roles and relationships; their interpretations of their personal history; and their ideas about how they would like to be in the future (Holland, Lachiotte, Skinner, & Cain, 1998; Wenger, 1998). One of the ways in which learners' identities can be seen as relevant to the disposition to understand is in how identities can frame what is meaningful or relevant for a student. Wenger (1998), for example, introduces the notion of learning trajectories, which form part of learners' identities. This notion of trajectories takes into account that identities can encompass both a sense of where an individual has been and a sense of where they are going in relation to particular communities of practice. Wenger contended that learners' perspectives on where they are going in relation to such communities helps them to decide what matters to them and what does not, and what they may incorporate in their developing identity and what will remain marginal for them.

This relationship between learning trajectories and the disposition to understand was seen in a recent interview study with final-year undergraduate students in the biosciences (McCune, 2007, in press). These students made clear links between their planned careers in the biosciences with the WTPs taught in the history settings. When engaging with primary sources in the biosciences, students were expected to understand how knowledge was generated in the subject area, as can be seen from this quote from a biosciences teacher:

> Students need to understand how things are known in this area, rather than simply being given lots of facts. So they need to know about experimental techniques and the interpretation of findings. Ultimately you want them to leave the programme being able to think about how to design their own experiments. You begin this by showing them how other people have designed experiments and tested things. (Hounsell & McCune, 2002, p. 17)

While the history students were also expected to develop an understanding of how knowledge was generated, the processes in which they were engaged and the sensitivities they were expected to have were quite different, as can be seen from this overview given by Hounsell and Anderson (2009):

> Another aspect of the diversity of historical knowledge is that within particular domains of historical study there typically are competing narratives and explanations. In engaging with these competing accounts, students need to be alert to authorial stance and the way in which this stance may be related to the historian's political, social and cultural positioning. (p. 77)

So the disposition to understand a particular subject area for oneself can be seen as developing over time as students come to grasp and identify with the forms of understanding, values, and practices of their academic disciplines. This emphasis on particular subject areas also raises the question as to how meaningful it is to speak of a disposition to understand for oneself in general terms. It may well be that a student with a strong disposition to understand in relation to one subject area might be either disinclined or insufficiently skilled to show such a disposition in relation to another academic discipline.

Hounsell and Anderson (2009) provide a number of examples of how the disposition to understand a particular subject area might be encouraged. Their examples often focus on students' active engagement in knowledge construction and teachers' efforts to make the tacit practices of the discipline more explicit. Considering further the difficulty of students gaining access to the tacit dimensions of academic disciplines, Northedge and McArthur (in press) argue that a novice in a

understand and to take the opportunity to modify her learning accordingly. Earlier in the year she had indicated that understanding was quite easy to achieve and the realization that it could be difficult to understand topics fully was an important shift in her sensitivity.

> I would just skim through it and got completely the wrong meaning, just because I assumed it would be a different meaning . . . So, I just read it through a second time, very slowly . . . I think actually this time I understood what they were talking about rather than just made up what they were talking about by making little references back to it.

These apparent changes in Leane's learning seemed to be partly supported by her perception of the role of higher education—that it was to help her develop her thinking. This was an unusual perspective for this cohort of students. She also had prior experience in high school of changing her ways of learning successfully. A critical incident in which her university tutor read her first essay aloud to her was described as a turning point, in that she came to realize that her work was not of as high a standard as she had thought and this seemed to feed into her realization of how difficult it can be to develop a more sophisticated understanding of a topic. Finally, Leane's sense of the personal relevance of psychology increased markedly over the year. Her experiences echo the overall findings of this study, that changes in the disposition to understand seemed to involve individual sensitivity to the opportunities for change afforded by particular incidents grounded in students' varied attitudes, goals, and learning histories.

The Disposition to Understand and the Cultures of Academic Disciplines

The development of the disposition to understand must also be understood in relation to the cultures of academic disciplines. These cultures have distinctive *ways of thinking and practicing* (WTPs), which shape what will be seen as ability and what students must attend to show effective sensitivity to context (McCune & Hounsell, 2005). The notion of WTPs in a subject area was developed to describe the richness, depth, and breadth of what students might learn through engagement with a given subject area in a specific context. This might include aspects that were explicitly taught, as well as more tacit norms and practices. This can be illustrated by contrasting some of the findings from the ETL research project concerning the WTPs taught in a range of course settings in the

understand the course material as presented by their lecturers; very few of them spoke of engaging widely with the literature or striving for more personal perspectives. This situation persisted throughout the year for most of the students despite assessment criteria for their coursework that emphasized the importance of forming a personal understanding through critical reflection on research findings. The students also attended lectures about student learning in which the deep approach and contextual influences on it were discussed at some length. Possible reasons for this lack of change seemed to include: a lack of explicit emphasis on developing new ideas about learning in the students' prior and current learning experiences; the relatively limited learning goals espoused by many of the students and their ease in reaching these goals; and, finally, students' difficulties in coming to terms with how to form a personal understanding in a manner that would be acceptable within the practices of the discipline of psychology. We shall return to this issue of disciplinary cultures and the disposition to understand later in the chapter.

Some of the students did describe departures from this typical pattern, apparently making more effort to develop ways of learning more aligned with the disposition to understand for oneself. One case study, Leane, is presented here to illustrate the complex and idiosyncratic interplay of factors that seemed to relate to the development of the disposition. She described a consistent intention to understand throughout her first year, although the depth of understanding she sought did depend to some extent on the learning task in which she was engaged at the time. Over the course of the year she began to describe a growing desire to develop a more personal understanding and to monitor the quality of her understanding for herself. Her account of her learning encompassed all three aspects of a disposition to understand for oneself: ability, inclination, and sensitivity to context—albeit in a more modest form than might be expected from more experienced students. The extract below suggests her sensitivity to how the learning context had changed to demand greater personal understanding.

> For [high school examinations] it seems to be more on style to get you through. But by the time you get to university, style isn't enough . . . I used to be a bit of a culprit for a waffly essay that I didn't know that much about what I was writing . . . It's actually getting into the realms of having to read those big books about it, and having to understand it yourself.

The following extract describes sensitivity to context in a different form. Leane discussed how she had come to notice when she did not

The research discussed thus far does not have a great deal to say about cultivating sensitivity to context. This issue has, however, been considered by David Perkins and his colleagues. These authors note the importance of avoiding performance on demand, where students only demonstrate their understanding when specifically cued to do so (Perkins & Ritchhart, 2004; Perkins & Tishman, 2006). They argue that, in order for students to be able to make use of their understanding in relation to complex, real-world problems, they need to have opportunities to engage with such authentic experiences and to identify for themselves when and how their understanding of a particular topic can be applied. Perkins and colleagues also suggest that it may, sometimes, be fruitful explicitly to teach alertness to the subtle signs that thinking of a particular kind is required. Much of Perkins and colleagues' work has been done with school children and—although many authors argue for the importance of authentic learning experiences in higher education (for example, Tenenbaum, Naidu, Olugbemiro, & Austin, 2001; Tynjälä, 1999)—there is little evidence available about the impact of such experiences on students' approaches to learning or other aspects of the disposition to understand.

Students' Sensitivity to Opportunities for Developing the Disposition to Understand

The literature suggests that students may differ in how prepared they are to take opportunities that might allow them to develop a stronger disposition to understand. For example, students who differ in their beliefs about learning and knowledge, their preferred approaches to learning, or their background knowledge of the subject area may also differ in their capacity to perceive or value opportunities for understanding that are presented (Crawford, Gordon, Nicholas, & Prosser, 1998; Entwistle & Tait, 1990; Perry, 1970, 1988; Säljö, 1982). A small-scale longitudinal study with first-year psychology students (McCune, 2000) allows us to develop this point further, as the students differed markedly in their development toward a disposition to form personal understandings and in the extent to which they responded to opportunities to change their perspectives on learning.

In this study, a small cohort of students participated in semi-structured interviews at three points during the academic year: once near the beginning of their time at university, once after their first assessment, and, finally, toward the end of their first year of undergraduate study. Most of the students in this cohort described a fairly limited intention to

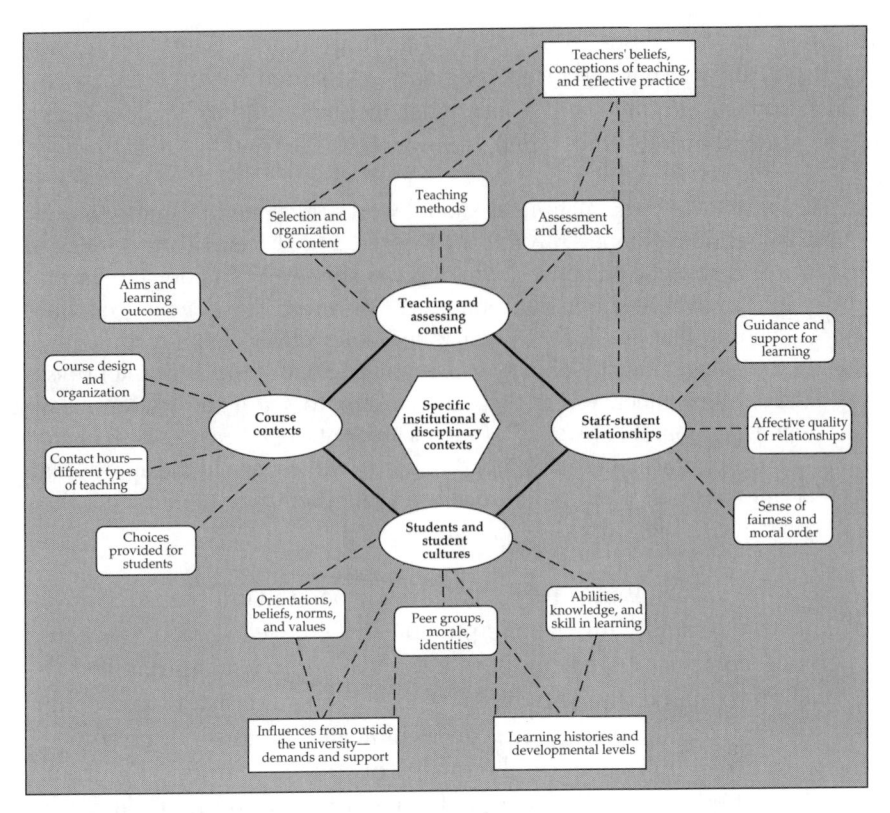

Figure 2.2 The inner teaching-learning environment influencing student learning. From "Investigating Ways of Enhancing University Teaching-Learning Environments: Measuring Students' Approaches to Studying and Perceptions of Teaching," by N. J. Entwistle, V. McCune, & J. Hounsell, 2003. In E. De Corte, L. Verschaffel, N. Entwistle, & J. van Merriënboer (Eds.), *Powerful Learning Environments: Unravelling Basic Components and Dimensions* (pp. 89–108). Oxford, UK: Elsevier Science.

ties suggests that it is possible to train students in the kinds of thinking processes and metacognitive reflection that would support the disposition to understand for oneself (Hattie, Biggs, & Purdie, 1996; Weinstein, Husman, & Dierking, 2000). Overall, the findings indicate that such efforts are more successful when the training is closely linked to students' academic work in their subject areas, rather than taught in a more decontextualized fashion (Hattie et al., 1996). While it has been more difficult to demonstrate the kinds of transfer of learning that would provide evidence for a lasting shift in disposition, some transfer does seem to be possible (Hattie et al., 1996; Masui & De Corte, 2005).

the learning processes involved in a deep approach. Biggs (2007), for example, argues that if the teaching and assessment within a course are *constructively aligned* to the aims that involve students in developing their understanding, then a deep approach will follow.

> It's easy to see why alignment should work. In aligned teaching there is maximum consistency throughout the system. The curriculum is stated in terms of clear objectives, which states the level of understanding required, rather than a list of topics to be covered. The teaching methods are chosen that are likely to realize those objectives; you get students to do the things that the objectives nominate. Finally, the assessment tasks address the objectives, so that you can test to see if the students have [achieved them] . . . [And so] students are "entrapped" in this web of consistency, optimising the likelihood that they will engage in the appropriate learning activities, but paradoxically leaving them free to construct their knowledge. (Biggs, 2003, p. 27)

However, Eizenberg (1988) had already pointed out that such a web of consistency is difficult, even impossible, to achieve in practice because even one component that induces a surface approach can damage the overall effect markedly. The difficulty in ensuring consistent and coherent support for a deep approach can be indicated by considering some of the most direct influences on the quality of student learning. Figure 2.2 was developed in the initial stages of a major project set up to find ways of enhancing teaching-learning environments in undergraduate courses (the ETL project) (Entwistle et al., 2003; also see TLRP, 2007). This was described as the "inner teaching-learning environment," as it was limited mainly to those influences likely to be directly experienced by the students.

The diagram focuses on four main groups of elements, course contexts, teaching and assessment content, staff-student relationships, and students and student cultures, and brings out some of the main aspects in those groups. The outlying boxes indicate some of the influences that lie outside this inner environment, while the central hexagon reminds us that in each institution and each subject area, the nature of the whole set of influences will differ.

In spite of this overall complexity, some attempts have been made to influence approaches to learning by working directly with students to develop learning strategies or self-regulation more explicitly, either through stand-alone study skills courses or by embedding reflection on learning within students' day-to-day studies. Research into such activi-

have shown, to varying degrees, elements of stability and change. We have to see how to capitalize on the change element to strengthen the disposition to understand for oneself.

Several bodies of literature provide insights into the ways in which these capacities may develop over time and into how such development might be supported. We will begin by considering research into teaching-learning environments (TLEs) in higher education and how students' dispositions to understand may develop within these contexts. This leads to questions as to why some students seem more prepared to respond to opportunities to develop their understanding and their disposition to understand, and findings from a small-scale longitudinal study with first-year undergraduates are used to consider this issue in more depth. The disposition to understand is also shaped by the culture of academic disciplines, and we will review research in this area before considering how learner identities may relate to the development of the disposition to understand.

Teaching-Learning Environments and the Disposition to Understand for Oneself

The impact of TLEs on approaches to learning is well established in the research literature (Biggs, 2007; Entwistle & Ramsden, 1983; Hounsell & Hounsell, 2007; Prosser & Trigwell, 1999). If students could have repeated experiences of TLEs that supported a deep approach, this might encourage a more lasting disposition to understand, although the kinds of longitudinal studies that might demonstrate this have yet to be carried out. Existing longitudinal research looking at approaches to learning presents a very mixed picture, with the deep approach increasing in some studies and decreasing in others (McCune, 2000; Nieminen, Lindblom-Ylänne, & Lonka, 2004). It would need studies that followed students throughout and beyond a program of study that consistently supported a deep approach to provide good evidence that the disposition to understand for oneself could be effectively developed.

Further, the main message from research into changing approaches to learning is that it is much easier to lead students into surface approaches, through assessments that appear to demand no more than factual responses (Scouller, 1998; Thomas & Bain, 1984), than it is to lead them into deeper approaches. Some researchers have suggested that it is possible, in principle, to design TLEs that entrap students in a web of teaching-learning activities, all of which require students to use

up their understanding. Whereas in the fixed form, a causal chain of evidence and conclusions was built up from a single perspective, the flexible form involved

> actively striving for a change in perspectives of the phenomenon and the use of multiple learning modalities. . . . These students actively exposed themselves to challenge and variation to acquire new perspectives of the phenomenon they were trying to understand, and the processes of developing understanding were considered to be an open-ended process. Understanding was continuously nuanced and refined by new information . . . [through] a continuous restructuring and reframing of facts and knowledge. . . . (Fyrenius, Silén, & Wirell, 2007, p. 368)
> It seems that [these] students continuously shift between details and wholes, and are simultaneously aware of the overall picture and details, even though their focus is on one of the two. (Fyrenius, Wirell, & Silén, 2007, pp. 160–161)

Moreover, the students who adopted this more active and flexible deep approach achieved an understanding that involved reaching out into new situations. As a result of their flexible understanding, students showed "awareness of conditions for the phenomena in various contexts. . . . [and] awareness of relevance of the phenomena in . . . therapy and/or disease" (Fyrenius, Silén, et al., 2007, p. 367)

This determination to go beyond the immediate demands of the syllabus to see how their understanding applied in practice, and to continuously refine their understanding again, seems consonant with their having a *disposition to understand* for themselves, adding to the growing, if still fragmentary, evidence of this description of a potentially important aspect of student learning.

EVOKING AND DEVELOPING THE DISPOSITION TO UNDERSTAND FOR ONESELF

As no empirical research has yet been carried out to describe the development of dispositions over the course of a degree, indications of what is likely to encourage the strengthening of that disposition come from existing studies on deep approaches and the related aspects mentioned previously. Although the term "disposition" implies an inclination to continue along a particular line, all the concepts describing student learning

surface. And once I started writing, it all just "welled up." I felt that I couldn't interrupt the argument half-way as it was developing.
I: Why did you feel you had to do that?
S: Basically, the way it ties together as a whole—it's very difficult to pick something like that apart, when you understand the theory like that. . . . I have to explain it in that way—you can't cut it up and avoid bits. Half an understanding doesn't make sense!
I: Are you saying that you have to explain it in the way you understand it for yourself?
S: Yes . . . It's *essential* to demonstrate your understanding of the whole, and its implications and limitations and you also need to demonstrate a critical approach to any evidence.
I: Might that insistence affect your exam marks?
S: You could say I shouldn't be [doing] that in an exam, but basically I *have* to do it that way, because that's me.
I: Is that what you want to get out of it?
S: Not necessarily. Among many of my friends it's more underlying than that; it's not even the will to succeed, it's almost an *obsession*.

The italicized words accurately reflect the strength of feeling put into these responses, and here we see a need both to understand and to demonstrate that understanding to others. This strong feeling of commitment to understanding puts it at the top end of Perry's traverse of epistemological development shown earlier in Figure 2.1, and so suggests that it had become a part of this student's sense of identity as a learner. It also implies a much stronger form of the idea of "willingness" than does the term "inclination."

Further evidence of such a strong sense of caring about understanding comes from a recent study of medical students, almost all of whom, within a long-established problem-based curriculum, were actively seeking understanding. But again the form of understanding differed, with some students feeling threatened by ideas that challenged their hard-won current understanding and so holding on to a fixed form of understanding that they believed was the "right" one. These students felt well able to explain their completed understanding, but were less comfortable when it came to using it in new situations. In contrast, students with a more flexible form of understanding actively sought to expand and refine it, and so welcomed new insights: they were also much more confident about *applying* their understanding to their work with patients. These students also differed in the way they used evidence in building

that encourages understanding has also been shown (Tait et al., 1998). These findings suggest that students are able, to some extent at least, to recognize what will help them in their intention to understand. The deep approach brings in the intention to understand for oneself, indicating an inclination or a willingness to learn, backed up by the alternating use of relating ideas and use of evidence (holist and serialist styles combined into versatility). Monitoring of understanding indicates elements of metacognition, in being ready to stand back from the learning process and reflect on it, but also the sensitivity to context needed in using the processes effectively in carrying out academic tasks. The correlation between the factors, and the item analysis, links monitoring understanding and deep intention with organized effort. In this way, there is cumulative evidence from the survey analyses of a grouping of related aspects going beyond the original definition of a deep approach. We can now draw on evidence from student interviews to broaden still further the elements linked to a deep approach to learning, using studies on students' experiences of developing their understanding through deep approaches.

Work in Edinburgh explored students' experiences of achieving understanding for themselves as they prepared for final examinations (Entwistle & Entwistle, 1991, 1997, 2003) and showed the understanding achieved to vary in terms of its breadth (how much material was integrated), depth (the amount of effort put into establishing patterns of relationship), and structure (the extent to which the understanding had been independently constructed). Some of the students reaching a deep and tightly integrated personal understanding showed a deep approach that seemed to have an additional feeling tone not reported in earlier work. Not only did these students feel strongly that they *had* to understand for themselves, but they also cared so strongly about what they had come to understand in their own way, they wanted to demonstrate the depth of that understanding in their examination answers, even within the severe time constraints of a 3-hour essay examination.

I: How well did you manage to demonstrate your understanding in the exams?

S: Well, there were cases where I knew too much . . . and I would spend half the essay giving the background and showing what I understood . . . I *had* to go through all the stages of working through [the topic] and showing that I had understood it. I couldn't gloss over the

Table 2.2

INTERCORRELATIONS BETWEEN DEFINING ITEMS OF DEEP APPROACH AND ORGANIZED EFFORT

ITEMS RELATING TO	MU	IU	UE	RI	EF	TM	OS
Deep approach							
Monitoring understanding (MU)	—						
Intention to understand (IU)	.35	—					
Using evidence (UE)	.21	.37	—				
Relating ideas (RI)	.23	.28	.33	—			
Organized effort							
Effort (EF)	.36	.26	.13	.15	—		
Time management (TM)	.38	.24	.13	.13	.53	—	
Organized studying (OS)	.31	.20	.09	.12	.52	.62	—

describing intention to understand and organized effort than with other items.

Taking the two tables together, we now have evidence of relationships linking the deep approach to intention, learning processes, organized effort, and monitoring understanding. But to what extent does this indicate the existence of a disposition to understand for oneself?

THE DISPOSITION TO UNDERSTAND FOR ONESELF

The work of Perkins and his collaborators on thinking dispositions suggests that, in relation to understanding, we should be expecting a combination of ability, willingness to put effort into learning, as well as sensitivity to situations that allow understanding to be used effectively. So, are all these elements to be found in the research on student learning?

The way in which the deep approach has shown consistent associations with a developed conception of learning as transforming reinforces the evidence for its partial stability (Lonka & Lindblom-Ylänne, 1996; Vermunt & Vermetten, 2004), while a link with preferences for teaching

Table 2.1

ITEMS LOADING HIGHLY ON THREE FACTORS EXTRACTED FROM AN ITEM ANALYSIS OF ASSIST

Deep approach (loadings over 0.47)

- I look at evidence carefully to reach my own conclusion about what I'm studying.
- Ideas I come across in my academic reading often set me off on long chains of thought.
- When I'm reading for a course, I try to find out for myself exactly what the author means.
- I try to relate ideas I come across to other topics or other courses whenever possible.
- In making sense of new ideas, I often relate them to practical or real-life contexts.
- I try to find better ways of tracking down relevant information in my subject.
- It's important for me to follow the argument, or to see the reason behind things.

Monitoring understanding (full scale, also loading on the deep factor)

- If I'm not understanding things well enough when I'm studying, I try a different approach.
- I go over the work I've done to check my reasoning and see that it makes sense.
- I pay careful attention to any advice or feedback I'm given, and try to improve my understanding.

Effort (full subscale)

- I try really hard to do just as well as I possibly can.
- I generally put a lot of effort into my studying.
- I generally keep working hard even when things aren't going all that well.
- Whatever I'm working on, I generally push myself to make a good job of it.

Organized studying (loadings over 0.47)

- I organize my study time carefully to make the best use of it.
- I carefully prioritize my time to make sure I can fit everything in.
- On the whole, I'm quite systematic and organized in my studying.
- I work steadily during the course, rather than just leaving things until the last minute.
- I'm quite good at preparing for classes in advance.

effort (Entwistle & McCune, 2004). Monitoring effectiveness was introduced into this version of the inventory to take account of what Vermunt (1998) has described as self-regulation in studying, which he uses in contrast to the extrinsic regulation that refers to the teacher's control of learning.

Relationships between these subscales of ASSIST were investigated in a factor-analytic study of 1,231 university students drawn from 10 contrasting departments in six British universities (Entwistle, 1998, p. 19). The analysis also included short scales describing the most striking differences in students' reasons for coming to university (intrinsic compared with extrinsic or no clear goal), in their conceptions of learning (reproducing versus transforming), and in their preferences for different kinds of teaching (encouraging understanding versus transmitting information). A factor interpreted as deep approach to learning was also found to load on intrinsic reasons for entering university, as well as on a transforming conception of learning and preferences for teaching that encourages understanding. It also had links with monitoring effectiveness, but this scale was equally split between deep and a different factor covering organized effort. An examination of the items making up monitoring effectiveness showed that two forms of monitoring were involved; monitoring understanding, which was part of the deep factor, and monitoring studying, which was linked to organized effort.

Looking at individual items provides a better idea of what lies behind the relationships between the subscales. An item factor analysis of an instrument similar to ASSIST, carried out on 3,778 students on 26 course units from 11 universities, produced four factors in a new analysis from the Enhancing Teaching and Learning project (ETL), mentioned later on (Entwistle et al., 2003; Teaching and Learning Research Programme [TLRP], 2007). One of these factors was interpreted as being deep approach (including monitoring understanding), with which the two others correlated positively, namely effort (0.42) and organized studying (0.38). The other factor was surface approach, which was negatively correlated with deep (–0.30). The items with the highest loadings on the three factors linked positively to the deep approach are shown in Table 2.1 in the order of reducing factor loadings.

A finer-grained analysis shows the correlations between the strongest items in the subscales related to the deep approach and enables us to probe the meaning of the relationships further. Table 2.2 shows closer relationships between monitoring understanding and the items

This distinction was initially linked, by analogy, to the two different levels of processing in the memory—deep and shallow processing, as identified by Craik and Lockhart (1972)—and a logical progression from intention, through learning processes, to outcome. Distinctive intentions evoke contrasting processes of learning and so produce qualitatively different outcomes of learning (Marton & Säljö, 1976). The intention to understand the material for oneself leads to meaningful learning (Ausubel, Novak, & Hanesian, 1978), while the concentration on spotting questions leads to rote learning or simple memorization.

The same data set was analyzed separately by Svensson (1977), who argued that intentions, process, and outcome were so tightly interwoven that it was impossible to separate them in discussing student learning. He saw the main distinction in terms of *cognitive approaches* described as *holist*, focusing on the article and its meaning as a whole, and *atomist*, concentrating on the parts, and these complementary descriptions of levels of processing and cognitive approaches came together as *approaches to learning* (Marton & Säljö, 1997).

Although Marton described approaches as being relational, inevitably affected by both content and context, Entwistle and Ramsden (1983) demonstrated that approaches involved a certain consistency, being a component of individual study habits, and also distinct variability, as different experiences of teaching or assessment are found to alter the approaches of a class as a whole (Thomas & Bain, 1984; Trigwell, Prosser, & Waterhouse, 1999). With approaches having elements of both variation and consistency, it made sense to measure them, and the interrelationships between their component parts, using self-report inventories. In one of the more recent instruments, the Approaches to Study Skills Inventory for Students (ASSIST; Tait, Entwistle, & McCune, 1998), subscales of a deep approach were constructed to cover its defining aspects, namely an intention (seeking meaning), and two processes reflecting holist and serialist learning processes (relating ideas and use of evidence), along with a more general motivational component (interest in ideas). And this description of the deep approach implies the use of both holist and serialist learning processes: these cannot be used simultaneously, and so we see again the alternation between broad relational thinking and narrowly focused critical thinking.

Besides the deep approach, the inventory included subscales measuring aspects of surface approach and also *strategic* ways of studying, which included subscales of monitoring effectiveness, organized studying, time management, and achieving, now described as organized

the addition of sensitivity to context strengthens that combination. And such sensitivity involves identifying situations in which specific abilities or learning strategies can be employed to deal with a specific problem in a particular context, but also the alertness to situations that will allow ability or knowledge to develop further, as we shall see in relation to learning and studying at university.

APPROACHES TO LEARNING AND STUDY STRATEGIES

One important strand in the conceptual and empirical work on student learning stems from the notion of *approach to learning* introduced by Marton and his colleagues in the 1970s and by later work looking at the study strategies used in tackling different kinds of academic work. This research has played a major part in explaining why students learn and study in the ways they do, and how teaching and learning environments affect those ways of learning (Biggs, 1987, 2007; Entwistle, 2007, 2008; Entwistle & McCune, 2004; Entwistle, McCune, & Hounsell, 2003; Entwistle & Ramsden, 1983). Here, we will consider the meaning originally given to the term "approach to learning," and how that meaning has gradually evolved into what we now see as a *disposition to understand for oneself.*

The origins of Marton's notion of approach to learning lie in an interview study with undergraduate students who had been asked to read an academic article on which they expected to be questioned (Marton & Säljö, 1976). The transcripts of the interviews were then analyzed, showing, initially, that there were wide qualitative variations in what the students had come to understand of the author's meaning. Seeking reasons for these differences in the students' descriptions of how they had gone about reading, the article led to an influential conclusion:

> All our readings and re-reading, our iterations and reiterations, our comparisons and groupings, finally turned into an astonishingly simple picture. We had been looking for the answer to the question of why the students had arrived at qualitatively different ways of understanding the text as a whole. What we found was that the students who did not get "the point," failed to do so simply because they were not looking for it. The main difference we found in the process of learning concerned whether the students *focused on the text itself or on what the text was about*—the author's intention, the main point, the conclusion to be drawn. (Marton & Säljö, 1997, p. 43, original emphasis)

single perspective. Being mindless, colloquially speaking, is like being on automatic pilot. (Langer, 1997, p. 4)

Langer sees education, even at university level, as encouraging mindlessness, as it fails to prepare students for ways of using ideas within new contexts, for thinking outside the box, for considering new situations in flexible and open-minded ways. And mindfulness, although a disposition, is not an unchangeable trait: it is a disposition, a habit of mind, and like all habits, it is open to change when circumstances become different.

So far, it is clear that students can be expected to differ in their predisposition to learn mindfully and that this tendency may well depend on their need for cognition as well as the sensitivity to context. But, as Perkins and Tishman (2001) argued, effective intelligent behavior involves another necessary component, namely the *inclination* to act in particular ways. They have been presenting evidence for the existence of a grouping of ability, inclination, and sensitivity to context within a *thinking disposition,* which goes beyond the stylist preference to process information in particular ways, to describe alertness to situations that allow critical and imaginative thinking to take place.

> The account of more or less intelligent behavior in terms of abilities alone leaves a logical gap. An ability to perform in a certain way—for instance to solve verbal analogy problems or to think about the other side of the case—does not itself guarantee that the person will marshal such abilities on appropriate occasions. To do so, the person has to detect these occasions and follow through with the appropriate effort. . . . [So,] a full account of intellectual behavior requires three logically distinct and separable components: *sensitivity, inclination* and *ability.* Sensitivity concerns awareness of occasion; inclination concerns motivation or leaning; ability concerns capability to follow through appropriately. . . . It is perfectly possible to detect a certain kind of situation (sensitivity) but not care to invest oneself in doing something about it (inclination). It is also perfectly possible for occasions to pass one by (sensitivity) even though in fact one cares quite a bit (inclination). Accordingly, an investigation of the dispositional side of good thinking needs to take into account [a triad of influences]. (Perkins & Tishman, 2001, pp. 236–237)

In a subsequent paper, Perkins and Ritchhart (2004) cite several empirical studies to show that this triad of ability, inclination, and sensitivity, while conceptually and empirically separable, are more potent when acting in consort. While ability and inclination have been frequently linked, *disposition* was seen in terms of its stability and motivational strength and direction. A wide range of studies were carried out into the *need for cognition,* seen alongside the need for achievement as one of an array of motivational needs affecting behavior generally, and covering learning behavior at university. From an extensive review, Cacioppo, Petty, Feinstein, and Jarvis (1996) concluded that need for cognition

> represents a personality variable reflecting individual differences in inclination to engage in and enjoy effortful cognitive activity: It can be reliably measured, is stable over time, . . . can account for significant variance beyond that explained by intellectual ability, and can be linked to important life outcomes such as academic achievement. . . . Individuals high in need for cognition tend to have active, exploring minds, and, through their senses and intellect, they reach and draw out information from their environment; accordingly, they are more likely to expend effort on information acquisition, reasoning, and problem-solving to cope with a wide variety of predicaments in their world. (p. 245)

This review also explored possible links with the so-called big five personality factors and concluded that it was, not surprisingly, most closely associated with openness—the receptivity to new ideas, preference for varied sensations, and intellectuality—but also with conscientiousness, with its will to achieve, self-control, persistence, and dependability. There was also a recognition that need for cognition was influenced by the situation, although that aspect had not been fully explored in the research reported. Rather, a lack of interest in situational influences had characterized the majority of the mainstream research into individual differences, whether intellectual, conative, or affective. In contrast, these effects have been given greater primacy in research on student learning.

From the review of work into need for cognition, it seems that the idea goes beyond the usual reach of ideas about personality in suggesting a tendency to "reach and draw out information from their environment" (Cacioppo et al., 1996, p. 245). And that extension implies a *sensitivity to context* that is also central to the work of Langer (1989, 1997) on mindfulness.

> A mindful approach to any activity has three characteristics: the continuous creation of new categories; openness to new information; and an implicit awareness of more than one perspective. Mindlessness, in contrast, is characterized by an entrapment in old categories; by automatic behavior that precludes attending to new signals; and by action that operates from a

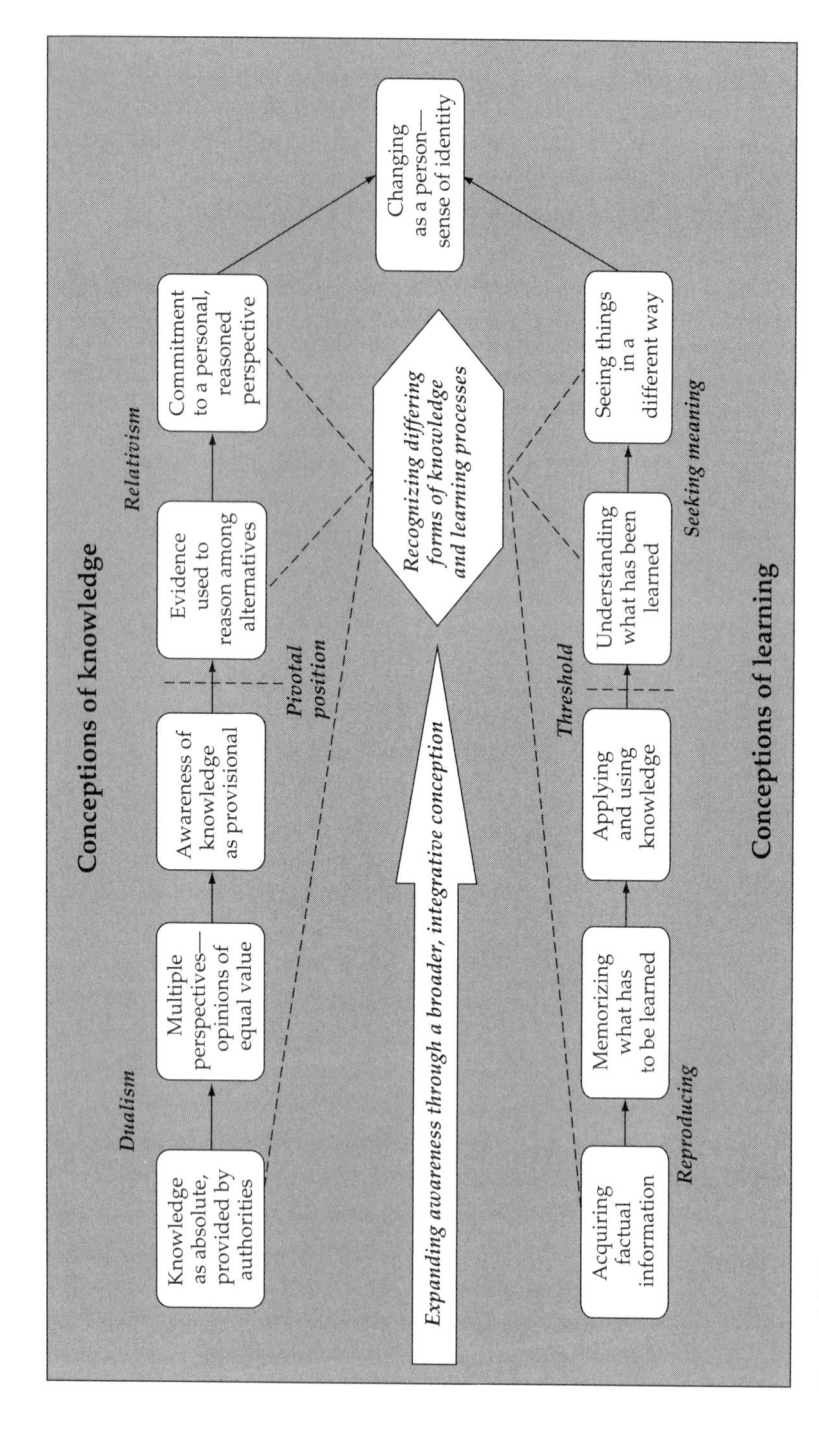

Figure 2.1 Categories showing the development of conceptions of knowledge and learning.

but has suggested gender differences in the extent to which the learning is seen through personal or impersonal referents (Belenky, Clinchy, Goldberger, & Tarule, 1986) and also led to debates about whether his scheme should be seen as a general trend or as differentiated across different facets of knowledge and across subject areas (Shommer-Aikins, 2002).

Changes in conceptions of knowledge are paralleled by equivalent development in students' *conceptions of learning*. Säljö (1979) found that students with little academic background saw learning in terms of memorizing and reproducing knowledge, whereas those who had experienced higher education had more sophisticated conceptions involving seeking personal meaning, suggesting the trend illustrated in Figure 2.1.

The diagram draws attention to a common feature of developmental schemes, namely that the more limited conceptions become integrated within the more sophisticated ones, so that, with the higher conceptions, students show a greater awareness of their own learning processes and how to use them effectively (*metacognition*), and are also better at monitoring their own ways of studying while carrying out academic tasks (*metalearning*—see Biggs, 1987). Figure 2.1 also highlights the parallel development of conceptions of knowledge and learning and shows the existence, in both, of a crucial threshold at which an important qualitative change in conception takes place, affecting the ways in which students subsequently tackle their academic work (Entwistle, 2007). Beyond that threshold the awareness of learning appears to broaden and involve the recognition of changing as a person. The similarity in these independent descriptions of conceptions suggests that the processes are intimately related within the experiences of students, even though they remain largely subconscious during the process of everyday studying. And they also seem to represent a fundamental change in their perceptions of the world around them, which leads to a different way of thinking along with changes in values and attitudes, suggesting another grouping of affect and cognition.

THINKING DISPOSITIONS

The description of developing conceptions begins the process of seeing how noncognitive elements work alongside abilities to affect learning, but we need to introduce other cognitive and affective aspects as well (Snow, Corno, & Jackson, 1996). In earlier research, the idea of a

Chapter 2 The Disposition to Understand for Oneself at University and Beyond

> Over the years, I have become increasingly impressed with the contextualisation of behavior and the idiosyncratic nature of individual perceptions of situations. I have been struck with the importance of cultural differences and taken seriously the suggestions . . . that meaning is all-important . . . and that meaning is highly idiosyncratic. . . . At the same time, . . . I believe that regularities can be found. . . . The person has a construct system, providing some stability (i.e. structure), but the system also is dynamic in that different constructs apply to different situations and become more or less important in different contexts. (pp. 313–315)

CONCEPTIONS OF KNOWLEDGE AND LEARNING

Research into student learning has also introduced broad concepts that, while suggesting relatively consistent thinking in the short term, clearly demonstrate change over time—a developmental sequence going beyond that described by Piaget and Inhelder (1969). An interview study by Perry (1970) was seminal in demonstrating that students developed *conceptions of knowledge* related to their academic studies, which progressed along common pathways during the college experience. The starting point involved seeing knowledge as either right or wrong and then moved, first, toward a recognition of how evidence is used to reach conclusions, and beyond that to an acceptance that knowledge is still developing and open to challenge, and so ultimately uncertain and socially constructed (relativism). The initial recognition of relativism takes students

> over a watershed, a critical traverse in our Pilgrim's Progress . . . In crossing the ridge of the divide . . . [students] see before [them] a perspective in which the relation of learner to knowledge is radically transformed. In this new context, Authority, formerly a source and dispenser of all knowing, is suddenly authority, ideally a resource, a mentor, a model, and potentially a colleague in consensual estimation of interpretations of reality . . . [Students] are no longer receptacles but the primary agents responsible for their own learning . . . As students speak from this new perspective they speak more reflectively. And yet the underlying theme continues: the learner's evolution of what it means to know. (Perry, 1988, p. 156)

Perry also showed that the acceptance of the implications of relativism came slowly and often with a difficulty not fully appreciated by faculty. Subsequent research has largely supported Perry's developmental scheme

globetrotting as they chase interesting but ultimately ephemeral relationships between ideas, while the serialists fall into the trap of *improvidence* as they fail to recognize critical connections among the various features.

> In the end, both groups of students can reach the same level of understanding, but their ways of reaching that understanding are very different. The serialists apparently put much more emphasis on the separate topics and logical sequences connecting them, forming an overall picture of what is being learned only rather late in the process. The holists try to build up that overall picture, as a guide to learning, right from the start and see where the details fit into that picture much later on. . . . Students who are readily able to adapt their learning strategy to the requirements of a particular task, emphasizing either comprehension or operation learning as appropriate, and using both in tandem wherever possible . . . Pask describes these students as having a "versatile" style of learning. (Entwistle, 1988, pp. 92–94)

We should thus expect to see in successful academic studying evidence of this versatility in using the two learning processes appropriately and interactively in tackling academic tasks, and that is indeed what has been found, as we shall see. In this work, it is recognized that there is a distinction between strategies, which are context dependent, and styles, which are more habitual, and this was also recognized by Rezulli and Dai (2001) in a review of studies bringing together abilities, interests and styles. The authors drew attention to the ways in which interest and motivation link with abilities to create strategies related to learning, and indicated that they could lead to habitual ways of processing information. They noted that interests are necessarily focused on a particular subject, topic, or task and so do not, in themselves, link with abilities to form styles; rather, they suggest strategies for tackling specific pieces of work. When used consistently, however, they do have the stable characteristic of styles or dispositions.

However, any attempt to describe this combination of ability and interest as being either stable or variable is misguided; a style or disposition certainly indicates consistency—a *tendency* to use one or other way of thinking, rooted in personality and continuing preferences. But an individual's reaction to a specific task or situation will still vary, depending on how that context is interpreted. The possibility that a concept can be both stable and variable seems, at first sight, to be a contradiction and yet, for some psychological concepts, it is almost certainly closer to everyday experience. Pervin (2001) reached a similar conclusion from his extensive research on personality.

The interplay between contrasting mental operations was found in practice in interviews carried out by Heath (1964), who followed a group of male undergraduates at Princeton and looked at their intellectual and personality development over the four years. He found three distinct personality types: the *noncommitter* with a marked tendency to avoid commitment; the *hustler* driven toward purposeful activity; and the overreacting *plunger* whose moods change quickly. And these personality characteristics were also reflected in their ways of thinking, being respectively cautious, competitive, and impulsive. Over time these initially opposed characteristics merged until a more integrated personality emerged, again with its own distinctive characteristics—the *reasonable adventurer*.

> The principal characteristic of Reasonable Adventurers is the ability to create their own opportunities for satisfaction. They seem to have their psychological house in sufficient order to release them to attack the problems of everyday life with zest and originality. And they seem to do so with an air of playfulness. . . . [They] are characterized by six attributes: intellectuality, close friendships, independence in value judgements, tolerance of ambiguity, breadth of interests, and sense of humor. . . . In pursuit of a problem [they] appear to experience an alternation of involvement and detachment, . . . the combination of two mental attitudes, the curious and the critical. These do not occur simultaneously but in alternation. (Heath, 1964, pp. 30–31)

This link between personality characteristics and distinctive ways of thinking helps to clarify where a cognitive style sits in relation to ability, and why the preferences they involve in handling information or problems appear to be relatively consistent yet also develop over time. But perhaps the most interesting aspect of Heath's research is its emphasis on the importance of using contrasting ways of thinking in alternation: they do not merge, but the interplay between them allows the students to reach an important integrated outcome—conceptual understanding. These reasonable adventurers proved to be academically the most successful students.

This idea of combining contrasting thinking processes or strategies can also be found in Pask's (1988) work on styles of learning. He described the distinctive strategies of *comprehension learning*, which, if used habitually, became a *holist* conceptual style, and *operation learning*, which might become a *serialist* style. Each style has its particular strength, but used exclusively it leads to a characteristic pathology—the holists indulge in

it within the different academic cultures encountered at university. The link between learner identities and the disposition to understand is explored before considering the potential importance of this disposition, with its emphasis on *sensitivity to context,* in preparing students for the super-complexity they will experience in their future lives.

LEARNING STYLES AND THINKING PROCESSES

The recent extensive review of the nature of intellectual styles by Zhang and Sternberg (2006) concluded that learning styles were essentially preferences for thinking or acting in particular ways. Earlier work describing the more general cognitive styles saw them as being preferences for distinctive ways of processing information, possibly indicating a preponderant use of left or right hemispheres of the brain. The left hemisphere was seen as specializing in semantic and logical thinking, while the right dealt with spatial and other visual aspects of thinking (Sperry, 1983). Neurologically, the hemispheric brain functions are no longer seen as being so distinct (Westen, 1999), but the psychological literature still echoes the hemispheric contrast, through dichotomies such as holist and serialist (Pask, 1976) and wholistic-analytic (Riding & Rayner, 1998). But even accepting hemispheric separation, most learning depends on an interplay between the two through the linking nerves of the corpus callosum (Westen, 1999).

One of the early contributions to the literature on cognitive styles as it relates to learning came from Witkin, Moore, Goodenough, and Cox (1977) in exploring the distinction between *field-independence* and *field-dependence* using the Embedded Figures Test (Witkin, Oltman, Raskin, & Karp, 1971). The test itself involved visual discrimination of simple figures embedded within complex patterns, which implies the ability to discern a simple image within a distracting background of similar designs. This can be seen as the perceptual version of Pask's holist style, but Witkin argued that the scores obtained in his perceptual test captured more fundamental thinking styles, with higher scores representing an *articulated* (or analytic) style and lower scores being interpreted as *global* (or holist) thinking. The test itself did not suggest any such general thinking style, yet the tendency to extract conceptual patterns and meaning from its background—discerning critical features within information presented—can also be seen as a crucial indicator of high-quality academic learning (Marton, 2007).

2

The Disposition to Understand for Oneself at University and Beyond: Learning Processes, the Will to Learn, and Sensitivity to Context

NOEL ENTWISTLE AND VELDA McCUNE

Cognitive styles have been viewed as melding together aspects of both personality and cognitive processes. In research into student learning in higher education, the notion of an approach to learning has brought together motivation and processes of learning, as well as monitoring the effectiveness of learning, making it a composite concept allied to styles but with strong contextual influences on it. Other research has identified dispositions as composites of ability, willingness to engage in learning, and sensitivity to contextual opportunities for learning. Research carried out in Edinburgh over many years enables us to align our work with a variety of related findings in the international literature on student learning to discuss the nature of dispositions, showing stability through a linking of cognitive and motivational characteristics, along with volitional states and experiences of the learning environment.

Setting the scene, we introduce earlier research looking at learning styles and thinking processes, before summarizing work on conceptions of knowledge and learning, which leads on to the general notion of *thinking dispositions*. We then consider the evidence on approaches to learning and study strategies to build up the idea of a disposition to understand for oneself. Possible ways of developing this disposition are then discussed, looking at teaching-learning environments designed to support understanding, and students' sensitivity to opportunities to develop

Shiffrin, R. M., & Schneider, W. (1977). Controlled and automatic human information processing: II. Perceptual learning, automatic attending, and a general theory. *Psychological Review, 84,* 127–190.

Segalowitz, S. J. (2007). Knowing before we know: Conscious versus preconscious top-down processing and a neuroscience of intuition. *Brain and Cognition, 65,* 143–144.

Shefy, E., & Sadler-Smith, E. (2006). Applying holistic principles in management development. *Journal of Management Development, 29*(4), 368–385.

Simon, H. A. (1987). Making management decisions: The role of intuition and emotion. *Academy of Management Executive, 12,* 57–64.

Sloman, S. A. (1996). The empirical case for two systems of reasoning. *Psychological Bulletin, 199,* 3–22.

Sloman, S. A. (2002). Two systems of reasoning. In T. Gilovich, D. Griffin, & D. Kahneman (Eds.), *Heuristics and biases: The psychology of intuitive judgment* (pp. 379–396). New York: Cambridge University Press.

Slovic, P., Finucane, M. L., Peters, E., & MacGregor, D. G. (2004). Risk as analysis and risk as feelings: Some thoughts about affect, reason, risk and rationality. *Risk Analysis, 24,* 311–322.

Smith, E. R., & DeCoster, J. (1999). Associative and rule based processing. In S. Chaiken & Y. Trope (Eds.), *Dual-process theories in social psychology* (pp. 323–336). New York: Guilford Press.

Sonenshein, S. (2007). The role of construction, intuition, and justification in responding to ethical issues at work: The sensemaking-intuition model. *Academy of Management Review, 32*(4), 1022–1040.

Stanovich, K. E. (2002). Rationality, intelligence, and levels of analysis in cognitive science. In R. J. Sternberg (Ed.), *Why smart people can be so stupid* (pp. 124–158). New Haven, CT: Yale University Press.

Stanovich, K. E., & West, R. F. (2000). Individual differences in reasoning: Implications for the rationality debate? *Behavioral and Brain Sciences, 23,* 645–665.

Sternberg, R. J. (1997). *Thinking styles.* Cambridge: Cambridge University Press.

Sternberg, R. J., & Zhang, L. F. (2001). Thinking styles across cultures: their relationships with student learning. In R. J. Sternberg & L. F. Zhang (Eds.), *Perspectives on thinking, learning and cognitive styles* (pp. 227–247). Mahwah, NJ: Erlbaum.

Taggart, W., & Robey, D. (1981). Minds and managers: On the dual nature of human information processing and management. *Academy of Management Review, 6,* 187–195.

Wagner, R. K. (2002). Smart people doing dumb things: The case of managerial incompetence. In R. J. Sternberg (Ed.), *Why smart people can be so stupid* (pp. 42–63). New Haven, CT: Yale University Press.

Wagner, R. K., & Sternberg, R. J. (1985). Practical intelligence in real-world pursuits: The role of tacit knowledge. *Journal of Personality and Social Psychology, 49,* 436–458.

Whetten, D. A., Cameron, K. S., & Woods, M. (1994). *Developing management skills for Europe.* London: Harper Collins.

Wilson, T. D. (2002). *Strangers to ourselves: Discovering the adaptive unconscious.* Cambridge, MA: Belknap/Harvard.

Zhang L. F., & Sternberg, R. J. (2005). A threefold model of intellectual styles. *Educational Psychology Review, 17*(1), 1–53.

Mitchell, J. R., Friga, P. N., & Mitchell, R. K. (2005). Untangling the intuition mess: Intuition as a construct in entrepreneurship research. *Entrepreneurship Theory and Practice, 30,* 653–679.

Myers, D. (2002). *Intuition: Its powers and perils.* New Haven, CT: Yale University Press.

Myers, I. B., & Briggs, K. C. (1976). *Introduction to type.* Gainesville, FL: Center for Application of Psychological Type.

Norris, P., & Epstein, S. (2007). *Intuition, imagination and feelings: Components and correlated of experiential processing.* Unpublished manuscript.

Paivio, A. (1971). *Imagery and verbal processes.* New York: Holt, Rinehart and Winston.

Peterson, E. R., Deary, I. J., & Austin, E. J. (2003). The reliability of Riding's Cognitive Style Analysis test. *Personality and Individual Differences, 34,* 881–891.

Policastro, E. (1995). Creative intuition: An integrative review. *Creativity Research Journal, 8,* 99–113.

Pollock, J. L. (1995). *Cognitive carpentry: A blueprint for how to build a person.* Cambridge, MA: MIT Press.

Posner, M. I., & Snyder, C. R. R. (1975). Attention and cognitive control. In R. L. Solso (Ed.), *Information processing and cognition: The Loyola symposium* (pp. 55–85). New York: Wiley.

Reber, A. S. (1993). *Implicit learning and tacit knowledge: An essay on the cognitive unconscious.* New York: Oxford University Press.

Riding, R. J., Glass, A., Butler, S. R., & Pleydell-Pearce, C. W. (1997). Cognitive style and individual differences in EEG alpha during information processing. *Educational Psychology, 17,* 219–234.

Riding, R. J., & Rayner, S. (1998). *Cognitive styles and learning strategies.* London: David Fulton Publishers.

Robinson, L. A. (2006). *Trust your gut: How the power of intuition can grow your business.* Chicago: Kaplan Publishing.

Sadler-Smith, E. (1998). Cognitive style: Some human resource implications for managers. *The International Journal of Human Resource Management, 9,* 185–202.

Sadler-Smith, E. (2002, August). *The role of cognitive style in management education.* Academy of Management Proceedings, C1–C6, Academy of Management Annual Meeting, Denver, Colorado.

Sadler-Smith, E. (2008). *Inside intuition.* Abingdon, UK: Routledge.

Sadler-Smith, E. (in press). Cognitive styles and learning strategies in management education. In S. J. Armstrong & C. Fukami (Eds.), *Sage handbook of management learning, education and development.* Thousand Oaks, CA: Sage.

Sadler-Smith, E., & Shefy, E. (2004). The intuitive executive: Understanding and applying "gut feel" in decision-making. *The Academy of Management Executive, 18*(4), 76–92.

Sadler-Smith, E., & Shefy, E. (2007). Developing intuitive awareness in management education. *Academy of Management Learning and Education, 6*(2), 186–205.

Sadler-Smith, E., & Sparrow, P. R., (2008). Intuition in organizational decision-making. In G. P. Hodgkinson & W. H. Starbuck (Eds.), *The Oxford handbook of organizational decision-making* (pp. 304–323). Oxford: Oxford University Press.

Salovey, P., & Meyer, J. D. (1995). Emotional intelligence. *Imagination, Cognition and Personality, 9,* 185–211.

Hogarth, R. M. (2006). Is confidence in decisions related to feedback? Evidence from random samples of real world behavior. In K. Fiedler & P. Justin (Eds.), *Information sampling and adaptive cognition* (pp. 456–484). Cambridge: Cambridge University Press.

Hogarth, R. M. (2008). On the learning of intuition. In H. Plessner, C. Betsch, & T. Betsch (Eds.), *Intuition in judgment and decision making* (pp. 91–105). New York: Lawrence Erlbaum Associates.

Kabat-Zinn, J. (1990). *Full catastrophe living: How to cope with stress, pain and illness using mindfulness meditation.* London: Piatkus.

Kahneman, D. (2000). A psychological point of view: Violations of rational rules as diagnostic of mental processes. *Behavioral and Brain Sciences, 23,* 683.

Kahneman, D., Krueger, A. B., Schkade, D. A., Schwarz, N., & Stone, A. A. (2004). A survey method for characterizing daily life experience: The Day Reconstruction Method. *Science, 306*(5702), 1776–1780.

Kahneman, D., & Tversky, A. (1982). The psychology of preferences. *Scientific American, 246,* 160–173.

Klein, G. (1998). *Sources of power: How people make decisions.* Cambridge, MA: The MIT Press.

Klein, G. (2003). *Intuition at work.* New York: Currency / Doubleday.

Kozhevnikov, M. (2007). Cognitive styles in the context of modern psychology: Toward an integrated framework. *Psychological Bulletin, 133*(3), 464–481.

Kozhevnikov, M., Kosslyn, S. M., & Shephard, J. (2005). Spatial versus object visualizers: A new characterization of visual cognitive style. *Memory and Cognition, 33,* 710–726.

Kruglanski, A. W., & Orehek, E. (2007). Partitioning the domain of social inference: Dual mode and systems models and their alternatives. *Annual Review of Psychology, 58,* 291–316.

Lakoff, G., & Johnson, M. (1999). *Philosophy in the flesh: The embodied mind and its challenge to Western thought.* New York: Basic Books.

Lave, J., & Wenger, E. (1991). *Situated learning: Legitimate peripheral participation.* New York: Cambridge University Press.

Lewicki, P., Hill, T., & Czyzewska, M. (1992). Non-conscious acquisition of information. *American Psychologist, 47,* 796–801.

Lieberman, M. D. (2007). Social cognitive neuroscience: A review of core processes. *Annual Review of Psychology, 58,* 259–289.

Lieberman, M. D., Jarcho, J. M., & Satpute, A. B. (2004). Evidence-based and intuition-based self-knowledge: An fMRI study. *Journal of Personality and Social Psychology, 87,* 421–435.

Louis, M. R., & Sutton, R. I. (1991). Switching cognitive gears: From habits of mind to active thinking. *Human Relations, 44,* 55–76.

MacLeod, C. M., Jackson, R. A., & Palmer, J. (1986). On the relation between spatial ability and field dependence. *Intelligence, 10,* 141–151.

McKenna, F. P. (1984). Measures of field dependence: cognitive style or cognitive ability? *Journal of Personality and Social Psychology, 47,* 593–603.

Meehl, P. E. (1954). *Clinical versus statistical prediction.* Minneapolis: University of Minnesota Press.

Messick, S. (1976). Personality consistencies in cognition and creativity. In S. Messick (Ed.), *Individuality in learning* (pp. 4–23). San Francisco: Jossey Bass.

Ericsson, K. A., & Charness, N. (1994). Expert performance: Its structure and acquisition. *American Psychologist, 49,* 725–747.

Ericsson, K. A., Prietula, M. J., & Cokely, E. T. (2007). The making of an expert. *Harvard Business Review, 85,* 115–121.

Evans, J. St. B. T. (2003). In two minds: Dual-process accounts of reasoning. *Trends in Cognitive Sciences, 7*(10), 454–459.

Evans, J. St. B. T. (2008). Dual-processing accounts of reasoning, judgment and social cognition. *Annual Review of Psychology, 59,* 255–278.

Flanagan, J. C. (1954). The critical incident technique. *Psychological Bulletin, 51,* 327–358.

Gardner, W. L., & Martinko, M. J. (1996). Using the Myers-Briggs Type Indicator to study managers: A literature review and research agenda. *Journal of Management, 22,* 45–83.

Gendlin, E. (1981). *Focusing.* New York: Bantam Books.

Gevins, A., & Smith, M. (2000). Neuro-physiological measures of working memory and individual differences in cognitive ability and cognitive style. *Cerebral Cortex, 10,* 829–839.

Gilovich, T., Griffith, D., & Kahneman, D. (Eds.). (2002). *Heuristics and biases: The psychology of intuitive judgment.* Cambridge, UK: Cambridge University Press.

Goldstein, K. M., & Blackman, S. (1978). *Cognitive style.* New York: Wiley.

Goleman, D. (1995). *Emotional intelligence.* New York: Bantam Books.

Goode, P. E., Goddard, P. H., & Pascual-Leone, J. (2002). Event-related potentials index cognitive style differences during a serial-order recall task. *International Journal of Psychophysiology, 43,* 123–140.

Haidt, J. (2001). The emotional dog and its rationalist tail: A social intuitionist approach to moral judgment. *Psychological Review, 108*(4), 814–834.

Hammond, K. R. (1996). *Human judgment and social policy.* New York: Oxford University Press.

Hayes, J., Allinson, C. W., Hudson, R. S., & Keasey, K. (2003). Further reflections on the nature of intuition-analysis and the construct validity of the Cognitive Style Index. *Journal of Occupational and Organizational Psychology, 76,* 269–278.

Hodgkinson, G. P., & Clarke, I. (2007). Exploring the cognitive significance of organizational strategizing: A dual-process framework and research agenda. *Human Relations, 60,* 243–255.

Hodgkinson, G. P., Langan-Fox, J., & Sadler-Smith, E. (2008). Intuition: A fundamental bridging construct in the behavioural sciences. *British Journal of Psychology, 99*(1), 1–27.

Hodgkinson, G. P., & Sadler-Smith, E. (2003). Reflections on reflections: On the nature of intuition, analysis and the construct validity of the Cognitive Style Index. *Journal of Occupational and Organizational Psychology, 76,* 279–281.

Hodgkinson, G. P., Sadler-Smith, E., & Sinclair, M. (2006, August). *More than meets the eye? Intuition and analysis revisited.* Paper presented at the Annual Academy of Management Meeting, Atlanta, Georgia.

Hodgkinson, G. P., & Sparrow, P. R. (2002). *The competent organization: A psychological analysis of the strategic management process.* Buckingham, UK: Open University Press.

Hofstadter, D. (2007). *I am a strange loop.* New York: Basic Books.

Hogarth, R. M. (2001). *Educating intuition.* Chicago: University of Chicago Press.

Backhaus, K., & Liff, J. P. (2007). Cognitive Style Index: Further investigation of the factor structure with an American student sample. *Educational Psychology, 27*(1), 21–31.

Bechara, A. (2004). The role of emotion in decision-making: Evidence from neurological patients with orbito-frontal damage. *Brain and Cognition, 55,* 30–40.

Bechara, A., Damasio, H., Tranel, D., & Damasio, A. R. (1997). Deciding advantageously before knowing the advantageous strategy. *Science, 275,* 1293–1294.

Betsch, C. (2004). Preference for Intuition and Deliberation (PID): An inventory for assessing affect- and cognition-based decision-making. *Zeitschrift für Differentielle und Diagnostiche Psychologie, 25,* 179–197.

Betsch, C. (2008). Chronic preferences for intuition and deliberation in decision making: Lessons learned about intuition from an individual differences approach. In H. Plessner, C. Betsch, & T. Betsch (Eds.), *Intuition in judgment and decision making* (pp. 231–248). New York: Lawrence Erlbaum Associates.

Bloom, B. S. (1956). *Taxonomy of educational objectives, the classification of educational goals—handbook I: Cognitive domain.* New York: McKay.

Browne, D. (1996). Cognitive versatility. *Minds and Machines, 6*(4), 507–523.

Burke, L. A., & Sadler-Smith, E. (2006). Instructor intuition in the educational context. *Academy of Management Learning and Education, 5*(2), 169–181.

Chaiken, S., & Trope, Y. (Eds.). (1999). *Dual-process theories in social psychology.* New York: Guilford Press.

Clarke, I., & Mackaness, W. (2001). Management "intuition": An interpretative account of structure and content of decision schemas using cognitive maps. *Journal of Management Studies, 38*(2), 147–172.

Coffield, F., Moseley, D., Hall, E., & Ecclestone, K. (2004). *Learning styles in post 16 learning: A systematic and critical review.* London: Learning and Skills Council.

Cools E., & Van den Broeck, H. (2007). Development and validation of the Cognitive Style Indicator. *The Journal of Psychology, 141*(4), 359–387.

Csikszentmihalyi, M., & Larsen, R. (1987). Validity and reliability of the experience-sampling method. *Journal of Nervous and Mental Disorders, 175,* 526–536.

Damasio, A. R. (1994). *Descartes' error: Emotion, reason and the human brain.* New York: HarperCollins.

Dane, E., & Pratt, M. G. (2007). Exploring intuition and its role in managerial decision-making. *Academy of Management Review, 32*(1), 33–54.

Dennett, D. (1987). *The intentional stance.* Cambridge, MA: MIT Press.

Dreyfus, H. L., & Dreyfus, S. E. (1986). *Mind over machine: The power of human intuition and expertise in the era of the computer.* New York: Free Press.

Emery, M. (1994). *Dr Marcia Emery's intuition workbook: An expert's guide to unlocking the wisdom of your subconscious mind.* Englewood Cliffs, NJ: Prentice Hall.

Epstein, S. (1994). Integration of the cognitive and the psychodynamic unconscious. *American Psychologist, 49,* 709–724.

Epstein, S. (2008). Intuition from the perspective of cognitive-experiential self-theory. In H. Plessner, C. Betsch, & T. Betsch (Eds.), *Intuition in judgment and decision making* (pp. 23–37). New York: Lawrence Erlbaum Associates.

Epstein, S., Pacini, R., Denes-Raj, V., & Heier, H. (1996). Individual differences in intuitive-experiential and analytical-rational thinking styles. *Journal of Personality and Social Psychology, 71,* 390–405.

NOTES

1. Coffield et al. (2004) reviewed 13 of the most influential style models and concluded that the Cognitive Style Index (CSI) had the best evidence for reliability and validity of all the models they studied.
2. Stanovich (2002) describes the two levels thus: (a) algorithmic level: concerned with computational processes; (b) intentional level: concerned with the goals of the computation (see Dennett, 1987).
3. The Pleistocene epoch stretched from 2×10^6 years ago to 10,000 years ago and saw the evolution of *Homo habilis, Homo erectus,* and, eventually, *Homo sapiens.*
4. Cools and Van den Broeck (2007) disaggregated the analytic cognitive style by splitting it into a knowing style and a planning style.
5. I have preferred the term *intuitive* over *experiential* for three reasons: The term intuition has greater currency in management research (see, for example, Dane & Pratt, 2007); intuition subsumes experientiality; and intuition is the operation of the experiential system (Epstein, 2004).
6. The term *analytical* is offered as an alternative to *rational* because there are strong elements of rationality in both systems (Slovic, Finucane, Peters, & MacGregor, 2004).
7. Analysis is defined as "The breakdown of a communication into its constituent elements or parts such that the relative hierarchy of ideas is made clear and/or the relations between the ideas expressed are made explicit" (Bloom, 1956, p. 205). However, it is interesting to note that Bloom may have been alluding to a form of intuition in his inclusion of the analysis of implicit structure present in a communication of which the producer him/herself "may not be aware" (p. 147) and expressed objectively as the learner's "ability to infer" (p. 148).
8. The popular Myers-Briggs Type Inventory (MBTI; Myers & Briggs, 1976) is excluded on the bases that: (a) it is a measure of personal style (rather than cognitive style per se); (b) its theoretical basis is in the Jungian psychoanalytic/psychotherapeutic tradition; and (c) there is ongoing controversy surrounding aspects of its construct validity (see Gardner & Martinko, 1996).
9. The simplest approach would be to sum intuition and analysis scores and to give an overall Cognitive Versatility Index (CVI)—see Equation 1; an alternative would be to compute the square root of the product of the values for each mode—see Equation 2. Equation 2 ameliorates the influence of any extreme values from either scale, but in this case the anchor for each scale score should be set to a nonzero value, otherwise the product of any calculation involving a zero term for either mode would be zero:

$$\text{CVI} = \text{Analysis}_{\text{CSI, PID or REI}} + \text{Intuition}_{\text{CSI, PID or REI}} \tag{1}$$

$$\text{CVI} = \sqrt{\{(\text{Analysis}_{\text{CSI, PID or REI}}) \times (\text{Intuition}_{\text{CSI, PID or REI}})\}} \tag{2}$$

REFERENCES

Agor, W. H. (Ed.). (1989). *Intuition in organizations: Leading and managing productively.* Newbury Park, CA: Sage.

Allinson, C. W., & Hayes, J. (1996). The Cognitive Style Index: A measure of intuition-analysis for organizational research. *Journal of Management Studies, 33,* 119–135.

valence). The role of affect as data has already been discussed, and individuals need to be aware of the adaptive role that affect, in the form of somatic markers (Bechara, 2004; Damasio, 1994), has evolved to play in stopping the "combinatorial explosion of possibilities that would occur" if System 2 tried to calculate all the options (Stanovich, 2002, p. 142). Equally, as well as not confounding emotions with intuitions, individuals need to be able to distinguish intuitive judgments (i.e., ones that are made on an informed basis and arise rapidly and involuntarily though nonconscious pattern recognition and wholistic associations) from biased social judgments made on the basis of individual or cultural prejudices, and from hopes, desires, and wishful thinking. Novel methods such as focusing (Gendlin, 1981) and mindfulness meditation (Kabat-Zinn, 1990) are of potential benefit for raising both cognitive and somatic phenomenal awareness. Preliminary steps have been taken using these and related techniques in order begin to understand how to enhance managers' intuitive awareness in a wholistic (mind/body) fashion (Sadler-Smith & Shefy, 2007; Shefy & Sadler-Smith, 2006).

CONCLUSION

Previous attempts at unification with the cognitive style paradigm were inhibited by weak theorization, dogged by controversy surrounding construct validity, and impeded by appeals to outdated notions of gross hemispheric dominances for left-brain (analytical) or right-brain (intuitive) processing (Kozhevnikov, 2007). As argued by Sloman (2002), an obvious solution to the conundrum of the either analysis or intuition dilemma is to conceive of the mind in both ways, that is, that it has dual aspects conforming to the processes of an associative system (characterized by intuition, fantasy, creativity, imagination, visual recognition, experientiality, and associative memory) and a rule-based system (characterized by deliberation, explanation, abstract symbolic representation, and formal analysis with verification and ascription of purpose). Dual-process theory offers cognitive styles researchers one way out of a sometimes bewildering maze of concepts, models, theories, and measures in a way that connects with other developments within the styles field (e.g., Zhang & Sternberg, 2005) and also with established and emerging insights from cognitive, evolutionary, and social psychology, and cognitive neuroscience. In the fullness of time, such developments may serve to reinvigorate this highly practice-relevant field in ways that are scientifically robust.

by participation in a community of practice (see Lave & Wenger, 1991), enlisting the assistance of expert mentors, coaches, and role models, consciously managing one's experience by choosing to inhabit environments in which one wants to develop intuition (Hogarth, 2008), and by exposure to difficult problems in those environments (preferably using simulations to minimize risk in hazardous situations). Notwithstanding these suggestions, research into the development of expert knowledge suggests a rule-of-thumb of 10 or more years of learning and practice in order to develop sufficiently complex schemas in a particular domain (see Ericsson & Charness, 1994) to support expertise-based intuition. The inevitable conclusion is that in order to develop intuitive muscle power (Klein, 2003), there can be no substitute for an extensive period of intensive learning, deep immersion, and sustained effort and practice: As Wagner (2002) noted, "expertise is not acquired cheaply" (p. 57) and neither is informed intuition.

Feedback

Given that the intuitive learning system is operating constantly and without conscious awareness, Hogarth (2001, 2008) emphasized the importance of feedback in the learning of intuitions. He drew a distinction between two contrasting types of learning structures for developing intuition: (a) favorable: environments that enhance intuition through good (i.e., timely, accurate, relevant, honest, constructive) feedback are "kind" structures for learning and (b) unfavorable: environments that lead to the development of poor intuitive awareness through little or low-quality feedback he termed "wicked" structures for learning.

Awareness

As noted previously, intuitions are affectively charged judgments (Dane & Pratt, 2007); therefore, becoming intuitively aware involves not only treating affect as a form of data but also being able to distinguish between different forms of affect (e.g., feelings, moods, and emotions). The term *affect*, when used in connection with intuition, refers to a nonemotional feeling (i.e., it does not encompass happiness or love, for example). Emotions (more intense) and moods (longer lasting) are distinct from the positively or negatively valenced "affective charge" that accompanies intuitive judgment, and the latter was referred to by Epstein (2008, p. 28) as "vibes," including feelings such as "disquietude" or "agitation" (negative

Taggart and Robey (1981) made a plea for the inclusion of intuition in the management education curriculum. However, little appears to have changed in the intervening decades in developing this aspect of management development. Sadler-Smith and Shefy (2004) argued that the rational model prevails in management education and training because it is safe, familiar, comforting, and reassuring, and in many situations (such as the computationally complex), it works perfectly well. Intuition, on the other hand, is unfamiliar, disconcerting, paradoxical, and ambiguous, and it may even be seen as a threat by the analytical mind; moreover, in many situations it is not needed (indeed machines, i.e., computers, can often outperform human judges in computationally complex and repetitive domains—see Meehl, 1954).

Sadler-Smith and Shefy (2004) argued, however, that intuition is pervasive, automatic, and involuntary and cannot be ignored; therefore managers have much to gain from being able to acknowledge and understand intuition (in much the same way that they appear to have embraced widely the concept and practices of emotional intelligence; see Goleman, 1995). Moreover, in certain situations (e.g., time-pressured decisions and creative problem solving), intuition is important and even necessary, and managers need to be able to harness its potential while being aware of its dangers. There are at least three ways in which managers may develop better intuitive judgment: (a) practice, (b) feedback, and (c) awareness (Burke & Sadler-Smith, 2006; Emery, 1994; Hogarth, 2001, 2008; Robinson, 2006; Sadler-Smith & Shefy, 2004).

Practice

Informed intuition is domain-specific and relies on pattern matching and pattern recognition using complex, domain-relevant schemas (Dane & Pratt, 2007) acquired by domain-general learning mechanisms (see Evans, 2008). These complex expert schemas support fast, nonconscious pattern recognition (Klein, 1998; Simon, 1987). An individual's level of expertise in a domain sets an upper limit on the extent to which he or she can exercise intuitive judgment (it is difficult, ill-advised, and probably perilous, for a novice to engage in intuitive judgment). The fact that intuition is exercised on the basis of implicit cognitive processes does not mean that it was acquired in this way (Hogarth, 2008). A corollary of this is that in order to become more intuitive in a specific domain, an individual must engage in explicit, focused, and deliberate practice (see Ericsson, Prietula, & Cokely, 2007). The process might be accelerated

be a potentially useful parameter not only for cognitive styles researchers but also for use by education and training practitioners.

Nonetheless, there has tended to be an overreliance on self-report methods of assessment in cognitive styles research. As a result, a whole body of work in this arena has developed founded on the bases of individuals' subjective perceptions of the ways in which they process information. How accurate these perceptions are is an open question, but what is clear is that in the future it will be important to employ alternative approaches in the study of intuitive processing style. This might include the critical incident technique (CIT; Flanagan, 1954) and the cognitive mapping techniques as used by Clarke and Mackaness (2001) to study managers' intuitions. Also, Hodgkinson, Langan-Fox, and Sadler-Smith (2008) saw potential in the use of the experience sampling method (ESM; Csikszentmihalyi & Larsen, 1987; Hogarth, 2006) and the day reconstruction method (DRM; Kahneman, Krueger, Schkade, Schwarz, & Stone, 2004) as means of exploring individuals' intuitive episodes. As is the case with self-report, the methods of CIT, cognitive mapping, ESM, and DRM are inherently subjective. Hence, it is all the more pressing that cognitive styles researchers use more direct methods in the assessment of intuitive processing and performance (e.g., the Tacit Knowledge Inventory for Managers; Wagner & Sternberg, 1985) in experimental and field settings. Moreover, in the brain sciences, a neuroscience of intuition is beginning to emerge with the application of fMRI to the study of intuitive processing in social cognition (Lieberman, 2007; Lieberman et al., 2004; Segalowitz, 2007), offering exciting prospects for future cognitive styles research.

IMPLICATIONS FOR LEARNING

The duplex model of style is parsimonious to the extent that it obviates any question of how our teaching could accommodate so many different styles (see Zhang & Sternberg, 2005, p. 43). It also provides a simple framework for educational and training practitioners to foster the development of cognitive strategies that enable learners to recognize the demands of a situation and be able to choose an appropriate information processing mode (analysis or intuition).

Traditional educational and training curricula and methods often aim to develop learners' rational and analytical reasoning skills. Over a quarter of a century ago, in the field of business and management,

Rational Experiential Inventory

Finally, the REI (Epstein et al., 1996) makes the conceptual presumption of individual differences in preferences for two modes (styles) of processing (intuitive and analytical); the issue of whether these styles are bimodal (i.e., intuitive versus analytical) or unimodal (i.e., intuitive and analytical) was left as an open question by Epstein and his colleagues, to be resolved empirically. Compelling evidence for unimodality was observed from Epstein et al.'s factor and correlational analyses. Specifically, correlations between scores on the intuitive ("Faith in Intuition") and analytical ("Need for Cognition") scales of the long (31-item) form of the REI were low and nonsignificant ($r = -0.07$), thus indicating that "rational [analytical] and experiential [intuitive] processing are independent" (Epstein et al., 1996, p. 395). A shorter 10-item version of the REI exhibited a similarly low scale intercorrelation ($r = -0.09$) (Epstein et al., 1996). An experiential (intuitive) thinking style was found to be positively associated with a variety of constructs, including esoteric beliefs, superstitious thinking, openness, positive thinking, naïve optimism, favorable interpersonal relationships, extraversion, agreeableness, favorable beliefs about the self and the world, sense of humor, creativity, social popularity, empathy, and aesthetic judgment, and negatively associated with categorical thinking (Epstein, 2008, p. 28). The content domain of the REI includes a verbal-visual facet of information processing (Paivio, 1971) to the extent that it aims to assess the role played by visualization in information processing (e.g., "I often have clear visual images of things" and "I am good at visualizing things").

Within a dual-process conceptualization of style, the CSI, PID, and REI are or may be used as modal measures (Coffield et al., 2004; Hodgkinson & Sadler-Smith, 2003); however, this raises the question of how to assess the versatile style. There are a number of possible approaches. The first, a computational approach, would be to combine intuition and analysis scores from the respective scales of the CSI, PID, or REI in a variety of ways to obtain an overall Cognitive Versatility Index (CVI).[9] A second approach, which may obviate any difficulties associated with respondents not discriminating sufficiently well between modes (i.e., indifferent or muddled responding), would be to develop a separate reliable and valid multi-item scale for the assessment of cognitive versatility per se. Sample items might include "I always run a 'gut check' on my analysis" and "I always check to see if my 'gut feel' squares with the available data." In either case, the computation or assessment of a CVI may

might emerge ontogentically from specialization, and how it may have emerged phylogenetically (see Browne, 1996), are questions for further theorizing and research.

ASSESSMENT WITHIN A DUPLEX MODEL OF COGNITIVE STYLE

Self-report, in spite of its inherent drawbacks, has been the mainstay of cognitive styles assessment as a means of eliciting individuals' subjective perceptions of their preferences for organizing and processing information. From the perspective of the duplex model of style, three candidate instruments may be considered: the Cognitive Style Index (CSI; Allinson & Hayes, 1996); the Preference for Intuition and Deliberation scale (PID; Betsch, 2004); and the Rational Experiential Inventory (REI; Epstein et al., 1996).[8]

Cognitive Style Index

The CSI (Allinson & Hayes, 1996) has been widely used, and its reliability is well-established (Coffield et al., 2004). However, the unifactoral structure of the intuition-analysis construct argued for by Allinson and Hayes is problematic in the present context in two respects. First, it is not fully compatible with a dual-process conceptual framework. Second, it fails to stand up to empirical scrutiny in that exploratory and confirmatory factor analytical studies suggest that—contrary to the guidance offered by Allinson and Hayes (1996) and the position adhered to by Hayes, Allinson, Hudson, and Keasey (2003)—it ought to be scored as two separate intuition and analysis factors (Backhaus & Liff, 2007; Coffield et al., 2004; Hodgkinson & Sadler-Smith, 2003).

Preference for Intuition and Deliberation

More recently, Betsch (2004) developed the PID for the "reliable, fast and economical" assessment of individual strategy preferences based on the presumption that intuition is not the opposite of deliberation (Betsch, 2008, p. 234). The PID consists of two slightly negatively correlated ($p < -0.20$) nine-item scales, PID-Intuition ($0.76 \leq \alpha \leq 0.81$) and PID-Deliberation ($0.76 \leq \alpha \leq 0.84$). Further concurrent and convergent validity studies of this instrument are required.

(see Robinson, 2006; Sadler-Smith & Shefy, 2007). In terms of the threefold model (Zhang & Sternberg, 2005), the versatile style corresponds to the notion of a Type III style: it is differentiated in that it can be exercised either with the characteristics of a Type I intellectual style (i.e., intuition) or with those of a Type II intellectual style (i.e., analysis).

3. Two fundamental aspects of human information processing are represented by similar constructs referred to under a variety of labels, namely: (a) intuitive: associative, heuristic, tacit, implicit, experiential, recognition-primed, automatic; wholistic; reflexive (System 1); (b) analytic: rule-based, explicit, rational, controlled, analytical, reflective (System 2) (see Evans, 2003; Stanovich & West, 2000, and Table 1.1). Statistically significant correlations have been observed between experientiality as measured by the Rational Experiential Inventory (REI; Epstein et al., 1996) and intuition as measured by the Cognitive Style Index (CSI; Allinson & Hayes, 1996), and between the corresponding rationality and analysis scales (Hodgkinson, Sadler-Smith, & Sinclair, 2006).

Cognitive style in terms of the duplex model of style has a hierarchical structure: At the specialized level, the intuitive mode and the analytic mode represent relatively stable preferences for intuitive processing or analytic processing; at the flexible level, the versatile style is such that intuitive or analytic processing is used interchangeably as the situation demands (see Figure 1.1). Individuals with a versatile style are able to engage in specialized intuitive or analytical processing (solid curved vertical arrows in Figure 1.1); individuals who operate with a preference for a specific mode may require education or training in order to acquire the necessary cognitive strategies to enable them to engage in a mode of processing complementary to their preferred mode and commensurate with the demands of the task they face; that is, analytics need to become more intuitively aware and vice versa (horizontal arrows in Figure 1.1). The issue of whether an individual with a relatively stable preference for intuitive or analytical processing can acquire a relatively stable versatile state is an open question (dashed curved vertical arrows in Figure 1.1) and is an important aim of metacognitive skills training programs (see the "Implications for Learning" section later in the chapter). Furthermore, the issues of the domain-specificity of intuition and analysis, the domain-generality of versatility, how versatility

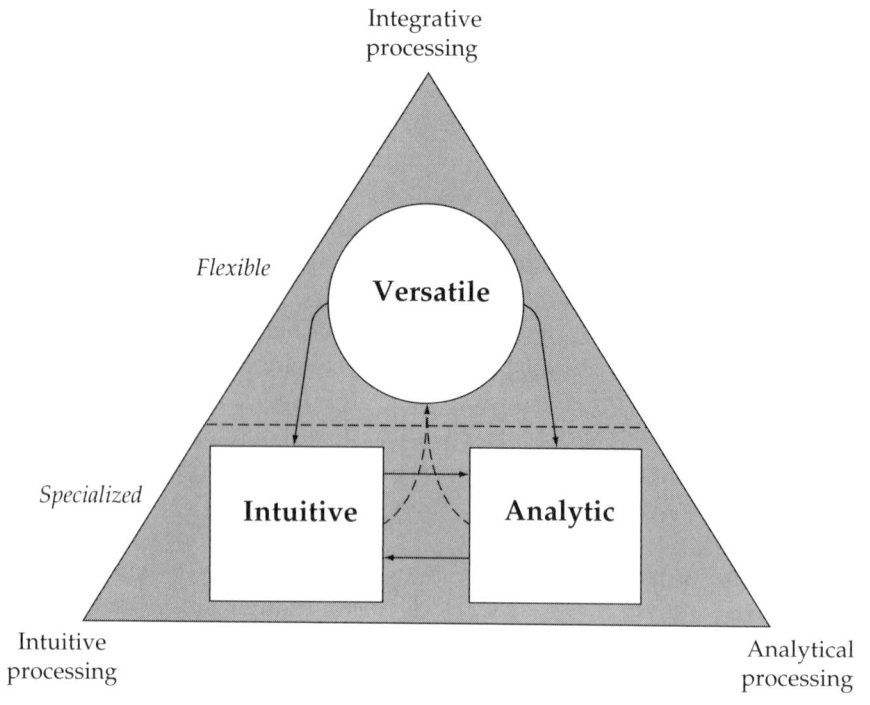

Figure 1.1 The duplex model of style.

(Triangle diagram with "Integrative processing" at top apex, "Intuitive processing" at bottom-left, "Analytical processing" at bottom-right. Inside: circle labeled "Versatile" at top, boxes labeled "Intuitive" and "Analytic" at bottom. Left side labeled "Flexible" and "Specialized".)

1. Everyone (except for individuals who have incurred damage through injury or disease to the neural circuitry that infuses decision making with affect—see Damasio, 1994) has access to the intuitive and analytical modes in greater or lesser degree. The modes are modifiable by learning, development, and socialization. For the majority of people, each mode is a propensity for which they express preferences, averaged out over tasks and the longer term.
2. Styles are value-free in general, and only value-laden under certain sets of circumstances. The analytical mode and the intuitive mode each has its strengths and weaknesses; each mode can be positive under particular sets of circumstances, and education and training interventions have been designed and applied that have striven to make individuals both more analytic (much of education is directed toward the development of analysis; Bloom, 1956)[7] and, admittedly to a lesser extent, more intuitive

Table 1.2

<table>
<tr><td colspan="3">**THE DUPLEX MODEL OF STYLE**</td></tr>
<tr><td colspan="3">**BASES OF THE DUPLEX MODEL OF STYLE**</td></tr>
<tr><td>*Intuitive and analytic modes*</td><td>1.</td><td>Intuition and analysis are two unipolar dimensions of information processing.</td></tr>
<tr><td></td><td>2.</td><td>Intuition and analysis are complementary information-processing modes to which most people have access.</td></tr>
<tr><td></td><td>3.</td><td>The intuitive and analytic modes are contextually appropriate and hence value-free.</td></tr>
<tr><td></td><td>4.</td><td>When averaged out over tasks there are differences between individuals in their propensity to deploy the analytic or intuitive mode; that is, they are relatively stable states.</td></tr>
<tr><td>*Versatile cognitive style*</td><td>5.</td><td>The extent to which an individual is able to deploy the intuitive or analytic mode in ways that are contextually appropriate is termed *cognitive versatility*.</td></tr>
<tr><td></td><td>6.</td><td>Cognitive versatility is: (a) differentiated and (b) value-laden.</td></tr>
<tr><td></td><td>7.</td><td>An individual's propensity to deploy the intuitive or analytic mode in contextually appropriate ways is developable and may lead to enhanced cognitive versatility.</td></tr>
</table>

"sequential," "adaptation," "impulsivity," "convergent thinking," "field dependent," "executive," "local," "conservative," and "monarchic") are *"predominantly* negative" (p. 40, emphasis added); (b) styles-as-traits versus styles-as-states: thinking styles represent states rather than traits because they can be socialized and modified; (c) styles-as-different-constructs versus styles-as-similar-constructs: styles constructs overlap to varying degrees—for example, any one of the 10 styles models Zhang and Sternberg (2005) included in their threefold model of intellectual styles has been shown to be correlated with at least one of the other style constructs. In the duplex model of style in terms of these three issues it is argued that:

and problem solving. The intuitive mode is affect-laden, comparatively fast in operation, slow in formation, parallel and wholistic, involuntary, cognitively undemanding, imagistic/narrative-based, and unavailable to conscious awareness. The analytic mode is affect free, comparatively slow in operation, fast in formation, serial and detail-focused, intentional, cognitively demanding, abstract/symbolic-based, and open to conscious awareness (Epstein, 1994; Lieberman, 2007; Sloman, 2002; Smith & DeCoster, 1999; Stanovich & West, 2000) (see Table 1.1).

When averaged out over a variety of tasks and the longer term, the majority of individuals have a proclivity to process information using either the intuitive mode or the analytic mode. These predispositions develop as a result of a variety of factors, including age, gender, personality, ability, education, and experience, and the nature of the task (Agor, 1989; Allinson & Hayes, 1996; Betsch, 2004, 2008). For example, Betsch (2004) found that people were able to adapt to the requirements of the situation by choosing the appropriate strategy (e.g., opting for intuition when intuitive judgments were appropriate), but preferences led certain individuals to choose intuition more frequently than deliberation (analysis) across all scenarios; that is, certain people tended to opt for their preference (intuition or analysis) in spite of the demands of the task (see Betsch, 2008). About two-thirds of Betsch's sample were either high on intuition and low on deliberation (analysis) or vice versa, while the remaining third were high or low on both scales, indicating that they use intuition or deliberation without clear preferences (Betsch, 2008). Similarly, Agor (1989), in his research with senior business executives, identified three different approaches to decision making: (a) giving intuition a free rein in order to foresee the correct path to follow and to avoid a rigorous step-by-step method (Agor described this group as "explorers"); (b) using a structured decision-making system that involved gathering and analyzing all the relevant data ("synthesizers"); and (c) cross-checking initial intuitive feelings against the data ("eclectics"). The duplex model of style, which shares some of the features both of Betsch's and Agor's conceptualizations as well as other two-dimensional frameworks (see Hodgkinson & Clarke, 2007; Sadler-Smith, 2002; Whetten, Cameron, & Woods, 1994), is summarized in Table 1.2 and Figure 1.1.

Zhang and Sternberg (2005) identified three controversial issues that are presented in the field of styles research, namely: (a) style as value-laden versus value-free: for example, they argue that the majority of styles that they identified as Type II (including those labeled as "surface," "conventional," "analytic," "sensing," "judging," "concrete,"

The Rational (Analytical) System

The rational (analytical)[6] system is an inferential logical system that operates consciously, primarily verbally, slowly, and effortfully; it is abstract, analytic, and affect-free, and it is evolutionarily the more recent of the two systems (Epstein, 1994, 2008). The operations of the rational system are analytic, intentional, effortful, logical, and mediated by conscious appraisal of events. It is slower, with a more delayed action than the experiential system but changes more rapidly on the basis of strength of argument and new evidence (Epstein, 1994; Epstein et al., 1996). The rational system is verbal (Paivio, 1971) in that it encodes reality in abstract symbols, words, and numbers.

CEST and related dual-process theories (e.g., Sloman, 2002) provide a simple yet compelling conceptual framework for cognitive style based on the parallel workings of an intuitive system and an analytical system. The two modes, which represent the operation of each system, are qualitatively different in terms of the type of data on which they draw, their operating principles, and their outcomes (Smith & DeCoster, 1999). The two systems interact both in their formation and in their operation. For example, in complex tasks under time-pressured conditions, intuitions—referred to by Simon (1987, p. 63) as "analyses frozen into habit and into the capacity for rapid response through recognition"—enable experts to arrive at involuntary, affectively charged, wholistic judgments (Dane & Pratt, 2007; Klein, 1998). Informed intuitive judgment draws on implicit and explicit knowledge that has become compressed into expertise through appropriate learning, exposure and practice, and feedback (see Hogarth, 2001, 2008) and is not something that a novice is able to execute effectively (Dreyfus & Dreyfus, 1986). Moreover, while microlevel neurobiological explanations of cognitive operations may be unnecessary for most purposes (Hofstadter, 2007), it is of interest and relevance that there is accumulating evidence indicating the brain structures that are activated when these modes of thought are engaged (see Kruglanski & Orehek, 2007; Lieberman, Jarcho, & Satpute, 2004).

A DUPLEX MODEL OF COGNITIVE STYLE

The duplex model of style based on dual-process theory in general, and CEST in particular, proposes two fundamental information-processing modes that individuals preferentially engage in during decision making

a hierarchical organization with various subcomponents including visualization, imagination, and aesthetic sensibility.[4] In spite of the fact that it shares many of the features of other dual-process theories, CEST also differs from them in a number of important respects:

1. *Role of affect:* CEST gives greater primacy to affect in its conceptualization of System 1; for example, Shiffrin and Schneider (1977) and Posner and Snyder (1975) emphasize automatic processing and activation rather than affect. Moreover, unlike models of emotional intelligence (Salovey & Meyer, 1995), the use of the term *affect* is not restricted to emotions per se.
2. *Dynamic interplay:* As argued by Evans (2008), each system in CEST has access to distinct forms of knowledge and is linked by two processing styles (modes) that may compete with or complement each other when they engage in what Epstein (2008) terms a "dance" between the two systems.
3. *Value-free:* Each system has its own strengths and limitations, and neither is innately superior to the other (Epstein, 2008, p. 27).

The properties of the rational and experiential systems are summarized in the following sections and in Table 1.1.

The Experiential (Intuitive) System

The experiential (intuitive)[5] system is a learning system that operates automatically, preconsciously, nonverbally, rapidly, effortlessly, associationistically and concretely. It is wholistic, associated with affect, and operates on the basis of schemas acquired from lived experiences. It is mediated by vibes from past events, concrete images, metaphors, and narratives, and it operates rapidly and with immediate effect. The experiential system is slower to form and more resistant to change than the rational system, and it changes with repetitive/intense experience (Epstein, 1994; Epstein et al., 1996). The experiential system is imagistic and nonverbal (Paivio, 1971) in that it encodes reality in concrete images, metaphors, and narratives. The experiential system is able to "effortlessly direct behavior in everyday life," is a source of "motivation and passion," and enables wholistic problem solving of a different order than that achievable by the rational system alone (Epstein, 2008, p. 26). The experiential system plays an important role in creativity, humor, and interpersonal functioning (Norris & Epstein, 2007). Intuition is a "subset of experiential processing" (Epstein, 2008, pp. 28–29).

> System 1 may have its own kind of *intuitive intelligence*. For example some people may have particularly nuanced and subtle representations of persons and social categories. These people will make better judgements by [the] representativeness [heuristic] than others, and consequently may achieve greater predictive accuracy than others. (p. 683, emphases added)

Compelling evidence for the utility of intuitive reasoning is to be found in research from several applied domains. For example, intuition has a significant and positive role to play in complex, difficult-to-quantify processes in loosely structured situations such as expert judgment under time-pressured conditions (Klein, 1998), creativity (Policastro, 1995), social judgment (Myers, 2002), entrepreneurship (Mitchell, Friga, & Mitchell, 2005), and moral judgment (Haidt, 2001; Sonenshein, 2007).

COGNITIVE-EXPERIENTIAL SELF-THEORY

Dual-process theory is an eclectic domain (see Table 1.1). For example, Stanovich and West (2000) listed a dozen different models, including associative/rule-based (Sloman, 1996), implicit cognition/explicit learning (Reber, 1993), intuitive cognition/analytical cognition (Hammond, 1996), recognition-primed decisions/rational choice strategy (Klein, 1998), and experiential system/rational system (Epstein, 1994). The latter, more properly termed cognitive-experiential self-theory (CEST), is described by Epstein, Pacini, Denes-Raj, and Heier (1996) as a global theory of personality that integrates the cognitive and psychodynamic unconscious. Two parallel interactive modes of information processing are posited, the rational (analytic) and the experiential (intuitive). The two modes are served by separate cognitive systems (Epstein, 1994). CEST helps to explain a variety of social behaviors as well as a person's receptivity to different kinds of complex cognitive tasks such as learning:

> Appeals to emotions, personal experience and the use of concrete examples could be more effective for people who process information primarily in the intuitive mode, whereas presenting facts and logical arguments could be more effective for individuals who process information primarily in the analytic mode. (Epstein et al., 1996, p. 390)

Epstein et al. (1996) speculated that in much the same way as rational processing can be disaggregated into various subcomponents (such as mathematical and verbal), the experiential (intuitive) system may have

rationality with the intentional level and intelligence with the algorithmic level opens the door to resolving the paradox of the seemingly conflicting roles of emotion and rationality. Consequently, identifying rationality with style (intentional level) rather than assuming it is synonymous with intelligence (algorithmic level) may help to resolve any paradox in the roles played by intuition and analysis in human reasoning: *Analysis* is not a synonym for *intelligence,* nor is it an antonym for *intuition.*

Affect (including emotion) is not necessarily the enemy of reason: Its adaptive function may be to truncate the "combinatorial explosion" of conscious reasoning that might occur if System 2 tried to compute all possible alternatives and their relative utilities (Stanovich, 2002, p. 145). This view squares well with the somatic marker hypothesis (SMH) proposed by Bechara, Damasio, and their colleagues (Bechara, 2004; Bechara, Damasio, Tranel, & Damasio, 1997; Damasio, 1994). Essentially the SMH posits that a gut feeling serves a computational role by intervening in order to provide a somatic signal of attraction toward (positive valence) or avoidance of (negative valence) a possible course of action (Bechara et al., 1997; Pollock, 1995; Stanovich, 2002). Hence, if certain aspects of a dual system of thinking (such as analysis and intuition) are adaptive under different sets of circumstances (i.e., contextually appropriate) one system could not, of necessity, be deemed superior to the other.

A further difficulty for a duplex model of style is encountered if intuitions are equated merely with heuristic judgments (see Sadler-Smith & Sparrow, 2008). As noted previously, System 1 processes are automatic, associative, and heuristic. It is well-established that errors of reasoning associated with heuristics such as representativeness, availability, and anchoring-and-adjustment can lead to judgments that violate the laws of probability and rationality (Kahneman & Tversky, 1982). However, Lakoff and Johnson (1999) argued that human reasoning is far richer than can be recognized in rational-actor models and probability theory. Metaphorical, frame-based, and prototypical reasoning mechanisms developed in the course of evolution enable *Homo sapiens* to function as effectively as possible in real-world, everyday life oblivious to the laws of probability and statistics (Lakoff & Johnson, 1999).

The operations of System 1 have their own rationality of purpose (Sadler-Smith, 2008), of the kind that was needed to survive (Lakoff & Johnson, 1999) in the social and natural environment of the Pleistocene.[3] However, the operation of System 1 is by no means redundant in the modern world; Kahneman (2000) himself noted that

Table 1.1

A SELECTION OF DUAL-PROCESS THEORIES IN RELATION TO INTUITIVE/ANALYTIC PROCESSING

SYSTEM 1	SYSTEM 2	SOURCES
Implicit cognition	Explicit learning	Reber, 1993
Associative system	Rule-based system	Sloman, 1996
Experiential system	Rational system	Epstein, 1994
Holistic; automatic, effortless; affective; associational; mediated by so-called vibes from past events; concrete images, metaphors, narratives; more rapid, immediate action; slower, more resistant to change; changes with repetitive/intense experience	Analytic; intentional, effortful; logical; mediated by conscious appraisal of events; abstract symbols, words, numbers; slower, delayed action; changes more rapidly; changes with strength of argument, new evidence.	
Intuitive cognition	Analytical cognition	Hammond, 1996
Recognition-primed decisions	Rational choice strategy	Klein, 1998
Unconscious cognition	Conscious cognition	Wilson, 2002
Reflexive (X–) system	Reflective (C–) System	Lieberman et al., 2004
Intuition	Deliberation	Betsch, 2004
Intuitive mode	Analytic mode	Allinson & Hayes, 1996; Epstein, 1994; Lieberman, 2007; Sloman, 2002; Smith & DeCoster, 1999; Stanovich & West, 2000
Affect-laden; comparatively fast in operation, slow in formation; parallel and holistic; involuntary; cognitively undemanding; imagistic/narrative-based; unavailable to conscious awareness	Affect free; comparatively slow in operation, fast in formation; serial and detail-focused; intentional; cognitively demanding; abstract/symbolic-based; open to conscious awareness	

Adapted from Evans (2003, 2008), Sadler-Smith (in press), Stanovich (2002), and Stanovich & West (2000).

specific knowledge acquired by domain-general learning mechanisms. Its workings are unconstrained by working memory capacity and it is independent of "general intelligence";
2. *System 2:* evolutionarily recent, heritable and distinctively human; its workings permit abstract, analytical and hypothetical reasoning processes constrained by working memory capacity and correlated with measures of general intelligence. (p. 454)

As Evans (2008) noted, the intuitive heuristic judgments researched by Kahneman, Tversky, and their colleagues (Gilovich, Griffith, & Kahneman, 2002) are associated with System 1 processing. In numerous rigorously executed experiments, such heuristics (essentially error-prone mental shortcuts) have been shown to lead to severe and systematic errors and biases in reasoning (Kahneman & Tversky, 1982). However, these arguably low-level heuristics deployed intuitively and with low cognitive effort are of a quite different and simpler order to the complex, nonconscious reasoning processes (see Lewicki, Hill, & Czyzewska, 1992) that result in intuition as defined by Dane and Pratt (2007, p. 40): "affectively charged judgments that arise through rapid, non-conscious and holistic associations." Table 1.1 presents a number of dual-process theories (see Evans, 2008; Stanovich & West, 2000).

Given that cognitive styles are qualitatively different forms of thinking unrelated to ability, and with a predictive power beyond general abilities (Kozhevnikov, 2007; Sternberg & Zhang, 2001), any correlation of System 2 (in general) with intelligence creates a difficulty regarding System 2 processes as a dimension of cognitive style. A similar issue proved all but fatal for one of the first dimensions of cognitive style to be systematically researched: The fact that measures of field independence (e.g., the Embedded Figures Test, EFT) are positively correlated with intelligence (Goldstein & Blackman, 1978; MacLeod, Jackson, & Palmer, 1986; McKenna, 1984) led Sternberg to argue that "a significant portion of the genetic variance in field dependence-independence [up to 60%] is explainable by genetic variation in intelligence" (1997, p. 7), thus undermining its status as a style.

Stanovich (2002) drew a conceptual distinction between algorithmic-level individual differences (intelligence) and intentional-level individual differences and observed that correlations between the two levels are less than unity; therefore it is entirely feasible for the intentional (e.g., a rational style of processing) and the algorithmic (intelligence) levels to dissociate.[2] Moreover, Stanovich (2002) also argued that identifying

cognitive styles—is beset by problems in relation to the four issues outlined in the preceding list. A continued proliferation of weakly theorized measurement instruments will inevitably further dilute the styles concept and consign it to applied fields and the margins of mainstream psychological and social scientific inquiry—very much a reversion to the position it occupied in the 1970s (see Kozhevnikov, 2007). In the fullness of time, this could sound the death-knell for cognitive styles as a field of research characterized by both scientific rigor and practical relevance.

A DUAL-PROCESS CONCEPTUALIZATION OF COGNITIVE STYLE

Conspicuous by its absence from the influential critical review of styles by Coffield and his colleagues is any mention of dual-process formulations of human reasoning, as discussed by researchers such as Chaiken and Trope (1999), Evans (2003), and Stanovich and West (2000). This is symptomatic not necessarily of an oversight on Coffield et al.'s part (given their aims), but of the fact that cognitive styles researchers themselves have ignored or overlooked a potentially important body of theory and research, for example as did Sadler-Smith (1998). It is an omission that is all the more surprising given the significance that cognitive and social psychologists have accorded dual-process theories (Evans, 2008) and the qualitative (i.e., stylistic) differences attributed to the different forms of reasoning posited therein (Epstein, 1994, 2008).

Two Systems of Reasoning

Stanovich and West (2000) distinguished between two fundamental types of human information processing for which they use the generic terms "System 1" (contextually dependent, associative, heuristic, tacit, intuitive, implicit/automatic, fast, and cognitively undemanding) and "System 2" (contextually independent, rule-based, analytic and explicit, slow, and cognitively demanding; Stanovich & West, 2000). Evans (2003) described such theories as essentially positing the existence of "two minds in one brain" and summarized the distinctions thus:

1. *System 1:* old in evolutionary terms, universal amongst humans and shared with other animals, it comprises a set of autonomous subsystems that includes innate input modules and domain-

emerged, including problematic issues of reliability regarding the Cognitive Styles Analysis (Peterson, Deary, & Austin, 2003) and construct validity of the Cognitive Style Index (Hodgkinson & Sadler-Smith, 2003).[1]

2. *Commonality of conceptual framework and shared theoretical basis:* The study of cognitive style would benefit considerably from a unifying model or conceptual framework (Sternberg, 1997, p. 149) underpinned by a coherent and current body of psychological theory.

3. *Integrated and interdependent nature of human thinking:* A problem with the notion of the polarization as opposites of contrasting styles (e.g., verbal *or* visual) is that complex, real-world tasks make demands on complementary modes of processing (e.g., visual *and* verbal, analytic *and* wholistic, intuitive *and* rational, divergent *and* convergent). In reality these are interdependent and integrated aspects of information processing that have each evolved for their own adaptive purposes. In the modern world a vital learning and managerial competence is the ability to take decisions and solve problems in cognitively versatile ways that integrate different modes of thinking (Coffield et al., 2004; Hodgkinson & Clarke, 2007; Hodgkinson & Sparrow, 2002; Louis & Sutton, 1991).

4. *Failure to draw on recent advances in cognitive and social psychology and cognitive neuroscience:* There were promising moves in the latter direction when in the 1990s Riding and his colleagues conducted research using electroencephalograph (EEG) techniques in an attempt to identify the neural correlates of the wholistic-analytical and verbal-imagery styles of processing (see Riding, Glass, Butler, & Pleydell-Pearce, 1997). However, with a small number of exceptions (Gevins & Smith, 2000; Goode, Goddard, & Pascual-Leone, 2002; Kozhevnikov, Kosslyn, & Shephard, 2005), the current generation of styles researchers has yet to take advantage of EEG or the more sophisticated imaging techniques such as PET and fMRI, which may help shed light on the neural correlates of differential processing modes and the biological nature of stylistic differences.

The inevitable conclusion is that cognitive styles research—including that which draws on the best of the available models and measures of

neural mechanisms, and their outcomes and effects. I will propose that a much-needed alternative to the dearth of theory and the plethora of measures that has dogged learning styles and cognitive styles research is to be found in a duplex model of style based on a distinction between an intuitive mode and an analytic mode of information processing (see Epstein, 2008) and a versatile style, which is a product of the interplay between these two modes.

BACKGROUND

Although many different labels are used for the concepts of style (see Riding & Rayner, 1998), *cognitive style* (rather than *thinking* or *learning* style) will be my preferred term since it is commensurate with the dual-process stance derived from social cognition research adopted in this chapter. I will use the term *cognitive style* to refer to relatively stable states that people have a proclivity to enter into that are more or less adaptive under different sets of circumstances (Zhang & Sternberg, 2005). Cognitive styles are malleable to the extent that they can be adapted to changing environmental demands and modified by life experiences (Kozhevnikov, 2007) and serve as "high level heuristics" that organize the deployment of strategies, operations, and propensities (including abilities) in complex processes such as "problem solving and learning" (Messick, 1976, p. 9). In spite of attempts to unify styles around one superordinate analytical-wholistic dimension (e.g., Allinson & Hayes, 1996), recent findings cast serious doubt on this dimension's unitary nature and suggest a more complex hierarchical organization of style consisting of at least two subordinate dimensions (Kozhevnikov, 2007).

In a review of cognitive styles from the perspective of business and management, Sadler-Smith (in press) concluded that if cognitive style is to achieve its potential in making a more meaningful contribution to management research and practice, there are a number of crucial issues that styles researchers must address:

1. *Reliability and validity of assessment:* It is axiomatic that the measurement of cognitive style must employ instruments that are not only reliable and valid but have a robust theoretical basis. Disappointingly, even among the models that were judged favorably in the critical review by Coffield, Moseley, Hall, and Ecclestone (2004), a number of weaknesses in this regard

1

A Duplex Model of Cognitive Style

EUGENE SADLER-SMITH

The question of whether human beings represent, organize, and process information in two contrasting modes has been debated in psychology for over a century, from Galton, James, Freud and Jung, up to the present (see Riding & Rayner, 1998). Such differences can be conceptualized in terms of cognitive style, defined by Messick (1976) as "consistent individual differences in preferred ways of organizing and processing information and experience" (p. 4). Styles have held particular allure for researchers and practitioners in a number of applied fields, including education and business management. The significance and popularity of cognitive styles as an area of research has waxed and waned, and it is regrettable that scientific progress has been impeded by a lack of coherent and useful theories (Kozhevnikov, 2007).

In this chapter I will argue that dual-process theories provide a simple and compelling conceptual framework for a model of cognitive style based on the workings of an intuitive (experiential) system and an analytical (rational) system (see Epstein, 2008). Within such a framework, affect and cognition may be thought of as parallel interacting processes that influence thought and behavior in an adaptive manner. The two modes of thought (intuitive and analytical) are qualitatively different in terms of, among other things, their perceptual processes, speed of operation, rate of formation, levels of conscious awareness, underlying

Models

PART I

Acknowledgments

Our very special thanks go to Philip Laughlin for contracting the book. We sincerely thank our production editor Mark Frazier for his unfailing support in the process of turning the manuscript into a published book. The first editor would like to thank her daughter Ashley, from whom she has learned much about the importance of understanding people's intellectual styles. The second editor would like to thank all the students he has advised over the years, from whom he, too, has learned a great deal about styles.

Sternberg, R. J., & Zhang, L. F. (Eds.) (2001). *Perspectives on thinking, learning, and cognitive styles.* Mahwah, NJ: Lawrence Erlbaum.

Zhang, L. F. (2005). Validating the theory of mental self-government in a non-academic setting. *Personality and Individual Differences, 38,* 1915–1925.

Zhang, L. F., & Higgins, P. (2008). The predictive power of socialization variables for thinking styles among adults in the workplace. *Learning and Individual Differences, 18*(1), 11–18.

Zhang, L. F., & Sternberg, R. J. (2005). A threefold model of intellectual styles. *Educational Psychology Review, 17*(1), 1–53.

Zhang, L. F., & Sternberg, R. J. (2006). *The nature of intellectual styles.* Mahwah, NJ: Lawrence Erlbaum.

The principal chapters in this volume are divided into two parts. Part I includes five chapters, each having its focus on a particular kind of model of styles. Part II comprises five chapters, each placing its emphasis on the application of styles. Together, the two parts provide a comprehensive overview of the field of intellectual styles as it exists today.

*Li-fang Zhang
and Robert J. Sternberg
The University of Hong Kong
and Tufts University*

REFERENCES

Betoret, F. D. (2007). The influence of students' and teachers' thinking styles on student course satisfaction and on their learning process. *Educational Psychology, 27*(2), 219–234.

Fan, W. Q. (2006). *Thinking styles among university students in Shanghai: Comparing traditional and hypermedia instructional environments.* Unpublished doctoral dissertation, the University of Hong Kong.

Grigoriadou, M., Papanikolaou, K., & Gouli, E. (2006). Investigating how to group students based on their learning styles. *Proceedings of the Sixth International Conference on Advanced Learning Technologies (ICALT'06).* IEEE Computer Society.

Hedlund, J., Wilt, J. M., Nebel, K. R., Ashford, S. J., & Sternberg, R. J. (2006). Assessing practical intelligence in business school admissions: A supplement to the graduate management admissions test. *Learning and Individual Differences, 16,* 101–127.

Kirton, M. J. (1976). Adaptors and innovators: A description and measure. *Journal of Applied Psychology, 61,* 622–629.

Myers, B., McCaulley, M., Quenk, N., & Hammer, A. (1998). *Manual: A guide to the development and use of the Myers-Briggs Type Indicator* (3rd ed.). Palo Alto, CA: Consulting Psychologist Press.

Nisbett, R. E. (2003). *The geography of thought: Why we think the way we do.* New York: The Free Press.

Sternberg, R. J. (1997). *Thinking styles.* New York: Cambridge University Press.

Sternberg, R. J. (2001). Epilogue: Another mysterious affair at styles. In R. J. Sternberg & L. F. Zhang (Eds.), *Perspectives on thinking, learning, and cognitive styles* (pp. 249–252). Mahwah, NJ: Lawrence Erlbaum.

Sternberg, R. J., & Grigorenko, E. L. (1997). Are cognitive styles still in style? *American Psychologist, 52*(7), 700–712.

Sternberg, R. J., & The Rainbow Project Collaborators. (2006). The Rainbow Project: Enhancing the SAT through assessments of analytical, practical and creative skills. *Intelligence, 34*(4), 321–350.

Sternberg, R. J., Wagner, R. K., & Zhang, L. F. (2003). *Thinking Styles Inventory—Revised.* Unpublished test, Yale University, New Haven, CT.

strengths and correcting or compensating for their weaknesses. As an example, someone in an auditing job will perform best if he or she is able to apply, as needed, a local style—concentrating on details—whereas someone in a top leadership position in any field will, for the most part, need a more global style—concentrating on large, long-term issues, while at the same time having advisors and subordinates who attend to local issues. CEOs and presidents with a local style risk getting enmeshed in details and losing the big picture of the work they are doing. They may under-perform because their style does not match their work.

Leaders in academic institutions and in business settings alike may be interested in the book because it is relevant to both successful recruitment and effective management of human resource portfolios. Undergraduate and graduate students in business management, education, and psychology (as well as those in other fields such as computer science, law, linguistics, and nursing) should be interested in the book because it will provide a window for them to see a more comprehensive and updated picture of the field of styles. Finally, laypeople may be interested in learning more about their own styles, how these styles affect their lives, and how they might use their knowledge of styles to improve their lives.

Existing work on styles should have exerted a stronger impact than it has on educators and human resource personnel. In educational settings, for example, knowledge about the match or mismatch of styles between teachers and students matters not only for students' academic achievement but also for their affective development. Such knowledge could help teachers to increase the effectiveness of their instruction and assessment. Moreover, teachers who take styles into account could be more confident in their ability to show sensitivity to the cultural and individual diversity that is so often absent in the classroom. For example, Nisbett (2003) found that North American students have a more linear style of thinking, whereas Asian students have a more dialectical style.

Although styles are primarily of interest in education, they are also of great interest in business. For example, the Myers-Briggs Type Indicator (MBTI; Myers, McCaulley, Quenk, & Hammer, 1998) and the Kirton Adaption-Innovation inventory (KAI; Kirton, 1976) are widely used in business as assessment tools for selection, placement, staff development, and organizational development. Laypeople may be interested in understanding their own styles and the effects of these styles on their daily life.

or develop particular styles would probably be in vain. If they are fluid, attempts at teaching and development might make good sense. Thus, addressing these issues has the potential for both advancing the field of styles and providing concrete guidelines for practitioners regarding how styles can be understood and used.

The main goal of this book is to integrate the most recent theories and research on intellectual styles. Specifically, the book intends to achieve five objectives: (a) to further distinguish styles from other constructs; (b) to foster a more profound internal dialogue among people in the field; (c) to situate the field of styles better within the larger context of the psychological, educational, and business literatures; (d) to present perspectives on the three controversial issues mentioned earlier; and (e) to provide more concrete guidelines for practitioners to apply the concept of styles to educational and business settings.

We asked leading worldwide experts in the field of intellectual styles to contribute chapters on topics that would facilitate the achievement of these objectives. We received an overwhelmingly positive response, enabling us to build a platform for leaders in the field to discuss various issues that are important from their perspectives. All the authors are scholars who have made major theoretical contributions, published important empirical data, or both. We attained international representation, including many of the major leaders who are currently active in the field of intellectual styles.

The book will be of interest to diverse audiences. Researchers in the field of intellectual styles and in related fields will be interested in the book as a basis for designing and conducting rigorous research projects. Educators will be interested in the book for ideas as to how to enhance their teaching and the psychological well-being of their students, as well as for providing means to foster their students' learning and development. Psychologists will be interested in the book because, more and more, researchers are looking for ways to integrate different fields, such as cognition and emotion, and cognition and personality. Because styles are at the interface of cognition and personality, the book provides one means for achieving such integration. Ideas in this book will be of interest to psychologists not only in the fields of cognition and personality but also in the fields of educational psychology, industrial/organizational psychology, consulting psychology, developmental psychology, and student development.

Consultants can help people to understand their own styles and to improve their studying or their job performance by capitalizing on their

freely and creatively. Someone with an "executive" style tends to prefer a multiple-choice test that is more constrained.

Since the 1930s, styles have been the focus of research by many scholars, though levels of interest have waxed and waned in the past 70 years. Several factors contributed to the lapse of interest (see Sternberg, 2001; Sternberg & Grigorenko, 1997).

First, some of the early theories proposed styles that were clearly distinguishable neither from abilities nor from personality traits. Second, many of the early theories not only were of isolated styles but also made little contact with other general literature in psychology and education. Third, the quality of some of the early empirical research was variable. Sternberg (2001) asserted that the major factor responsible for the untimely demise of styles research in the 1970s was the fact that the styles literature had failed to provide "any common conceptual framework and language for researchers to communicate either with one another or with psychologists in general" (Sternberg & Zhang, 2001, p. 250).

Styles have re-emerged as an area of interest because progress has been made in each of the aforementioned areas, although to varying degrees (see Sternberg, 2001). The field of styles has flourished in the past decade or so.

We had three motivations for editing this book. First, as just noted, after a quiescent period, the field of styles has become highly active. Even since the work of Zhang and Sternberg (2006), which covered research through 2005, substantial new empirical evidence has been accumulated. For example, in the last three years, the context of online learning environments has been a topic of special interest (e.g., Grigoriadou, Papanikolaou, & Gouli, 2006). As another example, empirical studies examining the nature of intellectual styles have been conducted (Betoret, 2007; Fan, 2006). Also, new inventories are being used in business settings (see Sternberg, Wagner, & Zhang, 2003; Zhang, 2005; Zhang & Higgins, 2008). Second, there is now more internal dialogue among workers in the field (Zhang & Sternberg, 2005).

Finally, in the field of styles, at least three major controversial issues are unresolved. The first is whether certain styles are better than others, that is, whether they are value laden. The second is whether styles are traits versus states. The third is the extent to which distinctly named styles are different constructs. These issues are important because the confusion over them has slowed the advancement of the field. Practitioners have also been more hesitant to use the concept of styles in their work. For example, if styles represent fixed traits, any attempt to teach

Preface

Rick and Rhea know the material they have learned for their business administration class equally well. Yet, Rick will get an A in the course and Rhea will get a B–. How is this possible? Does the teacher discriminate against women? Does Rhea fail to show up for classes? Was Rhea sick the day of the final exam?

What teachers assume is a difference in students' knowledge of course material may be nothing more than differences in styles of learning or thinking (Sternberg, 1997). For example, two students may know course material equally well, but one may have a style that thrives on multiple-choice testing and the other have a style that thrives on essay testing. In this case, if Rick and Rhea both take one or more multiple-choice tests, Rick may have a substantial advantage over Rhea.

Of course, this example is hypothetical and it may sound as though the whole concept of differences due to mode of testing is hypothetical as well. Yet, Hedlund, Wilt, Nebel, Ashford, and Sternberg (2006), studying the performance of students in a business school, found precisely the result described here for male versus female test takers. When the multiple-choice GMAT was used to assess students, men had a substantial advantage. When a supplementary, essay-based test was used instead, women had a substantial advantage. When both kinds of tests were used together, the two sexes did equally well. In other words, modality of testing made a large difference, a result comparable to that found by Sternberg and the Rainbow Project Collaborators (2006) when comparing results for different ethnic groups on college admissions tests.

Intellectual styles, an umbrella term for such constructs as cognitive styles, learning styles, teaching styles, and thinking styles, refers to people's preferred ways of processing information. One kind of preference is for mode of testing, which in turn can result from differences in thinking styles. Someone with what Sternberg (1997) calls a "legislative" style tends to prefer a free-form essay test whereby he or she can think

xi

Elizabeth R. Peterson, PhD
Lecturer
Department of Psychology
Faculty of Science
University of Auckland
Auckland, New Zealand

Steve Rayner, PhD
Professor of Leadership and
   Diversity
Department of Education
University of Gloucestershire
Cheltenham, Gloucestershire
United Kingdom

Joseph S. Renzulli, EdD
Board of Trustees Distinguished
   Professor
Director of the National Research
   Center on the Gifted and Talented
University of Connecticut
Storrs, Connecticut

Eugene Sadler-Smith, PhD
Professor of Management
   Development and Organizational
   Behavior
University of Surrey
Guildford
Surrey, England
United Kingdom

Erin E. Sullivan, PhD Cand.
University of Connecticut
Educational Psychology program
Storrs, Connecticut

Michael Waring, PhD
Senior Lecturer of Physical
   Education
School of Sport and Human
   Sciences
University of Loughborough
Loughborough, Leicestershire
United Kingdom

Contributors

Steve Armstrong, PhD
Director of Research and
 Professor of Organizational
 Behaviour
Hull University Business
 School
Hull, United Kingdom

John M. Baer, PhD
Professor of Educational
 Psychology
Rider University
Lawrenceville, New Jersey

Eva Cools, PhD
Vlerick Leuven Gent
 Management School
People and Organization
 Department
Ghent, Belgium

Noel Entwistle, PhD
Professor Emeritus
Bell Professor of Education
University of Edinburgh
South Bridge Edinburgh
Scotland, United Kingdom

Carol Evans, PhD
Assistant Director of
 Learning and
 Teaching (ITE)
Institute of Education
University of London
London, England
United Kingdom

Elena L. Grigorenko, PhD
Associate Professor of Child Studies
Dept. of Psychology, Epidemiology,
 and Public Health
Yale Child Study Center
New Haven, Connecticut

Kathryn W. Jablokow, PhD
Associate Professor of Mechanical
 Engineering and of Science
 Technology, and Society
Pennsylvania State University
State College, Pennsylvania

James C. Kaufman, PhD
Associate Professor
Learning Research Institute
Department of Psychology
California State University
San Bernardino, California

Michael J. Kirton, PhD
Director and Founder of the
 Occupational Research Centre,
Deputy Director of the Acton
 Society Trust, and Manager
 of Psychology
University of Hertfordshire
Hatfield, Hertfordshire
United Kingdom

Velda McCune, PhD
Senior Lecturer
Learning and Teaching Centre
University of Glasgow
Glasgow, United Kingdom

ix

7	The Place of Cognitive Style in Pedagogy: Realizing Potential in Practice 169
	Carol Evans and Michael Waring

8	Learning Styles Applied: Harnessing Students' Instructional Style Preferences 209
	Joseph S. Renzulli and Erin E. Sullivan

9	What Is So Stylish About Styles? Comments on the Genetic Etiology of Intellectual Styles 233
	Elena L. Grigorenko

10	Cognitive Styles and Their Relevance for Business and Management: A Review of Development Over the Past Two Decades 253
	Steven J. Armstrong and Eva Cools

Epilogue—Intellectual Styles: Nehru Jacket or Solid Blue Blazer? 291
Li-fang Zhang and Robert J. Sternberg

Index 299

Contents

Contributors *ix*
Preface *xi*
Acknowledgments *xvii*

PART I: MODELS   1

1   A Duplex Model of Cognitive Style   3
    Eugene Sadler-Smith

2   The Disposition to Understand for Oneself at University and Beyond: Learning Processes, the Will to Learn, and Sensitivity to Context   29
    Noel Entwistle and Velda McCune

3   Revisiting the Value Issue in Intellectual Styles   63
    Li-fang Zhang and Robert J. Sternberg

4   How Are Intellectual Styles Related to Creativity Across Multiple Domains?   87
    James C. Kaufman and John M. Baer

5   Reaffirming Style as an Individual Difference: Toward a Global Paradigm or Knowledge Diaspora?   107
    Steve Rayner and Elizabeth R. Peterson

PART II: APPLICATIONS   135

6   Problem Solving, Creativity, and the Level-Style Distinction   137
    Kathryn W. Jablokow and Michael J. Kirton

*This book is dedicated to Jerome Kagan,
a pioneer in the field of intellectual styles.*

Copyright © 2009 Springer Publishing Company, LLC

All rights reserved.

No part of this publication may be reproduced, stored in a retrieval system, or transmitted in any form or by any means, electronic, mechanical, photocopying, recording, or otherwise, without the prior permission of the publisher, or authorization through payment of the appropriate fees to the Copyright Clearance Center, Inc., 222 Rosewood Drive, Danvers, MA 01923, 978-750-8400, fax 978-646-8600, info@copyright.com or on the web at www.copyright.com.

Springer Publishing Company, LLC
11 West 42nd Street
New York, NY 10036
www.springerpub.com

Acquisitions Editor: Philip Laughlin
Project Manager: Mark Frazier
Cover design: Steve Pisano
Composition: Apex CoVantage, LLC

Ebook ISBN: 978-0-8261-0461-8

09 10 11 12 / 5 4 3 2 1

The author and the publisher of this Work have made every effort to use sources believed to be reliable to provide information that is accurate and compatible with the standards generally accepted at the time of publication. The author and publisher shall not be liable for any special, consequential, or exemplary damages resulting, in whole or in part, from the readers' use of, or reliance on, the information contained in this book. The publisher has no responsibility for the persistence or accuracy of URLs for external or third-party Internet Web sites referred to in this publication and does not guarantee that any content on such Web sites is, or will remain, accurate or appropriate.

Library of Congress Cataloging-in-Publication Data

Perspectives on the nature of intellectual styles / edited by Li-fang Zhang & Robert J. Sternberg.
　　p. cm.
　Includes bibliographical references and index.
　ISBN 978-0-8261-0460-1 (alk. paper)
　1. Cognitive styles.　2. Learning, Psychology of.　I. Zhang, Li-fang.
II. Sternberg, Robert J.

BF311.Z462　2009
153—dc22　　　　　2009005088

Printed in the United States of America by Hamilton Printing

Perspectives on the Nature of Intellectual Styles

EDITED BY

LI-FANG ZHANG, PhD, &
ROBERT J. STERNBERG, PhD

SPRINGER PUBLISHING COMPANY

New York

Li-fang Zhang, PhD, is currently associate dean of the faculty of education at the University of Hong Kong, where she is also associate professor. She is the author of nearly 100 peer-reviewed articles, books, and book chapters. Her recent book (with Dr. Robert J. Sternberg) is titled *The Nature of Intellectual Styles*. She serves on the editorial board of *Educational Psychology* and that of *Educational Psychology Review*. Her main research interests include intellectual styles, giftedness, personality, and student development in higher education.

Robert J. Sternberg, PhD, is currently dean of the School of Arts and Sciences at Tufts University, where he is also professor of psychology. He was previously IBM Professor of Psychology and Education at Yale University. Dr. Sternberg received his PhD from Stanford and is the recipient of 11 honorary doctorates. Moreover, he has won more than two dozen awards for his work. He is a former president of the American Psychological Association and the author of over 1,200 books, articles, and book chapters. His main research interests include intelligence, creativity, wisdom, intellectual styles, and leadership.

Perspectives on the Nature of Intellectual Styles

//
to a friend —
dear friend —
May the stars
be with you,
Sioux Rose

7-14-2008

Cassandra's Tale